Alexander Alekhine

My Best Games

1924-1937

EDITORA SOLIS

2023

© Garcez Leme & Associados Lda (Editora Solis), 2023.
Editors: Francisco Garcez Leme and Jussara Chaves Garcez Leme
Graphic and electronic publication project: Editora Solis
Layout: Heloísa Chaves Garcez Leme
Edited in Aveiro, Portugal, in September 2023.
ISBN: 9786598628024   comercial@editorasolis.pt

Alekhine, Alexander, 1892 -1946 - My Best Games 1924-1937 / Alexander Alekhine
©Translation and comments by Francisco Garcez Leme - 1. ed., Aveiro, Portugal , Editora Solis, 2023. Original title: *Mes meilleurs jeux d'echecs 1924-1937*

1. Chess, 2. Chess - Study and teaching 3. Teaching strategy in chess
ISBN 9786598628024

Alexander Alekhine

Summary

Page 5 - *Alekhine's Performance in Tournaments and Matches*

Page 9 - Chapter 1 - *Tournament Games and Match with Capablanca - 1924-1927*

Page 55 - Chapter 2 - *Tournament Games and Matches with Bogoljubov - 1929-1934*

Page 139 - Chapter 3 - *Tournaments Games and Matches with Dr. Euwe - 1934-1937*

Page 227 - Chapter 4 - *Simultaneous and Blind Games; Exhibitions and Games with Consultation*

Page 255 - *Appendix with biographical notes of Alekhine's opponents in this Book*

Page 321 - *Index of Openings*

Alexander Alekhine - My Best Games 1924-1937

Alekhine's performance in Tournaments

Year	City	Placement	Games	Wins	Draws	Losses
1909	St. Petersburg	1	16	12	2	2
1910	Hamburg	7	16	5	7	4
1911	Carlsbad	8	25	11	5	9
1912	Stockholm	1	10	8	1	1
1912	Vilna	6	18	7	3	8
1913	S. Petersburg	1	4	2	-	1
1913	Scheveningen	1	13	11	1	1
1913	St. Petersburg	1	17	13	1	3
1914	St. Petersburg	3	18	6	8	4
1914	Mannheim	1	11	9	1	1
1920	Moscow	1	15	9	6	-
1921	Triberg	1	8	6	2	-
1921	Budapest	1	11	6	5	-
1921	The Hague	1	9	7	2	-
1922	Pistyan	2	18	12	5	1
1922	London	2	15	8	7	-
1922	Hastings	1	10	6	3	1
1922	Vienna	4	14	7	4	3
1923	Margate	2	7	3	3	1
1923	Carlsbad	1	17	9	5	3
1923	Portsmouth	1	12	11	1	-
1924	New York	3	20	6	12	2
1925	Paris	1	8	5	3	-
1925	Bern	1	6	3	2	1
1925	Baden-Baden	1	20	12	8	-
1926	Hastings	1	9	8	1	-
1926	Semmering	2	17	11	3	3
1926	Dresden	2	9	5	4	-
1926	Scarborough	1	8	7	1	-
1926	Birmingham	1	5	4	-	1
1927	New York	2	20	5	13	2
1927	Kecskemet	1	16	8	8	-
1929	Bradley Beach	1	9	8	1	-
1930	San Remo	1	15	13	2	-
1930	Hamburg - Olympiad	-	9	9	-	-
1931	Nice - with consultation	1	8	4	4	-
1931	Prague - Olympiad	-	18	10	7	1
1931	Bled	1	26	15	11	-
1932	London	1	11	7	4	-
1932	Bern	1	15	11	3	1

Year	City	Placement	Games	Wins	Draws	Losses
1932	Mexico City	1/2	9	8	1	-
1932	Pasadena	1	11	7	3	1
1933	Folkestone - Olimpyad	-	12	8	3	1
1933	Paris	1	9	7	2	-
1933	Hastings	2	9	4	5	-
1934	Zurich	1	15	12	2	1
1935	Warsaw - Olympiad	-	17	7	10	-
1935	Orebro	1	9	8	1	-
1936	Bad Nauheim	1/2	9	4	5	-
1936	Dresden	1	9	5	3	1
1936	Podbrady	2	17	8	9	-
1936	Nottingham	6	14	6	6	2
1936	Amsterdam	3	7	3	3	1
1936	Hastings	1	9	7	2	-
1937	Margate	3	9	6	-	3
1937	Kemeri	4/5	17	7	9	1
1937	Bad Neunheim	2/3	6	3	1	2
1938	Montevideo	1	17	9	8	-
1938	Margate	1	9	6	2	1
1938	Plymouth	1/2	7	5	2	-
1938	AVRO	4/5/6	14	3	8	3
1939	Caracas	1	10	10	-	-
1939	Buenos Aires - Olympiad	-	10	5	5	-
1939	Montevideo	1	7	6	1	-
1941	Munich	2/3	15	8	5	2
1941	Krakow	1/2	11	6	5	-
1942	Salzburg	1	10	7	1	2
1942	Munich	1	11	7	3	1
1942	Krakow	1	10	6	3	1
1942	Prague	1/2	11	6	5	-
1943	Prague	1	19	16	3	-
1943	Salzburg	1/2	10	5	5	-
1944	Gijon	1	8	7	1	-
1945	Madrid	1	9	8	1	-
1945	Gijon	2/3	9	6	1	2
1945	Sabadell	1	9	6	3	-
1945	Almeria	1/2	8	4	3	1
1945	Melilla	1	7	6	1	-
1945	Cáceres	2	5	3	1	1

Alekhine's performance in Matches

Date	City	Opponent	Result	Score	+V-L=D
1908	Düsseldorf	Curt von Bardeleben	Won	4½/5	+4−0=1
1908	Munich	Hans Fahrni	Drew	1½/3	+1-1=1
1908	Moscow	Benjamin Blumenfeld	Won	4½/5	+4−0=1
1908	Moscow	Vladimir Nenarokov	Lost	0/3	+0−3=0
1913	Saint Petersburg	Stepan Levitsky	Won	7/10	+7−3=0
1913	Paris, London	Edward Lasker	Won	3/3	+3−0=0
1913	Saint Petersburg	José Raúl Capablanca	Lost	0/2	+0−2=0
1914	Saint Petersburg	Aron Nimzowitsch	Drew	1/2	+1−1=0
1916	Kiev	Alexander Evensohn	Won	2/3	+2−1=0
1918	Moscow	Abram Rabinovich	Won	3½/4	+3−0=1
1918	Odessa	Boris Verlinsky	Won	6/6	+6−0=0
1920	Moscow	Nikolay Pavlov-Pianov	Drew	1/2	+1−1=0
1921	Moscow	Nikolay Grigoriev	Won	4½/7	+2−0=5
1921	Triberg	Efim Bogoljubow	Drew	2/4	+1−1=2
1921	Berlin	Richard Teichmann	Drew	3/6	+2−2=2
1921	Berlin	Friedrich Saemisch	Won	2/2	+2−0=0
1922	Paris	Ossip Bernstein	Won	1½/2	+1−0=1
1922	Paris	Arnold Aurbach	Won	1½/2	+1−0=1
1922	Madrid	Manuel Golmayo	Won	1½/2	+1−0=1
1923	Paris	André Muffang	Won	2/2	+2−0=0
1926	Scarborough	Edgar Colle	Won	2/2	+2−0=0
1926/7	Amsterdam	Max Euwe	Won	5½/10	+3−2=5
1927	**Buenos Aires**	**José Raúl Capablanca**	**Won**	**18½/34**	**+6−3=25**
1927	New York	Charles Jaffe	Won	2/2	+2−0=0
1929	**Various cities**	**Efim Bogoljubow**	**Won**	**15½/25**	**+11−5=9**
1933	San Juan	Rafael Cintron	Won	4/4	+4−0=0
1933	Paris	Ossip Bernstein	Drew	2/4	+1−1=2
1934	**Various cities**	**Efim Bogoljubow**	**Won**	**15½/25**	**+8−3=15**
1935	**Various cities**	**Max Euwe**	**Lost**	**14½/30**	**+8−9=13**
1937	**Various cities**	**Max Euwe**	**Won**	**15½/25**	**+10−4=11**
1937	The Hague	Max Euwe	Lost	2/5	+1−2=2
1941	Vitoria	Lopez Esnaola	Won	2/2	+2−0=0
1943	Warsaw	Efim Bogoljubow	Drew	2/4	+2−2=0
1944	Zaragoza	Ramón Rey Ardid	Won	2½/4	+1−0=3
1946	Estoril	Francisco Lupi	Won	2½/4	+2−1=1

Alexander Alekhine

CHAPTER 1
Tournament Games and Match
with Capablanca - 1924 - 1927

Game 1
A.Alekhine - R.Réti
New York Tormament, March 1924
King's Indian Defense [E62]

1.d4 ♘f6 2.c4 g6 3.g3

Nowadays 3.♘c3 e5 4.♗f4 followed by e3 etc. is considered a promising line.

3...♗g7 4.♗g2 0-0 5.♘c3 d6 6.♘f3 ♘c6

If Black has nothing better (and this seems to be the case), than to induce White's pawn advance to d5 - where it will certainly reduce the reach of the bishop diagonal on g2 for the time being - but on the other hand it will bring considerable pressure to bear on Black's position - then his development plan should certainly not be recommended.

7.d5 ♘b8 8.0-0 ♗g4

Exchanging this bishop is unreasonable and simply diminishes Black's power of resistance in the position. Similarly, 8...e5 is unsatisfactory because of 9.dxe6 (ep) fxe6 10.♗g5 etc., as in my game against Sir G. Thomas at Carlsbad, 1923. On the other hand, you could consider 8...a5 to secure the c5-square for the knight for the time being. But in that case, White would maintain his superiority through the structure h3, ♗e3, ♕c2, b3, a3 and finally b4.

9.h3

It's important to clarify the situation before the opponent completes his development.

9...♗xf3 10.exf3

Much better than taking the bishop, which would keep the e pawn inactive for a long time and whose subsequent advance would restrict the action of White's own pieces. However, after the game move, the pawn will defend the important e5 square and more than that, Black will have to watch out for hostile actions on the open e column.

10...e6

The king's pawn must be exchanged, but it would be relatively better for Black to do so with 10...e5. White would then have only one good response (10...e5 11.dxe6) since 11.f4 exf4 12.♗xf4 ♘bd7 would clearly be tolerable for Black. On the other hand, after the opening move, White has a nice choice between two good continuations.

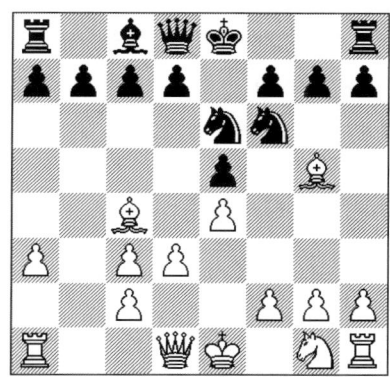

11.f4

Much more favorable than 11.dxe6 fxe6 12.♖e1 ♕d7 etc. After that it wouldn't be easy to take advantage of Black's central weaknesses.

11...exd5 12.cxd5

Now, however, Black will have to choose between three difficult paths: a. weakening on the c7 square, if he keeps the pawn structure intact; b. weakening the c6 square, if after ...c5 dxc5, he is forced to play ...d5; c. and, finally, the line they have played, through which they have obtained an isolated pawn on the queen column, difficult to protect from the hostile actions of the powerful joint operation of the opposing bishops, which will soon cause the decisive weakening of their queen wing.

12...c5 13.d×c6 ♘×c6 14.♗e3 ♕d7 15.♕a4

The most effective square for the queen, from where she will exert problematic pressure on black's queen wing.

15...♖ac8 16.♖ad1

Both players follow the same idea, i.e. their queenside pawns must be kept out of reach of the hostile bishops. Incidentally, 16.♗×a7 shouldn't be played, of course, because of 16...♖a8 etc.

16...b6 17.b3

This move has the additional aim of further protecting the Queen by anticipating subsequent complications. Its importance will soon become apparent.

17...♖fd8 18.♖d3

It would be premature to immediately play 18.♘b5 because of 18...e5 etc. Now, however, White is threatening to make his move after doubling the rooks and thus prevent Black's efforts through an exchange from relieving the pressure exerted by the white queen.

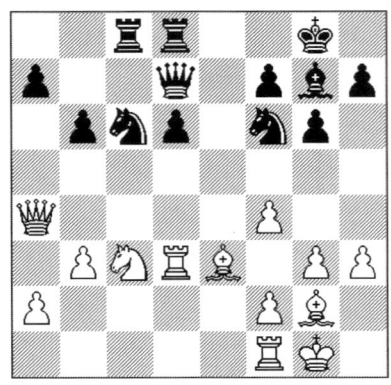

18...♘e7?

Not like that! This move leads Black to an immediate material disadvantage.

It would be a little better 18...♘d5 19.♕a3 ♗f8 20.♔fd1 with a game that is certainly difficult for Black, but still possible to defend.

19.♘b5 d5

Clearly forced.

20.♘×a7

This line also comes from White's 17th move.

20...♖a8 21.♗×b6 ♕×a4

Black has nothing better, as after 21...♖db8 White would simply continue with 22.♕×d7 ♘×d7 23.♗e3 ♔b7 24.♗×d5 ♘×d5 25.♖×d5 ♖×a7 26.♗×a7 ♖×a7 27.♖fd1 etc., with a decisive advantage.

22.b×a4 ♖d7 23.♘b5 ♖×a4

Also threatening 24...♖b4 25.♖b3 ♖×b3 26.a×b3 ♖b7 etc.

24.♘c3 ♖a6 25.♖b1 ♖b7 26.♗c5 ♖×b1+ 27.♘×b1 ♘c6

The position is now clear: White keeps his passed pawn while Black's d-pawn remains weak.

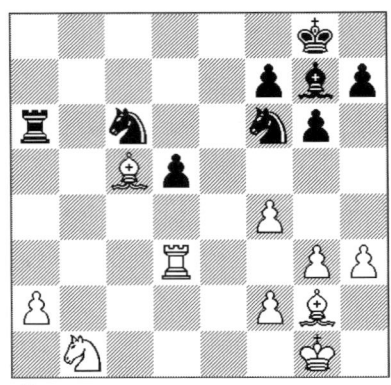

28.♘c3!

The quickest way to win. By giving up the a2 pawn, Black in return gains the possibility of forcing the rook into the enemy camp, where the decisive attack on the pawn will be possible. The quiet 28.a3 would allow the opponent more stubborn resistance after 28...♖a5 29.♗e3 ♖b5 etc.

28...♖a5 29.♗e3 ♘b4

After 29...e4 it wouldn't follow 29...d4 30.♗×d4 ♘×d4 31.♔×d4 ♘d5! with chances of a draw, but 30.♗×a5! d×c3 31.a4 winning.

30.♖d2 h6

If 30...♘e4, then 31.♘×e4 d×e4 32.♖d8+ ♗f8 33.f5 winning.

31.a4!

Threatening 32.♗b6 and thus forcing Black's next move.

31...♘e4 32.♘×e4 d×e4 33.♖d8+ ♔h7 34.♗×e4 ♖×a4

If 34...f5 35.♖d7 ♔h8 (or 35...f×e4 36.♗d4 ♖d5 37.♖×g7+ ♔h8 38.♖d7+ followed by the exchange of rooks and winning) 36.♗d4 ♗×d4 37.♖×d4 f×e4 38.♖×b4, winning.

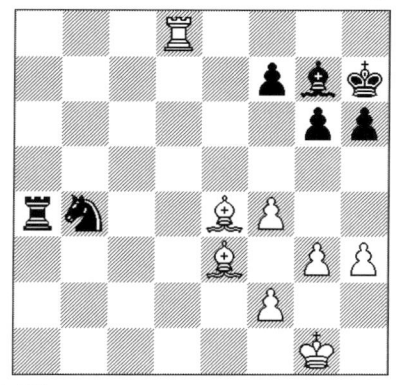

35.f5

The start of the pawns' decisive charge. At the moment 36.f×g6+ f×g6 37.♖d6 etc. is threatened.

35...♖a6 36.h4 h5

Forced by the threat 37.h5 etc.

37.g4! ♖a5

Or 37...h×g4 38.h5 winning.

38.f×g6+ f×g6 39.g×h5 ♖×h5 40.♗g5!

Gaining at least in quality.

40...♗c3 41.♖d7+ ♔g8 42.♗×g6

Now, after 42...♔h8 White wins immediately by advancing the h-pawn. Black has resigned.

Game 2
A.Alekhine – D.Janowisky
New York Tormament, March 1924
Irregular Defense [A53]

1.d4 ♘f6 2.c4 d6 3.♘c3 ♗f5?

This move would be reasonable if White had already developed his King's Knight, after which control of the e4 square would temporarily remain in Black's hands. But in the bishop's current situation, after e4 White has no future anyway. The veteran Janowski certainly had great skill in conducting the bishop pair, but he wasn't an expert in the openings compared to his contemporaries.

4.g3

Even 4.f3 and e4 would strategically refute Black's bishop move.

4...c6 5.♗g2 ♘bd7 6.e4 ♗g6 7.♘ge2 e5 8.h3

Preparing ♗e3. From that moment on Black only has the choice between unsatisfactory moves.

8...♕b6 9.0–0 0–0–0

This provides the opponent with an objective for a direct attack, which, due to the unfortunate position of the black pieces, will have catastrophic consequences for them. The move 9...♗e7 followed by 10.♗e3 ♕c7 would allow for more tenacious resistance.

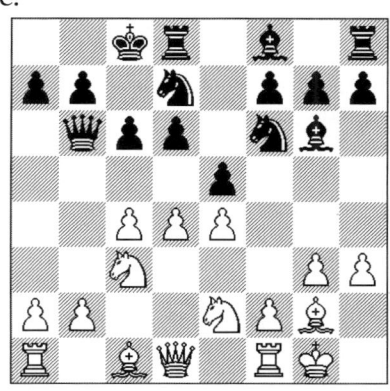

10.d5!

Demolishing all Black's hopes of eventual relief through the ...d5 move. The temporary liberation of the c5-square is, in comparison with this main theme, completely unimportant.

10...♘c5 11.♗e3 c×d5 12.c×d5 ♕a6

Accepting the pawn sacrifice would lead to a clear losing position, for example - 12...♕×b2 13.♗×c5 d×c5 14.♕a4 ♕b6 15.f4! e×f4 16.g×f4 etc. But the continuation of the game is just as hopeless.

13.f3

Simple and decisive. Black doesn't have a satisfactory defense against b4. If, for example, 13...♕d3, then of course 14.♕c1 etc.

13...♔b8 14.b4 ♘cd7 15.a4 ♕c4 16.♕d2

Good enough. But considering White's tremendous positional advantage, there's no need for combinations. The simple 16.♖b1, followed by ♕d2 and ♖fc1 would win with less effort.

16...♕×b4

In a position like this, you can eat anything!

17.♗×a7+ ♔a8 18.♖fb1 ♕a5 19.♗e3 ♘c5 20.♖b5 ♕c7 21.a5 ♘fd7

Black resisted with relative success in the first round, but since White can attack the opponent's King with all seven of his pieces, while Black's King's wing remains undeveloped and his Bishop has long since forgotten that he can move, White's victory is only a matter of time.

22.♘c1 ♖c8 23.♘b3 ♘a6

If 23...♘×b3, then 24.a6! forcing 24...b6 (24...♘×d2 or 24...♘×a1 25.e×b7 leads to forced mate).

24.♘a4 ♗e7

Black decides to give up quality, realizing that if 24...♔b8 White with 25.♗c1 ♕d8 26.♗c6 would make a decisive attack.

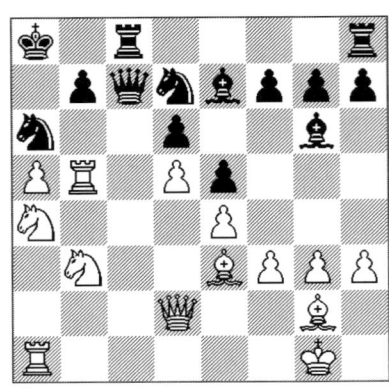

25.♘b6+

The crisis. After 25...♘×b6 26.a×b6 ♕ad lib. 27.♗×a6+ would win immediately.

25...♔b8 26.♖c1 ♘dc5 27.♘×c5 d×c5 28.♘×c8 ♖×c8 29.♗f1 ♕d7 30.♖b6 c4

Or 30...♗d8 31.♖b2, winning the pawn in the same way.

31.♖×c4 ♖×c4 32.♗×c4 ♕×h3 33.♕g2

Technically simpler than 33.♗×a6, which would also win.

33...♕×g2+ 34.♔×g2 ♗d8 35.♖b2 ♔c8 36.♗×a6 b×a6 37.♖b6 ♗g5 38.♖c2+ ♔b7 39.d6 f5 40.d7, and Black resigned.

Game 3
A.Alekhine - E.Colle
Paris Tormament, February 1925
Tchigorin Defense [D07]

1.d4 d5 2.c4 ♘c6 3.♘f3 ♗g4 4.♕a4

A new move that I've introduced here to avoid the usual variations derived from 4.c×d5 ♗×f3. I had reason to do so, since the former Belgian champion was an excellent player of this defense and achieved a large number of notable successes with it.

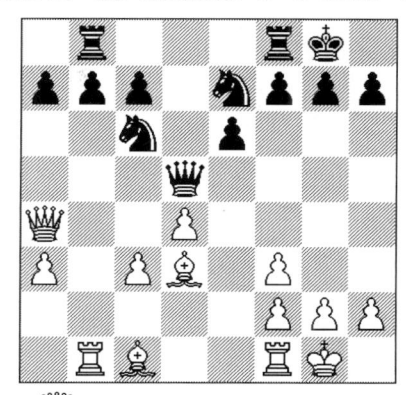

4...♗×f3 5.e×f3 e6

After 5...d×c4 White can play either 6.♗e3 or, even better, sacrifice a pawn for a big advantage in development by continuing with 6.♘c3 ♕×d4 7.♗e3 followed by ♗×c4.

6.♘c3 ♗b4 7.a3

It's worth taking the time to be immediately informed of the Bishop of Black's intentions.

7...♗×c3+ 8.b×c3 ♘ge7 9.♖b1 ♖b8 10.c×d5

In the Baden-Baden International Tournament, which was played shortly after the Paris Tournament, I played 10.♗d3 against the same opponent and obtained a more convincing positional advantage. I'm reproducing that game here because, in addition to White's more precise opening, it has a very instructive queen and rook ending, which probably prompted Dr. Lasker to select it among the few he included in his classic book "*Manual of Chess*". This was the sequence of that game: 10.♗d3 d×c4 11.♗×c4 0–0 12.0–0 ♘d5 13.♕c2 ♘ce7 14.♗d3 h6 15.c4 ♘b6 16.♖d1 ♘bc8 17.f4 b6 18.♗b2 c6 19.♕e2 ♘d6 20.♕e5 ♘e8 21.a4 ♖b7 22.♖e1 ♘f6 23.♖bd1 ♖d7 24.♗c2 a6 25.♕e2 ♕b8 26.d5 c×d5 27.♗×f6 g×f6 28.♕g4+ ♔h8 29.♕h4 ♔g7 30.♕g4+ ♔h8 31.♕h4 ♔g7 32.♕g4+ ♔h8 33.f5 ♘×f5 34.♗×f5 e×f5 35.♕×f5 ♕d8 36.c×d5 ♖d6 37.♕f4 ♔h7 38.♕e4+ ♔h8 39.♕e3 ♔g7 40.♕d3 a5 41.♖e3 ♖g8 42.♖h3 ♕d7 43.♕e3 f5 44.♖g3+ ♔h7 45.♖×g8 ♔×g8 46.♕g3+ ♔h7 47.♕b3 ♔g7 48.h3 ♕d8 49.♕g3+ ♔h7 50.♕e5 ♕d7 51.♖d3 f6 52.♕d4 ♕d8 53.♕c4 ♕d7 54.♖d4 ♔g7 55.♕d3 ♔f7 56.g4 ♔f8 57.g×f5 ♕e8 58.♖e4 ♕h5 59.♖g4 ♕f7 60.♕e3 ♕h7 61.♖g6, and Black resigned.

10...♕×d5 11.♗d3 0–0 12.0–0

12...♕d6!

A beautiful positional move, freeing up the d5 square for the knight and preventing White's ♗f4 move.

13.♕c2 ♘g6 14.f4 ♘ce7

Preparing central actions, starting with ...c5.

15.g3 ♖fd8 16.♖d1 b6 17.a4

This move weakens the b4 square and thus allows Black to gain some initiative in the center. 17.♗b2 would be correct, and if 17...c5 then 18.c4! c×d4 19.♗×d4 with some advantage, because if 19...♕×d4 20.♗×g6 (but not 19...♕×a3 20.♖a1 ♕b4 21.♖a4 ♕d6 22.♗e4! favoring White).

17...♘d5! 18.♗d2 c5 19.f5

Trying to maintain even a slight pressure. The variant 19.c4 ♘b4 20.♗×b4 c×b4 21.c5 b×c5 22.d×c5 ♕c7 would offer even less prospects of victory.

19...e×f5 20.♗×f5 c×d4 21.c×d4 ♘de7 22.♗b4 ♕f6 23.♗×e7

After 23.♗h3 ♘d5! the pair of Bishops would be of little use. So White tries to gain the advantage with his passed pawn in coordination with the open c-file.

23...♕xe7 24.♖bc1

The immediate consequence of 24.d5 would be to increase the prospect of a draw for Black with 24...b5!

24...♖d5 25.♗e4 ♖d7 26.d5 ♕f6 27.♖e1

The opening move of a well-hidden maté net.

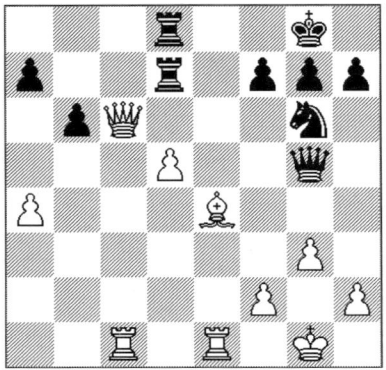

27...♖bd8 28.♕c6! ♕g5

Black is right to avoid exchanging queens with either 28...♕xc6 29.dxc6 or 28...♘e7 29.♕xf6 gxf6 and the move 30.d6 is decisive in White's favor. But oddly enough, the g5 square for the queen - which seems very natural - will prove fatal. The correct move would be 28...♕d4 after which there would still be nothing decisive for White.

29.♗xg6 hxg6

As the answer will show, it would be necessary to 29...fxg6 (of course not 29...♕xg6 30.♕xd7) 30.♕e6+ ♖f7 31.♖c8 ♖xc8 32.♕xc8+ ♖f8, after which White would have the pleasant choice between 33.♖e8 ♕f6 34.♖xf8+ ♕xf8 35.♕c6 or 33.♕c3; 33.♕e6+ ♔h8 34.d6 ♕d2 35.♖e2 ♕c1+ 36.♔g2 ♕c6+ 37.♔h3, with a winning position in both cases.

See the next Diagram

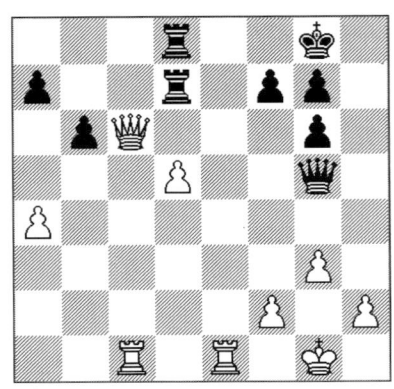

30.♕xd7!

This queen sacrifice was only possible because black's queen was on g5 and thus didn't allow black's king to escape from the doubled rooks on the eighth rank.

30...♔xd7 31.♖e8+ ♔h7 32.♖cc8 ♖d8 33.♖exd8, and Black resigned.

> **Game 4**
> **A.Alekhine - K. Opocensky**
> *Paris Tormament, February 1925*
> Slav Defense [D10]

1.d4 d5 2.c4 c6 3.♘c3

My second game against Dr. Euwe, in which the apparently promising response 3...dxc4 was convincingly refuted, proved that the text move is at least as good as the elegant 3.♘f3.

3...♘f6 4.e3 ♗f5 5.cxd5 ♘xd5

If 5...cxd5, then of course 6.♕b3 with advantage.

6.♗c4 e6 7.♘ge2

Played by Rubinstein against Bogoljubov in Hastings 1922, creating several difficulties for Black due to the inactive position of his queen bishop and not being able to return to the queen wing.

7...♘d7 8.e4 ♘xc3 9.♘xc3 ♗g6 10.0-0 ♕h4

After the more natural 10...♗b4

White would maintain his positional advantage with 11.f3. The queen move prepares the grand castling and at the same time guarantees the h5 square for the bishop, in case White plays f4 and f5.

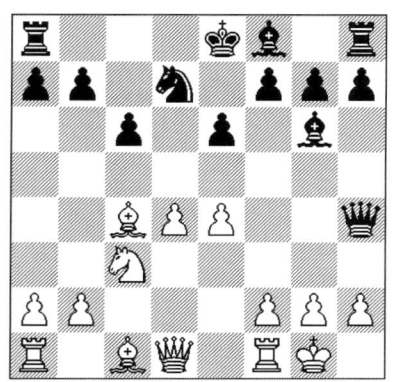

11.d5!

This central move was based on precise calculation, as Black would now force White to play the weakening g3. But in practice White had no other way of seizing the initiative - after 11.f3 0–0–0 Black's queen prospects would be excellent.

11...e×d5 12.g3 ♕f6 13.e×d5 ♗c5?

Black's first and already decisive mistake. Now they lose the possibility of castling and in the end succumb to their inability to coordinate the rooks' action. It would be necessary to first 13...♘e5 and only after 14.♗e2, ♗c5; in the case of 15.♔g2 renewing the threat f4 etc., then 15...h5! practically forcing the reply 16.h4 followed by ♗g5 etc. The position in this case would remain full of dynamite, but that doesn't mean no hope for Black.

14.♖e1+ ♔f8 15.♗f4 ♘b6 16.♗b3 h5 17.h4

From move 14 onwards, White has only one goal: to prevent Black's rooks from cooperating.

17...♔g8 18.♖c1 ♗d4 19.d×c6

After this move, White has no way to avoid exchanging one of his Bishops for the Knight.

19...b×c6 20.♘e4 ♗×e4 21.♖×e4 c5

Or 21...♗×b2 22.♖c5! ♘d5 23.♗×d5 c×d5 24.♖×d5 with a decisive advantage.

22.♕e2

Starting the final attack against the f7 square.

22...g6 23.♗g5 ♕d6

Attacking the g3 house.

24.♕f3 ♕f8

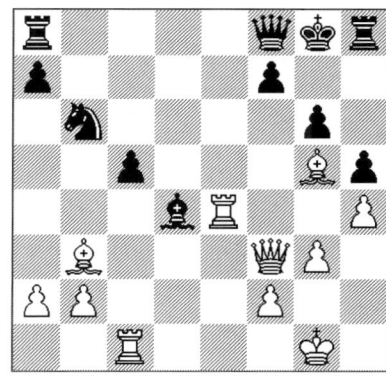

25.♖×d4!

Eliminating the only active enemy piece and thus breaking all resistance in practice.

25...c×d4 26.♖c6! ♔h7

After 26...♔g7 White could sacrifice another rook: 27.♗×g6+! ♔×g6 (or 27...f×g6 28.♕b7+ followed by mate) 28.♕f6+ ♔h7 29.♗×f7 ♔g8 30.♕f5+ ♔g7 31.♕g6+ ♔h8 32.♗f6+ and mate on the next move.

27.♗×f7 ♔c8 28.♖×g6, and Black resigned.

Game 5
S.Tarrasch-A.Alekhine
Baden-Baden Tormament, 1925
Giuoco Piano [C53]

1.e4 e5 2.♘f3 ♘c6 3.♗c4 ♗c5 4.c3 ♗b6 5.d4 ♕e7 6.0-0 ♘f6!

This move created by me instead of the usual 6...d6 leaves White little choice, since his e5 pawn is attacked.

7.♖e1 d6 8.a4 a6 9.h3

A necessary preparation for ♗e3.

9...0-0 10.♗g5

White has no advantage in provoking Black's next move and would do better to play 10.♗e3 directly.

10...h6 11.♗e3

If 11.♗h4, then of course 11...♔h8 followed by ...♔g8 and ...g5.

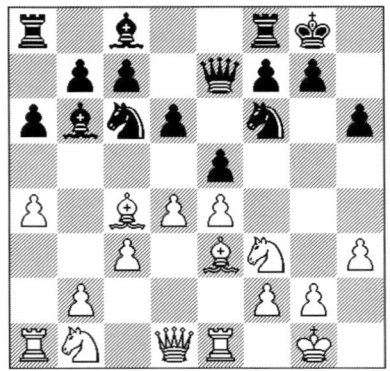

11...♕d8!

This paradoxical move - the most difficult in the game - is very effective. The double idea of preparing a central action with ...exd4 followed by ...d5 at the same time frees up the column for the Rook's action.

12.♗d3 ♖e8 13.♘bd2 ♗a7!

Played in view of White's possible ♘c4.

14.♕c2 exd4

At the right moment, Black can't take the Pawn because of ...♘b4.

15.♘xd4 ♘e5 16.♗f1 d5!

After this move Black becomes strong in the opponent's center. The tactical justification for this move is shown by the variant 17.f4 ♘g6 18.e5 ♘h5! etc.

17.♖ad1 c5 18.♘4b3 ♕c7 19.♗f4

Also after 19.exd5 ♘xd5 20.♘c4 ♘xc4 21.♗xc4 ♘xe3 22.♖xe3 ♖xe3 23.fxe3 ♕e7 Black would maintain somewhat better prospects.

19...♘f3+! 20.♘xf3 ♕xf4 21.exd5?

The decisive blunder, after which the game ends quickly. Instead I waited for 21.e5 and hoped that after 21...♗f5 22.♕d2 ♕xd2 23.♖xd2 ♘e4 24.♖de2 (24.♖xd5 ♗e6 25.♖ed1) 24...♖ad8 I could exploit the advantage of the bishop pair.

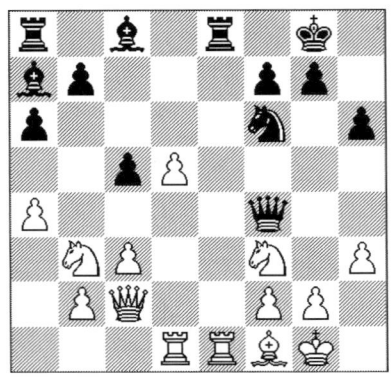

21...♗f5!

An important intermediate move, after which there is no longer enough defense. It would be much less convincing 21...♗xh3 due to 22.gxh3 ♕xf3 23.♗g2, etc.

22.♗d3

Or 22.♕d2 ♕xa4 23.♘c1 ♗c2! 24.♖xe8+ ♖xe8 25.♖e1 ♘e4 26.♕f4 c4 27.♘d4 ♗xd4 28.cxd4 ♕b4 with a decisive advantage for Black.

22...♗xh3

But not 22...♗xd3 23.♕xd3 c4 because of 24.♕d2.

23.gxh3 ♕xf3 24.♖xe8+

After the intermediate 24.♗f1 and Black's exchange of the rooks, White would of course lose his last hope - the passed pawn. But after the game move Black finishes with a mate attack.

24...♖xe8 25.♗f1 ♖e5 26.c4

The move 26.d6 obviously wouldn't change things.

26...♖g5+ 27.♔h2 ♘g4+ 28.h×g4 ♖×g4

With the threat of mate inevitable. The whites abandoned.

Game 6
R.Réti-A.Alekhine
Baden-Baden Tormament, 1925
King's Fiancheto [A00]

1.g3 e5 2.♘f3

An experience that Réti never repeated after that game. White intended to play the Alekhine Defense with the colors reversed, i.e., with an extra tempo. But the way they used this time (g3) became their disadvantage (see next comment).

2...e4 3.♘d4 d5

Black is satisfied with the free development of his pieces and the prospects of the middlegame. But they could achieve more by playing 3...c5! 4.♘b3 c4 5.♘d4 ♗c5 6.c3 ♘c6 having *ad absurdum* a development as if it were White.

4.d3 e×d3 5.♕×d3 ♘f6 6.♗g2 ♗b4+

Trying to get all the pieces into the game as quickly as possible. But nowadays I'd probably think more about the safety of the black squares in my position and thus avoid the exchange of bishops that followed.

7.♗d2 ♗×d2+ 8.♘×d2 0-0 9.c4!

With the exception of his eccentric first move, Réti plays the opening very well. Black would have no advantage with 9...c5 due to 10.♘2b3, threatening both 11.♘×c5 and 11.c×d5.

9...♘a6

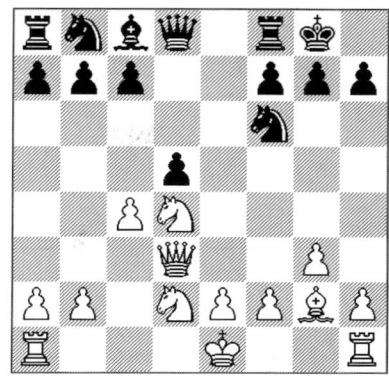

Relatively the best. But you can't deny that the whites have now gained a kind of pressure on the semi-open c-column.

10.c×d5 ♘b4 11.♕c4 ♘b×d5 12.♘2b3 c6 13.0-0 ♖e8 14.♖fd1 ♗g4 15.♖d2

After 15.h3 Black would bring his bishop to e4 via ...h5 and ...g6.

15...♕c8 16.♘c5 ♗h3! 17.♗f3

Through his previous move, Black offered a pawn, which if accepted could be fatal for White, for example: 17.♗×h3 ♕×h3 18.♘×b7 ♘g4 19.♘f3 ♘de3! 20.f×e3 ♘×e3 21.♕×f7+ ♔h8 22.♘h4 ♔f8, winning.

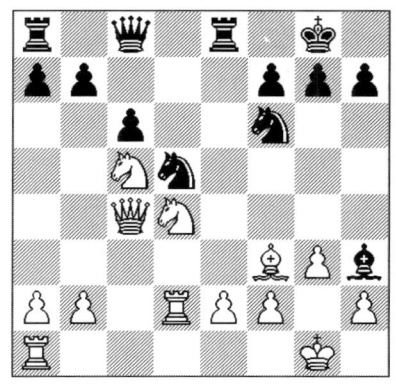

17...♗g4

Giving the opponent the choice between three possibilities: (1) to exchange his beloved bishop from the fianchetto; (2) to immediately accept a draw by repetition of moves - 18.♗g2 ♗h3 19.♗f3 etc. - which at this early stage of the game always means a moral defeat for White, and (3) placing the Bishop on a worse square (h1). Réti finally decides to play for a win and thus allows Black to launch a very interesting counter-attack.

18.♗g2 ♗h3 19.♗f3 ♗g4 20.♗h1

Finally!

20...h5!

To weaken White's g3 square by exchanging this pawn.

21.b4 a6 22.♖c1 h4 23.a4 h×g3 24.h×g3 ♕c7 25.b5

Consequential, but very risky to say the least. By playing 25.e3 ♘b6 26.♕b3 ♕b8 27.♕c2 White would face direct threats to his king, but the obstruction of the bishops' diagonal would at the same time be the end of his hopes on the other wing.

25...a×b5 26.a×b5

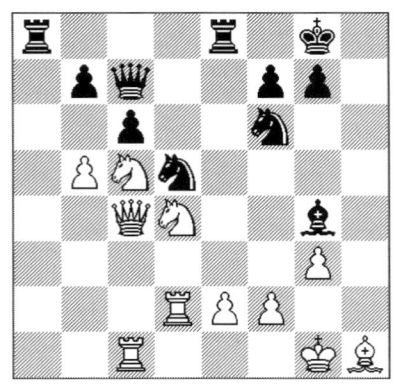

26...♖e3!

It seems almost unbelievable that this spectacular move should not only stop White's attack, but also cause them serious problems. And so it is! It's obvious that the Rook can't be taken due to 27...♕×g3+ followed by 28...♘×e3 winning. And also that White needs to do something to prevent 27...♕×g3+! etc.

27.♘f3

As the sequence will show, this natural move loses forcibly. Also insufficient would be 27.♔h2 due to 27...♖aa3 28.♘cb3 (not 28.f×e3 ♘×e3 followed by ...♘f1+ etc.) 28...♕e5! 29.b×c6 b×c6 with powerful attack, as 30.f×e3 would be bad due to 30...♕h5+ followed by 31...♖h3. The only chance of salvation would be 27.♗f3! ♗×f3 28.e×f3! c×b5 29.♘×b5 ♕a5! still with an advantage for Black, as 30.♔×d5 would lose immediately: 30...♖e1+ 31.♖×e1 ♕×e1+ followed by ...♖a1.

27...c×b5 28.♕×b5 ♘c3 29.♕×b7

After 29.♕c4 the reply 29...b5! would be decisive.

29...♕×b7

And not 29...♘×e2+ due to 30.♔×e2! ♕×b7 31.♖×e3! with some chances of salvation for White.

30.♘×b7 ♘×e2+ 31.♔h2

Or 31.♔f1 ♘g3+ 32.f×g3 ♗×f3 33.♗×f3 ♖×f3+ 34.♔g2 ♖aa3 35.♖d8+ ♔h7 36.♖h1+ ♔g6 37.♖h3 ♖fb3! winning.

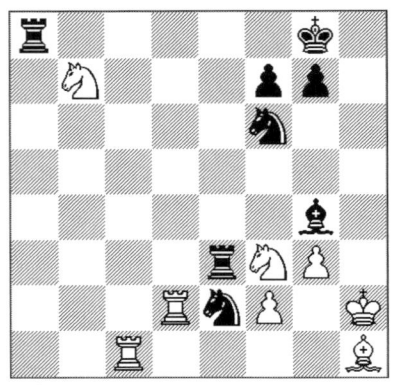

31...♘e4!

The start of a new combination - which, however, is the logical consequence of the previous maneuvers -

with the aim, after a series of twelve practically forced moves, of capturing the exposed white knight on b7. The capture of Black's Rook is still taboo because if 32.f×e3 White would lose quality with 32...♘×d2.

32.♖c4!

Relatively the best defense.

32...♘×f2

It would be insufficient 32...♘×d2 due to 33.♘×d2! or 32...♗×f3 due to 33.♔×e4! The situation is still very complicated.

33.♗g2 ♗e6!

One of the important moves of the game.

34.♖cc2

Here and in the sequence, as you can easily see, white has no chance.

34...♘g4+ 35.♔h3

But not 35.♔h1, due to 35...♖a1+.

35...♘e5+ 36.♔h2 ♖×f3 37.♖×e2 ♘g4+ 38.♔h3 ♘e3+ 39.♔h2 ♘×c2 40.♗×f3 ♘d4

And now if 41.♖e3 (or f2) then 41...♘×f3+ 42.♔×f3 ♗d5! (the final point!) winning a piece. White resigned.

I consider this and the game against Bogoljubov in Hastings 1922 (cf. the book *"My Best Games 1908-1923"*) to be the most brilliant tournament games of my chess career. And by a peculiar coincidence, neither of them won the beauty prize in any of those tournaments!

Game 7
A.Alekhine-K.Treybal
Baden-Baden Tormament, 1925
Orthodox Defense [D67]

1.c4 e6 2.d4 d5 3.♘c3 ♘f6 4.♗g5 ♘bd7 5.e3 ♗e7 6.♘f3 0-0 7.♖c1 c6 8.♗d3 d×c4 9.♗×c4 ♘d5 10.♗×e7 ♕×e7 11.♘e4

A very safe but harmless move, which I had a predilection for during a certain period of my career, including the game with Capablanca. Now I've concluded that the good old 11.0-0, although not extremely promising, still offers more fighting chances than the knight move.

11...♘7f6

After this response, however, Black will find it difficult to free up his game with ...e5 or ...c5 and so White's position will soon be preferable. Good methods of achieving equality would be 11...♘5f6 and after 12.♘g3 either 12...♕b4+ (Capablanca) or even 12...e5 (Dr. Lasker).

12.♘g3 ♕b4+ 13.♕d2 ♕×d2+ 14.♔×d2 ♖d8 15.♖hd1 ♗d7 16.♘e5 ♗e8 17.♔e2 ♔f8 18.f4 g6

It's rarely advisable in an endgame to place the pawns on squares the color of your own bishop. A more logical plan would be 18...♘d7, possibly followed by 3...f6.

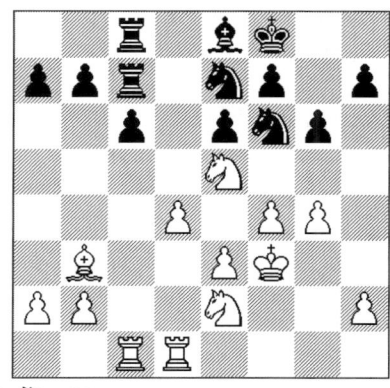

19.♔f3 ♖ac8 20.♗b3 ♖c7 21.♘e2 ♘e7 22.g4 ♖dc8

23.♘g3!

After this move, Black's preparation for ...f5 becomes useless, as it would have fatal consequences after 24.g5, for example: (I) 23...c5 24.g5 ♘fd5

25.dxc5 ♖xc5 26.♖xc5 ♖xc5 27.♘e4 ♔c7 28.♘d6 with an extremely advantageous position for White; (II) 24...♘d7 25.♘xd7+ ♗xd7 26.♖xc5 ♖xc5 27.dxc5 ♔e8 28.♔f2, and White would keep the advantage pawn.

23...♘fd5

With such a passive move, Black allows White the effective maneuvers of the following Knights.

24.♘e4 ♖d8

After 24...f6 White would exchange two minor pieces for a Rook and two Pawns, thus obtaining a winning position. For example: 25.♘c5! fxe5 26.♘xe6+ ♔g8 27.♘xc7 e4+ (otherwise 28.e4) 28.♔xe4 ♔xc7 29.♔f3, followed by e5, with a decisive advantage.

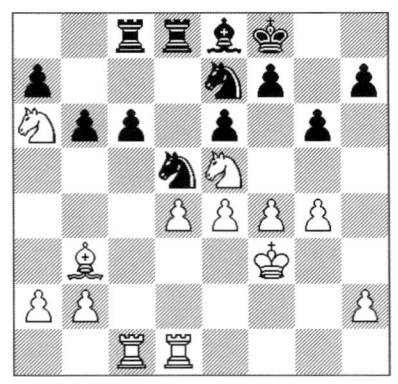

25.♘c5 b6 26.♘a6 ♖cc8 27.e4

27...f6

A desperate attempt to get some freedom for his pieces. After 27...♘f6 (or 27...♘c7 28.♘xc7 followed by d5 with a decisive advantage) 28.g5 ♘d7 29.♘g4 ♔g7 30.h4 Black would quickly die of suffocation.

28.exd5 fxe5 29.d6!

Forcing decisive material gain. If now 29...e4+, then 30.♔xe4 ♔xd6 31.♔e5! ♔cd8 32.♘c7, winning.

29...♖xd6 30.fxe5 ♖d5

If 30...♖dd8 31.♗xe6 would still leave us with no hope.

31.♗xd5 ♘xd5 32.a3

The start of a very instructive technical section. From now on White will force the exchange of the opponent's central knight.

32...g5 33.♘b4 ♘e7 34.♘d3 ♘d5 35.h4! gxh4

If 35...h6, then 36.hxg5 followed by ♘f2–e4 (or a3) etc.

36.♘f4 ♘xf4 37.♔xf4

White's next move will be to eliminate the h4 Pawn and return the King to the center to free the Rook from the protection of the d4 Pawn.

37...♖d8 38.♔g5 ♔g7 39.♔xh4 ♖d5 40.♔g5 ♖d8 41.♔f4 ♖d7 42.♔e3 ♖b7 43.b4

The start of the third phase: fixing Black's weak points.

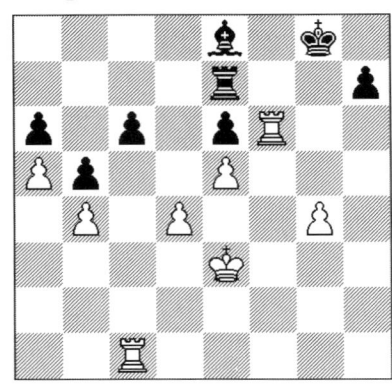

43...a6 44.♖f1 ♖a7 45.♖f6 ♖e7 46.a4 ♔g8 47.a5 b5

48.d5!

This sacrifice of the Pawn to allow the King to enter the opponent's rearguard victoriously is the logical conclusion of the whole procedure.

48...exd5

Or 48...cxd5 49.♖c8, followed by ♖a8, etc.

49.e6 ♔g7 50.g5 h5 51.♔d4 ♖c7 52.♔c5 ♖c8 53.♔b6 d4 54.e7!, and

Black resigned.

Although this game and the next one doesn't have any exciting points, I've decided to include them in this selection, as they convincingly illustrate the methods to be followed to exploit a space advantage gained in the opening stage.

> **Game 8**
> **G.Thomas-A.Alekhine**
> *Baden-Baden Tornament, 1925*
> Alekhine Defense [D67]

1.e4 ♘f6 2.d3

A very harmless sequel that doesn't promise any advantages in the opening.

2...c5 3.f4 ♘c6 4.♘f3 g6 5.♗e2 ♗g7 6.♘bd2?

After this apparently unnatural move, White's game is very restricted. It would be a lesser evil to play 6.c4, conceding the d4 square, but avoiding the double advance of Black's c5 pawn.

6...d5 7.0–0 0–0 8.♔h1 b6 9.e×d5 ♕×d5

Even better than 9...♘×d5, which allows the answer 10.♘e4.

10.♕e1

The pawn sacrifice through 10.♘e5 would prove insufficient after 10...♘×e5 11.f×e5 ♕×e5 12.♘c4 (or 12.♗f3 ♔b8 13.♘c4 ♕c7) 12...♕e6! 13.♗f3 ♘d5, etc.

10...♗b7 11.♘c4 ♘d4 12.♘e3 ♕c6 13.♗d1

See the next diagram

13...♘d5!

Practically forcing the exchange of three minor pieces, thus increasing the positional advantage already gained

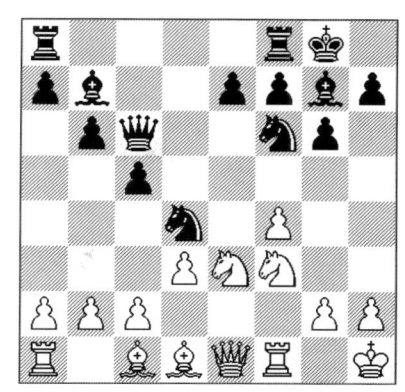

through the simplification method. I adopted a similar procedure in my game against A. Evenssohn (see *"My Best Games 1908 - 1923"*).

14.♘×d4

The consequences of trying to win a pawn with 14.♘×d5 would be sad: 14...♕×d5 15.♕×e7 ♖fe8 16.♕g5 ♘×f3 17.♗×f3 ♕×g5 18.f×g5 ♗×f3 19.g×f3 ♖e2 with a decisive advantage.

14...c×d4 15.♘×d5 ♕×d5 16.♗f3 ♕d7 17.♗×b7 ♕×b7 18.c4

Otherwise, the horrible weakness in c2 would remain.

18...d×c3 19.b×c3 ♖ac8 20.♗b2

20.♗d2 would be slightly better.

20...♖fd8 21.♖f3 ♗f6

Freeing the queen from the tedious defense of e7.

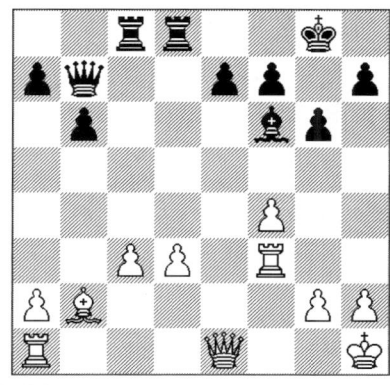

22.d4

The positional capitulation, after which Black will have a relatively easy game to win, as he has control of the white squares. With the threat of ...♕a6 combined with the doubled rooks on the d-file, White no longer has any real chances.

22...♕d5 23.♕e3 ♕b5! 24.♕d2 ♖d5 25.h3 e6 26.♖e1 ♕a4 27.♖a1 b5 28.♕d1 ♖c4

It would of course also be nice to have 28...♕xd1, but Black is in no hurry. The opponent won't be able to avoid the exchange.

29.♕b3 ♖d6 30.♔h2 ♖a6 31.♖ff1 ♗e7 32.♔h1 ♖cc6

With the aim of forcing White to exchange queens after ...♕c4 followed by ...♖a5 and ...♔c6.

33.♖fe1 ♗h4!

Hunting the Rook in column e. Because if for example 34.♖e2 then 34...♕xb3! 35.axb3 ♖xa1+ 36.♗xa1 ♖a6 37.♗b2 ♖a2 38.b4 (38.♔h2 a5) 38...♗g3 39.d5 ♗xf4 (or 39...exd5 40.c4!) etc., winning easily.

34.♖f1 ♕c4 35.♕xc4

Otherwise, Black would play, as already mentioned, 35...♖a4 etc.

35...♖xc4 36.a3 ♗e7 37.♖fb1 ♗d6!

Forcing the g2 pawn onto a black square.

38.g3 ♔f8 39.♔g2 ♔e7 40.♔f2 ♔d7 41.♔e2 ♔c6

After protecting his b-pawn, Black threatens ...♖ca4.

42.♖a2 ♖ca4 43.♖ba1 ♔d5 44.♔d3 ♖6a5 45.♗c1 a6 46.♗b2 h5

Threatening, of course, 47...h4.

47.h4 f6

After this move White has no defense against ...e5 etc.

48.♗c1 e5 49.fxe5 fxe5 50.♗b2

Or 50.dxe5 ♗xe5 51.♗f4 ♗xf4 52.gxf4 ♔e6! (the simplest), winning.

50...exd4 51.cxd4 b4!, and White resigned.

Later Nimzovitsch, who was always reluctant to comment on his colleagues' games, distinguished this game by including it as an example in his famous book *"My System"*.

Game 9
A.Alekhine-F.Marshall
Baden-Baden Tormament, 1925
Irregular Defense [D00]

1.d4 ♘f6 2.c4 d5

This move is very rarely adopted in games between Masters and in fact shouldn't be recommended. However, it was relatively successful in this game, thanks to the not very precise opening played by White.

3.cxd5 ♘xd5 4.e4

As this advance cannot be prevented by Black, it should only be made after the development of the pieces on the King's wing. A good plan here would be 4.g3 followed by ♗g2, leaving e4 for a more favorable moment.

4...♘f6 5.♗d3

Also after 5.♘c3 Black would get the same with 5...e5.

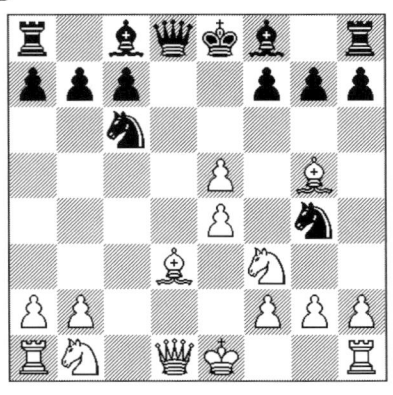

5...e5! 6.dxe5 ♘g4 7.♘f3 ♘c6 8.♗g5!

White imagines that he can't gain any kind of advantage by trying to keep the extra pawn. If, for example, 8.♗f4 then 8...♘b4 9.♗b5+ ♗d7 10.♗xd7+ ♕xd7 11.♕xd7+ ♔xd7 12.0-0 ♘c2 13.♖d1+ ♔c8 14.h3 (or 14.♘g5 ♘h6) 14...♘h6 and White's positional advantage doesn't compensate for the loss of quality.

8...♗e7 9.♗xe7 ♕xe7 10.♘c3 ♘cxe5 11.♘xe5 ♕xe5

But here Black has overestimated his position. Instead of the game move - which according to the evidence below only exposes his queen to the pawns' attack - they could get a game with better prospects through 11...♘xe5 12.0-0 0-0 13.♗e2 ♗e6 etc.

12.h3 ♘f6 13.♕d2!

It's certainly surprising how a simple maneuver with the queen - by which White strengthens the black squares in his position - increases his chances in the middlegame. From now on Black will gradually be dragged into a losing position without being able to make a move that could really be considered a blunder.

13...♗d7

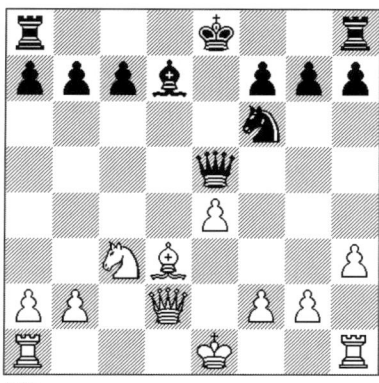

14.♕e3!

Not only by controlling the d4 and c5 squares, but above all by avoiding Black's big castling.

14...♗c6 15.0-0-0 0-0

As Black can't safely bring his King to the queen's wing (if 15...♕h5 then 16.♗c4) in practice they have no choice.

16.f4 ♕e6

After 16...♕a5 17.e5 Black would lose (just as played in the game) a Pawn if he continued with 17...♘d5 18.♘xd5 ♗xd5 19.♗xh7+, followed by ♕xd3+ and ♕xd5.

17.e5

With the main threat 18.f5.

17...♖fe8 18.♖he1 ♖ad8

It would be better 18...♘d7, after which White would continue the attack with g4, etc. The Rook move allows Black to win through a forced sequence of moves.

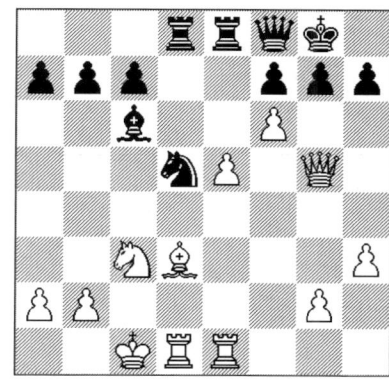

19.f5 ♕e7 20.♕g5 ♘d5 21.f6 ♕f8

22.♗c4!

The action of this Bishop on the a2–g8 diagonal is immediately decisive. It's important to note that Black doesn't have the intermediate move 22...h6 here due to 23.fxg7 winning a piece.

22...♘xc3 23.♖xd8 ♖xd8 24.fxg7!

Much more convincing than 24.e6 ♖d5!

24...♘xa2+

Or 24...♕e8 25.♗×f7+! ♔×f7 26.♕f1+ ♔e6 27.♕f6+ ♔d5 28.♕f8, winning.
25.♔b1!
Not 25.♗×a2 ♕c5+.
25...♕e8 26.e6!
Stronger now than 26.♗×f7+.
26...♗e4+ 27.♔a1
It would also be possible 27.♖×e4 ♖d1+ 28.♔c2 ♕a4+ 29.b3 ♘b4+ 30.♔×d1 etc., but the game move is simpler.
27...f5
Desperation. He would also lose 27...f×e6 28.♗×e6+ ♕×e6 29.♕×d8+ ♔×g7 30.♕d4+, followed by 31.♕×e4.
28.e7+ ♖d5 29.♕f6 ♕f7 30.e8♕+, followed by mate in two moves. Black resigned.

Game 10
J.Davidson-A.Alekhine
Semmering Tormament, 1926
Slav Defense [D46]

1.d4 d5 2.♘f3 ♘f6 3.c4 c6 4.e3 e6
The trendy moves these days is 4...♗f5, like the so-called Merano system initiated by the text move, which is considered very favorable for White.
5.♘c3 ♘bd7 6.♕c2
The natural and best move is 6.♗d3. But at the time the system mentioned had not yet been worked out in detail.
6...♗d6 7.♗d3 0-0 8.0-0 ♕e7 9.e4 d×c4 10.♗×c4 e5

See the next Diagram

Black thus obtained a position like the one Tchigorin considered perfectly playable, but with the considerable advantage that his queen already occupies the natural development square e7, while Black's queen is positioned on c2, a not particularly good square.
11.♖d1 e×d4 12.♘×d4 ♘b6!
Better than 12...♘e5 13.♗f1 ♘g6 14.♘f5 ♗×f5 15.e×f5 ♘e5 16.♗g5 with good play for White.
13.♗f1 ♖d8
Threatening 14...♗×h2+ 15.♔×h2 ♔×d4 16.♔×d4 ♕e5+ etc and thus inducing White to weaken his king's position.
14.h3 ♗c7
Threatening to win a piece through 15...♘×d4 followed by 16...♕e5.
15.♗e3 ♖e8!
Black's previous move attacked the Bishop on e3 and this forced the other Bishop to move to the third rank. As we'll see, both Bishops are now poorly positioned or obstructing the action of some other piece and can still be attacked by the enemy Knights.
16.♗d3 ♘h5 17.♘ce2 g6
Mainly to prepare the move ...♘g7 to protect the f5 square.
18.♖e1 ♘d7 19.♘f3
After this retreat Black gets a definitive push. Here I expected 19.f4 ♘df6 20.e5 ♘d5 21.♗d2 ♗b6, after which, although Black's game was still preferable, White wouldn't run out of fighting chances.
19...♗b6!

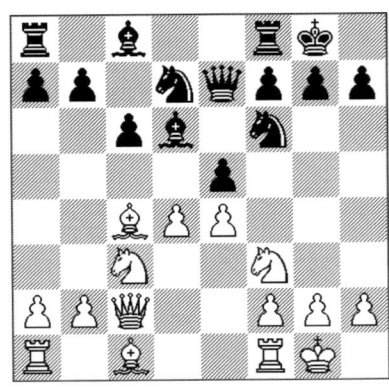

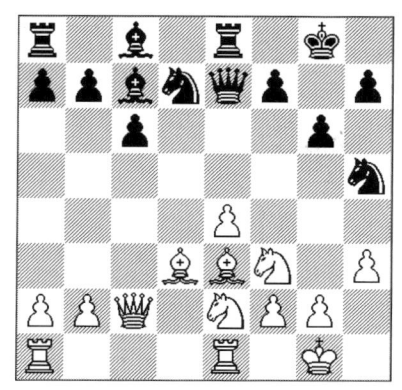

Hoping to increase the positional advantage already gained after 20.♗×b6 a×b6, opening up the a-file for the Rook's action. To avoid this unpleasant variant, White tries with his next two moves to complicate things, but all he achieves is the acceleration of his catastrophe.

20.♗g5 ♕c5!

If now 21.♕×c5 ♘×c5 22.♘c1 (forced), then 22...f6 23.♗d2 ♘×d3 24.♘×d3 ♘g3 25.e5 ♗f5 with winning positional advantage.

21.♘c3 ♘e5!

Forcing the exchange afterwards and thus renewing the attack on the b2–g7 diagonal that will prove decisive.

22.♘×e5 ♕×e5 23.♗e3 ♗c7 24.♘e2

Also 24.g3 ♗×h3 would lead to defeat in the long run.

24...♕h2+ 25.♔f1

See the next Diagram

25...♗×h3!

This combination with sacrifice isn't particularly complicated or unusual. But its value increases considerably since it is the logical conclusion of the previous positional game.

26.g×h3 ♕×h3+ 27.♔g1 ♗h2+ 28.♔h1 ♘f4!

Undoubtedly the shortest route to victory.

29.♘×f4

If 29.♗×f4, then 29...♗g3+ with mate in two moves.

29...♗×f4+ 30.♔g1 ♗h2+ 31.♔h1 ♕f3+!

The culmination of the whole combination, which forces the exchange of the queen for the rook and bishop.

32.♗×h2 ♖e5 33.♕c5

Only one move.

33...♖×c5 34.♗×c5 ♕h5+ 35.♔g2 ♕×c5

The rest is simply a matter of routine.

36.♖e3 ♖e8 37.♖ae1 ♕e5 38.♖1e2 ♖e6 39.b3 ♖f6 40.♖g3 ♔g7 41.♗b1 ♖f4 42.♗d3 ♖h4 43.♔f3 ♕f4+ 44.♔g2 ♕c1 45.♔f3 h5 46.♖c2 ♕d1+ 47.♔e3 ♖h1 48.♔d4 h4 49.♖e3 ♖e1 50.♖×e1 ♕×e1 51.♖e2 ♕a1+ 52.♔c4 b5+, and White resigned.

Game 11
A.Rubinstein-A.Alekhine
Semmering Tornament, 1926
Queen's Indian Defense [E16]
Beauty Award

1.d4 ♘f6 2.c4 e6 3.♘f3 b6 4.g3 ♗b7 5.♗g2 ♗b4+

This simplification is hardly advisable, as White's queen bishop could develop less in the future than Black's king bishop. This promises another 5...♗e7.

6.♘bd2

For the reasons mentioned, 6.♗d2 seems the most logical answer.

6...0–0 7.0–0 d5

As we'll see next, this is even good for equalizing. Also, good would-be 7...♖e8, followed by ...♗f8.

8.a3 ♗e7 9.b4 c5

The correct way to maintain central balance. It would be unsatisfactory for positional sense 9...a4 10.b5.

10.b×c5 b×c5 11.d×c5

It would also be satisfactory for Black 11.♖b1 ♕c8 12.♕b3 ♗a6.

11...♗×c5 12.♗b2 ♘bd7 13.♘e5 ♘×e5 14.♗×e5

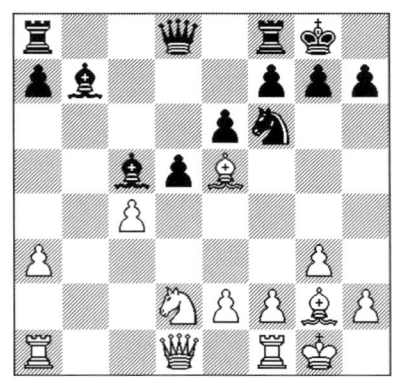

14...♘g4!

This distraction isn't as harmless as it seems. White will lose the game mainly because he underestimated its importance.

15.♗c3

And not 15.♗b2 ♕b6 etc.

15...♖b8

At that point 15...♕b6 could be answered with 16.e3. The move in the text prepares for the eventual advance of the d-Pawn.

16.♖b1

Although this move can't be considered a fatal mistake, it certainly facilitates the opponent's plans. It would also be unsatisfactory 16.h3 ♘×f2! 17.♔×f2 ♕g5! 18.♘f1 ♗×f2+ 19.♔×f2 d×c4 etc., with Black's advantage. But the continuation 16.c×d5 ♗×d5! 17.♘e4! (but not 17.e4 ♘×f2 18.♔×f2 ♗×f2+ 19.♔×f2 ♕b6+ 20.♔f1 ♗b7) with the consequent eviction of Black's threatening knight would still achieve a balanced game.

16...d4! 17.♖×b7?

Rubinstein didn't notice Black's surprising 18th move and will consequently be at a material disadvantage. The only possibility here would be 17.♗b4 ♗×g2 18.♔×g2 ♕c7, reaching a position which, although favorable to Black, would still not be decisive.

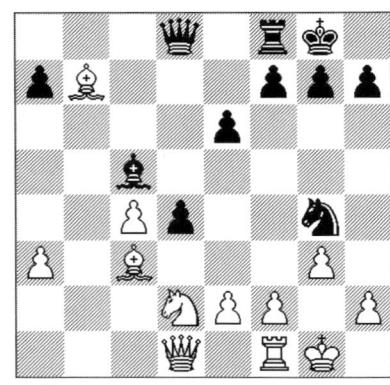

17...♖×b7 18.♗×b7

18...♘×f2!

By this pseudo-sacrifice Black forces the gain of at least one pawn with an overwhelming position. Of course, the immediate 18...d×c3 would be ineffective due to 19.♘e4 etc.

19.♔×f2

Other moves would be no better to say the least, for example: (I) 19.♕a1

(19.♖xf2? dxc3 winning) 19...dxc3 20.♘b3 ♘g4+ 21.♘xc5 ♕d4+; (II) 19.♗a5 ♘xd1 20.♗xd8 d3+ 21.e3 ♘xe3!, with an easy win for Black in both cases.

19...dxc3+ 20.e3

Or 20.♔e1 cxd2+ 21.♕xd2 ♕b6 with a quick decisive attack.

20...cxd2 21.♔e2 ♕b8 22.♗f3 ♖d8 23.♕b1 ♕d6

Winning the b4 square for the bishop.

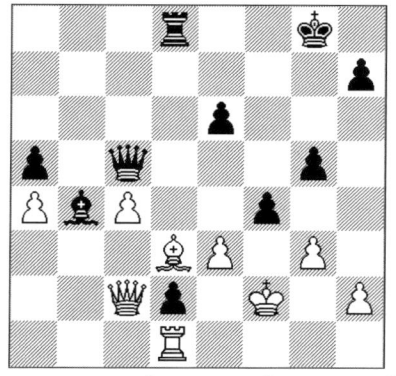

24.a4 f5 25.♖d1 ♗b4 26.♕c2 ♕c5 27.♔f2 a5 28.♗e2 g5 29.♗d3 f4!

If now 30.♗xh7+ ♔h8 31.♕e4, then 31...♕xe3+ 32.♔g2 f3+ 33.♔h3 ♕e2! 34.♕g6 g4+ 35.♔h4 ♗e7+ 36.♔h5 ♕xh2+, winning. White resigned.

Game 12
A.Alekhine–E.Gruenfeld
Semmering Tornament, April 1926
Queen's Gambit Accepted [D46]

1.d4 d5 2.c4 dxc4 3.♘f3 ♗g4

This move, recommended in the latest edition of *Collijn's Swedish Manual*, was introduced in masterly practice by Bogoljubov in his game against Vukovic at the Vienna Tournament, 1922. This game shows the danger of the early development of the Bishop in the event of a slight inaccuracy by Black.

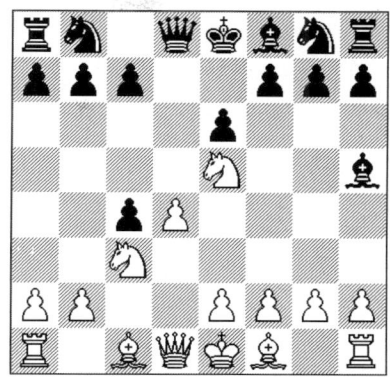

4.♘e5 ♗h5 5.♘c3 e6?

On the 5th move Black makes the decisive positional mistake! It would take 5...♘d7, after which I wanted to play 6.♕a4 c6 7.♘xd7 ♕xd7 (not 7...b5 8.♘xb5 cxb5 9.♕xb5 ♕xd7 10.♕xh5) 8.♕xc4 followed by e4 and ♗e3 with good play.

6.g4! ♗g6 7.h4 f6

A sad necessity!

8.♕a4+

It would also be good to 8.♘xg6 hxg6 9.e3.

8...c6 9.♘xg6 hxg6 10.♕xc4 ♔f7 11.e4 ♘d7 12.♗e3 ♕a5 13.a3

It was important to avoid ...♕b4.

13...♖e8 14.f4 ♘e7 15.0-0-0

Instead of 15.f5 ♘c8 etc., which would hardly be better than the simple move in the text.

See the next Diagram

15...♘c8 16.f5 ♘d6 17.♕a2!

After 17.♕b3 Black could play 17...c5, which would now lose a piece after 18.dxc5 and b4.

17...g5 18.h5 b5

Black no longer has any satisfactory moves.

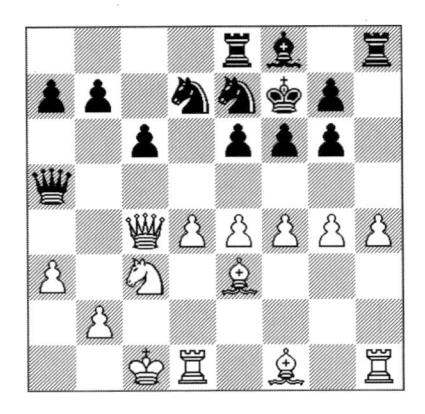

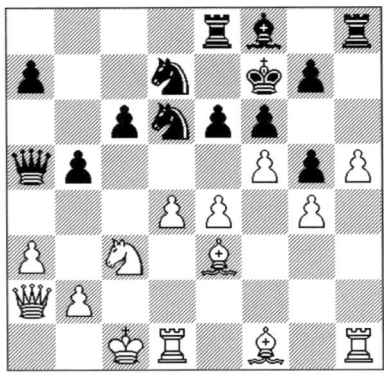

19.e5!

In conjunction with the next move, this advance is absolutely decisive. Not so good would be the immediate 19.♗d3 due to 19...b4.

19...fxe5

If instead 19...b4, then 20.exd6 bxc3 21.fxe6+ ♔xe6 22.♗c4, winning.

20.♗d3! e4

Or 20...♘c4 21.♗xc4 bxc4 22.♕xc4 etc., with an easily winning ending.

21.♘xe4 ♘xe4 22.♗xe4 ♘f6 23.fxe6+ ♖xe6 24.♗g6+!

Stronger than winning quality with 24.♗f5.

24...♔e7 25.♗xg5 b4 26.♗f5 ♖e2 27.♖he1

If now 27...♕b5, then 28.a4! ♕a6 29.♗d3 etc., and if 27...♖xe1, then 28.♔xe1+ ♔d8 29.♕f7! followed by mate. Black resigned.

> **Game 13**
> **F.Saemisch-A.Alekhine**
> *Dresden Tormament (1), May 1926*
> Queen's Indian Defense [E14]

1.d4 ♘f6 2.♘f3

The opinion that 2.c4 is better here is almost unanimous these days. But at the time of this game some Masters still feared the so-called "Budapest Gambit" (2...e5 as an answer to 2.c4).

2...b6 3.c4

If 3.g3, then 3...♗b7 4.♗g2 c5!.

3...♗b7 4.e3 e6 5.♗d3 ♗b4+ 6.♗d2 ♗xd2+ 7.♘bxd2 d6 8.0-0 ♘bd7 9.♕c2

White got a perfectly good position that could be improved by 9.♘g5 and if 9...h6, then 10.♘ge4 0-0 11.f4 d5 (or 11...♘xe4 12.♗xe4) 12.♘g3 c5 13.♕e2 followed by ♖ad1. The text move, while not bad, is aimless and allows Black to keep his bishop well placed.

9...0-0 10.♖ad1 ♕e7 11.♘g5

Two moves too late!

11...h6 12.♘h7

Or 12.♘ge4 ♔fd8, similarly to the game.

12...♖fd8 13.♘xf6+ ♘xf6 14.♘e4 c5 15.♘xf6+ ♕xf6 16.dxc5

White has managed to exchange almost all the minor pieces, but he is still a long way from achieving the draw he is obviously playing for, as the position of the black pawns is much more elastic. The exchange of the text has the obvious disadvantage of opening up the b-file for the opponent, but on the other hand the alternative 16.♗e4 would not be satisfactory either due to 16...d5! 17.♗f3 (or 17.c×d5 e×d5 followed by ...c4 with Black's advantage) 17...♗a6 18.b3 ♖ac8 etc., with Black's advantage.

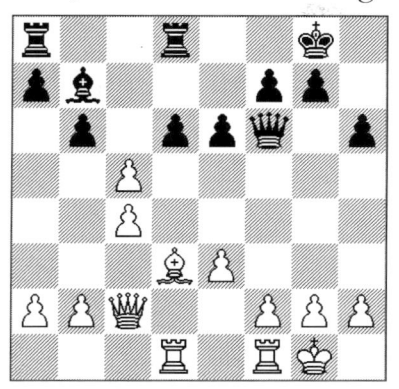

16...b×c5!

After 16...d×c5 Black, due to the symmetrical position of the Pawns, could hardly avoid a draw.

17.♖d2 ♖ab8 18.♖fd1 ♗c6! 19.b3

Of course, not 19.♗h7+ ♔h8 20.♖×d6? ♕×d6 21.♕×d6 ♗×b2 and Black wins. But now White threatens the pawn win as much as 19.♗e4, which would lead to further simplifications.

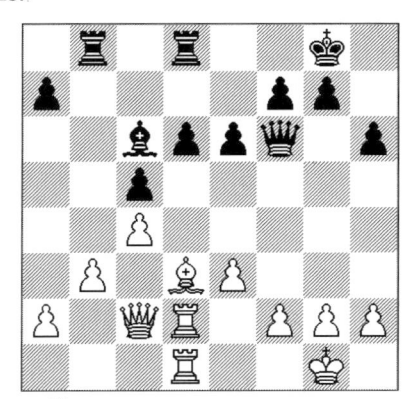

19...♕e5!

A very important move, which not only stops the threats mentioned, but also prepares for Black's later improvement of the position with ...f5. White then has nothing better to offer than the exchange of queens, resulting in an ending that will prove (due to the typical Pawn formation) to be very instructive, despite its apparent simplicity.

20.♕b2 ♕×b2 21.♖×b2 a5 22.♖bd2 ♔f8 23.♗c2 ♔e7

The first result of Black's strategy in the middlegame. The so-called weakness at e6 is purely illusory, and White's problems on the opposite a and b columns are very real.

24.f3 a4! 25.♔f2 a×b3 26.♗×b3

After 26.a×b3 Black would take full control of the a–file.

26...f5

It can be useful to avoid e4.

27.♔e2 ♖b4 28.♔d3 ♗a4

The only, but effective, method of proving the weakness of White's a2 and c4 squares.

29.♗×a4

Or 29.♔c3 ♖db8! 30.♖b2 (30.♖×d6? ♖×b3+! winning) 30...d5! etc., with an advantage for Black.

29...♖×a4 30.♖b1

He loses the Pawn, which in this kind of position is usually decisive. But also 30.♖c1 ♖a3+ 31.♔e2 ♖da8 32.♖cc2 ♖d8 followed by ...♔f6 and ...d5 would leave no hope in the long run.

30...♖a3+ 31.♔e2

After 31.♔b3 ♖da8 Black's win would be even simpler.

32...♖c3 32.a4 ♖a3!

Much better than 32...♖×c4 33.♖a2, after which the passed pawn could create some problems for Black.

33.♖b7+ ♖d7 34.♖db2 ♖×a4 35.♖×d7+ ♔×d7 36.♖b7+ ♔c6 37.♖×g7 ♖×c4 38.♖g6

White recovers the Pawn, but this has no effect as Black's Rook occupies the second row, and the King supports the passed Pawn. The rest is pure routine.

38...♔d5 39.♖xh6 ♖c2+ 40.♔f1 c4 41.♖h8 c3 42.h4

Or 42.♖c8 f4 43.exf4 ♔d4 44.h4 ♔e3 45.♔g1 ♔xf4 46.h5 ♔g5 47.g4 d5, winning easily.

42...♖d2 43.♔e1 ♖xg2 44.♖c8 c2 45.h5 ♖h2 46.h6 ♖xh6 47.♖xc2 ♖h1+ 48.♔d2 ♖h2+ 49.♔d3 ♖xc2, and White resigned.

Game 14
A.Rubinstein-A.Alekhine
Dresden Tormament (6), May 1926
Queen's Indian Defense [A47]
Beauty Award

1.d4 ♘f6 2.♘f3 e6 3.♗f4 b6 4.h3

It's certainly not necessary to avoid Black's knight on a5 at this point. The weakening of the g3-square gave me the idea of an unusual development system, but as it will prove, a very effective one.

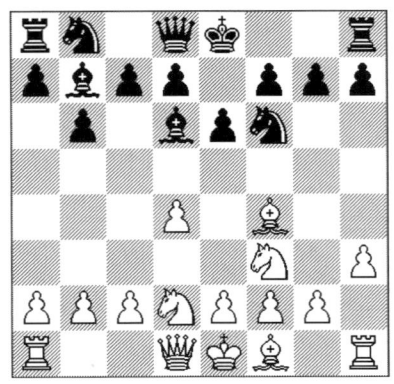

4...♗b7 5.♘bd2 ♗d6!

After this move, Black has the unpleasant choice between (1) the exchange, with the strengthening of Black's central position; (2) 6.e3, which would spoil his pawn structure after 6...♗xf4; and (3) 6.♗g5 by which Black would have the advantage of the bishop pair through ...h6.

6.♗xd6 cxd6 7.e3 0-0 8.♗e2

And not 8.♗d3, because he wants to play ♘xe4 after ...d5, followed by ...♘e4.

8...d5 9.0-0 ♘c6 10.c3

If 10.♘e5, then 10...♘e7 followed by ...d6.

10...♘e4!

Black has already taken the initiative.

11.♘xe4 dxe4 12.♘d2 f5 13.f4

Otherwise, Black would play ...♕g5 and avoid the text move for a long time.

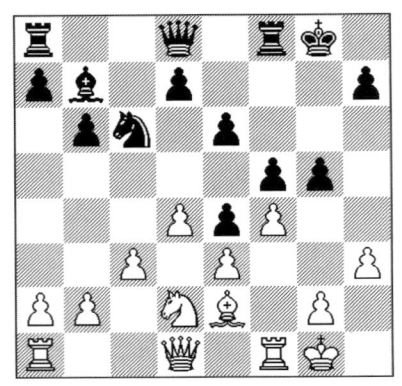

13...g5!

Black needs to play energetically before his opponent finds time to coordinate the activity of his pieces.

14.♘c4 d5 15.♘e5 ♘xe5

Much better than 15...gxf4 16.♘xc6! followed by ♖xf4.

16.dxe5

In the case of 16.fxe5 Black would eventually break through with ...f4.

16...♔h8 17.a4?

White has no time for this counterattack. Their only chance of a successful defense would be 17.g3 followed by 18.♔h2 etc. After losing this opportunity, Black will gradually exert overwhelming pressure.

17...♖g8 18.♕d2 gxf4!

The timing is right, because White

can't retake the pawn with 19...♕h4 with the double threat of 20...♕×h3 or 20...♔×g2+!

19.♖×f4 ♕g5 20.♗f1 ♕g3!

Forcing White's next kingside move and thus preparing to gain time on the 23rd move.

21.♔h1 ♕g7 22.♕d4 ♗a6! 23.♖f2

The white Queen obviously have no choice.

23...♕g3!

See the commentary on Black's 20th move.

24.♖c2 ♗×f1 25.♖×f1 ♖ac8

Always working with time gains, Black now threatens 26...♔c4.

26.b3 ♖c7 27.♖e2 ♖cg7 28.♖f4

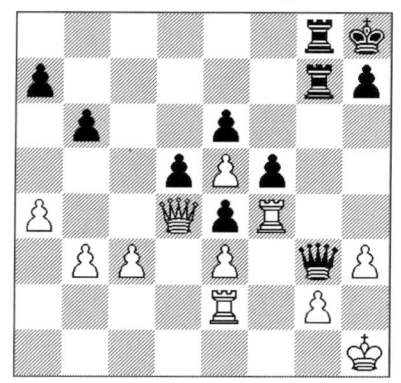

28...♖g6!

After this move we arrive at a highly original position, the exceptional particularities of which are as follows: Black's immediate threat is 29...♖h6 30.♕d1 ♕g7 winning the e5 Pawn, as 31.♕d4 would be answered by 31...♖×h3+. If Black tries to stop this attack with 29.♕d1, Black would likewise play 29...♖h6!, putting his opponent in a position of complete *zugzwang*.

In fact, (1) The Rook on f4 cannot move due to 30...♕×e5. (2) The Rook on e2 is tied to the defense of squares e3 and g2. (3) The King cannot move due to 30...♖ (or ♕) × h3. (4) The Queen cannot move to the first row due to 30...♕g7! etc., nor to the d-file due to 30...♖×h3+! etc. (5) Finally in the case of 30.b4 Black would win through 30...♕g6 31.♕d4 ♔c8! followed by 32...♔c4.

White then offers a pawn in the hope of exchanging the pair of rooks and thus weakening the enemy's attack.

29.♕b4 ♖h6 30.h4

Again, absolutely forced.

30...♕g7!

Much better than the prosaic 30...♖×h4+. If now 31.♕d6, then 31...♔g6 32.♖ff2 f4! 33.e×f4 e3! winning.

31.c4 ♖g6 32.♕d2 ♖g3!

Threatening 33...♖h3+ 34.♔g1 ♕g3; and if immediately 33.♔g1, then 33.d4! 34.e×d4 e3! 35.♕c2 (or b2) 35...♔h3, followed by ...♕g3 winning. White has no salvation.

33.♕e1 ♔×g2, and White resigned.

Game 15
A.Alekhine–A.Nimzowitsch
New York Tormament (3), March 1927
Nimzowitsch Defense [E32]

1.d4 ♘f6 2.c4 e6 3.♘c3 ♗b4 4.♕c2 d6

The only modern move these days (see, for example, my second game with Dr. Euwe) is 4...d5.

5.♗g5 ♘bd7 6.e3 b6 7.♗d3 ♗b7 8.f3

By maintaining control of the e4 square, White makes it very difficult for his opponent to formulate an adequate plan for further development.

8...♗×c3+ 9.♕×c3 c5 10.♘h3!

White here expected 10.♘e2 or

10.♖d1, both of which simplified things with 10...♘♕5! The chosen move allows White to make effective use of his Bishops.

10...h6 11.♗f4

And not 11.♗h4 because of the possibility of ...g5 and ...g4.

11...♕e7 12.♗g3!

Black threatened 12...e5, followed eventually by ...e4.

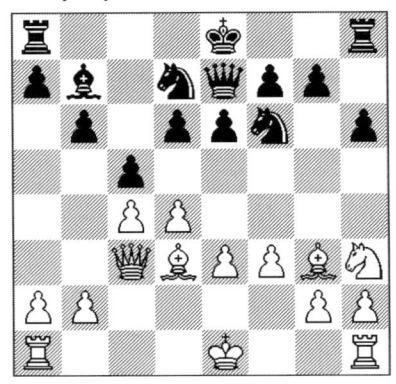

12...e5?

This move is not only an unnatural attempt to define the central situation, but it is also almost the decisive blunder. After the simple 12...0-0 White would have no easy time exploiting the clear weakness of the black squares in the enemy position.

13.d×e5 d×e5 14.0-0-0 g6

14...e4 15.♗e2 would be useless and the immediate 14...0-0-0 would be answered by 15.♗f5 g6 16.♗×e5! g×f5 17.♔×d7 followed by 18.♗×f6 or 18.♗×h8 etc., with a decisive advantage.

15.♗c2

This Bishop will prove very useful on the a4–e8 diagonal.

15...0-0-0 16.♗a4 ♖he8 17.♘f2 ♕e6

Black wants to dislodge his opponent's threatening white bishop, but his plan will take time, which White will use to strengthen his pressure on the d-file decisively. A slightly better chance of salvation would be 17...♘h5, and if 18.♖d2 then 18...♘×g3 19.h×g3 ♖h8! 20.♖hd1 ♘b8 etc.

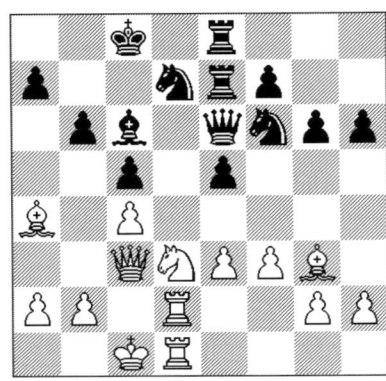

18.♘d3 ♖e7 19.♖d2 ♖de8 20.♖hd1

If now 20...♘h5 then simply 21.♗×d7+ ♔×d7 22.♘×c5 winning.

20...♗c6

21.♗c2! ♘h5

In this rather harmless-looking position - only one Pawn has been exchanged and none of White's pieces are situated beyond the third row - Black is already completely defenseless against the threats of 22.♘×c5 followed by 23.♖d6, or alternatively 22.b4. If for example 21...♔c7 (to protect d6), then 22.b4! c×b4 23.♘×b4 ♘c5 24.♘d5+ ♗×d5 25.c×d5 ♕d6 26.f4!, winning. And after the text move Black loses the Queen and Pawn for a Rook and Knight, after which the rest will be a matter of technique.

Although this game is one of my happiest achievements in the strategic realm of the opening, it went almost unnoticed simply because of its length and the preference of many chess journalists for short, flashy games. It's certainly not my fault that Nimzovitsch (who was fighting for second place, which would be heavily compromised by this defeat) decided to fight a desperate battle to its bitter end.

22.♘xc5! ♘xc5 23.♖d6 ♘xg3 24.hxg3 ♕xd6 25.♖xd6 ♖c7 26.b4 ♘b7 27.♖xc6

It's obvious that any decrease in material on the board from now on will favor White.

27...♖xc6 28.♗a4 ♖ee6 29.♗xc6 ♖xc6 30.♕xe5

This exchange in particular opens new fronts for action by both the Queen and the White King.

30...♖xc4+ 31.♔d2 h5 32.a3

White's next objective will be to tie up Black's Rook and Knight. They will succeed by bringing their queen to a very strong position in the middle of the board (see the 43rd move).

32...♖c7 33.♕e8+ ♘d8 34.e4 ♖d7+ 35.♔e3 ♖c7 36.♔f4

Also good would be 36.♔f2, followed by ♔g1, ♔h2 and eventually f4, f5 etc. But White wants his king to take part in the final battle.

36...♖c3 37.a4 ♖c2 38.♕e7 ♖c7 39.♕f6 ♖c2 40.♕e7 ♖c7 41.♕d6 ♘e6+ 42.♔e5

Or 42.♔e3–f2–g1 etc., as mentioned in the previous comment.

42...♘d8 43.♕d5! ♖c6 44.♔f4

From now on White decides to provoke the move ...a5 which will create a new weakness in Black's point b6.

44...♘e6+ 45.♔e3 ♖c3+ 46.♔e2 ♖c7 47.f4 ♘d8 48.♔e3 ♖c3+ 49.♔d4 ♖c7 50.♔e5! a5

Practically forced, because after 50...♔c6 51.f5! etc., and there would be no more satisfactory moves.

51.♕a8+ ♔d7 52.b5 ♔e7

If instead 52...♖b7, 53.♔f6 etc.

53.f5!

And not 53.♕b8? due to 53...♘e6! winning the queen thanks to the threat of mate on c5.

53...f6+ 54.♔d4 ♖d7+ 55.♔e3 gxf5 56.exf5

After this move Black's h5 pawn will fall quickly.

56...♘f7 57.♕f3 ♘e5

The position of this Knight is very good, but not enough to compensate for the loss of material afterwards.

58.♕xh5 ♖d3+ 59.♔f2 ♖d2+ 60.♔f1 ♖d4 61.♕h7+ ♔d6

If 61...♘f7, then 62.♕g8, followed by ♕b8 with the Pawn winning b6.

62.♕b7 ♘d7 63.♕c6+ ♔e7 64.♕e6+ ♔d8 65.♕b3 ♖b4 66.♕d1 ♔e7 67.♕e2+ ♔d8 68.♕a2 ♔e7 69.♔e2! ♖e4+

Or 69...♔d8 70.♕g8+, followed by 71.g4 etc.

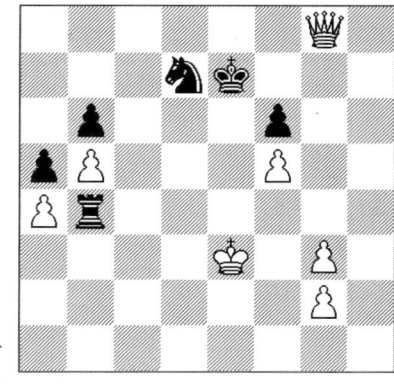

70.♔f3 ♖b4 71.♔e3 ♘c5 72.♕g8 ♘d7

73.g4!

Now the decision will be quick.

73... ♖xa4 74.g5 fxg5 75.♕xg5+ ♔d6 76.♕g6+ ♔c7 77.♕c6+ ♔d8 78.f6 ♖a1 79.g4 ♖f1 80.g5 ♖f5 81.♕a8+ ♔c7 82.♕c6+ ♔d8 83.g6!

If now 83...♔xf6, then 84.g7 and if 83...♘xf6 then 84.♕d6+ followed by

85.g7 etc. Black resigned.

> **Game 16**
> **A.Alekhine-F.Marshall**
> *New York Tormament (4), March 1927*
> Queen's Pawn Opening [E10]
> Brilliance Award

1.d4 ♘f6 2.c4 e6 3.♘f3 ♘e4

This unnatural move and waste of time can be successfully responded to in several ways. One of the simplest is 4.♕c2, and in the case of 4...d5 or 4...f5, 5.♘c3 etc.

4.♘fd2

With the obvious idea of exchanging on e4 and developing the other knight on c3. This game proves the soundness of this scheme quite convincingly.

4...♗b4

A typical Marshall trap: if now 5.a3 then 5...♕f6! with an immediate win.

5.♕c2 d5

Or 5...f5 6.a3 forcing the exchange of both of Black's active pieces.

6.♘c3 f5 7.♘d×e4

After this move White will easily force open the central columns with f3 and eventually e4. And since they have better development, this opening gives them a substantial positional advantage.

7...f×e4 8.♗f4

This Bishop will protect the King's position against any unexpected attacks.

See the next Diagram

8...0-0 9.e3 c6

White threatened with 10.a3 to force the exchange of the Bishop for his Knight (10.a3 ♗d6? 11.♗×d6 followed by 12.c×d5 e×d5 13.♘×d5! etc.).

10.♗e2 ♘d7 11.a3

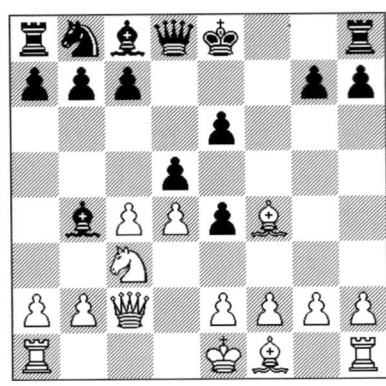

I consider this move to be healthier than 11.0-0 ♘f6 12.f3 ♘h5! 13.f×e4 ♘×f4 14.♔×f4 ♗×f4 15.e×f4 d×c4 etc.

11...♗e7

After the exchange on c3 the black squares would remain hopelessly weak.

12.0-0 ♗g5

It's hard to find anything better.

13.f3 ♗×f4 14.e×f4 ♖×f4

Instead, 14...e×f3 15.♔×f3 ♘f6 16.f5! would be a rather sad alternative due to the weakness of the e6 square. With the move in the text, together with the next two, Marshall will try to save his already compromised game through combinatorial play.

15.f×e4 ♖×f1+ 16.♖×f1 e5

Or 16...d×c4 17.♗×c4 ♘b6 18.♕f2! etc., with a clear advantage.

17.♕d2!

The initial move of the decisive maneuver. If now 17...♕b6 then 18.c5 ♕a5 19.e×d5 e×d4 20.b4! d×c3 21.♕g5 ♕c7 22.d6 h6 23.♕e7, winning.

17...c5

Trying to increase the pressure at any cost, but the exchange of pawns will quickly prove disastrous.

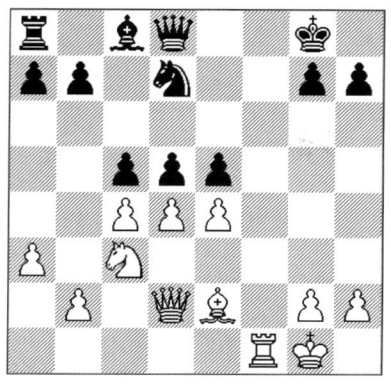

18.d×e5!

It would be wrong instead 18.♘×d5 c×d4 19.♕b4 due to 19...♘f6.

18...d4 19.♕f4!

This sacrifice in connection with the "quiet" 21st move is undoubtedly the quickest and safest method of forcing victory. Not 19.♘d5 due to 19...♘xe5 followed by 20...♕d6 etc.

19...d×c3

Forced.

20.♕f7+ ♔h8 21.b×c3!

This alone proves the correctness of the sacrifice. It was tempting, but premature, to instead 21.e6 due to 21...♘f6 22.e7 ♕g8 23.♖×f6 ♗g4! 24.♕×g8+ ♔×g8 25.♖d6 ♖e8!, etc. with Black's advantage.

21...♕g8 22.♕e7 h6 23.♗h5!

And not 23.e6 ♘f6 24.e5 ♘h7!, etc.

23...a5

If 23...♕×c4, then of course 24.♗f7.

24.e6 g6 25.e×d7 ♗×d7 26.♖f7, and Black resigned.

Game 17
A.Alekhine–L.Asztalos
Kecskemet Tormament (9), July 1927
Queen's Gambit Declined
Orthodox Defense [D43]
Brilliance Award

1.♘f3 d5 2.c4 e6 3.d4 ♘f6 4.♗g5 h6

This move is rightly considered unsatisfactory since Black's pair of Bishops does not compensate for White's advantage in space. The modern line 4...♗b5+, connected with 5...d×c4 (forming the so-called Vienna Variant) has not yet been fully analyzed, but in any case, it offers more fighting chances than the one chosen in the game.

5.♗×f6 ♕×f6 6.♘c3 c6 7.♕b3

The right preparation for e4.

7...♘d7 8.e4 d×e4 9.♘×e4 ♕f4 10.♗d3 ♗e7 11.0–0 0–0 12.♖fe1 ♖d8 13.♖ad1 ♕c7

Because of the variant employed, Black has some difficulties in developing his pieces, especially the Queen's Bishop. The queen's retreat is practically forced, if 13...♘f8 for example, then 14.♕c3 with the threat of 15.♘e5.

14.♘g3 ♘f8

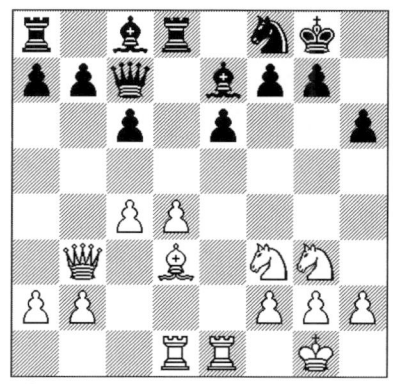

15.♕c3!

White intends to continue with ♘h5 followed by d5, which will force a fatal weakness in Black's King position. Black's maneuver then stops this danger, but at the cost of disordering the Pawns on the Queen's wing.

15...a5 16.a3 a4 17.♘e5

After 17.♘h5 the reply 17...♕a5 would force the exchange of queens.

17...♕a5 18.♕c1 ♗d7 19.c5!

The logical response to Black's Pawn advance. White now threatens to install his knight on b6 and thus force the next moves of the pawns, which will remove the natural protection of Black's c6 pawn.

19...b5 20.♗e4 ♕c7 21.♕c3

Threatening 22.♕f3 etc.

21...♗e8 22.♘e2!

The start of a series of maneuvers against which Black has no adequate defenses. First, White threatens to bring the knight via c1 to b4 and to avoid this Black is forced to exchange his valuable knight, thus leaving the h7 square undefended.

22...♖a6 23.♘c1 ♘d7 24.♘×d7 ♖×d7 25.♘d3 ♖d8 26.♘e5 ♗f8

With the hope of building a new defensive position through ...g6 followed by ♗g7. But White's next move leaves no time for that.

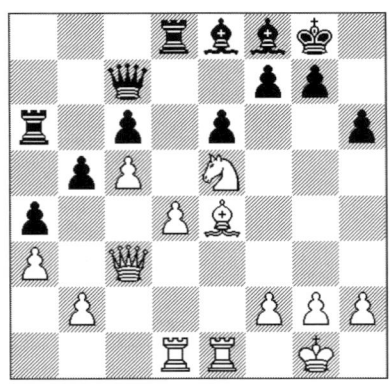

27.h4! ♖aa8

If 27...g6, then 28.h5 g5 29.f4! with the rapid demolition of Black's last bastion.

28.♗b1

Threatening 29.♕c2 g6 30.h5, etc.

28...h5 29.♕f3 g6 30.g4 h×g4 31.♕×g4 ♗g7 32.♗a2!

An important move that prevents the advance of Black's f-Pawn. Black can't prepare this advance with 32...♕e7 due to the reply 33.♘×g6!, with immediate victory.

32...b4!

An ingenious but insufficient resource: if 33.a×b4, then 33...a3 34.b×a3 ♗×a3 etc., with some counterplay.

33.♗c4! b×a3 34.b×a3 ♕a5 35.♕e4

The best. It would be premature to 35.♘×g6 ♗×d4!, or 35.h5 g×h5 36.♕×h5 ♗×d4! etc.

35...♕c7 36.♕f4

Preparing the Pawn's next move, against which there is no defense.

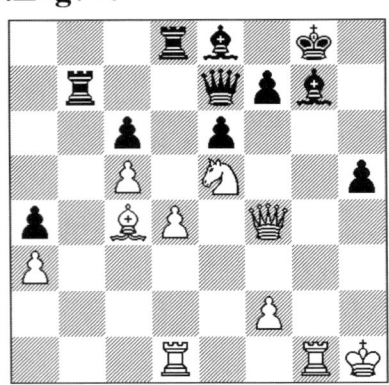

36...♖ab8 37.h5! g×h5 38.♔h1 ♖b7 39.♖g1 ♕e7 40.♖×g7+!

Black had hoped to have fended off this possibility with his last move. But the combination still works because of the unexpected point on the 42nd move.

40...♔×g7 41.♖g1+ ♔h7 42.♘×f7!!

Only like this! If now 42...♕×f7, then 43.♗d3+ ♕g6 44.♗×g6+ ♗×g6 45.♔×g6! ♗×g6 46.♕e4+ ♔g7 47.♕e5+! and Black, after a few more checks, will realize the inevitable loss of one of his rooks.

> **Game 18**
> **A. Alekhine – S. Tartakower**
> *Kecskemet Tormament, July 1927*
> Caro-Kann Defense [B15]

1.e4 c6 2.d4 d5 3.♘c3 d×e4 4.♘×e4 ♘f6 5.♘g3

In the Hastings International Tournament 1936-1937 I successfully tried against W. Winter the pawn sacrifice 5.♗d3 recommended by Dr. Tarrasch shortly before his death. That game continued with 5...♕×d4 6.♘f3 ♕d8 7.♕e2 ♘×e4 (here it would be slightly premature 7...♘bd7 as four (!) amateurs with consultation played against me in Majorca, January 1935 - due to the unpleasant response 8.♘d6 mate...) 8.♗×e4 ♘d7 9.0-0 ♘c5 10.♖d1 ♕c7 11.♘e5 ♘×e4 12.♕×e4 ♗e6 13.♗f4 ♕c8 14.♘c4! g5!? 15.♗×g5 ♔g8 16.♗f4 ♗×c4 17.♕×c4 ♕g4 18.g3 e5 19.♖e1 (a more elegant solution would be 19.♕b3! as 19...e×f4 or 19...♕×f4 would lead to an immediate disaster after 20.♕×b7) 19...0-0-0 20.♔×e5 and Black resigned a few moves later.

5...e5

Most likely enough to balance. But to achieve this, Black must play the next moves carefully.

6.♘f3 e×d4 7.♘×d4

Nor does 7.♕×d4 ♕×d4 8.♘×d4 ♗c5 9.♘df5 0-0 10.♗e3 played by me against Capablanca in New York, 1927, give any serious chance of favorable complications.

7...♗c5

Already a serious waste of time. The immediate 7...♗e2 was indicated, followed by castling with a satisfactory position.

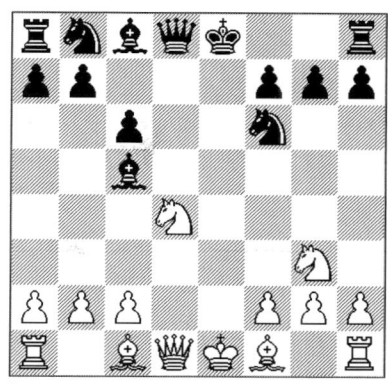

8.♕e2+! ♗e7

Or 8...♕e7 9.♕×e7+ ♗×e7 10.♘df5 with some advantage for White.

9.♗e3 c5?

This attempt to avoid castling on Black's queen's wing fails completely. A much lesser evil would be 9...0-0 10.0-0-0 ♕a5 11.♔b1 ♘d5 12.♕f3 with no immediate danger to Black.

10.♘df5 0-0 11.♕c4!

An important move, which prepares the development of the king's bishop with a tempo gain (by attacking Black's c5 pawn).

11...♖e8

Also, after the immediate 11...b6 White would gradually get a winning attack by playing 12.♖d1 followed by ♕h4 etc.

12.♗d3 b6 13.0-0-0 ♗a6

It's obvious that other moves would also lead to a rapid catastrophe.

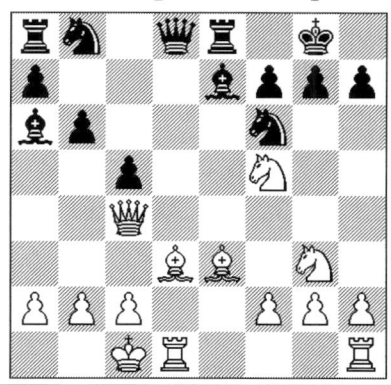

14.♘h6+!

In making this forced combination, White calculated that his opponent wouldn't get three pieces for the queen, but - because of the weakness of his a8–h1 diagonal - only two; the rest is forced to Black.

14...gxh6 15.♗xh7+! ♘xh7

If 15...♔h8, then 16.♕xf7 followed by 17.♘f5 with a mate attack.

16.♕g4+ ♔h8 17.♖xd8 ♖xd8

Or 17...♗xd8 18.♕f3 etc.

18.♕e4 ♘c6 19.♕xc6 ♗f8 20.♘f5 ♗c4 21.♗xh6 ♗d5 22.♕c7 ♖ac8 23.♕f4 ♖c6 24.♗xf8 ♖xf8 25.♕e5+ ♘f6 26.♘d6!, and Black resigned.

Game 19
H.Kmoch-A.Alekhine
Kecskemet Tornament, (1) July 1927
Queen's Pawn Opening [D12]

1.e4 e5 2.♘f3 c6 3.e3

After this harmless move Black will have no difficulty with his Queen Bishop. More common and better would be 3.c4, leading to the Slav Defense of the Refused Queen's Gambit.

3...♗f5 4.♗d3 e6 5.0–0

You certainly can't recommend switching now or in the next bid.

5...♘d7 6.c4 ♘gf6 7.♕c2

It's easily understandable that White wants to clarify the central situation as quickly as possible. The move 7.♘c3 would be answered simply by 7...♗e7.

7...♗xd3 8.♕xd3 ♘e4

To eliminate as many smaller pieces as possible, because White will sooner or later get some extra space by playing e4.

9.♘fd2 ♘df6 10.♘c3

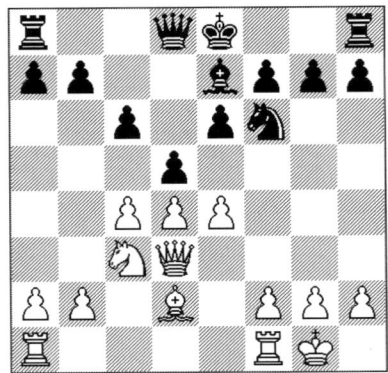

After 10.♘xe4 ♘xe4 11.f3 ♘f6 12.e4 dxc4 13.♕xc4 ♕b6 14.♘c3 ♖d8 15.♖d1 ♗e7, followed by 16.0–0 0–0 etc., White's position would remain quite unstable.

10...♘xd2 11.♗xd2 ♗e7 12.e4

The excessive freedom that White gained with this move will be neutralized by the need to permanently protect his d-pawn. But they would hardly have any other plan at their disposal, as an attempt to block would fail, for example: 12.c5 e5! or 12.f4 c5!, both of which are very favorable to Black.

12...dxe4 13.♘xe4 0–0 14.♗c3 ♕c7

The b6 square would also be good for the queen.

15.♖ad1 ♖ad8 16.♖d2?

White lost this game not because of the opening, which was satisfactory, but mainly because of his play, which was both passive and conventional. Here, for example, they had the perfectly saving move 16.f4, preventing the opponent's queen from occupying that square. From now on, the second player's chances can be considered the best.

See the next Diagram

16...♕f4! 17.♘xf6+ ♗xf6 18.♖fd1 ♖d7 19.♕g3

Exchanging queens would undoubtedly increase white's chances of a draw. But Black quickly avoids this.

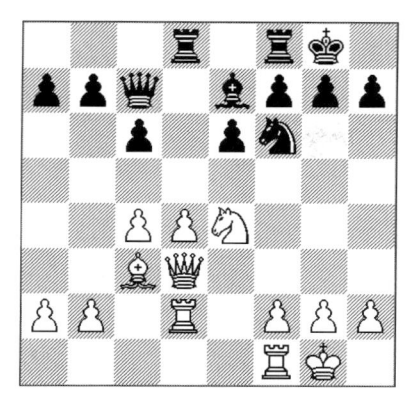

19...♕f5 20.f4

The aim of this move seems to be to prevent the possible responses ...♗b4 or ...b4.

20...♖fd8 21.♕e3 h5!

Not only giving the King a way out, but also blocking White's King's wing (22.h3 h4 etc.).

22.b4

This makes it easier for Black, who will immediately eliminate the opponent's c4 pawn, thus gaining full control of the d5 square.

22...b5! 23.♕f3

This attempt to save a very sick strategic position with tactical means quickly leads to collapse. But also, after the quieter 23.c5 ♖d5 followed by 24...g5 the game would hardly go far.

23...b×c4 24.♕×c6 ♕×f4 25.♕×c4 e5!

Gaining a decisive material advantage.

26.♕e2 e×d4 27.♖d3

If such a block were possible, Black would face some technical difficulties. But as it is, Black can force an immediate victory through an intensely calculated combination.

See the next Diagram

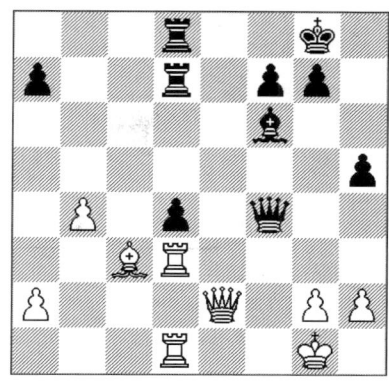

27...d×c3!

The main variant of this exchange is both beautiful and convincing: 28.♗×d7 ♔×d7 29.♖×d7 29.♕e8+ ♔h7 30.♕×d7 ♕e4!! 31.♕×f7 (or 31.♕d5 ♕×d5 32.♖×d5 c2, winning, as 33.♖c5 is refuted via 33...♗d4+) 31...c2 32.♕×h5+ ♔g8 winning.

28.♖×d7 ♖×d7 29.♖×d7

This lose immediately.

29...♗d4+ 30.♔h1

Or 30.♔×d4 ♕×d4+ 31.♔f1 ♕f4+ 32.♔e1 ♕×b4 etc.

30...♕c1+, and White resigned.

Game 20
J.Capablanca-A.Alekhine
World Championship, Buenos Aires (1), September 1927
French Defense [C01]

1.e4 e6 2.d4 d5 3.♘c3 ♗b4 4.e×d5 e×d5 5.♗d3 ♘c6 6.♘ge2 ♘ge7 7.0-0 ♗f5 8.♗×f5

Other moves such as 8.a3 or 8.♘g3 also proved harmless. This game shows once again that White has no ambition to fight and should avoid exchanging pawns on the 4th move in this variant.

8...♘×f5 9.♕d3 ♕d7 10.♘d1

The start of a long series of slightly inferior moves. The natural development move, 10.♗f4, which Black intended to answer with 10...0-0-0

41

would lead to a more vivid battle.

10...0-0 11.♘e3 ♘xe3 12.♗xe3

The smaller white pieces are now obstructing the vital column e. This is convincing proof of the inaccuracy of the opening strategy.

12...♖fe8 13.♘f4

The answer will show that the knight has no future in this house. Natural and good enough for a draw would be 13.♗f4, followed by c3 etc.

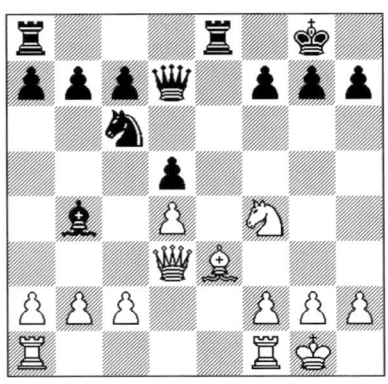

13...♗d6!

So Black proposes an exchange, the results of which will be very satisfactory for himself. If, namely, 14.♘xd5 ♗xh2+ 15.♔xh2 ♕xd5 16.c4, then 16...♕h5+ 17.♔g1 ♖ad8 18.d5 ♖d6 and the white King would be in a dangerous position.

14.♖fe1

White continues to play superficially. The first move was 14.c3.

14...♘b4 15.♕b3?

After this move White will be forced to at least corrupt his pawn structure in a very ugly way. The lesser evil would be 15.♕d2 ♕f5 16.♖ec1 g5! (threatening ...♖e5 followed by ...h4) with some positional advantage for Black.

15...♕f5 16.♖ac1?

After this blunder, the game can hardly be saved, as Black now wins a pawn in a very good position. It would take 16.♘d3 after which Black, it's true, would get a much better ending by continuing with 16...♘xd3 17.♕xd3 ♕xd3 18.cxd3 ♗b4 19.♖ec1 c6, possibly followed by ...a5!, etc.

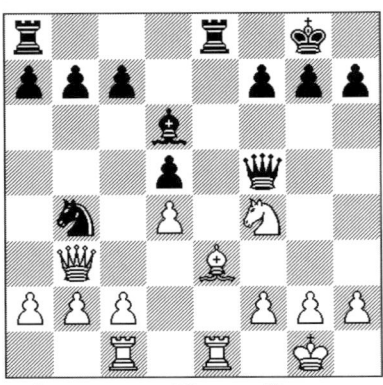

16...♘xc2! 17.♖xc2 ♕xf4!

This was the possibility that Capablanca missed on his 16th move. He only expected 17...♗xf4, after which White would restore the balance with 18.♔c5, etc.

18.g3

It's simply a matter of taste to choose between this move or 18.♕xd5 ♕xh2+ 19.♔f1 c6 as the preferred one.

18...♕f5

It was also tempting 18...♕f6 19.♕xb7 h5 20.♕b5 h4 21.♕e2 ♕f5, etc., with a good attack. But the decision to return the material advantage gained didn't excite me.

19.♖ce2 b6 20.♕b5 h5 21.h4 ♖e4

Threatening 22...♖xh4!, etc.

22.♗d2!

See the next Diagram

This temporary sacrifice of a second pawn allows for relatively better chances of salvation, should Black accept it. It would be totally hopeless

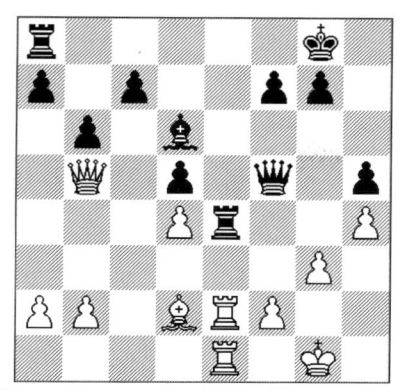

22.♕d3 ♖ae8 23.♗d2 ♕e6, etc.

22...♖×d4

This acceptance - which was very calculated - was not absolutely necessary. Simple and convincing instead would be 22...♖ae8, with the possible exchange of White's queen for two rooks via 22...♖ae8 23.♕×e8+ ♖×e8 24.♖×e8+ ♔h7 etc. Black, due to his considerable positional advantage, would have very little difficulty in forcing a win.

23.♗c3 ♖d3

Also, after 23...♔g4 (23...♔f4? 24.♖e5! etc.) 24.♗e5 White would finally get one of his pawns back.

24.♗e5 ♖d8 25.♗×d6 ♖×d6

Technically simpler than the non-aesthetic 25...c×d6 26.♕c6! etc.

26.♖e5 ♕f3

Of course, not 26...♕g6 27.♔g5, etc.

27.♖×h5 ♕×h5

And here 27...♖e6 would be another form of suicide (28.♕e8+! etc.).

28.♖e8+ ♔h7 29.♕×d3+ ♕g6 30.♕d1

See the next Diagram

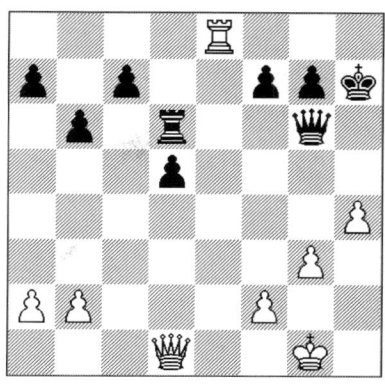

31...♖e6!

An interesting conception. Black returns his two extra Pawns to combine the advantage of his passed Pawn d with a mate attack. Much less convincing would be 30...d4 due to the reply 31.♕f3, threatening both ♕a8 and h5.

31.♖a8 ♖e5!

With the intention of putting the queen behind the rook and at the same time preparing the formation of the pawn chain b6–c5–d4.

32.♖×a7 c5 33.♖d7?

Shortening the agony. Instead I expected 33.♔g2 d4 34.♖a3 ♕e6! 35.♕f3 c4 followed by the decisive advance of the d-pawn.

33...♕e6 34.♕d3+ g6 35.♖d8 d4 36.a4

Despair!

36...♖e1+

This direct attack is quite convincing. But Black could also get an immediate advantage from the exposed position of the adventurous Rook, for example: 36...♕e7! 37.♔b8 ♕c7 38.♕b3 ♖e6 39.♖a8 ♕b7 and the Rook would be lost due to the threat of 40...♖e1+, etc.

37.♔g2 ♕c6+ 38.f3 ♖e3 39.♕d1 ♕e6 40.g4 ♖e2+ 41.♔h3 ♕e3 42.♕h1 ♕f4!

After this move, there's no avoiding the Rook's next move.

43.h5 ♔f2, and White resigned.

> **Game 21**
> **J.Capablanca-A.Alekhine**
> *World Championship, Buenos Aires (11), October 1927*
> Queen's Gambit Declined
> Cambridge Springs Defense [D52]

1.d4 d5 2.c4 e6 3.♘c3 ♘f6 4.♗g5 ♘bd7 5.e3 c6 6.♘f3 ♕a5 7.♘d2 ♗b4 8.♕c2 d×c4 9.♗×f6 ♘×f6 10.♘×c4 ♕c7 11.a3 ♗e7 12.♗e2

White doesn't need to rush to prevent ...c5 by playing 12.b4, as this advance would be premature due to 13.♘b5 ♕b8 14.d×c5 ♗×c5 15.b4 ♗e7 16.♘a5, etc., with White's advantage.

12...0–0 13.0–0 ♗d7

And here too 13...c5 would not be advisable for the same reason.

14.b4 b6

It would be safer to first 14...♖fd8 followed by ...♗e8. Black's plan continuing through 15...a5 16.b×a5 b5 would then stop White's reply.

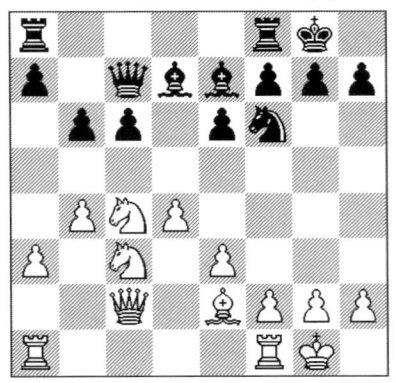

15.♗f3!

If now 15...a5 then 16.♘e5! a×b4 17.♘b5, etc., with advantage.

15...♖ac8 16.♖fd1 ♖fd8 17.♖ac1 ♗e8 18.g3

A good positional move, whose immediate aim is to prevent ...♕f4 in the case of e4.

18...♘d5 19.♘b2 ♕b8

Immediate 19...♕b7 would be more accurate, given the possibility of ...♕a6.

20.♘d3 ♗g5

With the possible threat of ...♘×e3 etc.

21.♖b1 ♕b7 22.e4 ♘×c3 23.♕×c3 ♕e7?

Disadvantageous, as the King's Bishop will now be temporarily out of the game. It would be correct to 23...♗c7 and if 24.♗g2 then 24...♗f6 25.e5 ♗e7 26.♖bc1 ♕c8, after which Black would wait patiently for events to unfold.

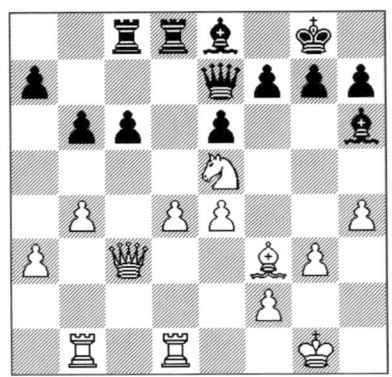

24.h4! ♗h6 25.♘e5

Threatening 20.♘g4.

25...g6 26.♘g4?

Now it's White's turn to waste the best move! After 26.♘c4! ♗g7 27.e5 h5 28.♘d6, Black would have nothing better than to start a fight for a draw by sacing the quality for a pawn: 28...♖×d6 29.e×d6 ♕×d6 30.♕c4! etc., with an advantage.

26...♗g7 27.e5 h5 28.♘e3 c5!

Black seizes the great opportunity to finally release his queen bishop, correctly imagining that White won't be able to gain a real advantage by opening the b-file.

29.b×c5

If 29.d×c5 then 29...b×c5 30.♔×d8

♕xd8 31.b×c5 ♕c7, etc.

29...b×c5 30.d5

This attempt to complicate things - quite unusual for Capablanca - works in Black's favor. An easy draw would be obtained through 30.♗b7 ♗d7 31.♗×d7 ♘×d7 32.d5 (or 32.d×c5 ♗e8 33.c6 ♕c7, etc.) 32...e×d5 33.♘×d5 ♕e6 34.♘f4 ♗×e5, followed by a general liquidation and Bishops of opposite colors.

30...e×d5 31.♘×d5 ♕e6

Of course, not 31...♕×e5 32.♕×e5 ♗×e5 33.♘e7+, etc.

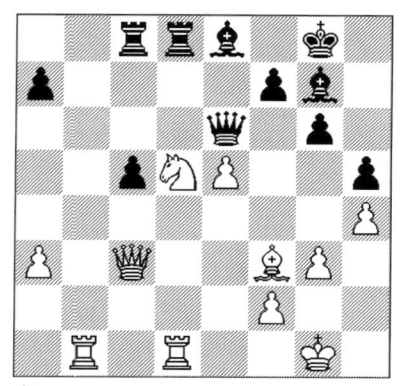

32.♘f6+?

As the sequence will show, the exchange forced in this way will only make things easier for Black, whose passed Pawn from now on will easily compensate for the problems related to the appearance of White's Pawn on the f6 square. It would be relatively better 32.♖b7 ♗×e5 33.♕a5 ♔g7 34.♖×a7 and Black's advantage - the pair of Bishops - is still not decisive.

32...♗×f6 33.e×f6 ♖×d1+ 34.♖×d1 ♗c6!

White can't exchange the Bishop - in that case he would lose his only pride, the Pawn on f6.

35.♖e1 ♕f5 36.♖e3 c4! 37.a4

Realizing the inferiority of their position, White begins to "scratch". If now 37...♗×a4, then 38.♗e4 ♕g4 (38...♕d7 39.♔f3 ♔h7 40.♕e5, etc., and may even lose) 39.♗f3 ♕d7 40.♖e7 ♕d3 41.♕×d3 c×d3? 42.♖×a7 etc., with a draw in sight. But after the simplest response, Black's position is even better than before, as he gets control of the b4 square.

37...a5 38.♗g2 ♗×g2 39.♔×g2 ♕d5+ 40.♔h2 ♕f5 41.♖f3 ♕c5 42.♖f4

After 42.♖e3 ♕b6 White has no useful moves at his disposal (43.♖f3 ♕c6! etc.).

42...♔h7

That wasn't necessary here: it would be much more important to prevent White's next move with 42...♕b6. But the tempting 42...♕b4 would be insufficient: 42...♕b4 43.♕e3 ♕×a4 due to 44.♔f5! ♕b4 45.♖×h5 g×h5 46.♕h6 ♕f8 47.♕g5+ etc., with perpetual check.

43.♖d4 ♕c6?

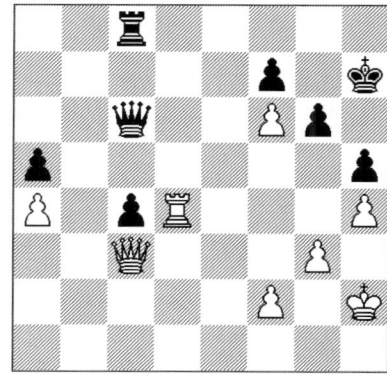

A miscalculation, after which White saves the game. It would still be correct 43...♕b6! and if 44.♔f4 then 44...♔g8 would reach the same position it could have reached two moves ago.

44.♕×a5

Forced, but good enough.

44...c3

If instead 44...♛×f6 then 45.♔f4 with the following possibilities: (a) 45...♛g7 46.♛d5; (b) 45...♛e6 46.♛c3 followed by e5, in any case without risk for White.

45.♛a7! ♔g8

Other moves also don't force a win against correct answers, for example:
I. 45...♛×f6? 46.♔f4 ♛×f4 47.g×f4 c2 48.♛×f7+ ♔h6 49.f5! etc..;
II. 45...♛c7 46.♛×c7 ♜×c7 47.♜d1 etc..;
III. 45...♜c7 46.♛b8 c2 47.♜d8 ♛×f6! 48.♔h8+!! (this was the move I didn't see when I started the combination by playing 43...♛c6) ♛×h8 49.♛×c7 etc., with salvation in all cases.

46.♛e7

If now 46...c2 47.♜d8+ ♜×d8 48.♛×d8+ ♔h7 49.♛e7 ♛e6 50.♛c7 etc., forcing a draw.

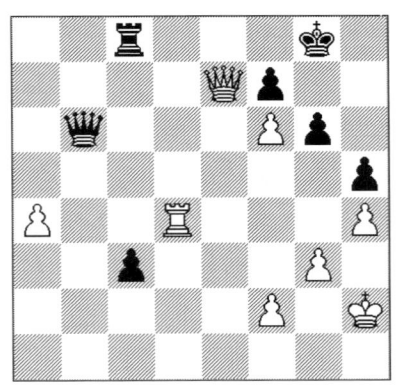

46...♛b6

47.♛d7?

Capablanca doesn't exploit all the advantage given to him by my 43rd move and the game again takes its normal course. By playing 47.♜d7! White would get a draw, because after 47...♛×f2+ (if 47...♔f8 then 48.a5 ♛×a5 49.♜a7 ♛d5 50.♜d7 ♛a5 51.♔c7 and the white Rook due to the ♛×f8+! threat will eternally chase the Queen) 48.♔h1! (48.♔h3 would lose, as in most variants where Black's queen reaches the e6 square with check) 48...♛a2; 49.♜d8+ ♜×d8 50.♛×d8+ ♔h7 51.♛f8 and Black would have nothing better than perpetual check, the white Pawn on f6 remaining invulnerable. A very unusual escape!

47...♛c5! 48.♜e4

Now the only way to stop 48...c7.

48...♛×f2+ 49.♔h3 ♛f1+ 50.♔h2 ♛f2+ 51.♔h3 ♜f8 52.♛c6

Again, the only move.

52...♛f1+ 53.♔h2 ♛f2+ 54.♔h3 ♛f1+ 55.♔h2 ♔h7 56.♛c4

If 56.♛×c3, then 56...♛f2+ 57.♔h1 ♜d8 58.♛e1 ♛f3+ 59.♔h2 ♜d1 winning.

56...♛f2+ 57.♔h3 ♛g1!

The decisive move. Alternatively 57...c2 would be insufficient due to 58.♔f4! followed by ♔f1.

58.♜e2

If instead 58.g4 would lead to a nice ending: 58...c2! 59.♛×c2 ♜e8!! etc.

58...♛f1+?

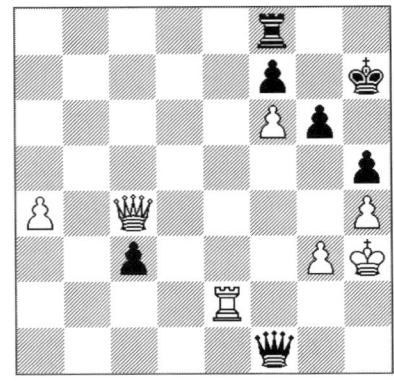

For the second time Black wasted an easy win! The right sequence of moves (which I intended by playing 57...♛g1!) was 58...♛h1+ 59.♜h2 ♛f3! after which White couldn't play

60.♔c2 due to 60...♛f5+; and would be defenseless against the threat of 60...♛×f6, etc. (if 60.♛f4, then 60...♛d1!).

59.♔h2 ♛×f6 60.a5?

Instead of securing a draw with 60.♖c2 ♖e8 61.♔g2! (threatening both 62.♖×c3 and 62.♖f2) Capablanca makes another mistake and could lose instantly.

60...♖d8?

An immediate definition would be obtained through 60...♛f1! 61.♛e4 ♖d8. After the text move, victory will once again become quite problematic.

61.a6?

After 61.♔g2 they could only get a checkers ending with three pawns against two, which with the right defense would most likely end in a draw. Now we're finally at the end!

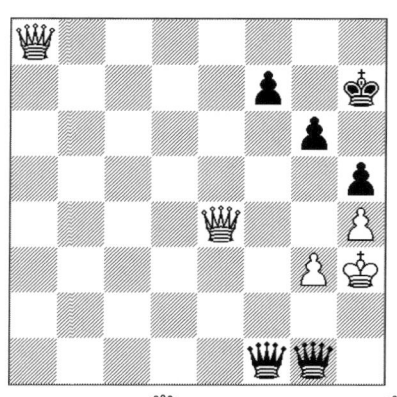

61...♛f1 62.♛e4 ♖d2 63.♖×d2 c×d2 64.a7 d1♛ 65.a8♛ ♛g1+ 66.♔h3 ♛df1+

If now 67.♛g2 then 67...♛h1 mate. White resigned.

In my opinion, this game was praised far too much all over the world. It was certainly very exciting for both players - who were constantly pressed for time - and for the audience. But the final half was a real comedy of errors in which my opponent wasted the equalizer several times and I missed almost as many chances to win. In short, if it weren't for its great sporting importance (it became, in fact, the crucial point of the game), I would hardly include it among my best games.

> **Game 22**
> **J.Capablanca-A.Alekhine**
> *World Championship, Buenos Aires (21), October 1927*
> Queen's Gambit Declined
> Orthodox Defense [D63]

1.d4 d5 2.c4 e6 3.♘c3 ♘f6 4.♗g5 ♘bd7 5.e3 ♗e7 6.♘f3 0–0 7.♖c1 a6

Although with this less usual defense I was quite successful in the game (+1 =7 -0), I now consider it to be unsatisfactory due to the possible response 8.cxd5, adopted by Capablanca in the 23rd, 25th and 27th games.

8.a3?

This harmless rejoinder will be convincingly refuted (as a winning attempt, of course) in the current game. Since then, it has completely disappeared from masterly practice.

8...h6 9.♗h4 d×c4 10.♗×c4 b5!

More natural and better than 10...b6, which in the 13th, 15th, 17th, and 19th games proved sufficient to maintain the balance of the position.

11.♗e2 ♗b7 12.0–0

In the case of 12.b4 Black would gain the initiative through 12...a5! 13.♛b3 a×b4 14.a×b4 g5 15.♗g3 ♘d5, etc.

12...c5 13.d×c5 ♘×c5 14.♘d4

As White doesn't have an atom of advantage, the natural course for him would be to simplify things by 14.♛×d8 ♖f×d8 15.♖fd1, etc.; completely wrong would be to instead bid

47

14.♗×f6 ♗×f6 15.♘×b5 due to 15...♕×d1 16.♖f×d1 ♘b3 17.♖c2 ♗×f3 18.♗×f3 a×b5 19.♗×a8 ♖×a8 with Black's advantage.

14...♖c8

Avoiding ♘×b5 once and for all.

15.b4

Weakening the c4 square unnecessarily. It would be simpler 15.♗f3 ♕b6 16.♕e2, etc.

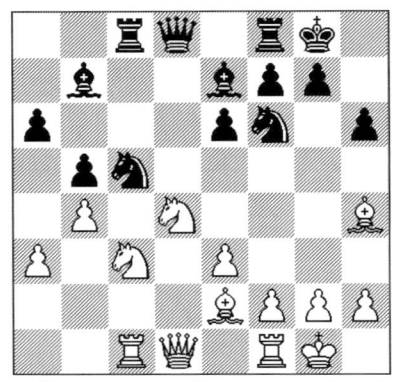

15...♘cd7! 16.♗g3

In the case of 16.♗f3 I intended to play 16...♕b6 17.♘e4 ♗×c1 18.♕×c1 ♗c8, after which the white queen would have no good squares available, for example: (I) 19.♕b1? or 19.♕d2 19...♘×e4, etc.; (II) 19.♕b2 g5 20.♘×f6+ ♗×f6 with an advantage for Black; (III) 19.♕d1 or 19.♕e1, 19...g5, also with an advantage for Black. The text's move is therefore relatively the best.

16...♘b6 17.♕b3

To answer 17...♘c4 with 18.♖fd1 ♕b6 19.a4, etc.

17...♘fd5

A good move, connected with the positional threat 18...♘×c3 19.♖×c3 ♗d5 20.♕b2 ♖×c3 21.♕×c3 ♕a8 followed by ...♗c8, with advantage. White's reply is practically forced.

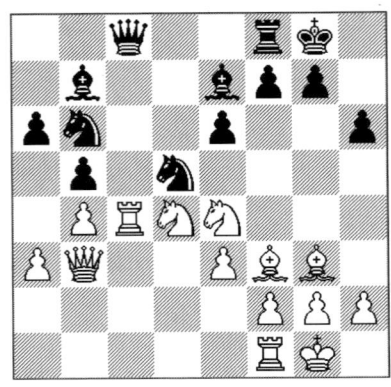

18.♗f3 ♖c4 19.♘e4 ♕c8 20.♗×c4

I'm inclined to consider this exchange as the decisive positional error, because from now on Black, taking the advantage with his Knight's formidable position on c4, will be able to gradually concentrate all his pieces to force the central action. White's correct move would be 20.♕b1, threatening both ♘d6 and ♗d6. In that case, if 20...♖d8 then 21.♘d2 ♗×c1 22.♖×c1 ♕a8 23.♗c7, and White would be able to exchange more material without compromising his position. Still, the move in the text can in no way be considered the decisive blunder. Capablanca lost this game only because he didn't realize the dangers of his position in time and was regularly outplayed in this respect.

20...♘×c4 21.♖c1 ♕a8!

Threatening ...♘×b4 or ...♘×e3, thus forcing White to relinquish control of the central white squares.

22.♘c3

If 22.♘c5, then 22...♗×c5 23.b×c5 ♗c8 24.♗e2 ♖×c5 25.♗×c4 ♕c8 etc., winning a pawn.

22...♖c8

Threatening 23...♘d2, etc.

23.♘×d5 ♗×d5 24.♗×d5 ♕×d5 25.a4

The desire to reduce the Pawns on the Queen's wing is natural, but

White's position remains compromised, as his b-Pawn will become a welcome object of attack at the end of the game.

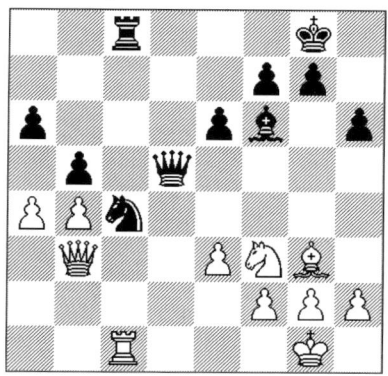

25...♗f6 26.♘f3

Of course, not 26.♖d1 due to 26...b×a4 27.♕×a4 ♘b2 28.♕×a6 ♖a8, winning.

26...♗b2!

To play ...e5 without restricting the Bishop's activity. The tactical justification for this move is demonstrated by the following variants:

(I) 27.♖d1 b×a4! 28.♕×a4 ♘b6 29.♖×d5 ♘×a4 30.♖d1 ♘c3 31.♖e1 ♖c4 32.♗d6 ♘e4 33.♗e7 f6 34.♖b1 ♔f7 35.♔f1 ♗c3 etc., with an easy win in the end;

(II) 27.♖b1 ♘a3! 28.♕×b2 ♘×b1 29.♕×b1 ♕b3 30.♕f1 b×a4 31.h3 a3, winning.

27.♖e1 ♖d8 28.a×b5 a×b5 29.h3

This emergency exit is necessary.

29...e5 30.♖b1 e4!

The beginning of the end.

31.♘d4

Or A. 31.♘e1 ♕d2 32.♕c2 (32.♔f1 ♖a8 33.♖d1 ♖a3 winning) 32...♕×c2 33.♘×c2 ♖d2 34.♘e1 ♘a3 winning; B. 31.♘h2 ♕d3! 32.♖×b2! ♕×b3 33.♖×b3 ♖d1+ 34.♘f1 ♘d2 35.♖a3 ♘×f1, and White would be defenseless.

31...♗×d4 32.♖d1

He loses immediately. But also after 32.e×d4 d×d4 the game wouldn't go far.

32...♘×e3!, and White resigned.

That and the 34th game were, in my opinion, the most valuable of the game.

Game 23
A.Alekhine-J.Capablanca
World Championship, Buenos Aires (32), November 1927
Queen's Gambit Declined
Orthodox Defense [D35]

1.d4 ♘f6 2.c4 e6 3.♘c3 d5 4.♗g5 ♘bd7 5.e3 c6 6.c×d5 e×d5 7.♗d3 ♗e7 8.♘ge2

This development of the Knight was played here for the first time. Due to White's success in this game, it came into fashion in the following years. In my opinion, it's no better or worse than the usual ♘f3; only in the case of castling to the queen's wing, White must be especially careful, as Black's counterattack on that wing can easily become more dangerous than his own initiative on the king's wing.

8...0-0

In this kind of position, ...h6 is usually played before castling so as not to allow White to respond to this pawn move with h4. If Black had done this, my answer wouldn't have been 9.♗h4, but 9.♗f4.

9.♘g3 ♘e8

There is hardly any other form of emancipation, such as 9...♖e8 which would be answered very strongly by 10.♘f5.

10.h4

The natural consequence of the whole opening plan.

10...♘df6 11.♕c2 ♗e6 12.♘f5

♗xf5 13.♗xf5 ♘d6 14.♗d3

Of course, not 14.♗xf6 ♘xf5, with equality. The text move forces Black to weaken his king's position.

14...h6 15.♗f4

In the case of 15.0-0-0 Black could try a counterattack from 15...b5 etc.

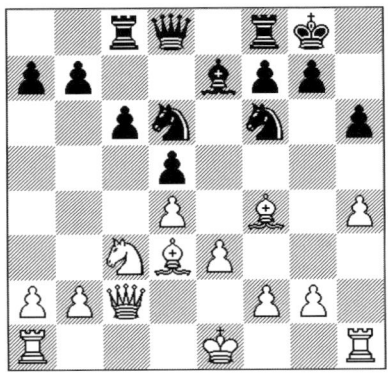

15...♖c8

Black wants to start an action on the c-file as soon as his opponent castles on the queen's wing, and here he misses the combinatorial answer. A more logical course would be 15...♖e8, with the idea of ...♘fe4.

16.g4!

This advance was made possible by the fact that after 16...♘xg4? 17.♗xd6 followed by 18.♗f5 etc., Black would lose quality, considerably strengthening White's position, leaving Black with few choices.

16...♘fe4 17.g5 h5 18.♗xe4

White decides to accept the pawn's (forced) sacrifice, although he imagines that the ending will be extremely difficult to win - due to the very effective position of Black's rook on the second rank. A promising alternative would be 18.♗xd6 ♘xd6 19.0-0-0 (not immediately 19.g6 due to 19...♗xh4 with counterplay) 19...♘b5 20.♔b1 ♘xc3+ 21.♕xc3, and despite the oppositely colored Bishops, Black would not find it easy to get a draw.

18...♘xe4 19.♘xe4 dxe4 20.♕xe4 ♕a5+ 21.♔f1

White can't risk the variant 21.♔e2 ♕b5+ 22.♔f3 ♖fe8, etc.

21...♕d5!

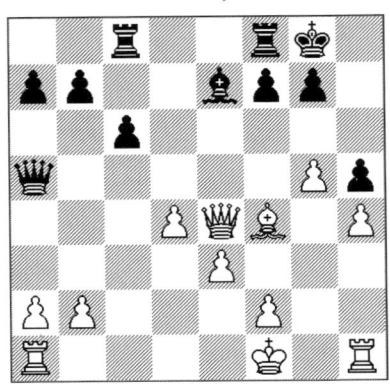

The point of Black's counterplay: after Queen's forced exchange, the only open column will become an especially crucial factor in its favor.

22.♕xd5 cxd5 23.♔g2 ♖c2 24.♖hc1

The importance of eliminating a pair of rooks is obvious. If now 24...♖xb2, White would secure a strong advantage in the end with 25.♔cb1! etc.

24...♖fc8 25.♖xc2 ♖xc2 26.♖b1 ♔h7

Black is preparing to take the advantage of the fact that the white squares in White's position are insufficiently protected. White's next moves show the only appropriate defense against this plan.

27.♔g3 ♔g6 28.f3 f6!

And not 28...♔f5? because of 29.e4+ etc. Both sides have so far tried to make the ending difficult in the right way.

29.gxf6 ♗xf6 30.a4

Preparing to relieve the Rook from the defense of the Pawns on the Queen's wing.

30...♔f5 31.a5 ♖e2

Black now threatens (in the case of 32.b4 for example) 34...g5! 33.h×g5 ♗×g5 34.♗×g5 ♔×g5, after which 35.f4+ ♔f5 36.♔f3 ♖h2 37.♖g1 ♖h3+ 38.♖g3 ♖×g3+! etc., which would only lead to a Pawn ending with a draw.

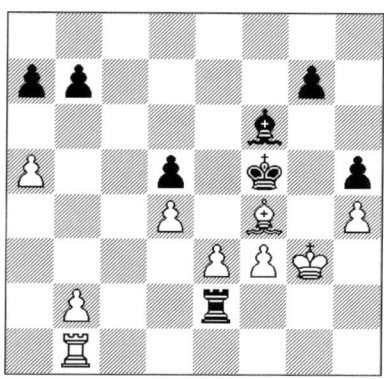

32.♖c1

If White wants to play for a win, he must give back the advantage pawn (at least temporarily). But the most efficient and logical way to do this, considering their last two moves, would be 32.a6! After 32...b×a6 (32...b6 33.♗b8 etc.) the reply 33.♖a1! would prevent 33...g5 due to 34.h×g5 ♗×g5 35.e4+! etc., while after 33...♖×b2 34.♖×a6 ♖b7 35.♖a5 etc., White's positional advantage would prove decisive. After the chosen move, Black will be able to offer a long and not entirely hopeless resistance.

32...♖×b2 33.♖c5 ♔e6 34.e4 ♗×d4

Here, as many times during this game, Black could play differently, but it's doubtful whether this would alter the final result. If, for example, 34...d×e4 35.d5+ ♔f5 36.d6+ ♔e6 37.f×e4 ♖b3+ 38.♔g2 ♗×h4 39.♖×h5 followed by 40.♖h7 and the fight against the passed central pawns would prove extremely difficult.

35.♖×d5 ♗c3

By playing 35...♗f2+ 36.♔h3 ♖b3 37.♖e5+ ♔f7 Black would temporarily save the pawn, but his position after 38.♗g5 still looks very compromising.

36.♖×h5 a6

If 36...♗e1+ 37.♔h3 ♔f2, then 38.♖e5+!, followed by 39.♖f5+ or 39.♖d5+ – d3, still keeping the Pawn advantage.

37.♗c7 ♗e1+

Or 37...♖b5 38.♔g4! etc.

38.♔g4 ♖g2+ 39.♔h3

Of course, not 39.♔f4 ♗d2 mate!

39...♖f2 40.♔g4 ♖g2+ 41.♔h3 ♖f2 42.f4! ♖f3+ 43.♔g2

Here is another form of suicide: 43.♔g4 ♖g3 mate.

43...♖f2+ 44.♔h3 ♖f3+ 45.♔g2 ♖f2+ 46.♔g1 ♖c2 47.♗b6 ♖c4

This makes White's task easier, as it allows his King to give effective support to the central Pawns. It would be better to 47...♗g3 after which White would try to win with 48.♖e5+ (48...♔d6 49.♔g5 or 48...♔f7 49.h5! etc.).

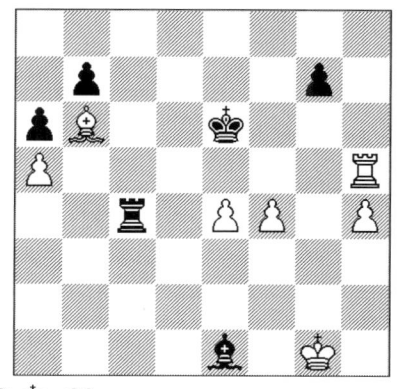

48.♔g2!

With this move, White finally has a

clear winning position. It's obvious that after 48...♔xe4 49.♔f3 Black would lose immediately.

48...g6 49.♖e5+ ♔d7 50.h5! gxh5 51.♔f3 h4

Wouldn't 51...♔c3+ 52.♔e2 ♗g3 53.♗e3 h4 54.♖h5, etc. be better?

52.♖h5 ♖c3+ 53.♔g4 ♖c4 54.♔f5!

Seemingly falling into the trap, but in reality, choosing the quickest and safest way to make their past Pawns count.

54.♗xa5 55.♖h7+

Of course not 55.♗xa5 ♔c5+ 56.♔g4? due to 56...♔xh5 followed by 57...a3, winning.

55...♔c6 56.♗xa5 ♖c5+ 57.♔e6! ♖xa5 58.f5 ♖a3 59.f6 ♖f3 60.f7 b5 61.♖h5!

The last detail of that flashy finale.

61...h3 62.♖f5 ♖xf5 63.exf5

If now 63...h2 64.f8♕ h1♕, then 65.♕a8+ etc., winning. Black resigned.

Game 24
A.Alekhine–J.Capablanca
World Championship, Buenos Aires (34), November 1927
Queen's Gambit Declined [D51]

1.d4 d5 2.c4 e6 3.♘c3 ♘f6 4.♗g5 ♘bd7 5.e3 c6 6.a3

This quiet move, whose main goal is to avoid the Cambridge Springs Defense, hardly promises White more than a comfortable balance. I chose it here simply to get out of the book variants as quickly as possible.

6...♗e7 7.♘f3 0–0 8.♗d3 dxc4

A more solid alternative would be 8...h6 9.♗h4 c5.

9.♗xc4 ♘d5 10.♗xe7 ♕xe7

10...♘xe7 was also possible.

11.♘e4 ♘5f6 12.♘g3 c5

It's worth considering 12...b6 followed by ...♗b7 as Maroczy played against me in San Remo, 1930. The maneuver in the text has the small defect of not solving the development problem of Black's queen bishop.

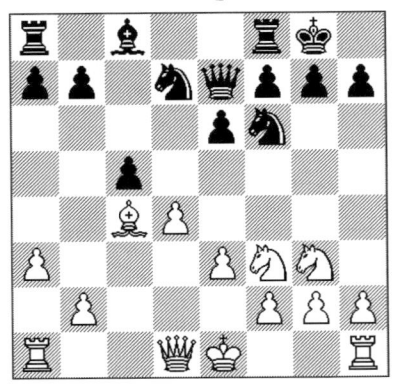

13.0–0 ♘b6 14.♗a2 cxd4 15.♘xd4 g6

To be able to answer e4 with ...e5 without ceding the f4 square to White's knights.

16.♖c1

Eventually threatening ♘b5.

16...♗d7 17.♕e2 ♖ac8 18.e4 e5 19.♘f3 ♔g7

Black here could exchange both rooks through 19...♖xc1 20.♖xc1 ♗c8 21.♖xc8+ and after 21...♘xc8 the move 22.♘g5 would be sufficiently answered by 22...♗e8, etc. The move in the text, and especially the next one, suddenly puts his position in danger.

20.h3 h6?

See the next Diagram

21.♕d2!

This harmless move is actually difficult to respond to. White's main threat is 22.♕a5, and if Black tries to stop it by counter-attacking 21...♗c6 (or 21...♗b5), then an unexpected diversion on the kingside would lead to a quick ending: 22.♘h4! ♘xe4 (or 22...♗xe4 23.♕e3!; or 22...♗d7 23.♕a5 etc.) 23.♘hf5+ gxf5 24.♘xf5+ ♔f6 25.♕xh6+ ♔xf5 26.g4 mate!.

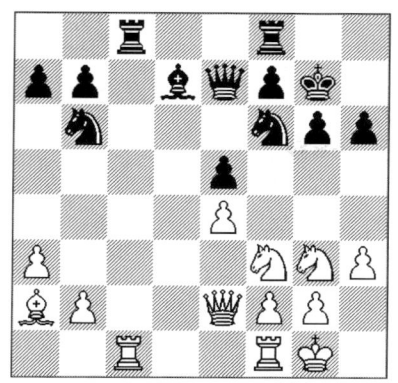

The only move that offered any prospect of a successful defense was suggested by Dr. Lasker, 21...♘a4! In that case, White would simply continue strengthening his position, for example with 22.♖fd1.

21...♗e6?

The position proved difficult for Black. They now lose a pawn and after a desperate struggle, the game, and the game. The sharp combination afterwards, as well as the subsequent Queen and Rook ending, are exciting and instructive.

22.♗xe6 ♕xe6 23.♕a5 ♘c4

Or 23...♕b3 24.♕xe5 ♘c4 25.♕d4, etc., with an advantage for White.

24.♕xa7 ♘xb2 25.♖xc8 ♖xc8 26.♕xb7 ♘c4 27.♕b4 ♖a8 28.♖a1 ♕c6!

Threatening to block White's Pawn with 29...♖a4 and also (at least apparently) win the King's Pawn. But White's next two moves set the record straight.

29.a4! ♘xe4 30.♘xe5

Thus avoiding the quagmire 30.♘xe4 ♕xe4 31.♖c1 ♔c8 32.♘xe5? ♘e3! 33.♕xe4 ♖xc1+ 34.♔h2 ♘f1+ followed by ...♘g2+ and ♘xe4, after which Black can even win.

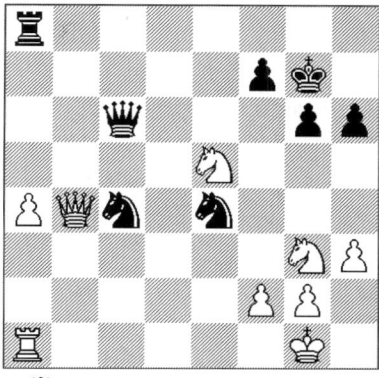

30...♕d6!

The better comparatively under the circumstances, as both pairs of Knights will soon disappear from the board.

31.♕xc4 ♕xe5 32.♖e1 ♘d6 33.♕c1! ♕f6 34.♘e4 ♘xe4 35.♔xe4

The winning procedure that follows is quite elaborate and consists of a combination of threats connected to the passed pawn and an attack on Black's somewhat exposed king. First, White will succeed in controlling the important a1–h8 diagonal.

35...♖b8 36.♖e2 ♖a8 37.♖a2 ♖a5 38.♕c7! ♕a6

Obviously, the only way to prevent the advance of the passed pawn.

39.♕c3+ ♔h7 40.♖d2

With the deadly threat 41.♖d8.

40...♕b6 41.♖d7

The secret move. Black's next move offers the only chance, if not to save the game, at least to allow a long resistance.

41...♕b1+ 42.♔h2 ♕b8+ 43.g3

♖f5 44.♕d4

Threatening 45.a5! followed by ♖d8.

44...♕e8 45.♖d5 ♖f3

Damas' end would, of course, be tantamount to resignation.

46.h4

White doesn't need to avoid Black's Queen's next move, which will finally lead to an easily winning Rook ending for them.

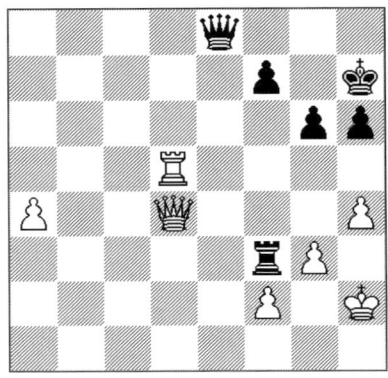

46...♕h8 47.♕b6!

The exchange would be premature at this point, as it would allow Black to place the Rook behind the passed Pawn.

47...♕a1 48.♔g2 ♖f6

If 48...♖a3 White wins with 49.♖d7 ♔g8 (or 49...♔g7 50.♕e6!; or 49...♕a2 50.♕f6 etc.) 50.♕d8+ ♔g7 51.♕e7 ♕a2 52.♕e5+ ♔h7 53.♕f6, etc.

49.♕d4

Now the time is right for the exchange, and it will be the *white* rook that will be behind the passed pawn.

49...♕×d4 50.♖×d4 ♔g7

Instead, 50...♖a6 would lose immediately after 51.♔f3, followed by ♔-e4–d5 etc.

51.a5 ♖a6 52.♖d5 ♖f6 53.♖d4 ♖a6 54.♖a4 ♔f6 55.♔f3 ♔e5 56.♔e3 h5 57.♔d3 ♔d5 58.♔c3 ♔c5 59.♖a2 ♔b5 60.♔b3

White uses any opportunity, by repeating moves, to gain time on the clock, thus avoiding a slip-up that could let the title slip away.

60...♔c5 61.♔c3 ♔b5 62.♔d4

If now 62...♔b4, then 63.♖a1! etc.

62...♖d6+ 63.♔e5 ♖e6+ 64.♔f4 ♔a6 65.♔g5 ♖e5+ 66.♔h6 ♖f5 67.f4

The simplest method of forcing the capitulation would be 67.♔g7 ♖f3 68.♔g8 ♖f6 69.♔f8! ♔f3 (or 69...♔f5 70.f4) 70.♔g7 ♔f5 71.f4 etc.

67...♖c5! 68.♖a3 ♖c7 69.♔g7 ♖d7 70.f5

Another inaccurate move. The most direct path would be first 70.♔f6 and only after 70...♔c7 71.f5 g×f5 72.♔×f5 ♔c5+ 73.♔f6 ♔c7 74.♖f3 ♔×a5 75.♖f5+, winning.

70.g×f5 71.♔h6 f4 72.g×f4 ♖d5 73.♔g7 ♖f5 74.♖a4 ♔b5 75.♖e4! ♔a6 76.♔h6 ♔×a5

Or 76...♔b7 77.♖e5 ♖×f4 78.♔g5! ♖f1 79.♔×h5 f5 80.♔g5 f4 81.♖f5 f3 82.♔g4, winning.

77.♖e5 ♖a1 78.♔×h5 ♖g1 79.♖g5 ♖h1 80.♖f5 ♔b6 81.♖×f7 ♔c6

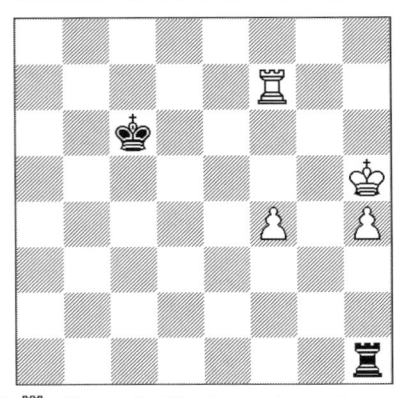

82.♖e7, and Black resigned.

Alexander Alekhine

CHAPTER 2
Tournaments Games and Matches with Bogoljubov - 1929 - 1934

Game 25
A.Alekhine-H.Steiner
Bradley Beach Tournament, June 1929
Queen's Gambit Accepted [D28]
Beauty Award

1.d4 ♘f6 2.♘f3 d5 3.c4 dxc4 4.e3 e6 5.♗xc4 c5 6.0-0 a6 7.♕e2 ♘bd7

If 7...♘c6, the best answer according to the most recent practice (Euwe-Alekhine, 5th Game of the match, 1937) would be 8.♘c3!

8.♘c3 ♕c7

If Black doesn't want to risk fianchetto development, which isn't really advisable (for example, 8...b5 9.♗b3 ♗b7 10.♖d1 ♗e7 11.e4! b4 12.e5 bxc3 13.exf6 etc...), he could simply play 8...Be7; square c7 for the queen, with an advantage for White, as in the Alekhine-Letelier game, Montevideo 1938), they could simply play 8...♗e7; the c7 square for the queen, in the event of the d-pawn advancing, will then prove very uncomfortable.

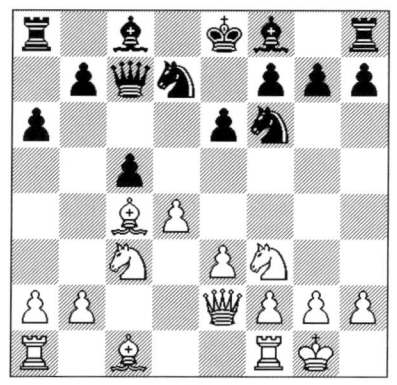

9.d5! exd5 10.♗xd5

One of Black's problems from now on is that if this bishop is exchanged, White will always recapture, gaining time.

10...♗d6 11.e4 0-0 12.♗g5 ♘g4

In order to develop their queen wing, Black's pieces are forced to waste time with this knight, and more than that, facilitate the dangerous advance of White's f-pawn.

13.h3 ♘ge5 14.♘h4!

In view of Black's restricted position, the correct policy is to avoid exchanges. In addition, Black is now forced to avoid the ♘f5 move and consequently has even fewer choices than before.

14...♘b6 15.f4 ♘c6 16.f5!

A paradoxical but very effective attacking continuation, through which White "sacrifices" the central square e5. The "natural" advance 16.e5 could instead leave White - oddly enough - with an insignificant positional advantage after 16...♗e7.

16...♘e5 17.♕h5 ♖e8

Stalling the threat 18.f6 would now be answered by 18...g6 10.♕h6 ♗f8.

18.♖f4 ♗e7

This move will be refuted by a beautiful combination, but as Black still can't take the powerful Bishop - after 18...♘xd5? follows 19.♘xd5 ♕c6 20.♘f6+! gxf6 21.♗xf6 – there soon won't be enough defense.

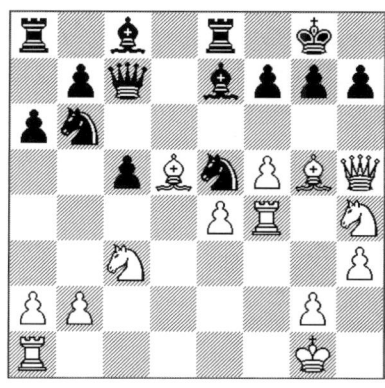

19.f6!

Because of Black's last move, White is able to make this breakthrough *despite the possible defense 19...g6*

20.♘xg6 h×g6 20.♕h6 20...♗f8 - and that's because of the following combination: 19...g6 20.♘xg6!! h×g6 (or A) 21.♗×f7+! ♔×f7 22.f×e7+ ♔e6 (or 22...♔g8 23.♖f8+ ♖×f8 24.e×f8♕+ ♔×f8 25.♕h8+ ♔f7 26.♕h7+ winning the Queen) 23.♖f6+ ♔×e7 (or 23...♔d7 24.♖d1+ etc.) 24.♕h7+ ♔d8 25.♖d6 mate.

(A) 20... ♘×g6 21.♗×f7+ ♔×f7 22.♕×h7+ ♔e6 23.♕×g6 winning. After the next retreat, which allows the f-file to open, the game is practically over.

19...♗f8 20.f×g7 ♗×g7 21.♖af1 ♗e6 22.♘f5

Also threatening ♖h4 etc.

22...♗×d5 23.♘×g7 ♘g6 24.♘×e8 ♔×e8 25.♘×d5, and Black resigned.

Game 26
A.Alekhine-E.Bogoljubov
World Championship (1)
Wiesbaden, September 1929
Queen´s Gambit Declined , Slav Defense [D16]

1.d4 d5 2.c4 c6 3.♘f3 ♘f6 4.♘c3 d×c4 5.a4 e6

I was peculiarly fortunate that this illogical move (instead of the natural 5...♗f5) was adopted against me, with disastrous effects, on no less than four occasions, namely (in addition to the present game) again by Bogoljubov (Nottingham 1936), by Dr. Euwe (19th Game of the 1935 game) and later by the German master Helling, in Dresden 1936.

6.e4 ♗b4 7.e5 ♘d5

In the three other games mentioned, the answer was 7...♘e4, which is at least as bad as the move in the text.

8.♗d2 ♗×c3

If instead 8...b5, then 9.♘e4 ♗e7 10.b3! etc., recovering the pawn with a decidedly better position.

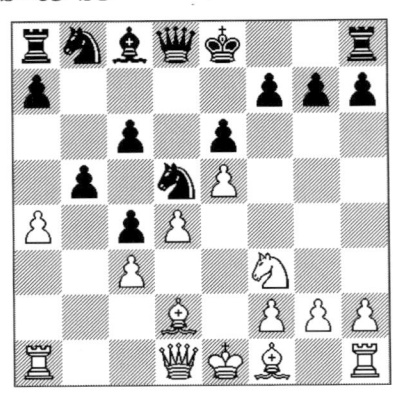

9.b×c3 b5

10.♘g5!

An important move with multiple objectives, not least to avoid 10...0-0 due to 11.♕b1!, followed by 12.a×b5 etc., with an advantage for White.

10...f6

Preventing the ♘e4 – d6+ maneuver, but at the cost of seriously compromising the central position.

11.e×f6 ♘×f6

Or 11...♕×f6 12.a×b5 c×b5 13.♘e4 ♕e7 14.♗g5, followed by ♕h5+, etc., with White's advantage.

12.♗e2 a6

The move 12...0-0 13.a×b5 g6 (if 13...c×b5 then 14.♗f3 ♘d5 15.♕b1, etc.) 14.b6! ♕×b6 15.♘f3 would prove hopeless in the long run.

13.♗f3!

With the threat 14.a×b5, which is difficult to stop, for example: 13...♘d5 then 14.♕b1! g6 15.♘×h7 ♖×h7 16.♕×g6+ ♖f7 17.♗h5 followed by 18.♕g8 winning. Or 13...♖a7 14.♗f4 ♖b7 15.a×b5 a×b5 16.♖a8 etc., also with a winning attack.

13...h6

It's mere desperation.

14.♗h5+ ♘×h5 15.♕×h5+ ♔d7 16.♘f7 ♕e8 17.♕g6 ♖g8 18.♗f4

♗b7

Or 18...♔f8 19.♘e5+ ♔d8 20.♕e4, etc.

19.♗g3 ♔e7 20.♗d6+

A bit of a game of cat and mouse.

20...♔d7 21.0–0 c5 22.d×c5 ♗d5 23.a×b5 a×b5 24.♖×a8 ♗×a8 25.♖a1 ♘c6

26.♘e5+!

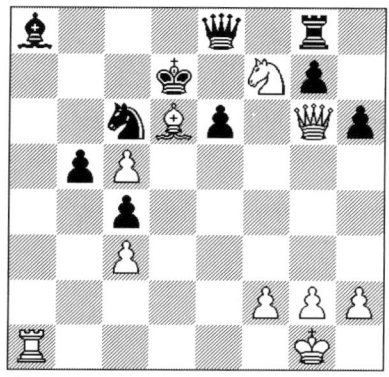

If now 26...♘×e5 27.♖a7+ ♔c6, then 28.♕e4 mate. Black resigned.

Game 27
A.Alekhine-E.Bogoljubov
World Championship (5)
Wiesbaden, September 1929
Queen's Gambit Declined, Slav Defense [D17]

1.d4 d5 2.c4 c6 3.♘f3 ♘f6 4.♘c3 d×c4 5.a4 ♗f5 6.♘e5 e6

A simple and good move. But in making it here (and in Game 3 of the game, in which I adopted the less logical answer 7.f3), Bogoljubov, as will be shown below, didn't fully understand its real value.

7.♗g5 ♗e7

Decidedly too passive. The correct continuation is 7...♗b4 (introduced by me in a game with consultation against Bogoljubov and Dr. Seitz immediately after the game) 8.f3 h6! (as in my 11th Game in the game against Dr. Euwe, Groningen 1937), obtaining at least a balanced game.

8.f3 h6

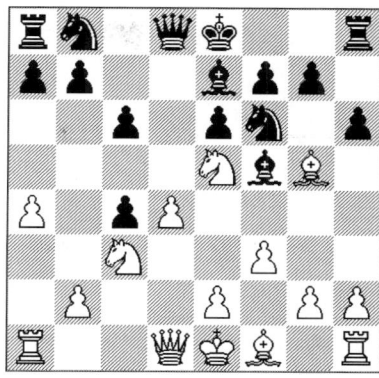

9.e4!

This move, which with Black's Bishop on b4 would be answered by 9...h×g5 10.e×f5 b5! 11.a×b5 c×b5 12.♕c2 0–0! etc., with better play for Black, in the current position practically puts the opponent's queen bishop out of play for the rest of the game.

9...♗h7

Or 9...h×g5 10.e×f5 e×f5 11.♗×c4 0–0 12.h4! etc., with an advantage for White.

10.♗e3 ♘bd7 11.♗×c4 0–0 12.♗e2 c5

The exchanges that follow decisively favor White, as they don't eliminate the main flaw in Black's position, the clumsy situation of his queen bishop.

13.d×c5 ♗×c5 14.♗×c5 ♘×c5 15.b4 ♘a6

It would also be unsatisfactory 15...♕×d1+ 16.♔×d1 ♘×a4 17.♘×a4 b5 18.♘cb6! a×b6 19.♗×b5 etc., with an advantage for White.

16.♕×d8 ♖f×d8

See the next Diagram

17.♘a2!

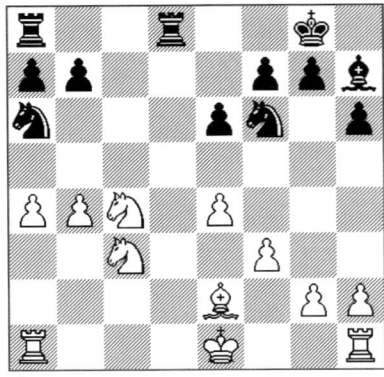

The only way to take the positional advantage, since 17.b5 would concede the important c5 square and 17.♖b1 would allow the promising counterattack initiated by 17...♘d5!

17...♘b8

White threatens 18.♘a5 ♖ab8 19.♘×b7, etc.

18.♔f2 ♘c6 19.♖hd1 ♘d4

If instead 19...♔×d1 20.♔×d1 ♖d8, it would quickly be fatal 21.b5 ♔×d1 22.♗×d1 ♘d8 23.♘d6 followed by 24.♘b4 and 25.♘c8! etc.

20.♖ac1 ♔f8

The first step is to release the Bishop on h7 via ...♗g8, ...♘e8, ...f6 etc. But this plan will obviously take a lot of time, which White will use for the decisive strengthening of the pressure on the queen's wing. From now on the game develops in a perfectly logical way.

21.♗f1 ♘e8 22.♘c3

A strong alternative here would be 22.♘a5, for example:

I. 22.♘a5 ♖ab8 23.♘c3 b6 24.♖×d4! ♖×d4 25.♘c6 ♖bd8 26.♔e3 ♖4d6 27.♘×d8 ♖×d8 28.♘b5

II. 22...b6 23.♘b7 ♖d7 24.♗b5! ♔×b7 25.♗×d4, with a tremendous positional advantage in both cases.

22...f6 23.♘a5 ♖ab8

This seemingly natural response gives White the opportunity for the next combination, which forcibly wins a pawn. It would be better 23...b6 24.♘b7 ♖d7 25.♗b5 ♖×b7 26.♖×d4 ♖c7 27.♘e2 ♖×c1 28.♘×c1 ♖c8 29.♘d3 with some defensive chances, despite White's undoubted advantage.

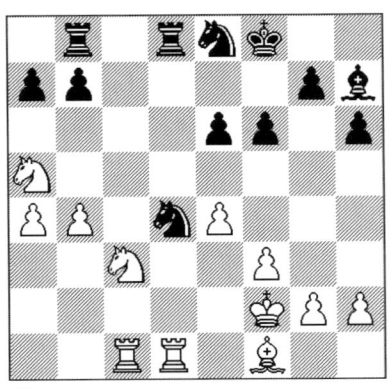

24.♘b5!

Eliminating the enemy's central knight at the right moment: if Black found time for a later consolidation with ...e5, there would be very little pressure resigned from White on the queen's wing.

24...♘×b5

Obviously forced.

25.♖×d8 ♖×d8 26.♘×b7! ♖b8

Or 26...♖d2+ 27.♔e3 ♘bd6 28.♔×d2 ♘×b7 29.♖c8 followed by ♖a8 and ♖×a7, winning.

27.♘c5 ♔e7

Due to the threat 28.♘d7+ the Knight still had to stay put. The ending then, with an extra Pawn and a much better position, will be a walkover for White.

28.a×b5

Much more effective than 28.♗×b5, because now Black's a-pawn becomes extremely weak.

29...♘d6 29.♖a1 ♘c8 30.♗c4

♔g8

After 30...e5 White would win immediately with 31.♗e6, etc.

31.f4 ♗f7 32.e5

All of Black's pieces will gradually be immobilized, and soon White's King will be able to pay a meaningful visit to the opposing knight in its own residence.

32...fxe5 33.fxe5 ♖b6 34.♔e3 ♗e8 35.♖a5 ♗d7 36.♔d4 ♗e8

Black has nothing else to do and patiently awaits the execution.

37.h4 ♗d7 38.♗e2 ♖b8 39.♘xd7 ♔xd7 40.♗f3!

Avoiding the maneuver ...♖–b7–c7 would allow Black to prolong the agony.

40...♖b6 41.♔c5 ♖b8 42.h5 ♔d8 43.♗c6 ♔e7 44.♖a3 ♔f7 45.♗e4 ♔e7 46.♔c6!

Now the Knight will perish.

46...♔d8 47.♖d3+ ♔e7 48.♔c7, and Black resigned.

Game 28
E.Bogoljubov-A.Alekhine
World Championship (8)
Wiesbaden, September 1929
Queen's Indian Defense [D50]

1.d4 ♘f6 2.c4 b6

Although this system of development is not easy to refute, it can hardly be considered absolutely correct because it allows White to have total control over the central squares at an early stage in the game. And the fact that Black can attack the central Pawn with ...c5 doesn't give him full compensation for the lack of space he'll suffer after the next 10 to 15 moves. Without a doubt, the safest move is 2...e6.

3.♘c3 ♗b7 4.f3 d5 5.cxd5 ♘xd5 6.e4 ♘xc3 7.bxc3

White's position now looks very promising. But by adopting a completely wrong half-game plan, White will spoil it.

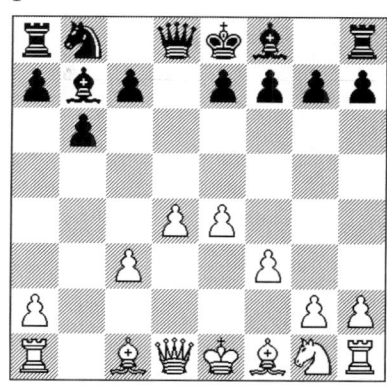

7...e6 8.♗b5+

No better or worse than the immediate 8.♗d3, as ...a6 won't prove to be a weakness in Black's position throughout the game.

8...♘d7 9.♘e2 ♗e7 10.0–0 a6 11.♗d3 c5 12.♗b2?

A bad move, which demonstrates a total misconception of the needs of the position. White instead had the choice between two good bishop moves: 12.♗e3 and 14.♗f4. Also 12.a4 (to fix Black's slight weakness on b6) could be considered. From now on Black will gradually seize the initiative.

12...♕c7 13.f4

This allows Black to gain a couple of tempo points by attacking the insufficiently defended central Pawns. A lesser evil would be 13.e5, temporarily restricting Black's knight's field of play.

13...♘f6 14.♘g3

See the next Diagram

White's last aimless moves provoke

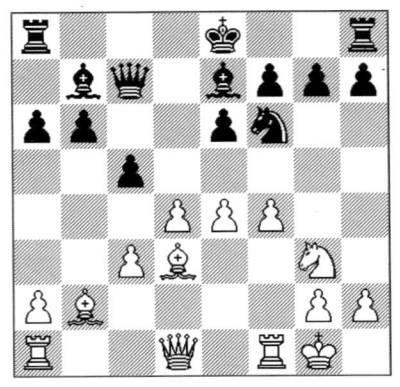

an immediate attack on his king.

14...h5! 15.♕e2 h4 16.♘h1 ♘h5 17.♕g4

Despite their previous indifferent play, White could still retake the game if he recognized his mistake on the 12th move and took his bishop to c1. The seemingly more aggressive move made in the game instead relieves Black of the worry about being a d-pawn and thus allows him, through castling, to have an overwhelming position.

17...0-0-0 18.♖ae1

If 18.f5 then 18...♘f6 (19.♕xg7? ♖h7) followed by 19...e5 with advantage.

18...♔b8 19.f5

This attempt to block the center fails, as Black can secure strong diagonals for both Bishops. But the game is already lost from a strategic point of view.

19...e5 20.d5 c4!

Securing the future of the Bishop of Kings.

21.♗c2 ♗c5+ 22.♘f2 g6!

After this move the queen bishop will also carry out a killing move on the c8–h3 diagonal.

23.fxg6 ♖dg8 24.♗c1

A sign of belated remorse!

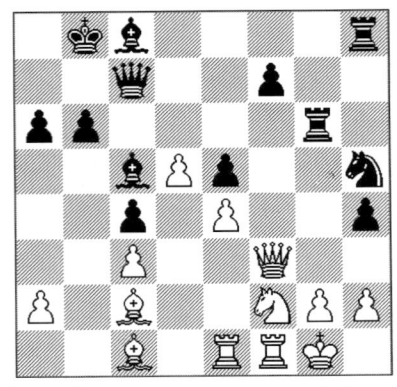

24...♗c8 25.♕f3 ♖xg6 26.♔h1

White is eager to save his queen (which Black threatens to win with 26...♗g4) and doesn't notice the mate combination that follows. However, their position was already hopeless anyway - if, for example, 26.♗e3, then 26...♗xe3 27.♔xe3 ♘f4 28.g3 hxg3 29.hxg3 f5, followed by 30...♕h7 and mate.

26...♘g3+! 27.hxg3 hxg3+ 28.♘h3 ♗xh3 29.gxh3 ♖xh3+ 30.♔g2 ♖h2 g mate.

Game 29
A.Alekhine-E.Bogoljubov
World Championship (17)
Berlin, October 1929
King's Indian Defense [D70]

1.d4 ♘f6 2.c4 g6 3.f3 d5

Although this system isn't very solid, it doesn't mean that it's as easy to play as it seems at first glance, as White's central position can eventually become weak. The first player therefore needs to be careful.

4.cxd5 ♘xd5 5.e4 ♘b6 6.♗e3 ♗g7 7.♘c3 ♘c6?

See the next Diagram

But Black also needed to get the opening moves right, which he didn't do this time. What was needed was

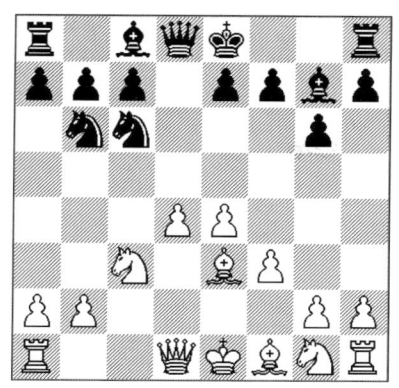

7...0-0, as played by Bogoljubov against me in Bled 1931. In that case, the correct answer for White would be 8.f4!. The move in the text is already almost a decisive positional blunder.

8.d5 ♘e5 9.♗d4 f6

Practically forced, because after 9...0-0 10.f4 ♘ed7 11.♗×g7 followed by 12.♕d4+, 13.0-0-0 and a4 etc., White would get a winning attack on the King.

10.f4?

This is enough to have some advantage in the opening, but it would be much more unpleasant for Black in the first place 10.a4! as in this case they can't play ...e5, which in this game would relieve their restricted position.

10...♘f7 11.a4 e5

Otherwise, the "hole" in e6 would quickly prove fatal.

12.d×e6 ♗×e6 13.a5 ♘d7 14.a6

Through an analogous maneuver on the King's wing, I obtained a winning position in the decisive game against Rubinstein in Prague 1921. In the present position it's certainly not as forceful, but still strong enough.

14...b6 15.♗b5

Threatening 16.♗c6 followed by 17.♘b5, etc.

15...♕e7

To answer 16.♗c5 with 16...0-0-0.

16.♘ge2 c5 17.♗f2 0-0-0

By making this risky move, Bogoljubov was probably already planning the sacrifice on e5, which would undoubtedly give him some fighting chances. He can hardly be blamed for this decision, since the alternative 17...0-0 18.♘d5 ♗×d5 (or 18...♕d6 19.♗g3, with White's advantage) 19.♕×d5 ♔fd8 20.0-0-0 ♘f8 21.♕b7 would leave very few chances of salvation.

18.♕a4 f5 19.e5

At that point the move 19.♗c4 would lead to nothing in particular after 19...♘b8 20.♗×e6+ ♕×e6 21.♘b5 ♘c6 (or 21...♖d7), etc.

19...g5

Forcing White to show his hand, because after 20.g3 g×f4 21.g×f4 the sacrifice 21...♘d×e5 etc. would be more than unpleasant.

20.♗c4! ♘d×e5!

A passive resistance started by 20...♘b8 would soon prove hopeless after 21.♗×e6+ ♕×e6 22.0-0 with the strong threat 23.b4, etc. But now White will be forced to play very precisely to get any advantage.

21.♗×e6+ ♕×e6 22.f×e5 ♘×e5 23.0-0 ♕c4!

The sacrificial point! After 24.♕×c4 ♘×c4 25.♘b5 ♔b8 etc., Black hopes to get some further advantage for his piece, after which the endgame would offer them not such bad prospects; and if 24.♕c2 then 24...♕d3 with roughly the same result. White's next move, however, comes unexpectedly for Black.

See the next Diagram

24.b4!

White sacrifices another Pawn - thus re-establishing the balance of power -

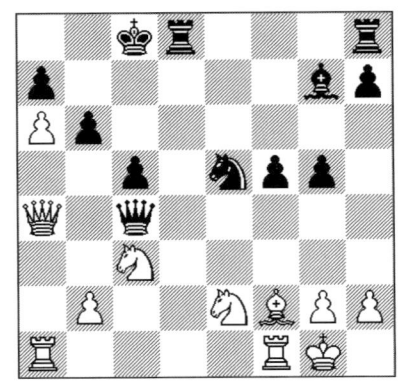

just to avoid the exchange of Queens. If now 24...c×b4 then 25.♘b5! ♕×e2 26.♔fe1 ♕d2 27.♘×a7+ ♔b8 28.♘c6+! etc., winning.

24...♕×b4 25.♕c2 ♘d3

The only defense against the double threat 26.♖a4 and 26.♕×f5+.

26.♖fb1 ♕c4 27.♖a4 ♕e6

If instead 27...♕f7 then 28.♗d4! c×d4 (or 28...♗×d4+ 29.♘×d4 ♖×d4 30.♖×d4 c×d4 31.♕×d3 d×c3 32.♕×c3+, winning) 29.♘d5+! ♘c5 30.♘×b6+! a×b6 31.♔×b6 followed by 32.a7 winning.

28.♘b5 ♔b8

A longer resistance would be possible after 28...♘×f2 29.♔×f2 (and not 29.♘×a7+ ♔b8 30.♕×c5? ♖d1+! etc.) 29...♔b8 but continuing with 30.♘g3 ♔hf8 31.♖a3! (followed by 32.♖e3 or 32.♖d3 etc.), White would still increase his pressure decisively.

29.♘ed4! ♕e4

Or 29...♗×d4 30.♗×d4 ♔×d4 31.♖×d4 ♕e3+ 32.♔f1e the Rook is taboo because of the mate in two in the event of its capture.

30.♘c3 ♕e8 31.♕×d3 c×d4 32.♗×d4 ♕e6 33.♕f3! ♕f7 34.♗×b6

See the next Diagram

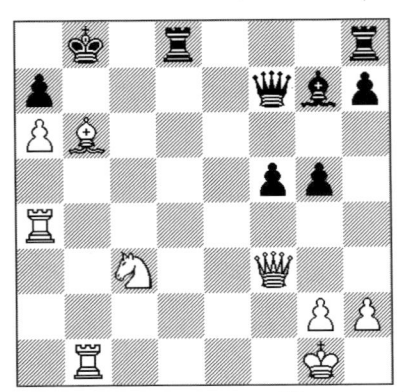

If now 34...a×b6 35.♖×b6+ ♔c8, then 36.♕c6+ ♕c7 37.♖b8+ ♔×b8 38.a7+ and mate in two moves. Black resigned.

Game 30
E.Bogoljubov-A.Alekhine
World Championship (22)
Amsterdam, November 1929
King's Indian Defense [D17]

1.e4 e5 2.♘f3 ♘c6 3.♗b5 a6 4.♗a4 d6 5.c3

The fashionable move here - especially after Keres' victory against me in Margate, 1937 - is 5.c4. But for how long? Black seems able to get a fairly satisfactory position by continuing 5...♗d7 6.♘c3 ♘f6 7.d4 ♘×d4 8.♗×d7+ ♕×d7 9.♘×d4 e×d4 10.♕×d4 ♗e7 followed by ...0-0, etc.

5...♗d7 6.d4 g6 7.♗g5

As the continuation shows, White has no means of exploiting the b3-g8 diagonal, and on the other hand, the f7 square will prove to be a suitable square for Black's knight. It seems, however, that after 5.c3 White's advantage in the opening is about to disappear in a few moves and that therefore the usual 5.♗×c6+ followed by 6.d4 offers them more fighting chances.

7...f6 8.♗e3 ♘h6 9.0-0 ♗g7

10.h3

To avoid ...♘g4 in the case of ♘bd2.

10...♘f7 11.♘bd2 0-0 12.d×e5

White - rightly - recognizes that prolonged maintenance of the central tension can be somewhat favorable to Black and aims for simplification. The defense problem in this game was solved in a very satisfactory way.

12...d×e5

It could also be played 12...f×e5, hoping to exploit the f-file. White in this case could try to bring the knight to d5 after the moves 13.♗b3 h6 14.a4, followed by ♘c4, ♗d2, ♘e3, etc. I preferred the text move because of the tempting possibility of briefly attacking White's central position with ...f5.

13.♗c5

To provoke the move ...b6 which slightly weakens Black's queen wing.

13...♖e8 14.♗b3 b6 15.♗e3 ♕e7 16.♕e2

Or 16.♗d5 ♖ad8 17.♕e2 ♘b8 followed by ...♗e6.

16...♘cd8 17.♗d5

Still playing for simplicity, which Black can't avoid with 17...c6, as he would lose a Pawn after 18.♗×f7+ followed by 19.♗×b6.

17...♗c6 18.c4?

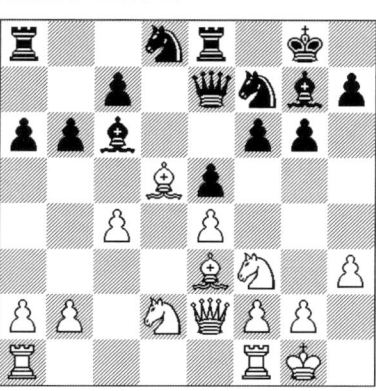

But this is certainly not in line with the requirements of the position, as the Pawn on d5 after ...f5 will become very weak. It would require 18.♗×c6 ♘×c6 19.♔f1, etc., with only a slight advantage for Black due to the possibility (after proper preparation) of the f-awn advancing.

18...♗×d5 19.c×d5

It would be even worse 19.e×d5 f5, etc.

19...f5 20.♘c4 ♘b7

Black is in no hurry to play ...f5 because the threat combined with this advance and the eventual ...f×e4 will limit White's choice of moves much more than any direct attack.

21.♖ac1 ♖ad8!

Deliberately allowing exchanges afterwards, which only seem to relieve White of his problems in the center. If instead 21...♖ed8 would leave the queen unprotected, and thus allow the reaction 22.e×f5 g×f5 23.♗d4! (if 23...♗×d5 24.♖fe1 e4 25.♗×g7 ♔×g7 26.♘e3 with White's advantage) etc.

22.d6 ♘b×d6 23.♘×d6 ♖×d6 24.♕×a6

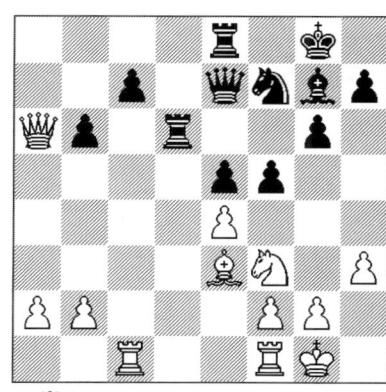

24...♕d7!

An important intermediate move, securing with time (the threat ...f4) control of the open column.

25.♖c2 c5 26.a4 f4!

Now it's time, because the Pawn's next advance will connect with the formidable threat 28...g4 29.h×g4 ♕×g4 etc., with a mate attack.

27.♗d2 g5 28.♕b5

Although practically forced, this move is of little help here, because after the proposed exchange of queens, Black not only gets a much better ending, but also - a very rare case considering the reduced material - a direct attack on the enemy king.

28...♕×b5 29.a×b5 ♖d3!

Freeing up the important d6 square for the knight.

30.♖a1 ♘d6 31.♖a6 ♖b8

If now 31.♘×g5, then simply 32...♗f6 32.♘f3 ♘×e4; with sufficient positional advantage. And if 31.♔c3 then 32...c4! 32.♖×d3 c×d3 33.♖a3 ♘×e4 34.♖×d3 ♖a8! 35.♖a3 ♖d8, etc., winning.

32.♗c3

Just as ineffective as the rest.

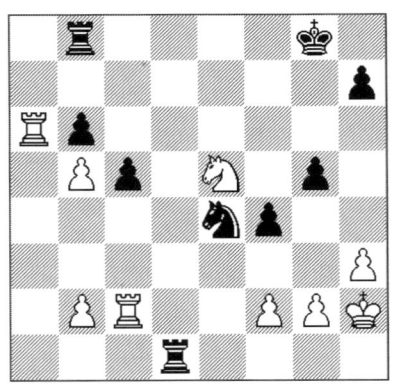

32...♘×e4 33.♗×e5 ♗×e5 34.♘×e5 ♖d1+ 35.♔h2

35...♘d2!

This sudden blow - the threat of mate in three through 36...♘f1+ etc. at least wins the quality. But Bogoljubov, as so often, prefers suicide to a long agony.

36.h4 ♖e8! 37.♘f3

Or 37.♘g4 ♖ee1 38.♔h3 ♖h1+ 39.♔h2 h5! 40.h×g5 ♘f1, with mate following.

37...♘×f3+ 38.g×f3 ♖ee1 39.♔h3 h5!, and White resigned.

> **Game 31**
> **F.Yates-A.Alekhine**
> *San Remo Tournament, January 1930*
> Spanish Opening [D71]

1.e4 e5 2.♘f3 ♘c6 3.♗b5 a6 4.♗a4 d6 5.♘c3

An unusual way to fight the delayed Steinitz Defense. White's idea was probably to play c3, after bringing his queen knight to d5. But in the meantime, Black managed to play the "Spanish" Bishop, and thus gained the advantage of the pair of Bishops with a more elastic Pawn structure.

5...♗d7 6.d3

Logical - but still more promising would be 6.♗×c6 followed by 7.d4.

6...g6 7.♘d5 b5!

It was necessary, because if White managed to complete his plan (8.c3) he would in fact have a space advantage.

8.♗b3 ♘a5 9.♗g5!

The weakening of the a2-g8 diagonal, provoked in this way, may become of some importance, especially if White decides to keep the corresponding Bishop.

9...f6 10.♗d2 c6

Necessary, because after the intermediate 10...♘×b3 White, after 11.a×b3 would threaten 12.♗a5, etc. with an advantage.

See the next Diagram

11.♘e3?

It would be relatively better

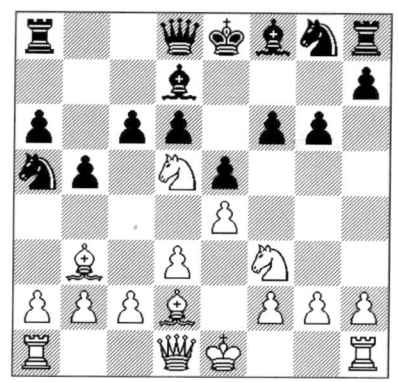

11.♗xa5 ♕xa5+ 12.♘c3, after which Black would be forced, before taking any action in the center, to complete his development with ...♘–h6–f7, followed by ...♗e7 and ...0–0. After the text move their task of increasing their space advantage will, on the contrary, be relatively easier.

11...♘xb3 12.axb3 ♘h6 13.b4

White's real problem lies in the fact that they don't have safe houses for their Knights and, on the other hand, if you try to open the position Black's Bishops will become super powerful.

13...f5

If White's previous move had been 13.d4, this response would have proved even more effective.

14.♕e2 ♘f7 15.♘f1 ♕e7

A quiet positional move. Black is in no hurry to play ...f4 and White has nothing to do but try to stabilize the situation in the center - even at the cost of some time.

16.♘g3 f4 17.♘f1 g5 18.♗c3

See the next Diagram

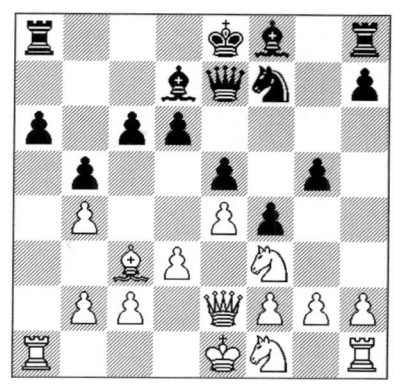

18...h5!

Planning 19...h4 and only after 20.h3 g4 21.hxg4 ♗xg4 followed by ...♘g5, ...h3 etc. To avoid this pinning, White decides to weaken his black squares by playing f3.

19.♘3d2 ♗g4 20.f3 ♗e6 21.d4

If 21.♘c3 Black wouldn't exchange his valuable queen bishop for the knight, but would play 21...c5 followed by ...♘–d8–c6–d4.

21...♗g7 22.♕d3

The "combination" 22.d5 cxd5 23.♗xa6 ♗xa6 24.♕xb5+ ♕d7 25.♕xa6 d4 etc. would lose a piece.

22...exd4 23.♗xd4 ♘e5

The occupation of this powerful central house signifies a strategic decision.

24.♕e2 0–0

As the position will now become even more open, cooperation between the Rooks will be vital.

25.h3 c5!

The start of the decisive action.

26.♗c3

Instead 26.bxc5 dxc5 27.♗xe5 ♗xe5 would be completely hopeless.

26...cxb4 27.♗xb4 ♘c6 28.♗c3 ♗xc3

The advantage is now so definite that the combined action of the two Bishops is no longer necessary.

29.bxc3

See the next Diagram

29...♕f6

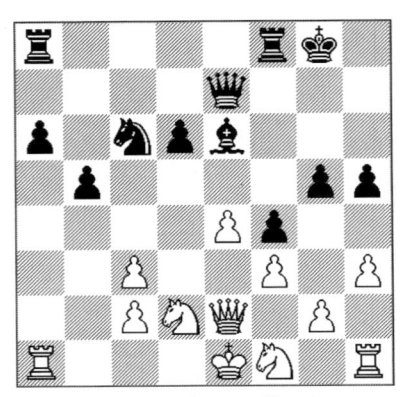

This move can't really be severely criticized, as it wins a Pawn and allows Black to simplify things after a few moves, obtaining an ending that is technically quite easy to win. Furthermore, Black doesn't have to give up the e5 square to his opponent, even temporarily, for the Knight. It would be logical in the meantime to 29...♕g7 (if 30.e5 then 30...d5! etc.) after which all Yates' tenacity wouldn't be able to prolong the game for long. I didn't play my queen to g7 to avoid the possibility of 30.♕d3 ♘b4 31.♕xd6 attacking the bishop, but 31...♘xc2+ 32.♔d1 ♘xa1 (or even 32...♔f6) in that case would be decisive in Black's favor. White's game from now on is an example of defensive patience and ingenuity in a theoretically lost position.

30.e5! ♘xe5 31.♘e4 ♕e7 32.♘fd2 ♗c4 33.♘xc4 ♘xc4

Threatening 34...d5 as well as 34...♘e3. One could imagine that the game would last a couple more moves.

See the next Diagram

34.♖d1!
Threatening 35.♖d5.
34...♕e5 35.♕d3!
Avoiding 35...♘b2 again due to 36.♕xd6 etc. In addition, White now threatens 36.♕d5+ etc.

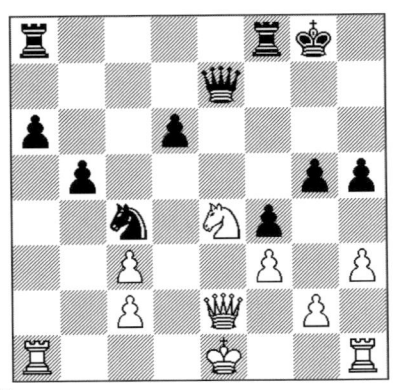

35...♖f5 36.0–0!
So White has saved himself from a middlegame disaster, and strange as it may seem, Black is unlikely to get enough of an advantage by playing 36...♘e3. The continuation could be 37.♘xd6! ♖d8 (or 37...♖f6 38.♖fe1 ♖d8) 38.♖fe1 ♖f6 39.♕e4! (the defense point) after which 39...♕xc3 could be a mistake due to 40.♘xb5! etc.; and also 39...♕xe4 40.♘xe4 ♔xd1 41.♘xf6+ ♔f7 42.♔xd1 ♘xd1 43.♘e4 would still not be convincing enough (43...a5 44.♘d6+ or 43...♔e6 44.♘c5+). Therefore, Black's next move is the simplest method of obtaining a winning advantage in the end.

36...d5!
Not only returning the advantage pawn, but even the passed pawn will be sacrificed to establish the Rook on the 7th rank. The ending is then sharp and full of tactical points.

37.♕xd5+
Obviously, there is no other choice.
37...♕xd5 38.♖xd5 ♖xd5 39.♘f6+ ♔f7 40.♘xd5 ♖d8
Instead, 40...a5 41.♘c7 ♔b8 42.♔b1 would not be convincing.
41.♘b4 ♖d2 42.♖a1

The main variant I was hoping for was 42.♘xa6 ♘e3 43.♖b1 ♖xg2+ 44.♔h1 ♖xc2 45.♖xb5 g4! 46.hxg4 hxg4 47.fxg4 f3, winning.
42...a5 43.♘c6 ♖xc2 44.♘xa5 ♘e3 45.♖b1 ♖xg2+ 46.♔h1 ♖g3

It's not as simple as it sounds instead 46...g4 due to 47.hxg4 hxg4 48.♘c6! etc.

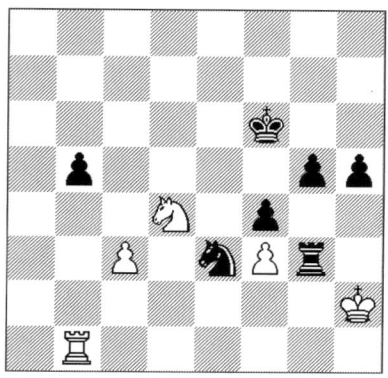

47.♘c6 ♖xh3+ 48.♔g1 ♖g3+ 49.♔h2 ♔f6 50.♘d4

50...g4!

Advancing at just the right moment saves the g Pawn due to the strong threat involved.

51.fxg4 ♘xg4+ 52.♔h1 f3

Threatening to kill in two and thus forcing an answer.

53.♖f1 ♖h3+ 54.♔g1 f2+ 55.♔g2 ♖xc3 56.♖h1

Yates is still fighting! Instead 56.♘xb5 would lose quickly after 56...♖b3 57.♘d4 ♖d3 58.♘c2 ♖d2 etc.

56...♖d3! 57.♘e2

Or 57.♘xb5 ♖d2 58.♖h3 ♖d1, etc.

57...♖d2 58.♘g3 ♖b2!

Starting the final combination. The immediate 58...♘h2 would, of course, be a mistake, due to 59.♘e4+.

59.♘xh5+ ♔e5 60.♘g3 ♘h2!

An elegant move, through which Black forces the exchange of knights and keeps his two extra pawns.

61.♘f1 ♘xf1 62.♖h5+ ♔d4 63.♔xf1 b4 64.♖h8 ♖c2 65.♖b8 ♔c3 66.♖b7 b3, and White resigned.

Game 32
A.Alekhine–A.Nimzowitsch
San Remo Tournament, January 1930
French Defense [C17]

1.e4 e6 2.d4 d5 3.♘c3 ♗b4 4.e5 c5 5.♗d2

This rather harmless move in connection with the Knight's next maneuver shouldn't cause too many problems for Black. More promising - only perhaps because it's less exploited - seems to be 5.♕g4 or even 5.dxc5.

5...♘e7 6.♘b5 ♗xd2+ 7.♕xd2 0–0 8.c3 b6

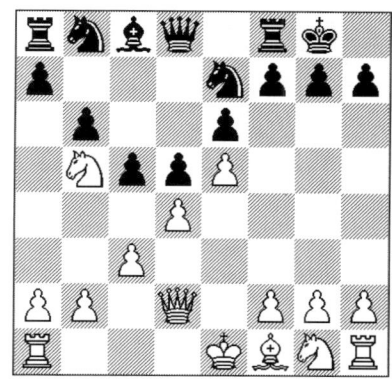

The desire to solve the Queen's Bishop problem as quickly as possible is, for the second player in the French Defense, very legitimate, - but in this position the attempt will prove to be a failure, *as Black can't exchange this piece for Black's King's Bishop.* Good - and quite natural - instead would be 8...♘f5! (preventing ♘d6) as successfully played by the same Nimzowitsch against Dr. Lasker in Zurich 1934.

9.f4 ♗a6

Trying to force White's a4 move and

then play ...♘c6–a5 etc. But, as we'll see, the second part of this plan can't be carried out.

10.♘f3 ♕d7 11.a4 ♘bc6 12.b4!

Rather strangely, this conventional move (whereby White avoids ...♘a5 and at the same time forces a clean-up of the central situation) created something of a minor sensation at the time. Later Dr. Tarrasch, for example, classified it in his comments as "highly original". More surprising to me than the move was the fact that a player of Nimzowitsch's class, in adopting the plan initiated by 8...b6, didn't take the possibility seriously.

12...cxb4

Relatively better than 12...c4, after which White would have little technical difficulty in decisively exploiting his space advantage on the kingside.

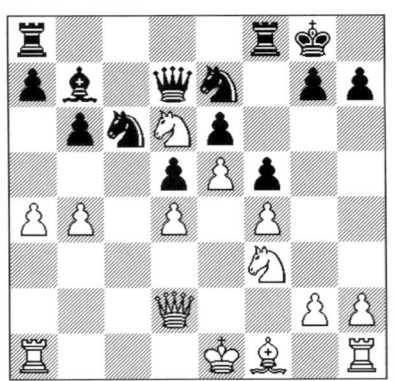

13.cxb4 ♗b7 14.♘d6 f5?

The decisive strategic blunder in an already compromised situation. In view of the threat of the advance of White's a-♙awn, the only chance of gaining a little more space lay in 14...a5 15.♗b5 (better than 15.b5 ♘b4) 15...axb4 16.0–0, after which White's initiative - which needs to spend some time recovering the b-Pawn - would not develop so quickly. By playing his f5 Pawn, Nimzowitsch obviously feared an attack on his King - and that was the only thing in this game he didn't have to worry about!

15.a5!

As 15...bxa5 16.b5! followed by 17.♖xa5 is now obviously bad for Black, this advance secures the very important b5 square for the white Bishop.

15...♘c8

The elimination of the terrible knight on d6 - which in other circumstances would mean complete emancipation - doesn't really bring any relief to Black.

16.♘xb7 ♕xb7 17.a6 ♕f7

To their chagrin 17...♕e7 doesn't work due to 18.♗b5! ♘xb4? 19.♔b1 etc.

18.♗b5

From now on Black can play all he wants - he'll be unable to sufficiently protect his c6 and c7 squares. The hopeless coup de grace that follows is just the inevitable consequence of this organic maneuver.

18...♘8e7 19.0–0 h6

Although ♘g5 is not yet a threat, it could become one soon. Besides, the immediate 19...♔c8 wouldn't change the situation at all: Black loses not because of a lack of time, but because of a lack of space.

20.♖fc1 ♖fc8 21.♖c2

If now 21...♘d8 22.♖ac1 ♖xc2 23.♖xc2 ♖c8 24.♖xc8 ♘xc8 25.♕c3, followed by 26.♕c7 winning.

21...♕e8 22.♖ac1

This and the next moves are not the most accurate, because the winning formation ♕c1, ♖5–c2 and ♖–c3 will be achieved not after three moves, but five, as happened in this game: 22.♖a3! followed by ♖ac3 and ♕c1.

22...♖ab8 23.♕e3 ♖c7 24.♖c3!

From now on, White will win with the fewest moves.

24...♕d7

To give the King the chance to protect the Rook on c7. A desperate idea in a desperate position.

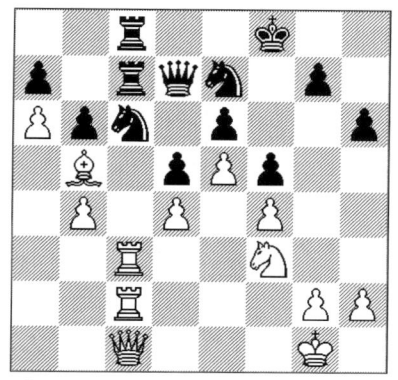

25.♖1c2 ♔f8 26.♕c1 ♖bc8

27.♗a4!

The last link in the positional attack started with 15.a5! To save the piece threatened by 28.c5 Black must sacrifice his b-pawn. After that, they manage to protect the important square with the King, but still must resign as a result of a complete *zugzwang*. An instructive ending!

27...b5 28.♗×b5 ♔e8 29.♗a4 ♔d8 30.h4!

After a couple of irrelevant Pawn moves, Black will be forced to play ...♕e8, after which White's lace b5 will immediately win. Black has resigned.

Game 33
M.Vidmar-A.Alekhine
San Remo Tournament, January 1930
Nimzowitsch Defense [E37]

1.d4 ♘f6 2.c4 e6 3.♘c3 ♗b4 4.♕c2 d5 5.a3 ♗×c3+ 6.♕×c3 ♘e4 7.♕c2 ♘c6

According to the current stage of theory, 7...c5 8.d×c5 ♘c6 is enough to equalize. The move in the text - in connection with the Pawn sacrifice that follows - was introduced by me in the present game and was considered for a long time to be a kind of refutation of 5.a3. Only recently have some tournament games taken place, and subsequent analysis has cast doubt on the effectiveness of Black's counterplay. As the idea only occurred to me during that game and I haven't tested it since, I wouldn't be surprised if further detailed analysis definitively proved its inadequacy.

8.e3

After 8.♘f3 e5 9.d×e5 ♗f5 10.♕b3 ♘a5 11.♕a4+ c6 12.c×d5 ♕×d5 etc., Black would get good positional compensation for the Pawn down.

8...e5 9.f3?

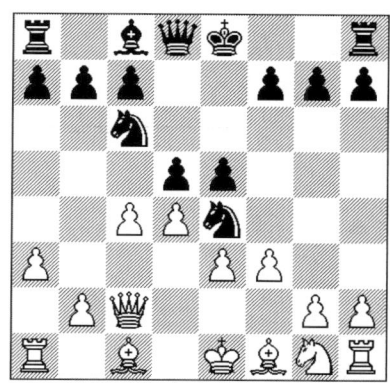

Very harmless, to say the least. White would enter the main variant by playing 9.c×d5, which would bring them, after a rather daring King's journey it's true, two minor pieces for the Rook and a safe enough position. The game could be 9...♕×d5 10.♗c4 ♕a5+ 11.b4! ♘×b4 12.♕×e4 ♘c2+ 13.♔e2 ♕e1+ 14.♔f3 ♘×a1 15.♗b2 ♗e6! (Fine's move) 16.d5 0-0-0

17.dxe6 fxe6 18.♕g3! after which the few threats Black still has hardly compensate for his material loss. After the text move, Black gets an advantage in development without any sacrifice in return.

9...♘f6

It would be a premature attack 9...♕h4+ 10.g3 ♘xg3 11.♕f2 ♘f5 12.cxd5 etc., with an advantage for White.

10.cxd5 ♕xd5 11.♗c4

This gain in time is not enough compensation for all the time wasted previously.

11...♕d6 12.dxe5 ♘xe5 13.♗d2

Not satisfied with the result of the opening, White began to set small traps, which, however, proved to be quite ineffective. Relatively better than this artificial development would be 13.♘e2 followed by 0–0.

13...0–0!

Correctly ignoring the white combination.

14.♗b4

Also 14.♖d1 ♕b6 would be favorable to Black.

14...c5 15.♖d1

Of course not 15.♗xc5 ♕xc5 16.♗xf7+ ♔xf7 17.♕xc5 ♘d3+, etc. But also, the intermediate move of the text, which White obviously trusts, is of little help.

15...♕c6!

The point of Black's active defense: if now 16.♗xc5, then 16...♘xc4 17.♕xc4 (or 17.♗xf8 ♔xf8, etc.) 17...b6 etc., winning a piece. This way, White needs to take his Bishop.

16.♗d2 ♗f5!?

From now on, Black's problem will be that they will have many promising continuations at their disposal, so it will be extremely difficult to decide which one is best at any given moment. As the game went on, they managed to win through an interesting tactical game, with the initial sacrifice of a Pawn and finally of quality - but White maintained, almost until the end, excellent chances of a draw! So something must not have worked in Black's method of exploiting his considerable positional advantage. More likely, the rational way is not to try to take advantage of the insufficient protection of White's King's Pawn, but to increase two already existing advantages: (1) the majority of Pawns on the Queen's wing, and especially (2) the weakness of White's squares in the White camp. Thus, the tempting move with the Bishop should be exchanged for the simple variant 16...♘xc4 17.♕xc4 ♗e6 18.♕c2 ♕b5! etc., after which White would hardly be able to get the King to safety.

17.♕xf5 ♘xc4 18.♗c1 ♖fe8

In no way would 18...♖ad8 19.♔xd8 ♖xd8 20.♘e2 ♘d5 21.♘g3! followed by 22.e4, etc. be convincing.

19.♔f2 ♖e6

Planning the next intermediary, who necessarily wins a Pawn.

20.♘h3!

Relatively better than 20.♘e2, as the knight can eventually be useful on g5. After the unfortunate opening Dr. Vidmar defends his compromised position with extreme care and determination.

20...♘e4+! 21.♔e1

Of course, the knight can't be taken due to 21...♔f6.

21...♘ed6 22.♕d3!

If 22.♕d5 Black would naturally avoid exchanging queens with 22...♕b5.

22...♘xe3!

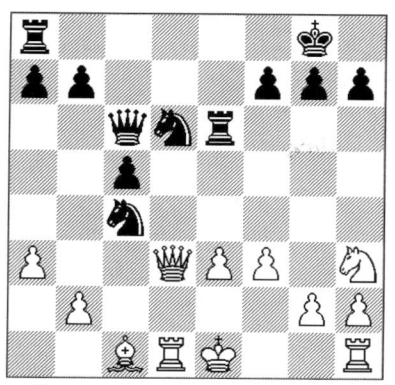

The point of Black's previous moves, which aim not to exchange the two Rooks for the Queen, but simply to win the Bishop, remaining with the Pawn advantage. However, as White can now force the exchange of Queens, the fight is by no means over.

23.♗xe3 c4! 24.♕d5

Otherwise, Black plays 24...♘f5.

24...♖xe3+ 25.♔f2 ♕xd5

After that, Black has almost no choice in the next 10-12 moves, when it comes to an extremely difficult ending between Rook+2 Pawns against Knight+3 Pawns. Possibly a slightly more promising alternative was then 25...♖e6 26.♕xc6 (Black avoided exchanging) 26...bxc6 27.♖he1 ♖xe1 28.♔xe1 ♘f5! followed eventually by ...♘e3. But at this stage it wasn't easy to decide which line would leave White with the least chances of a draw.

26.♖xd5 ♖d3

This was, of course, planned in the previous move. After 26...♖e6 27.♖hd1 etc., White would easily draw.

27.♖xd3 cxd3 28.♖d1 ♘c4 29.♖xd3 ♘xb2 30.♖b3 ♘c4 31.♖xb7 ♘xa3 32.♘g5

Finally White manages to justify the move 20.♘h3!. It's obvious enough that Black doesn't have time to protect his Pawn f, since after 32...c6 the move ♘–e6–c7 would immediately force a draw.

32...a5 33.♘xf7 a4

It would be pointless to 33...♘c4 because of 34.♘c7.

34.♘d6 ♘c2 35.♖b2

Otherwise, the past Pawnbroker will leave.

35...a3! 36.♖xc2 a2 37.♖xa2?

It's hard to explain why White took the Pawn instead of playing 37.♖c1 a1♕ 38.♖xa1 etc., which would have given them the option of playing the King on g3 (as in the game) or making another move. In fact, after 38...♖xa1 39.g4! Black's win, if possible, would be more remote than in the chosen line.

37...♖xa2+ 38.♔g3 ♔f8

Black's plan obviously consists of restricting the activity of both of White's pieces and trying to create a weakened Pawn in the enemy structure. Whether this can be achieved against an impeccable defense is another matter. Having not seen a game ending like this in the literature dedicated to this branch of chess, I confess that I rather hoped that my opponent would manage to find an impregnable defensive position for his Knight and King.

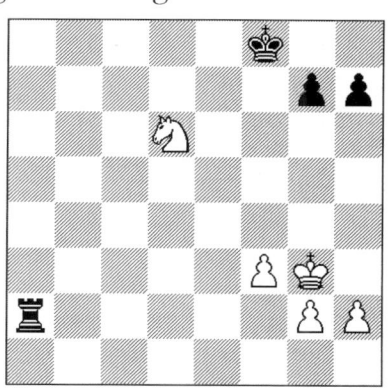

39.h4

It's difficult to suggest exactly what maneuvers White needs to make to prevent the gradual advance of Black's King, but one positional consideration is beyond discussion: *White's Pawns cannot be moved without necessity or without a real prospect of exchange.* Although the text move can hardly be considered the decisive blunder, it certainly helps the execution of the first part of Black's plan, because from now on White's King will have to watch out not only for g2 but also eventually for h4.

39...♔e7 40.♘e4 h6

Necessary to allow the King to advance.

41.♘f2 ♔e6 42.♘d3 ♔f5 43.♘f4 ♖a4 44.♘d3 ♖c4 45.♘f2 ♖c6 46.♘h3 ♔e5

Black now threatens to bring his King to f1, for example: 47.♘f4 ♔d4 48.♔f2 ♖c2+ 49.♔g3 ♔e3 50.♘d5+ ♔e2 51.♘f4+ ♔f1; after that, the next step would be to secure the f2 square for the King, through *zugzwang*, even if not now, but at the end of the winning procedure! One can then imagine how welcome the Pawn's next move was, which provided me with several new attacking possibilities.

47.h5?

Apart from Black's control of the g6 square, but as we shall see, the control of g5 was much more important.

45...♖c2 48.♘f4 ♖d2! 49.♘h3

There is no longer a choice.

49...♔d4 50.♘f4 ♔e3

See the next Diagram

51.♘e6?

Impatience or desperation? If it's the latter, it's justified, since the return

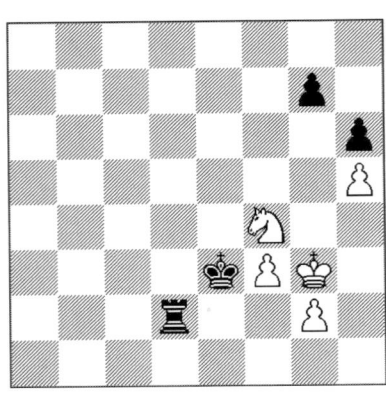

51.♘h3 would mean certain defeat: 51...♖a2! 52.♘f4 ♖a5, winning White's adventurous Pawn h in the first place.

51...♖d5

The beginning of the end, as 52.♔h4 doesn't help much due to 52...♖e5! 53.♘xg7 ♔g5 followed by ...♔g2, etc.

52.f4 ♖f5!

Pawn f is much more important than pawn g, which is bound to be captured sooner or later anyway.

53.♔g4 ♖f6!

Preventing White from protecting the f-pawn with 53.g3, which could be played against 53...♔e5.

54.f5 ♖f7

Not the shortest way, which would be: 54...♔e4 55.♘xg7 ♔f7 56.♘e6 (or 56.♘e8 ♔e5!) 56...♔xf5 57.g3 ♖e5 58.♘f4 ♔g5+ 59.♔h4 ♔f3, winning.

55.g3

Precipitating the end. After 55.♘d8! ♔f6 56.♘e6 Black would adopt the variant shown above, starting with 55...♔e4!

55...♔e4 56.♘c5+ ♔d4! 57.♘b3+ ♔e5, and White resigned.

My games with Dr. Vidmar are usually full of life and struggle.

Game 34
A.Alekhine-G.Maroczy
San Remo Tournament, January 1930
Queen's Gambit Declined [D67]

1.d4 d5 2.c4 e6 3.♘c3 ♘f6 4.♗g5 ♗e7 5.e3 ♘bd7 6.♘f3 0-0 7.♖c1 c6

Recent practice seems to show that the intermediate move 7...h6 gives Black greater opportunities to solve the central problem more satisfactorily than this old-fashioned and so-called "Capablanca release maneuver" (although it had already been played, for example by Mason in Hanover 1902).

8.♗d3 d×c4 9.♗×c4 ♘d5 10.♗×e7 ♕×e7 11.♘e4 b6

An attempt to solve the queen bishop problem immediately. Although it was partially successful in this game (at least in the opening stage), it can hardly be indicated if White plays the next moves more energetically. Instead, Dr. Lasker's idea 11...♘5b6 12.♘g3 e5! (see *game 70*) seems to be enough to equalize.

12.0-0 ♗b7 13.♘g3 c5 14.e4

An interesting alternative here would be 14.♗b5 to answer 14...c×d4 with 15.e4 followed by ♖c7. Black in this case would have to deal with the usual problems caused by this variant arising from an insufficiently prepared advance of the c-Pawn.

14...♘5f6 15.♖e1

White's previous move would find its logical justification here if it continued with 15.d5, for example: 15...e×d5 16.e×d5 ♕d6 17.♘f5 ♕f4 18.♘e7+ ♔h8 19.♗b5! after which the d-pawn would remain an important factor in White's favor. By choosing the smooth continuation (mainly since by starting the tournament with five wins in a row, I didn't want to give away any chances in the sixth round), White still maintained a slight positional advantage - but against an expert endgame player like Maróczy, White's chances became quite problematic.

15...c×d4

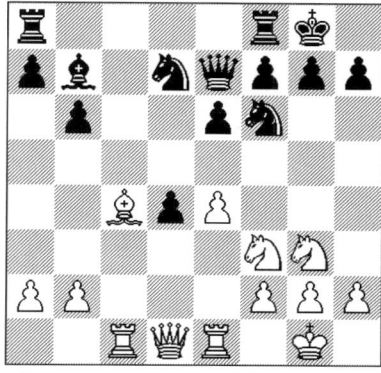

16.♗b5!

If instead 16.e5, then 16...♘g4! 17.♕×d4 ♗×f3 18.g×f3 ♘g×e5! 19.♔×e5 ♘×e5 20.♕×e5 ♖ac8 etc., with an advantage for Black.

16...♖fc8 17.♕×d4 ♖c5 18.♗×d7 ♘×d7 19.b4 ♖×c1 20.♖×c1 ♖c8 21.♖×c8+ ♗×c8 22.♕c3

The position is not a dead draw, as one might imagine at first glance. Now, for example, Black will have to waste time to stop White's threats on the c-column.

22...♕d8 23.♘d4 ♗b7 24.f3

One of White's advantages is that Black's Bishop, due to the general structure of the Pawns, has very modest prospects.

24...♘f6

To be able to oppose the queen on c7 - undoubtedly the correct scheme.

25.♘f1

This knight obviously has nothing to do in g3.

25...♘e8 26.♘e3 a6

Maróczy seems unwilling to play a purely passive ending - otherwise logical - which would be achieved through 26...♕c7 27.♕xc7 ♘xc7 28.♘c4 ♘e8! White's space advantage in this variant would be evident, but the direct threat 29.♘b5 would be stopped by 25...♗a6 and a draw would still be likely. After the move made in the game, Black on the other hand is unlikely to offer the exchange of queens due to his weakness on the b6 square.

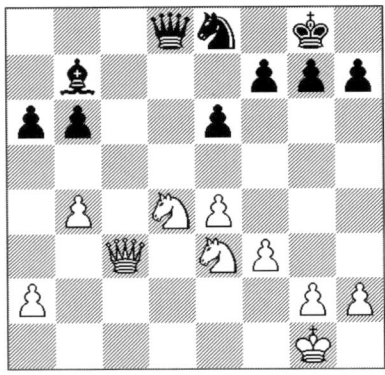

27.a4!

The intention a5 will serve a double purpose: (i) to fix Black's weakness on the b6 square; (ii) to secure the strong c5 square for the knight.

24...h6 28.h3

Not to give the King an escape square - unnecessary here - but simply by planning to move this piece eventually to the center, and thus placing the h Pawn on a protected square.

28...h5?

Black's 26th move, although not completely logical (avoiding the exchange of queens and creating a weakness on the queen's wing), was hardly enough to seriously jeopardize the situation. But this Pawn move - the significance of which will not be explained by Black's next moves - by creating a new (although one might say, at the moment, almost imperceptible) weak point on the g5 square, produces unmistakable winning chances for White.

29.a5 bxa5 30.bxa5 ♕d6 31.♘b3 ♗c6

The desire to bring the Bishop to a more active square (b5) is reasonable; but White takes the opportunity to advance his central Pawns, and in this way limits the action of the hostile Knight.

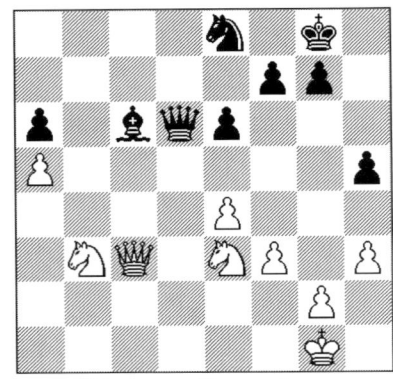

32.e5! ♕c7 33.♘c5 ♗b5 34.f4

The slight weakening of the white squares caused by this advance no longer matters, as the Bishop is stuck defending the Pawn a.

34...♕d8 35.f5

White's only chance of victory consists of combining pressure on the queen's wing with direct threats to Black's king.

35...exf5 36.♘xf5 ♕g5 37.♘d4!

An important technical detail: 37...♕xe5 38.♘xb5, etc.

37...♘c7 38.♘f3

From now on, Black will imagine that he made a mistake by playing 28...h5.

38...♕f4 39.♔f2

Thus, showing that White is almost willing to exchange the queen. In fact, the resulting ending after 39...♘d5 40.♕d4 ♕×d4+ 41.♘×d4 ♗c4 42.♘c6! followed by ♘d6 would be extremely critical, if not hopeless for Black.

39...♕f5 40.♕d2 ♔h7

If instead 40...♘e6 41.♘b7! followed by ♘d6 it wouldn't allow Black to hold out any longer. The winning procedure that follows is instructive.

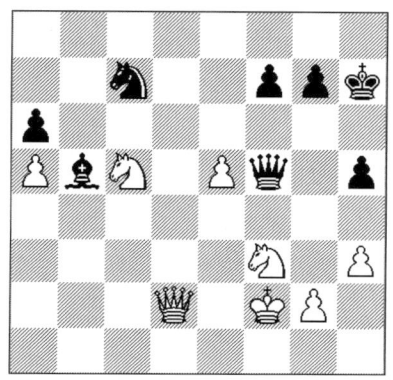

41.♘e4!

If now 41...♘e8, then 42.♘b3 ♕g6 43.♕d8 etc., with gradual strangulation. Black then prefers to sacrifice a Pawn to get rid of at least the boring Knight.

41...♘e6 42.♘d6 ♕b1

If 42...♕g6 White wins with 43.♘×b5 a×b5 44.a6 because 44...♘c5 doesn't work due to 45.♘g5+ ♕×g5 46.♕×g5 ♘e4+ 47.♔e3 ♘×g5 48.a7.

43.♘×f7 ♗c6 44.♘7g5+ ♘×g5 45.♘×g5+ ♔g6 46.h4

So White took maximum advantage of Black's weakness on g5!

46...♔f5

The threat was 47.♕d6+ ♔f5 48.♕e6+ ♔f4 49.g3 mate.

47.e6 ♕b5 48.♕c2+

The aim of the following checkers is to avoid the move ...♕c5+ in *time* and thus make the future advance of the passed Pawn possible.

48...♔e5 49.♕c3+ ♔d6 50.♕g3+ ♔d5 51.♕f3+ ♔e5 52.♕e3+ ♔f6

Or 52...♔d6 53.♕f4+! etc.

53.♕c3+ ♔g6 54.e7 ♕f5+ 55.♔e3

The king is certainly safer here than on the wing (55.♔g1 ♕b1+ etc.).

55...♗e8 56.♕d4 ♗b5 57.♕d6+ ♕f6 58.♘e4!, and Black resigned.

> **Game 35**
> **A.Alekhine–S.Tartakower**
> *San Remo Tournament, January 1930*
> Dutch Defense [A90]

1.d4 e6 2.c4 f5 3.g3 ♘f6 4.♗g2 ♗b4+ 5.♘d2 ♘e4

Black wants to exchange pieces right from the opening - a dubious strategy, to say the least. It would be more in the spirit of the chosen opening 5...0–0 6.a3 ♗e7, etc.

6.a3 ♘×d2 7.♗×d2 ♗×d2+ 8.♕×d2 0–0 9.♘h3

Mainly to reinforce the control of the d5 square in case Black chooses the development ...d6 and ...e5.

9...d5

From now on the black squares in the black position will sooner or later become very weak. And White, to exploit these weaknesses, decides to free up the Pawn center as quickly as possible. Although it's very difficult to judge at this point, if after the projected exchanges Black would have adequate defense at his disposal against the many threats, a slower policy would be more appropriate - like 10.♔c1 c6 11.0–0 ♕e7 12.♕e3 followed by ♘f4, etc. to take advantage of Black's maneuver between moves 5-7.

10.c×d5 e×d5 11.♘f4 c6 12.0–0

♕e7

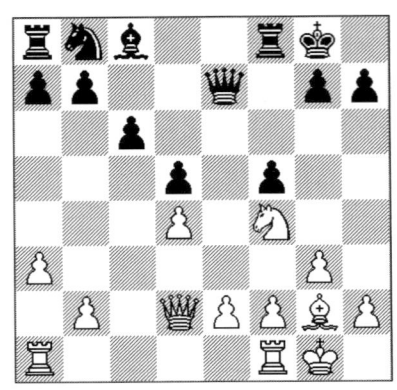

13.b4!

The real purpose of this move - apart from a minority attack which through it makes the a4 continuation also quite possible - is to open for the queen the way to a2. The sequel will prove the importance of this diversion.

13...a6 14.f3

All according to the plan initiated by his 10th move. But Black, keeping a cool head, manages to get out of the skirmish without too much damage.

14...♘d7 15.e4 fxe4 16.fxe4 dxe4 17.♕a2+

Sadly the tempting 17.♗xe4 doesn't work - for example 17...♕xe4 18.♖ae1 ♕f5 19.♕a2+ (or 19.♘e6 ♕g6 20.♘xf8 ♘xf8, with Black's advantage) 19...♔f7 20.♖e8+ (or ♖e7) 20...♘f8 - and Black escapes.

17...♔h8 18.♘e6

It's unconvincing 18.♕e6 ♖e8! etc.

18...♖xf1+ 19.♖xf1 ♘f6 20.♘g5 h6

See the next Diagram

21.♕f7!

This strong move, which forces the exchange of queens due to the threat of 22.♗xf6!, etc. had to be foreseen when the action in the center began, otherwise Black would have had a better game.

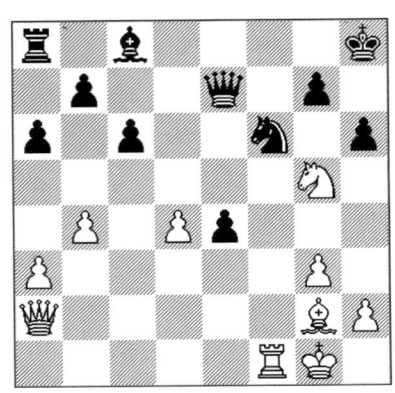

21...♕xf7 22.♘xf7+ ♔h7 23.♘d6

This threatening position of the knight ensures that white can recapture the sacrificed pawns. But on the other hand, Black can meanwhile find the opportunity to complete his development and obtain equality.

23...♗e6?

Obviously overestimating the value of his central Pawn. The correct path was 23...a5! 24.♘xe4 (if 24.b5 then simply 24...cxb5) 24...axb4 25.♘xf6+ (or 25.axb4 ♘d5) 25...gxf6 26.axb4 ♔g7 with a probable draw in sight.

24.♘xb7 ♗d5 25.♖e1!

Otherwise, in many cases Black can play ...e3.

25...♖a7 26.♘c5 a5

Giving White a passed Pawn. But the Rook, of course, cannot defend the Pawn a forever.

27.bxa5 ♖xa5 28.a4 ♖a8

With the aim of occupying the b column, or as it happens, reducing White's pressure on the e Pawn a little.

29.♖a1 ♖a5

See the next Diagram

30.♖a3!

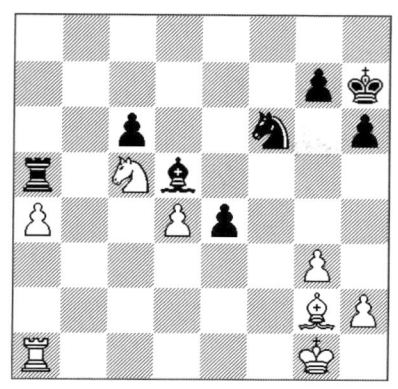

Also with the aim of avoiding ...e3.
30...♔g6
Black hoped to have the exact time to execute the move ♘–e8–d6 but was prevented from doing so by what Dr. Tartakower himself called a "combinatorial marvel".
31.h3 ♔f5 32.♔f2 ♘e8
All according to plan. Instead, 32...h5 would avoid the surprise to follow, but after 33.♔e3 etc., the loop in all of Black's pieces would lead to material loss anyway.

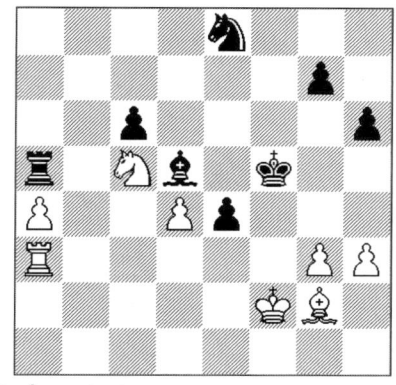

33.♗xe4+!
At first glance, given the very simple exchange 34.♘xe4 ♔xe4 35.♖e3+ ♔xd4 36.♖xe8 ♖xa4 etc.; but in fact forcing a technically very easy winning ending with a Pawn advantage.
33...♗xe4 34.g4+
The simple but very unpleasant point: if 34...♔f4 35.♘e6 mate!
33...♔f6 35.♘xe4+ ♔e6 36.♔e3 ♘d6 37.♔d3 ♘xe4 38.♔xe4 h5
Black realizes that a calm game would leave him no chances - for example 38...♔d6 39.♔d3 ♔d5 40.♖a1 c5 41.dxc5 ♔xc5 42.♔c3 etc., as I did in my last game against Capablanca. They then try to create attacking objectives on the King's wing, but only speed up the ending by accepting the Pawn sacrifice afterwards.
39.g5! ♖xg5
After 39...♔d6 40.h4 his situation would be even worse than before.
40.a5 ♖b5 41.a6 ♖b8 42.a7 ♖a8 43.h4! g5 44.hxg5 h4 45.♖a6 ♔f7 46.♔f4 h3 47.♔g3 ♔g6 48.d5! ♔xg5 49.dxc6 ♔f5 50.c7 and Black resigned.

Game 36
C.Ahues-A.Alekhine
San Remo Tournament, January 1930
Indian Queen's Defense [A47]

1.d4 ♘f6 2.♘f3 b6 3.e3 ♗b7 4.♘bd2
This system of development was favored by Rubinstein and the late Belgian champion Colle. It's not particularly aggressive, but it does have its dangers - especially if White manages to get an opening for his queen bishop on the right diagonal in time.
4...c5 5.♗d3 e6 6.c3 ♗e7 7.♕e2
White is very cautious. It would be more in the style of the chosen variant 7.e4, and only after 7...d6 8.♕e2, because with the move made Black can then come up with an original response to prevent the advance of the Pawn e.
7...♘d5!

No hidden intentions: if e4, then ...♘f4; if c4, then ...♘b4, etc.

8.d×c5

With this exchange White begins an elaborate maneuver, with the goal of bringing the queen's bishop to the a1–h8 diagonal. In fact, there's hardly a more promising line to recommend here.

8...b×c5 9.♘f1

White hasn't played ♘c4, as he wants to dislodge Black's central knight with c4.

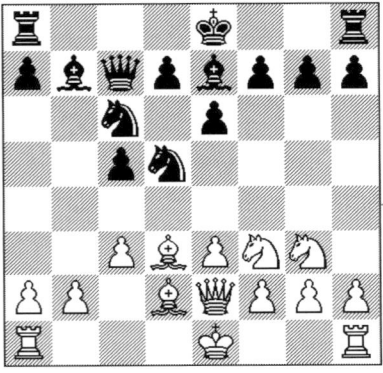

9...♕c7 10.♘g3 ♘c6 11.♗d2

11...g5!

A brave idea, connected with the offer of a Pawn and the following general considerations: Black has an elastic mass of Pawns on the King's wing, not obstructed by his own pieces; the natural thing to do then is to try to gain space by gradually advancing these Pawns. But which Pawn to start with? The move 11...h5 would be answered by 12.h4! which would stop any further action on that wing. On the other hand, 11...f5 would also be premature, as it would allow White to open up the position through 12.e4 f×e4 13.♕×e4! etc. That leaves the text move, which, by the way, is more effective than the preparatory 11...0–0, which would allow White to respond with 12.a3! followed by c4, etc.

12.c4 ♘db4 13.♗c3

It must be admitted that White is at least playing logically - the diagonal a1–h8 is currently his only counterchance.

13...♘×d3+ 14.♕×d3 ♘b4 15.♕e2

The main variant considered by Black when he played 11...g5 was 15.♕b1 f6 16.♘×g5 (or 16.a3 ♘c6 17.♘×g5 ♘e5, with Black's advantage) 16...♗×g2 17.♖g1 ♗b7 18.♘×h7 0–0–0!, with more than enough positional advantage to compensate for the material sacrificed.

15...♖g8 16.a3 ♘c6 17.♘d2 ♘e5 18.♕h5

White is obviously not satisfied with his position and is looking for complications. Of course, Black's chances would also be higher (mainly due to the possibilities offered by the pair of Bishops) after the quiet 18.f3.

18...0–0–0

Even more energetic would be 18...♗×g2 19.♔g1 ♗c6 20.♕×h7 0–0–0 etc., with an advantage for Black. After the move in the text, White decided to give up - at the cost of two moves! - to make this compromising exchange.

19.0–0 f5

Threatening 20...g4.

20.♕e2

See the next Diagram

20...h5!

There's no reason to give your opponent any moment's relief!

21.♘×h5

White is forced to take this Pawn, otherwise his advance would be very painful.

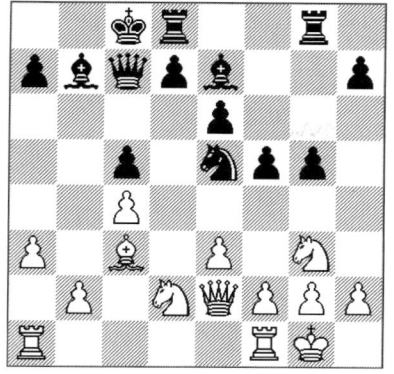

21...♖g6

Threatening 22...♖h6 followed by ...♖d1h8 etc., with deadly effect.

22.f4

The exchange proposed in this way will put the Knight in an excellent defensive position - but, unfortunately for White, only for a very short time. However, as White doesn't even have a shadow of a counterplay, his King's long-term position was indefensible anyway.

22...g×f4 23.♘×f4 ♖h6 24.h3 ♖g8

With the strong threat of 25...♘g6, etc.

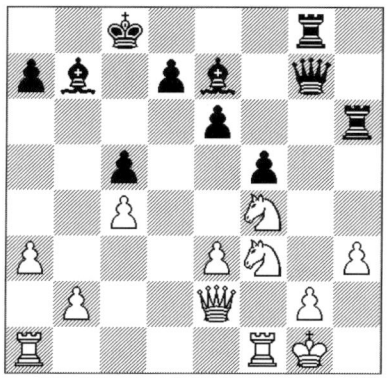

25.♗×e5 ♕×e5 26.♘f3 ♕g7

27.♖ad1

After this move, Black recovers the Pawn and at the same time demolishes the last protective fortification of the enemy King. But also protecting the h Pawn through 27.♔h1 would lead to an untenable position after 27...♗d6 28.♕f2 ♕g4! (threatening 29...♗×f4 30.e×f4 ♖×h3+! etc.) 29.♔g1 ♖×h3! 30.♘×h3 ♕×h3, etc.

27...e5! 28.♘d5 ♖×h3 29.♕d2 ♗×d5 30.c×d5 e4 31.d6 e×f3 32.♖×f3 ♖×f3 33.d×e7 ♕×e7, and White resigned.

Game 37
A.Alekhine-H.Kmoch
San Remo Tournament, January 1930
Nimzowitsch Defense [E51]

1.d4 ♘f6 2.c4 e6 3.♘c3 ♗b4 4.♗d2

One of the most harmless responses to Black's 3rd move. This game also shows that Black, even with the simplest moves, can get a half-game with the same prospects.

4...0–0 5.e3 d5 6.♘f3 c5 7.a3

Again, a passive move. When I played the opening of this game, I was not in the best of moods! First 7.♕c2 and only after 7...♘c6 8.a3 ♗×f3 9.♗×f3 etc., which would lead to a more picturesque game.

7...♗×c3 8.♗×c3 ♘e4

Perfectly logical, as the simplification below only favors the second player.

9.♖c1

Even now 9.♕c2 was more promising.

9...♘×c3 10.♖×c3 c×d4 11.e×d4

See the next Diagram

11...♘c6!

Black doesn't rush with 11...d×c4, because after 12.c5 he will be able to start a successful battle in the center

81

Alexander Alekhine

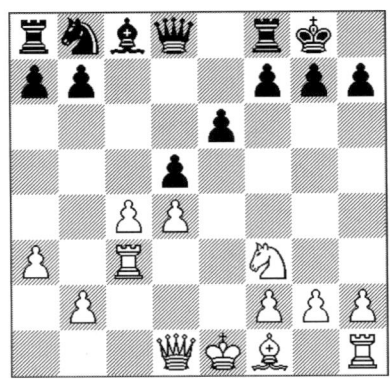

by answering 12...e5!
12.♗e2 dxc4 13.♗xc4

It's not hard to see that the opening battle has turned out quite favorably for Black, as White's isolated Pawn doesn't decorate this position and, on the other hand, the space advantage White has at the moment doesn't matter much, due to the lack of vulnerable points in the enemy position. White's only chance, therefore, is to try to create an attack on the kingside - and the reader will see how difficult this will prove against the author of *Die Kunst der Verteidigung* (The Art of Defense).

13...♕f6 14.0-0 ♖d8 15.♖d3 ♗d7 16.♖e1

Despite their lackluster prospects, White still decides to play to win, and so doesn't try to trade the isolated Pawn. Otherwise, they would play 16.♕d2, preparing d5, whose move at this point would not be good, due to the response ...♘a5!

16...♗e8 17.♕d2 ♘e7

Now Black also becomes ambitious and avoids d5 for the time being.

18.♘g5! ♘d5

But not 18...♘f5 due to 19.♘xe6! fxe6 20.♗xe6, winning.

19.♖f3 ♕e7 20.♖g3

White is eager to provoke a weakening Pawn move on Black's King's wing, so he protects the Knight to play ♕d3.

20...h6 21.♘f3

It's hard to decide which Knight move would be better. I finally rejected 21.♘e4 because of the possible reply 21...♕h5; however, in that case too, White, after 22.h3! ♕f4 23.♕e2 etc., would also maintain quite reasonable attacking chances.

21...♕f6 22.♖e4

Defending d4 and f4 and eventually threatening ♖3g4. But Black's next knight move again protects everything.

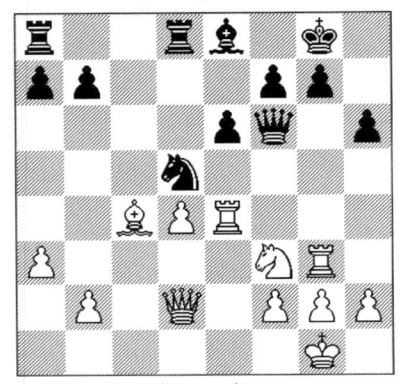

22...♘e7 23.♘e5 ♘f5 24.♖d3

It would be a mistake 24.♔f3 due to 24...♗c6 25.♘xc6 bxc6 etc., with Black's advantage.

24...♖ac8 25.h3!

White takes advantage of the fact that his opponent doesn't threaten anything important to secure an escape square for the king. The next part of this game will clearly show the significance of this quiet preparatory move.

25...♘d6?

Taking advantage of the first opportunity for a later simplification, which, however, at that moment will prove to be perfectly good for White. In fact, the knight at this point is too important a defensive piece to be eliminated.

Instead, 25...♗c6! would offer at least one quite sufficient defense, for example: 26.♘xc6 bxc6 (not 26...♖xc6 due to 27.d5!), or 26.♖e1 ♗d5 etc., with equality.

26.♖f4 ♘xc4 27.♘xc4 ♕g5

This move was generally criticized as a waste of time, but also after 27...♕e7 28.♘e5 White would get better fighting chances. If in that case 28...f6 then 29.♘g4 threatens possible sacrifices on f6 or h6. From now on Black's king has rather insufficient protection.

28.♖g3 ♕d5 29.♘e3 ♕c6

The exchange of the Ladies here would be a paradise for the black ones!

30.♔h2

The pleasant consequence of White's 25th move.

30...♕c1

Waiting for 31.♕a5 ♕c7 etc. But White chooses the right square for his queen.

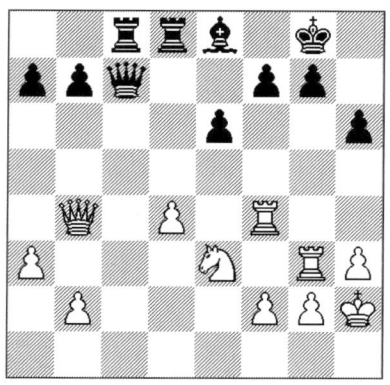

31.♕b4! ♕c7

32.d5!

Such an effective advance of the powerful weakness would certainly please the great friend of the isolated queen pawn, the late Dr. Tarrasch! It's obvious that in the case of ...exd5 (here or in the next move) the ♕d4 response would lead to a rapid collapse of Black's position. But also because of the chosen defense, they will also be forced to deliver at least the quality.

32...a5 33.♕e4

Of course not 33.♕d4 e5.

33...♖d6! 34.♕e5 g6 35.♕h5!

Instead of the tempting 35.♔c4 which would lead to nothing after 35...♔c6! and also 35.♘g4 which after 35...exd5 would only bring the exchange of a Pawn.

35...♖xd5

Instead of resigning. I would have preferred 35...♔h7 36.♘g4!! gxh5 37.♘f6+, followed by mate.

36.♘xd5 exd5 37.♕xh6, and Black resigned.

Game 38
G.Stahlberg-A.Alekhine
Hamburg Olympiad, July 1930
Nimzowitsch Defense [E23]

1.d4 ♘f6 2.c4 e6 3.♘c3 ♗b4 4.♕b3 c5 5.dxc5 ♘c6 6.♘f3 ♘e4 7.♗d2 ♘xc5

This move came into fashion in the Bogoljubov-Nimzowitsch game at the San Remo Tournament, a beauty prize for Black. It's certainly more logical than the old 7...♘xd2 8.♘xd2 after which White, playing 0-0-0, will soon get strong pressure on the open column.

8.♕c2 f5 9.a3

So White got - at least temporarily - the pair of Bishops. Rather strangely, Bogoljubov, in the game mentioned above, delayed this move until it became a blunder, at which point he handed the game to his opponent! This happened as follows: 9.e3 0-0 10.♗e2 a6 11.0-0-0 b5 12.b3 a5! etc., with Black's advantage.

9...♗xc3 10.♗xc3 0-0 11.b4 ♘e4 12.e3 b6 13.♗d3

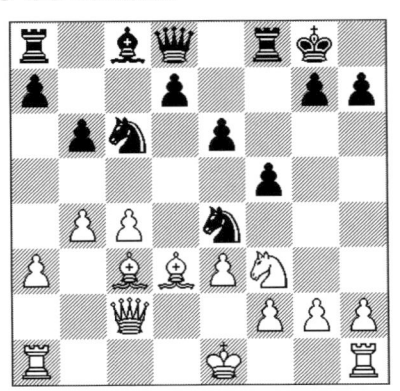

White could also play 13.♗b2 but he wouldn't get any advantage from it, for example: 13...♗b7 14.♗d3 ♕e7! and 15.♗xe4 fxe4 16.♕xe4 would turn the advantage to Black after 16...♘b4 17.♕xb7 ♘d3+ etc.

13...♘xc3 14.♕xc3 ♗b7 15.0-0 ♘e7

It certainly seems risky to leave Black's central squares without adequate protection - but I thought that something should be done to prevent increased pressure on the center by White through c5.

16.♗e2

Threatening to bring the Rook and Queen into the open column, with unpleasant consequences for Black.

16...♕e8 17.♖fd1 ♖d8

Not yet 17...f4 due to 18.exf4 ♔xf4 19.♕d2, etc.

18.a4

See the next Diagram

The serious flaw of this advance, otherwise justified from a strategic point of view, is that it takes up too much time, and thus allows Black to build up the instructive attack afterwards. Undoubtedly, 18.♕e5 would be better here with the strong threat 19.♕c7. In that case, the game would continue 18...f4! 19.♕c7! (and not 19.exf4 ♘g6 20.♕c7 ♘xf4 with Black's advantage) 19...♗xf3 20.♗xf3 fxe3 21.fxe3 ♘f5, with the double tendency 22...♘xe3 and 22...♘h4. Although White in this variant didn't have time to exploit Black's weaknesses on the queen's wing, he would have been perfectly capable of protecting his king - and that was his most important problem now!

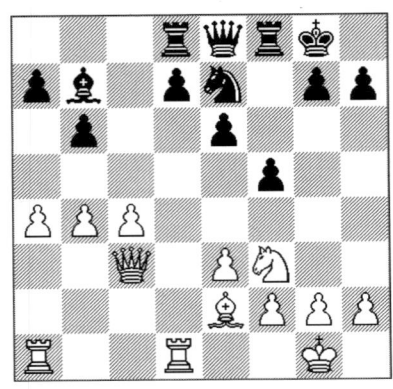

18...f4!

From now until the end, all of Black's moves are precise and at the right time. You can hardly exchange any of them for a better one.

19.a5 fxe3 20.♕xe3 ♘f5 21.♕c3 d6!

A simple but very effective defense against White's ♖a7 move.

22.axb6 axb6 23.♘e1

If 23.♖a7, then of course 23...♖d7 threatens to win a piece with ...♗xf3 etc.

23...e5

Securing the d4 square for the knight. As you can see, the weaknesses of the black squares were, without any apparent effort, transformed into strengths.

24.♖a7

Hoping to complicate things after 24...♖d7 25.c5 with the threat 26.♗b5. But Black had an important intermediate move at his disposal.

24...♘d4! 25.♕e3 ♖d7

Threatening ...♗c6 etc.

26.♖a2 ♖df7 27.f3

One would assume that this pawn, protected by its neighbor and easily supported by 3-4 pieces, would not be the target of an attack by Black. And even if the f3 pawn couldn't be captured almost inevitably. It was certainly this unusual winning stratagem that led the judges to award this game the beauty prize.

27...♖f4 28.♗d3 ♕h5

Threatening 29...e4!.

29.♗f1 ♕g5!

With the main threat of 30...♘xf3, forcing a queen win. White's reply is forced.

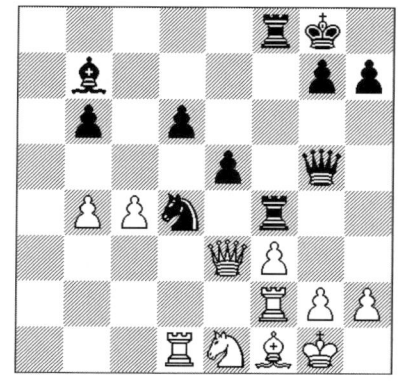

30.♖f2

30...h6!

A terrible move in its simplicity. Black threatens 31...♘xf3! 32.♕xg5 ♖xf2 etc., and if 31.♕d2 (relatively the best) they would play 31...♗xf3 32.♘xf3 ♘xf3+ 33.♖xf3 ♖xf3 34.♕xg5 ♖xf1+ 35.♖xf1 ♖xf1+ 36.♔xf1 hxg5 37.♔e2 ♔f7 38.♔f3 ♔e6 39.♔e4 b5!, with a winning Pawn ending. White's next move in practice changes nothing.

31.♔h1 ♗xf3! with the same point as above. White resigned.

Game 39
A.Alekhine-E.Andersen
Team Tournament, Prague July 1931
Queen's Indian Defense [A50]

1.d4 ♘f6 2.c4 b6

I tried this development in fianchetto (before ...e6) on several occasions at the start of my professional career in the early 1920s and played it successfully in the 1929 game against Bogoljubov (see *Game 28*). Its disadvantage is that it allows White considerable central freedom. Its merit in forcing the opponent to choose a definitive opening plan earlier than he would probably like.

3.♘c3 ♗b7 4.♕c2

On 4.f3, see the game mentioned above.

4...e6?

But this is not in line with 2...b6. The only logical continuation consists of 4...d5 5.cxd5 ♘xd5 6.♘f3 (in the case of 6.e4 Black can play 6...♘xc3 7.bxc3 e5) 6...e6 7.e4 ♘xc3 8.bxc3 ♗e7 followed by ...♘d7, and eventually ...c5, etc, with fighting chances.

5.e4 ♗b4 6.f3!

Avoiding doubling the Pawns on column c. Black now has a slight compensation for White's central dominance.

6...0–0 7.♗d3

Threatening 8.e5, etc.

7...h6 8.♘ge2 d5

Something had to be done to increase the activity of the minor pieces - and the path chosen was probably no worse than any other. At least Black will now briefly have the illusion of a "counterattack" starting with ...c5.

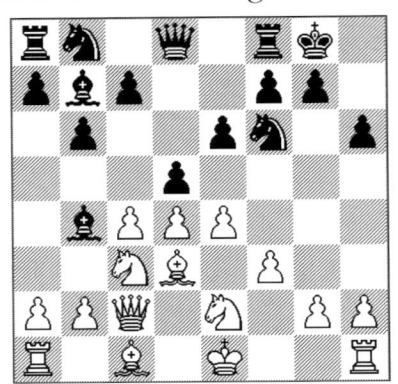

9.cxd5 exd5 10.e5 ♘fd7 11.0–0 c5

If instead 11...♗e7, then 12.♘f4 with an advantage for White.

12.a3 ♗xc3

After 12...♗a5 the Pawn sacrifice 13.b4! cxb4 14.♘b5, etc. would bring Black to a hopeless position.

13.bxc3 ♘c6 14.♗e3

The combination starting with 14.e6 in connection with ♘f4 etc. is also quite strong, but the simple concentration of forces to guard the intact Pawn structure in the center will lead to a quick decision.

14...cxd4 15.cxd4 ♖c8 16.♕d2!

As Black's response to this move is obvious, it should be considered the start of the final combination. Another method, purely positional and much slower, of taking some advantage consisted of 16.♕b1 ♘a5 17.f4 ♘c4 18.♗c1, etc.

16...♘a5

Intending, if nothing special happens, to force the exchange of one of White's bishops with 17...♘c4.

See the next Diagram

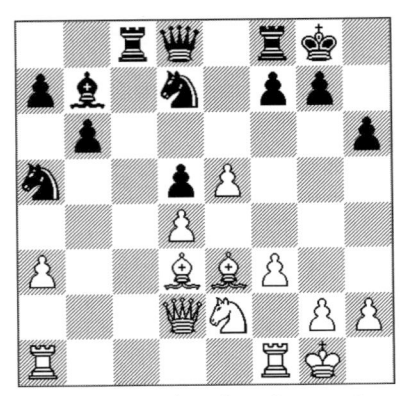

17.♗xh6!

Of course, the offer cannot be accepted: this is by far the easiest part of the combination. But the complications arising from the best defense, in fact the one chosen by Black, require careful analysis.

17...♘b3 18.♕f4 ♖c6!

If instead 18...♘xa1, then 19.♕g3 g6 20.♗xg6 ♔h8 21.♗f5 ♔g8 22.♕h3, winning.

19.♗g5 f6

White also threatened 20.♕h4.

20.exf6 ♘xa1

His last chance, which would then be annihilated by the intermediate sheikh.

21.♗h7+! ♔h8

The alternative was 21...♔xh7 22.♕h4+ ♔g6 (or 22...♔g8 23.f7+) 23.♘f4+ ♔f5 24.g4 mate.

22.♕h4! ♘xf6 23.♘f4

If now 23....g6 then 24.♕h6! with the collapse. Black resigned.

Game 40
A.Alekhine–H.Weenink
Team Tournament, Prague July 1931
Slav Defense [D12]

1.d4 d5 2.c4 c6 3.♘f3 ♘f6 4.e3 ♗f5

As my first game with Dr. Euwe proved, this move happens to be enough for equality, and so White would do better to play 4.♘c3 instead of 4.e3.

5.c×d5 ♗×b1?

But the exchange of the developed Bishop is completely out of place. Rather strangely, this move was warmly recommended by the great openings expert, Dr. Tarrasch, although its defects (the cession of the center and the pair of Bishops to White) are obvious at first glance. Instead, it would be much better to play 5...c×d5 6.♕b3 ♕c7, etc.

6.♖×b1 ♕×d5 7.a3

It was also tempting to sacrifice the Pawn 7.♕c2 ♕×a2 (or 7...e6 8.b4!) 8.♗c4 ♕a5+ 9.♗d2 ♕c7 10.e4, etc. But why give chances if the simple continuation ensures an unquestionable positional advantage?

7...e6 8.♕c2 ♗e7

It would be a mistake 8...c5 due to 9.b4! etc.

9.♗d3 h6

The immediate 9...0–0 would be refuted by 10.e4 followed by e5.

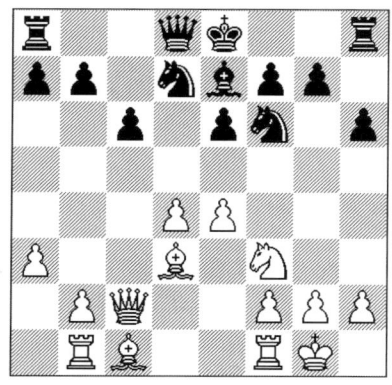

10.e4 ♕d8 11.0–0 ♘bd7

12.b4!

Not only by avoiding ...c5 for a long time, but also by preparing the development of the queen's rook afterwards.

12...0–0 13.♕e2 ♖e8

To have the ♘f8 defense in case White plays 14.e5 followed by ♕e5.

14.♖b3!

Although this Rook won't move until the end of the game, it will play an important role in the attack that follows. But the move in the text also has another purpose - to free up the b1 square for the Bishop.

14...♕c7 15.♗b1 ♘h7

This induces White to finally clarify the situation in the center, since there won't be time to install Black's knight on d4. But also the demonstration on the queen's wing through 15...a5 would end up in White's favor: 16.♕c2 (threatening e5) 16...♘f8 17.e5, etc.

16.e5 f5

Black decides to make this breakthrough sooner rather than later, since after 16...♘hf8, for example, it would be prevented by 17.g4! The exchange then gives their pieces a little more freedom - at least temporarily; but, on the other hand, the e6 square and other white squares in their position remain weaker than ever.

17.e×f6 ♗×f6 18.♕e4

With this and the next two moves, the queen will bring out a very strong attacking position without wasting any time.

18...♘hf8 19.♕g4

Threatening, of course, 20.♗×h6.

19...♔h8 20.♕h5 ♘h7

White now threatened 21.♗×h6! g×h6 22.♕×h6+ ♔g8 23.♘g5 etc., with a quick win.

21.♖e1

Bringing into play the only inactive piece, and at the same time avoiding 21...e5 due to the possible reply 22.♗g4!

21...♖ad8

There's not much use in such a "development", but the position was already hopeless anyway.

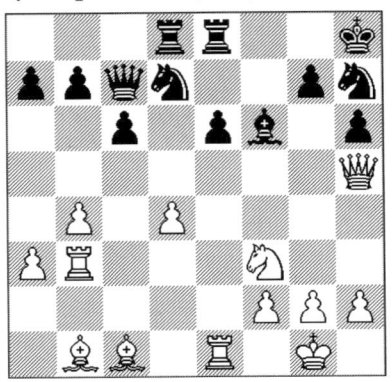

22.g4!
This small threat from Pawn, through further advancement, will set fire to the residence of the King of Black - and it won't be possible to stop him in his cruel plan.

22...♕d6
Hoping to stop 23.g5 through 23...♕d5. But White had an intermediate move in reserve.

23.♗g6! ♖f8 24.g5 ♗×d4
There was no choice.

25.g×h6 ♘df6
White threatens mate in three moves.

26.h×g7+ ♔×g7 27.♕h6+ ♔h8
Or 27...♔g8 28.♘×d4 ♕×d4 29.♔g3, winning.

28.♘×d4 ♕×d4 29.♗b2!
If now 29...♕d7 (the only possible defense), then 30.♖d3 ♕g7 31.♗×f6, followed by mate in three moves. Black resigned.

Game 41
A.Alekhine-E.Steiner
Team Tournament, Prague July 1931
Réti Opening [A32]

1.♘f3 ♘f6 2.c4 c5 3.d4

Something premature. White doesn't need to worry about the 3...d5 response in the case of 3.♘c3 (due to 4.c×d5 ♘×d5 5.e4 ♘b4 6.♗c4, with advantage), he must choose this move in order to be able to respond to 3...♘c5 through 4.d4 and 3...e6 with 4.e4.

3...c×d4 4.♘×d4 e6 5.a3
I didn't like after 5.♘c3 the possibility of 5...♗b4 6.♕b3 ♗c5 - and decided simply not to allow the Bishop's unpleasant move. But even if you're playing White, you can't afford to lose such important time in the opening stage without the risk of giving your opponent the initiative. So, although in this game the move 5.a3 proved to be a success, I must emphatically recommend to the reader *not to make it*, but instead to try, for example 5.♘c3 ♗b4 6.♗d2.

5...♘e4
To one eccentricity Black responds with an even greater one, which allows White to take the lead once again in the fight for the central squares. The natural 5...d5 would be correct 6.c×d5 ♗c5 7.♘c3 ♗b6, followed by ...e×d5 and ...0-0, with a splendid development.

6.e3 f5 7.♘d2 ♘f6 8.b3 ♗e7 9.♗b2 0-0 10.♗d3
Despite the delay on the 5th move, White has already gained an appreciable advantage in the build-up. It's clear that something went wrong with 5...♘e4.

See the next Diagram

10...♘c6 11.0-0 ♘e5
A tricky maneuver to prevent White from playing e4, which would happen for example after 11...b6 12.♘×c6

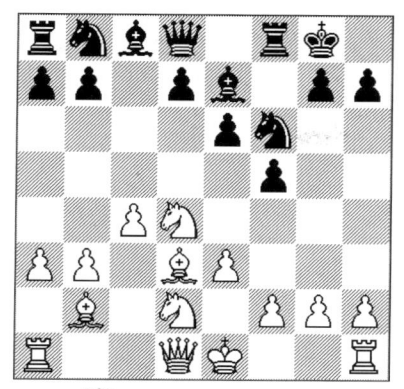

dxc6 13.♕e2 c5 14.e4, with an advantage.

12.♗c2 ♘g6

Hoping to counter-attack after 13.e4 fxe4 14.♘xe4 d5 15.♘xf6+ ♗xf6, etc. But White is in the fortunate position of being able to increase his pressure without prematurely opening the central columns.

13.f4! ♘g4

After 13...b6 the advance 14.e4 would become much more effective than before, for example 14...fxe4 15.♘xe4 ♗b7 16.♘b5, etc. with advantage.

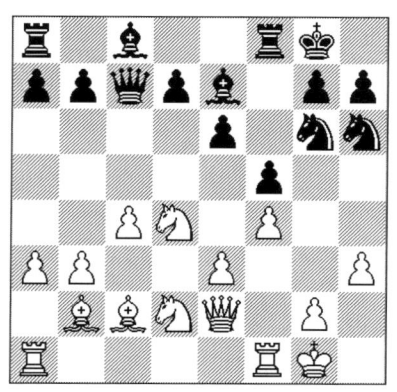

14.♕e2 ♕c7 15.h3 ♘h6

Black has succeeded in banning e4, but at what a price! Both their knights are out of the game and their queenside remains undeveloped. No wonder White soon acquired more and more space and gradually drove his opponent to despair. The reader can compare this game with some other chokes in his collection - for example, those against Nimzowitsch and Yates (San Remo), Mikenas (Folkestone), Winter (Nottingham). In all of them the losers became victims of their passivity and the absence of a defined plan in the opening stages.

16.g4 b6 17.g5 ♘f7 18.♘2f3 ♗b7 19.h4 ♗c5

An attempt to create complications in the immediate case of 20.h5, which would be answered with 20...♘xf4! 21.exf4 ♕xf4 to Black's advantage. But White doesn't need to rush!

20.♕h2! ♖ae8 21.h5 ♘e7 22.♖ae1

Preparing ♘b5 followed by b4.

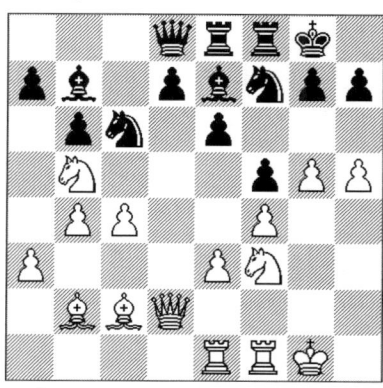

22...♘c6

If 22...a6, then 23.b4 ♗xd4 24.♗xd4 ♕xc4 25.♗xb6 etc., with an advantage for White.

23.♘b5 ♕d8 24.b4 ♗e7 25.♕d2!

Suddenly g7 turned into a deadly weakness - an unusual phenomenon in restricted positions!

25...♗xg5

This kind of desperate sacrifice should, as a rule, be approached with the utmost caution, as it may contain more poison than it first appears. In view of the threat 26.♕c3, Black in fact had practically no choice: 25...d6 26.♘bd4 ♘xd4 27.♘xd4 ♕d7 28.♕c3 would, if possible, be even more welcome for White.

26.fxg5 ♘xg5 27.♕g2!

The most convincing rebuttal to the "offer".

27...♘xf3+ 28.♖xf3 ♖e7 29.♘d6 ♗a8 30.e4

Putting an end to all kinds of "scratches" on the a1–h8 diagonal.

30...♕b8 31.♖g3 e5 32.♘xf5 ♖xf5 33.exf5 ♘d4 34.♗e4 ♘xf5 35.♗xa8 ♘xg3 36.♗d5+, and Black resigned.

Game 42
A.Alekhine-G.Stoltz

Bled Tournament, August 1931
Slav Defense [D17]

1.d4 d5 2.♘f3 ♘f6 3.c4 dxc4 4.♘c3 c6 5.a4 ♗f5 6.♘h4

The main objection that could be raised against this move is that White is wasting time to exchange a piece that is already developed. However, (Dr. Klause's) idea of eliminating Black's sinister queen bishop at any cost is not anti-positional as is generally thought, and at least it has never been refuted in the few games in which it has been tried.

6...e6

Natural and good enough. White, it's true, will enjoy the pair of Bishops, but since Black will be able to control the central squares for a long time, he won't have much to fear. Less satisfactory for them, on the other hand, would be 6...♗c8 (as played for example by Dr. Euwe in the 15th Game of our game in 1935). In that case White (apart, of course, from the draw opportunity 7.♘f3) would have the choice between 7.e3 e5 8.♗xc4 (of course, not 8.dxe5? ♕xd1+ 9.♘xd1 ♗b4+ with an advantage for Black, as played - to my chagrin - in the aforementioned game) 8...exd4 9.exd4 with slightly better prospects, or 7.e4 e5 8.♗xc4 exd4 9.e5, etc. leading to the same complicated situations as in Game 6 of the 1937 game. In any case, an interesting field for investigation.

7.♘xf5 exf5 8.e3 ♘bd7 9.♗xc4 ♘b6

The knight has little to do here - but something that can be done is to avoid 10.♕b3.

10.♗b3 ♗d6 11.♕f3 ♕d7

Black will lose this game mainly because from now on he decides to avoid the "weakening" move ...g6 and tries to protect his Pawn f5 through artificial methods. As a matter of fact, there's not much to say against 11...g6 since 12.e4? would be refuted by 12...♘xe4 13.♘xe4 ♕e7! and 12.a5 answered by 12...♘bd5 13.♘xd5 ♘xd5, etc.

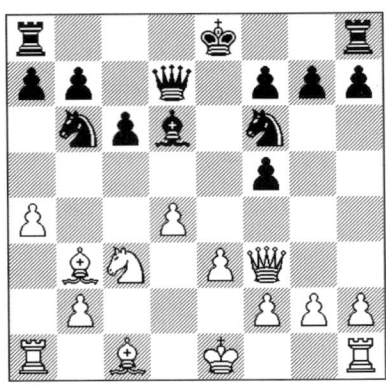

12.h3!

Threatening 13.♗c2 g6 14.g4 etc., with advantage. Black's next move averts the danger.

12...♘c8 13.a5

Playing simultaneously on both sides of the board - my favorite stra-

tegy. The threat now is 15.a6 b6 16.d5! etc.
13...♘e7 14.♗d2

Instead, White could once again try 14.g4, but by playing that way he would lose the bishop development move he had now made. Besides, it wasn't unimportant to prepare for certain eventualities, such as castling.
14...♖b8

This plausible move - made to weaken the effect of the possible a6 advance - will prove to be an important, if not decisive, waste of time. The only possibility of offering serious resistance consisted of 14...h5!

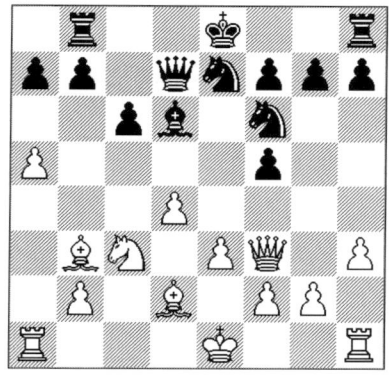

15.g4!

With this move White has at least the extremely important square e4.
15...b5

In keeping with his aggressive style, Stoltz tries to solve the difficult problem by the purely tactical route - as a result, his queen's wing will soon become pitifully weak. Also 15...f×g4 16.h×g4 ♕×g4 17.♕×g4 ♘×g4 18.♖g1 f5 19.f3 ♘f6 (after 19...♘h2 20.♔e2, etc., the Knight won't make it out alive) 20.♖×g7, etc. would have been rather unsatisfactory for Black; but the quiet 15...0-0 (for which White's best response would be 16.♖g1) would give them some defensive possibilities.
16.g×f5

The move 16.g5 would be answered by 16...b4! through which Black would get the central squares for his knights.
16...♕×f5 17.♕×f5 ♘×f5 18.♗c2!

White will succeed in exploiting the weaknesses of the queen's wing before his opponent finds time to concentrate his forces on defense. The following part of the game is convincing and easy to understand.
18...♘h4 19.♔e2 0-0 20.♘e4 ♘×e4 21.♗×e4 c5

The exchange of this Pawn brings Black a slight relief, but the fatal weaknesses in the Queen's wing remain.
22.d×c5 ♗×c5 23.♖ac1 ♗d6

Or 23...♖bc8 24.a6 threatening 25.♗b7 followed by 26.♗a5 etc.
24.♖c6 ♖bd8 25.♖a6 ♖fe8 26.♗c6 ♖e7

For the time being everything is more or less in order, as 27.♗×b5 ♖b7 etc. would not be convincing. But White's next move - through which the lack of coordination of Black's pieces is underlined more drastically - brings the fight to a quick end.

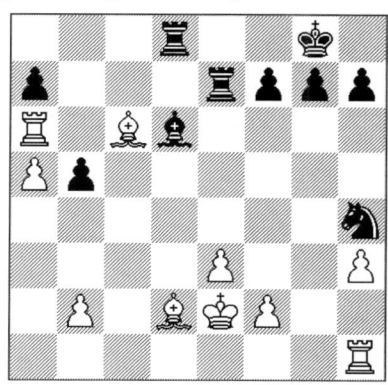

27.♖d1! ♘f5

The Bishop has no square suitable for retreat. If for example 27...♗b8,

then 28.♗b4 ♔×d1 29.♗×e7! and they win.
28.♗b4 g6 29.♗c5!
Threatening to confiscate the queen's rook as well as black's b-pawn. Black, in desperation, sacrifices quality.
29...♗×c5 30.♖×d8+ ♔g7 31.♖d5!
31.♖d7 or 31.♗×b5 would be faulty due to 31...♘d4+, etc.
31...♗d4 32.♖d7
Now, after the d4 house has been taken by the Bishop, this bid is strong.
32...♖e5 33.♔d3 ♗×b2 34.♖a×a7 ♖c5 35.♖×f7+ ♔h6 36.♖×h7+ ♔g5 37.♖af7!
With the unpleasant threat 38.f4+, etc. Black resigned.

Game 43
A.Alekhine-A.Nimzowitsch
Bled Tournament, September 1931
French Defense [C15]

1.e4 e6 2.d4 d5 3.♘c3 ♗b4 4.♘ge2
This move, which is quite satisfactory in the Mac Cutcheon Variant (1.e4 e6 2.d4 d5 3.♘c3 ♘f6 4.♗g5 ♗b4 5.♘ge2) is perfectly harmless at the moment. I chose it, however, in the present game because I knew that already on one occasion (against Sir G. Thomas in Marienbad, 1925) Nimzowitsch had shown an exaggerated voracity (6...f5) without being duly punished for it.
4...d×e4 5.a3 ♗×c3+
Also 5...♗e7 is good enough for equality.
6.♘×c3 f5
Played against all the principles of healthy opening strategy, as Black's squares in the position will be very weak, especially due to the exchange of his King's Bishop. The correct answer, which ensures Black at least a balanced game is 6...♘c6! and if 7.♗b5 then 7...♘ge7, followed by ...0–0, etc.

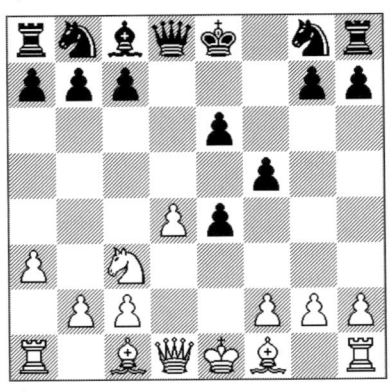

7.f3
The sacrifice of the second Pawn is tempting, probably correct - and already unnecessary, as White can get an excellent game without giving any chances by first playing 7.♗f4, and if 7...♘f6 then 8.f3 e×f3 9.♕×f3, after which 9...♕×d4 would be refuted by 10.♘b5.
7...e×f3 8.♕×f3 ♕×d4
Contrary to the opinion of theoreticians, this move is as good or as bad as 8...♕h4+ 9.g3 ♕×d4: in this case White could play 10.♘b5 and Black wouldn't have - as in the current game - the defense ...♕h4+, g3; ♕e7 etc.
9.♕g3!
An attacking continuation by no means obvious. White's main threats are 10.♘b5 (10...♕e4+ 11.♗e2) and 10.♗f4 or ♗e3.
9...♘f6
This brave move is relatively Black's best chance. It would be insufficient 9...♘e7 due to 10.♗e3! ♕f6 11.0–0–0, etc.
10.♕×g7 ♕e5+?
Inconsequential and therefore fatal. Black - in order to keep a fighting

game - should also give up the c-pawn, because after 10...♔g8 11.♕×c7 ♘c6 there wouldn't be a win for White through 12.♘b5 due to 12...♕h4+! 13.g3 ♕e4+ 14.♔f2 ♕×c2+, followed by ...♘e5, etc. The check of the text allows White to gain time in the development - and time in such a tense position *is* a decisive factor.

11.♗e2 ♖g8 12.♕h6 ♖g6 13.♕h4

White doesn't need to protect his g-Pawn with 13.♕h3, because after 13...♔×g2 the reply 14.♗g5 would be decisive.

13...♗d7 14.♗g5 ♗c6 15.0–0–0 ♗×g2

Under normal circumstances this capture would be considered another blunder, but - due to White's tremendous advantage in development - Black's game is hopeless (if, for example, 15...♘bd7 – then also 16.♖he1 followed by a move with the King's Bishop) and his morbid appetite can't spoil anything else.

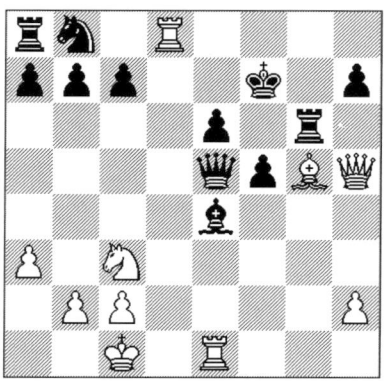

16.♖he1 ♗e4 17.♗h5 ♘×h5 18.♖d8+ ♔f7 19.♕×h5

Nimzowitsch quite rightly resigned here, where there is no longer a decent move for Black - even 19...♔g7 would lose the queen after 20.♘×e4 f×e4 21.♗h6+!.

It was, I believe, the shortest defeat of his career.

> **Game 44**
> **A.Alekhine-M.Vidmar**
> *Bled Tournament, September 1931*
> Queen's Gambit Declined, Lasker Defense
> [D55]

1.d4 d5 2.♘f3 ♘f6 3.c4 c6 4.♘c3 e6

This is not accurate, since the Orthodox Defense move ...c6 is not always used. So far (summer 1939) no clear way has been found for White to gain an advantage after 4...d×c4.

5.♗g5

5.e3 is also considered to be good for white.

5...♗e7 6.e3 0–0 7.♕c2 ♘e4 8.♗×e7

Has anyone tried this type of h4 position? The pitch could be taken into consideration.

8...♕×e7 9.♗d3 ♘×c3

After 9...f5 10.♘e5 ♘d7 11.0–0 the exchanges in the center would favor White, as he has a smaller piece than his opponent.

10.b×c3

In this particular case it's more promising than 10.♕×c3, as Black will be forced to lose time to protect his Pawn h.

10...♔h8

As the sequence will prove, this is only a temporary defense (11.♗×h7? g6) which allows White to build his attacking plans from now on. It was less compromising anyway 10...h6.

See the next Diagram

11.c×d5!

Logical and psychological chess. The aim of this exchange is first of all to prevent Black from obtaining the a1–h8 diagonal for his Bishop through ...d×c4 followed by ...b6. But regardless of these considerations, *White could assume that having avoided weakening his square g6 by not playing ...h6, Black would now try to take advantage of this and bring his Bishop to g6 via g4 and h5.* By provoking this last maneuver, White correctly considered that the opening of the columns on the King's wing - followed by the eventual capture of Black's Pawn h - would only be favorable for the better-developed side.

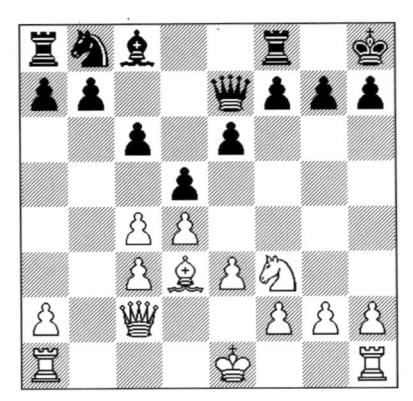

11.e×d5 12.0–0 ♗g4

If 12...♘d7, White would start a promising central plan with 13.♖ae1 ♘f6 14.♘g5 followed by f4, etc. The move in the text is the start of an adventure.

13.♘e5 ♗h5 14.♗×h7!

This Bishop will now be at no greater risk than his colleague in black.

14...g6 15.g4 ♗×g4

In this way, Black avoids material loss for the moment - but his knight remains in the stable and White's defensive moves have attacking purposes at the same time.

16.♘×g4 ♕g5 17.h3 ♔×h7 18.f4 ♕h4 19.♔h2 ♘d7

Finally!

See the next Diagram

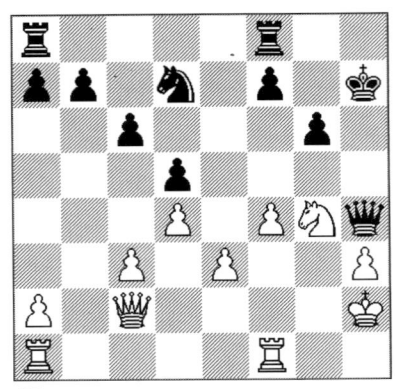

20.♖ab1!

Provoking the response that weakens Black's c pawn. How important this detail is will appear half a dozen moves ahead.

20...b6 21.♖g1 ♘f6 22.♘e5

Threatening 23.♘×g6 and the Pawns c and f.

22...♘e4

Not only interrupting the threats (20.♘×c5 ♖ac8) but also aiming to simplify with 23...♕f2+.

23.♖bf1 ♔g7

Black's possible threats in column h are insignificant compared to White's attack along columns e and f.

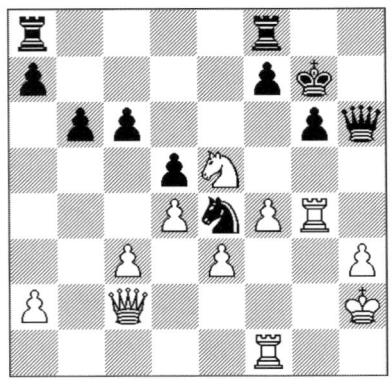

24.♖g4 ♕h6

25.f5!

The tactical justification for this energetic advance is based on two variants - the one played in the present game, and another that starts with 25...g5. In this case, I didn't intend to exchange two rooks for the queen by continuing with 26.f6+ ♘xf6 27.♖xg5+ ♕xg5 28.♖g1 ♕xg1+ 29.♔xg1 ♘e4 (which would be good, but still not decisive enough) - but to sacrifice quality: 26.♖xe4! dxe4 27.f6+ ♔h8 (or 27...♔g8) 28.♕xe4 etc., with a winning positional advantage. Dr. Vidmar thus chose the most promising line of resistance.

25...♕xe3!

This finally loses *only* quality for the Pawn and leads to a difficult ending. It's easy to see that, apart from 25...g5, there's nothing resigned to do.

26.♕g2 ♕d2

Or 26...g5 27.f6+ ♔h7 28.♖h4+! ♔g8 29.♘xc6 etc., with more tragic consequences.

27.f6+ ♔g8 28.♘xc6

The deserved reward for the 20th move.

28...♕xg2+ 29.♔xg2 ♖fe8

There is no other reasonable defense against the threat of mate in two moves.

30.♘e7+ ♖xe7

And now 30...♔f8 would be answered victoriously by 31.♘xd5 (not 31.♖h4? ♘xf6) threatening both 31.♖h4 and 31.♘f7.

31.fxe7 ♖e8

Again forced, as 31...♘xc3 would be quickly lost after 32.♔c1 followed by ♖c7 or possibly ♖c6.

32.c4!

Without this possibility, such as securing a past Pawn, victory would still be very much in doubt.

32...♖xe7 33.cxd5 ♘c3 34.d6 ♖d7 35.♖c1 ♘b5

If 35...♘xa2, White would choose the following sharp continuation to force victory: 36.♖c8+ ♔g7 37.d5 (threatening to win the ♘night) 37...a5 38.♖c7 ♖xd6 39.♖f4 ♖f6 (otherwise White has a mate attack) 40.♔f3 ♘b4 41.♖xf6 ♔xf6 42.♔e4 and despite the level of material, Black will lose, as his two Pawns on the Queen's wing will be short-lived.

36.♖g5 ♘xd6

After 36...♘xd4 the win would technically be easier: 37.♖d5 ♘f5 38.♖c7! ♔xd6 (or 38...♔d8 39.d7) 39.♔xd6 ♘xd6 40.♔xa7, etc.

37.♖d5!

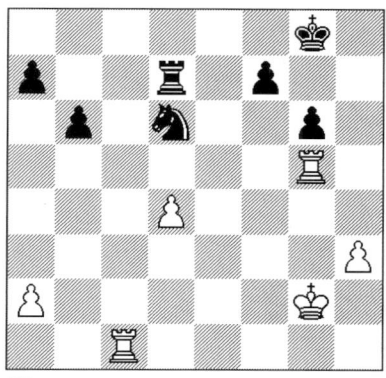

From now on, the purely technical part of the endgame begins. By combining the play of their two rooks and king, White must do his utmost to limit the hostile knight's movements.

37...♔f8 38.♖e1!

Black's king cannot be allowed to approach the center until all of White's units have been taken to the most effective squares.

38...♖d8 39.♔f3 ♖d7

It's obvious that the exchange of the rooks after 39...♘b7 wouldn't put up any serious resistance.

40.♔f4 ♔g7 41.♖e8!

An additional restriction on Black's ability to move.

41...♔f6 42.h4 ♔g7 43.a4 ♔f6 44.♖c8!

With the intention of replacing vertical crimping with a more effective horizontal crimping.

44...♔e6 45.♖e5+ ♔f6 46.♖c6 ♖d8 47.a5! b5

Black must lose a Pawn and prefers to do it this way, because after 47...b×a5 48.♖×a5 ♔e7 49.♖ca6 etc., Black would also force the exchange of the Rooks.

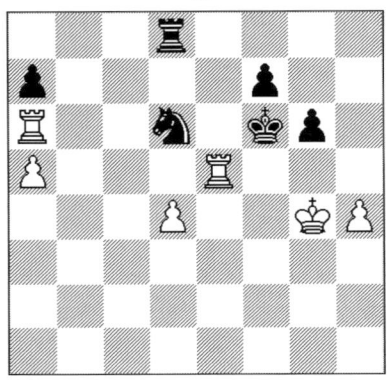

48.♖×b5 ♔e6 49.♖e5+ ♔f6 50.♖a6 ♖d7 51.♔g4 ♖d8

52.♔f3!

A small subtlety: it's more advantageous for White to make the h5 advance when Black's Rook is on d8, because then he'll capture Pawn a with the other Rook on e5.

52...♖d7 53.♔f4 ♖d8 54.h5 g×h5 55.♖×h5 ♖d7 56.♖e5 ♖d8 57.♖×a7

Now White takes the Pawn without allowing the ...♘f5 response that would have been possible before the exchange of the g-Pawn.

57...♘c4 58.♖a6+ ♔g7 59.♖g5+ ♔f8 60.♔e4

The rest is easy.

60...♔e7 61.♖c5 ♘d6+ 62.♔d3 ♔e6 63.♖cc6 ♔d5 64.♖×d6+ ♖×d6 65.♖×d6+ ♔×d6 66.a6, and Black resigned.

Appendix to Game 44 - Alekhine-Vidmar

Endgames with two rooks against a rook and knight are relatively uncommon, and the manuals dedicated to endgames - even the most up-to-date ones, such as the recent edition of E. Rabinovitsch's excellent work - don't give any convincing examples. The materially stronger side should win in most cases, but not without experiencing serious technical difficulties.

According to general opinion, I succeeded against Vidmar by finding the shortest and most instructive winning method, and to a large extent I owe this achievement to the practical lessons I received at the beginning of my career (in St. Petersburg 1914) from the great endgame artist, Dr. Lasker. That lesson cost me a whole point, because I happened to be the man with the Knight! Dr. Lasker, to everyone's surprise, demonstrated that even with a Pawn on each wing (and *not* a passed Pawn) the stronger side is able to force the decisive exchange of the Rook.

Since the game against Dr. Vidmar, I've had the opportunity to play the same type of ending twice, and the procedures for winning have had the same characteristics: (1) Restricting the Knight through compulsory moves or possibly pinning. (2) Gradually weakening the strong points, which usually occur in the center of the board. (3) Threatening exchanges of the Rook, which always mean a step forward - especially if the side with the Knight has no passed Pawns. Other tactics, such as centralizing the King, freeing Pawns, etc. are, of course, common to all types of endgames.

I haven't fully commented on the

next two games in this collection, because although they are interesting, I don't include either of them in my best achievements. Kashdan, to his misfortune and without knowing it, entered on the 15th move in a variant known to be a loser since the 1929 Carlsbad Tournament; and against Dr. Bernstein, instead of the winning exchange, I forced the win by winning all the pieces and, consequently, his resignation. Even so, I believe that these two endgames - in connection with the previous one - can be useful for the student.

Alekhine,A - Kashdan,I
Pasadena Tournament 1932

The characteristic ending began after the moves **1.d4 ♘f6 2.c4 e6 3.♘c3 d5 4.♗g5 ♘bd7 5.c×d5 e×d5 6.e3 c6 7.♗d3 ♗e7 8.♕c2 0-0 9.♘ge2 ♖e8 10.0-0-0 ♘e4** (the same mistake was made by Spielmann against Nimzowitsch, Kissingen 1928 and by Sir G. A. Thomas against Spielmann, Carlsbad 1929) **11.♗×e4 d×e4 12.h4 f5 13.♕b3+ ♔h8 14.♘f4 ♘f6 15.h5 h6 16.♕f7 ♘g8 17.♘g6+ ♔h7 18.♘×e7 ♖×e7 19.♗×e7 ♕×e7 20.♕×e7 ♘×e7 21.d5 ♗d7 22.d×c6 ♗×c6 23.♖d6 ♖c8 24.♖hd1 ♘g8 25.♖d8 ♖c7 26.♖f8 ♘f6 27.♖dd8 ♘×h5 28.♖×f5 ♘f6 29.♔d2 ♔g6 30.♖c5 ♖f7 31.♖d6 ♔h7 32.♖f5 ♔g6 33.♖a5 a6 34.♘d5 ♗×d5 35.♖a×d5 ♔h7** - when the following position was reached:

See the next Diagram

36.♖f5

The combination of vertical and horizontal moves is like what happened in the game against Vidmar.

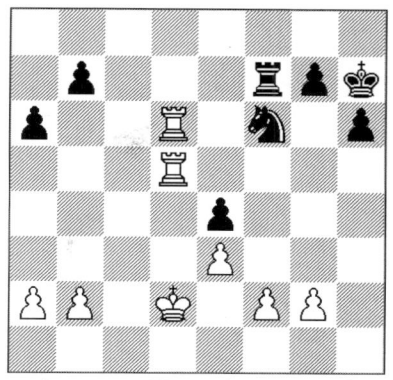

36...♔g6 37.♖c5 ♔h7 38.♔e2

To avoid the move ...♘g5 via f3. If Black now remains passive, White will advance his Pawn to b6 after the exchange on b5, and then play ♖c7.

38...g5 39.b4 ♔g7 40.a4 ♘g4

The only possible attempt.

41.f3 e×f3+ 42.g×f3 ♘h2 43.f4! g×f4 44.e×f4 ♘g4

The old story! It would be fatal 44...♔×f4, because 45.♔c7+ would force the exchange of the Rooks.

45.♔f3 ♘f6 46.b5 ♘d7 47.♖cd5 ♘f6 48.♖f5!

Once again, the pin as a method of gaining important time.

48...♔g6 49.♖c5 a×b5 50.♖×b5

Here it's even more effective than 50.a×b5.

50...♖c7 51.♖bb6 ♖f7 52.a5 ♔g7 53.♖b5 ♖c7 54.♖db6 ♖c3+ 55.♔e2 ♖c4 56.♖×b7+ ♔g6 57.f5+ ♔g5 58.a6 ♖a4 59.a7 ♘e4 60.♔e3!

If now 60...♘d6, then 61.f6+ ♘×b5 62.f7, etc. Black resigned.

Against Dr. Bernstein the task was even more difficult, as his Knight was strongly positioned on d4, protected by a Pawn. The previous moves before the final position under discussion were as follows:

Alekhine,A - Bernstein,O
Zurich Tournament, 1934
1.d4 d5 2.c4 e6 3.♘c3 ♘f6 4.♗g5 ♗e7 5.e3 h6 6.♗f4 c6 7.♘f3 ♘bd7 8.c×d5 ♘×d5 9.♗g3 ♕a5 10.♕b3 0-0 11.♗e2 ♘7f6 12.♘d2 c5 13.♘c4 ♕d8 14.d×c5 ♗×c5 15.♗f3 b6 16.0-0 ♕e7 17.♘b5 a6 18.♘bd6 ♗d7 19.e4 b5 20.e×d5 b×c4 21.♘×c4 ♘×d5 22.♖fe1 ♕d8 23.♖ad1 ♕c8 24.♖c1 ♖a7? (a blunder in an already almost compromised position) 25.♘d6 ♕c6 26.♘e4 ♖b7 27.♖×c5 ♖×b3 28.♖×c6 ♖×f3 29.♖d6 ♖×g3 30.h×g3 ♗b5 31.♘c5 ♖c8 32.♖c1 g5 33.♘b3 ♖b8 34.♘d4 ♔g7 35.♘×b5 a×b5

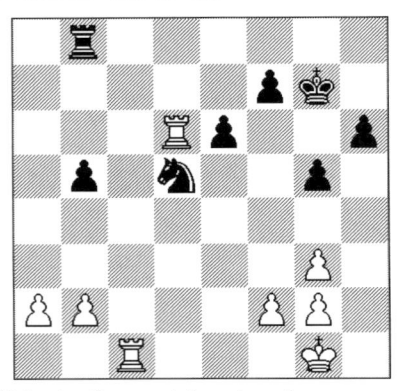

White's first objective is to prevent Black's king from approaching the center, which is achieved by the move:
36.♖c5!
Which now was also Black's rook. But after the answer
36...b4
White needs to stop the threat 37...♖a8 playing.
37.♖a6
And now everything is ready for the centralization of the King, which will allow the advantage on the Queen's wing to be exploited.
37...♘f6
An attempt to stop the normal course of things through tactical threats.
38.♔f1 ♘e4 39.♖c7 ♔g6 40.♔e2 ♖b5 41.♔e3

This dissolves the counterattack started by Black's 37th move. If now 41...♖e5?, then 42.f4, etc.
41...♘f6 42.♖c4
Also avoiding 42...♘g4+.
42...h5 43.f3 ♔f5
Now, the king's advance towards the center isn't as important as his white counterpart's advance.
44.♔d3 ♘d5 45.♖a7 f6 46.♖e4
Giving space to the King.
46...♖b6 47.g4+!
The beginning of the decisive part of this ending. To have free hands on the queen's wing, White needs to eliminate any danger on the other wing, and the move in the text responds to this purpose, as it puts an end to Black's possible threat ...h4; g×h4 g×h4 followed by ...♘f4 etc.
47...♔g6 48.g×h5+ ♔×h5 49.g3 ♔g6 50.♔c4 f5
Something needs to be done about the threat 51.♔c5.
51.♖e2 ♔f6 52.♔c5
With the intention of ♖-d7-d6 etc.
52...♖b8 53.♖a6 ♖e8 54.♖d6!
Threatening 55.♖e2×e6+ ♖×e6 56.♔×d5 etc., finally forcing the King out of the central square.
54...f4 55.g×f4 ♘×f4 56.♖ed2
Forcing the exchange of rooks - or winning the Pawn b.
56...♖a8 57.b3 ♔e5 58.♖d8 ♖a7 59.♔×b4 ♘d5+ 60.♔c5 ♖c7+ 61.♔b5 ♖c3 62.♖e2+ ♔f4 63.♖f8+ ♔g3 64.♖e5!
But not 64.♔×e6?, because 64...♘c7+ and Black will take two Rooks for one.
64...♘f4 65.♖×g5+ ♔×f3 66.♖e5

♖e3 67.♖×f4+!, and Black resigned.

I believe that these three examples taken represent a very important contribution to the chapter two Rooks against Rook and Knight (with Pawns).

Game 45
V.Pirc-A.Alekhine
Bled Tournament, August 1931
Queen's Gambit Refused,
Tarrasch Defense [D32]

1.d4 d5 2.c4 e6 3.♘c3 c5 4.c×d5 c×d4

This interesting Pawn offer (instead of the usual 4...e×d5) was analyzed by some German amateurs and introduced into international practice - if I'm not mistaken - by Dr. Tartakower. As subsequent research proved, Black, despite the superiority of his development, may not be able, against an adequate defense, to prevent the opponent from emerging after the opening with an extra Pawn and a secure position.

5.♕a4+

Better than 5.♕×d4 ♘c3.

5...♗d7

A mistake here would be 5...♕d2 due to 6.♘b4! with advantage.

6.♕×d4 e×d5 7.♕×d5 ♘c6

Black can also play 7...♘f6, after which 8.♕×b7 ♘c6 etc. would definitely be too risky for White; but 8.♕d1 followed by e3 etc. would lead to the same variant that occurred more easily after the text move.

8.♗g5

Due to the delay in development, it would be safer for White to use this Bishop for defensive purposes on the queen's wing, and instead play 8.e3 (...♘f6 9.♕d1). However, the move in the text can't really be considered a blunder.

8...♘f6 9.♕d2 h6

This rather harmless attempt to create (in the case of the natural response 10.♗h4) new threats in connection with ...♗b4 followed by ...g5 and ...♘e4, had unexpected and pleasant consequences.

10.♗×f6

This certainly gives Black more attacking chances than the retreat, but it won't prove so bad if White takes full advantage of the d5 square he wins with this exchange.

10...♕×f6 11.e3 0-0-0 12.0-0-0?

The decisive mistake, which allows Black to recover the gambit Pawn with persistent pressure. 12.♘d5! was needed and if 12...♕g6 (the best), then 13.♘e2 followed by 14.♘2f4 or 14.♕b3 with defense possibilities. Black now can conduct an attack on the King in the "good old style".

12...♗g4 13.♘d5

Too late!

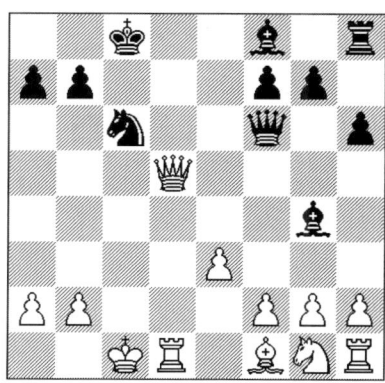

13...♖×d5! 14.♕×d5

14...♗a3!

After 14...♗×d1 15.♕×d1 ♕×f2 16.♕g4+ f5 17.♕e2 ♕×e2 followed by ...♗c5, Black would probably win after a long ending. The move they chose shows their decision, clearly justified under the circumstances, to find a winning solution in the middlegame.

15.♕b3

There's nothing better: if, for example I. 15.b×a3, then 15...♕c3+ 16.♔b1 ♖d8! 17.♕×d8+ ♘×d8, with the double threat 18...♗×d1 and 18...♗f5+; II. 15.♖d2, then 15...♗×b2+! 16.♔×b2 ♕c3+ 17.♔b1 (or 17.♔c2 ♕a1+ followed by ...♖d8) 17...♕e1+ 18.♔c2 ♖d8 winning.

15...♗×d1 16.♕×a3 ♕×f2 17.♕d3 ♗g4!

And not 17...♖d8 due to 18.♘h3! ♕f6 19.♕c3 etc., with chances of salvation.

18.♘f3 ♗×f3

Here too 18...♖d8 would be out of place because of 19.♕e2, etc.

19.♕f5+ ♔b8 20.♕×f3 ♕e1+ 21.♔c2

If White gave up the Pawn, the agony wouldn't be any greater: 21.♕d1 ♕×e3+ 22.♕d2 ♕e6! 23.♔b1 ♖d8 24.♕f4+ ♔a8 etc., with some deadly threats.

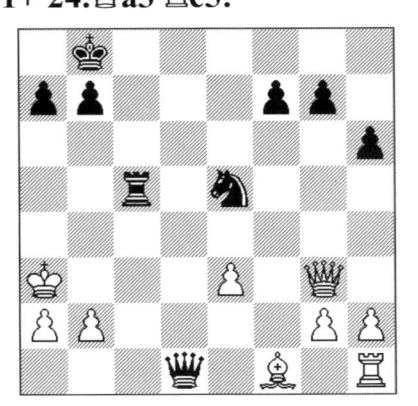

21...♖c8 22.♕g3+ ♘e5+! 23.♔b3 ♕d1+ 24.♔a3 ♖c5!

A quick death is now inevitable, for example: **A.** 25.b4 ♘c3+ 26.♔b2 ♕c1 mate; **B.** 25.b3 ♖a5+ 26.♔b4 ♕d2 mate; and most beautifully, **C.** 25.♔b4 ♕d2+! 26.♔×c5 b6+ 27.♔b5 ♕a5 mate.

The whites resigned.

> **Game 46**
> **A.Alekhine-S.Flohr**
> *Bled Tournament, August 1931*
> Queen's Gambit Accepted [D28]

1.d4 d5 2.c4 d×c4 3.♘f3 ♘f6 4.e3 e6 5.♗×c4 c5 6.0–0 ♘c6 7.♕e2 a6 8.♖d1

Quite peculiarly, this move - which contains no real threat and is therefore at this moment, to say the least, inaccurate - was almost unanimously adopted at the time this game was played. After Euwe's win against me in Game 5 of the game in 1937, and my win against Böök in Margate 1938, "theory" probably recognized that the natural development move 8.♘c3! is the best.

8...b5 9.d×c5

The positional rebuttal to 9.d5 consists of 9...e×d5 10.♗×d5 ♘×d5 11.e4 ♕e7! 12.♔×d5 ♗e6 etc., with advantage.

9...♕c7 10.♗d3 ♗×c5 11.a4

Hoping to disrupt Black's position on the queen's wing and succeeding in doing so because of the following inferior response.

11...b4?

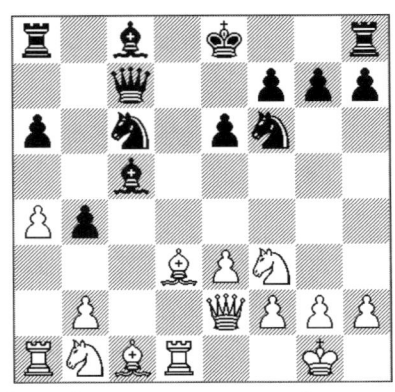

After this move, several squares in this sector will be insufficiently protected and, what's worse, Black will have no hope of counterattacking, since White's position has practically no weaknesses. A very different situation would result from the correct answer 11...b×a4!, which would give Black compensation for the Pawn's weakness with a counter-attack against White's b–♙awn.

12.♘bd2 0-0

Slightly better, though not entirely satisfactory would-be 12...♘a5, as played, for example, by Flohr in the game against Dr. Euwe in 1932.

13.♘b3 ♗e7 14.e4 ♘d7

The possibility of 15.e5 in connection with ♕e4 was certainly unpleasant.

15.♗e3 ♘de5

The intended exchange of the Knights won't bring relief, as it doesn't help solve the important problem of the coordination of the black rooks. So 15...♗b7 16.♖ac1 ♕b8 would be slightly preferable.

16.♘xe5 ♘xe5 17.♖ac1 ♕b8

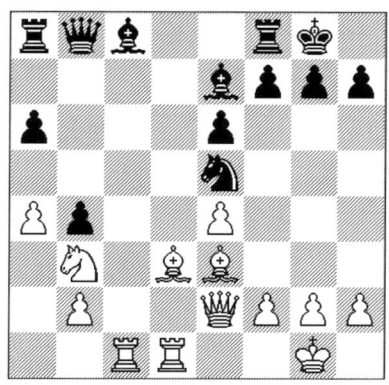

18.♗c5!

From now on, all exchanges will favor exploiting the Pawns' organic weaknesses created by Black's 11th move.

18...♗xc5 19.♘xc5 ♕b6 20.♕h5! ♘d7

As the knight was Black's only active piece, it would be advisable not to remove it unnecessarily. Playing 20...f6 could offer more resistance, although White's advantage after 21.♗f1 ♖d8 22.♖d4!, followed by ♕d1 etc., would still remain considerable.

21.♗e2 g6

To open a "hole" for the King without wasting time; but, as the sequel will show, this move weakens the King's wing, *especially since White is in no hurry to exchange queens.* Black should take the Knight immediately.

22.♕g5 ♘xc5 23.♖xc5 a5

One of White's positional threats was also 24.a5.

24.h4

The punishment for 21...g6.

24...♗a6 25.♗f3!

White's Bishop here is stronger than Black's. White now threatens everything everywhere (26.h5; 26.♗xa5; 26.♔d7, etc.).

26...f6 26.♕e3

From now on, White begins to speculate on the unprotected position of the enemy queen!

26...♖ad8 27.♖xd8 ♖xd8

Or 27...♕xd8 28.e5 f5 29.♗c6 ♗c8 30.♕c5 etc., with a winning position.

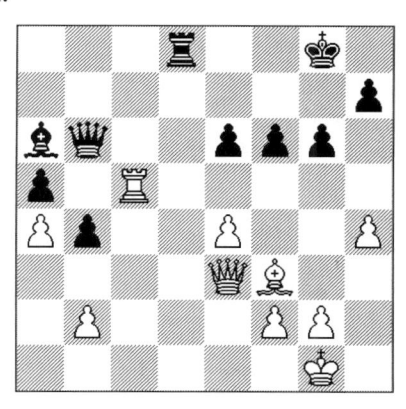

28.e5!

Either threatening to win the Pawn with a devastating position after 28...fxe5 29.♕xe5 (perhaps even stronger is 29.h5 first!), or the catastrophe that actually occurred in this game. The immediate 28.♔c8 was not convincing due to 28...♕d6.

28...f5 29.♖c8!

Winning at least the Rook. Black abandoned.

Game 47
G.Stoltz-A.Alekhine
Bled Tournament, September 1931
Spanish Opening [C71]

1.e4 e5 2.♘f3 ♘c6 3.♗b5 a6 4.♗a4 d6 5.d4 b5 6.♗b3 ♘xd4 7.♘xd4 exd4 8.♗d5

If White's unusual 5th move had an objective in any case, it would only be the offer of the Pawn 8.c3, after which Black's acceptance would have some difficulties in developing. The text move with the Bishop, in connection with the exchange that follows, finally gives Black an advantage in space.

8...♖b8 9.♗c6+

Obviously, White is in a hurry to "simplify things". If they've been told that this is the easiest way to get a draw, they've certainly been badly advised.

9...♗d7 10.♗xd7+ ♕xd7 11.♕xd4 ♘f6 12.♘c3

The move 12.♕a7 would lead to nothing after 12...♕c8.

12...♗e7 13.0–0 0–0 14.♗d2

This bishop doesn't have good development squares. In a clock practice game played in Paris in 1933, Dr. Bernstein tried 14.♗g5 against me, but after 14...b4 15.♘d5 (15.♘e2 ♘xe4 loses a Pawn) 15...♘xd5, he had to resign, because 16.♕xd5 would be answered by 16...♔b5.

14...♖fe8 15.♕d3 b4 16.♘e2

Inconsequential, because here White had more reason than before to pursue his exchange policy. After 16.♘d5 ♘xd5 17.♕xd5 (or 17.exd5) 17...♕b5 etc., Black would only have a slightly more comfortable ending, which, however, with White's correct play, would eventually end in a draw. After the text move, White's task becomes much more complicated.

16...♕c6 17.f3

In the case of 17.♘g3 the reply 17...♘g4 followed by ...♘e5 or ...♗f6 would be strong. The Pawn move, however, weakens Black's squares (especially e3) and thus gives Black the initiative with a concrete goal.

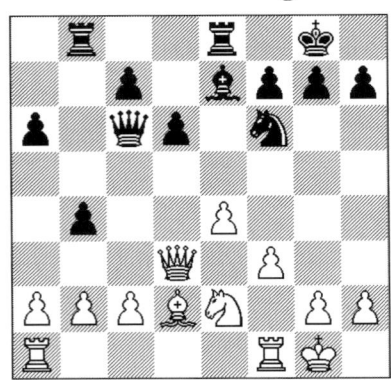

17...d5! 18.exd5

Otherwise, they would lose that Pawn in practice without compensation.

18...♘xd5 19.♖ae1 ♗f6 20.c4

Also 20.c3, which was slightly preferable, would not prove satisfactory after 20...♕c5+ 21.♘d4 ♖ed8 etc., with an advantage for Black.

20...♕c5+ 21.♖f2 ♘e3 22.b3 ♖bd8 23.♗xe3 ♖xe3 24.♕c2

As is easy to see, the last 3-4 moves were practically forced. Black not only gained total control of the board, but even a position to gain a material advantage. In the final part of the fight, however, there is no shortage of piquancy.

24...♗h4! 25.g3 ♖×f3 26.♖ef1 ♗g5 27.♔g2 ♖×f2+ 28.♖×f2 ♕c6+ 29.♔h3

Forced, as Black threatens 30...♖d2 or 30...♗e3.

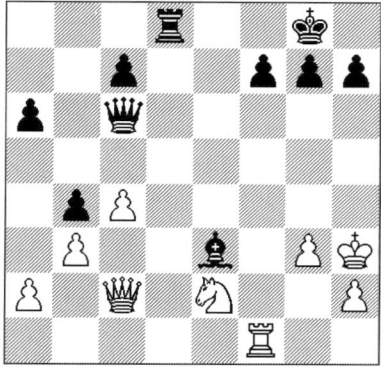

29...♗e3 30.♖f1

30...♖d5!

It still wouldn't be decisive 30...♖d6 or 30...♖d2, because of 31.♕f5 with counterplay. But after the text move, cooperation with the Rook will leave White defenseless.

31.♘f4 ♕d7+ 32.g4 ♖d4 33.♕g2

The Whites can still find defensive moves, but obviously they can't go on like this.

33...c6 34.♘h5 ♗g5!

After that there is no remedy against 35...g6, etc.

35.♕e2 g6 36.♘g3 h5 37.♘e4 ♕×g4+!

Only apparently allowing White to reach a bookend with a Pawn less. What Black wants is to take White's Rook.

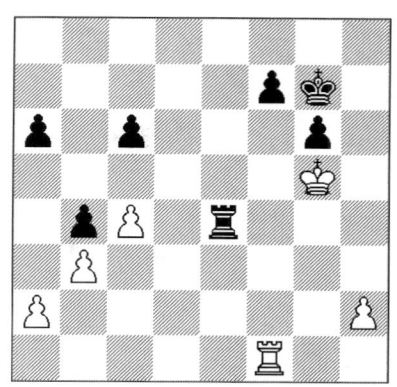

38.♕×g4 h×g4+ 39.♔×g4 ♖×e4+ 40.♔×g5 ♔g7

Black's next move would now be 41...f6+! followed by 42...♖e5+, winning the Rook. Then - White resigned.

Game 48
A.Alekhine-G.Maroczy
Bled Tournament, September 1931
Orthodox Defense [D66]

1.d4 d5 2.♘f3 ♘f6 3.c4 e6 4.♗g5 ♘bd7 5.e3 h6 6.♗h4 ♗e7 7.♘c3 0-0 8.♖c1 c6 9.♗d3 a6

The continuation of the fashion, whereby Black actually has very little to fear after 9...d×c4 10.♗×c4 b5 11.♗d3 a6 and if 12.a4 (12.e4? ♘×e4, with Black's advantage: Euwe-Alekhine, 28th Game of the game, 1935), then simply 12...b×a4.

10.0-0 d×c4 11.♗×c4 c5

It's too risky to delay development on the queen's wing. Instead, 11...b5, followed by ...♗b7 and ...c5 would still be a very good alternative.

See the next Diagram

12.a4!

This move, in connection with the isolation of the central Pawn, gives the game its characteristic. After 12.♗d3 or 12.♕e2 b5, etc., it would develop in conventional lines - and probably end in an honorable draw.

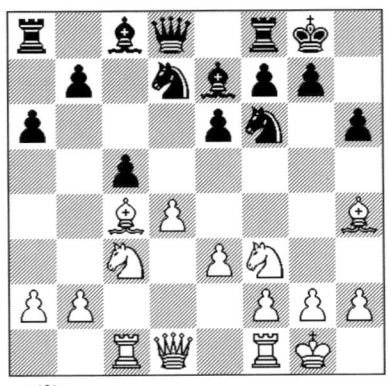

12...♕a5

Maróczy now plays very enterprising chess, combining defensive moves with counterattacks against White's weaknesses on a4 and d4.

13.♕e2 cxd4!

At the right moment, because 14.♘xd4 ♘e5 15.♗b3 ♘g6 16.♗g3 e5 etc. would favor Black.

14.exd4 ♘b6 15.♗d3!

Practically leaving the Pawn at its destination. At this point, it's true, it can't be taken due to 16.♘e4! with a very strong attack. But it will remain weak almost until the - dramatic - end.

15...♗d7 16.♘e5

Threatening 17.♗xf6 followed by 18.♕e4, etc.

16...♖fd8 17.f4

White had already decided, with 12.a4!, to conduct the whole game in *fortissimo* style. Although the result justifies this method, I'm by no means sure that it was the most logical way to exploit the - unquestionable - advantage in space. Here, for example, the simple move 17.♕f3 must seriously be taken into account, since (1) 17...♘xa4 would still be answered by 18.♘e4!, with an advantage for White; (2) 17...♗xa4 would obviously be unsatisfactory due to 18.♕xb7; and (3) after 17...♗c6 18.♘xc6 bxc6 19.♖fd1 etc., Black's pawn weaknesses would be at least as vulnerable as White's. The game would be played in the same way.

17...♗e8 18.♘g4

The logical consequence of the previous move. White offers the d-Pawn, because its defense with 18.♖cd1 or 18.♗f2 would allow Black to stop important threats with ...♘(b or f)d5.

18...♖xd4

Black, on the other hand, has nothing better to do than accept the offer, as White's other attacking moves would remain - with more material - at least as strong as in the game.

19.♗xf6 ♗xf6 20.♘xf6+ gxf6 21.♘e4

Black's kingside position is now dangerously compromised, especially as they can't adequately protect the f6 square (if 21...♘d7, then 22.f5! with a strong attack).

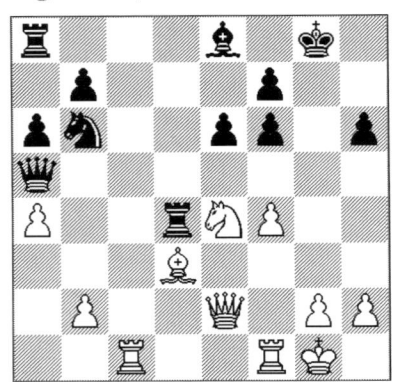

21...♖ad8?

But Black could - and should - save the c6 Pawn by playing 21...f5 to which White would respond 22.♘f6+ ♔f8 (or 22...♔g7 23.♘h5+ followed by b3) 23.b3! and try to exploit the weaknesses of his opponent's black squares later - with an uncertain outcome. The counterattack initiated by the text move will be refuted mainly due to the fact that White will be able to protect his Bishop *indirectly*, without wasting any time.

22.♘xf6+ ♚f8 23.♘h7+!

Perhaps Maroczy underestimated this check. If now 23...♚g8, then 24.♕g4+ ♚h8 25.♕h4! ♚xd3 26.♕xh6 winning.

23...♚e7 24.f5!

The first indirect defense: if 24...♚xd3? then 25.f6+ followed by 26.♕xd3+, etc.

24...♖8d6

But after this move everything seemed to be in order again, as the King achieved a comfortable escape on d8. However, the next response, which was by no means easy to find, turned the tables.

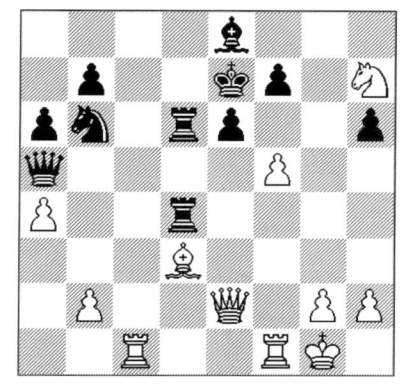

25.b4!!

A surprising solution to the attacking problem, the idea of which was as follows: White succeeds (in the case of 25...♚xb4) by playing 26.♕h5! without allowing the strong reply 26...♚d2! or (as happened in the game) by getting the queen into Black's position via e5.

25...♕xb4

An interesting ending would occur after 25...♖xb4 26.♕h5! e5! 27.f6+ ♚d8 28.♕xh6! ♚xd3 29.♕f8 ♖d7 30.♚c5 ♕xa4 31.♖xe5 winning.

26.♕e5!

Threatening 27.♕f6+ ♚d7 28.♘f8 mate.

26...♘d7

It protects both the critical house and - apparently - finally wins the Bishop.

27.♕h8! ♖xd3

Losing a move earlier than he could. The best answer 27...♕b6 would force White to reveal the last point of the combination started on his 25th move - 28.a5! (the triumph of the neglected Pawn!) with two variants: (a) 28...♕xa5 29.♚c8, or (b) 28...♕a7 29.c6+ etc., as played in the game.

28.f6+!

If 28...♘xf6, then 29.♕xf6+ ♚d7 30.♘f8 mate; if 28...♚d8 29.♕xe8+! followed by 30.♚b8 mate. Black resigned.

Game 49
A.Alekhine-W.Winter
London Tournament, February 1932
Caro-Kann Defense [B13]

1.e4 c6 2.d4 d5 3.exd5 cxd5 4.c4

One of the best ways to tackle Caro-Kann. It's a bit out of fashion these days, in my opinion without much reason and probably only temporarily.

4...♘f6 5.♘c3 ♘c6 6.♘f3

If 6.♗g5 (Botvinnik's move) 6...e6 7.♘f3 ♗e7, with slightly restricted but very solid defensive play.

6...♗g4 7.cxd5 ♘xd5 8.♗b5 ♕a5

Introduced by me in the game against Nimzowitsch (Bled, 1931), in which my opponent after 9.♕b3! ♗xf3 10.gxf3 ♘xc3 made the curious mistake 11.♗xc6+ bxc6 12.♕b7? – and after 12...♘d5+ 13.♗d2 ♕b6! 14.♕xa8+ ♚d7 15.0-0 ♘c7 he was forced to give up a piece via 16.♗a5, rendering any future resistance hopeless in practice. However, the move with the queen is - as this game shows - decidedly too risky. The correct line is 8...♔c8 9.h3 ♗×f3 10.♕×f3 e6 etc., with equal prospects.

9.♕b3! ♗×f3 10.g×f3 ♘×c3 11.b×c3 e6

Black has, it is true, obtained the best Pawn position, but the efficient Pawn sacrifice that follows will show that his King's position is by no means secure. The next phase of the game is highly instructive, as White's attack needs a particularly accurate calculation for its success.

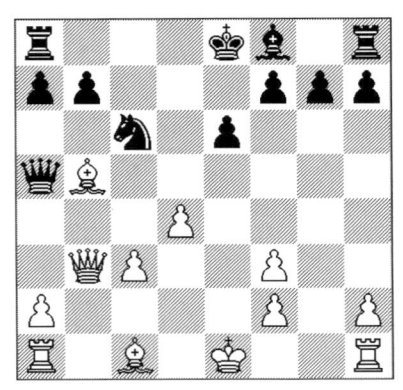

12.d5

It's necessary to sacrifice the Pawn at once, because after 12.0–0 ♖d8 Black would have a satisfactory position.

12...e×d5 13.0–0 0–0–0

The only move. After 13...♗e7 14.♖e1 the King pin would be deadly.

14.♗×c6 b×c6 15.♖b1 ♕c7

Or 15...♔d7 16.c4! etc., with a tremendous attack.

16.♕a4 ♖d7 17.♗d2!

A difficult move, much more effective than 17.♗f4 or 17.♗e3. Despite his precise defense, Black will be unable to prevent a future gradual demolition of his royal residence.

17...♗c5 18.c4 ♔d8

Again, relatively the best, as 18...♗b6 would fail due to 19.c5! ♗×c5 20.♕a6+ ♔d8 21.♗a5 ♗b6 22.♖×b6 etc.

19.♗a5 ♗b6 20.♗×b6 a×b6 21.♕a8+!

The objectives of this very deep Queen maneuver are as follows:

(1) If White plays 21.c×d5 straight, Black can answer 21...♔×d5 22.♖fd1 ♔e7! 23.♖×d5 c×d5 24.♖e1+ ♔f6 25.♕h4+ ♔g6, and White has no more than perpetual check. So, they must prevent Black's king from escaping via e7.

(2) In some important variants the white rook must be placed on a4 - so the queen frees up this square in view of this eventuality.

21...♕c8 22.♕a3 ♕b8 23.c×d5 c×d5

After 23...♔×d5 24.♖fd1 ♔e8 25.♖×d5 c×d5 26.♖d1 ♕e5 27.f4 Black would have no adequate defense.

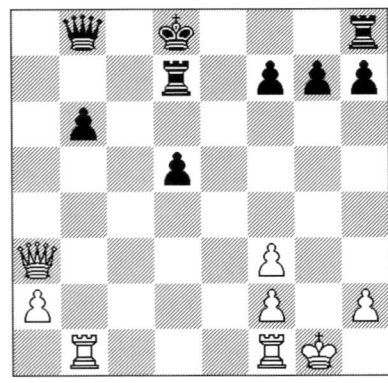

24.♖b4!

The winning move, because Black doesn't have time to play 24...♖e8 due to 24.♖a4, etc.

24...♕d6 25.♖e1! ♖c7

Or 25...♖e7 26.♖d1 etc., with a

winning attack.

26.♕b3 ♖e8 27.♖d1 ♖e5

Obviously Black can't protect both Pawns.

28.♖×b6 ♖c6 29.♖×c6 ♖g5+

Forced - 29...♕×c6 30.♕b8+, etc.

30.♔h1 ♕×c6

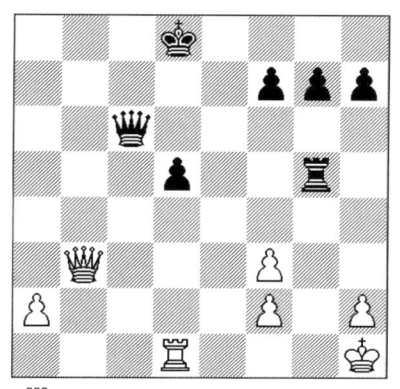

31.♖e1!

Beginning the final attack.

31...♕f6 32.♕b8+ ♔d7 33.f4 ♖g6

Here I expected 33...♖h5 34.♕e8+ ♔d6 35.♖c1! ♖×h2+ 36.♔g1!, forcing a win.

34.♕e8+ ♔c7 35.♖c1+ ♔b6 36.♖b1+ ♔c5 37.♕b5+, and Black resigned.

Game 50
V.Menchik-A.Alekhine
London Tournament, February 1932
Queen's Indian Defense [E14]

1.d4 ♘f6 2.c4 e6 3.♘f3 b6 4.e3

A harmless development system, which doesn't mean it's bad. Black in this way has no difficulties in the opening, if he doesn't overestimate his position, and realizes that although he has enough strength to control the e4 square, he hasn't yet developed enough to *occupy it*.

4...♗b7 5.♗d3 ♗b4+ 6.♗d2 ♗×d2+ 7.♘b×d2

This knight is not very happily positioned on d2. More promising then would be 7.♕×d2 followed by ♘c3.

7...d6 8.0-0 ♘bd7 9.♕c2 ♕e7 10.♖fd1 0-0 11.♘e4 g6

A good move, the aim of which is, as the sequel will show, to avoid the exchange of the queen's bishops. Since the Pawn position is much more elastic than the opponent's, it's interesting for Black to keep as many pieces on the board as possible.

12.♖d2 ♘×e4 13.♗×e4 c6! 14.♕a4

Probably hoping to provoke the response 14...b5, which would be advantageous for White after 15.♕b3!

14...♖fc8 15.♗d3 c5 16.♕d1

None of White's pieces has a suitable square. But it will be some time before Black can get a serious initiative.

16...♘f6 17.d×c5 b×c5

The correct way to recapture, as the rear of Pawn d is very easy to protect in this type of position.

18.♕e2 ♘h5 19.♖ad1

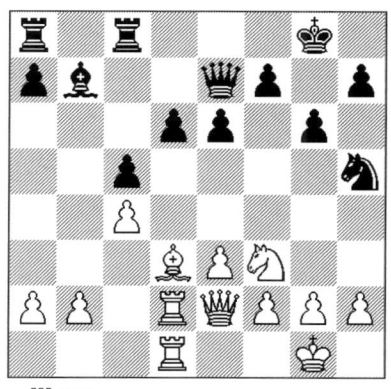

19...♖f8!

Preparing the pawns' e and f advances.

20.e4 ♘f4 21.♕e3 e5 22.♗f1 ♖ad8

107

From this point on Black's tactics are impeccable, but here ♖fd8, followed by ♘–e6–d4 would be more convincing, as it would prevent White's next attempt.

23.b4!

An interesting pawn sacrifice in a difficult position. If now 23...c×b4, then 24.♕×a7 ♖a8 25.♕b6 ♗×e4 26.♕×d6 ♕×d6 27.♔×d6 ♗×f3 28.g×f3 ♔×a2 29.♔b6, with good chances of a draw for White.

23...♘e6 24.♖b2 ♗a8 25.b×c5 ♘×c5 26.♘d2 f5 27.e×f5 g×f5

With the opening of the g column, Black finally has the basis for a powerful attack on the king.

28.f3 ♕g7

Threatening 29...f4 followed by ...e4.

29.♖db1 ♔h8 30.♘b3 ♘e6 31.♖d2 ♘g5 32.♔h1 ♖g8 33.♖f2

The only defense against 33...♘×f3.

33...♖de8 34.♖d1 ♖e6

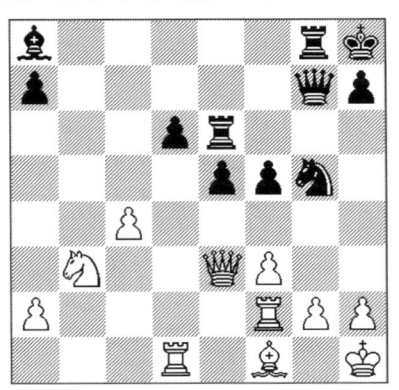

Despair, as Black threatened 35...♔h6 followed by 36...♔×h2+ 37...♕h6+ 38...♘h3+, etc. And after 35.b5 d5 etc., they would win by simply advancing their central Pawns.

35.f4 e×f4 36.♕d4 ♖e5! 37.c5 d×c5 38.♘×c5 ♘h3 39.♖c2 f3! 40.g3 f2+

That was the farthest bishop check I've ever given in my life! White gave up.

> **Game 51**
> **A.Alekhine–G.Koltanowski**
> *London Tournament, February 1932*
> Spanish Opening [C73]
> **Beauty Award**

1.e4 e5 2.♘f3 ♘c6 3.♗b5 a6 4.♗a4 d6 5.♗×c6+ b×c6 6.d4 e×d4

The usual defensive scheme here is 6...f6, followed by ...♘–e7–g6, etc. But White in this game obviously wants a free diagonal for his King's Bishop.

7.♘×d4 ♗d7 8.0–0 g6 9.♘c3

White has nothing better than this quiet development of forces - hoping that sooner or later the slight weakening of the black squares in the opponent's camp will give them real chances.

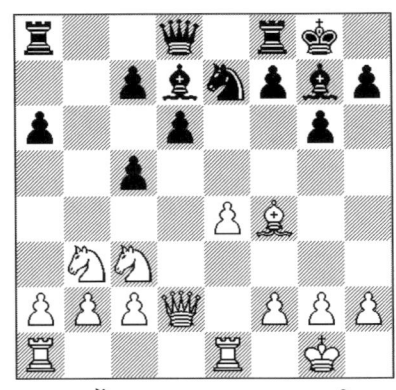

9...♗g7 10.♖e1 ♘e7 11.♗f4 0–0 12.♕d2 c5 13.♘b3

Not 13.♘f3 due to 13...♗g4. But 13.♘de2 comes into serious consideration.

13...♘c6 14.♗h6 ♗e6 15.♗×g7 ♔×g7 16.♘d5 f6 17.♖ad1 ♖b8 18.♕c3 ♕c8 19.a3 ♕b7 20.h3!

This and the next move were by no means easy to find because, in preparing the final combination, I had to keep in mind at the same time the possibility of the simplifying variant starting with ...♗×d5.

20...♖f7 21.♖e3 ♕b5

As the continuation shows, Black could play 21...♗×d5 here - but after 22.e×d5 ♘d4 23.♘×d4 c×d4 24.♔×d4 ♕×b2 25.♕d2 White would still retain a real positional advantage, although not easily achievable.

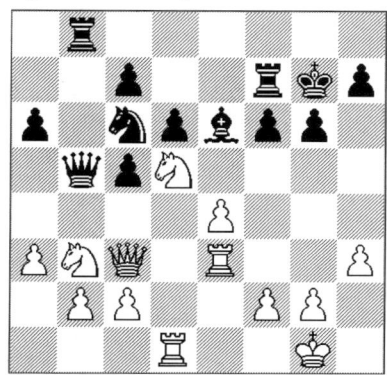

22.♘×c7!

As a rule, so-called "positional" sacrifices are considered very difficult, and therefore more praiseworthy than those based exclusively on exact calculations of practical possibilities. The present position offers, I believe, an exception, because the quantity and complexity of the variants arising from the sacrifice of the Knight requires much more intense mental work than any generic assessment of reciprocal possibilities.

22...♖×c7 23.♖×d6 ♗c4

Black has many other answers, but all of them would ultimately lead to defeat, as shown below: (I) 23...♗×b3? 24.♕×f6+ followed by 25.♖×b3 etc.; (II) 23...♘d4 24.♘×d4 etc.; (III) 23...♕c4 24.♘×c5! etc.; (IV) 23...♘d8 24.♖f3 ♖f7 25.♘×c5 etc.; (V) 23...♗f7 24.♖×f6! ♘d4 25.♘×d4 c×d4 26.♕×c7 ♔×f6 27.♖f3+ etc.; (VI) 23...♖e8 24.♘×c5 ♘d8 25.b4 ♗f7 26.♖×e6 etc.; (VII) 23...♔f7 24.♖f3 ♔e7 25.a4 ♕b6 (the best) 26.♖×e6+ ♔×e6 27.♘×c5+ ♔d6 (or 27...♔f7 28.♕×f6+ ♔g8 29.♘e6! etc.) 28.♕×f6+ ♔×c5 29.♖c3+ ♔b4 30.♕d6+, winning.

24.a4! ♕×a4 25.♘×c5 ♕b5 26.♕×f6+ ♔g8 27.♘d7! ♖d8

Or 27...♖e8 28.♕c3, winning.

28.♖f3 ♕b4 29.c3 ♕b5 30.♘e5! ♖dc8 31.♘×c6

If now 31...♔×c6, then 32.♖d8+ winning. Black resigned.

Game 52
A.Alekhine–S.Tartakower
London Tournament, February 1932
Budapest Defense [A51]

1.d4 ♘f6 2.c4 e5 3.d×e5 ♘e4

Less usual, but no better than 3...♘g4, against which I've had (except in the game against Gilg, Semmering 1926) rather pleasant experiences too. Here, for example, are two short stories from "Budapest":

(I) Alekhine - Rabinowitsch, Baden-Baden 1925. 1.d4 ♘f6 2.c4 e5 3.d×e5 ♘g4 4.e4 ♘×e5 5.f4 ♘g6 6.♘f3 ♗c5 7.f5 ♘h4 8.♘g5! ♕e7 9.♕g4 f6 10.♕h5+! g6 11.♕×h4 f×g5 12.♗×g5 ♕f7 13.♗e2 0-0 14.♔f1 ♘c6 15.♘c3 ♘d4 16.f×g6 ♕×g6 17.♖×f8+ ♗×f8 18.♗h5 ♕b6 19.0-0-0 ♗g7 20.♖f1 ♘e6 21.♗f7+ ♔h8 22.♗×e6 ♕×e6 23.♗f6!, and Black resigned.

(II) Alekhine - Dr. Seitz, Hastings 1925-1926. 1.d4 ♘f6 2.c4 e5 3.d×e5 ♘g4 4.e4 ♘×e5 5.f4 ♘ec6 6.♗e3 ♗b4+ 7.♘c3 ♕e7 8.♗d3 f5 9.♕h5+ g6 10.♕f3 ♗×c3+ 11.b×c3 f×e4 12.♗×e4 0-0 13.♗d5+ ♔h8 14.♘h3 d6 15.0-0 ♗×h3 16.♕×h3

My Best Games 1924-1937

109

♕d7 17.f5 g×f5 18.♖ab1 f4 19.♗×f4 ♕×h3 20.♗e5+, and Black resigned.

4.♘d2 ♘c5

If 4...Bb4+, then 5.♘c3 followed by a3, to get the advantage of the pair of Bishops.

5.♘gf3 ♘c6 6.g3 ♕e7 7.♗g2 g6

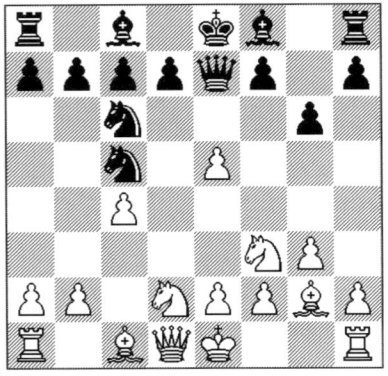

8.♘b1!

At first glance this move is surprising, but in reality, it's perfectly logical. After Black has clearly demonstrated his intention to develop the King's Bishop on g7, White can no longer count on any action on the e1–a5 diagonal. So, there's no point in delaying the knight's placement on the dominant square d5.

8...♘×e5 9.0-0 ♘×f3+ 10.e×f3 ♗g7 11.♖e1 ♘e6 12.♘c3 0-0 13.♘d5 ♕d8 14.f4 c6

For better or worse, the teats dislodged White's knight - thus creating a dangerous weakness on d6, because after the immediate 14...d6 the temporary sacrifice 15.f5 etc. would be very dangerous for them.

15.♘c3 d6 16.♗e3 ♕c7 17.♖c1 ♗d7 18.♕d2 ♖ad8 19.♖ed1 ♗c8 20.♘e4 ♘c5

This will finally be refuted through the combination started on White's 24th move - but due to the weakening mentioned above, Black's position is already very difficult. It would be unsatisfactory, for example, 20...d5 21.c×d5 ♖×d5 22.♘f6+ followed by 23.♗×d5 etc., winning the quality; or 20...c5 21.f5! g×f5 22.♘c3 ♘d4 23.♘d5 ♕b8 24.♗g5 etc., with an advantage; and after the relatively safer 20...b6, White would easily increase his advantage in space by continuing with 21.b4, etc.

21.♘×d6! ♘a4 22.c5 ♘×b2 23.♖e1

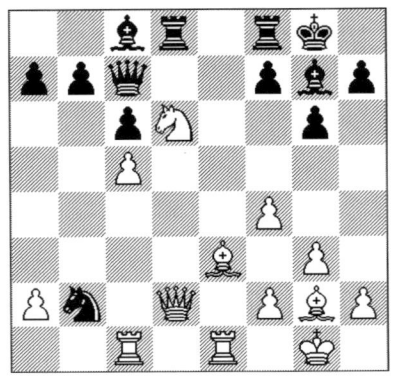

23...b5

This response - the logical consequence of the three previous moves - will prove insufficient. But Black had no way out, for example: 23...♗e6 24.♗d4! or 23...♗f5 24.g4!24...♗×g4 25.♗d4, in both cases with a decisive advantage for White.

24.c×b6!

A surprising combination, but not too complicated. The only difficulty consisted in the need to plan this possibility many moves before, when the capture 21.♘×d6 was made.

24...♕×d6 25.♕×d6 ♖×d6 26.b×a7 ♗b7 27.♗c5 ♖dd8 28.♗×f8 ♔×f8 29.♗×c6 ♗×c6 30.♖×c6 ♖a8

Black's moves were practically forced and, as their position is absolutely hopeless, they prefer a quick

110

endgame. If instead 30...♗d4, then 31.♖d6, also winning immediately.

31.♖b6 ♖×a7 32.♖b8 mate.

Game 53
A.Alekhine-M.Sultan Khan
Bern Tournament, July 1932
Caro-Kann Defense [B13]

1.e4 c6 2.d4 d5 3.e×d5 c×d5 4.c4 ♘f6 5.♘c3 ♘c6 6.♘f3 ♗g4 7.c×d5 ♘×d5 8.♗b5 a6

On 8...♕a5 see *Game 49* against Winter. The point of the move in the text is the positional offer of the Pawn, which is by no means easy to refute on the board.

9.♗×c6+ b×c6 10.♕a4! ♘×c3

The logical consequence of his 8th move, since 10...♗d7 11.♘e5 would obviously be in White's favor.

11.♕×c6+ ♗d7 12.♕×c3 ♖c8 13.♕e3 ♗b5

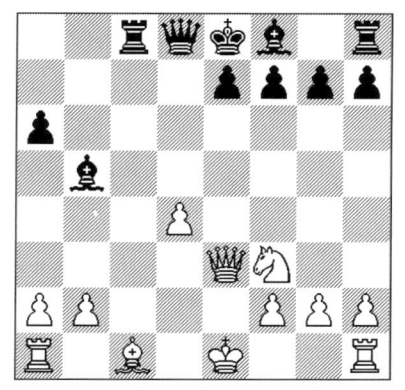

It's clear that Black has no compensation for the Pawn less: White's d-Pawn is isolated and - more importantly - Black will be forced to weaken his Queen's wing over the next few moves if castling is to be possible.

14.a4 ♗c4 15.b3 ♗d5 16.0-0 ♕b6 17.♗d2!

It would be a weak strategy to protect the b-♙awn with 17.♔b1, after which Black would find time to finish his development with 17...e6, ...♗d5 or ...♗e7 and ...0-0.

17...e6

If instead 17...♕×b3, then 18.♖fc1! ♖×c1+ 19.♖×c1 ♕×e3 20.f×e3 e6 (or 20...♗×f3 21.g×f3 ♔d7 22.♗a5, etc.) 21.♖c7, followed by ♖a7 with advantage.

18.♖fc1 ♖b8

Relatively better than the exchange.

19.♘e5 f6

Probably underestimating the strength of the reply; but also 19...♗e7 was not satisfactory, for example: 20.♘c4 ♕×b3 21.♕×b3 ♗×b3 22.♘d6+! etc., with advantage.

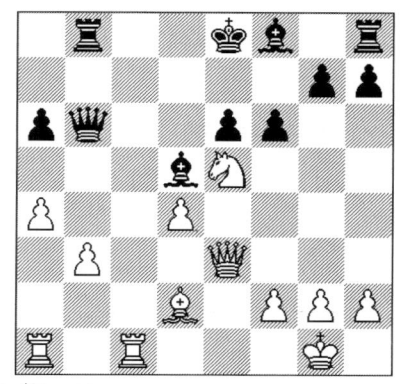

20.♘c6!

The aim of this Knight manoeuvre is to put an end to Black's attacks on the b Pawn.

20...♖a8

The only move, as 20...♔c8 would be inferior due to 21.♘b4!

21.♘a5

Eventually 22.♖c6!.

21...♔f7

This position of the King in the early stages of the game is more familiar to Sultan Khan than to European and American players, because in Indian chess castling is carried out in three moves: (1) ♔e7 – d7 or f7; (2)

the Rook moves from its original square; (3) a Knight move, with the King returning to the first rank to the side of the Rook that moved - without the King being in check during this process. Returning to our game, it can be assumed that Black, due to the threats mentioned above, doesn't really have anything better than the King's move.

22.♘c4 ♕b7 23.♕g3 ♗e7 24.a5

The opening move of the decisive scheme: the establishment of the knight on b6 will allow White to take complete advantage of the c-file.

24...♖ad8 25.♘b6 ♗c6 26.♖c4!

This had to be calculated exactly, because if the possible answer was 26...e5 White had decided to give back the extra Pawn to get a strong direct attack. The continuation would be 27.♖ac1! ♔xd4 28.♖xc6 ♔xd2 29.♕g4! ♖hd8 30.♕e6+ ♔f8 31.h3 ♖d1+ 32.♖xd1 ♖xd1+ 33.♔h2 etc., with an advantage.

26...♖he8 27.♖ac1 ♗b5 28.♖c7 ♕e4

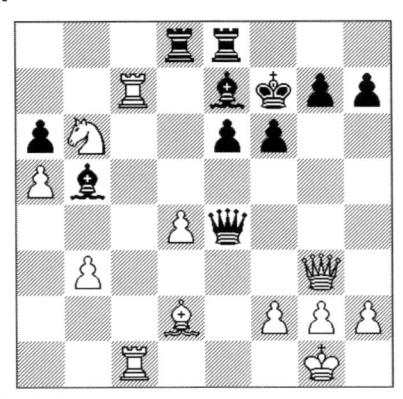

now tried his best practical chance through 29...exd5 the following variant would have occurred: 30.♖e1 ♗e2 31.♘a4! (one of the important links in White's combination) 31...d4 32.♘c5 ♕c2 33.♖xe2 ♕d1+ 34.♖e1 ♕xd2 35.♔f1! and Black would have had no defense against the many threats. The remaining moves would probably be 35...♔g8 36.♘e6 g6 37.♘xd8 ♕xe1+ 38.♔xe1 ♗d6+ 39.♔d2 ♗xg3 40.hxg3 ♖xd8 41.♖c6 ♖d5 42.b4, after which Black would have to resign.

29...♔g8

It leads to collapse even more quickly because of White's 31st move.

30.♖e1 ♕f5 31.♗b4! ♖d7

As useless as any other move.

32.♖xd7 ♗xd7 33.♗xe7 exd5

Or 33...♔xe7 34.♕d6 winning.

34.♕d6, and Black resigned.

Game 54
A.Alekhine-H.Grob
Bern Tournament, July 1932
Spanish Opening [C84]

1.e4 e5 2.♘f3 ♘c6 3.♗b5 a6 4.♗a4 ♘f6 5.0-0 d6 6.c3

Here it's also good to 6.♗xc6+ bxc6 7.d4 ♘xe4 8.♕e2 f5 9.♘bd2 ♘xd2 10.♘xd2!, and White will get the Pawn back with an advantage, for example: 10...e4 11.f3 d5 12.fxe4 dxe4 13.♘xe4!, with an advantage.

6...♗g4 7.d4 b5 8.♗b3 ♗e7 9.♗e3

Instead, the wing game 9.a4 would be quite good. The chosen continuation leads to a very complicated game in the center.

9...0-0 10.♘bd2

See the next Diagram

10...d5!

29.d5!

Instead of the simple 29.♗c3 - which would probably also prove sufficient in the long run - White decides to force the game through a strongly calculated combination. If Black had

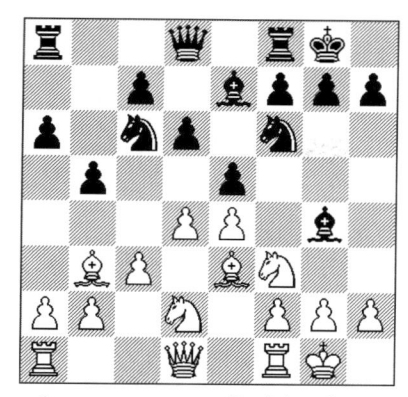

At that moment I felt that I had been drawn into a variant prepared in advance by my opponent. Here's what happened: a few years before the Bern Tournament - to be exact, in 1925 - I gave an exhibition in Bessel with time advantage, with clocks, against 10 top-class amateurs, where the following game, identical to the present one up to the 10th move, including White's, was played and published (because of its instructive attack and beautiful ending) by the Swiss press, as well as in my German books: Alekhine-Meck: 10...♘a5 11.♗c2 c5 12.h3 ♗xf3 13.♕xf3 ♘d7 14.♖ad1 ♕c7 15.♗b1 ♖ad8 16.♕g3 ♖fe8 17.f4 ♘c6 18.fxe5 dxe5 19.d5 ♘a5 20.♘f3 ♘c4 21.♗h6 g6 22.♖f2 ♗f8 23.♕h4 ♗e7 24.♘g5 ♘d6 25.♖df1 ♗xg5 26.♗xg5 ♖c8 27.♖xf7 ♘xf7 28.♖xf7 h5 29.♖f3 ♖f8 30.♖g3 ♖f7 31.♗e7 ♔h7 32.♗d3 c4 33.♗e2 ♕b6+ 34.♔h2 ♘f6 35.d6 ♖xe7 36.♕xf6 ♖g7 37.♗xh5 ♖cg8 38.♕h4 g5 39.♗g6+, followed by mate in two. It's certainly to the credit of the talented Swiss master to have found the exact moment when his countryman went wrong - and one can also consider it his bad luck that the whole variant (as the present game proves) is still not quite satisfactory, despite the improvement. In any case, I spent a few rather anxious minutes before discovering the path that finally secured the advantage for me.

11.exd5 exd4 12.cxd4 ♘xd5

White now must solve a double problem: free his King's Knight from the nasty pin, and at the same time take the necessary measures to effectively confront the threatening advance of Black's f-Pawn.

13.♕b1!

That's the hidden solution! White wants to protect his queen bishop by counter-attacking Black's central knight.

13...f5

Not only an attack, but also a defense against the possibility of ♕e4.

14.a3!

Freeing up square a2 for (a) the Bishop, in the case of 14.♘a5; (b) the Queen - as played in the current game.

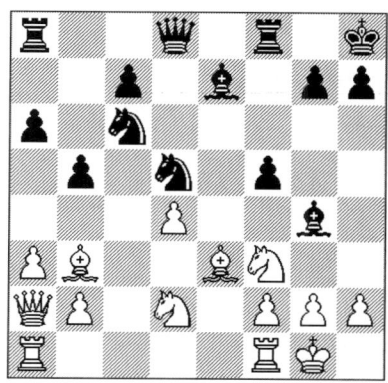

14...♔h8 15.♕a2

15...♘db4!?

Black continues to speculate but will soon be forced to recognize that he is out of the game in the battle for the central squares. Also after 15...♘b6 16.♗e6! followed by d5 etc., White would easily get the best position.

16.axb4 ♘xb4 17.♕b1 f4

The material balance is thus re-

113

established, but not for long, as White's knight on e5 will exert tremendous pressure.

18.♘e5 ♗f5

Or 18...♗h4 19.♕e4! fxe3 20.fxe3 ♗f6 21.♘f5! etc., with an overwhelming position.

19.♕d1 fxe3 20.fxe3 ♘d5 21.♘c6!

The simplest, because you get two minor pieces for a Rook, thus avoiding the complications of the middlegame. Instead, it wouldn't be convincing 21.♔xf5 ♔xf5 22.g4 due to 22...♔xe5, etc. - but 21.♕h5 g6 (not 21...♘xe3? 22.♔xf5 winning) 22.♘xg6+ ♗xg6 23.♕xd5 would be an equally pleasant alternative.

21...♘xe3 22.♘xd8 ♘xd1 23.♘c6 ♗g5 24.♖fxd1!

Instead, 24.♖axd1 would - rather strangely - allow a convincing escape for Black via 24...♗e3+! 25.♔h1 ♗xd2 26.♖xd2 ♗d3!, etc.

24...♗e3+ 25.♔h1 ♗g4 26.♘f1

Of course not 26.♘f3 ♖xf3!, etc.

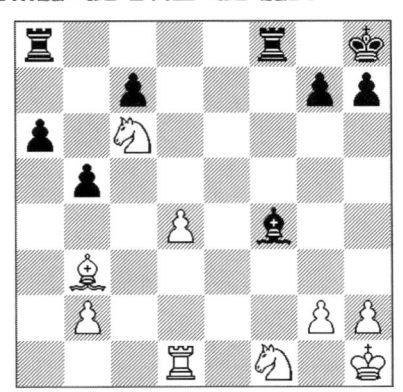

26...♗xd1 27.♖xd1 ♗f4

28.♗d5!

The Bishop's maneuver prevents ♖a8–e8–e7.

28...♖ae8 29.♗f3 ♖f6 30.♔g1 g6

Obviously losing time, if you compare that to the next move; but in this position, one more or less time has no influence on the result. If, for example, 30...g5, then 31.h3 ♗e3+ 32.♘xe3 ♖xe3 33.d5 ♖b3 34.♖d2 with a technically easy job for White.

31.♖a1 g5 32.h3 ♗e3+ 33.♘xe3

Of course, not 33.♔h1 g4!, etc.

33...♖xe3 34.♖xa6 ♖b3 35.♗d5!

The start of a successful mate attack.

35...♖xb2 36.♖a8+ ♔g7 37.♖g8+ ♔h6 38.♘e5 ♔h5 39.♖g7 ♔h4 40.♔h2! h6

Obviously forgetting to leave.

41.♗f3 ♖d2 42.♖g6 g4 43.♖xg4+ ♔h5 44.♖g3+ ♔h4 45.♘g6+ ♖xg6 46.♖xg6 b4 47.♖g4+ ♔h5 48.♔g3 ♖d3 49.♖g7+ ♖xf3+ 50.♔xf3, and Black resigned.

Game 55
A.Alekhine–S.Flohr
Bern Tournament, July 1932
Colle System [D05]

1.d4 d5 2.♘f3 ♘f6 3.e3

This tranquil move, whose idea is to postpone the fight for the center until White gets his King to safety - has managed to grace the Belgian champion with a long series of brilliant victories. Its objective value has almost been called into question by the variant 3...♗f5 4.♗d3 e6! introduced by me in San Remo 1930, against the same player, and since then adopted, for example, by Dr. Euwe against me in our 1935 game. The defense chosen here by Flohr allows White to fulfill his development plan.

3...e6 4.♗d3 c5 5.c3 ♘c6 6.♘bd2 ♗e7 7.0–0 ♕c7 8.♕e2 0–0 9.e4

As I found out later, this rather natural move hadn't been tried before. By adopting the usual 9.dxc5 ♗xc5

10.e4 I arrived at a not entirely pleasant position, having to fight another innovation of mine (game against Gilg, Kecskemet 1927), i.e. 10...♗d6 11.♖e1 ♘g4! etc., with roughly the same prospects.

9...d×e4

It would be unsatisfactory 9...c×d4 due to 10.e5! ♘d7 (or 10...♘h5 11.♘b3, threatening g4) 11.c×d4 ♘b4 12.♗b5! a6 13.♗a4, etc., with advantage.

10.♘×e4 c×d4 11.♘×d4

Not 11.c×d4, because it's in White's interest to exchange as many pieces as possible to attack his isolated Pawn.

11...♘×d4 12.c×d4 ♘×e4

Instead, 12...♘d5 13.♕f3! etc. would lead to a very complicated middlegame position. However, the move in the text could be enough for equality.

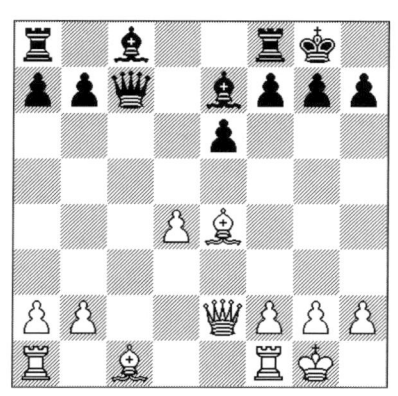

13.♗×e4

13...f5

But from now on Flohr decidedly overestimates his position, which he very rarely does. After the simple 12...♗d7 13.♕f3 ♗c6, the natural result would be a draw.

14.♗f3 ♗f6

This move and the next are the logical consequence of trying to exploit the "weakness" in d4. Relatively better still would be 14.♗d7.

15.♖d1 ♖d8 16.♗e3 f4?

Suicide. But also after the relatively better 16...g5 17.h3 ♕g7 18.♖ac1 it will soon become clear that White's d-pawn can only be captured at the price of a decisive further compromise in Black's position.

17.♖ac1 ♕d6 18.♗d2 ♗×d4

That Pawn is poisoned, as the answer shows. But also 18...♔b8 19.a3! threatening 20.♗b4 etc. would be almost hopeless.

19.♗a5! ♖d7

If the Rook resigned the d-file, then 20.♕c4! would win immediately.

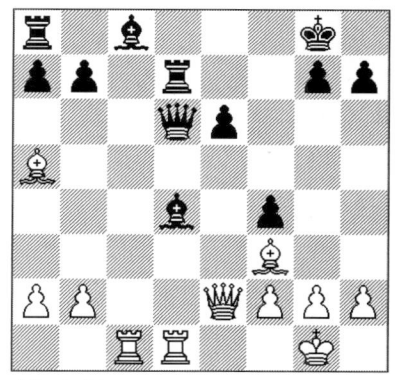

20.♖×d4!

The convincing rebuttal to Black's ultra-materialistic tendency in this game.

20...♕×d4 21.♕×e6+ ♖f7

After 21...♔f8 22.♖e1 g6 23.♗c3 Black would lose the queen.

22.♖×c8+ ♖×c8 23.♕×c8+ ♖f8 24.♕×b7 ♖e8 25.h3

But not 25.♗c3? because of 25...♕×c3!

25...♕c5 26.♗c3 ♕e7 27.♗d5+ ♔h8 28.♕×e7, and Black resigned.

> **Game 56**
> **A.Alekhine–H.Steiner**
> *Pasadena Tournament, August 1932*
> Spanish Opening [C78]

1.e4 e5 2.♘f3 ♘c6 3.♗b5 a6 4.♗a4 ♘f6 5.0–0 ♗c5

Having been rather partial to this move for a while (see *"My Best Games - 1908 - 1923"*), I must, much to my chagrin, now admit that it's not enough against an accurate game. And since 5...d6 has recently been somewhat discredited, Black has practically brought back the old choice between the speculative 5...♘xe4 and the cautious 5...♗e7.

6.c3 ♘xe4 7.d4 ♗a7 8.♕e2

Here I decided to follow the line of play adopted by Yates against me in Hastings 1922: although in that game Black only got a draw, I was hoping to find some better moves on the board than those made by Yates, but there really weren't any. It's much better than Queen's move 8.♖e1 (which is also more logical and brings another piece into the action), and if 8...f5, then 9.♘bd2 0–0 10.♘xe4 fxe4 11.♗g5, followed by 12.♖xe4 with a clear advantage.

8...f5 9.dxe5 0–0 10.♗b3+ ♔h8 11.♘bd2 ♕e8

An interesting idea *à la* Marshall: Black sacrifices 1-2 Pawns for a quick development, after which White's position will seem somewhat critical for a while. However, the attempt can, and should, be refuted; much more preferable is then (as happened in the aforementioned Hastings Tournament) 11...d5 12.exd6 ♗xd6 13.♘c4 f4! 14.♘ce5 (or 14.♘xd6 cxd6! 15.♖d1 ♗g4) 14...♘xe5 15.♘xe5 ♕g5 etc., with very good prospects for Black.

12.♘xe4 fxe4 13.♕xe4 13...d5!

The point of the first sacrifice - Black will develop his queen bishop in time.

14.♗xd5

Better than 14.♕xd5 ♗g4 15.♘g5 ♘xe5 etc., with unpleasant threats.

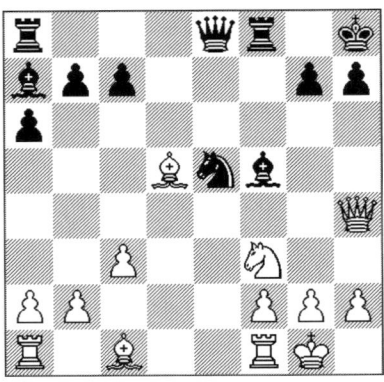

14...♗f5 15.♕h4 ♘xe5

16.♗xb7!

The only way to successfully counter Black's attack on the f2 square. Instead, it would be unsatisfactory 16.♘xe5 ♕xe5 17.♗xb7 due to 17...♗d3! 18.♗xa8 ♗xf2+! 19.♔h1 ♕e8! (stronger than 19...♗xf1 20.♕e4) etc., with strong pressure from Black.

16...♖b8 17.♘xe5 ♖xb7

If now 17...♕xe5, then 18.♗xa6! stops Black's main threat ...♗d6. That was the point of White's 16th move.

18.♖e1!

Black can in no way take advantage of the momentary weakening of the f2 square.

18...♖b5 19.♘f3 ♕c8 20.c4 ♖b7 21.b3

In connection with the next move, a much faster solution than the passive 21.h3.

21...♗g4

22.♗a3!

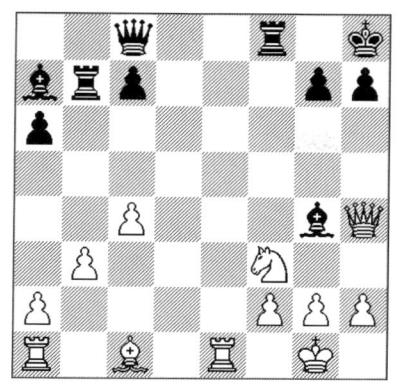

Practically forcing the reply that puts an end to Black's hopes on his diagonal h7–g1.

22...c5

Of course, not 22...♔f6 due to 23.♕×g4.

23.♘e5

From here on in, the Whites have their work cut out.

23...♗f5 24.g4!

To force Black's bishop to abandon the home defense g6.

24...g5

Despair.

25.♗b2

A spectacular move (25...g×h4 26.♘f7+ ♔g8 27.♘h6 mate), but the simpler 25.♕h5 would also be good enough. Not so convincing, on the other hand, would be 25.♕×g5 ♔g7 26.♗b2 ♔g8! etc.

25...♔g8

With the hope of after 26.♕×g5+ ♖g7 entering the last mentioned variant.

26.♕h5! ♗e6

See the next Diagram

27.♘d7!

A kind of "partner" to the final move of *Game 117* against Borochow.

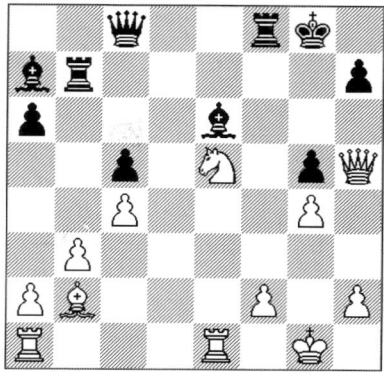

In the case of 27...♕×d7 White forces a win this way: 28.♕×g5+ ♔f7 29.♕f6+ ♔g8 30.♕h8+! ♔f7 31.♕×h7+ ♔e8 32.♕g6+ ♔e7 33.♖ad1! ♕c6 34.♕g5+ ♔f7 35.♕f6+ and mate in two moves.

The Blacks abandoned.

Game 57
A.Alekhine-V.Mikenas
Folkestone Team Tournament, July 1933
King's Fianquet [B06]

1.e4 g6

This move is rightly considered inferior, as it gives White total control of the central squares. This, however, doesn't make it very easy for the first player to turn this space advantage into a decisive one.

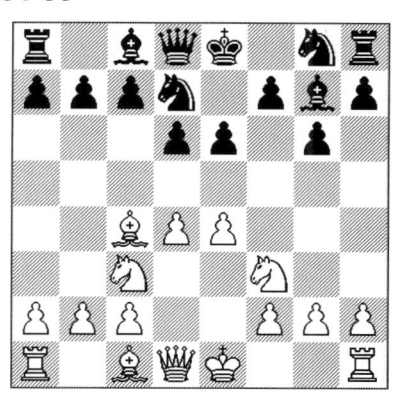

2.d4 ♗g7 3.♘c3 d6 4.♘f3 ♘d7 5.♗c4 e6

By choosing this Pawn structure, Black strategically avoids the future central advance of White's Pawns at this stage of the game, since either e5, d4 or d5, e4 would allow the second player to later gain the initiative in the center through ...c5 or ...f5. White's strategy in the next stage of the game will then consist of restricting more and more - leaving the central position intact - the already almost limited field of action of the enemy pieces.

6.0–0 ♘e7 7.a4!

A very important move in this type of position, worth noting by the student. Its purpose is to prevent Black's queen bishop pin (if ...b6 a5, with advantage) or to induce the weakening of Black's b5 square - by responding ...a5.

7...0–0 8.♗e3 h6

Avoiding 9.♕d2 followed by ♗h6, which would eliminate Black's only more or less active piece.

9.♕d2 ♔h7 10.h3

To avoid the possibility of ...♘f6 and if e5, then ...♘g4 etc.

10...c6

This obviously weakens his d6 - a circumstance that, however, shouldn't have been decisive. Besides, it's already extremely difficult to indicate a suitable plan for Black's future development.

11.♗f4 d5

It would also be unsatisfactory to play 11...e5 12.d×e5 d×e5 (in the case of resuming with pieces on e5, Black would lose his Pawn f) 13.♗e3 with an advantage. But by playing 11...♘b6 12.♗d3 a5 Black would obtain a relatively more stable position than after the compromising move in the text.

12.♗d3 a6?

Black can't imagine that his d6- move must be protected at all costs. From now on, only the dominant position of White's queen bishop would prove sufficient to decide the battle. Thus, 12...♘f6 –...e8 was needed with a playable game, although White could easily still find a way to increase his pressure - for example, through 13.a5 etc.

13.♗d6 f5

Or 13...♘f6 14.e5 ♘fg8 15.♗a3, followed by h4, with an easy attack on the King.

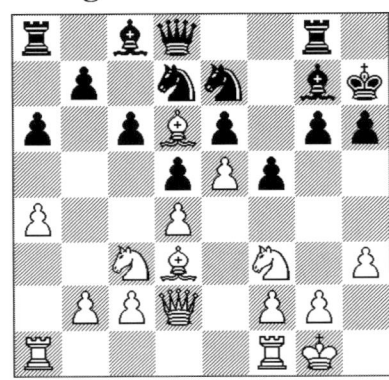

14.e5 ♖g8

15.h4

White's overwhelming positional advantage allows them to choose whichever method they prefer to enter the not-so-well-protected enemy fortress. In addition to the text move, which opens up an irresistible plan (*status quo* on the King's wing; opening a column on the other wing), they can also start an attack on the King, with the spectacular move 15.♕g5, which however will not give any immediate result after the correct defense 15...♗f8 and if 16.♘e2 (or 16.♕h4 g5 17.♕h5 ♘g6) then 16...♔g7 with at least a temporarily sufficient defense.

15...b6!

Preparing ...♘f8, which would be a

mistake here due to 16.♕g5! etc. But from now on this queen move can be answered with ...♖a7!

16.♘e2 ♘f8 17.a5

Before breaking through, White weakened the black squares in Black's position as much as possible; the final phase of the game will illustrate the usefulness of this procedure.

17...b5 18.g3!

In connection with the next two moves, a prophylactic maneuver, by which White prevents once and for all any serious attempt by Black to get an attack on his King.

18...♖h8 19.♔g2 ♔g8 20.♖h1 ♔f7

The King is no better here than on h7. But Black is still not in the mood to give up with unmade moves...

21.♘f4 ♖g8 22.b3

After that, White's strategic scheme becomes obvious - there is no more defense against c4 in connection with the opening of the b or c columns.

22...♘h7 23.c4 ♗d7 24.♖ac1 ♗f8

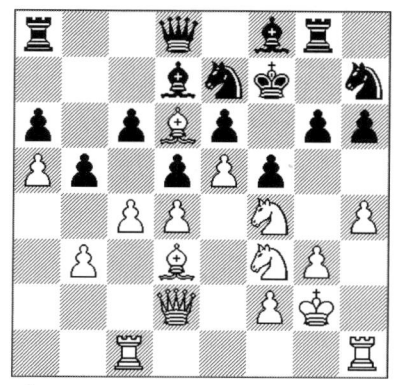

25.♗e2!

Freeing up the d3 square for the knight, and at the same time preventing Black's g-pawn from advancing - for example, 25...g5? 26.h×g5 ♘×g5 27.♘×g5+ h×g5 (or 27...♖×g5 28.♘h3 followed by ♗h5+ winning)

28.♗h5+ ♔g7 29.♘×e6+ ♗×e6 30.♕×g5+, then mate.

25...♘c8 26.c×d5

It's not often that a game is strategically decided long before the first catch, which here doesn't mean the start, but practically the end of the fight.

26...c×d5

Or 26...♘×d6 27.d×e6+ ♗×e6 28.♘×e6 ♔×e6 29.♖×c6 winning.

27.♗×f8

The Bishop has done far more than his duty and can now disappear quietly.

27...♘×f8 28.♖c5 ♘a7 29.♘d3 ♔g7

As a result, on White's 18th to 20th moves the reply ...g5 would obviously be completely in his favor.

30.♖hc1 ♖c8 31.♖×c8 ♗×c8 32.♕c3

All the black houses in the black camp are like so many open wounds. No wonder they decided to try the desperate diversion next.

32...♔h7 33.♕c5 ♖g7 34.♕b6!

All very simple, but with deadly effects. The knight, after being taken to c5, will command the execution.

34...♕e7 35.♘c5 g5

At last! But as the sequel will convincingly show, this attempt is now harmless.

36.h×g5 h×g5 37.♘e1!

To answer 37...f4 with 38.♗g4! and 37...g4 with 38.♘ed3 followed by ♘f4.

37...♘g6 38.♘ed3 f4 39.♖h1+ ♔g8 40.♗g4 f×g3 41.f×g3

The agglomeration of forces in column g is quite picturesque. Instead of the "sacrifice" afterwards, the Blacks would do well to abandon it.

41...♘h4+ 42.g×h4 g×h4 43.♘f2

119

♔f7 44.♘xe6 ♔h7 45.♕d6, and Black resigned.

A game with a stranglehold a *la* Rubinstein or Dr. Tarrasch from the early days.

Game 58
L.Steiner-A.Alekhine
Folkestone Team Tournament, July 1933
Spanish Opening [C86]

1.e4 e5 2.♘f3 ♘c6 3.♗b5 a6 4.♗a4 d6 5.c3 ♗d7 6.d4 ♘f6 7.♕e2 ♗e7 8.0-0 0-0

Now threatening 9...♘xd4.

9.♗b3 ♕e8

Rightly or wrongly, this move is my invention, one of whose ideas is to exert pressure on the back and after ...♗d8. Before it is called by the name of a particularly hospitable city or a particularly generous chess patron (as happened, for example, with the move "Kecskemet" ...♗e8) I suggest calling it the variant "Timbuktu". At least that would be the author's choice.

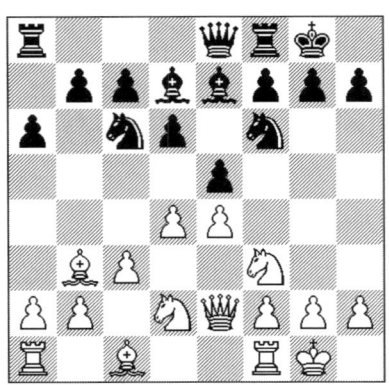

10.♘bd2

10...♔h8!

Black hasn't played 10...♗d8 yet, as there is still hope of using this piece more effectively. With the text move, Black eventually prepares ...♘g8, followed by ...♗f6 or ...f6, etc.

11.dxe5

Not 11.♘c4, due to 11...exd4 12.cxd4 d5 etc. But the simplifying variant 11.♖e1 is relatively better, followed by ♘f1-g3 etc.

11...dxe5 12.♘c4 ♗c5 13.a4

Quite interestingly, this apparently normal move creates - as will be shown as the game continues - a slight weakness in the b3 square. 13.♗c2 (threatening to gain ground through 14.b4 etc.) 13...a5 14.♗e3 etc. would have been preferable, with equal prospects.

13...a5

Prophylactic. White's bishop on c2 cannot be accompanied by the expansion b4!

14.♗g5

A rather superficial development move. Instead, 14.♗e3 was still preferable.

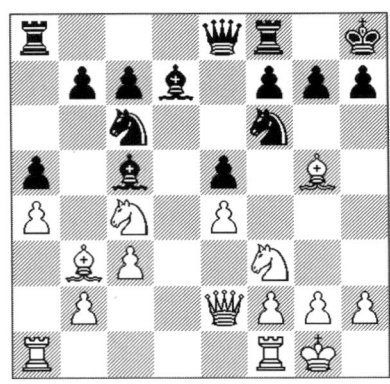

14...♘h5!

With this energetic response (instead of the quiet 14...♘g8 that White probably expected), Black gets a solid initiative. White's relatively better response was now 15.♘fxe5 - after which an ending would be reached with better prospects for Black: 15...♘xe5 16.♕xh5 (not 16.♘xe5 due to 16...♕xe5 followed by 17...f6 winning a piece) 16...♘xc4 17.♗xc4 -

and now *not* 17...♕×e4 as suggested by the commentators), but 17...f6! 18.♕×e8 ♖f×e8 19.♗e3 ♗×e3 20.f×e3 ♖×e4 - to White's displeasure, for example: 21.♗d5 then 21...♖×e3 22.♗×b7 ♖b8 23.♖ad1 ♗e8 etc., with a clear advantage.

In view of these rather grim prospects, it's not entirely surprising that Steiner chose a risky counter-demonstration, the consequences of which were by no means easy to calculate.

15.♘h4 ♘f4 16.♕f3

If 16.♗×f4 e×f4 17.♕h5 Black would have the good answer 17...f5!

16...f6!

This was the move that was probably underestimated by White. After the forced exchange that followed, the knight on h4 will be exposed to attacks and Black's domination of e4 will soon prove decisive.

17.♗×f4 e×f4 18.♘f5 g6!

Gaining important time compared to the immediate 18...g5.

19.♘h6 g5 20.g4

Black threatened 20...♕g6 21.♘g4 h5 and also - as happened in the game - 20...♗e6, etc.

20...♗e6

Planning 21...♗×c4 22.♗×c4 ♘e5 23.♕e2 f3.

21.♘d2 ♘e5 22.♕h3 ♖d8 23.♗×e6

If this Bishop could be protected by the Pawn a (see the commentary on White's 13th move), White would still temporarily have a defense in 23.♖ad1. But now this move would simply be answered by 23...♗×d2, etc.

23...♕×e6 24.♘b1

If 24.♖ad1, then 24...♖d3 followed by 24...♔fd8, winning a piece.

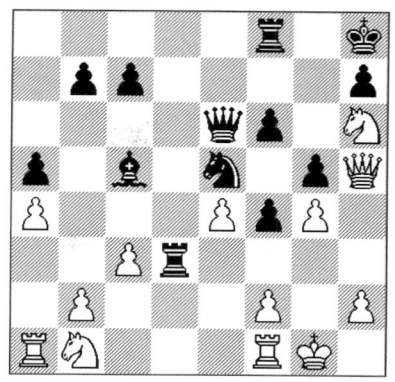

24...♖d3 25.♕h5

It's almost unbelievable that such a position occurred in a modern master-class after 25 moves in a Ruy Lopez!

25...♘f3+

If now 27.♘f7+, then 27...♔×f7 28.♕×f7 ♘h4+ 29.f3 ♕×f3+, followed by mate in two.

The whites resigned.

Game 59
A.Alekhine-B.Zuckierman

Paris Tournament, October 1933
Queen's Gambit Declined,
Orthodox Defense [D63]

1.d4 d5 2.c4 e6 3.♘c3 ♘f6 4.♗g5 ♗e7 5.e3 ♘bd7

Nowadays (1939) it's fashionable to play 5...h6.

6.♘f3 0–0 7.♖c1 b6

This old-fashioned fianchetto defense can't be considered very satisfactory because Black won't be able to avoid some Pawn weaknesses in the center.

8.c×d5 e×d5 9.♗b5

The most logical way to exploit the slight weaknesses on Black's queen's wing. Instead, a "game for attack" by placing this Bishop on the b1–h7 diagonal would be rather out of place, as Black's King position now is quite secure.

9...♗b7 10.0–0 a6 11.♗a4 c5

This move, at first glance logical, finds a decisive refutation here. But even after the more cautious 11...♔c8 and 12.♗b3! etc., Black's position would remain unsatisfactory.

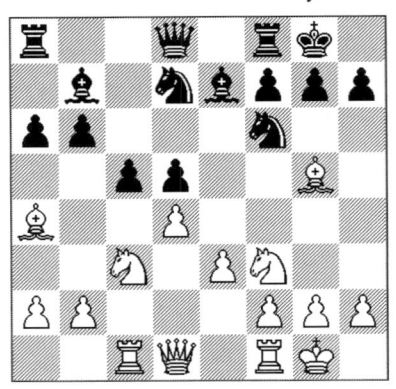

12.♗×d7!

Much more accurate than 12.d×c4 ♘×c4 etc., with a playable position for Black, as happened in the Capablanca-Teichmann game in 1913. If now 12...♕×d7, then 13.d×c5 b×c5 14.♘a4!, with a decisive positional advantage.

12...♘×d7 13.♗×e7 ♕×e7 14.d×c5 ♕×c5

In order not to lose the Pawn immediately, Black is forced to expose his Queen in a dangerous way - and this circumstance, coupled with the Bishop's most unfortunate position, will allow White to discover the winning procedure without too much difficulty.

15.♘d4

Threatening 16.♘cb5 followed by 17.♘c7, etc.

15...♖ac8 16.♘f5 ♔h8!

A defense against 17.♘×d5 and at the same time a trap: that is, if 17.♘×g7, hoping to win a Pawn after 17...♔×g7 18.♕g5+, etc. - then 17...d4 18.e×d4 ♕g5 or 18.♕×d4 ♕×d4 19.e×d4 ♔g8 etc., with Black's advantage.

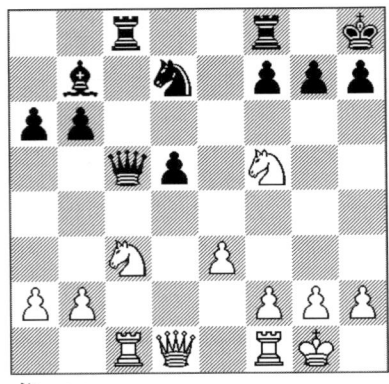

17.♘e2!

To force the exchange of queens on d4 with no change in the pawn constellation. It's remarkable how hopeless Black's position will be in the endgame after that!

17...♕b4 18.♕d4 ♕×d4 19.♘e×d4 ♖×c1

Or 19...♘c5 20.♘d6 ♖b8 21.b4 etc., with an advantage.

20.♖×c1 ♘c5

If instead 20...♗c8? 21.♖×c8+ followed by 22.♘d6 he would have lost a piece immediately.

21.♘d6 ♗a8

Again forced, as can easily be seen.

22.b4 ♘d3 23.♖c7

Of course, not 23.♘×f7+, ♔g8 etc., with an advantage.

23...♔g8

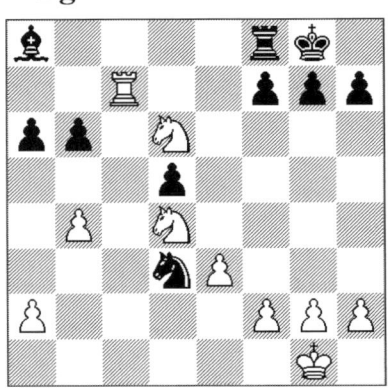

24.♘c8!

After 24.a3, Black could easily save his Bishop by playing 24...♘e5 followed by ...♘c4, after which a long resistance would have been possible. With the text move, White launches an attack on the unfortunate Bishop, who is obviously unable to escape his fate.

24...♘×b4 25.♘×b6

Threatening 28.♖a7, etc.

25...♖b8 26.♘d7

But not 26.♖a7 ♗b7 27.♘d7 ♔c8 followed by 28...♘c6 saving the piece.

26...♖d8 27.a3 ♘d3 28.♖a7 ♖c8 29.♔f1

After that it's inevitable 30.♘b6, etc. Black is out.

Game 60
E.Znosko-Borovsky-A.Alekhine
Paris Tournament, October 1933
Spanish Opening [C87]

1.e4 e5 2.♘f3 ♘c6 3.♗b5 a6 4.♗a4 ♘f6 5.0–0 d6

It's safer to play 5...♗e7 first, because after the text move, according to the latest research, White can get an advantage by playing 6.♗×c6+ b×c6 7.d4 ♘×e4 8.♖e1 f5 9.d×e5 d5 10.♘d4 c5 11.♘e2 followed by ♘f4, etc.

6.c3 ♗d7 7.♖e1 ♗e7 8.d4 0–0 9.♘bd2 ♗e8

This original move (whose idea is to keep the central position intact by means such as ...♘d7 and to use - after f6 - the queen's bishop on the e8–h5 diagonal) was introduced by me (after 9...♔h8 10.h3) in my game against Steiner in Kecskemet, 1927.

It was later baptized (not by me) as the Kecskemet Variant. Such a name is illogical, since the move ...♗e8 is the key not to a "variant", but to a System!

This game is of some theoretical interest because it shows how White, even if he's only playing for a draw, can't get an absolute equality by settling the central tension after the text move.

10.♗×c6 ♗×c6 11.d×e5 d×e5 12.♘×e5 ♗×e4 13.♘×e4 ♕×d1!

It would be a mistake 13...♘×e4 because of 14.♘d7! etc.

14.♘×f6+

After 14.♔×d1 ♘×e4 there would still be enough material to complicate the fight. After exchanging the knights, White hopes to reach a "dead draw" position (14...♗×f6 15.♔×d1 ♗×e5 16.♗e3, etc.). But...

14...g×f6!

The only way - and a safe one - is to "play to win".

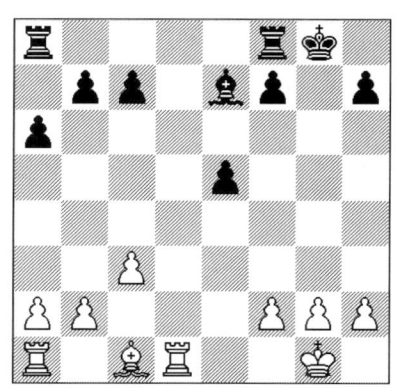

15.♖×d1 f×e5

The endgame thus achieved is by no means easy to navigate - especially for the first player, as it turns out. Black's plan for the campaign - which will prove to be a complete success - is divided into the following parts:

(1) The exchange of a pair of Rooks.

(2) Bring the King to e6 where it will be protected from a frontal attack by the Pawn and can be used to protect the entrance to White's remaining Rook on the d7 square.

(3) When operating with the Rook on the open column g and advancing the Pawn h, force the opening of column h.

(4) After that, White's King - and possibly also the Bishop - will be very busy preventing Black's Rook from entering squares h1 or h2.

(5) Meanwhile Black, by advancing Pawns a and b, will sooner or later be able to open a column on the Queen's wing. E...

(6) As White's king will still be on the other wing at that point, the first player won't have enough strength to prevent the enemy rook's final entry into his first or second row.

If White had, from the outset, imagined that there really was a danger of losing this ending, he would probably have saved it through extremely careful defense. But as it happened, Black played with a definite plan, and White only with the conviction that the game would be a draw. And the result was a very instructive series of typical stratagems, much more useful for inexperienced players than so-called "brilliance".

16.♗h6

Certainly not a mistake, but proof that White hasn't yet understood the spirit of the position. Otherwise, they wouldn't be eager to "force" the exchange of a pair of rooks which, as mentioned, will be very welcome by the opponent.

16...♖fd8 17.♔f1

A more aggressive line starting with 17.g4 might be advisable. But then Black would also can complicate things with 17...f6, followed by ♔f7-e6, etc.

17...f5 18.♖xd8+ ♖xd8 19.g3

Move 19...f4 was a serious threat.

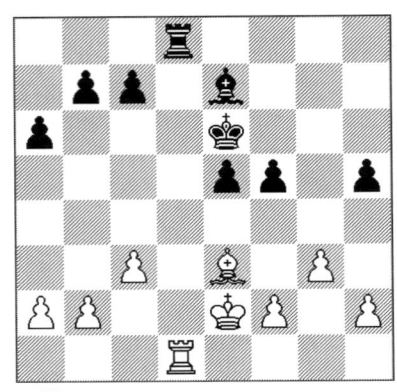

19...♔f7 20.♗e3 h5 21.♔e2 ♔e6 22.♖d1

22...♖g8!

If now 23.h4, then 23...♔g4, with the strong threat 24...f4. White is therefore forced to allow the opening of the h-file.

23.f3 h4 24.♗f2 hxg3 25.hxg3 ♖h8 26.♗g1 ♗d6 27.♔f1

To answer 27...e4 with 28.fxe4 gxe4 29.♔g2 etc.

27...♖g8 28.♗f2 b5!

Now Black shows his cards. In the event of White leaving his Pawns' position on the Queen's wing intact, the plan of attack would be ...c5–c6, followed by a5 and b4. White's next move shortens this procedure.

29.b3? a5 30.♔g2 a4 31.♖d2

In the case of 31.b4, the intention was 31...♔c8 32.♗c5 ♖a8! followed by ...♖a6 and ...♔c6 etc., with an advantage.

31...axb3 32.axb3 ♖a8

See the next Diagram

So, Black has reached the position he was aiming for when he started the ending. Their positional advantage from now on will prove sufficient for victory, especially as they will be able to successfully force the advance of their King by pinning White's Rook through the defense of one of their weak Pawns.

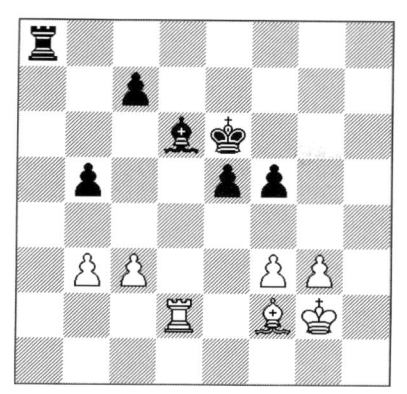

33.c4

Probably the only attempt, as 33.b4, for example, would immediately prove fatal: 33...♖a1 33.♖d3 ♖a3, etc.

33...♖a3!

The road to victory.

34.c5 ♗e7 35.♖b2 b4 36.g4

One of the last resorts: White tries to create a passed Pawn that *could* become a force if the Bishops are exchanged. But Black doesn't need to rush with this pawn.

36...f4 37.♔f1 ♖a1+ 38.♔e2 ♖c1

With the main objective of 39...♔c3, definitively pinning all the enemy pieces. White's next rook expedition in this way will be pure despair.

39.♖a2 ♖c3 40.♖a7 ♔d7 41.♖b7 ♖xb3 42.♖b8 ♖b2+ 43.♔f1 b3 44.♔g1 ♔c6 45.♔f1 ♔d5

Of course, no 45...♗xc5? 46.♗xc5 ♔xc5 47.g5 etc., with chances of a draw. But a slightly faster procedure would be 45...e4! 46.fxe4 f3, etc.

46.♖b7 e4 47.fxe4+ ♔xe4 48.♖xc7 ♔f3 49.♖xe7 ♖xf2+ 50.♔e1 b2 51.♖b7 ♖c2 52.c6!

See the next Diagram

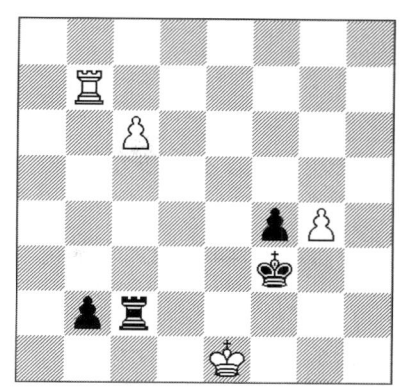

A good final joke: 52...♖c1+ 53.♔d2 b1♕ 54.♖xb1 ♖xb1 55.c7, etc. But Black accurately calculated that his other passed Pawn would force the win.

52...♔g3! 53.c7 f3 54.♔d1 ♔xc7 55.♖xb2 f2, and White resigned.

> **Game 61**
> **A.Alekhine-E.Bogoljubov**
> *World Championship (2), Baden-Baden, April 1934*
> Queen's Gambit Declined,
> Slav Defense [D48]

1.d4 ♘f6 2.c4 c6 3.♘f3 d5 4.e3 e6 5.♗d3 ♘bd7 6.♘c3 dxc4 7.♗xc4 b5 8.♗d3 a6 9.0–0

Nowadays, top masters consider 9.e4 c5 10.e5 cxd4 11.♘xb5 ♘xe5 12.♘xe5 axb5 13.♕f3! etc. to be decidedly advantageous for White. But in 1934 White's 13th move in this variant was not yet sufficiently considered and the Merano Variant's stock was on the rise. Because of this, the move in the text.

9...c5 10.a4

Instead, the move 10.♕e2, played experimentally in the games Šaemisch-Capablanca (Moscow, 1925) and Dr. Vidmar-Bogoljubov (Bled, 1931) brought the first players - at least at the opening stage - only disappointment.

10...b4 11.♘e4 ♗b7 12.♘ed2

After their 9th harmless move, White hardly had any other way to complicate things without a disadvantage, apart from this attempt to block the opponent's queen wing.

12...♗e7

Black doesn't need to prevent his opponent's next move because he's developed enough to start a central counteraction almost immediately.

13.a5 0-0 14.♘c4 ♕c7 15.♕e2 ♘g4

Black's position is quite good, but from now on he's starting to overestimate his chances. Instead of the adventurous move in the text, which in the end leads to a Pawn but allows White's Knight to enter on e6 with a powerful effect, they would do better to simplify things - for example, with 15...♗e4.

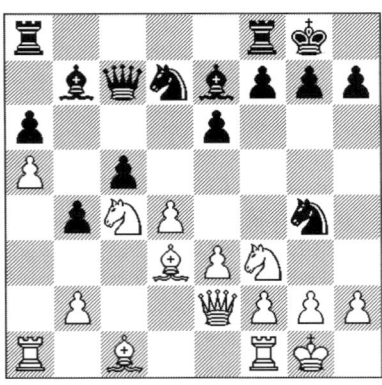

16.e4!

A surprise for Black, who probably only expected the almost suicidal 16.g3...

16...c×d4 17.h3 ♘ge5

To 17...♘gf6 White would reply 18.♗g5 ♘c5 19.♘b6 ♖ad8 20.♖ac1 ♕b8 (these moves were recommended by Bogoljubov in the game book as the best for Black) and now not 21.e5? (Bogoljubov) but 21.♗×f6! g×f6 22.♖c4 e5 23.♘h4 etc., with ample positional compensation for the Pawn down.

18.♘f×e5 ♘×e5 19.♗f4 ♗d6 20.♗×e5 ♗×e5 21.♘b6

The point of the sacrificial combination started on the 16th move. From now on the Knight will paralyze the whole of Black's queen's wing.

21...♖a7

In the case of 21...♖ad8, White wouldn't take the Pawn directly, but would prevent the eventual advance of Black's d-Pawn by playing 22.♖ad1! with a different positional advantage.

22.♖ac1 ♕d6

Or 22...♕d8 23.♕d2! ♗d6 24.f4 etc., with an advantage.

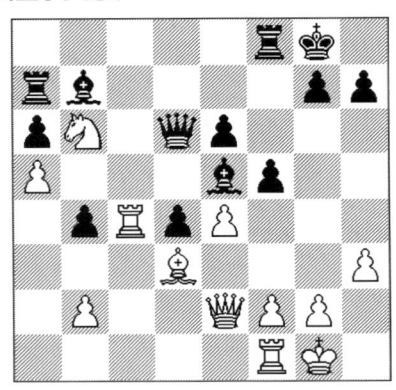

23.♖c4 f5?

The opening of the King's column leads, due to Black's multiple Pawn weaknesses, to a quick catastrophe. But even the quieter 23...♗f4 recommended by Bogoljubov is not satisfactory, because after 24.♖d1 e5 25.♕e1 etc., White would recover the Pawn, still maintaining strong pressure.

24.e×f5 e×f5 25.♖e1!

The threat of the exchange of queens on e6 with an easily winning ending causes Black despair, and he tries to devise a complicated attacking combination, which however is on the verge of failure due to the uselessness of his queen rook.

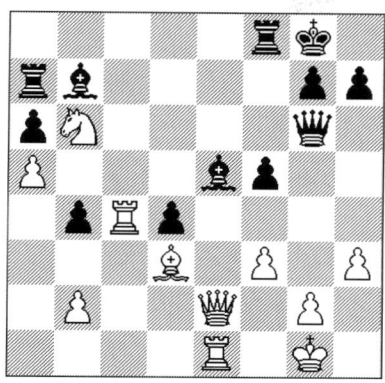

25...♕g6 26.f3

26...♖e8

In the case of bids with the Bishop, Bogoljubov gives the following variants:

I. 26...♗g3 27.♕e6+ ♔h8 28.♕xg6 hxg6 29.♖e6 ♖d8 30.♖xg6 f4 31.♖e6.

II. 26...♗f4 27.♔xd4 ♕g3 28.♗c4+ ♔h8 29.♕e7, with White winning in both eventualities.

27.f4 ♕g3 28.fxe5 ♖xe5 29.♖c8+!

The rebuttal.

29...♔f7 30.♕h5+

The alternative 30.♔c7+ was not as elegant, but slightly faster; for example: 30...♔g6 31.♖xg7+! or 30...♔g8 31.♗c4+ ♔h8 32.♗c8+, followed by 33.♕xe5, etc.

30...g6 31.♕xh7+ ♔f6 32.♖f8+ ♔g5 33.h4+ ♔f4 34.♕h6+ g5 35.♖xf5+! ♔xf5 36.♕d6+ ♔g4 37.♗xf5+ and mate in three. Black resigned.

Game 62
A.Alekhine-E.Bogoljubov
World Championship (4), Villingen, April 1934
Queen's Gambit Declined,
Slav Defense [D31]

1.d4 d5 2.c4 c6 3.♘c3 ♘f6 4.e3 e6 5.♗d3 ♘bd7 6.f4

Not a very happy opening idea, as it allows Black to quickly make a successful move in the center. Even so, as the game really developed, White had the opportunity to equalize without too much difficulty.

6...dxc4

This, in connection with the next four moves, is a good and natural method of development.

7.♗xc4 b5 8.♗d3 ♗b7 9.♘f3 a6 10.a4

The idea of advancing this Pawn to a5 - analogous to the previous game - is, in this position - very elaborate. The natural path was 10.0–0 c5 11.f5, etc.

10...b4 11.♘e2 c5 12.0–0 ♗e7 13.a5?

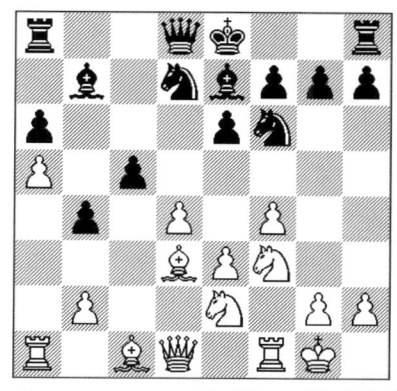

And even now 13.f5 exf5 14.♗xf5 0–0 15.♘g3 would lead to a picturesque game, with chances for both sides. After the move has been made, White can only hope, through careful play, to equalize the game.

13...0-0 14.♘g3 g6!
Now it was vital to prevent 15.f5.
15.♕e2 cxd4 16.exd4
Isolating the central pawn is certainly a brave decision, but - as the course of the game shows - more likely to equalize the chances than the alternative 16.♘xd4 ♘c5, etc.
16...♘b8
Threatening to win a Pawn with impunity with 17...♘c6.
17.♘e5!
If 17.f5!? Black could hardly accept the sacrificed piece, because after 17...exf5 18.♗xf5 gxf5 19.♘xf5 White's threats become very strong; but by answering 17...♗xf3 18.♕xf3 ♕xd4+ 19.♔h1 ♘bd7 with the threat 20...♘e5 Black would get the best cards. After the text move, on the other hand, they could get into big trouble by playing 17...♕xd4+ 18.♗e3 followed by 19.♘f4 or ♖fd1 etc., with White's advantage.
17...♘c6!
It's undoubtedly the best response, and it kills off White's hopes of attacking. The next hole is practically forced.
18.♘xc6 ♗xc6 19.♗c4?

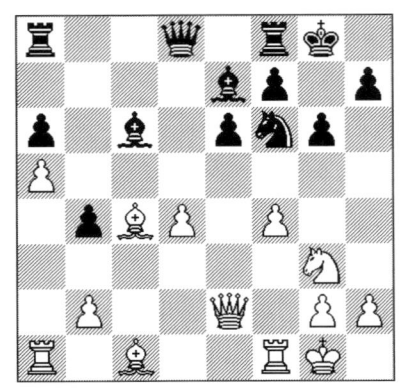

But this is decidedly too optimistic, as after Black's single next defensive move White will have no compensation for the permanent weakness in his central position. Good enough for a draw was 19.♗xa6 - which was, by the way, the only logical consequence of the previous knight move. If in that case 19.♗xa6 ♗xa6 20.♕xa6 ♕xd4+ 21.♔h1 ♕d5 22.♕e2 ♗b5 23.♕f3 ♗xf1 24.♕xd5 ♘xd5 25.♘xf1 and White, to say the least, had nothing to fear. Bogoljubov in the game book also indicates two other moves, which I believe are equally harmless. These are (a) 19...♖a7 20.♖d1 ♕a8 21.♗b5; (b) 19...♘g4 after which White would get several counter-attacking possibilities through 20.♕xg4 ♗xa6 (or 20...♕xd4+ 21.♔h1 ♗xa6 22.♕e2 followed by 23.♗e3, etc.) 21.f5!, etc.

19...♗b7 20.♗e3 ♕d6
Dr. Lasker, in his excellent booklet on this game, claims (in my opinion quite correctly) that Black already has a strategically winning position. Furthermore, he tries to prove that a *forced win* can be achieved here with 20...♘d5, and he gives such long variants with this line of play that they go up to the 35th move! But, rather strangely, in doing so he doesn't consider the simple move that I would certainly make in response to 20...♘d5. That move is 21.♘e4, possibly followed by ♘c5, etc. And it's more than likely that Bogoljubov didn't choose the otherwise natural 20...♘d5 because he didn't want to allow White's Knight with an unfortunate position to take an active part in the battle.

21.♖ad1 ♖fe8 22.b3
Since both the queen's bishop and white's knight have no future, they want to at least strengthen the other bishop's position. Moreover, the text

move, as we shall see, makes it easier to protect the a-pawn.

22...♗f8 23.♖d3

Because of their many weaknesses, White is reduced to complete passivity. Fortunately for them, Black doesn't prove to be a game for the situation, either strategically or tactically.

23...♕c7 24.♕a2 ♗d6 25.♗d2 ♕c6

The pressure against the g2 square is very painful for the first player - and would become even greater if Black didn't deliberately remove his queen from this dominating position (see the 29th move)...

26.♗e1 ♖ad8 27.♖d2 ♗e7

A strange move. Why not the obvious 27...♗b8 followed by 28...♗a7?

28.♕b2 ♖d7 29.♖c2

"A tactical error," says Dr. Lasker. But in this desperate position I was curious to see which move in the subsequent analysis wouldn't look like "a tactical error"! In other words, White is lost whatever move he plays.

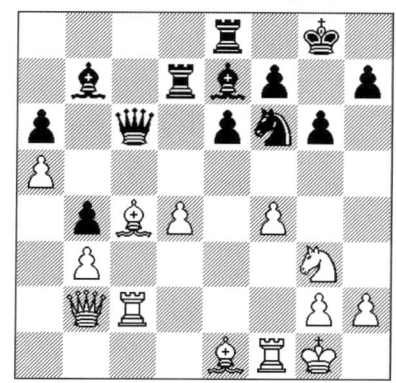

29...♕d6?

Since White isn't threatening anything, there's no reason to delay things. Move 29...♘g4! would win at least a Pawn, with a still dominant position.

This game - more than any other - proves how pointless the arrangements for this second game were from a sporting point of view, and at the same time explains my indifferent play on several occasions. I was sure that Bogoljubov was no longer able to take advantage of the opportunities my game could present him with, and - very unfortunate for the artistic value of this game - the 7-1 score in my favor after the 22nd game completely justified my optimistic observation.

30.♘e2

At least poor Knight is starting to contribute to the defense. But the outlook for the Whites is still bleak.

30...♘d5 31.♕c1 ♗d8 32.♗g3 ♕e7

Bogoljubov claims - and he's probably right - that 32...♕c6 would lead to complications favorable to Black. But 32...f5 was also good enough. On the other hand, the queen maneuver, initiated by the move in the text, only leads to the exchange of queens and thus relieves White of worrying about the g2 square. An unfortunate strategy!

33.♖a2 ♕f6 34.♕d2 ♕f5 35.♗d3 ♕f6 36.♗c4 ♗e7 37.♕d3 ♖ed8 38.♗e1 ♕f5 39.♕d2 ♕e4

Finally deciding to simplify things and implicitly admitting that nothing has been achieved in the last 20 moves.

40.♗d3 ♕e3+ 41.♗f2 ♕×d2 42.♖×d2

The position thus achieved is still naturally in Black's favor. But to win it would require the artistry of a Lasker or a Capablanca from the old days, even because the game was postponed at this point. But if it's not easy for Black to win, it's hard to imagine how he could lose it.

See the next Diagram

42...♖c8 43.♗c4 ♔g7 44.g3

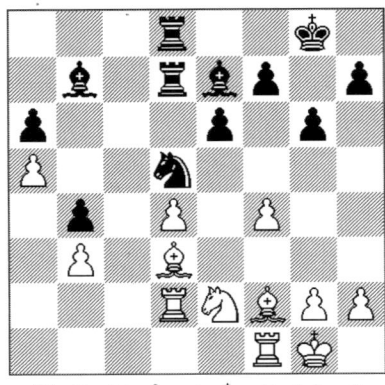

The possibility of this defensive move is the result of checkers disappearing, because before that the weakening of the g1–a8 diagonal would quickly prove fatal.

44...♖cd8 45.♖c1 h6

The start of a dangerous plot against his own position. Instead, 45...♘c3! would still hold the positional advantage.

46.♗d3 f5 47.♖dc2 g5?

As the surprising answer shows, this advance at best only leads to equality. But 47...♔f7, suggested later by Bogoljubov, wouldn't prove effective, as White in that case plays, for example, 48.♔f1 eventually followed by ♘-g1-f3-e5, etc.

48.g4!

Black can't quite accept the Pawn sacrifice offered in this way - for example 48...fxg4 49.f5 ♔f7 50.fxe6+ ♔xe6 51.♘g3 followed by 52.♖e1+ etc. with an advantage. But they could - and should - play 48...gxf4 49.gxf5 ♔f7 etc., with an approximately balanced position.

48...♘xf4?

This exchange of his best-placed piece against the cripple on e2 spoils Black's position. It's interesting to note from now on the joyful revival of all the white pieces, which had been unable to move for hours.

49.♘xf4 gxf4 50.gxf5 e5

In the vain hope that White would be satisfied with different colored Bishops after 51.dxe5 followed by 52.f6+, etc.

51.♖e1! exd4

Without foreseeing the beautiful combination that followed. His only chance of salvation was 51...♗f6, which White answered with 52.♔c4! exd4 53.♔xb4 etc., with much better prospects.

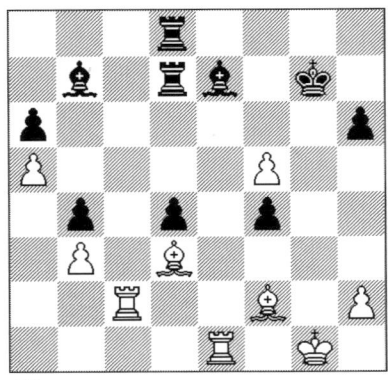

52.♖xe7+!

The unexpected point of this at first sight harmless exchange is the inevitable promotion of the f pawn. As you can see, Black now has an absolutely forced line of play.

52...♖xe7 53.♗h4 ♔f7

Otherwise, 54.f6+.

54.♗xe7 ♔xe7 55.♖c7+ ♖d7 56.f6+ ♔e8 57.♗g6+!

More accurate than 57.f7+ ♖xf7 58.♗g6 ♗d5, etc.

57...♔d8 58.f7 ♗xc7 59.f8♕ f3 60.♕xb4 ♖d6 61.♗d3, and Black resigned.

Game 63
E.Bogoljubov-A.Alekhine
World Championship (9), Pforzheim, April 1934
Benoni Defense [A44]

1.d4 c5

I consider the choice of this move (which, because of my success in that game, became something of a fashion for a while) to be one of my chess sins. Because if a champion, being human, can't sometimes help adopting inferior opening moves, he should at least avoid those that he himself considers to be not satisfactory enough.

2.d5 e5 3.e4 d6 4.f4

This decidedly premature response can only be explained by the fact that Bogoljubov had again squandered a win in the previous game and was particularly eager to make a better showing in this one. A natural and good line is instead 4.♘c3 and in the case of 4...a6 5.a4, followed by ♘–f3–d2–c4 etc., which would secure the initiative for White for a long time.

4...e×f4 5.♗×f4 ♕h4+

It wasn't worth provoking the weakening move g3 at the cost of development time. A simple 5...♘e7 followed by ...♘g6 etc. would take control of the e5-square with a very good game.

6.g3

The pawn sacrifice 6.♗g3 would not be correct because of 6...♕×e4+ 7.♗e2 ♗f5, etc.

6...♕e7 7.♘c3?

It was essential to prevent Black's next move with 7.♘f3! after which 7...♕×e4+ 8.♗e2 would be too risky. Black could instead play 7...♗g4 8.♘c3 a6 followed by ...♘b8d7 with roughly the same chances.

7...g5!

The strong position of his King's Bishop on the grand diagonal ensures that Black will have an easy and enjoyable game from now on.

8.♗e3 ♘d7 9.♘f3 h6 10.♕d2

Instead, it would be aimless 10.♘b5 ♔d8! etc.

10...♘gf6 11.0–0–0 ♘g4 12.♗e2

Also 12.♗h3 - recommended by Bogoljubov - ♘×e3 13.♕×e3 ♗g7 wouldn't relieve White of his problems.

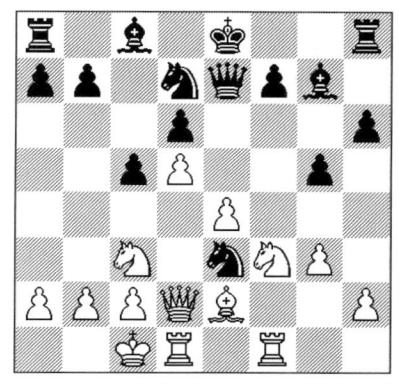

12...♗g7 13.♖hf1 ♘×e3

It was certainly tempting to add the advantage of the two Bishops to the one already acquired. But since the knight on g4 is well placed and the queen's bishop is harmless now, the immediate 13...a6 might even be more consequential.

14.♕×e3 a6 15.♘g1 b5 16.♖de1 ♗b7 17.♘d1

This knight needs to be brought to f5 - the only strong point in White's position.

17...0–0–0 18.♗g4

As the Bishop doesn't have many prospects, his switch to the dangerous Black Knight is difficult to criticize.

18...♔b8 19.♗×d7 ♖×d7 20.♕d2

Again, the natural consequence of the maneuver that began on his 17th move.

20...g4!

Immobilizing White's King's Knight and thus securing the important e5 square for the Queen.

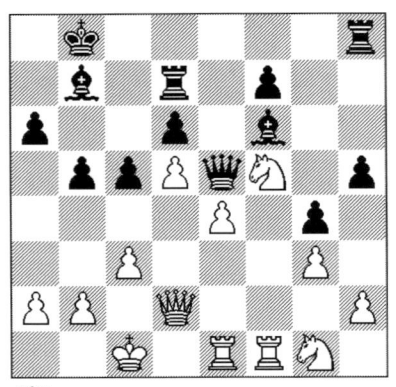

21.♘e3 ♕e5 22.c3 h5 23.♘f5 ♗f6

24.♕f4?

The exchange of the queens turns a difficult but by no means hopeless position (White could try, for example, 24.♔b1 as a preparation for 24.♘h4) into a losing one.

It's interesting that Bogoljubov is quite prone to making this mistake. For example, in the 11th Game of the same game, Bogoljubov with White, in the position reached after Black's 34th move, as shown in the diagram below:

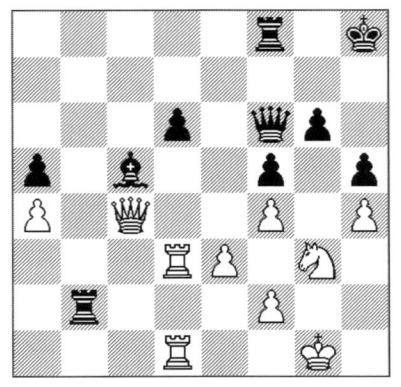

Bogoljubov, instead of trying a counter-attack with an uncertain outcome with 35.♕a6, preferred to exchange the queens: 35.♕c3? ♕×c3 36.♖×c3 ♖a2 37.♖c4 ♖b8, and had to resign after a few more desperate moves.

This same theme, although not in such a typical way, also occurred in the 5th and 22nd Games of our first game (see *Games 27* and *30 in* this collection) But also, rather strangely, my other game opponent, Dr. Euwe, also has a peculiar tendency to exchange queens at inappropriate moments. Compare, for example, the 7th (*Game 75*) and 24th Games of the 1935 game and especially the third exhibition game of 1937.

I don't mention these coincidences in any way to place undue blame on my opponents, but simply to remind the average amateur of how particularly difficult the question of the timing of the exchange of queens is, and how much attention it deserves. If even the greatest exponents of our game are often inclined to fail to appreciate the correctness of their choice of endgames, what can we expect from the "*di minores*"?

24...♕×f4+ 25.g×f4 ♖dd8!

Threatening to dislodge the Knight on f5, whose position has been weakened by the Pawn's obstruction of the f-file. In addition to their other advantages, Black now also has the majority of Pawns on the wing opposite White's King. The game is strategically closed.

26.c4

This attempt to find another safe square (c4) for the knight will be refuted by Black's 27th move. But on the other hand, 26...♗c8 etc. would quickly prove fatal for White.

26...b×c4 27.♘e3 c3! 28.b3 ♗d4 29.♘c4 f5!

Finally bringing the second Bishop

into play, after which White would do well to abandon.

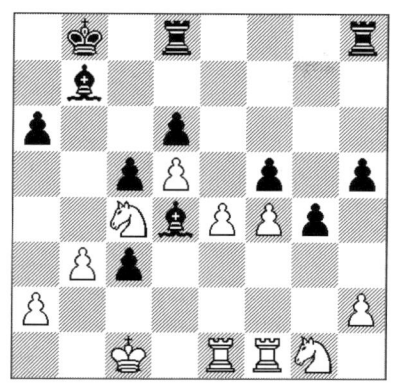

30.e5 dxe5 31.fxe5 ♗xd5 32.♖xf5 ♖df8 33.♖xf8+ ♖xf8 34.e6 ♖e8 35.e7 ♗xc4 36.bxc4 ♗xg1 37.♖xg1 ♖xe7 38.h3 gxh3 39.♔c2 h2 40.♖b1+ ♔b7 41.♖h1 ♖b2+ 42.♔xc3 ♖xa2 43.♔d3 ♔c7 44.♔e4 ♔c6 45.♔f5 a5 46.♔g5 a4, and White resigned.

Game 64
A.Alekhine-E.Bogoljubov
World Championship (16), Bayereuth, May 1934
Spanish Opening [C77]

1.e4 e5 2.♘f3 ♘c6 3.♗b5 a6 4.♗a4 ♘f6 5.♗xc6 dxc6

I believe Bogoljubov is right in saying that 5...bxc6 is an even more convincing response to White's artificial fifth move. In fact, I chose the Ruy Lopez exchange variant in this game mainly because, although I was playing with White, I had no ambitions. As a result of the game rules, I'd spent the whole of the previous night driving from Munich to Bayereuth and I was finding it difficult to do intensive mental work.

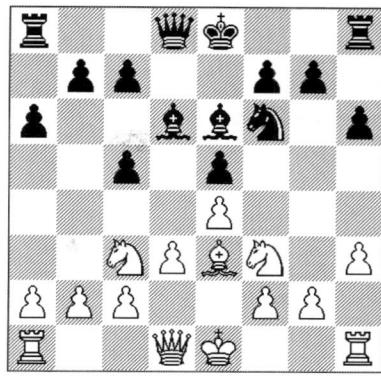

6.♘c3 ♗d6 7.d3 c5 8.h3 ♗e6 9.♗e3 h6

10.a4!
If immediately 10.♘d2, then 10...b5 11.a4 c6, etc. But now White "threatens" to get a safe position through ♘–d2–c4, etc.

10...c4?
By opening the position in the center at this particular moment, Black only increases the activity of the opposing pieces. Instead, a reasonable maneuver would be 10...♘d7, followed by ...♘b8–♘c6, etc.

11.d4 exd4
If 11...♗b4, then 12.d5, with advantage.

12.♗xd4 ♗b4 13.0–0 c6?
A strange move, which weakens his b7-square unnecessarily. Instead, Black could roll and probably get a draw after 14.e5 ♗xc3 15.♗xc3 ♘d5 16.♕d2, etc.

14.e5 ♘d5
Now practically forced, as 14...♗xc3 15.exf6! ♗xd4 16.♘xd4 ♕xf6 17.♘xe6 fxe6 18.♕h5+! followed by 19.♕c5 etc. would have been decidedly in White's favor.

15.♘e4 ♘f4
It would be a lesser evil 15...0–0.

16.♗c5!
The natural exploitation of weak black houses in the black position.

16...♗xc5 17.♕xd8+ ♖xd8

18.♘xc5 b6?

A miscalculation. 18...♔b8 was necessary, although after 19.♘xe6 ♘xe6 (no better 19...fxe6) 20.a5! (threatening both 21.♖a4 and 21.♘d2) his position would remain unpleasant.

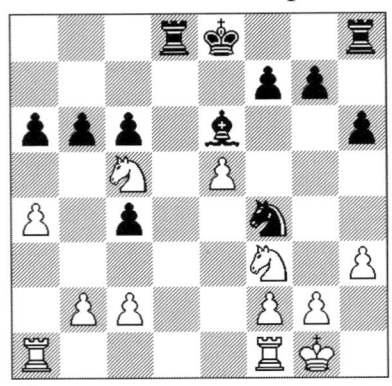

19.♘b7?

Black's a-pawn is by no means poisoned, and its capture would quickly prove decisive. For example: 19.♘xa6 ♗c8 20.♘c7+ ♔d7 21.♘a8 (this was the move I didn't see in my calculations) 21...♘d5 22.a5 (also quite good 22.♔fd1) 22...bxa5 23.♖xa5 ♗b7 24.♖a7 ♖b8 25.♖e1 c5 26.e6+, and Black obviously doesn't succeed in capturing the opponent's Knight. After the text's timid move Black temporarily recovers.

19...♖d7 20.♘d6+ ♔e7 21.♘d4 ♗d5 22.g3!

The value of this bold move - that by making it White, after having squandered the win on move 19, was only playing for a draw - was completely misinterpreted by my critics - Bogoljubov, Nimzowitsch, Dr. Lasker and others. They all claimed that White was taking risks unnecessarily and would now get into difficulties. In reality, *(a) the defense of the g Pawn would prove unsatisfactory, because* (I) 22.f3 would be answered by 22...g6!, threatening both 23...c5 and 23...f6; (II) After 22.♘6f5+ ♔f8, Black would again threaten 23...c5, etc.; (III) In the case of 22.♘4f5+ Black would have every right to play 22...♔e6! 23.♘xg7+ ♔xe5 and if 24.♘de8 then simply 24...♘xg2! etc., with an advantage. *(b) After the opponent's acceptance of the sacrifice, White, even though adequate defense, would have no problem obtaining a draw.*

22...♘xh3+ 23.♔h2 ♘g5 24.f4 ♘e4 25.♘6f5+ ♔d8?

Playing for a counterattack and obviously not taking into account White's interesting 27th move. 25...♔f8 was needed, which would probably be answered by 26.♘e3 ♔g8 27.f5 ♔h7 28.e6 etc., with ample compensation for the Pawn less.

26.♘xg7 f6 27.♖ad1!

This time gained (27...♔xg7 28.♘e5+) gives White a net, if not yet decisive, advantage.

27...♔c8 28.♘df5 fxe5

The alternative 28...♔g8 would also leave White with better chances in the ending: for example, 29.♘h5 fxe5 30.fxe5 ♖e8 31.♘f6 ♘xf6 32.exf6 ♖e2+ 33.♔h3, and now both (A) 33...♗e6 34.g4 ♗xf5 35.gxf5, and (B) 33...♗g2+ 34.♔g4 ♗xf1 35.♔xd7 ♔xd7 36.f7 ♖e8 37.fxe8♕+ ♔xe8 38.c3! followed by ♘xh6 etc..., would be in White's favor.

29.fxe5 ♖g8?

After the previous exchange, this move is already the decisive blunder, unlike 29...♘g5 30.♖xd5! ♔xd5 (better than 30...cxd5 31.e6) 31.♘e7+ ♔d7 32.♘xd5 cxd5 33.♖f6 ♖g8 etc., which would still offer chances of salvation.

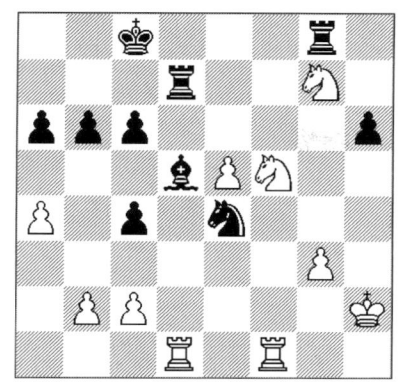

30.e6!

This short, sharp combination with a promotion point is partnered by the final attack in the 4th Game of the game (*Game 62*).

30...♖dxg7 31.♘xg7 ♖xg7 32.♖xd5

The bishop needs to be eliminated as it protects the f7 square.

32...cxd5 33.♖f8+ ♔c7 34.♖f7+ ♔d6

A sad necessity, because after 34...♖xf7 35.exf7 this Pawn couldn't be stopped.

35.♖xg7 ♔xe6 36.♖g6+ ♔e5 37.♔g2

The black pawns won't run away!

37...b5 38.a5 d4 39.♖xa6 b4 40.♔f3 c3 41.bxc3 bxc3 42.♖e6+! ♔xe6 43.♔xe4, and Black resigned.

Game 65
E.Bogoljubov–A.Alekhine
World Championship (17), Kisingen,
May 1934
Queen's Gambit Accepted [D24]

1.d4 d5 2.c4 dxc4 3.♘f3 ♘f6 4.♘c3

Unusual, but playable. The logical course is, however, the immediate retaking of the gambit Pawn (4.e3 followed by 5.♗xc4).

4...a6 5.e4?

But this is merely an adventure, which would only be chosen by a player who already had very little to lose (the game situation was then 5-1 in my favor). It required 5.a4 followed by 6.e3, etc.

5...b5

Of course! Black doesn't really have any weak points and White's next attacking moves are easy to deal with.

6.e5 ♘d5 7.♘g5 e6 8.♕f3

Also 8.♕h5 ♕e7 would prove harmless.

8...♕d7 9.♘xd5 exd5 10.a3

It's certainly unpleasant to be compelled to make such defensive moves while at a material disadvantage. But the threat of 10...♗b4+ was very strong.

10...♘c6 11.♗e3 ♘d8

As the sequence will show, this relieves the queen of defending pawn d.

12.♗e2 ♕f5!

Because of 13.♕xd5? then 13...♗b7 wins the queen.

13.♕g3 h6 14.♘h3

Or 14.♘f3 ♕g4, etc.

14...c6

Prepare the next successful getaway.

15.f4 ♕c2! 16.♕f2

Apparently defending everything, since both 16...♕xb2 17.0–0 and 16...c3 17.b4! etc. would be dangerous for Black. But here comes a big surprise.

See the next Diagram

16...♗xa3!

It's becoming increasingly difficult to find original combinations in chess, especially in the early stages of the game. This, I think, is one of them: although the Bishop move *has already* been made in analogous positions (for example, with White's Pawn on a2 and his Bishop on c1), it hasn't previously, as far as I know, had a sacrifice combined with the idea of capturing the ♖ook after ♖×a3, ♕×b2, etc.

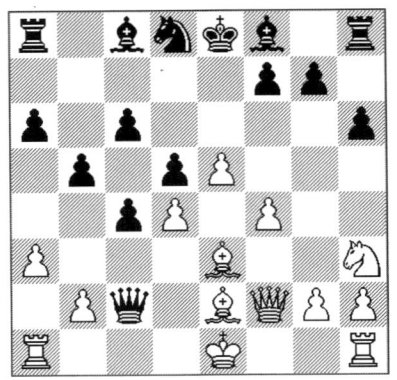

17.0–0

There's no choice here, as 17.♖×a3 ♕×b2 18.♖a5 ♕b4+ 19.♗d2 c3 etc. would lose quickly.

17...♗×b2 18.♖ae1 ♗f5

The idea of putting that Bishop on e4 and rooting for the queen's wing afterwards is certainly a good one. But with Black's overwhelming material advantage (three Pawns!), they had every reason to simplify things: 18...♗×h3 19.g×h3 ♘e6, and if 20.f5 ♘g5 etc., it would probably settle things even more quickly.

19.g4 ♗e4 20.f5 ♘b7 21.♘f4

If 21.♕h4 to prevent Black's next move - the reply 21...c5! would be too strong.

See the next Diagram

21...0–0–0! 22.♕g3 g5

One of the easiest methods, as White's activity on the f-file will still be paralysed by the threat of the inevitable counterattack ...c5.

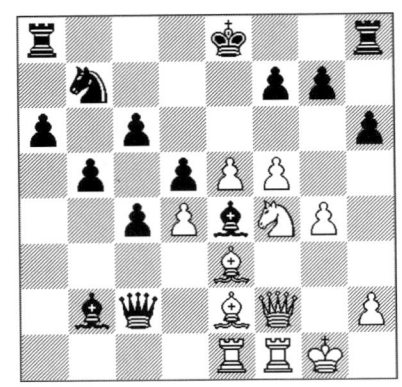

23.f×g6 f×g6 24.♗d1 ♕c3 25.♘e6 ♖de8 26.♖f6 ♖e7 27.♖ef1 ♖he8 28.♘f4

After 28.♘c5 ♘×c5 29.♖×c6+ ♔b7 30.♖×c5, the queen sacrifice 30...♕×d4! etc. would end the game.

28...♘d8 29.♕f2

Or 29.♘×g6 ♗×g6 30.♖×g6 c5! etc., winning easily.

29...♕a3 30.♗f3 ♗×f3 31.♕×f3 g5 32.♘e2 ♖e6 33.♖f5 ♕d3 34.h4 ♖g6 35.h5 ♖ge6 36.♕f2 c5!

Finally!

37.♖f3 ♕c2 38.♕e1 ♘c6 39.♖1f2 ♕e4 40.♘g3 ♕×g4 41.♔g2 ♗×d4, and White resigned.

Game 66
E.Bogoljubov-A.Alekhine
World Championship (25), Belin, June 1934
Queen's Gambit Accepted [D11]

1.d4 d5 2.♘f3 c6 3.c4 d×c4

An unusual line of play (instead of ...♘f6) that is certainly not refuted in this game.

4.e3 ♗g4 5.♗×c4 e6 6.♘c3

Bogoljubov thought that here he could get some advantage for the endgame by continuing 6.♕b3 ♕b6 7.♘g5; but after 7...♗f5 8.♘c3 ♘f6 9.f3 ♘fd7! etc., there wasn't much for White to hope for.

6...♘d7 7.h3 ♗h5 8.a3

Very slow. But since the Black women don't plan any action in the center, such a preventive move can't be criticized.

8...♘gf6 9.e4 ♗e7 10.0–0 0–0 11.♗f4 a5

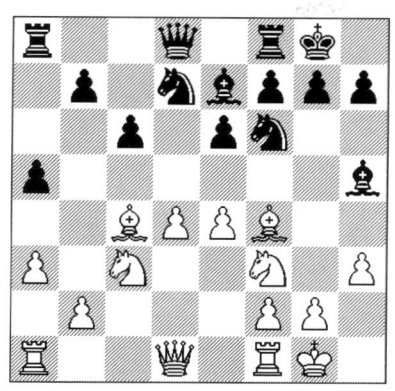

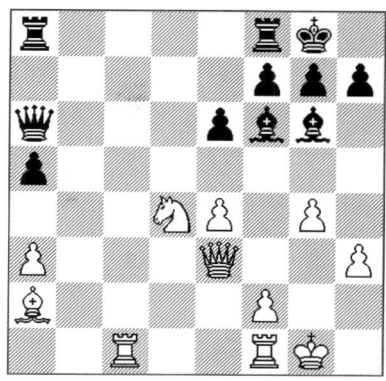

The whites are strong in the center for now. Black is looking for a diversion on the queen's wing. This will result in the exchange of a couple of pieces that will gradually ease their somewhat restricted position.

12.♗a2 ♕b6 13.g4 ♗g6 14.♕e2 ♕a6! 15.♕e3

Exchanging the queens would obviously remove any serious hope of victory for White.

15...b5 16.♘e5 ♘xe5

It was also possible 16...b4 17.♘xg6 hxg6 18.♘e2 c5, but I wasn't particularly enthusiastic about the variant 19.e5 ♘d5 20.♗xd5 exd5 21.♗g3, followed by f4, etc. And besides, I believed in the future of my temporarily caged queen bishop.

17.♗xe5 b4 18.♗xf6 ♗xf6 19.♘e2

After that, Black takes the initiative, which he will keep until almost the end. But also after 19.♘a4 (recommended by Nimzowitsch and Bogoljubov) 19...bxa3 20.bxa3 e5! 21.d5 ♗e7 etc., their prospects would remain satisfactory.

19...bxa3 20.bxa3 c5 21.♖ac1 cxd4 22.♘xd4

22...♗xd4!

The exchange of the active King's Bishop seems surprising at first glance, but in reality, it offers a great opportunity to exploit the weak points in White's position, both in the center and on the kingside.

23.♕xd4 ♖fd8 24.♕c4! ♕b7

The interesting variant 24...♕xc4 25.♖xc4 ♖d3 26.f4 ♖xa3 27.♖f2 ♖xh3 28.f5 ♗g3+ 29.♔h2 ♖xg4 30.fxg6 ♖xg6 etc. would give Black 4 Pawns for the piece, but no real chances of winning.

25.f3 h5

Without making a hole for their King, Black can't dream of launching a serious offensive. At the same time, this Pawn move is the first step towards the emancipation of the prisoner on g6.

26.♕e2 ♖d4 27.♕e3

Instead, Dr. Lasker suggested 27.♖fd1, which, however, after the exchange of the rooks, would lead to roughly the same position we reached after the 33rd move.

27...♖d7

After 27...♖ad8, White would have forced an exchange of queens by playing 28.♗d5 ♕b2 29.♔b1, etc.

28.gxh5

White hopes to get some counterplay on the c-file and to buy time to double the rooks, he gives the poor bishop some fresh air. Bogoljubov indicated as the best line 28.♔fd1 ♖ad8 29.♔xd7 ♔xd7 30.♗c4, but after 30...a4! followed by ...h4 the black squares in his position would still remain very weak.

28...♗xh5 29.♖c5 ♗g6 30.♖fc1 ♖ad8! 31.♗c4

White can't take the a5 Pawn due to 31...♕b2, with an immediate win.

31...♖d1+ 32.♗f1 ♖xc1 33.♖xc1 a4!

Despite the fact that this Pawn cannot, at least at the moment, be supported by the Bishop, it is by no means weak, as Black will be perfectly capable of protecting it with a counterattack.

34.♖c4 ♖d1 35.♖b4

Not 35.♔xa4 ♔xf1+ due to 35...♔xf1+ followed by 36...♕b5+.

35...♕c7

Threatening mate in three with 36...♕g3+, etc.

36.f4 ♕d8 37.♕f2

The move 37.♔xa4 would be refuted by 37...♔xf1+ and 38...♕d1+. The end is approaching.

37...f5!

which not only rescues the Pawn but also contributes to an effective exploitation of the disorganized position of White's King.

38.e5 ♗e8 39.♖b6 ♕c8 40.♖d6

Or 40.♔h2 ♕c3!, winning.

40...♖c1 41.♕d4

There is no more defenses. If for example 41.♔h2, then 41...♖c2 42.♖d2 ♖xd2 43.♕xd2 ♕c5! winning a Pawn and the game.

41...♔h7

To answer 42.♖d8 with 42...♕a6!, etc.

42.♔f2 ♕c2+ 43.♕d2

Or 43.♗e2 ♗b5 44.♕d2 ♗xe2! 45.♕xe2 ♕c5+ etc., winning.

43...♕c5+ 44.♕e3

If 44.♕d4, then 44...♕xa3 after which White can resign with ease.

44...♔xf1+, and White resigned.

That game finished the match and gave me 15 points against my opponent's 10.

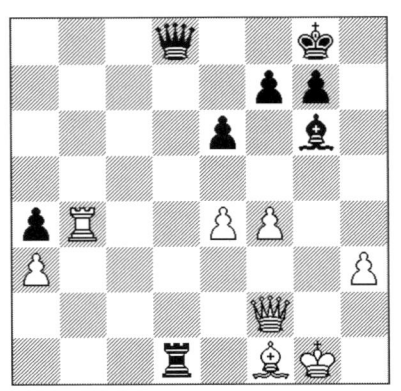

The resurrection of the Bishop,

Alexander Alekhine

CHAPTER 3
Tournaments Games and Matches with Dr. Euwe - 1934 - 1937

Game 67
A.Alekhine-S.Rosseli del Turco
Zurich Tournament, July 1934
Queen's Pawn Opening [D05]

1.d4 d5 2.♘f3 ♘f6 3.e3 e6

It's not a mistake, of course, but 3...♗f5 4.♗d3 e6! would solve the otherwise annoying problem of the queen's bishop development without disadvantage.

4.♗d3 c5 5.b3

An old - and rather harmless - mobilization method, rather than the Colle System, which starts with 5.c3 and offers more attacking possibilities. This is because Black responds with an unjustified central clarification.

5...cxd4?

Curiously, this exchange - which opens the central column for White without compensation (because there's nothing for Black to do with the c column) - is often made even by very experienced players. The course of this game illustrates in typical fashion the irresponsibility of this strategy.

6.exd4 ♗d6 7.0-0 0-0 8.♗b2 ♘c6 9.a3

More accurate than the intermediate 9.♘bd2, because after 9...♕c7! Black would threaten both 10...♘b4 and 10...e5.

9...b6 10.♘bd2 ♗b7 11.♕e2 ♕c7 12.♘e5 ♘e7 13.f4 ♖ac8 14.♖ac1

See the next Diagram

To add to the already existing advantages (more space in the center and more chances on the King's wing) another trump - the dynamization of the Pawn c. However, the general situation after the wrong exchange on the 5th move is so favorable for White that an attack on the King can be developed *without using this trump*. A characteristic example of such an attack is my game with Asgeirson (Black), shown below, played at the Folkestone Team Tournament in 1933, which, with a slight reversal of moves, soon reached the same kind of position as the present game: 1.d4 ♘f6 2.♘f3 e6 3.e3 c5 4.♗d3 ♘c6 5.a3 cxd4? 6.exd4 d5 7.0-0 ♗d7 8.b3 ♗d6 9.♖e1 ♔c8 10.♗b2 0-0 11.♘e5 ♗b8 12.♘d2 g6 13.♕f3 ♘h5 14.♕e3 ♘g7 15.♕h6 ♘e7 16.g4! ♔h8 17.♘df3 ♘g8 18.♕h3 ♗e8 19.♗c1 ♗d6 20.♘g5 h5 21.gxh5 ♘xh5 (or 21...gxh5 22.♘h7, winning the quality) 22.♘gxf7+! ♗xf7 23.♗xg6 ♗xg6 24.♘xg6+ ♔g7 25.♘xf8!, and Black resigned.

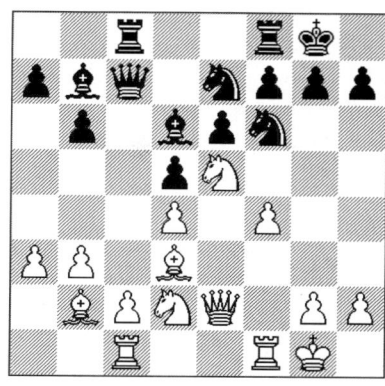

14...g6

This, in connection with the next two moves, will not prove sufficient to deal with the threatening advance of White's g-Pawn. But in the same way, Black's attempt to position his Knight on e4 would be unsuccessful, for example: 14...♕b8 15.♔f2! ♕a8 16.♖e1 followed by g4, with advantage.

15.g4 h5 16.h3 ♔g7

As we'll see, this only makes it easier

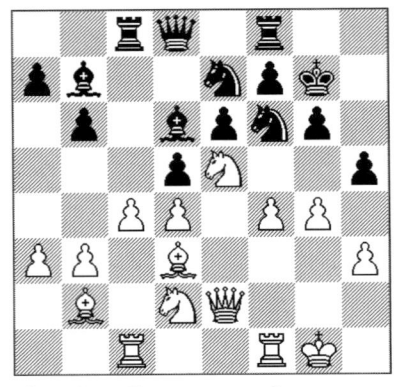

for White's c Pawn to advance.
17.c4 ♕d8
18.c5!

This is the strategic decision, as White's forces here protect the passed Pawn on the Queen's wing without weakening his pressure on the other wing. Black obviously can't play 18...b×c5 19.d×c5 ♗×c5+ now due to 20.♖×c5! followed by 21.g5 etc. winning.

18...♗×e5 19.f×e5 ♘d7 20.b4 h×g4 21.h×g4 ♖h8

The occupation of this column is unimportant, as the light pieces cannot cooperate.

22.♘f3 b×c5 23.b×c5 ♘c6 24.♕e3!

Threatening 25.♘g5.

24...♕e7 25.♔g2

Now threatening 25.♖h1! followed by ♖c–f1 and ♗c1 etc., and thus inducing Black to take desperate action in the center.

25...f5 26.e×f6+ ♘×f6 27.♕g5 ♖h6 28.♖h1 ♖ch8 29.♖×h6 ♖×h6 30.♖e1!

Even stronger than 30.♖h1, which would only win a Pawn.

30...♘d8 31.♘e5 ♘g8

Or 31...♘f7 32.♘×f7 followed by 33.♕e5 etc., with an easy win.

32.♗c1!

One of the points of 30.♖e1.

32...♕e8 33.♖f1 ♗c6 34.♖f6! ♘×f6 35.♕×h6+ ♔g8 36.♗g5, winning at least two minor pieces. Black resigned.

Game 68
A.Alekhine–H.Johner
Zurich Tournament, July 1934
Spanish Opening [C79]

1.e4 e5 2.♘f3 ♘c6 3.♗b5 a6 4.♗a4 ♘f6 5.0–0 d6

This allows White to start an immediate action in the center without having to first protect the Pawn and through ♖e1 or ♕e2, which would be the case after ...♗e7.

6.c3 ♗d7 7.d4 ♗e7 8.d5

This blocking maneuver was introduced by Bogoljubov against me in our game in Rotterdam, 1929. Its characteristic is that it usually leads to slow, high-caliber positional battles.

8...♘b8 9.♗c2 ♗g4

Keres tried against me in the Team Tournament in Warsaw 1935 a more aggressive line of play, involving giving up castling and starting with 9...h6. The continuation 10.c4 ♕c8 11.♘e1 g5 12.♘c3 ♘h5 13.♘e2! (of course, not 13.♕×h5 ♗g4) 13...♘f4 14.♘g3 c6 15.♘f5 c×d5 16.♗×f4 g×f4 17.c×d5 ♗×f5 18.e×f5 proved, however, to be favorable to the first player, who, taking advantage of the open c-file, succeeded in forcing Black's resignation after the 37th move. For ...a5 in conjunction with ♘a6–c5, see my game with consultation against Kashdan (*Game 119*).

10.c4 ♘bd7

See the next Diagram

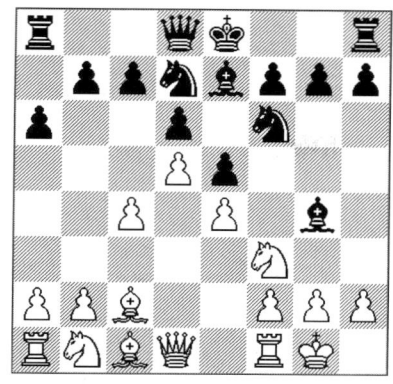

My Best Games 1924-1937

11.h3!

In the game mentioned above, Bogoljubov here played 11.♘c3, and after 11...♘f8 12.h3? – this is now out of place, as simply after 12...♗d7 Black is able to launch an attack on the King via a Pawn sacrifice, ...g5!, and soon obtain a winning position.

11...♗h5 12.♘c3 0-0 13.g4 ♗g6 14.♕e2

Preparing ♘a4, which if played immediately would be answered by 14...♗xe4, etc.

14...♘e8 15.♗d2 h6

The apparently more aggressive 15...h5 would be answered favorably by the move ♘-d1-e3-f5.

16.♔g2 ♗h7 17.♖h1 g5!

By building this Pawn-barricade, Black has at least eliminated the immediate danger threatening his King.

18.h4 f6 19.♘d1 ♖f7 20.♘e3

This knight needs to be exchanged on c5 before Black can find the time to bring the knight to c4 via g6.

20...♘f8 21.♘f5 ♗xf5 22.gxf5 ♖h7

See the next Diagram

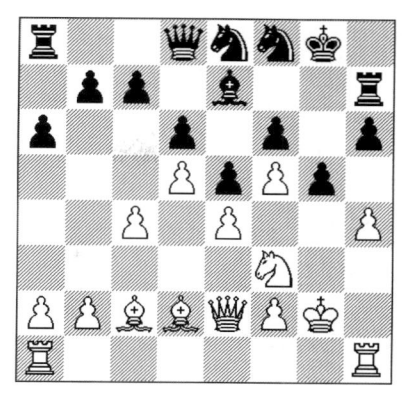

23.♖ag1 ♘g7 24.♔f1 ♕e8 25.♘h2 ♘h5 26.♘g4 ♘f4 27.♕f3!

Threatening 28.♗xf4 exf4 29.♕xf4! gxf4 30.♘xh6+ followed by mate.

27...♔g7!

The only defense; for 27...♔h8 the defeat would come through 28.♘xh6! ♔xh6 29.hxg5, etc.

28.hxg5 hxg5 29.♖xh7+ ♘xh7 30.♖h1 ♔h8 31.♖h6 ♕f7 32.♗d1 ♖g8 33.♕b3!

As all of Black's pieces are occupied on the King's wing, the Queen undertakes a short walk on the other wing, not just for the sake of sightseeing, but to grab anything insufficiently protected. This material gain, by no means accidental, is the logical consequence of a persistent initiative, which has prevented Black from simultaneously protecting his vulnerable spots.

33...b6 34.♕a4 ♗f8

If 34...a5, then 35.♕d7 etc., winning quickly.

35.♕xa6 ♗xh6 36.♘xh6 ♕g7 37.♘xg8 ♔xg8 38.♕c8+ ♘f8 39.♗xf4 exf4 40.♕e8

After gaining a material advantage, the attack, as so often, disappears, and White now needs to be particularly careful against a possible counterattack. For example, Black's strong threat was 40...♕e7 and ...♕e5.

40...g4! 41.♕h5 f3 42.♗a4 ♘h7 43.♗c2

The necessary preparation for the

143

surprising assault in the center.

43...♞f8

If 43...♞g5, White would win with 44.♕×g4 ♕h6 45.♔g1! – for example: (I) 45...♔f8 46.♗d1 ♞h3+ 47.♔f1 ♕d2 48.♕×f3; (II) 45...♕g7 46.♕g3 with technically easy work in both cases.

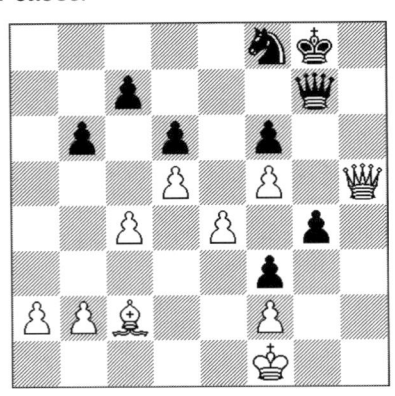

44.e5!!

The secret bid for postponement, which turns a technically complicated problem into a short, sharp winning procedure.

44...d×e5

Or 44...f×e5 45.f6! ♕×f6 46.♕×g4+ followed by 47.♗e4, with no fight resigned.

45.d6! c5

After 45...c×d6, the third point, 46.c5! threatening 47.♗b3+ etc. would bring the work to a successful close.

46.♗e4 ♕d7 47.♕h6!

More precise than 47.♕×g4+. Black resigned.

Game 69
F.Gygli–A.Alekhine
Zurich Tournament, July 1934
Benoni Defense [A44]

1.d4 c5 2.d5 e5 3.e4 d6 4.g3

An elaborate method of development, which doesn't cause too many problems for Black. White should, in my opinion, try this opening combining the following two strategic ideas: (1) occupation of the c4 square by a Knight and strengthening that position, and (2) preparation for the f4 advance, *which should however only be carried out as an immediate reaction to Black's move ...f5*. In the latter case, the opening of the central position always favors the side that already has a superiority in space.

4...f5 5.♞c3 ♞f6 6.♗g2 ♗e7

The immediate 6...b5 (7.♞×b5 ♞×e4, etc.) also comes into consideration. Since Black doesn't take advantage of this possibility, White would do better to avoid it now by playing 7.a4.

7.♞ge2 b5!

The tactical consequences of this strategically justified advance had to be carefully examined, as shown below.

8.e×f5 b4 9.♞e4 ♗×f5 10.♞×c5

A tempting but unsatisfactory deal, as it only helps Black's strength to develop. It's also a harmless alternative, which only accentuates the inefficiency of the opening's first moves.

10...d×c5 11.d6

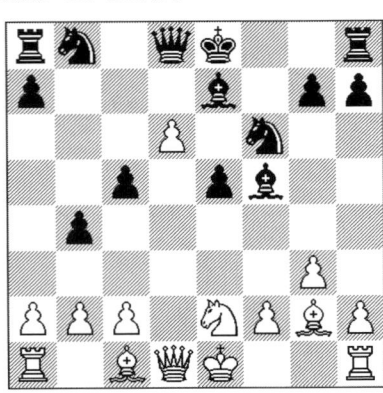

11...e4!

And not 11...♗e4 12.♗xe4 ♘xe4 13.♕d5 with advantage.

12.dxe7 ♕xd1+ 13.♔xd1 ♔xe7 14.♗e3 ♘bd7

The middlegame without the queens, the result of the central exchanges, favors Black - mainly because of the uncomfortable position of White's king, preventing the combined action of the rooks.

15.h3 h5 16.a3 a5 17.axb4 axb4 18.♔d2 ♔f7!

An important move, the aim of which is to prevent the capture of the c-awn *with check* if ...♘e5.

19.♘f4?

This proves to be an important, if not decisive, waste of time, and was obviously based on a tactical miscalculation. By playing 19.b3 White would still have maintained a playable game, albeit an inferior one.

19...g5 20.♘e2

White probably intended to play 20.♖xa8 ♖xa8 21.♘xh5 and now realized that this would lead to a hopeless position after 21...♘xh5 22.g4 ♘f4 23.♗xf4 gxf4 24.gxf5 f3 25.♗f1 ♔f6, etc. But what will happen after the removal of the text won't be much better for them.

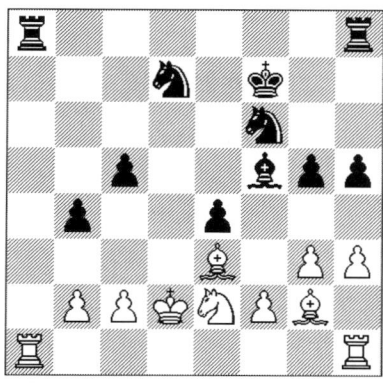

20...♘e5!

With the threats ...♘c4+ and ...♘f3+, both can't be stopped.

21.♖xa8 ♖xa8 22.♖d1 ♘f3+

Even more convincing than 22...♘c4+ 23.♔e1 ♘xb2 24.♖b1, etc.

23.♗xf3 exf3 24.♘c1 c4!

Putting White's knight in a drowned position, in which it will remain until almost the end of the game.

25.♔e1 g4

There's no hurry to take the c-pawn, as White's response is compulsory: if 26.hxg4 hxg4, followed by 27...♔h8 and ...♘e4 with a mate attack.

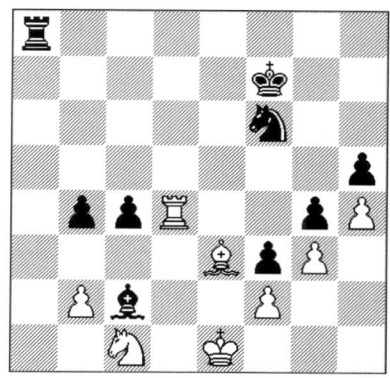

26.h4 ♗xc2 27.♖d4

27...c3!

Forcing a powerful passed Pawn and at the same time ending the siege of the enemy King. White now can't play 28.♔xb4 due to 28...♖d8 29.♗d4 ♔xd4! 30.♔xd4 cxb2 winning.

28.bxc3 bxc3 29.♖f4 ♔e6 30.♖c4 ♘d5 31.♗g5 ♔d6 32.♗h6

White has fewer and fewer moves at his disposal.

32...♖e8+ 33.♔f1 ♗d1 34.♖d4 ♗e2+ 35.♔e1

Or 35.♔g1 ♗b5! followed by ...♖e1+, ...♗f1, ...♗g2 and ...♖h1 mate.

35...♔c6 36.♗g5 ♗c4+ 37.♔d1 ♔c5!

Capturing the Rook, right in the

middle of the board!
38.♔xd5+ ♔xd5 39.♔c2 ♖e2+! 40.♔xc3 ♖xf2, and White resigned.

> **Game 70**
> **A.Alekhine-Dr.E.Lasker**
> *Zurich Tournament, July 1934*
> Orthodox Defense [D67]

1.d4 d5 2.c4 e6 3.♘c3 ♘f6 4.♘f3 ♗e7 5.♗g5 ♘bd7 6.e3 0–0 7.♖c1 c6 8.♗d3 dxc4

As mentioned elsewhere, this exchange gives Black more defensive resources if preceded by ...h6 ♗h4.

9.♗xc4 ♘d5 10.♗xe7 ♕xe7 11.♘e4

This move, "patented" by me, is just as good as the more common 11.0–0, but probably not better. In both cases White usually gets an advantage in space and doesn't have to worry about a possible loss.

11...♘5f6 12.♘g3 e5

An interesting attempt by Lasker to quickly solve the Queen Bishop problem. Capablanca regularly in our game here played 12...♕b4+ and, after exchanging queens, managed to draw, but not without difficulties.

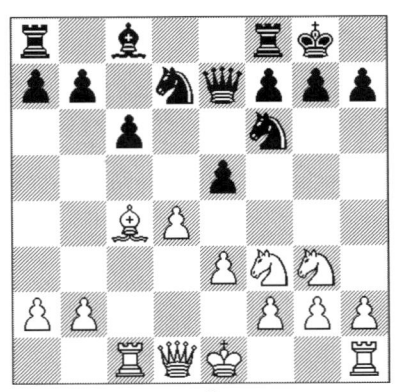

13.0–0 exd4 14.♘f5

This apparently sharp move is actually less aggressive than the direct 14.exd4, which, due to the opening of the column, would cause real problems for Black's development - for example, 14...♘b6 15.♖e1 ♕d6 16.♗b3, and if 16...♗g4 then 17.h3 ♗xf3 18.♕xf3 etc., offering the d-Pawn for a strong attack. After the text move, White will be practically forced to take on d4 with a piece and consequently allow an unwelcome simplification.

14...♕d8 15.♘3xd4

If 15.♕ (or e3)xd4, then 15...♘b6.

15...♘e5 16.♗b3 ♗xf5 17.♘xf5 ♕b6?

Underestimating, or not realizing, the reply, which gave White a strong and hardly resistable attack. The right move, sufficient for balance, is 17...g6, played by Flohr against Euwe in Nottingham, 1936. Neither 18.♕d6 (♖e8!) nor 18.♘d6 (♕e7) would succeed.

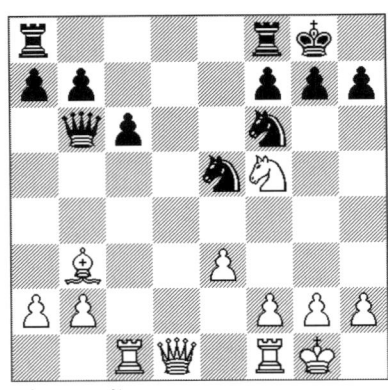

18.♕d6! ♘ed7

Also 18...♘g6 19.♘h6+ gxh6 20.♕xf6 ♕d8 21.♕f3 would be pretty bad.

19.♖fd1 ♖ad8 20.♕g3 g6 21.♕g5!

With the main threat 22.♖d6, Black no longer has any real chances of defense.

21...♔h8 22.♘d6 ♔g7 23.e4!

Not only to use this Pawn as an attacking factor, but also, as we shall see, to free up the third row for the Rooks.

23...♘g8 24.♖d3 f6

The move 24...h6 would lead to a similar variant, that is 25.♘f5+ ♔h7 26.♘xh6! f6 27.♘f5! fxg5 28.♖h3+ with mate following.

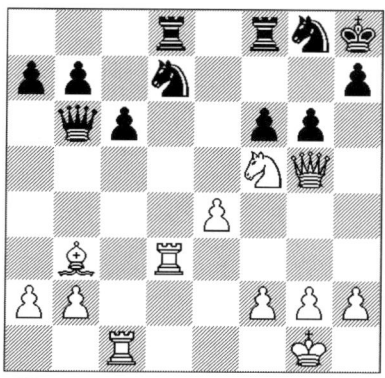

25.♘f5+ ♔h8

26.♕xg6!

The spectacular final blow of an attack that would hardly have been conducted so effectively had it not been for Black's shallow 17th move.

Game 71
A.Alekhine-E.Lundin
Orebro Tournament, May 1935
Orthodox Defense [D51]

1.d4 d5 2.c4 e6 3.♘c3 ♘f6 4.♗g5 ♘bd7 5.♘f3 c6 6.e4

This old move - a radical method of avoiding the Cambridge Springs Defense - was successfully adopted by me on two occasions in the game with Bogoljubov in 1929 and on a few occasions afterwards. Its advantage is gaining some space in the center and its defect - not allowing the exchange of the minor pieces early on, which facilitates the mobilization of Black's pieces.

6...dxe4 7.♘xe4 ♗e7

In addition to this simple development move, Black has at least three other continuations at his disposal, each involving a different development plan:

I. 7...♕b6. This counterattack is aimed at immediate material gain at the cost of time, and possibly space - a dangerous idea, and in my view, contrary to good chess principles, which however, in this particular case, is by no means easy to refute. In Game 11 of the game against Bogoljubov, I adopted the ultra-cautious 8.♘xf6+ gxf6 9.♗c1 - and soon had a winning attack, but only because of my opponent, who with his typical overestimation of his resources, replied 9...e5? instead of 9...♕c7, thus opening up the position before finishing the development. The continuation was 10.♗d3 exd4 11.0–0 ♗e7 12.♖e1 ♘f8 13.♘h4! ♗e6 14.♘f5 ♗b4 15.♘g7+ ♔d7 16.♖e4! ♗g8 - after which White was able to finish quickly by playing 17.♘f5!, with the threat ♖xd4, etc.

Also successful, but not quite convincing, was another attempt of mine against Colle in Bled 1931, where after 7...♕b6 I played 8.♗d3. My opponent decided to accept the Pawn offer, but he did it in a way that wasn't the safest: instead of 8...♘xe4 8.♗xe4 ♕b4+! - successfully introduced by Dr. Euwe in a game with consultation against Flohr - he immediately played 8...♕xb2, allowing White to get his King to safety. The attack that followed - based first on the space advantage and then on the supremacy of the two Bishops - was both typical and instructive. The game continued as follows: 9.0–0 ♘xe4 10.♗xe4 ♘f6 11.♗d3 ♕b6 12.♖e1 ♗e7 13.♕c2 h6 14.♗d2 c5 15.♗c3 cxd4 16.♘xd4 0–0 17.♘f5 ♕d8 18.♘xe7+ ♕xe7 19.♖ab1 ♖d8 20.♖e3 b6 21.♕e2! ♗b7 22.♖g3 ♘e8 23.♖e1 ♔f8 24.♕b2 f6 25.♗b4 ♘d6 26.♖ge3 ♔f7 27.f4! ♕d7 28.♕e2 ♖e8 29.♕h5+ ♔g8 30.♕g6 f5 31.♗xd6 ♕xd6 32.♗xf5 ♕xf4 33.♕h7+ ♔f8 34.♗g6 ♕d4 35.♗xe8 ♔xe8 36.♔h1 ♕f6 37.♕h8+ ♔f7 38.♕xe8+! and Black resigned.

Since no attempt can be considered satisfactory from a theoretical point of view, White should, after 7...♕b6, complete his development in a way that doesn't allow an undesirable reduction of the fighting units. With this idea, I would recommend the continuation that was tried by Marshall against Tchigorin in Hanover 1902, and completely forgotten since then: 8.c5! ♕xb2 - and only now 9.♗d3 followed by 10.0–0, with ample material compensation for the Pawn.

II. 7...♗b4+, with the aim of temporarily exploiting the e8–a4 diagonal and at the same time preparing a central break through ...e5. The idea is, however, too artificial with too much wasted time to become a success. The following game, played by me at the Team Tournament in Warsaw 1935, dramatically illustrates White's possibilities in this variant: Black, Silbermann (Romania) 8.♘c3 ♕a5 9.♗d2 ♕c7 10.♗d3 e5 11.dxe5 ♘xe5 12.♕e2 ♘fd7 13.0–0 0–0 14.♘d5 (a very original combination in which White finally wins the quality by a Pawn) 14...cxd5 15.♗xb4 ♘xd3 16.♕xd3 dxc4 17.♕e3! ♕b6 (if 17...♖d8, then 18.♕e7 with a winning position) 18.♗xf8 ♕xe3 19.fxe3 (the following ending was harder to win than you might think, especially as Black defended with great determination) 19...♔xf8 20.♖ad1 ♔e7 21.♖d5 f6 22.♖fd1 b6 23.♖d6 ♘c5 24.♖d8 ♗b7 25.♖xa8 ♗xa8 26.♘d4 ♗e4 27.♖c1 ♗d5 28.♘f5+ ♔e6 29.♘xg7+ ♔e5 30.♘h5! ♗f7 31.♘f4 ♘e4 32.a3 b5 33.♖d1 ♘c5 34.♖d8 a6 35.♔f2 ♘a4 36.♖d7 ♗g6 37.♖d5+ ♔e4 38.♖d2 ♗f5 39.h3 c3 (this breakthrough attempt is answered with a mate threat, which decides the game once and for all. Compare with the same endgame stratagem in the games against Tartakower in San Remo and the 24th Game of the 2nd game with Euwe) 40.♖d4+ ♔e5 41.♔f3! ♘b6 42.bxc3 ♗d7 43.♘d3+ ♔f5 44.♖d6, and Black resigned.

(III) 7...h6!, practically forcing the exchange of White's queen bishop. Although, after 8.♗xf6 ♘xf6 9.♘c3 b6 followed by ...♗b7 etc., White would still enjoy more freedom, at least temporarily, Black's chances for the future, due to his pair of Bishops, would be quite satisfactory, which is why I recently abandoned the otherwise playable 6.e4.

8.♘c3 0–0 9.♕c2

This move in connection with the great castling was, I believe, never played before my game with Bogoljubov in 1929. On a previous occasion Gilg played Spielmann 9.♗d3 and castled for the kingside, after which Black equalized easily with ...c5.

9...e5!

A new and interesting attempt to free up the queen bishop, which forces White to play very carefully in order to maintain the space advantage. It's too passive, instead 9...b6 10.0–0, as for example my next two games show very convincingly:

I. Black, Bogoljubov, 19th Game, 1929. 10...♗b7 11.h4 ♕c7 12.♗d3 ♖fe8 13.♔b1 ♘f8 14.♗×f6! ♗×f6 15.♘e4 c5 16.♘×f6+ g×f6 17.♕d2 ♘g6 18.h5 ♘f4 19.♖h4 ♗×f3 20.g×f3 e5 21.d5 ♕d6 22.h6 ♔h8 23.♕c2 ♘×d3 24.♕×d3 ♖g8 25.f4! ♔g6 26.♕f5 a6 27.♖e1 e×f4 28.♔×f4! (by giving up the h-pawn White takes full control of the central column and gradually develops an irresistible attack on the king) 28...♖×h6 29.♖fe4 ♖g8 30.♖e7 ♖f8 31.a4 ♖h4 32.♖e8 ♖×e8 33.♖×e8+ ♔g7 34.♕c8 ♔h6 35.♖g8 ♕e7 36.♔a2 b5 37.♖g3 f5 38.♕×f5 f6 39.♖e3 ♕f7. Here I played 40.♖e6 and casually won in 77 moves. But 40.♕e6! would force an almost immediate resignation.

II. Black, J. Vasquez, Mexico City Tournament, September 1932: 10...c5 11.h4 ♕c7 12.d5 e×d5 13.c×d5 a6 14.♗d3 h6 15.♗h7+ ♔h8 16.♘e4! ♗d6 17.♗f5 ♘×e4 18.♕×e4 ♘e5 19.♘×e5 ♗×e5 20.d6 ♗×d6 21.♕×a8 ♗×f5 22.♕f3 ♗g6 23.h5 ♗h7 24.♗×h6! ♗e5 25.♗g5 f5 26.h6 f4 27.♕d5! f3 28.h×g7+ ♕×g7 29.♖×h7+ ♔×h7 30.♖h1+ ♔g6 31.♗h6 ♗f4+ 32.♗×f4 ♖×f4 33.g×f3 ♕d4 34.♕g8+ ♔f6 35.♖h6+ ♔e7 36.♖e6+, and Black resigned.

10.0–0–0

Accepting the offer would be in Black's favor, for example: 10.d×e5 ♘g4 11.♗f4 ♗c5 12.♘e4 ♗b4+ or 10.♘×e5 ♘×e5 11.d×e5 ♘d7 12.♗×e7 ♕×e7 13.f4 f6 - in both cases with sufficient compensation for the Pawn.

10...e×d4 11.♘×d4 ♕a5 12.h4

As the reader can see from the games above, this move is an important link in the plan begun with 9.♕c2.

12...♘c5 13.♔b1 ♖d8

If 13...♗e6, White wouldn't exchange that bishop directly, but would first finish the development as in the current game - ♗–e2–f3, etc.

14.♗e2 ♕c7

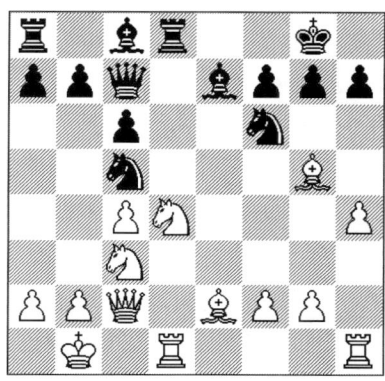

15.♗f3!

Judiciously resisting the temptation to dislodge the Knight with 15.b4, because after 15...♘e6 16.a3 c5! Black would get a counterattack that can't be made after the text's positional move.

15...a5 16.♖he1

At this moment the Rook is more useful in the center, especially since the attack on the King is very slow to develop due to Black's precise preventive maneuvers.

16...g6

Almost necessary if Black wants to dislodge White's central knight with ...♘e6. Moreover, the move also involves the direct threat 17...♘×e4, followed by 18...♗f5.

17.g4 ♘e6 18.♘×e6 ♗×e6 19.h5!

Threatening 20.h×g6 h×g6 21.♖×e6! etc., and not worrying about the c-pawn, as 19...♗×c4 is answered by 20.♖×e7! ♕×e7 21.♘e4 ♔×d1+

22.♕xd1 etc., with a decisive advantage.

19...♖xd1+ 20.♘xd1 ♘e8
To avoid sacrificing quality in e6.
21.♗h6 ♗f6 22.h×g6 h×g6

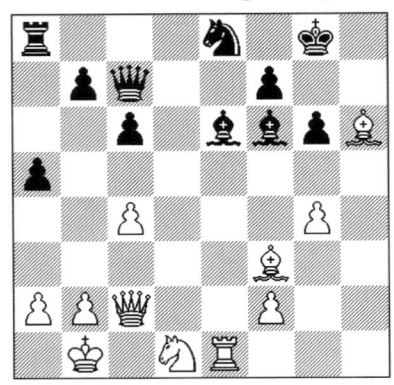

23.♘c3!
I count this Pawn sacrifice among my most difficult combinations, as it was extremely hard to calculate how little material resigned in the main variant would prove sufficient to increase the pressure definitively. And victory was necessary for both players, as we had 7 ½ points out of 8 and this was the last round!

23...♗×c4
Otherwise, after 24.♘e4, White would have an easy attacking game.

24.♘e4 ♕e5
This counterattack will be refuted by White's next two moves. The main variant mentioned arises from 24...♗d5 and the real difficulty lies in finding after 25.♘×f6+ ♘×f6 26.♕c3 ♕d6 27.♗×d5 c×d5 the two quiet moves 28.♖h1 ♕e6 (if 28...d4, then 29.♕h3, etc.) *29.f3!*, with the main threat ♕–d2–h2, after which the open h-column will sooner or later be decisive.

25.g5!
The Bishop thus attacked cannot move due to 26.♘f6+.

25...♕b5
That was obviously the point of the previous move. The piece is temporarily saved, but now Black loses due to the weakness of his g7 square.

26.♘×f6+ ♘×f6 27.♕c3! ♖e8 28.♖c1
And not 28.g×f6 ♕f5+ 29.♔a1 ♗×e1+ followed by 30...♕×f3.

28...♕f5+ 29.♔a1 ♔h7 30.♕×c4, and Black resigned.

Game 72
A.Alekhine–M.Euwe
World Championship (1), Amsterdam
October 1935
Slav Defense [D17]

1.d4 d5 2.c4 c6 3.♘f3 ♘f6 4.♘c3 d×c4 5.a4 ♗f5 6.♘e5

It was proven in our second game that this aggressive move, which has been in fashion for about ten years, is decidedly less promising than the natural 3.e3. Black's best response to the move in the text, however, is not 6...♘bd7, but 6...e6 and if 7.♗g5 ♗b4 8.f3, then 8...h6! etc., (11th Game of the 1937 game).

6...♘bd7 7.♘×c4 ♕c7 8.g3 e5 9.d×e5 ♘×e5 10.♗f4 ♘fd7 11.♗g2 ♗e6

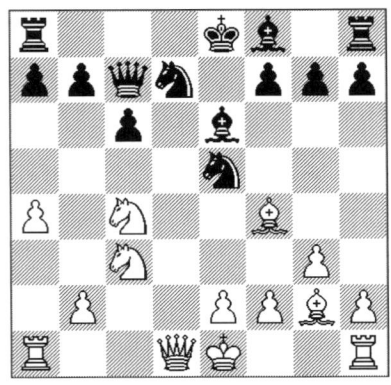

Black doesn't have to concede the

c7 square to White, but as the 1st Game of the 1937 game convincingly demonstrated - even through the best continuation 11...g6 12.0-0 ♖d8 13.♕c1 ♗e6 White gets a clear positional advantage with 14.♘e4!

12.♘xe5 ♘xe5 13.0-0 ♗e7

Then Black tries to avoid weakening the e6 square with ...f6 and gradually gets into great difficulty due to insufficient protection for his knight.

14.♕c2

Threatening both ♘d5 and ♘-b5-d4, etc. Black is unlikely to succeed in holding the pair of Bishops for long.

14...♖d8

Also 14...♕a5 15.♘b5! would be advantageous for White.

15.♖fd1 0-0 16.♘b5 ♖xd1+

If immediately 16...♕a5 17.♗xd8 ♔xd8 18.♗xe5 cxb5 19.♗xb7 ♖d2 20.♕c6 etc., with advantage.

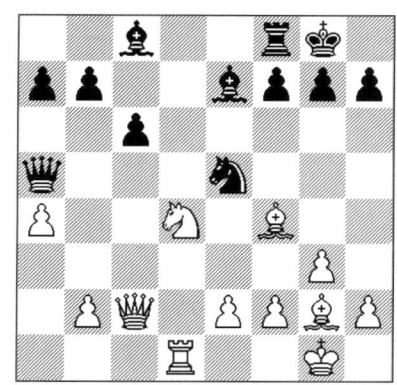

17.♖xd1 ♕a5 18.♘d4 ♗c8

19.b4!

The spectacular start of a "minority attack" that will immediately result in the conquest of the important d5-square. The tactical justification for the move in the text is shown in the following variant: 19...♗xb4 20.♘b3 ♕c7 21.♕e4 ♗c3 (or 21...♗d6 22.♕d4 winning) 22.♔c1 ♗b2 (or 22...c5 23.♕c2; 22...f5 23.♕c2 etc.) 23.♔c2 f5 24.♕b4! etc., with a winning position.

19...♕c7 20.b5 c5 21.♘f5 f6

After that, the weakening of the white squares would soon prove fatal. But also after 21...♗f6 22.♘d6 ♖d8 23.♘c4! etc., the realization of White's positional advantage would have been merely a matter of time.

22.♘e3 ♗e6 23.♘d5!

Even more effective than 23.♖d5.

23...♗xd5 24.♖xd5 ♕a5

There's no defense resigned for long. If, for example 24...♖d8, then simply 25.♗xe5 fxe5 26.♕c4 etc., winning easily.

25.♘f5 ♕e1+ 26.♔g2 ♗d8 27.♗xe5 fxe5 28.♖d7!

Ending the game with a mate attack.

28...♗f6 29.♘h6+ ♔h8 30.♕xc5

If now 30...♖e8 then 31.♕d5 gxh6 32.♕f7 ♗e7 33.♗xe7 followed by mate. Black resigned.

Game 73
A.Alekhine-M.Euwe
World Championship (3), Amsterdam
October 1935
French Defense [C15]

1.e4 e6 2.d4 d5 3.♘c3 ♗b4 4.a3

This rarely played move is certainly better than its reputation and was not even close to being refuted, both in the current game and in its subsequent analysis. Less recommended, despite its practical success, is another attempt I made in Game 9 of the same game, the continuation of which was: 4.♕g4 (very risky due to the already messy situation on the queen's wing) 4...♘f6 5.♕xg7 ♖g8 6.♕h6 ♖g6 7.♕e3 ♘xe4? (by playing 7...c5! Black would get a solid initiative) 8.♗d3 f5 9.♘ge2 c5 10.♗xe4 fxe4 11.♕h3 ♘c6 12.♕xh7 ♕f6 13.♘f4 cxd4

14.♘xg6 dxc3 15.b3 ♘e7 16.♘xe7 ♗xe7 17.h4 ♕f7 18.♕h8+ ♕f8 19.♕xf8+ ♔xf8 20.♗g5 e5 21.f3 exf3 22.gxf3? (after 22.♗xe7+ ♔xe7 23.gxf3 etc? White would have little trouble forcing victory; the less exact move in the text leads to an interesting ending with bishops of opposite colors) 22...♗a3! 23.f4! ♗f5 24.fxe5 ♗xc2 25.0–0+ ♔g8 26.♖ac1! ♗xc1 27.♖xc1 ♗f5 28.♖xc3 ♖c8 29.♖f3 ♖f8 30.♗f6 ♗e4 31.♖g3+ ♔f7 32.h5! ♖c8 33.♖g7+ ♔e6 34.h6! d4 35.h7 ♖c1+ 36.♔f2 ♖c2+ 37.♔g3 ♗xh7 38.♖xh7 ♖xa2 39.♔f4 b5 40.♔e4 ♖e2+ 41.♔xd4 and Black resigned.

4...♗xc3+ 5.bxc3 dxe4 6.♕g4 ♘f6

A safer alternative was 6...♔f8 7.♕xe4 ♘d7 - followed by ...♘dg6, etc. After the text move, the black squares in Black's position become decidedly weak.

7.♕xg7 ♖g8 8.♕h6 c5 9.♘e2 ♘bd7

To relieve the queen of the other knight's protection. If 9...♘f6 White's simplest answer would be 10.dxc5! but also 10.♗g5, as played by Romanovski against Botvinnik in the semi-final of the 1938 Soviet Championship, would be enough to equalize, although White had lost that game due to only being outplayed in the last stages.

See the next Diagram

10.♘g3 ♔g6?

After this waste of time Black's game becomes very difficult. Comparatively better would be to play for complications after 10...♕a5, although White's prospects would remain better even then after 11.♗d2 ♕a4 12.dxc5!, etc.

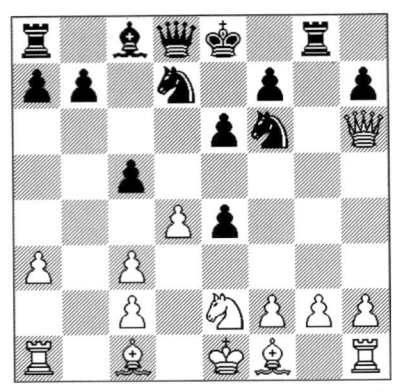

11.♕e3 ♘d5

Black already needs to look at compensation for his Pawn on e4 which is now close to being lost.

12.♕xe4 ♘xc3 13.♕d3 ♘d5

Also 13...cxd4 14.♕xd4 ♕f6 15.♕xf6 ♘xf6 16.♗d3 ♔g7 17.♗d2 etc. would not be satisfactory. In fact, Black's game after his reckless tenth move could hardly be saved.

14.♗e2 ♕f6 15.c3 cxd4 16.cxd4 ♘7b6

Exchanging Black's best-placed pieces with 16...♘f4 17.♗xf4 ♕xf4 18.0–0 would only make things easier for White.

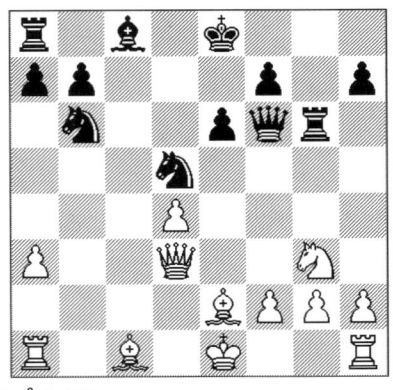

17.♗h5!

The Bishop's maneuver, consisting of four successive moves, forces a practically decisive weakening in the position of Black's Pawns. The following game on both wings is very instructive and, I believe, typical of my style.

17...♖g7 18.♗f3

Threatening 19.♘h5.

18...♕g6 19.♗e4! f5 20.♗f3 ♔f8 21.a4!

The diagonal a3–f8 is here the best path of activity for the Bishop.

21...♖c7 22.0–0 ♗d7 23.♗a3+ ♔g8 24.a5 ♖c3

This leads to the loss of a Pawn without any improvement in Black's position. But the apparently better move 24...♘c4 wouldn't save the day either. The continuation could be 25.♗c5! (stronger than 25.♘×f5 ♔h8! etc.) 25...♘e5 26.d×e5 ♖×c5 27.♖fc1 ♖ac8 28.♖×c5 ♖×c5 29.♕d4! winning at least the a-Pawn in an overwhelming position. The remaining part is - despite Black's desperate efforts to "nibble" something - quite easy.

25.♕b1! ♘a4 26.♗×d5 e×d5 27.♕×b7 ♕c6 28.a6!

If now 28...♕×b7 29.a×b7 ♔b8, then 30.♖fb1 ♘b6 31.♗b4 followed by ♖×a7, winning.

28...♘b6 29.♗c5 f4 30.♘f5!

More accurate than 30.♘e2, which would also be sufficient.

30...♔h8 31.♘e7 ♕e6 32.♗×b6 ♗c6

More despair.

33.♘×c6 ♖g8

Threatening perpetual check with 34...♗×g2+, etc.

34.♘e5! ♖g7 35.♕b8+?

In many games of this unfortunate game, I played very quickly after the decision had practically been reached - without, however, in this case, affecting the final result. Instead, 35.♗×a7! would have forced Black to resign immediately.

35...♖c8 36.♘g6+ ♖×g6 37.♕×f4 ♕×b6 38.♕e5+ ♖g7 39.♕×d5 ♖d8 40.♕e5 ♕×d4 41.♕×d4, and Black resigned.

Game 74
M.Euwe-A.Alekhine
World Championship (4), Hague
October 1935
King's Indian Defense [D81]

1.d4 ♘f6 2.c4 g6 3.♘c3 d5 4.♕b3

Practice over the last two to three years has proven that this queen move is less effective than 4.♗f4 ♗g7 5.e3 0–0 6.♕b3 c6 7.♘f3 etc., with an unquestionable space advantage.

4...d×c4 5.♕×c4 ♗g7

Also playable is 5...♗e6 6.♕b5+ ♘c6 7.♘f3, but not 7...♔b8 (as in Game 2 of the 1935 game), but 7...♘d5! etc., with reasonably good counter-chances.

6.♗f4 c6 7.♖d1?

An artificial and unnecessary move instead of the indicated 7.♘f3 0–0 8.e4, etc. Black can now get at least an equal game.

7...♕a5

Threatening 8...♗e6.

8.♗d2 b5?

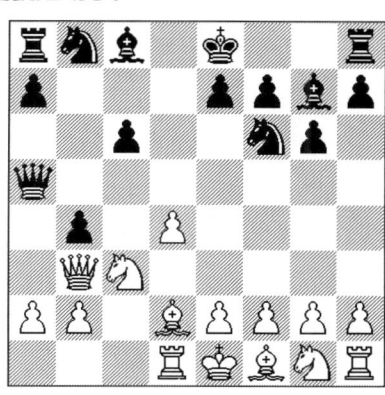

There are some moves of mine in the first game with Euwe that I really can't understand. Neither before nor since have I played such decidedly unstable chess, especially in the openings! Here, for example, the damage to the Pawn structure on the Queen wing cannot be excused even by the absence of other promising continuations. The simple 8...♕b6 9.♗c1 ♗f5 followed by ...0-0 would ensure a distinct development advantage for Black. I have, however, included the present game in this collection, despite the poor opening strategy of both sides - due to the particularly interesting tactical complications in the well-played middlegame.

9.♕b3 b4

The advantage is at least consistent. Black avoids e4 - but at what a price!

10.♘a4 ♘a6 11.e3 ♗e6

Black could also immediately play 11...0-0 12.♗xa6 ♗xa6 13.♕xb4 ♕d5 or 13.♗xb4 ♕b5 would be in his favor. But then they wouldn't like the answer 12.♗c4.

12.♕c2 0-0 13.b3

If instead 13.♕xc6 then 13...♘c7 with the threats 14...♗d7 or 14...♗xa2.

13...♖ab8 14.♗d3

Due to their slightly delayed development White decides not to take the c-pawn correctly. After 14.♕xc6 ♗c8! The open c-column would become a dangerous weapon in Black's hands - for example, 15.♘f3 ♗b7 16.♕c2 ♔fc8 17.♕b1 ♘d5 eventually followed by ...♘c3, etc.

14...♖fc8 15.♘e2

Obviously underestimating the value of the Pawn offer afterwards. Otherwise, White would continue with 15.♗xa6 ♕xa6 16.♘c5 ♕b5

17.♘f3! (but not 17.♘xe6 fxe6 followed by ...e5 etc., with good play for Black) 17...♘d7 18.♔c1 etc., with better prospects in the end. This possibility clearly proves the fragility of Black's 8th and 10th moves.

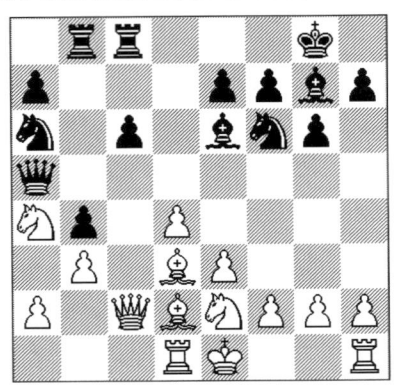

15...c5!

An absolutely correct combination that - against White's best defense - would easily give me equality. But in fact, my opponent, fortunately for me, underestimated the danger.

16.♗xa6 ♕xa6 17.♘xc5 ♕b5 18.♘f4?

Allowing Black to open the center and thus set fire to his opponent's square. The correct defense consisted of 18.e4! ♘d7 19.♗e3 ♗xd4 20.♘xd4 ♕xc5 21.♕xc5 ♘xc5 etc., with a probable draw as a result.

18...♗g4! 19.f3

If 19.♔c1 the reply 19...e5 would also be strong.

19...e5! 20.♘fd3

It would be equally unsatisfactory 20.fxg6 exf4 etc. with an advantage.

See the next Diagram

20...exd4!

A beautiful and well-calculated piece offer, which White is practically obliged to accept, as both 21.exd4

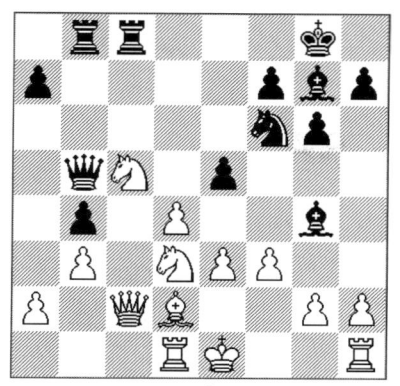

♘d5! and 21.e4 ♘d7 would leave them with even fewer chances of salvation.

21.fxg4 dxe3 22.♗xe3

A relatively more difficult variant for White would be 22.♗xb4 ♘d5 23.a3 a5 24.♕c4! axb4! 25.♕xd5 bxa3 26.♖f1 (or 26.b4 ♗c3+ followed by ...♗xb4) 26...a2 27.♖xf7 ♗c3+ 28.♔ moves ♖xf5, winning.

22...♘xg4 23.♗f4

Anything else would be equally unsatisfactory, for example: I. 23.♗g1 ♗c3+ 24.♔f1 ♖b6 etc.; II. 23.♗f2 ♗c3+ 24.♔f1 ♖c6! 25.♔g1 ♘xf2 26.♕xf2 ♖d8 etc., with a winning position.

23...♗c3+ 24.♖d2

Obviously forced.

24...♖xc5! 25.♘xc5

If 25.♗xb8 then 25...♕e8+ wins immediately.

25...♕xc5

Black finally has enough of all the complications and chooses the clearest variant, which assures him a slight material advantage (Queen and Pawn against two Rooks) with persistent attacking. A shorter path to victory, however, would be 25...♖e8+! with the following main variant: 26.♘e4 f5 27.♔d1 ♗xe4 28.♖d8+ ♔f7 29.♗g5 f4! 30.♔c1 ♖e2 31.♕d3 ♕xg5!, win-

ning.

26.♗xb8 ♕e7+ 27.♔d1 ♘e3+ 28.♔c1 ♘xc2 29.♖xc2 h5!

A necessary preparation for ...♗g7.

30.♖d1 ♗g7 31.h3 a5

Black's main trump cards - which used correctly guarantee victory - are (1) the permanent insecurity of White's King; (2) the unprotected position of the Bishop, whose efforts to find a safe home are on the verge of failure. The game remains vivid and instructive until almost the end.

32.♗f4 ♕e4 33.♗c7 ♕e3+ 34.♔b1 a4!

Through this rupture, which could not be avoided in the long term, the blacks are forcing at least a gain in quality.

35.bxa4 b3 36.axb3 ♕xb3+ 37.♔c1 ♗h6+ 38.♖dd2 ♕xa4 39.♗e5

Instead, 39.♔d1 would slightly prolong the game, as Black would have to first force White's King back to the Queen's wing through 39...♗xd2 40.♔xd2 ♕e4! 41.♔c1 ♕e1+ etc., and only after that decide the game on the other wing through the gradual advance of their Pawns supported by the King.

39...♔h7 40.♗c3 ♕b5!

Avoiding 41.♔d1.

41.♗d4

White has no more satisfactory moves. If, for example, 41.♗a1, then 41...♕f1+, followed by ...♗g7+, etc.

41...♕e2! 42.g4 ♕e1+ 43.♔b2 ♗xd2 44.♖c8 ♗c1+!, and White resigned.

155

Game 75
A.Alekhine-M.Euwe
World Championship (7), Utrecht
October 1935
French Defense [C15]

1.e4 e6 2.d4 d5 3.♘c3 ♗b4 4.♘ge2 d×e4 5.a3 ♗e7

Even more convincing is 5...♗×c3+ 6.♘×c3 ♘c6, with at least one equal game. This possibility practically refutes White's fourth move.

6.♘×e4 ♘c6

Here too the Knight move is quite good. In Game 5 of this game I tried 7.♗e3 here (if 7.c3 then 7...e5) but got nothing more after 7...♘f6 8.♘2c3 0-0 (already threatening ...♘×e4 followed by ...f5) than equality. So, I decided to try the following apparently paradoxical Pawn move in the present game, with the obvious idea of combining the development of the King's Bishop's pincer with a possible Pawn attack on the King's wing.

7.g4!? b6

This isn't even an attempt at refutation, and White will soon get the kind of position he wanted. It's true that the more natural answer 7...e5 wouldn't be convincing either, due to 8.d5 ♘d4 9.♘2c3 (but not 9.♘×d4 ♕×d5! with advantage) - and if 9...f5 then 10.g×f5 ♗×f5 11.♗e3 etc., with good fighting chances for White; but 7...♘f6! 8.♘×f6+ ♗×f6 9.♗e3 ♕d5 etc. would ensure that Black could comfortably develop all his forces, thus proving the inefficiency of White's 7th move.

8.♗g2 ♗b7 9.c3 ♘f6 10.♘2g3 0-0?

See the next Diagram

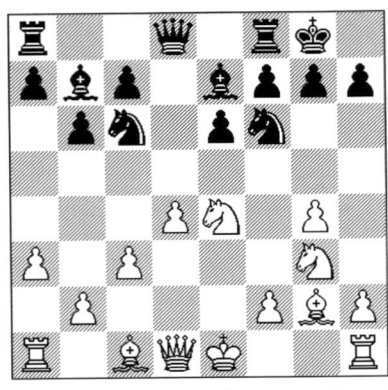

Even if they could prove it - Black could find an adequate defense against the attack on the King afterwards - the move in the text can still be condemned for endangering Black's game without any advantage or necessity. After the simple 10...♕d7 followed by ...0-0-0 White would remain with an unimportant space advantage, but without any real prospect of attacking.

11.g5 ♘×e4 12.♘×e4 ♔h8

Preparing for ...f5, which Black avoids with the next strong move.

13.♕h5!

If now 13...f5, then of course 14.g6 with deadly effect.

13...♕e8

Threatening again ...f5 but allowing the promising combination afterwards. In any case, 13...♘a5 14.b4 was safer, as the variant 14...♘b3 15.♘f6 g×f6 16.♗×b7 f5! etc. would not be dangerous for Black. In that case White would improve his pressure by finishing his development - 14.♗f4, followed eventually by 0-0-0, etc., with an advantage.

See the next Diagram

14.♘f6!

A correct Pawn offer, giving White a strong and probably irresistible offensive.

14...♗×f6

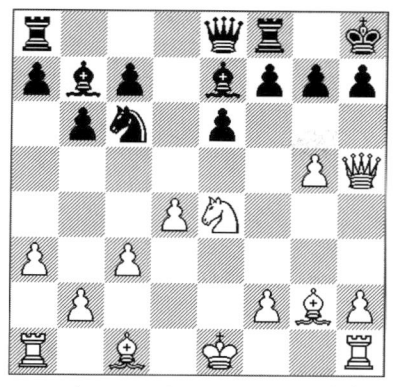

My Best Games 1924-1937

The alternative was 14...g×f6 15.g×f6 ♘a5 (if 15...♗×f6? then 16.♗e4 followed by mate) 16.f×e7 ♕×e7 17.♗×b7 ♘×b7 18.♗g5 f6 19.♗h6 ♖g8 20.0-0-0 ♘d6 21.♖hg1 etc., with a clear advantage for White.

15.g×f6 g×f6 16.♕h4 ♕d8

Forced, because 16...♕e7 would lose a piece after 17.♗e4! etc.

17.♗f4!

This continuation of the attack - the point of which is the removal of the Bishop in the next move - was by no means easy to find. Black's relatively better chance was to return the extra Pawn now by playing 17...f5 - although after 18.♕×d8 ♖a×d8 19.♗×c7 ♖d7 20.♗f4 ♘a5 21.♔g1! etc., White's advantage at the end of the game would be quite obvious.

17...e5 18.♗g3! f5

Now there's hardly anything better. If, for example, 18...exd4, then 19.0-0-0! etc., with an easy attacking game.

19.d×e5

Here too, 19.0-0-0 was strong. But the simple recovery of the sacrificed material is, considering the possibilities of White's powerful attack, quite convincing.

19...♖g8 20.♗f3?

But this inaccurate move allows Black to open up a saving counterattack. Instead, 20.♕h3 would be practically decisive, after which 20...♕d3 would be refuted by 21.♗h4! and 20...♔g4 by 21.0-0! threatening 22.f3 with material gain and persistence in the attack.

20...♕d3!

An ingenious resource. But as the sequence shows, the black women, by adopting it, didn't really imagine how many interesting possibilities opened for them.

21.♗e2

White has nothing better, as 21.♗×c6? would be fatal, due to 21...♗a6! 22.♕h5 ♔g4!, etc.

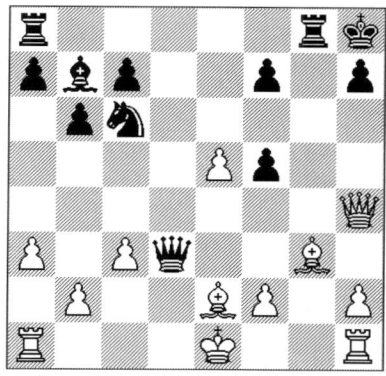

21...♕e4?

Leading to a lost ending. From an objective point of view, it's certainly a shame that Black avoided the fantastic complications arising from *21...♕c2!* - a move that through correct continuation would have secured them a draw. Here follows the main variant as well as some minor possibilities:

22.♕f6+ ♖g7 23.♖g1! (a) *♕×b2 24.e6!! ♕×a1+ 25.♗d1 ♘d4!!* (b) *26.♕×g7+!* (c) *♔×g7 27.♗h4+ ♔h6!* (d) *28.♗g5+ ♔ move 29.♗h4+, etc.* draw by perpetual check.

(a) The plausible 23.e6 due to 23...♖e8! 24.♖g1! ♗a6!! (24...♖×e6

157

25.♗e5! winning) 25.♗×a6 ♖×e6+ 26.♗e5 ♕e4+ 27.♔f1 ♕×e5 etc., with Black's advantage.

(b) But not 25...♖d8 or 25...♕b1 because of 26.♗d6!! with White winning.

(c) There is no chance of victory for White through the continuation 26.♕×d4 f6! 27.♕×f6 ♗f3 28.♔d2 ♕a2+ 29.♔c2 ♗e4 etc.

(d) Instead, 27...♔f8 loses: 28.e7+ ♔e8 29.♖g8+ ♔d7 30.♖d8+ winning.

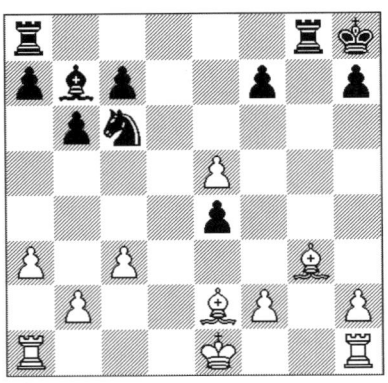

22.♕×e4 f×e4

23.♗h4!

The winning move, probably not seen by Black when he played 21...♕e4. After 23.0–0–0 they would get excellent drawing chances by continuing 23...♔×g3! 24.h×g3 ♘×e5 etc.

23...h6 24.0–0–0 ♖ae8 25.♗f6+ ♔h7 26.f4 e×f3 27.♗×f3

Of course, much stronger than winning the quality by a Pawn through 27.♗d3+ etc. The white Bishops now dominate the board and Black is unable to avoid the intrusion of the hostile Rook on the seventh rank.

27...♘a5

The change of Bishops, which would probably have saved the battle at the start of the half, brings no relief at this stage of the game.

28.♗×b7 ♘×b7 29.♖d7

The start of the execution.

29...♘c5 30.♖×f7+ ♔g6 31.♖×c7 ♘d3+ 32.♔b1

The simple 32.♔c2 was also quite good.

32...♔f5 33.♖d1 ♘×e5 34.♖f1+ ♔e4 35.♖×a7 ♘c4

Or 35...♘f3 36.♖a4+ ♔e3 37.♗d4+ etc. Black's game is totally hopeless.

36.♖d7 ♔e3 37.♖e1+ ♔f3 38.♖×e8 ♖×e8 39.♖d4 ♘e3 40.♖h4, and Black resigned.

Game 76
A.Alekhine–M.Euwe
World Championship (27), Hague
December 1935
Viennese Opening [C27]

1.e4 e5 2.♘c3 ♘f6 3.♗c4 ♘×e4 4.♕h5 ♘d6 5.♗b3

Instead 5.♕×e5+ ♕e7 etc. would lead to a perfectly equal game. Being obliged to play for a win at any price, I decided to allow my opponent to make the offer of an exchange, which for about 30 years has been known to give Black excellent attacking chances. It goes like this: 5...♘c6! 6.♘b5 g6 7.♕f3 f5 8.♕d5 ♕f6 9.♘×c7+ ♔d8 10.♘×a8 b6 (or 10...♕g5) followed by ...♗b7, after which they would have to suffer, a little at least. However, from a psychological point of view, it's easy to understand that with two points ahead Euwe didn't want to take this chance.

5...♗e7 6.♘f3 ♘c6

Instead, 6...0–0 would be slightly premature due to the possibility of 7.h4.

7.♘×e5 ♘×e5?

An instructive opening blunder.

Black underestimated the potential power of his opponent's King's Bishop which could be eliminated after 7...0-0 8.♘d5 ♘d4! 9.0-0 ♘xb3 10.axb3 ♘e8 etc., with roughly the same prospects. After the text move, White manages to avoid the normal development of Black's queenside for a long time and maintains a gradual increase in pressure.

8.♕xe5 0-0

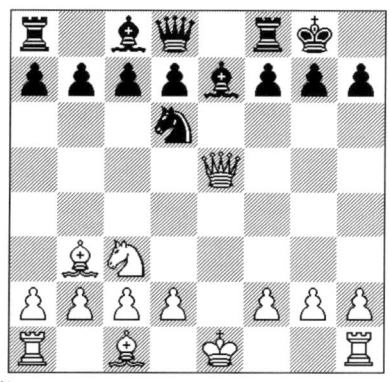

9.♘d5!

It was important to avoid 9...♗f6.

9...♖e8 10.0-0 ♗f8 11.♕f4 c6

Since Black couldn't play ...d5, this move doesn't make things any easier for him. Instead, 11...b6 deserves consideration, as 12.♘xc7 (12...♕xc7? 13.♗xf7+ with advantage) would be a blunder due to 12...♖e4!.

12.♘e3 ♕a5 13.d4

Mainly to prevent 13...♕e5. That Black has temporary control of the e4 square is relatively unimportant.

13...♕h5

Of course, not 13...♖e4 due to 14.♗xf7+, etc.

14.c3 ♘e4

If 14...♘b5, then 15.a4 ♗d6 16.♕xf7+ ♕xf7 17.♗xf7+ followed by axb5 etc., with advantage.

See the next Diagram

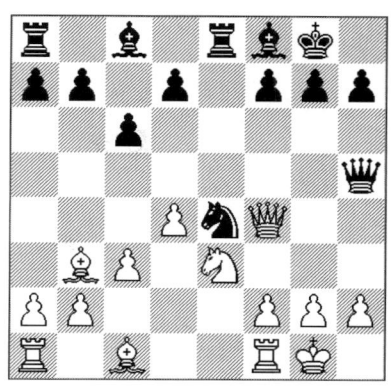

15.f3!

Through this important intermediate move, White practically forces the isolation of Black's Pawn and thus obtains an appreciable advantage in the endgame.

15...♘g5

There is nothing better. If, for example, 15...♗d6, then 16.♕xf7+! etc., finally winning the Pawn, and if 15...♘f6 16.♘g4! etc., also with a strong advantage.

16.d5!

Threatening, of course, 17.h4.

16...cxd5 17.♘xd5 ♘e6 18.♕g4

The apparently more energetic move 18.♕g3 ♕g6 19.f4 would in fact not be so clear, due to 19...♗c5+ 20.♔h1 ♕xg3 21.hxg3 ♖b8 22.f5 ♘f8, etc.

18...♕g6 19.♗e3 b6 20.♖ad1 ♗b7 21.♕xg6

After all, White's forces were mobilized in time to turn the battle into an endgame in which Black's pawn weaknesses will become more apparent than they are at the moment.

21...hxg6 22.♖fe1 ♖ac8 23.♔f2 ♗c5

What else? If, for example, 23...♘c5, then 24.♗c2 followed by the Rook doubling against Black's weakness on d7.

24.♗xc5 ♗xd5

If 24...bxc5 then 25.♘e3 followed by ♘–c4–d6 etc., with a big advantage. But 24...♔xc5 would probably allow more stubborn resistance.

25.♗xd5 ♘xc5 26.♖xe8+ ♖xe8 27.b4!

The point of the previous exchanges. White, correctly, considered that in the endgame of the following Rooks his majority of Pawns on the Queen's wing, supported by the King and strengthened by the fact that the enemy King is completely out of the game, will become decisive. Black obviously can't avoid exchanging his minor pieces as 27...♘a4 28.♗b3 followed by ♔xd7 would be hopeless.

27...♘e6 28.♗xe6 dxe6 29.♖d7

After 29.c4 ♔c8 30.♔c1 ♔f8 etc., White's advantage wouldn't be decisive.

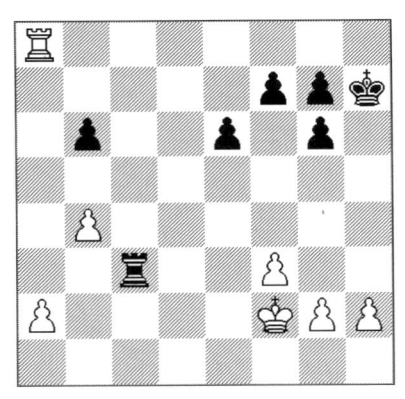

29...♖c8 30.♖xa7 ♖xc3 31.♖a8+ ♔h7

32.a4?

This rather obvious blunder in a technically winning position has not - as far as I know - been reported by any of the eminent critics who have devoted many pages to analyzing the possibilities offered by this ending. The main disadvantage of the text's move is that it leaves squares a3 and b3 free for Black's rook, which from now on can only be moved from the third row at the cost of valuable time. It was correct - and quite simple - *32.♔e2!*, after which Black's rook could (1) be dragged into a purely passive position - as in the current game - after 33.♔d2, etc.; (2) or forced to immediately launch the counterattack 32...♔c2+ with the result 33.♔d3 ♔xg2 34.♔c4! – and you don't need to count the *tempi* to imagine that the passed Pawns, if necessary with the support of the King, will be faster by far. The fact that I lost this simple win, deserved for the previous difficult positional play, proves once again how bad I was in 1935. In the second game, fortunately, I took the advantage on such occasions regularly and without hesitation (compare, for example, King's analogous maneuver connected with the offer of the whole Queen's wing in Game 2 of the 1937 game - *Game 97*).

32...♖b3

It would be hopeless 32...♔c2+ 33.♔e3 followed by the King's march to the Queen's wing. But after 32...e5! (certainly, a difficult move to find in practice in a game) there is, according to several Soviet masters - supported by Dr. Lasker - no forced win for White. Even if that were the case (some of the variants are by no means convincing), it would only prove that White's earlier move was a bigger omission than it really appeared to be. But for the general appreciation of the *characteristic* Torres ending arrived at after Black's 28th move, all these analyses are of no importance.

33.b5 g5 34.♔e2

Due to Black's loss of time on his 32nd move, King's trip will be successful even now.

34...e5 35.♔d2 f6 36.♔c2 ♖b4 37.♔c3 ♖d4

Black managed to avoid the formation of *two* passed Pawns, but to his misfortune, *a* Pawn supported by the King is amply sufficient!

38.♖a6 ♔g6 39.♖×b6 ♖×a4 40.♖a6 ♖d4 41.b6, and Black resigned.

Game 77
C.Ahues-A.Alekhine
Bad Nauheim, May 1936
Queen's Gambit Accepted [D24]

1.d4 d5 2.c4 d×c4 3.♘f3 a6

This move, in connection with the next one, was introduced by me in Game 3 of the game with Bogoljubov in 1934. Even if it can be convincingly proved (which it hasn't yet) that the development of the Bishop on g4 isn't good for Black, the move in the text will still be used by those who prefer to avoid the variants started with ♕a4 by White.

4.a4

White has no reason to avoid ...b5, as the variant 4.e3 b5 5.a4 ♗b7 6.a×b5 a×b5 7.♖×a8 ♗×a8 8.b3 is to their advantage. In addition, the text's move wastes time, also weakening Black's b5 square, and should therefore be definitively condemned. The following two positional struggles can give an idea of Black's possibilities after 4.e3 ♗b4. The characteristic of the resulting conflict depends on whether White leaves the Pawn structure in the center intact (as in I) or tries to solve the central problem in a dynamic way (as in II).

I. White: E. Zinner (Podebrad 1936): 4.e3 ♗g4 5.♗×c4 e6 6.h3 ♗h5 7.♕b3 (or 7...♗×f3 8.g×f3 b5) 7...♖a7 8.a4 ♘c6 9.♗d2 ♘f6 10.♗c3 ♘d5 11.♘bd2 ♘×c3 12.b×c3 ♘a5 13.♕a2 ♘×c4 14.♕×c4 ♗d6 15.♖b1 0-0 16.0-0 ♗g6 17.♖b2 c6 18.♕b3 b5 19.c4 ♖b7 20.♖a1 ♖b8 21.♖aa2 ♗c7 22.♕d1 ♗d3! 23.c×b5 c×b5 24.♘e1 ♗g6 25.♕e2 ♕d6 26.♘df3! b4 27.♘d3 ♗e4 28.♘c5 ♗d5 29.♘b3 ♖fc8 30.♖a1 a5 31.♖c1 ♗b6 32.♖bc2 ♖×c2 33.♕×c2 ♕d7 34.e4 ♗×b3 35.♕×b3 ♖c8 36.♖c4 ♖×c4 37.♕×c4 h6 38.d5 ♕×a4 39.♕c8+ ♔h7 40.♕b7 ♗d8! 41.♕×f7 ♕a1+ 42.♔h2 ♕f6 43.♕d7 b3 44.h4 b2 45.♕b5 e×d5, and White resigned.

II. White: Axelsson (Orebro, 1935) (the first five moves as in the previous game): 6.0-0 ♘f6 7.h3 ♗h5 8.♘c3 ♘c6 9.♗e2 ♗d6 10.b3 (better than 10.a3 played in an analogous position by Bogoljubov in the game mentioned above) 10...0-0 11.♗b2 ♕e7 12.e4 ♗×f3 13.♗×f3 ♖ad8 14.♘e2 ♗c5 15.♕c2 ♗b6 16.♖ac1 e5 17.d5 ♘b4 18.♗a3! a5 19.♕c4 ♘e8 20.♖fd1 ♕h4! 21.♗×b4 ♕×f2+ 22.♔h2 a×b4 23.♕×b4 ♘d6 24.a4 ♖a8 25.♖f1 ♕h4 26.♕d2 g6! 27.g3 ♕e7 28.♘c3 f5 29.e×f5 g×f5 30.♖ce1 ♕g7 31.b4 e4 32.♗d1 ♘c4 33.♕c1 ♘e5 34.♗e2 c6! 35.d×c6 b×c6 36.♖d1 ♔h8 37.a5 ♖g8 38.♕f4 ♗c7 39.♕f2 ♘d3!, and White resigned.

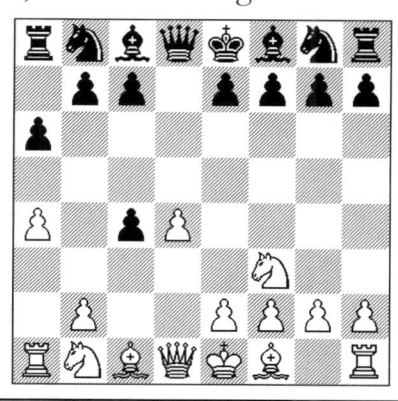

4...♘f6 5.e3 ♗g4 6.♗×c4 e6 7.♘c3 ♘c6

As you can see from the games above, this development of the knight belongs to the system inaugurated with ...♗g4. In this particular position, it's more appropriate than ever for Black to have the b4 square at his disposal, if necessary.

8.♗e2 ♗b4 9.0–0 0–0 10.♘d2

White is too eager to simplify and allow, to his disadvantage, the Pawn and Black to advance next. The quieter 10.♗d2 would probably give them more chances of equalizing.

10...♗×e2 11.♘×e2 e5!

Since the opening of the central columns through d×e5 here or in the next moves would obviously be favorable to the more developed side, White is practically obliged to allow a later advance of this Pawn, after which the activity of his Bishop will be limited to a minimum.

12.♘f3 ♖e8 13.♗d2 ♗d6

Exchanging the opponent's poorest piece would, of course, be a serious strategic error.

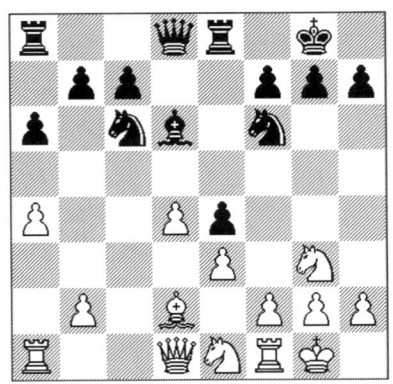

14.♘g3 e4 15.♘e1

15...♗×g3!

After this exchange, the immobilized mass of Pawns on the King's wing will be unable in the long term to prevent the formation of ...♘g4 and ...♕f5 (or a5). The small counter-demonstration that White will now launch on the open c-file can be stopped without effort or wasting time.

16.h×g3 ♘e7

Total control over the d5 square is the key to the situation.

17.b4 ♕d7 18.♘c2 ♘ed5 19.♘a3 b5!

Restricting the mobility of the hostile knight.

20.a×b5 a×b5 21.♕e2 c6

That Pawn could eventually become weak - Black hadn't yet prepared a plan for an irresistible mate attack!

22.♘c2 ♕f5

White can't even respond to this move with f3 - with his knight unprotected - and he has nothing better to do than prepare a desperate escape from the king.

23.♖fc1 h6

A useful precaution - especially as white has very little choice of moves.

24.♖a5 ♖ac8 25.♘a1

The Knight dreams of reaching a more suitable home (c5), but it's too late!

25...♘g4

With the strong threat 26...♕h5.

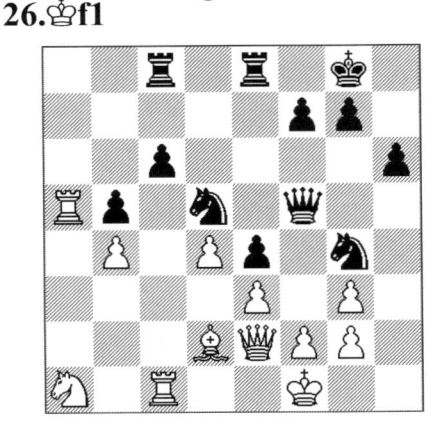

26.♔f1

26...♖e6!

A stratagem like that of the game in Dresden against Bogoljubov (*Game 79*): Black gives up a useless unit to win the f-Pawn and thus strip the enemy King.

27.♖×b5 ♖f6 28.♖bc5 ♘×f2 29.♔e1

Or 29.♔g1 ♘g4 followed by ...♕h5 and mate.

29...♘d3+ 30.♔d1 ♕f1+ 31.♗e1 ♖f2!

Waiting for 32.♕×f1, after which I had a nice choice between mate with the knight on b2 and e3. White resigned.

Game 78
A.Alekhine–E.Bogoljubov
Bad Nauheim, May 1936
Cambridge Springs Defense [D52]

1.d4 e6 2.c4 ♘f6 3.♘f3 d5 4.♘c3 c6 5.♗g5 ♘bd7 6.e3 ♕a5 7.♘d2

The most logical response to Black's 6th move, to reduce his chances on the a4–e8 diagonal to a minimum.

7...♗b4 8.♕c2 d×c4

Obtaining the pair of Bishops, however, is hardly sufficient compensation for abandoning the center. The older 8...0–0 in conjunction with ...♘g4 is relatively more promising.

9.♗×f6 ♘×f6 10.♘×c4 ♕c7 11.g3 0–0

11...c5 would be useless due to 12.♗g2, after which 12...c×d4 would be answered with 13.♕a4+.

12.♗g2 ♗d7

Here too 12...c5 would lead nowhere after 13.0–0 c×d4 14.♘b5, etc. But after the text move, White must consider the possible advance of the c-Pawn, which explains his next two moves.

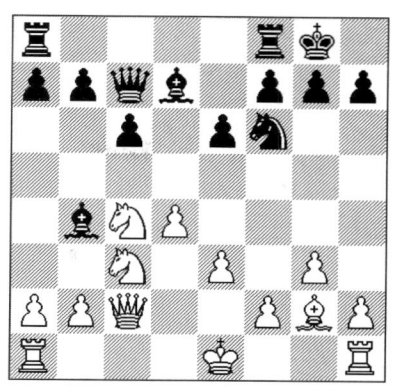

13.a3 ♗e7 14.b4 ♘d5 15.0–0

It also takes into account 15.♘e4, but I estimated that White's advantage after the exchange of the knights would be quite convincing and so there was no need to try to complicate things by avoiding it.

15...♘×c3 16.♕×c3 ♖fd8 17.♖ac1

The correct use of the pair of rooks in the semi-open columns often presents very difficult problems. Here, for example, it's obvious that *a* Rook should be placed on the c column to make the realization of ...c5 even more difficult, but where to develop the other Rook - on b1 or d1? As the reader will see, I didn't choose the most effective method here, thus allowing my opponent to have an even game for a moment. The correct scheme was ♖c1 and ♖b1.

17...♗e8 18.♖fd1 ♖ac8 19.♘a5

Trying to provoke Black's next move by threatening b5. But even more important would be 19.♖b1! b6 20.♖dc1, avoiding the liberating ...c5.

19...a6 20.♘c4 b6 21.♖b1

Too late!

21...♗f6

Black is still preparing ...f5, not imagining that he could - and should - play it straight away. White would have no advantage either in I. 21...c5

22.♘xb6?! cxb4! 23.♕xc7 ♖xc7 24.axb4 ♖b8 25.♘a8 ♖cb7 or in II. 22.bxc5 bxc5 23.♖b7 cxd4 24.♖xd4 ♗xd4 25.♖xc7 ♖d1+ followed by ♖xc7, with an advantage. White would have nothing better than 22.bxc5 bxc5 23.d5! exd5 24.♗xd5 ♗a4 25.♖d3 ♗f6 26.♕d2 ♗b5 etc., with a draw in prospect due to the oppositely colored bishops. Now White can take full advantage of his opportunity.

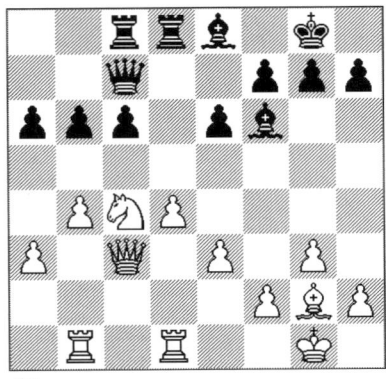

22.♖dc1

It protects the knight once again, to make it possible, after 22...f5?, to move 23.bxc5 bxc5 24.♖b7, etc.

22...♕a7 23.♕c2!

Avoiding ...f5 and threatening to advance the Pawn a to win the square b6 for the Knight.

23...♖c7 24.a4 ♗e7

Or 24...c5 25.a5!, etc.

25.a5 bxa5 26.bxa5 c5

Now this move no longer has any effect, as White's pieces have meanwhile taken control of the command points. It's instructive to see how little the famous "pair of Bishops" has to say here, mainly due to the earlier inaccurate handling of the heavy pieces.

27.♘b6 ♗b5 28.d5 exd5

See the next Diagram

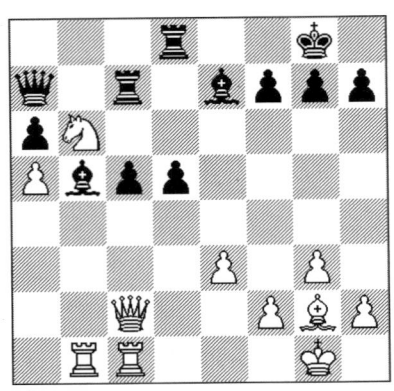

29.♗xd5!

Much stronger than 29.♘xd5, due to the fact that the Bishop will be very useful on c4 to block the passed Pawn.

29...♗f8 30.♖d1 ♖d6 31.♗c4

At the same time, White takes control of the open column, his powerful Knight preventing Black's Queen and Rook from freely maneuvering. The second player deservedly pays the penalty for the short-term vision of his 21st move.

31...♖xd1+ 32.♖xd1 ♕b8 33.♕d3 ♕e8 34.♕d8

From now on, simplicity is an asset!

34...♖e7 35.♕xe8 ♗xe8

After 35...♔xe8 there would be a sharp and quick win: 36.♗xb5 axb5 37.a6 c4 38.a7 c3 39.♖d7! ♗c5 40.a8♕ ♖xa8 41.♘xa8 followed by 42.♖d8+ and 43.♖c8.

36.♖d8 ♗c6

See the next Diagram

37.♗xa6

The first material gain is absolutely decisive, as Black can't even seek compensation with 37...♖a7 due to 38.♘c8! etc. Despite the inaccuracy of moves 17 and 19, the game is a pretty good illustration of the Cambridge Springs Defense with

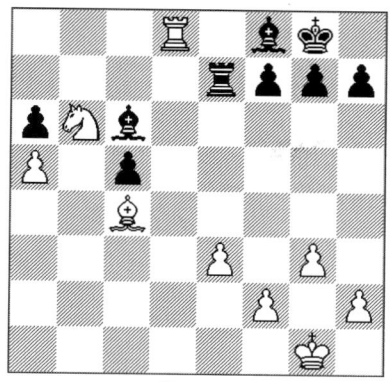

White's move 7.♘d2.

37...g6 38.♗c4 ♖b7 39.♔f1 ♗g7 40.♔e2 ♗e7 41.♖c8 ♗g2 42.f3 h5 43.e4 ♗h3 44.♖e8 ♗f8 45.a6 ♖c7 46.e5!

Preventing ...♗d6 and now threatening 47.♔b8 followed by ♔b7, etc.

46...♗d7 47.♘xd7 ♖xd7 48.♖b8, and Black resigned.

> **Game 79**
> **A.Alekhine-E.Bogoljubov**
> *Dresden Tournament, May 1936*
> Three Knights Opening [C46]

1.e4 e5 2.♘f3 ♘c6 3.♘c3 g6

Playing at his best Bogoljubov would hardly have chosen such an obviously inferior defense - since he knew very well how to play the Four Knights Opening with Black (see, for example, his game against Maróczy, London 1922).

4.d4 exd4 5.♘d5 ♗g7 6.♗g5 ♘ce7

This seemingly unnatural move is almost the only one, because after 5...f6 6.♗f4 d6 the a2–g8 diagonal would become a fatal weakness.

7.e5

White has the choice between this only in appearance aggressive move - which in fact leads to a favorable ending - and the simple 7.♘xd4, with excellent possibilities in the middlegame after 7...f6 8.♘xe7 ♘xe7 9.♕d2 followed by 0-0-0, etc. Possibly this path would be the most logical.

7...h6!

Otherwise 8.♘f6+ would be too strong.

8.♗xe7

The sacrifice of a Pawn through 8.♗f6 ♗xf6 9.♘xf6+ ♘xf6 10.exf6 ♘g8 followed by ...♕xf6 wouldn't be worth it.

8...♘xe7 9.♕xd4 ♘xd5 10.♕xd5

White's advantage in space is becoming alarming, so Black must try to exchange queens as quickly as possible to avoid an uncontested attack on the king.

10...c6

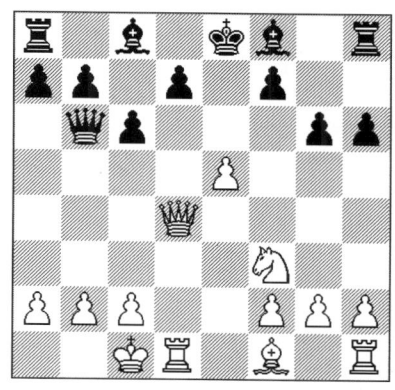

If 10...d6, then 11.0-0-0 ♗e6 12.♕b5+ etc., with advantage.

11.♕d6 ♗f8 12.♕d4 ♕b6 13.0-0-0!

By offering their Pawn f, White gains important development time. Black rightly refuses this offer, as after 13...♗c5 14.♕c3 ♗xf2 15.♘d4! his position would quickly be shattered.

13...♕xd4 14.♘xd4

An interesting and difficult moment. White decided not to avoid the opening of the center followed by the emancipation of the Bishop, with the right to expect appreciable advantages for the two central columns dominated by his Rooks. The consequences of the alternative 14.♖xd4 ♗e7 15.♖e4 b5 followed by ...♗b7 and ...0-0-0 are, to say the least, not obvious, especially since it could be Black who takes the initiative by opening the position.

14...d5

It was almost forced, as White threatened ♙-f4-f5 in addition to other mischief.

15.exd6 ♗xd6 16.♗c4 0-0 17.♖he1

The white pieces are beautifully positioned while Black's queen bishop is still looking for a suitable home. The next excursion is the best proof of the difficulties he must deal with.

17...♗g4 18.f3 ♗c8 19.g3

Holding f4 and now threatening 20.♘xc6.

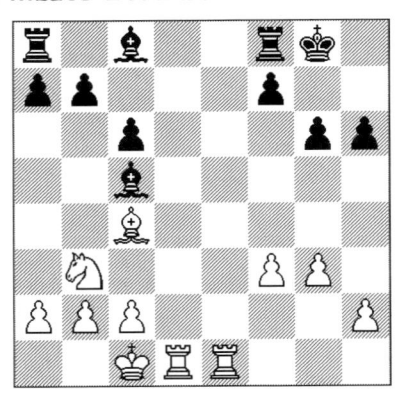

19...♗c5 20.♘b3

The start of an interesting move by the knight to strengthen the pressure against the g5 square. Also good was 20.g4 followed by h4(5), etc.

20...♗b6 21.♘d2

If 21.♖e7, then 21...♔g7 eventually followed by ...♔f6.

21...♗h3 22.♘e4 ♗a5

To save the b Pawn with ...b5.

23.c3 ♖ad8 24.♘d6

If 24.♔xd8 the answer could not be 24...♗xd8 25.♘f2! followed by ♖e7 with advantage, but 24...♗xd8 25.♘d6 b5 26.♗b3 ♗f6 etc., with equality.

24...b5 25.♗b3 ♖d7

He's protecting all the vulnerable points for the time being. It can be admitted that, after his extravagant opening, Bogoljubov defended his position very carefully and still has a fighting chance.

26.♘e8

A solid alternative would be 26.♘e4 ♖xd1+ 27.♔xd1 ♔g7, although Black would still have a temporary defense through ...♔g7, etc. The maneuver in the text relates to a temporary sacrifice of a Pawn leading, with the best defense, finally to the capture of Black's f-Pawn.

26...♖xd1+ 27.♔xd1 ♗g2

This counterstroke is Black's best chance. After, for example, 27...♗d8, White would increase the pressure without too much trouble with 28.♘d6 ♗f6 29.♔e2, etc.

28.♘f6+

White imagines that Black's king will finally be no better on h8 than on g8, so he takes the opportunity to gain time on the clock. If Black, in his 28th move, had played ...♔g8, I would have wanted to continue as in 29...♔h8 30.♔c2 ♗xf3 31.♘d7, leading to the variants examined below.

28...♔g7 29.♘e8+ ♔h8 30.♔c2! ♗xf3 31.♘d6 ♗d5?

See the next Diagram

After Black's hitherto stubborn

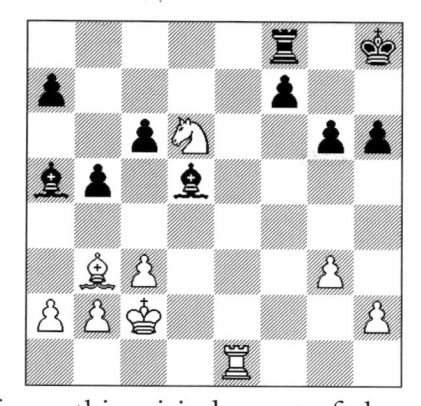

defense, this misjudgment of the position seems unbelievable, since after the exchanges White gets: (1) The elimination of Black's pair of Bishops; (2) The majority of Pawns on the Queen's wing; (3) The central square d4 for his Knight; (4) Play against the isolated Pawn d; (5) The possibility of Rook penetration via d7 or d8. Each of these considerations taken separately should dissuade Bogoljubov from choosing the move in the text, and in fact he could set his opponent some not-so-easy tasks by playing 31...♔g7. My intention was to continue with 32.♖e7 and, if 32...♗b6 (the best), then 33.♗xf7 ♗c5 34.♗b3+ ♔h8 35.♘f7+ ♔g7 (but not 35...♔h7 36.♘g5+, followed by mate) 36.♗b7! ♗e4+ 37.♔d1 ♔f6 38.♘xh6 ♖d8+ 39.♔e2 and Black wouldn't find enough compensation for the Pawn less. Still, now there would be a kind of fight that merely resembles one executed with precision by a butcher!

32.♗xd5 cxd5 33.♘xb5 ♗b6 34.♔d3 ♔g7 35.b4

Now white's game continues its own.

35...♖d8 36.a4 a6 37.♘d4 ♖d6 38.♖e8 h5

If instead ...♔f6, White would play a5 first.

39.♖a8 ♖f6

A hopeless trap. Anything else is just as hopeless.

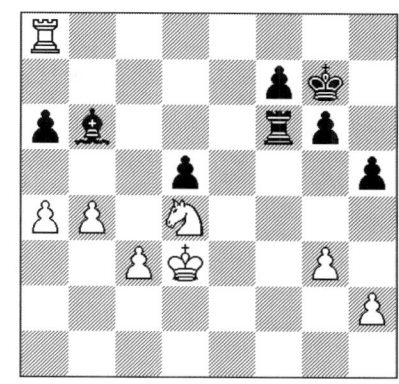

40.♖xa6!

White walks into the trap and proves that this is the quickest way to win!

40...♗xd4 41.♖xf6 ♗xf6 42.a5

The extra Bishop is unable to stop the two passed Pawns. If, for example, 42...♗d8, then simply 43.♔d4, followed by ♔xd5, ♔c6, etc.

42...♗e5 43.b5! h4

Or 43...♗c7 44.b6 ♗d8 45.♔d4, etc.

44.a6

Resolving the issue, because 44...hxg3 would be answered by 45.hxg3 and if 45...♗xg3 then 46.a7. Black resigned.

Game 80
A.Alekhine–E.Eliskases
Podebrad Tournament, June 1936
Spanish Opening [C90]

1.e4 e5 2.♘f3 ♘c6 3.♗b5 a6 4.♗a4 ♘f6 5.0–0 ♗e7 6.♖e1 b5 7.♗b3 d6 8.c3 ♘a5 9.♗c2 c5 10.d3

See the next Diagram

167

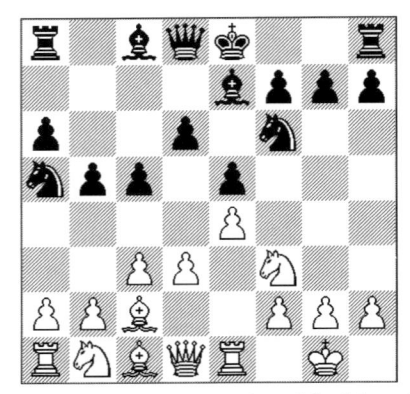

It's more usual to play **10.d4**, which allows White - if he wants - to block the position in the center with d5 to start a not very promising attack on the King's wing. The aim of the move in the text is first to finish off the development on the queen's wing and only after that to play d4 - when, or if, it seems appropriate.

10...♘c6 11.♘bd2 0-0 12.♘f1 ♖e8

Quite an acceptable plan - if it was conceived solely for defensive purposes. Another plausible way to finish the development without too many inconveniences was 12...♗e6 13.♘g3 h6 followed by ...♕c7 and ...♖ad8.

13.♘e3 d5?

A typical mistake: Black is in a hurry to "punish" White for having delayed d4, and starts a central operation himself - but, as will be shown shortly, at a very unfortunate moment. It was logical to 13...♗f8, especially since 14.♘d5 wouldn't then be fearsome: 14...♘xd5 15.exd5 ♘e7 16.d4 exd4 17.cxd4 c4! etc. In this case, the chances would be roughly the same.

14.exd5 ♘xd5 15.♘xd5 ♕xd5 16.d4!

The rebuttal: White opens the position in the center at the moment when his opponent hasn't finished his development and, in this way, manages to take full advantage of the various insufficiently protected points (Knight on c6 the first) in Black's territory.

16...exd4 17.♗e4 ♕d7

Or 17...♕d6 18.♗f4.

18.cxd4 ♗f6

Otherwise, the Pawn's subsequent advance in the center would prove devastating - for example, 18...♗b7 19.d5 ♘d8 20.♘g5 ♕d6 21.♗f4 etc., with all the positional trumps in hand.

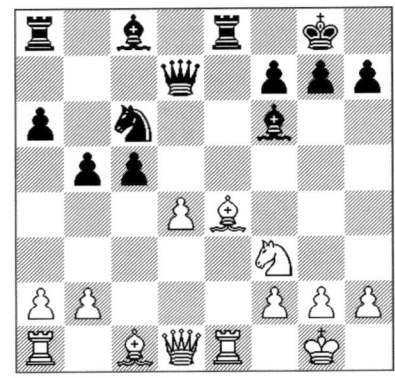

19.♗g5!

The main idea of this move is shown through this small variant: 19...♗xd4 20.♗f5! ♔xe1+ 21.♕xe1 ♕d6 22.♕e8+ ♕f8 23.♗xh7 winning the queen; and since 19...♗xg5 20.♘xg5 g6 21.dxc5 leads to a hopelessly lost ending, Black, *nolens volens*, must try the quality sacrifice next.

19...♖xe4! 20.♖xe4 ♗xd4 21.♘xd4 ♘xd4

If Black had found time to finish the development on the queen's wing, White's slight material advantage would have been very difficult to exploit. White would then need to act with extreme energy.

22.♕h5!

The point of this rather difficult attacking move can be seen in the continuation: 22...♗b7 23.♖h4! ♕f5

23...h6 24.♗×h6 ♘f5 25.♗×g7! and Black is mate in two if 25...♔×g7.

22...♗b7

Also 22...♕c6 23.♖ae1 ♗e6 24.♖h4 ♗f5 25.♗e7! would not prove sufficient.

23.♖h4 ♕f5

Since 23...h7 loses immediately (cf. comment above), Black has no choice.

24.♗e3!

Another surprising point of the attacking maneuver: White forces the exchange of the queens and at the same time dislodges the knight from its strong central position. After the "normal" moves, 24...♕×h5 25.♖×h5 ♘c2 26.♖d1 ♘×e3 27.f×e3 c4 28.♖c5 followed by 29.♖d7 the ending would be won very easily. In this way, Black's next blunder only makes the agony shorter.

24...♖d8? 25.♖×d4, and Black resigned.

Game 81
A.Alekhine-P.Frydman
Podebrad Tournament, June 1936
Sicilian Defense [B63]

1.e4 c5 2.♘f3 ♘c6 3.d4 c×d4 4.♘×d4 ♘f6 5.♘c3 d6 6.♗g5

The idea of this move is to eliminate the possibility of ...g6 and ...♗g7 (the Dragon Variant) and practically forces Black to adopt the so-called Scheveningen Variant, one of the characteristics of which is the exposure - albeit perfectly defensible - of the d Pawn on the open column. White would be mistaken, however, to think that from now on they can count on a serious advantage in the opening. For my part, despite 100% success with the text move, I'm very far from that illusion.

6...e6 7.♘b3

This harmless retreat, typical of many variants of the Sicilian, contains - as this game, among others, shows - more poison than you might think. For 7.♗b5, see my game against Foltys in Margate (*Game 92*).

7...♗e7 8.♕d2

This attempt to reinforce the pressure against d6 can be answered with 8...g6! and - only after 9.♗h4 - ...0–0, with the threat of 10...♘×e4, easily equalizing. White could then play 9.♗e3 (instead of 9.♗h4), but in any case Black doesn't need to worry about his d-Pawn at the moment.

8...0–0?

Strangely enough, this plausible answer is already a decisive mistake, and from now on the black women will only have the choice between different evils.

9.0–0–0

Threatening 10.♗×f6 ♗×f6 (10...g×f6 would allow a winning attack on the King, starting with 11.♕h6) 11.♕×d6, etc. This way, Black doesn't even have time for the preventative ...a6 or the simplifying ...h6.

9...♘a5

Hoping, after 10.♗×f6 ♘×b3+ 11.a×b3 ♗×f6 12.♕×d6, to get a counterattack through 12...♕a5 etc. But White's strong next move stops this plan.

See the next Diagram

10.♔b1! ♘×b3 11.a×b3

The point of the 10th move is that Black can no longer play 11...♕a5 due to 12.♘d5 and likewise 11...♕b6 would lead to a quick collapse after 12.♗×f6 ♗×f6 13.♕×d6 ♕×f2 14.e5

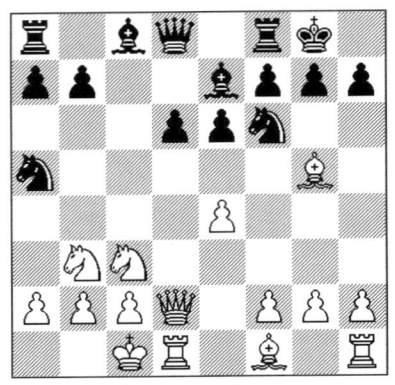

♗g5 15.h4! ♗f4 16.♗b5! threatening 17.♕xf8+ with mate in two. His next move is the only way which, if it doesn't save the day, at least prolongs the struggle.
11...♘e8 12.♗xe7 ♕xe7 13.♘b5 ♗d7
Expecting, not without reason, that White's doubled pawns will cause them some technical problems in the search for the winning procedure.
14.♘xd6 ♘xd6 15.♕xd6 ♕xd6 16.♖xd6 ♗c6 17.f3 ♖fd8 18.♖xd8+ ♖xd8 19.♗d3
The following endgame is highly instructive. First, White wants to take full advantage of the trumps he already has: the open column a and especially the domination of point a5.
19...e5
Gaining some space in the center and eventually using the Rook in the 3rd row.
20.♔c1 ♔f8 21.♔d2 ♔e7 22.♖a1 a6 23.♔e3 ♖d6 24.♖a5!

See the next Diagram

At the right moment, it's your job to defend the Pawn and prevent Black from launching the planned fun with the Rook.
24...f6 25.b4 ♔d7 26.g3!

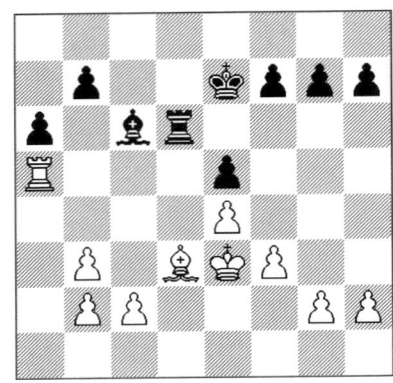

Of course, 26.b5 axb5 27.♗xb5 would be premature due to 27...♖d1, etc. The central advance, initiated by the text move, will force Black's rook to leave the column open.
26...g5 27.f4 gxf4+ 28.gxf4 ♖e6
After 28...exf4+ 29.♔xf4 followed by ♖h5 etc., White's job would be easier.
29.f5! ♖e7
If 29...♔d6, then ♖–a1–g1 etc., and the white Rook would have an easy game on the King's wing. Now, on the other hand, the doubled Pawn can finally be dissolved.
30.b5! axb5 31.♗xb5 ♖g7 32.♗xc6+ ♔xc6 33.♖a8 ♖g2
This counter-attempt is Black's only chance, as 33...♔f7 34.♖e8 followed by ♖e6+ would be fatal.
34.♖f8 ♖xh2 35.♖xf6+ ♔c5
With the threat 36...♖h3+ followed by ...♔d4

See the next Diagram

36.b4+!
The first link in the final combination: White wins the d6 square for his Rook.
36...♔c4!
If 36...♔xb4, then 37.♖e6 etc., winning easily.

37.♖d6

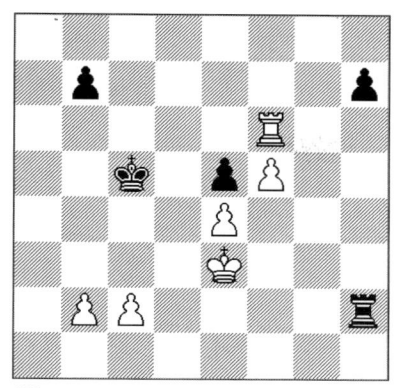

Threatening 38.♖d5, which, however, Black tries to avoid in an ingenious way.

36...♖h3+ 38.♔e2 ♖h4 39.♔f3 h5!

Still making efforts - which is in fact crowning with a kind of "moral" success in complicating things. By making this move, Black suggests that White can't win via the natural 40.♖d5 - and the opponent believes them!

40.♖e6

This can hardly be called a blunder since it wins forcibly and is coupled with another fine point. But with 40.♖d5! White proves to his opponent that the trap... isn't a trap at all! The continuation would be: 40...♔f4+ 41.♔e3 ♔xf5 42.exf5 ♔xd5 43.c4+ ♔d6 44.b5 b6 (or 44...h4 45.♔f3, etc.) 45.f6 ♔e6 46.c5, winning. The idea behind this Pawn ending is that while Black's passed Pawns are separated by two columns and can then be stopped by the enemy King, White is able to get passed Pawns within three columns of each other. This example is worth noting.

40...♖f4+

If 40...♔d4, then 41.c3+ (a second deviation bid) followed by 42.♔xe5, etc.

41.♔e3 h4 42.♖xe5 h3!

Very elegant - but the material advantage of the whites ensures that they can defend themselves against such tactical tricks.

43.♖d5 ♖h4 44.♖d4+! ♔c3 45.♖d1 h2 46.♖h1 ♖h3+ 47.♔f4 ♖h4+ 48.♔e5 ♔d2 49.f6 ♔e3 50.♔d6! ♔xe4 51.♖xh2 ♖d4+ 52.♔e5, and Black resigned.

Game 82
A.Alekhine-J.Foltys
Podebrad Tournament, June 1936
Queen's Gambit, Orthodox Defense
[D61]

1.d4 e6 2.c4 d5 3.♘c3 ♘f6 4.♗g5 ♗e7 5.e3 ♘bd7 6.♘f3 0–0 7.♕c2

This elegant move - which for unknown reasons has been overlooked for about a quarter of a century - allows Black to initiate a counterattack in the center through ...c5; but since this action cannot be supported by the Rooks, the resulting opening of the columns returns in White's favor. Therefore, in my opinion, the following system could be considered instead of 7...c5: 7...c6 8.a3 (preventing ...♘b4) 8...h6 9.♗h4 ♘e8 10.♗xe7 (or 10.♗g3 ♘d6) 10...♕xe7, followed by ...♘d6 etc.

7...c5 8.♖d1

As Black's response proved sufficient to equalize, it would have been better to play as I did in two games in Buenos Aires - 8.cxd5 ♘xd5 9.♗xe7 ♕xe7 10.♘xd5 exd5 11.dxc5, followed by ♗e2 and 0–0, with a slight advantage safe for the endgame.

8...♕a5 9.♗d3 h6 10.♗h4 ♘b6

A good move, forcing White to clarify the central situation before castling.

11.c×d5 c×d4

Although not directly bad, this intermediate move certainly can't be recommended, as it allows White to complicate things without giving too many chances. It would be incisive and good enough to equalize 11...♘b×d5, threatening 12...♘b4 or eventually ...c×d4.

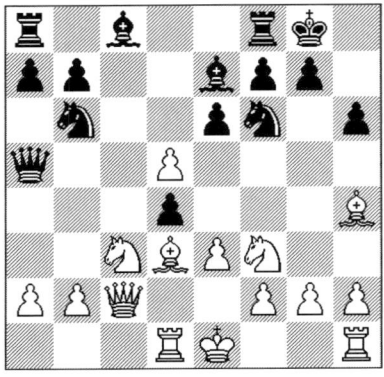

12.d6!

This may not bring much, but it's still a relief for White to get out of the rut, the "theoretical" rut, and force his opponent to find the best answer for himself.

12...♗×d6

Better than 12...d×c3 13.d×e7 c×b2+ 14.♖d2 ♖e8 15.♗×f6 g×f6 16.♕×b2 etc., with advantage.

13.♗×f6 g×f6?

But this weakening of the King's wing was certainly unnecessary. After 13...d×c3 14.♗×c3 ♗b4! 15.♗×b4 ♕×b4+ 16.♕d2 etc., White's positional advantage was negligible.

14.♘×d4 ♗b4

The Bishop's position on d6 was unsafe, and besides, the exchange afterwards will give Black some kind of compensation for the King's disorganized wing.

15.0–0 ♗×c3 16.b×c3 ♗d7 17.c4!

This Pawn is almost a weakness when it was on c3 - but now, at least, it makes the important d5 square inaccessible to Black's Knight.

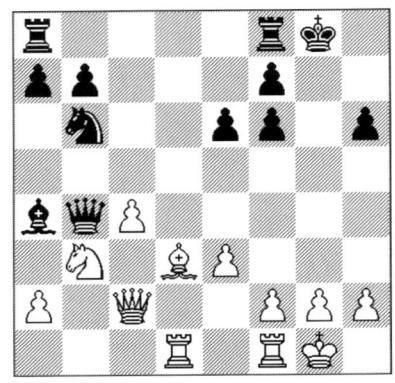

17...♗a4 18.♘b3 ♕b4

19.♕e2!

A move for both attack and defense. If now 19...♗×b3, then first 20.♔b1.

19...♖fc8 20.♖b1 ♘×c4

That sounds very dangerous, and in fact it will prove fatal. But as Black's King has been abandoned to his fate by all his troops, it's too late to avoid a direct attack through passive tactics. If, for example, 20...♗×b3, then 21.♔×b3 ♕e7 (or 21...♕f8 22.♕f3 etc.) 22.♕g4+ ♔f8 23.♕h4 ♔g7 24.f4 with an easy attack.

21.♘d4 ♕c5

When he took the Pawn on the previous move, Black probably calculated that he would have a saving defense if White made the natural move 22.♔×b7. In fact, the second player's position would be quite precarious even then, especially in view of the threat of White's 23.♘×e6, which would win promptly, for example, after 22...♔c7, or 22...♘d6, or 22...♗e8. Also 22...♘e5 would lose quickly after 23.♕h5 ♕f8 24.f4 ♘×d3 25.♘×e6 etc. - but *22...♕d5* to answer 23.♘×e6 with 23...♕×e6 and 23♖b4 via 23...♘b6 etc. would still prolong the battle. White's following combination is, however, the most convincing way of forcing a decisive advantage.

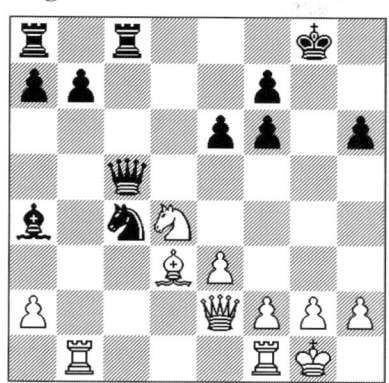

22.♘×e6!

It finally leads "only" to winning the Pawn - but by weakening Black's King position, it *allows White to force advantageous exchanges*, which will prove to be amply sufficient.

22...f×e6 23.♕g4+ ♔h8

After 23...♔f8, death would be quicker: 24.♗×b7 ♕g5 25.♕×e6 ♘e5 26.f4!, etc.

24.♖×b7

Threatening mate on g7 and h7.

24...♖c7 25.♖×c7 ♕×c7 26.♗×c4 e5 27.♕h4 ♕g7 28.♗d5

As Black's king is now conveniently protected, White rightly decides to simplify things.

28...♖d8 29.♕×a4 ♖×d5 30.♕c6!

It was important to prevent the blacks from bending the pieces in the central column.

30...♕f7 31.h3

To also make the Rook active.

31...♔g7 32.♖b1 ♖d7 33.a4!

That Pawn now threatens to get as far as a6, after which ♖b7 will be decisive. Black is then practically forced to offer the exchange of queens.

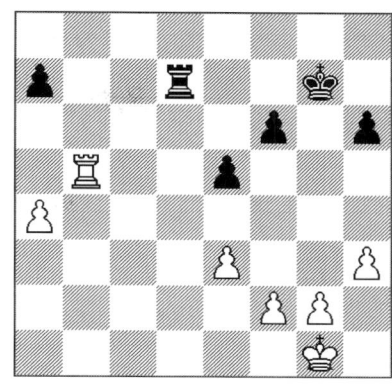

33...♖c7 34.♕b5 ♕d7 35.♕×d7+ ♖×d7 36.♖b5!

The end of the game will then be easy to win, mainly due to the dominant position of the Rook.

36...♔g6 37.g4 h5 38.♔g2 h×g4 39.h×g4 ♖d6 40.♖a5 a6 41.♔g3 ♖c6 42.f4! e×f4+ 43.e×f4 ♖b6 44.♖c5!

The Rook will prove even more effective on the 7th rank than on the 5th. If now 44...♔b4 then simply 45.♔c6 ♔×a4 46.g5, winning.

44...♔g7 45.♖c7+ ♔h6 46.♖a7 ♖b3+ 47.♔h4 ♖b4

Or 47...♖b6 48.a5 ♖c6 49.♖f7! ♔g6 50.♖b7 followed by 51.♖b6, winning.

48.♔×a6, and Black resigned, since if 48...♔×f4 then 49.♔×f6+! etc.

Game 83
V.Menchik-A.Alekhine
Podebrad Tournament, June 1936
Queen's Indian Defense [A46]

1.d4 ♘f6 2.♘f3 b5

In such early stages, it's a healthy principle not to give the opponent a goal, like this one: the venture can succeed, as here, but only if the opponent continues to develop his pieces without trying to take advantage of unusual situations. Instead of the fianchetto development chosen by the

Women's World Champion, a good method would have been, for example, 3.♗f4 ♗b7 4.e3 a6 5.a4 b4 6.c4, and, whether Black takes *en passant* or not, his position remains slightly inferior.

3.g3 ♗b7 4.♗g2 e6 5.0-0 ♗e7 6.♘bd2

Because of their aimless mobilization plan, White didn't get the advantage in the opening. The text move, which prepares for the exchange of Black's exposed b–Pawn, is no worse than 6.a4 (...a6 etc.) and certainly better than 6.e3 (...b4! etc.).

6...♕c8!

Protecting the Bishop to respond to 7.♖e1 with 7...♘e4! and after 7.c4 the Queen will obviously find a large field of action on the Queen's wing.

7.c4 b×c4 8.♘×c4 0-0 9.b3

As is often the case with the Queen's Indian Defense, White can't find a suitable square for his Queen's Bishop. It's relatively better than the move in the text, which weakens the queen's wing, 9.♘e5, to clarify the situation on the h1–a8 diagonal as soon as possible.

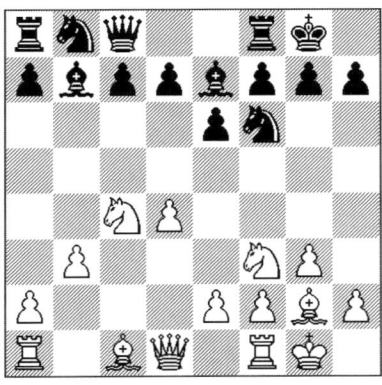

9...a5!

Not only avoiding ♘a5 once and for all (which in the previous move would have been answered with ...♗d5), but also eventually threatening ...a4.

10.a3?

A decisive strategic mistake in an already delicate position. White could take advantage of the fact that the threat mentioned was not immediate, and propose exchanging the bishops with 10.♗a3. After 10...♗×a3 11.♘×a3 ♘c6, followed eventually by ...♘b4, Black's position, although superior, would not be as easy to improve as after the text move, which creates an incurable weakness on b3.

10...♗d5 11.♕c2 ♕b7 12.♗b2

White only has the choice between a few evils; for example, after 12.♗d2 ♘c6 Black would already threaten 13...♘×d4.

12...♘c6 13.♘e1 ♖ab8 14.♗×d5

The only way to save the pawn temporarily.

14...e×d5!

Much stronger than 14...♘×d5 - the point of Black's next move.

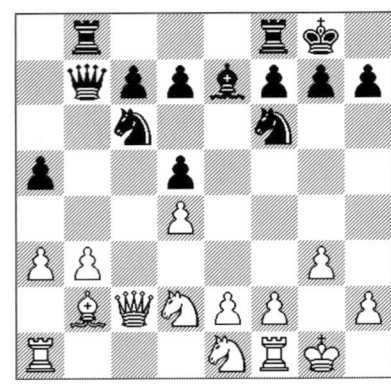

15.♘d2

15...♘e4!

Black has thus become master of the central sector. The b-pawn isn't lost immediately, but it can't escape its fate. This purely positional battle is, in my opinion, remarkable mainly because of the method Black adopted to exploit his advantage in the opening. This method, unusual at first glance, was in fact quite simple.

16.♘ef3 f5 17.♖fb1 ♕b5!

If now 18.e3 (which was relatively the best), then 18...♕e2 19.♖e1 ♕b5 20.♘xe4 dxe4 21.♘d2 d5 22.♖ec1 ♖b6 and White would finally be played in the open King. But Miss Menchik prefers to succumb in open combat.

18.♘xe4 fxe4 19.♘e5 ♘xe5

The simplest. The move 19...♕xb3 would probably also win, but after 20.♕c1 more resistance would be possible than in the ending forced by the maneuver in the text.

20.dxe5 ♕c5

Rough, but extremely solid.

21.♕xc5 ♗xc5 22.e3 ♖xb3 23.♗d4 ♗xd4 24.exd4 ♖ff3!

Forcibly winning a second Pawn.

25.♖xb3 ♖xb3 26.♖c1 c6 27.e6 dxe6 28.♖xc6 ♔f7 29.♖c7+ ♔f6 30.g4 h6 31.h4 ♖xa3, and White resigned.

Game 84
A.Alekhine–M.Euwe
Nottingham Tournament, August 1936
French Defense [C02]

1.e4 e6 2.d4 d5 3.e5

I adopted this favorite move of Nimzowitsch's for the first time in my career only because I thought that Dr. Euwe, after his failure in the 1935 game games (continuing with 3.♘f3 ♗b4), had in the meantime made a careful private study of this line of play. Although the result of the opening game of the present game was quite favorable to me, I would hardly repeat an experiment allowing Black to assume a kind of initiative right from the start and obtain (admittedly, at the cost of his Pawn setup) a free development of his pieces.

3...c5 4.♘f3

In the last years of his activity, Nimzowitsch preferred the peculiar move 4.♕g4, thus showing the clear project of exploiting the space advantage obtained on the kingside. The idea has some drawbacks, however, such as the following short game in which I had to fight against this idea in the Montevideo Tournament (White: J.Canepa), shown in characteristic fashion: 4...♘c6 5.♘f3 ♘ge7 (if this move hasn't been played before, it would only be further proof of Queen Theory's short-sightedness: the problematic development of this Knight, *being the most elaborate so far,* needs to be solved at the next opportunity) 6.c3 ♘f5 7.♗d3 cxd4 8.0–0 ♗d7 9.♖e1 dxc3 10.♘xc3 g6 11.♗g5 ♗e7 12.♕f4 ♘cd4! 13.♗f6 ♘xf3+ 14.gxf3 ♖g8 15.♔h1 ♗c6 16.♗xf5 gxf5 17.♗xe7 ♕xe7 18.♘e2 d4! 19.♘xd4 ♕b4! 20.♖g1 ♖xg1+ 21.♖xg1 0–0–0 22.♖d1 ♕xb2 23.♖d2 ♖xd4! 24.♖xd4 ♕xf2, and White resigned.

4...♘c6 5.♗d3

The central Pawn is only sacrificed temporarily, but its recovery will cost White some precious time. The whole plan, then, is unlikely to lead to more than a balanced position.

5...cxd4 6.0–0 f6

If 6...♕b6 White would turn the game into a regular gambit with 7.c3 dxc3 8.♘xc3, with some chances of success.

7.♗b5

There's nothing better than re-establishing the material balance. If, for example, 7.♗f4, then 7...g5, followed by ...g4.

7...♗d7 8.♗xc6 bxc6 9.♕xd4

f×e5 10.♖×e5

It's by no means easy to decide which is the better move: that or 10.♘xe5. My choice was determined by the consideration that if I took the knight in many variants, I would be practically obliged to exchange Black's "bad" bishop on d7; while here I already expected to be able to hunt down his black squares partner successfully.

10...♘f6 11.♗f4

Preventing ...♕b8 and preparing the protection of the Pawn f through ♗g3.

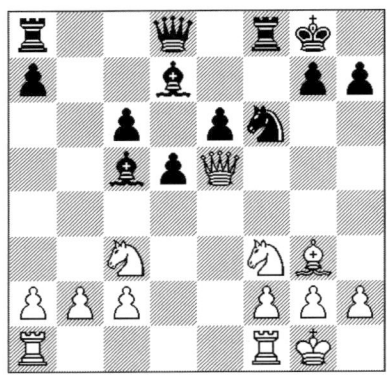

11...♗c5 12.♘c3 0–0 13.♗g3

White's slight advantage (control of the e5 square) is extremely difficult to exploit - especially as Black still has the pair of Bishops and two open columns for his Rooks. In the next section of the game, however, neither player will take full advantage of their opportunities.

13...♕e7

Here, for example, 13...♕e8, to be able to answer 14.♘a4 with 14...♗e7 was decidedly more promising.

14.a3?

White should persist in attacking the Bishop with 14.♘a4, for example, 14...♗b6 (14...♗b4 15.a3 ♗a5 16.b4 ♗d8 17.♘c5 etc. would definitely be too artificial) 15.♘xb6 a×b6 16.♕c7!, with advantage. The move in the text allows Black to "save" his Bishop.

14...a5 15.♖fe1

I didn't occupy this open column with the other Rook because of the possible reply 15...♗b8, which, however, wouldn't be dangerous: 15.♖ae1 ♗c8 16.♖d1!,followed by ♖fe1 etc., with advantage.

15...♖a7?

It would be relatively better 15...♗b6, to answer 16.♘a4 with ...♗d8.

16.♘a4 ♖b7

It would be a mistake 16...♘e4 due to 17.♘×c5 ♘×c5 (17...♕×c5 18.♔×e4) 18.♕d6! winning.

17.♕c3

Even this rather risky and complicated maneuver finally results in White's advantage. But even more convincing was the simple 17.♘×c5 ♕×c5 18.♖e2 followed by the exploitation of the black squares.

17...♗a7 18.♕×a5

Due to Black's counterattack against f2, this gain in material is only temporary.

18...♘e4 19.♕a6!

But from his intermediate move White really had the worst of it, as Black threatened to eventually ...♖a8, etc.

19...♗e8 20.b4

He then prepares a counter-sacrifice, which puts an end to Black's intermediate threats.

See the next Diagram

20...g5?

This move has generally been accused, and rightly so, as Black will soon regret compromising his King's position. But many of the critics are mistaken in believing that instead 20...e5 would be not only satisfactory but even advantageous for Black. In this case, I intended to sacrifice quality, thus obtaining winning prospects - for example, 21.♖xe4! dxe4 22.♕c4+ ♗f7 23.♕xe4 ♗d5 24.♕xe5 ♗xf3 25.♕xe7 ♖xe7 26.gxf3 ♖xf3 27.♘b2 ♖f8 28.c4 ♗d4 29.♖d1 etc., with advantage. Black would then have a relatively better counter-chance with 20...♗h5 21.♘c5! (but not 21.♕xc6 ♗e8 22.♕a6 ♗b5 23.♕a5 ♕e8 etc., with Black's advantage) 21...♗xc5 22.bxc5 ♗xf3 23.gxf3 ♖xf3 24.♕xc6 ♘xc5 etc., still with a fighting chance. It must be admitted, however, that even after the lower move in the text the second player will retain some practical chances of salvation for a long time, which he will try to exploit with the energy of desperation.

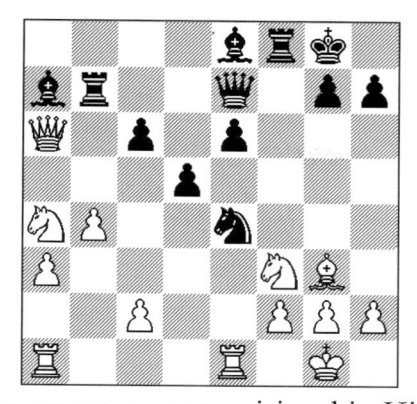

21.♘c5!

According to the program and very efficient, because now the strongest Bishop of Black will disappear.

21...♗xc5

No 21...♘xc5 22.bxc5 ♗xc5 due to 23.♖xe6! etc.

22.bxc5 ♘xc5 23.♕e2 ♘e4 24.♕e3

White's superiority is now evident. Their Pawns are much more securely placed; they still have control of e5, typical in this variant; and, finally, they have the very threatening a-Pawn.

24...♗g6

Even against the somewhat better 24...c5 White would maintain his advantage simply by advancing his passed Pawn. But the exchange of two minor pieces, possible after the text move, makes their task considerably easier.

25.♘e5! c5 26.♘xg6 hxg6 27.f3 ♘xg3 28.hxg3 ♔f7 29.a4!

To exploit Black's weaknesses in the center and on the King's wing, White first makes a demonstration on the other wing, forcing his opponent to leave some points vulnerable.

29...♖a8 30.♔f2

With the sudden threat of a mate attack starting with ♖h1.

30...♖b2 31.♖e2 c4

Under the circumstances, the best, although not enough. In fact, no human being could hope to protect at the same time: (1) the a column; (2) the e column; (3) the c-Pawn; (4) the e-Pawn; (5) the g-Pawn; and (6) the e5 square. It really is a bit much!

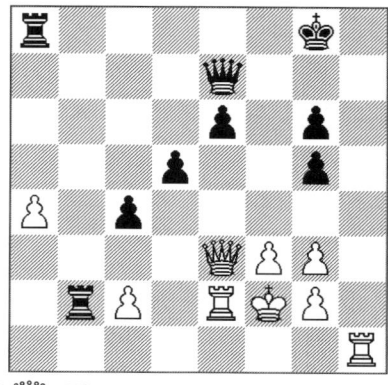

32.♖h1 ♔g8

33.♕e5!

From now on, both players produce - in a different way from the first phase of the game - top-class chess. Particularly interesting is the method Dr. Euwe adopts to avoid a rapid collapse and the chances he manages to find, despite the inevitable loss of two Pawns.

33...♕a7+ 34.♔f1 ♖b1+ 35.♖e1 ♖xe1+ 36.♔xe1 ♕g7!

It is, of course, the only move after which White, if he wants to play to win, must act with exceptional care.

37.♕xe6+ ♔f8 38.♕d5!

Instead of 38.♕d6+ ♕e7+ etc., which only leads to a draw. But now Black's king seems to be in greater danger than Black's.

38...♕c3+

The alternative was 38...♖e8+ 39.♔d2! (not 39.♔f2 ♕a7+ 40.♔f1 ♔g7! threatening ...♕e3) 39...♕f6 40.♖h7 after which 40...♖d8 would lose directly due to 41.♖h8+, etc.

39.♔f2! ♖e8

It would be hopeless 39...♕xc2+ 40.♔g1 ♕b1+ 41.♔h2 ♕b8 42.♕xc4, etc.

40.g4!

Check on d6 and then d7 would be useless. The queen is better placed in the center.

40...♕e3+ 41.♔g3 ♕f4+ 42.♔h3 ♖e7

If 42...♔g7, then 43.♕d7+.

See the next Diagram

43.♕c5!

The right move. After 43.g3 ♕e3!. Victory was in doubt.

43...♕f6 44.g3

No 44.♖e1 ♕h8+ 45.♔g3 ♕h4 mate!

44...♕h8+

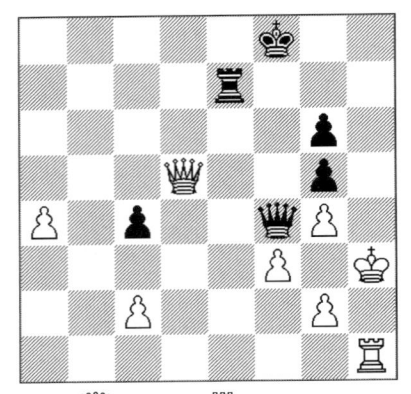

If 44...♕xf3 45.♖e1 is winning.

45.♔g2 ♕c3 46.♖h7 ♕xc2+ 47.♔h3 ♕e2 48.♖xe7 ♕xe7 49.♕xc4

In the difficult Queen ending that follows, Black's chances of a draw are based mainly on the fact that White's King cannot be put to safety. If, however, White's Pawn on g4 were on f2, Black's game would be ripe for abandonment. But not only that: by sheer chance, Black could even, in certain circumstances (for example, if White's passed Pawn got as far as a7) speculate a drowned mate by moving his King to h6. No wonder this game has thirty more moves, and if it weren't for Black's inaccuracy on his 61st move, it would have many more!

49...♕e1 50.♕c5+ ♔f7 51.♔g2 ♕a1 52.♕c2 ♔f6 53.♕b3 ♔e5?

Here we were both in time trouble, which explains the bidding of the text and its inadequate response. The King could, of course, return to g7.

54.♔f2?

The last move before the time control, instead of 54.♕b8+ ♔d5 (or 54...♔e6 55.♕e8+) 55.♕g8+, winning both g-Pawns for the a-Pawn - ending the game quickly.

54...♔f6 55.♕b6+ ♔g7 56.♕b4 ♕e1

178

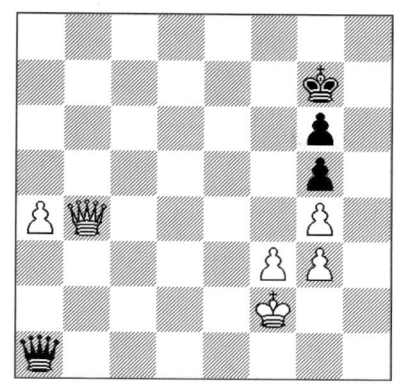

The game here was postponed for the second time, and White began a serious endgame task. Their plan was: (1) to play a5 as quickly as possible; (2) after that to eliminate once and for all any mate-drowning combinations by playing f4.

57.♕e1 ♕h2+ 58.♔e3 ♔h7 59.a5 ♕a2 60.♕d2 ♕a1 61.♔e2 ♔h6

The best chance of a prolonged resistance consisted of 61...♕h8. After the text move, White gets c4 in more favorable circumstances, leaving no difficulties for the King's final move, which will make his passed Pawn irresistible.

62.f4! g×f4 63.g×f4 ♕a4 64.♔f2!

To play g5 now when Black can't respond with ...♔h5.

64...♔h7 65.g5 ♕a3 66.♕d7+ ♔h8 67.♕c8+ ♔h7 68.♕c7+

So the queen protects both the pawn a and f and the king is ready for the final move.

68...♔h8 69.♔e2 ♕a2+ 70.♔e3 ♕b3+ 71.♔d4 ♕b4+ 72.♔d5 ♕b5+ 73.♔d4

The third postponement. White could also have played 73.♔e6, and after 73...♕f5+ 74.♔e7 ♕f8+! 75.♔d7. But they didn't need to.

See the next Diagram

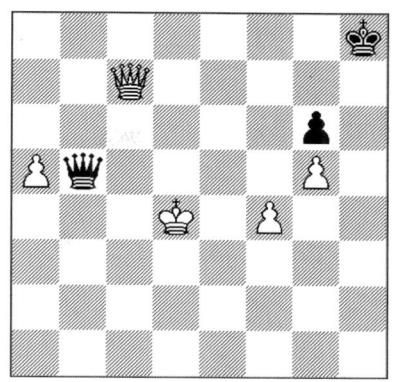

73...♕a6 74.♕b6 ♕c8 75.♕d6!

The simplest scheme.

75...♕c2 76.a6 ♕d2+ 77.♔e5 ♕c3+ 78.♔e6 ♕c8+ 79.♔e7 ♔h7 80.♕d7! ♕c3 81.♔e6+, and Black resigned.

Game 85
W.Winter–A.Alekhine
Nottingham Tournament, August 1936
French Defense [C01]

1.d4 e6 2.e4 d5 3.e×d5

This move is usually adopted to show that White is only playing for a draw. But in fact, Black will at least have fewer opportunities for complications if he wants to do this than in many of the other French variants.

3...e×d5 4.♗d3 ♘c6 5.♘e2 ♗d6 6.c3

Giving Black a welcome chance to seize the initiative. However the alternative 6.♘bc3 ♘b4 would lead either to the exchange of White's King's Bishop, or to its removal to outlying squares after 7.♗g5 f3.

6...♕h4!

It was important to avoid 7.♗f4.

7.♘d2 ♗g4!

A correct offer of a Pawn. After 8.♕b3 0-0-0 9.♕×d5 ♘f6, followed by ...♖he8, Black would have an over-

whelming advantage in development.
8.♕c2 0-0-0 9.♘f1
If 9.♗f5+ then simply 9...♔b8.
9...g6
Preparing for the exchange of White's "good" Bishop (d3) after which the white squares in his position would become a little weak.
10.♗e3 ♘ge7 11.0-0-0 ♗f5 12.♘fg3 ♗×d3 13.♕×d3 h6
To secure his queen's position, which could become uncomfortable after the ♕d2 move.

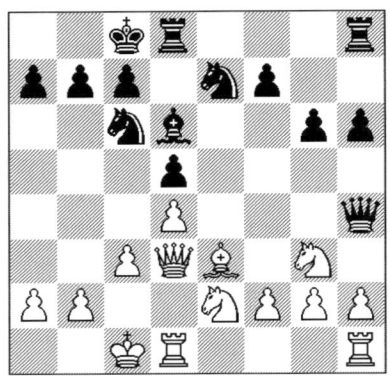

14.f4?
This move, weakening important squares on the e column without compensation, could be considered the decisive strategic error. It was relatively better 14.♘g1, followed by ♘f1, with a rather restricted but still defensible position.
14...♕g4
Black is aiming - and succeeding - to keep the f5 square under control. How important that will be will become clear in the second half of the game.
15.h3 ♕d7 16.♖hf1 h5!
If now 17.f5, then 17...h4 18.f6 ♘g8 19.♘h1 ♖e8 and White's f-pawn will fall.
17.♘g1 h4 18.♘3e2 ♘f5 19.♘f3 f6
All the smaller white pieces from now on will suffer from an obvious lack of space and will then be unable to prevent an increase in pressure in the e-column.
20.♘h2 ♖de8 21.♗d2 ♖e6 22.♘g4 ♖he8 23.♖de1 ♖8e7 24.♔d1 ♕e8 25.♕f3
To move the knight from e2, which now is impossible due to 25...♖×e1 followed by ...♗f4.
25...♘a5!
Through this maneuver Black quickly gains decisive material superiority. White now can't play 26.♕×d5 due to 25...♗×e2 27.♔×e2 ♖×e2 28.♕×a5 ♘g3 29.♔f3 ♕e4! winning.
26.b3

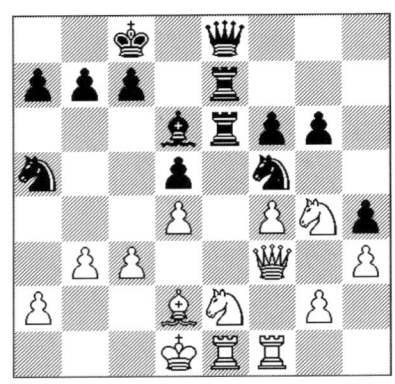

26...♘c4!
An energetic ending. If 27.b×c4, then 27...♕a4+ 28.♔c1 ♗a3+ 29.♔b1 ♖b6+ 30.♔a1 ♕c2 and mate in two.
27.♗c1 ♘ce3+ 28.♗×e3 ♘×e3+ 29.♘×e3 ♖×e3 30.♕f2 ♕b5!
Threatening 31...♕d3+ 32.♔c1 ♗a3 mate. White is then forced to give up a Pawn.
31.♘c1 ♖×c3 32.♖×e7 ♗×e7 33.♕e1 ♔d7
If ♕×c3 on this or the next move, Black responds with ...♕×f1+ followed by ...♕×f4 or ...♕×g2 winning.
34.f5 ♖e3! 35.♕f2 g5 36.♖e1 ♖e4

37.♖×e4

This exchange, which gives Black a strong passed Pawn, cut things short. But White had no salvation in any case.

37...d×e4 38.♔d2 ♗d6

Threatening 39...e3+!

39.♔c2 ♗f4, and White resigned.

Game 86
A.Alekhine-C.Alexander
Nottingham Tournament, August 1936
Queen's Indian Defense [E16]
Beauty Award

1.d4 ♘f6 2.c4 e6 3.♘f3 ♗b4+ 4.♘bd2

The usual move is 4.♗d2 to develop the knight on the most natural square c3 after the bishops' den. By avoiding the exchange White tries to complicate things, without having many chances.

4...b6 5.g3 ♗b7 6.♗g2 0–0 7.0–0 ♗×d2?

Instead of this exchange, which gives White the advantage of the pair of Bishops unnecessarily, Black should play either 7...d5 (Rubinstein-Alekhine, Semmering 1926) or even 7...♗e7, followed by ...d6, ...♘d7, etc. In both cases they would have better prospects of equality than in the current game.

8.♕×d2

The correct recapture because the Bishop's Queen is wanted on the big diagonal.

8...d6 9.b3 ♘bd7 10.♗b2 ♖b8

Black shows his hand too early. The obvious aim of the text move is to play ...♘e4, followed by ...f5, which is why the Bishop needs to be protected, to avoid the possible ♘g5 reply. But the same idea could be combined with a mobilization of forces through 10...♕e7; 11...♖ad8 and eventually ...♗a8.

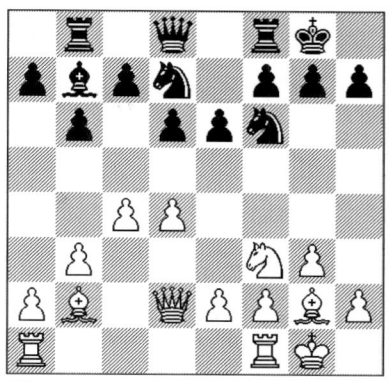

11.♖ad1!

An interesting and effective way of tackling Black's plan. White's queen bishop will play a very important and practically decisive role in the development that follows.

11...♘e4

If 11...♕e7, then 12.♕e3 (...♘e4 13.d5).

12.♕e3 f5 13.d5!

This Pawn is only weak in appearance, as White can easily protect it with counterattacks.

13...e×d5

If instead 13...e5 Black would lose a Pawn through 14.♘h4.

14.c×d5 ♘df6 15.♘h4 ♕d7

If 15...♘×d5 then 16.♗×d5! ♗×d5 17.♕d4 would win a piece.

16.♗h3

Again avoiding ...♘×d5, this time due to 17.♕×d4.

16...g6 17.f3 ♘c5 18.♕g5

Threatening not only 19.♗×f6 but also 19.♗(or ♘)×f5; and if 18...♘×d5, then 19.♘×g6 winning. Black's reply is therefore forced.

18...♕g7 19.b4 ♘cd7

It would be equally hopeless 19...♘a4 20.♗a1, etc.

20.e4!

The initial move of the final combination with sacrifice.

20...♘xe4

Black is clearly basing his last hopes on this ingenious move. If now 21.♗xg7, then 21...♘xg5 22.♗xf8 ♘xh3+ 23.♔g2 ♔xf8 24.♗xh3 ♘f6 followed by ...♘xd5 with good fighting chances.

21.♕c1!

Much more effective than 21.fxe4 ♕xb2 22.exf5 ♕f6 etc., giving White only a possible win after a laborious ending.

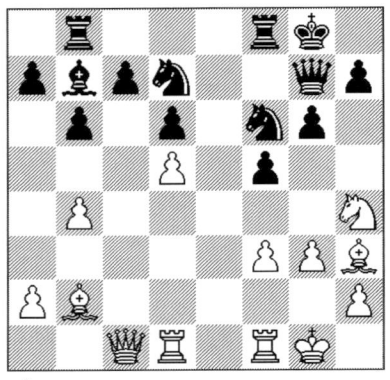

21...♘ef6

22.♗xf5!

The surprising continuation of 20.e4. After 22...gxf5 23.♘xf5 Black would lose the queen or take mate - 23...♕h8 24.♘h6+ ♔g7 25.♕g5 mate.

22...♔h8 23.♗e6

Pawn d is finally safe.

23...♗a6 24.♖fe1 ♘e5 25.f4!

The simplest way to force abandonment.

25...♘d3 26.♖xd3 ♗xd3 27.g4

There's no remedy against f5. Black resigned.

Game 87
A.Alekhine-E.Bogoljubov
Nottingham Tournament, August 1936
Queen's Gambit Declined
Slav Defense [D16]

1.♘f3 d5 2.d4 ♘f6 3.c4 c6 4.♘c3 dxc4 5.a4 e6?

That was the third time in a year that I've had the pleasure of encountering the indifferent bidding of the text - and taking advantage of it. It's much better, of course, 5...♗f5.

6.e4 ♗b4

Relatively better, although not enough to game, is 6...c5.

7.e5

Also very promising is 7.♕c2 b5 8.♗e2 and 9.0-0 with more than enough positional compensation for the Pawn.

7...♘e4

For 7...♘d5, see *Game 26*.

8.♕c2 ♕d5 9.♗e2 c5

The game with Helling, Dresden 1936, continued as follows: 9...0-0 10.0-0 ♘xc3 11.bxc3 ♗e7 12.♘d2 c5 13.♗xc4 ♕d8 14.♕e4 cxd4 15.cxd4 ♗d7 16.♗d3 g6 17.♗a3 ♗c6 18.♕g4 ♖e8 19.♘c4 h5 20.♕f4 ♗g5 21.♕g3 ♗h4 22.♕e3 ♕d5 23.f3 ♗d8 24.♘d6 ♖e7 25.♗c5! – and Black, whose queen was trapped in a rather spectacular way, resigned a few moves later.

10.0-0 ♘xc3 11.bxc3 cxd4 12.♘xd4

The 19th Game of my 1935 game with Dr. Euwe went like this: 12.cxd4 c3 13.♗d2 ♕a5 14.♗xc3! ♗xc3 15.♖a3 ♘c6 (if 15...♗d7 then 16.♖xc3 ♗xa4 17.♗b5+!! winning) 16.♖xc3 ♗d7 17.♖b1 0-0 18.♖c5 ♕d8 19.♖xb7 ♗c8 20.♖b1 ♘xd4 21.♘xd4 ♕xd4 22.♗f3 and with the advantage of quality White had a technically easy win.

By recapturing here with the Knight, I wanted to satisfy myself that this line is stronger than the one I adopted previously. As this game proves, White also recaptures the sacrificed Pawn, while maintaining excellent attacking chances. The question of which of these moves gives the greatest advantage is therefore rather academic.

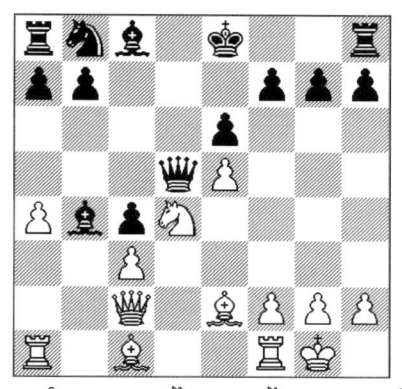

12...♗c5 13.♘f3! ♘d7 14.♖d1 ♕c6 15.♗×c4 0–0

The King must fly, because after 15...♗×f7+ 16.♕×f7 and 17.♗a3 Black would quickly succumb.

16.♘g5

Forcing a weakening of Black's position on the King's wing.

16...g6 17.♗b5 ♕c7 18.♘e4 ♗e7

Of course, not 18...♘×e5, due to 19.♘×c5 followed by ♗a3, etc.

19.f4

This is not the strongest attacking continuation. The correct idea of exploiting Black's restricted position is to force the exchange of his King's Bishop through 19.♗h6 ♖d8 20.f4 followed by ♗g5 etc., after which Black's square weaknesses would quickly become fatal for the second player. The move in the text was based on a slightly overestimated assessment of the attacking possibilities in the position that occurred after Black's 21st move.

19...♘c5 20.♘f6+

Under the circumstances more promising than 20.♘d6, which was actually quite playable.

20...♗×f6 21.e×f6 ♗d7 22.♗e3?

I made that move instantly, having calculated the whole variant on the 19th move. Instead, 22.♗a3! ♖fd8 23.♖d4 etc., would keep the space advantage without any bidding.

22...♗×b5 23.a×b5 ♘d7! 24.g3

Relatively the best, since 24.♗d4 ♕×f4 25.♔f1 ♕g4 would give Black, in addition to his material gain, attacking prospects (...e5).

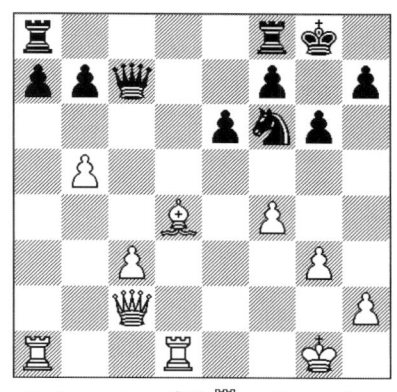

24...♘×f6 25.♗d4

Realizing that 25.♖×a7 – planned a few moves ago, could be answered not by 25...♖×a7 26.b6 etc., with an advantage for White, but by 25...♘d5! 26.♖×a8 ♘×e3 27.♖×f8+ ♔×f8 28.♕d3 ♘×d1 29.♕×d1 ♕c5+ etc., with a better queenside ending for Black. After the text move White gets enough compensation for the Pawn, due to his powerful Bishop - but that's almost all. Through the following moves Black could force simplifications, which would most likely lead to a draw.

25...♘d7 26.♕f2 b6 27.♖e1

Avoiding 27...f6 followed by ...e5.

27...♕c4 28.♖ab1 ♖ac8 29.♕e3 ♖fe8 30.♕f3 f6

Black is starting to play with fire. Here, or even in the next move, they could offer to exchange the queens with ...♕d5, as they would still be able to protect their Pawn late on. The variant 30...♕d5 31.♕×d5 e×d5 32.♗×e8+ ♔×e8 33.♖a1 ♖a8 would, as mentioned, result in a peaceful draw. After the text move and the next one White manages to develop a formidable attack on the kingside.

31.♖b4 ♕c7? 32.♖b2!

Now Black's pawn becomes weak.

32...♖e7 33.♖be2 ♔f7 34.g4 ♖ce8 35.g5!

With a hidden intention that the black women ignore entirely.

35...f×g5

His only chance of salvation was 35...f5 when White would still have excellent winning prospects by continuing with h4–h5, etc.

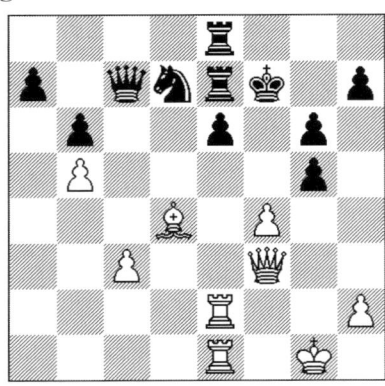

36.f5!!

A problem move, which forces victory in all variants. In addition to the continuation of the text, the following possibilities come into consideration:

I. 36...e×f5 37.♕d5+ ♔f8 38.♗g7+!, winning.

II. 36...g×f5 37.♕h5+ ♔f8 38.♕h6+ ♔g8 39.♕×g5+, winning.

III. 36...e5 37.♕d5+ ♔f8 38.♕c6! ♕×c6 39.b×c6 e×d4 40.♖×e7 ♖×e7 41.♖×e7 ♔×e7 42.c7, winning.

36...♕f4

No better, no worse than the variants already given.

37.f×e6+ ♖×e6 38.♕d5

Another winning line was 38.♕h3 ♕h4 39.♔f1+ ♔g8 40.♔×e6!, winning.

38...♘f6

White also threatens 39.♔f1, etc.

39.♗×f6 ♕g4+ 40.♖g2 ♕f5 41.♗e5

But not 41.♕c4? ♕c5+ and Black would win!

41...♔g8 42.♖f2 ♕g4+ 43.♔h1 h5 44.♖g1 ♕h4 45.♖f6 ♔h7 46.♖×e6 ♖×e6 47.♕d7+, and Black resigned.

Game 88
S.Tartakower–A.Alekhine
Nottingham Tournament, August 1936
Catalan Defense [D02]
Quality Award

1.d4 ♘f6 2.g3 c5

Intending, if 3.d5, to play a kingside pin. But a more solid answer to White's unusual second move is 2...d4.

3.♘f3 d5 4.♗g2

Giving Black predominance in the center. A safer line was 4.c3, entering the Schlechter Variant of the Slav Defense with an extra tempo.

4...c×d4 5.0–0 ♗g4

And not 5...♘c6 6.♘×d4 e5 7.♘×c6 b×c6 8.c4 etc., with better fighting chances for White.

6.♘×d4?

This is perfectly in line with Black's

wishes. Instead, 6.♘e5! would maintain the balance of the position, since after 6...♗h5 7.♕×d4 winning a Pawn via 7...♗×e2 would prove decidedly risky after 8.♖e1 ♗h5 (or a6) 9.♕f4 etc., with advantage.

6...e5 7.♘f3 ♘c6 8.h3 ♗f5

It was even more accurate 8...♗d7 (but not 8...♗e6 9.♘g5) after which 9.c4 would simply be answered by 9...d×c4, with an advantage. But the text move, after all, is also quite good.

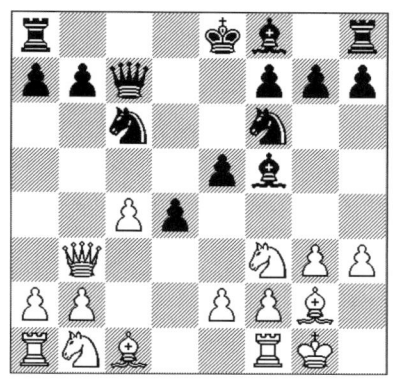

9.c4! d4 10.♕b3 ♕c7?

But after that, White acquires the opportunity to equalize the chances. The most natural 10...♕d7 (but not 10...♕c8 11.♘×e5 followed by 12.♗×b7) would also be the best; if 11.e3, then 11...♗e7 12.e×d4 e×d4 followed by ...0–0 etc., with a clear advantage.

11.e3 ♗e7

Black now needs to get his King to safety as quickly as possible.

12.e×d4 e×d4 13.♗f4

This very important gain in time is a direct consequence of the inaccuracy of Black's 10th move.

13...♕c8 14.♖d1 0–0

Fortunately for Black, he doesn't need to worry about his center Pawn, so he'll seek compensation by capturing White's h Pawn. If now 15.g4, then 15...♗e4! 16.♘fd2 ♗g6 etc., with a tricky but not disadvantageous middlegame position.

15.♘×d4 ♗×h3 16.♘×c6 b×c6 17.♗×h3?

Here and later, White makes some indifferent moves, which quickly wreak havoc on his defensible position at the time. It was obviously inadvisable to bring Black's queen into a strong attacking position through this exchange. They needed first and foremost to finish their development with 17.♘c3.

17...♕×h3 18.♕f3 ♘g4 19.♘c3

Again, underestimating Black's attacking chances. It was better 19.♘d2 and if 19...f5 then 20.♘f1.

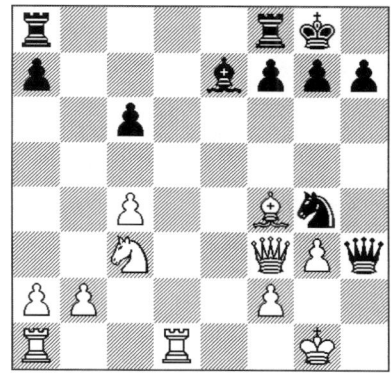

19...f5!

With the powerful threat of 20...♗c5, at the moment premature due to 20.♘e4. From here on in, Black's handling of the attack on the King is impeccable and explains the distinction given to this game.

20.♕g2 ♕h5 21.♖e1

Equally unsatisfactory would be 21.♗d6 ♗×d6 22.♖×d6 f4 etc., with an advantage for Black.

21...♗c5 22.♘d1 g5 23.♗e5

The variant 23.♗e3 ♗×e3 24.♘×e3 ♘e5 followed by ...c5 would give Black an equally easy attack.

185

23...♖ad8
After that there is no defense against ...♖xd1 etc.
24.♗c3 ♖xd1!
Not only winning a Pawn, but demolishing what was resigned of White's fortress.
25.♖axd1 ♗xf2+ 26.♔f1 ♗xe1
Tempting, but less convincing would be 26...♗e3 due to 27.♔e2!
27.♖xe1 f4 28.gxf4
The desperate resource 28.♖e7 would prove insufficient because of 28...♘e3+ 29.♔g1 ♕d1+ 30.♔h2 fxg3+, etc.
28...♖xf4+ 29.♔g1

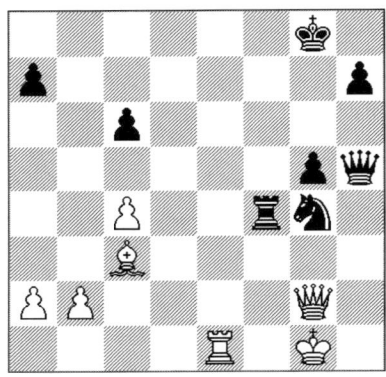

29...♘h2!
The killing blow. If 30.♕xh2, then 30...♔g4+ 31.♔h1 ♔h4, etc. White chooses another method of giving up his Queen but will soon be persuaded that further resistance is rather hopeless.
30.♖e3 ♔f1+ 31.♕xf1 ♘xf1 32.♔xf1 ♕f7+ 33.♔g2 ♕xc4 34.♖e7 ♕d5+ 35.♔h3 h5, and White resigned.

Game 89
A.Alekhine–M.Vidmar
Hastings Tournament, December 1936
Queen's Gambit Declined
Orthodox Defense [D65]

1.d4 ♘f6 2.c4 e6 3.♘c3 d5 4.♗g5 ♘bd7 5.e3 ♗e7 6.♘f3 0–0 7.♖c1 c6 8.♕c2
Nowadays Rubinstein's move is considered quite harmless because of the response 8...♘e4!; but since Dr. Vidmar had had an unpleasant experience with this move (in a very analogous position) in our game in Bled (see *Game 44*), he decided to adopt the old, more complicated defensive method.
8...a6 9.cxd5
Rarely played at that moment, but very much in line with modern trends: against the more natural response 9...exd5, White plans a minority attack on the queen's wing.
9...♘xd5
And after that the position will have the characteristics of the so-called Capablanca Defense, but with the important difference in White's favor, that Black has trouble holding his game with ...e5.

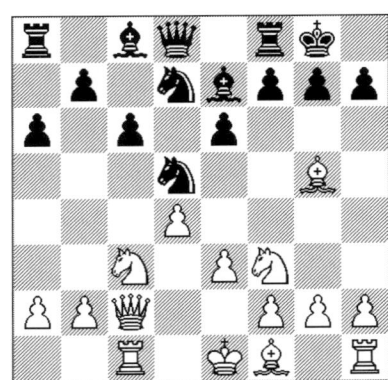

10.♗xe7 ♕xe7 11.♗c4
Of course, not 11.♗d3 due to 11...♘b4, but 11.a3 also comes into consideration.
11...♘xc3 12.♕xc3 c5
As 12...♖e8 (with the aim of ...e5) would be efficiently answered by 13.♖d1!, Black decides to start opera-

tions on the queen's wing. After the text move, they threaten, of course, 13...b5 etc., with very satisfactory play.

13.dxc5

A difficult move in its simplicity: White temporarily sacrifices space to recover it with some additional advantages. Not so convincing would be 13.♗e2 cxd4 14.♘xd4 ♘f6 or 14.♕xd4 e5 etc., with more chances for Black to equalize than in the game.

13...♕xc5

As Black wants to avoid exchanging queens, it would be more logical to 13...♘xc5 14.♗e2 ♘e4 15.♕d4 ♘f6 16.0-0 etc., with only a slight superiority for White.

14.♗b3! b6

Certainly the endgame after 14...♕xc3 ♔xc3 would offer little chance of salvation due to the possible entry of White's Rook on the 7th rank and the position of his King in the middle. But now Black's queen will be chased until White gains a material advantage.

15.♕d2 ♕h5

It would even be less satisfying 17...♕e7 18.♖c7 etc.

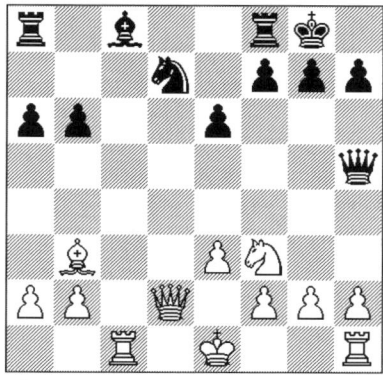

16.♗d1!

This seemingly modest retreat practically decides the game. White not only threatens 17.♗xc8 followed by 18.♕xd7 - which would be wrong at this point due to 17...♖fd8 18.♕e7 ♗c1+ 19.♔e2 ♕b5+ with mate on the next move - but also eventually dislodges Black's queen with 18.♘d4 and then occupies the large diagonal with ♗f3. As a result, Black is forced to waste time with the Knight *tour* next, which as a direct consequence - will lead to the loss of a Pawn.

16...♘c5 17.b4!

But not 17.♘d4, because 17...♕g6 threatens 18...♘d3+.

17...♘e4 18.♕d4 ♗b7

Dr. Vidmar tries, as he usually does in compromised positions, to complicate things. If White took the Pawn immediately, Black could get some kind of counterattack after (19.♕xb6) ♗d5 20.a3 ♘f6! (21.0-0 ♘d7!) etc. But twenty-five years' experience with the Yugoslav Grandmaster (see, for example, my game with him in Carlsbad 1911 in *My Best Games, 1908-1923*) taught me to be very careful after strategically outplaying him. In fact, my next simple move will leave him with no hope of further "scratches".

19.0-0 b5

Instead, 19...♗d5 would be hopeless: 20.♘d2 ♕g6 21.♗c2 f5 22.♘xe4 fxe4 23.f3! etc.

20.♘e5 ♕h6 21.♘c6

Then forcing the exchange, after which the Bishop will prove to be much more powerful than the Knight in both the mid-game and the endgame.

21...♗xc6 22.♖xc6 ♘f6 23.♗f3

This is the kind of position I was aiming for when I played 16.♗d1! It becomes obvious that Black's off-center queen is unable to cooperate in protecting the threatened queen's wing.

23...Rad8 24.Rd6

White women are in the pleasant position of being able to use the simplest methods - a reward for adopting the right strategic plan.

24...Rxd6 25.Qxd6 Qh4 26.a3

Black's Pawn is now about to fall, and to avoid further damage, they must allow the queens to be exchanged. The endgame that follows, tough and theoretically winning for White, is still highly instructive, especially as Dr. Vidmar defends with extreme care and resourcefulness.

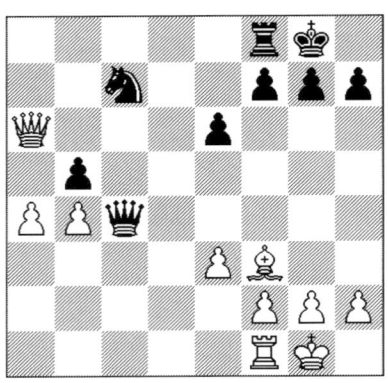

26...Qc4 27.Qxa6 Nd5 28.a4! Nc7

After 28...Qxb4 29.Bxd5 exd5 30.Qxb5 etc. White would win quickly.

29.Qc6 Qxc6 30.Bxc6 bxa4 31.Ra1 Rb8 32.Rxa4 Kf8 33.g4

The winning plan is easy to explain, but technically quite difficult to execute. White takes advantage of the fact that Black's pieces are occupied on the Queen's wing with the passed Pawn *to create* - with the gradual advance or eventual exchange of Pawns - *permanently vulnerable points in the center and on the King's wing on Black's side*; and only after this preliminary work can the final assault begin.

33...Ke7 34.b5!

Obviously the last chance to secure a stable position for this Pawn.

34...e5

Black faces two evils: surrendering control of d4, as in the game, or allowing his Pawn to be isolated e.

35.f4 f6 36.fxe5 fxe5 37.Ra2

Frustrating 37...Kd6 due to 38.Rd2+ etc.

37...Rb6 38.Rb2 h6 39.Kf2 Ke6 40.Kf3 Nd5 41.h4

The exchange of minor pieces, here or on moves 42 and 43, would naturally increase Black's chances of a draw considerably.

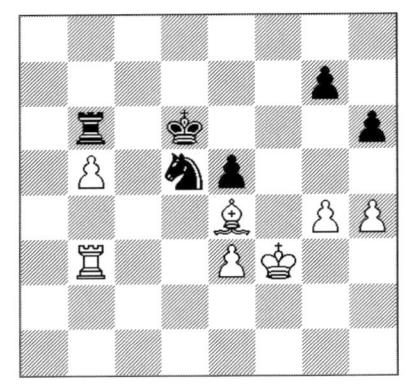

41...Ne7 42.Be4 Nd5 43.Rb3 Kd6

44.g5!

It avoids ...Nf6 and reduces the mobility of Black's g-awn. The endgame crisis is approaching.

44...hxg5 45.hxg5 Ke6 46.Bd3

The Rook will gradually regain its freedom of movement.

46...Kd6 47.Ra3 Ne7 48.Ra7 Rb8 49.Ke4

Threatening 50.Kf5 and this practically forces the Pawn's weakening move next.

49...g6 50.Ra3!

The time has come to dislodge the King on d6.

50...♖b6 51.♗c4 ♖b8 52.♖d3+ ♔c5

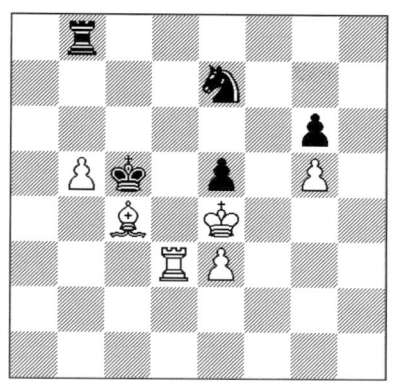

53.♖d7!

After about twenty preparatory moves, the Rook enters the enemy formation with decisive effects. Black's desperate struggle afterwards is good and futile, as they won't be able to offer the exchange of the minor pieces for long without losing both remaining Pawns.

53...♘c8 54.♗f7 ♘d6+ 55.♔×e5 ♖b6 56.e4

Of course, not 56.♗×g6 ♘c4+ 57.♔f5 ♘×e3+, etc.

56...♘×b5

That Pawn is of no importance now because the fight is decided on the other wing. The rest is agony.

57.♖d5+! ♔b4 58.♖d8 ♘a7 59.♖d6 ♘c6+ 60.♔d5 ♘e7+ 61.♔e6 ♘c6 62.♔f6 ♔c5 63.♖d5+ ♔b4 64.e5! ♔c4 65.♖d1+ ♔c5 66.♖c1+ ♔d4 67.e6 ♔e3 68.♗×g6 ♘d4 69.♗f7 ♘e2 70.♖e1 ♔f2 71.♖×e2+, and Black resigned.

Game 90
A.Alekhine-R.Fine
Hastings Tournament, January 1937
Spanish Opening [C90]

1.e4 e5 2.♘f3 ♘c6 3.♗b5 a6 4.♗a4 ♘f6 5.0-0 ♗e7 6.♖e1 b5 7.♗b3 d6 8.c3 ♘a5 9.♗c2 c5 10.d4 ♕c7 11.♘bd2 0-0

So far everything is conventional, but here the move usually adopted is 11...♘c6, trying to force White into a central decision. The most promising continuation for White would then be 12.a4 ♔b8 13.a×b5 a×b5 14.d×c5 d×c5 15.♘f1 followed by ♘g3 etc.

12.♘f1 ♗g4

The continuation of this game will prove convincingly that the premature exchange of this bishop gives White promising attacking opportunities on the kingside - but a completely satisfactory plan is not easy to find. The relatively most logical method seems to be 12...♗d7 followed by ...♔fc8 and ...♗f8.

13.♘e3!

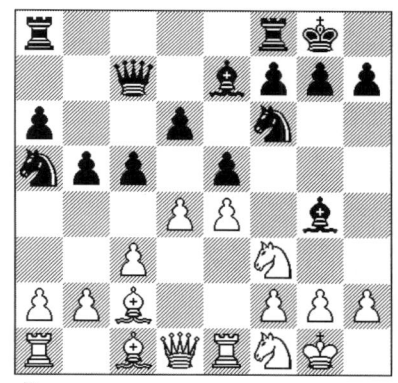

The most convincing response, which only doesn't force White to sacrifice something in the next few moves if he doesn't want to.

13...♗×f3 14.♕×f3!

After the simple 14.g×f3 White would have the pair of Bishops and some attacking chances at the base of the open column g; but the text move, with which they preserve their Pawn structure intact, is stronger and more precise.

14...c×d4 15.♘f5?

But this risky offer, explained mainly by my being half a point behind Fine and having to win at all costs to be first - can't objectively be recommended, even though White seized the initiative for a long time. The right move was 15.c×d4!, because after 15...e×d4 16.♘f5 ♕×c2 17.♘×e7+ ♔h8 18.♘f5! (threatening 19.♘×g7 ♔×g7 20.♗h6+, etc.) Black would have gained a decisive advantage. Also 15...♘c6 (the answer I was really hoping for to 15.c×d4) 16.d5! ♘d4 17.♕d1 ♘×c2 18.♘×c2 (threatening 19.♘b4, etc.) 18...a5 19.♗d2 followed by ♔c1 etc. would have been favorable for White. Fine's next defensive moves are not only good, but unique.

15...d×c3 16.♕×c3! ♖fc8!

Protecting the Knight on a5 by attacking White's King's Bishop.

17.♕g3 ♗f8 18.♗d3

If instead 18.♗g5, then simply 18...♕×c2 19.♗×f6 g6, etc.

18...♘c6 19.♗g5 ♘e8 20.♖ac1?

Since an eventual exchange of the rooks would be entirely to Black's advantage, there is no need for White to play his rook on the open column. It was directly indicated 20.♖ad1, (see the 24th move) followed by a3 and ♗b1–a2, etc. The extra time would probably have been of great importance. From now on, on the other hand, Black has a relatively easier defensive game.

20...♕b7 21.a3

The maneuver attempted here induces Black to start a counter-demonstration on the queen's wing and, in order to do this, they must first force the exchange of White's knight.

21...g6 22.♘h6+ ♗×h6 23.♗×h6

Black's black squares are now a little weakened - but his knight on e8 is a sturdy defender.

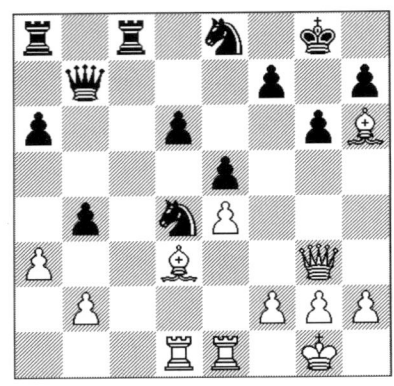

23...♘d4 24.♖cd1 b4

25.f4!

The opening of this column offers good prospects for equality - but with more difficult right answers.

25...e×f4

The defense of e5 with 25...f6 would be advantageously answered by 26.f5! etc.

26.♕×f4 b×a3 27.b×a3 ♖c3!

An ingenious drawing combination: if you know 28.e5, then 28...♔×d3! 29.♔×d3 ♘e2+ 30.♖×e2 ♕b1+ 31.♔f2 ♕×d3 32.e6! ♕f5 33.♕×f5 g×f5 34.e7 f6 35.♔e3! and the presence of White's king on the queenside would eliminate the danger of his defeat. But since a draw meant much more to me than a loss, I didn't even take this continuation seriously.

28.♕f2 ♘e6?

From here on Fine's resistance gradually began to weaken. The game didn't develop quite according to his expectations (i.e., the frustrated chance of simplification via 28...♔×d3, etc.). After the natural 28...♘c6 29.♗c1! ♘e5 30.♗f1 (♘g4 31.♕d4), Black would have slight winning chances, although White's

Bishops would almost compensate for the not very important extra Pawn.

29.a4

This seemingly insignificant Pawn will now support White's threats in a very efficient way.

29...♖ac8

Again, out of place, as it will immediately become clear that his Pawn needs more protection. The other Rook should have returned to f8.

30.♖f1

Threatening 31.♗×a6, etc.

30...♖3c7 31.♖b1 ♕c6 32.a5!

Incredible but true - White suddenly got strong pressure on the queen's wing. A rather confusing result of Black's maneuvers in that sector of the board.

32...♘c5?

This knight's development has been decidedly unlucky, and after his last move he won't be saved. Comparatively better would be 32...♖a8, after which White would increase his positional advantage with 33.♖bc1 followed by 34.♗c4, etc.

33.♗c4

If now 33...♘×e4, then 34.♗×f7+ ♔h8 35.♕d4+ winning. Black's reply is therefore forced.

33...♕d7

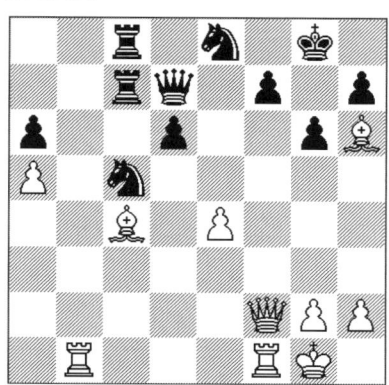

34.♕a2!

It's strange how sometimes the same attacking ideas are repeated in a short space of time! You can compare the move in the text, for example, with 37.♕d2 in my game against Tylor (*Game 91*) where the transposition of a vertical attack by the queen into a diagonal one brought a quick denouement in the same way.

34...♘×e4

Or 34...♘e6 35.♗×e6, etc.

35.♗×f7 ♕×f7 36.♗×f7+ ♔×f7 37.♕e6, and Black resigned.

An interesting fight, but certainly influenced by the exceptional importance of the result.

> **Game 91**
> **A.Alekhine-T.Tylor**
> *Margate Tournament, April 1937*
> Spanish Opening [C86]

1.e4 e5 2.♘f3 ♘c6 3.♗b5 a6 4.♗a4 ♘f6 5.0-0 ♗e7 6.♕e2 0-0?

A very common mistake: White doesn't threaten anything at this point (e.g. 7.♗×c6 d×c6 8.♘×e5 ♕d4 9.♘f3 ♕×e4, easily equalizing) and so Black thinks it's time to roll - and forgets that precisely after this move White can win a Pawn, the Bishop on e7 is no longer protected by the King! The correct move is, of course, 6...d6.

7.c3?

An exaggerated belief in the knowledge of my opponents has always been the vulnerable point of my opening game. For example, in San Remo 1930, I didn't take a Pawn on the tenth move that my opponent, Rubinstein, resigned *en prise in* an even more obvious way than in this game! It's quite obvious that 7.♗×c6 d×c6 8.♘×e5 can and should be played, because 8...♕d4 9.♘f3 ♕×e4? It costs a piece after 10.♕xe4 ♘xe4 11.♖e1. The slight advantage in development that Black would get after, for example, 8...♖e8 9.d3 ♗c5 10.♘f3 ♗g4, would in no way compensate for the lost material. After the harmless text move, well-known positions will be reached.

7...d6 8.d4 ♗d7 9.d5 ♘b8 10.♗c2 ♘e8

The maneuver 10...a5 followed by ♘–a6–f5 played by me in a game with consultation against Kashdan (see Game *119*), proved quite successful. But also, the move in the text with the aim of a quick counterattack in the center can hardly be criticized.

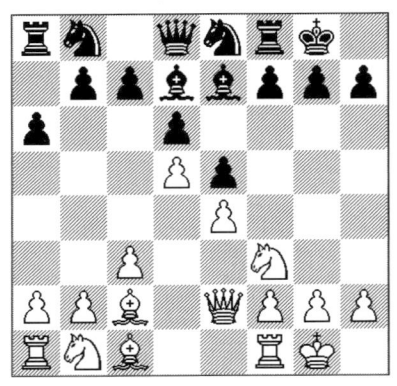

11.c4 f5

But here Black needs to prepare this advance with 11...g6 eventually followed by ...♘g7 so as not to completely surrender control of the e4 square. From now on White has a clear positional advantage, which he will exploit impeccably until an advanced stage of the middlegame.

12.exf5 ♗xf5 13.♗xf5 ♖xf5 14.♘c3 ♘d7 15.♘e4 ♘f8!

Tylor from then on defended his difficult position extremely well until the fateful 32nd move. White would have no advantage now playing 16.g4 ♖f7 17.♘fg5 ♗xg5 18.♘xg5 ♖e7 or 18.♗xg5 ♕d7, etc.

16.♗e3 ♘g6 17.g3 h6

To be able to play the Knight or Queen without allowing White's ♘g5 move.

18.♘fd2

Threatening 19.♕g4.

18...♔h7 19.♕d3 ♕d7

Preparing a possible demonstration on the kingside starting with ...♔h5 and ...♕h3. So White has no time for the logical advance b4, c5, etc.

20.f4

White correctly calculated that by this means he would win the e6 square for his knight and that Black's possible queen move against his king wouldn't improve his opponent's chances much.

20...♔h8

White's threat was 21.fxe5 ♘xe5 22.♘f6+, etc.

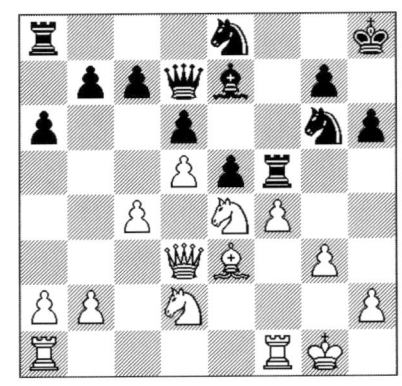

21.♘f3!

An important intermediate move that allows the central tension to relax without ceding the important e5 square to Black's knight.

21...exf4 22.♘d4 ♖f7

It would be very pointless 22...♖h5 23.♕c2, etc.

23.♗xf4?

A slight strategic mistake that prevents White from taking full advantage of his strong position. The following two important considerations speak in favor of resuming with the Pawn: (1) As Black's position is somewhat restricted, White should avoid any further exchanges. (2) White's Bishop is particularly useful for protecting Black's squares. In fact, the entire next section of the game (up to the 32nd move) is influenced by the potential power of Black's Bishop, unleashed by his main antagonist.

23...♘xf4 24.gxf4

It's hard to decide how advisable it was to provoke the exchange of a pair of rooks through 24.♔xg4: Black's rook on g7 has considerable defensive power, but on the other hand, the prospect of playing both rooks on the open columns was also tempting.

24...♕g4+ 25.♔h1!

White had already calculated this Pawn offer when he played 20.f4. Of course, the simple 25.♕g3 was also playable and would have ensured a comfortable endgame.

25...♘f6!

Quite rightly refusing the Danaian gift, because 25...♖xf4 26.♖xf4 ♕xf4 27.♖f1 would have catastrophic consequences for Black: I. ♕e5 28.♔f5 II. 27...♕h4 28.♘f5. III. 27...♕g4 28.♔f7! ♕h5 29.♘c3 - with an easy win in all cases.

26.♘f2

A seemingly artificial retreat which, in fact, should only have led to an equal game. Either 26.♖ae1 or immediately 26.♘e6 was appropriate; in the latter case, the following curious variant would be possible: 26...♕f5 27.♖ae1 c6 28.♖g1! cxd5 29.♘xd6! ♕xd3 30.♘xf7+ and mate on the next move.

26...♕h5

White's previous move would only prove strong after 26...♕xf4 27.♘e6 ♕h4 28.♘h3! threatening ♘f4-g6 etc., with an advantage.

27.♖g1

Now 27.♘e6 is not effective due to the simple 27...c6 etc.

27...♘d7!

Again, a very good maneuver, which practically forces the desirable change of knights.

28.♘e6 ♘c5 29.♕e3

Instead, 29.♕g3 would avoid the immediate exchange on e6, but on the other hand it would allow 29...♗f6.

29...♘xe6 30.dxe6

White's still existing advantage in space is here compensated by the attack to which this Pawn can be subjected, while its neighbor on f4 will need permanent defense. The chances are now almost equal.

30...♖f6 31.♖ae1 ♖af8

This Rook is necessary for guarding your g Pawn and should have been moved straight to g8. But the text doesn't spoil anything yet.

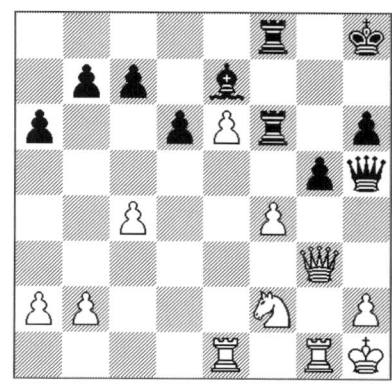

32.♕g3 g5?

A mistake, but an excusable one, because White's tactical attack afterwards was really hard to see. It was correct 32...♔g8 33.♖e4 ♕f5 34.♕e3 followed by ♘d3 etc., with an open fight in progress.

33.♘h3

Although there is no direct threat with this move, (34.fxg5 ♗f3 etc.), Black's game now becomes more problematic: he can no longer dream of a successful attack on White's Pawn.

33...♖f5 34.♔g2!

A good preparatory move for the Rook's next maneuver, against which Black won't be able to find an adequate defense.

34...c6 35.♖e3!

Only after this move does White begin to threaten. Black now needs to find something against 36.♘xg5! ♗xg5 37.♖h3! followed by 38.fxg5, etc.

35...♔g7!

A seemingly paradoxical defense, but sufficient for the moment.

36.♖g3

Taken separately, this move - like many of its immediate predecessors - seems quite harmless. In fact, after 37.fxg5 hxg5 38.♘xg5 ♗xg5 39.♖xg5+ ♖xg5 40.♕xg5+ ♕xg5 41.♖xg5+ ♔f6 etc., the game would end in a draw. And only the next smooth move gives the whole attacking scheme its real meaning.

36...d5 37.♕d2! ♗d6

After 37...♗c5 38.♖e1 (the simplest), White's win would be easy.

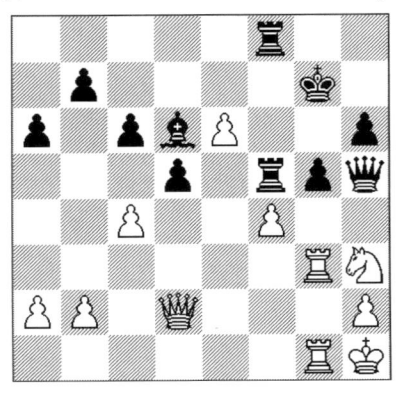

38.♘xg5!

The immediate aim of this pseudo-sacrifice is obvious - Black can't take the Knight without losing his Queen; but the consequences of Black's response are misleading, as is often the case when there are many possibilities for uncovered checkers.

38...♗xf4! 39.♕c3+!

The first point - White delays the "revelation" and rejects the tempting 39.e7 which would prove to be a hallucination after 37...♗xd2 40.♘e6+ ♔h8! etc.

39...♖8f6

If 39...♗e5, then 40.♘f3+, etc.

40.♘e4+! ♗xg3 41.♖xg3+ ♔h8

Or 41...♔f8 42.♕b4+! and mate in a few moves.

42.♕xf6+

The final point, reminiscent of a composition by Greco or Stamma.

42...♖xf6 43.♖g8+!

After 43...♔xg8 44.♘xf6+ ♔f8 45.♘xh5 dxc4 46.♔g2 White doesn't even need his extra knight to stop the pawn on the queen's wing. Black therefore resigned.

Game 92
A.Alekhine-J.Foltys
Margate Tournament, April 1937
Sicilian Defense [B62]

1.e4 c5 2.♘f3 ♘c6

If someone wants to play the "Dragon Variant" (the flank development of the King's Bishop), they would do better to start with 2...d6, since White would then not have the opportunity to play ♗g5 before ...g7, for example 2...d6 3.d4 cxd4 4.♘xd4 ♘f6 5.♘c3 g6 etc. Also, if no improvement can be found for Black in the variant of my game against

Botvinnik (6.♗e2 ♗g7 7.♗e3 ♘c6 8.♘b3 ♗e6 9.f4 0–0 10.g4 d5! 11.f5 ♗c8 12.e×d5 ♘b4 13.d6 ♕×d6 14.♗c5 ♕f4! 15.♖f1 ♕×h2! 16.♗×b4 ♘×g4 17.♗×g4 ♕g3+ 18.♖f2 ♕g1+ etc. - draw), it hardly seems tempting for them to adopt this line of play - considering, of course, that they play to win.

3.d4 c×d4 4.♘×d4 ♘f6 5.♘c3 d6

Here 5...g6 is inadvisable, due to 6.♘×c6 followed by e5.

6.♗g5 e6

Black can also delay this move by playing, for example, 6...♗d7, as 7.♗×f6 g×f6 etc. would have both advantages and disadvantages - but such a delay would be pointless for ...e3 is still inevitable. My game against Silva Rocha (Black) (Montevideo, March 1938, continued as follows: 6...♗d7 7.♗e2 a6 8.0–0 e6 (what else?) 9.♘b3 b5 10.a3 ♘a5 11.♘×a5 ♕×a5 12.♕d4! ♗e7 13.♔fd1 ♕c7 14.a4 b4 15.♗×f6 g×f6 16.♕×b4, with a decisive advantage for White.

7.♗b5

To induce Black to place his queen bishop on d7 and thus eliminate the possibility of kingside development. This system at least deserves consideration as 7.♘f3 in conjunction with ♕d2 (see my game against P. Frydman, *Game 81*)

7...♗d7 8.0–0 h6 9.♗h4

The present game shows that this apparently logical retreat is not without danger. Since the main objective of 6.♗g5 - the prevention of the "Dragon Variant" - has been achieved, 9.♗e3 is quite good.

9...a6 10.♗e2 ♗e7 11.♘b3

Trying to exploit the weakness on d6 in a similar way to the game with Frydman; but the Czechoslovak master, having played in Podebrad, also knew that game and had taken advantage of its lesson.

11...♕c7 12.f4

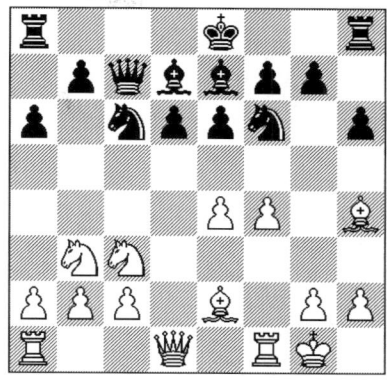

Further pressure on the d-Pawn would prove ineffective - for example 12.♕d2 ♖d8! (not 12...0–0 13.♖ad1 ♘×e4 14.♘×e4 ♗×h4 15.♕×d6 etc., with an advantage) 13.♖ad1 ♗c8 etc., with a solid position. So White decides to prepare an attack on the King, relying mainly on 12...0–0 13.♕e1! b5 14.♗f3 and eventually g4. But Black's next move gives the battle quite another aspect.

12...g5!

Brave and effective, Black secured the powerful central square for his knight, and one could say until the end of the game. It's interesting to note that this move - solely because Black lost the game - was completely misjudged by critics. For example, one of the most famous modern commentators wrote: "This move was mainly of psychological value, because as it is known that Alekhine does not like defensive positions, there was little chance that he could choose the variant 13.f×g5 h×g5 14.♗×g5 d5 15.h3, etc.". I confess that I didn't accept the Pawn's offer quite independently of what would be a distinction

195

for defensive play, but because I *really don't like taking mate,* and this dislike would probably occur after 15...♔×h3! etc.

These incursions into the psychology of other masters are unpleasant!

13.♗g3!

The only way is to take the balance of the position, as White now gets some pressure on the column and in compensation for Black's strong home for his knight.

13...g×f4 14.♖×f4 ♘e5 15.♕f1 ♘h7 16.♖f2!

Threatening 17.♗×e5 followed by ♖×f7, thus forcing 16...0-0, after which the presence of his King will prevent Black from increasing his initiative on that wing.

16...0-0 17.♗h5 f6

Also almost forced, but not as disadvantageous, because in exchange for the weakness on e6 Black increases the strength of his knight's position.

18.♗f4 ♔g7 19.♖e1

Dreaming of seriously upsetting Black's king after 20♕e3 and ♕g3+; but his opponent avoids this in a simple and efficient way.

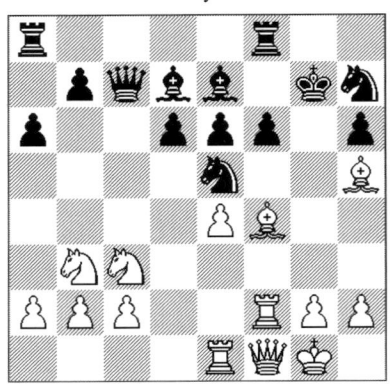

19...♕c4!

Threatening the exchange of the queens and thus obtaining a good endgame due to his well-protected center. The safest thing for White would have been to repeat moves through 20.♗e2 ♕c7 21.♗h5 etc., but they preferred to risk the tricky middlegame next, relying less on the strength of their position than on their greater experience.

20.♖ee2 ♗e8 21.♗×e8 ♖a×e8 22.♕c1 ♘g5 23.h3 ♔h7 24.♔h1 ♖g8

Black's King is now completely safe, the open e-column is a factor in his favor, and even on the Queen's wing Black has some initiative prospects due to the c-column. Folty is conducting the game very well so far and would certainly not have lost it through correct play.

25.♕e3 ♖g7 26.♘d4 ♖eg8?

But this small oversight allows White to gain a serious initiative. Obviously Black only saw that b3 **wasn't** a direct threat - because the queen would protect the pawn and from c8 - and underestimated the importance of 28.♘a4! If they had played 26...b5! instead, the chances would have remained almost equal.

27.b3 ♕c8

Otherwise 28.♗×g5 and 29.♘×e5.

28.♘a4!

With the strong threat 29.♗×g5 followed by 30.♘b6 and 31.♘×e5.

28...♗d8 29.c4

Now White has managed to gain considerable space in the center and threatens to improve his position later through 30.♔c2 followed by c5, etc. Black's next move facilitates the realization of this plan.

29...♕d7 30.c5!

If now 30...d×c5, then 31.♘×c5 ♕e7 32.♗×g5 followed by 33.♘d×e6 or 33.♗×h6 etc.

30...d5 31.♗×g5 ♖×g5

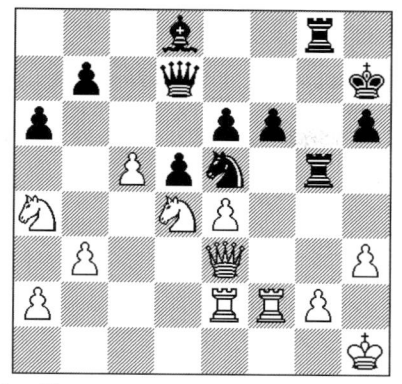

32.c6!

Allowing the Knights to menacingly enter the enemy fortress. In addition to this real strategic value, the whole maneuver also had a strong psychological effect (since "psychology" seems to be the fashion in chess these days): bewildered by the complete change of situation, Black will undoubtedly not offer the most effective resistance in the final phase that follows.

32...b×c6 33.♘c5 ♕d6 34.♘c×e6 ♖g3

Allowing the exchange to go ahead, after which White's knights "fold" in an original way on the 6th rank, quickly making any further resistance useless. Also after the best 34...♔5g6 (35.e×d5 c×d5 36.♘×d8 ♔×d8 37.♔c2 ♖e8 38.♕f4, etc.) White would win due to the various weaknesses in the opponent's position.

35.♕×h6+!

Much less because of the importance of this Pawn than because of the possibility of the second Knight entering.

35...♔×h6 36.♘f5+ ♔h7 37.♘×d6 ♘d3 38.♖f1 d×e4

The loss of a second pawn is inevitable.

39.♘×e4 ♔3g6 40.♘×d8, and

Black resigned.

> **Game 93**
> **A.Alekhine–S.Reshevsky**
> *Kemeri Tournament, June 1937*
> Alekhine Defense [B05]

1.e4 ♘f6 2.e5 ♘d5 3.d4 d6 4.♘f3 ♗g4 5.c4

There's no hurry to dislodge the knight. The immediate 5.♗e2 would allow White, in the event of 5...d×e5, to retake the knight without being forced to sacrifice a pawn.

5...♘b6 6.♗e2 d×e5 7.♘×e5

That was my intention when I adopted 5.c4; but - although White did indeed get *some* compensation for the Pawn sacrifice, it was hardly advisable to make a considerable effort to probably get equality. In the 29th Game of my first game with Dr. Euwe, here I played 7.c5 and got an advantage in the opening, but only because my opponent after 7...e4 8.c×b6 e×f3 9.♗×f3 ♗×f3 10.♕×f3 a×b6 instead of 10...♘c6 chose the harmless move 10...a×b6.

7...♗×e2 8.♕×e2 ♕×d4 9.0-0

Allowing the exchange of the central knight and thus facilitating Black's defense. More to the point would be 9.♘a3! ♘8d7 10.♘f3, or 9...e6 10.♘c2 preserving in both cases three minor pieces for attacking purposes.

9...♘8d7 10.♘×d7

Sacrificing the c-Pawn with 10.♘f3 would be pointless.

See the next Diagram

10...♘×d7?

Rather strangely, Reshevsky decided to make this inferior move after a particularly close examination of the situation. One might think that

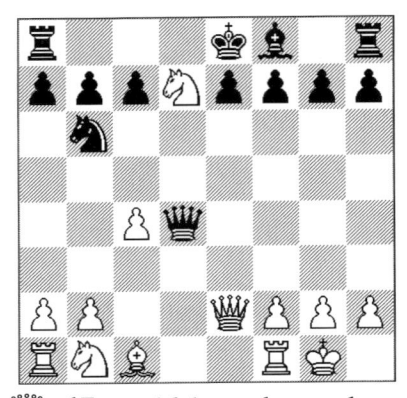

10...♕xd7 could have been the move chosen automatically because it's a general consideration that the Queen exposed in the center would then allow White to gain time and thus obtain real compensation for the sacrificed Pawn. If Black had taken back the queen, my intention would have been to continue with 10...♕xd7! 11.a4 ♕c6 (not 11...♘xa4 12.♕f3!) 12.♘a3 e6 13.a5 ♘d7 14.♘b5 after which Black's defensive problem would remain far from easy. The text move puts his game in danger and only the greatest circumspection will save Black from a quick collapse.

11.♘c3 c6

The threat of 12.♘b5 was very strong.

12.♗e3 ♕e5 13.♖ad1 e6 14.♕f3!

An important move, which practically forces Black to give back his extra pawn, as his King must be removed from the center of the board under any circumstances. For example, 14...♗d6 15.g3 or 14...♗e7 15.♗xd7! followed by 16.♕xf7 or 14...♘f6 15.♘b5! would be insufficient with a winning attack.

14...0-0-0! 15.♗xa7

It would be a serious mistake instead for 15.♕xf7 due to 15...♗d6 followed by ...♔hf8 to win. But now White, having equalized the forces, retains a clear positional advantage, and Black's kingside position is anything but safe.

15...♕a5 16.♗d4

Avoid 16...♘e5.

16...♕f5

Trying to make the best of it. The endgame after the Ladies' exchange certainly looks pretty bad, but that doesn't mean *entirely* hopeless.

17.♕g3

A former Champion's decision... Before 1935 - and now - I would undoubtedly adopt the simple line starting with 17.♕xf5 which would virtually guarantee me an extra Pawn on the Queen's wing and eliminate any shadow of danger. But throughout the period leading up to the regame, I simply couldn't rely on my patience and nerves, which would certainly be needed to win the endgame in question.

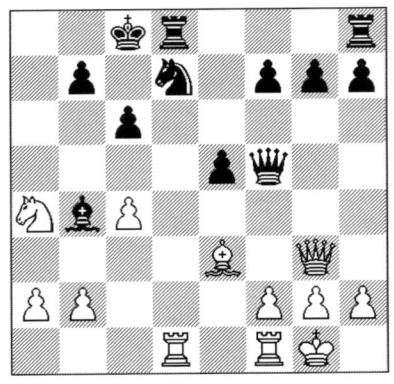

17...e5 18.♗e3 ♗b4 19.♘a4

19...♗a5! 20.f4!

Otherwise Black would even get the initiative after 20...♗c7 and ...e4.

20...♗c7 21.b3

It was important to prevent Black from playing ...♕c2 in *time*.

21...f6 22.fxe5 ♕e6

Of course, not 22...♕xe5 23.♗f4 winning.

23.h3!

A good positional move, which, however, isn't particularly deep or difficult to find. Its main aim is to avoid the possibility of ...♕g4 after 23...♘xe5 24.♘c5, and also in some other variants the protection of the g4 Pawn was essential. I wasn't at all surprised to read all the praise heaped on this modest move in the text by the critics, and to be asked - in all seriousness - after the game was over, if with 23.h3 I planned to play my queen on h2 in the 33rd move...

23...♖hg8

At this moment the g-Pawn is not yet in danger - but after the exchange of a pair of Rooks on the Queen's wing it could possibly be taken.

24.♗d4

With the clear purpose of reducing the central tension through 25.♕e3 or ♕c3.

24...♘xe5

This looks quite promising, as 25.♘c5 can be met with 25...♕e7 and 25.♘b6+ ♔b8 26.♕c3? - through 26...c5 etc., with an advantage; but a slight transposition of moves completely changes the situation in White's favor. Relatively better then would be 24...fxe5 25.♕e3 e4 26.c5 ♔de8, after which Black's passed Pawn could somehow counterbalance White's threats on the Queen's wing.

25.♕c3!

Threatening both 26.♘c5 and 26.♘b6+. Black's response is practically forced, because after 25...♔b8 26.♘c5 ♕d6 27.♕b4! etc., White's threats would prove stronger.

25...♘d7 26.c5!

This Pawn will then fill various roles in the game for the Bishop, who from now on will merely oversee the progress of events.

26...♖ge8 27.b4!

A Pawn offer, whose idea is (27...♕xa2) 28.♖a1 ♕e6 (or 28...♕d5 29.♖fd1) 29.b5! threatening 30.♘b6+ etc., with a very strong attack.

27...♘b8

Also, after this retreat White gets a winning game - but not so much through the direct attack, but through the fact that after the next forced exchange his Bishop will become considerably stronger than Black's Knight. A satisfactory defense, however, is not visible. Black's decisive mistake - although not at all obvious - was probably 24...♘xe5.

28.♘b6+ ♗xb6 29.cxb6 ♕xa2

After their counter-chances on the b8–h2 diagonal have disappeared, Black correctly estimates that his only slight chance of salvation consists of extreme recklessness. In fact, I confess that at that moment I didn't even consider the possibility of capturing the text...

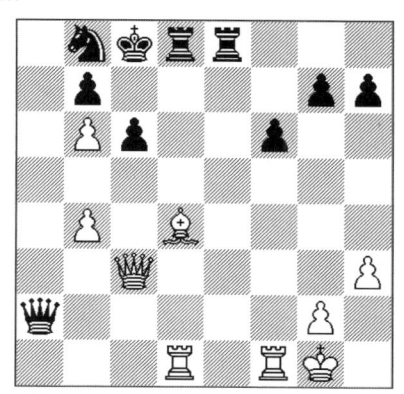

30.♕g3!

More accurate than 30.♖a1 ♕d5.

30...♖d7

Or 30...♕f7 31.♖a1! ♔xd4 32.♖a8 ♖e5 33.♕xe5, winning.

31.♗c5

Quite good, but 31.♗×f6! was simpler: if 31...g×f6, then 32.♕×d7 ♔×d7 33.♕c7+ ♔e6 34.♖e1+ winning.

31...♕f7 32.♖a1 ♕g6 33.♕h2!

After that Black can't avoid the unwelcome visit of the Rook on a8 for long.

33...♖e5

Or I. 33...♕g5 34.♖a8 ♕e5 35.♗f2! ♕×h2+ 36.♔×h2 and after ♗g3 Black would lose quality with a hopeless position. II. 33...♘a6 34.b5! ♕g5 35.♔fc1! winning.

34.♖a8 ♖d2

Black didn't see the main threat. But after a defensive move like 34.♕e8 White would also win quickly with 35.♕g3 followed by 36.♕a3 etc.

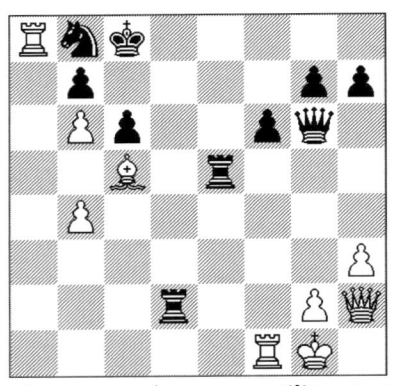

35.♔×b8+! ♔×b8 36.♕×e5+! and mate in two moves.

Although I objectively must blame my 17th move (which, by the way, in the Tournament Book is accompanied by an exclamation mark), I must admit that the final attack of that game gave me (and I hope it gave the readers) much more pleasure than a scientifically correct but purely technical exploration of the Pawn majority on the Queen's wing would have. After all, chess isn't *just about* knowledge and logic!

> **Game 94**
> **A.Alekhine–R.Fine**
> *Kemeri Tournament, June 1937*
> Queen's Gambit Accepted [D23]

1.d4 d5 2.c4 d×c4 3.♘f3 ♘f6 4.♕a4+

This Queen maneuver is more effective than in the Catalan system (after g3) because White can in some variants wish to develop the Bishop on the g1–a6 diagonal. But also, after the more usual 4.g3 White's prospects are considered by far the most promising, and this is not due to any particular variant, but to the modern method of handling the Accepted Queen's Gambit with the white pieces: advancing the central Pawns at the earliest opportunity, possibly at the cost of heavy sacrifices. The Reshevsky-Vidmar games (Nottingham 1936), Euwe-Alekhine (5th Game of the 1937 game), and even the older Opocensky-Rubinstein (Marienbad 1925) are characteristic of this. In my recent practice, the following two examples, illustrating this new white trend, are, I believe, remarkable:

I. Black: R. Letelier, Montevideo 1938: 4.♗×c4 e6 5.d4 ♘f6 6.0–0 a6 7.♕e2 b5 8.♗b3 ♗b7 9.♘c3 ♘bd7 10.♖d1 ♗e7 11.e4! b4 12.e5 b×c3 13.e×f6 ♘×f6 14.♗a4+ ♔f8 15.d×c5 ♕a5 16.c6 ♕×a4 17.c×b7 ♖b8 18.b×c3 ♖×b7 19.♘e5 ♕e4 20.♕×a6 ♖c7 21.♗a3! g6 22.♗×e7+ ♖×e7 23.♕d6, resign.

II. Black: E. Böok, Margate 1938: 4.e3 e6 5.♗×c4 c5 6.0–0 ♘c6 7.♕e2 a6 8.♘c3 b5 9.♗b3 b4 (in the above Euwe-Alekhine game the continuation was 9...♗e7 10.d×c5 ♗×c5 11.e4! with an advantage for White) 10.d5! ♘a5 11.♗a4+ ♗d7 12.d×e6 f×e6

13.♖d1! b×c3 14.♖×d7 ♘×d7 15.♘e5 ♖a7 16.b×c3 ♔e7 17.e4! ♘f6 18.♗g5 ♕c7 19.♗f4 ♕b6 20.♖d1 g6 (or) 21.♗g5 ♗g7 22.♘d7! ♔×d7 23.♖×d7+ ♔f8 24.♗×f6 ♗×f6 25.e5!, they resign.

4...♕d7

As White's queen wouldn't be particularly in danger on c4, there's no reason to try to force its exchange. Instead, a safe line is 4...c6 5.♕×c4 ♗f5, etc.

5.♕×c4 ♕c6 6.♘a3

There is little difference between this move and 6.♘bd2 as Black has nothing better to justify his previous move than to exchange queens in both cases.

6...♕×c4 7.♘×c4 e6 8.a3

It was very important to avoid ...♗b4+.

8...c5?

A dogmatic move, after which White manages to gain a clear positional advantage. In their haste to counterattack in the center, Black for a moment forgot the importance of each d6. A brave but not at all antipositional scheme would instead be 8...a5 (avoiding b4) and if 9.♗f4 then 9...b5 followed by ...♗d6. At least White wouldn't get the advantage of the bishop pair so easily.

9.♗f4 ♘c6

It was slightly better 9...♘bd7 10.♘d6+ ♗×d6 11.♗×d6 ♘e4 12.♗c7 b6 followed by ...♗b7, etc. But the weaknesses on the black squares would remain in any case.

10.d×c5 ♗×c5 11.b4 ♗e7 12.b5 ♘b8 13.♘d6+ ♗×d6 14.♗×d6 ♘e4

See the next Diagram

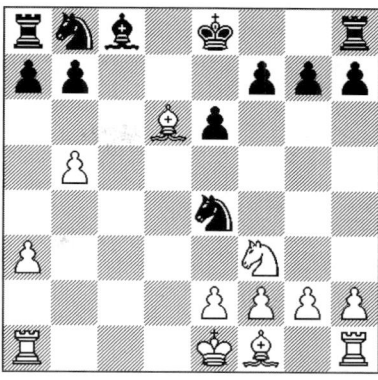

15.♗c7!

This Bishop is practically White's only chance of victory at this stage and should be played very carefully to avoid its exchange. Instead, it would be inadvisable to play 15.♗b4 a5! 16.b×a6 ♘×a6, etc. or 15.♗f4 f6! followed by ...e5 etc., with almost equal prospects in both cases.

15...♘d7 16.♘d4!

Again, an important move, the idea of which is to form the Pawn chain e4–f3–g2. This wasn't very easy to find, especially as the two alternatives 16.e3 and 16.g3 also offer some interesting possibilities.

16...♘b6 17.f3 ♘d5 18.♗a5 ♘ef6

Another important variant was 18...♘d6 19.e4 (not 19.♘c2 ♘c4 etc.) 19...♘e3 20.♗b4! e5 21.♗×d6 e×d4 22.♗d3! ♘×g2+ 23.♔f2 ♘e3 24.♗e5 etc., with advantage.

19.♘c2!

The real point of the maneuver initiated by 16.♘d4: Black's knight is prevented from entering e3 and will henceforth be forced to play a secondary role. The hunt for the bishop by the two knights in this way proved to be a complete failure.

19...♗d7 20.e4 ♖c8

This intermediate move is also perfectly harmless, as White's king on d2 can't be seriously bothered by Black's almost crippled strength.

21.♔d2! ♘b6 22.♘e3 0-0

All of Black's moves after 18...♘ef6 are virtually forced.

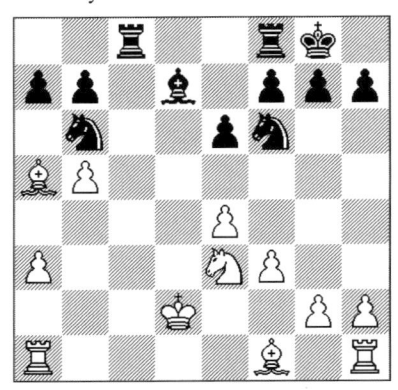

23.a4!

Much stronger than the conventional 23.♗d3 which would allow the liberating move ...♘–a4–c5, etc.

23...♖fd8 24.♗d3 e5

After this weakening of the d5 and f5 squares the game can hardly be saved. The only slight chance consisted of 24...♗e8 eventually followed by ...♘fd7. White's tactics in this case would remain almost the same - exchange a pair of rooks, remove the bishop on a5 and dislodge Black's knight on b6.

25.♖hc1 ♗e6 26.♖xc8 ♖xc8 27.♗b4

Both prevent Black's king from approaching the center and eventually threaten ♗d6.

27...♘e8 28.a5 ♘d7 29.♘d5!

This had to be calculated exactly as the passed Pawn resulting from the exchange would be slightly exposed. Due to the formidable threat 30.♘e7+ Black must now take the Knight.

29...♗xd5 30.exd5 ♘c5

The "little combination" thus initiated finds a convincing rebuttal in White's 32nd move. But what could Black really do? The Tournament Book's recommendation, 30...g3 would be completely hopeless in the long run after 31.d6 f5 32.♗b1! ♔g7 33.♗a2 ♔f6 (or 33...♘ef6 34.♖e1) 34.♗d5, etc.

31.♗f5! ♖d8

Or 31...♘b3+ 32.♔d3 ♘c1+ 33.♔e3 ♔c4 34.d6 winning.

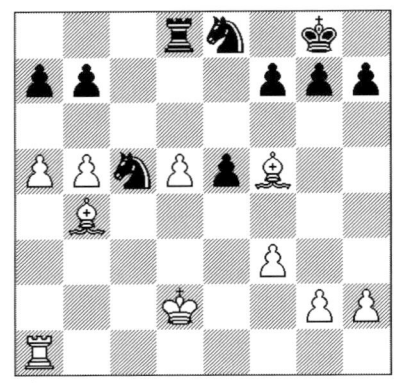

32.♔c3!

This beautiful move eliminates both threats 32...♘b3+ and 32...♔xd5+, the latter due to the reply 33.♔c4! winning a piece. White's overwhelming advantage in space now decides the battle in a few moves.

32...b6

Or 32...♘d7 33.♗e7 winning.

33.axb6 axb6 34.♗xc5!

The Bishop has done more than his duty in this game and can now withdraw, as the passed Pawn b can only be stopped with heavy losses.

34...bxc5 35.b6 ♘d6 36.♗d7! ♖xd7

Instead of abandoning.

37.♖a8+ and mate in two.

This game is probably my best achievement in recent years.

Game 95
A.Alekhine-E.Bogoljubov
Quadrangular Tournament, Bad Nauhein
July 1937
Queen's Gambit Declined,
Orthodox Defense [D58]

1.d4 d5 2.c4 e6 3.♘c3 ♘f6 4.♗g5 ♗e7 5.♘f3 h6 6.♗h4 0-0 7.e3 b6

In conjunction with ...h6, this flanking development has quite often been adopted by Dr. Tartakower with success. The first player has several plausible ways of tackling this, but no convincing rebuttal. I decided to allow Black to complete his mobilization plan or - to be more precise - the first part of it, consisting of ...♗b7, ...♘bd2, ...c5 – and try to take advantage of just one detail of the position, namely the fact that Black's queen is deprived of the d8–a5 diagonal and cannot easily find a suitable square. The course of the game will show to what extent the idea proved successful. It lacks tactical points, is emotionless - but not dull - and is of use to the student.

8.♖c1 ♗b7 9.♗e2

Inducing Black to gain time by exchanging Pawns afterwards.

9...d×c4 10.♗×c4 c5 11.0-0 ♘bd7

If 11...♘c6, then 12.d×c5 ♕×d1 13.♖f×d1 and Black would be in trouble due to the possible entry of the Rook on the 7th rank.

12.♕e2 ♘e4

I suppose many masters would have made this move because, by forcing the exchange of two minor pieces, it frees up Black's game and provides a safe point for the queen. It's still questionable whether the more complicated 12...a6 13.♖fd1 b5 wouldn't have offered more prospects of equality. After Black's queen's bishop hole, the white squares on the queen's wing suddenly become weak.

13.♘×e4 ♗×h4

Or 13...♗×e4 14.♗g3! etc., with an advantage.

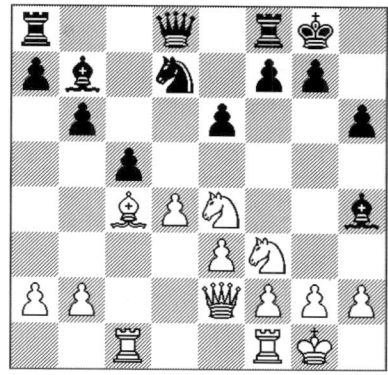

14.♘c3!

This simple retreat is more effective than 14.♘d6 ♗×f3 15.♕×f3 ♗e7 etc., forcing White to waste more time, or 14.♗d3 ♗f6, after which Black would avoid exchanging his queen bishop.

14...♗f6 15.♖fd1 ♕e7

Finally, the intercom between the Rooks has been established, but now the real point of White's last maneuver begins.

16.♗a6 ♖ab8 17.♗×b7 ♖×b7 18.♘e4!

To gain full control along column c, which, as the following will clearly show, is by no means weak.

18...c×d4 19.e×d4

Instead, 19.♘×d4 ♗×d4 20.♖×d4 ♘f6 etc. would be good enough for a comfortable draw.

19...♖d8

His position becomes difficult. By playing 19...♘b8 20.♘e5!, etc. Black could at least temporarily avoid compromising the Pawn structure on the King's wing - but a suitable subsequent

203

plan of defense is harder to find after the chosen move.

20.♕a6! ♘b8

After 20...♖db8 21.♖c8+ would be too strong - and 20...♘f8 21.♘xf6+ etc. would leave the c6 square defenseless.

21.♘xf6+ gxf6 22.♕e2

White now has two important trump cards: the open back rank and Black's weakness on the kingside. Through rational exploitation this will be enough.

22...♖bd7 23.♖d3 ♖d5 24.♖dc3

As the weak pawn needs only one protector, the rook can - and should - be used to exert strong pressure on the c-column.

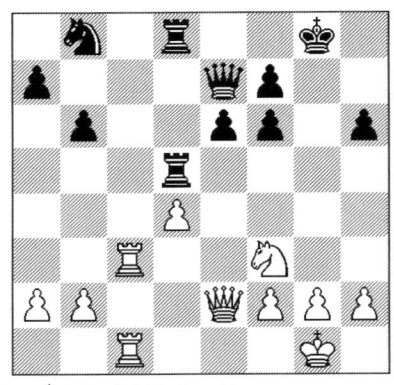

24...♔h7 25.h3 a5

Weakening Pawn b - but otherwise Pawn a would need permanent defense. Black almost only has a choice of evils.

26.a3

Since the opponent has no useful moves at his disposal, White can easily correct the small defects in his Pawn structure.

26...♖g8 27.♖c7 ♘d7 28.♖1c6 ♕f8 29.♕c2+!

More accurate than 29.♔c8 ♕g7! 30.♕c2+ when Black would have the answer 30...♕g6.

29...f5

Otherwise 30.♖c8 would be even more effective.

30.♖c8 ♕e7 31.♖xg8

Black's rook must be exchanged to prevent the queen's possible activity on the king's wing.

31...♔xg8 32.♕c1 ♔g7 33.♕f4

Threatening 34.♕g3+, followed by ♔c8+.

33...♕d8 34.a4!

Avoiding ...♖b5 once and for all and putting Black in a kind of *zugzwang* position.

34...b5

This seemingly natural response is quickly lost. By comparison it would be better to 34...♔h7, after which White finally forces the denouement by playing the queen to the queenside: ♕c1–♕c4–♕a6.

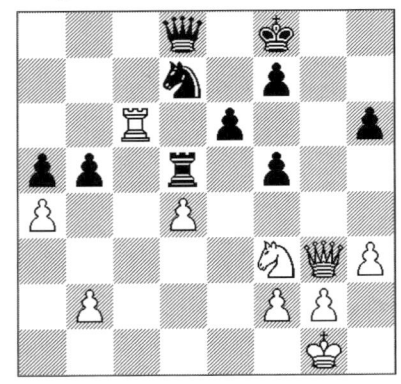

35.♕g3+ ♔f8

36.♖d6!

This gains at least a Pawn by practically forcing the exchange of Queens. The resulting endgame won't present much difficulty, as it will have even more weaknesses to exploit than - for example - Black's h6 square.

36...♕a8

Equally hopeless would be 36...bxa4 37.♔xd5 exd5 38.♕d6+ ♕e7 39.♕xd5 etc.

37.a×b5 ♕b7 38.♖×d5 ♕×d5 39.b6! ♕c6 40.♕c7 ♕×c7 41.b×c7 ♘b6 42.♘e5 ♔e7 43.♘c4

Then the passed Pawn b will force at least one Black piece onto the Queen's wing and meanwhile White's King will become master on the other side of the board.

43...♘c8 44.♘×a5 ♔d7 45.♔h2 ♔×c7 46.♔g3 ♔d6 47.♔h4 ♔d5 48.♔h5 ♔×d4 49.♔×h6 e5 50.♔g5 f4 51.h4 f6+

The last "try", which the whites face in the simplest way.

52.♔×f6 e4 53.♘b3+! ♔d5

Or 53...♔d3 (c4) 54.♘c5+ (d2+), followed by 55.♘×e4 and h5, winning.

54.h5 e3 55.f×e3 f×e3 56.♘c1, and Black resigned.

Game 96
A.Alekhine-F.Saemisch
Quadrangular Tournament, Bad Nauhein
July 1937
Spanish Opening [C86]

1.e4 e5 2.♘f3 ♘c6 3.♗b5 a6 4.♗a4 ♘f6 5.0–0 ♗e7 6.♕e2 b5 7.♗b3 d6 8.c3 0–0

A safer course is 8...♘a5 9.♗c2 c5 etc., similar to the variant starting with 6.♖e1.

9.a4! ♗g4

This is comparatively better than 9...b4 10.a5, or 9...♖b8 10.a×b5 a×b5 11.d4 etc., with an advantage, but still has the disadvantage of putting the Bishop out of play if White, as in the current game, doesn't accept the Pawn offer.

10.h3

More common is ♖d1 followed by d4. The move in the text is the start of a quite different plan, aimed at limiting the activity of Black's queen bishop to a minimum. It would be inadvisable instead to play 10.a×b5 a×b5 11.♗×a8 ♕×a8 12.♕×b5 ♘a7!, after which Black recovers the Pawn with a good position.

10...♗h5 11.g4

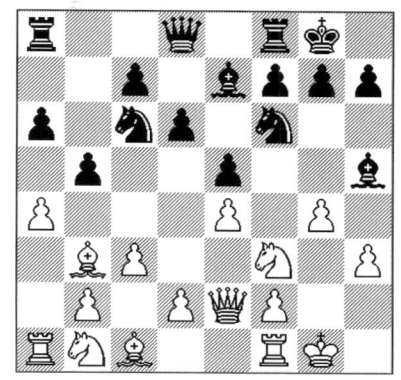

The main objections against advancing in this type of position are usually: (1) The possibility of the Knight being sacrificed on g4. (2) The disruption of the Pawn structure through ...h5. Neither of these eventualities is feared here (for example, *11...♘×g4 12.h×g4 ♗×g4 13.♕e3* - or *11...♗g6 12.d3 h5 13.♘g4*, with advantage) - there's no reason to delay trapping the Bishop.

11...♗g6 12.d3 ♘a5 13.♗c2 ♘d7?

The full value of the system adopted by White could only be estimated if Black had constructed the classic defensive position by playing 13...c5 followed by ...♕c7. The inconsequential move in the text - probably dictated by an exaggerated fear of White's move ♘h4 - resigned White with free hands, both in the center and on the queen's wing. The first victim of this strategy will be the queen's knight, which will be removed directly to a purely passive square, making the next

205

part of the game merely an object for White's combinatorial play.

14.b4 ♘b7 15.♘a3 c6 16.♗b3 ♘b6

White eventually threatens c4, which would force Black to exchange his Pawn b, thus further weakening the overall situation on the Queen's wing. The move in the text, which avoids this danger at the cost of time, cannot therefore be condemned.

17.a5 ♘d7 18.♗e3

In making this last move in preparation for their intended advance on the queen's wing, White had considered the counterattack 18...d5!? 19.exd5 c5, which they intended to counter with 20.d6! ♗xd6 21.♗d5 or 20...♘xd6 21.bxc5 etc., in both cases with an advantage.

18...♔h8

Sooner or later, it is obligatory to bring the Bishop of the Queen to life.

19.c4!

As we'll see, White's next tactics are based on the Knight's weakness on b7.

19...♘f6

Initiating an ingenious counterattack, although not enough. In fact, Black desperately had little choice.

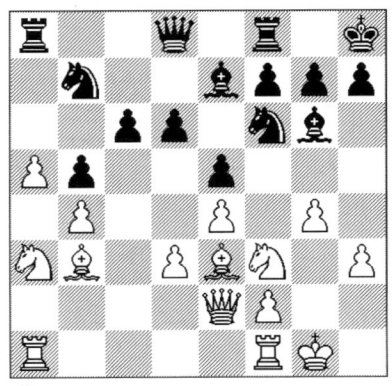

20.cxb5 axb5

21.♘xb5!

A purely positional offer, or rather an exchange combination, which in the main variant would go like this: 21...cxb5 22.a6 ♕c7 23.axb7 ♕xb7 24.g5 ♖xa1 25.♖xa1 ♘d7 (otherwise 26.♖a7 would win) 26.♘h4 ♖a8 27.♖a5, and Black would finally perish mainly due to his helpless queen bishop. No wonder then that Saemisch preferred to continue the exploitation of White's slightly exposed kingside and gain important time by leaving the hostile knight *en prise*.

21...♕d7! 22.a6 ♘d8 23.♘c3 ♘xg4!

The interesting point of Black's active defense, however, proves comparatively harmless, as White can simply continue his "work" on the other side.

24.b5!

Instead, 24.hxg4 ♕xg4+ 25.♔h1 ♗h5! etc. would have ensured Black at least a draw. But now things become very difficult for them, due to the formidable threat of b6 and the possibility of ♗d5 in the case of cxb5.

24...♘xe3 25.fxe3

After this forced exchange, the King's position again is quite secure.

25...cxb5 26.♗d5 ♘e6

Delivering a Pawn via 26...♘c6 27.♘xb5 would certainly not be a better alternative, while 26...♖a7 27.♖fb1 ♕c8 28.♘xb5 ♖xa6 29.♘a7! would lose quality in the same way.

27.♗xa8 ♖xa8 28.♕b2 ♘c7 29.♔g2 f6

Exchanging the b-Pawn for the white a-Pawn - here or on the next move - would certainly mean death after a rather prolonged agony.

See the next Diagram

30.♕b3!

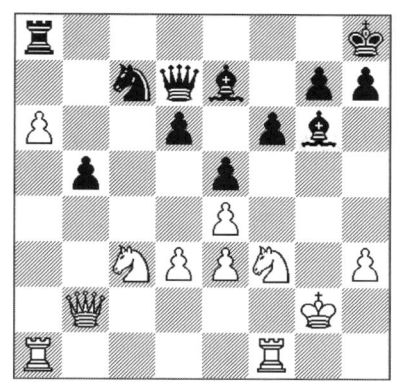

Taking control of the d5-square and at the same time avoiding ...♗f7.

30...♗e8 31.a7 g6 32.♖a5 ♔g7 33.♖fa1 ♗f7 34.♘d5!

Otherwise Black would get some counter-chances after ...d4; but now he is almost forced to force the exchange on d4, as 34...♕c6 would be answered by 35.♘xe7 and 34...♗d8 through 35.♘b6! ♕c6 36.♘xa8! etc.

34...♘xd5 35.exd5 ♗e8 36.e4 f5

These anemic last-ditch efforts will be brought to a swift halt by an energetic final combination.

37.♖a6 g5 38.♕c3! g4

This would finally show something like the following drastic blow.

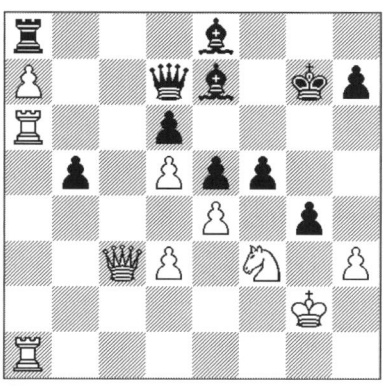

39.♘xe5!

The Knights certainly did their best in this fight: the first contributed to smashing the pieces on the Black King's wing, and his colleague could die happily after opening the way to the heart of the enemy fortress. The rest is easy.

39...dxe5 40.♕xe5+ ♔g8 41.d6!

Also threatening 42.♕d5+.

41...♕c8 42.dxe7 ♕c2+ 43.♔h1 ♕f2 44.♕xf5, and Black resigned.

Game 97
A.Alekhine-M.Euwe
World Championship (2), Rotterdam
October 1937
Slav Defense [D17]

1.d4 d5 2.c4 c6 3.♘f3 ♘f6 4.♘c3 dxc4 5.a4 ♗f5 6.♘e5

The discovery that the text move is not enough to secure White an opening advantage was one of the legacies of this game.

6...e6

Played twice by Bogoljubov against me in the 1929 game. As the experiment was unsuccessful (he only managed to draw one game with great difficulty and lost the other) the move 6...e6 disappeared from master practice. But, as proved especially by the 11th Game of that game, it is in fact much safer than the Kmoch Variant (6...♘bd7) then in vogue, in conjunction with ...♕c7 and ...e5.

7.♗g5

Since, after 7.f3 ♗b4, the move 8.e4? would provoke the safe sacrifice 8...♘xe4! (first played by Chéron against Przepiorka in The Hague 1928), White needs to be in no hurry to form a Pawn center. Still, after the next response, they have no better move than 8.f3.

7...♗b4

Much more logical than 7...♗e7 as played by Bogoljubov in our 5th game of the 1929 game (see Game *27*).

8.♘×c4

Very harmless, because Black, instead of the complicated variant chosen here, could simply play 8...h6, and if 9.♗h4 then 9...g5 10.♗g3 ♘e4 11.♔c1 (or 11.♕b3 ♘a6) 11...c5 etc., with at least the same prospects.

8...♕d5

It's also a good move, leading after a short, sharp *intermezzo* to a balanced position.

9.♗×f6

The alternative 9.♘e3 ♕a5 10.♘×f5 ♕×f5 etc. was even less promising. And if 9.♕b3, then 9...♘a6, with advantage.

9...♕×c4

Better than 9...g×f6 10.♘e3 ♕a5 11.♕b3 with slightly better prospects for White.

10.♕d2

The only move, since 10.♔c1? would be refuted by 10...g×f6 11.e4 ♕a2! etc.

10...g×f6

It was more promising 10...♕b3 11.♗×g7 ♔g8 12.♗h6 ♘d7 etc., with a strong initiative for the Pawn.

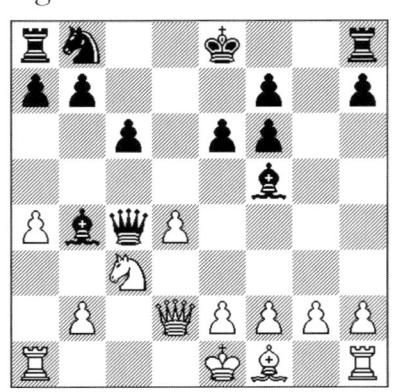

11.e4 ♕b3 12.e×f5 ♘d7 13.f×e6 f×e6 14.♗e2 0-0-0 15.0-0

The final moves were practically forced and the position thus achieved offers practically equal attacking possibilities for both sides.

15...e5

This logical move - which brings the knight into a strong position and opens up the d-file to Black's advantage - has, in my opinion, been unduly criticized. In any case, 15...♘b6, which was recommended instead, would expose Black to dangerous threats after 16.a5 ♘a4 17.♕e3 ♘×b2 18.♔fc1- and that without offering them any real prospect of winning.

16.d×e5 ♘×e5 17.♕c1 ♗×c3

Since 18.♘e4 really wasn't a strong threat, this exchange could be postponed until an appropriate moment. Black should have played 17...♔hg8, and if 18.♘e4 (18.♕e3 ♕×b2), then 18...♘f3+ 19.♗×f3 ♕×f3 20.♘g3 ♕g4 etc., with a very satisfactory position. After the text move White gets the best chances because his Bishop will prove superior to the Knight as soon as Black's piece is dislodged from e5.

18.b×c3 ♖hg8 19.♕e3 ♔b8

Not absolutely necessary, as they could indirectly protect their Pawn by playing 19...♕d5 20.g3 ♕d2; but after 21.♕×d2 ♖×d2 22.♖ae1 (22...♘d3 23.♖d1!) White's chances in the end would still be better.

20.g3

As this defensive move is inevitable anyway, it's best to play it straight away.

20...♖d7 21.♖ab1 ♕c2

See the next Diagram

22.♖fe1!

The most subtle move of the game! With this, White prepares the important f4. The immediate advance of

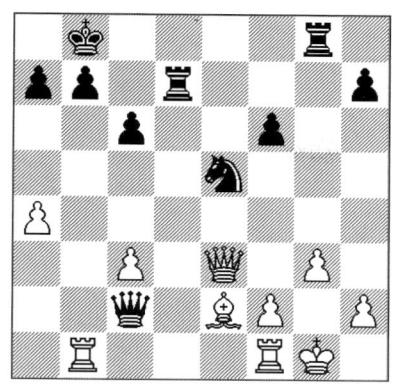

this Pawn would be refuted by 22...♖d2! 23.♖fe1 ♘d3, etc.
22...♕d2 23.♕×d2 ♖×d2 24.f4 ♘g6 25.♗c4 ♖gd8

Or 25...♔g7 26.♖e8+ ♔c7 27.♖a1! with an advantage for White.

26.♖e6!

To exchange a pair of rooks. It should be noted that Black can't play 26...♔c2 due to 27.♗a6 b6 28.♖×c6.

26...♖8d6 27.♖be1 ♔c7 28.♖×d6 ♖×d6

If 28...♔×d6 then 29.♗g8 threatens both ♗×h7 and ♖e6+.

29.h4

To play the King at f2 undisturbed by the Rook check on the second row.

29...♔d7 30.♔f2 ♘e7 31.♔f3 ♘d5?

Allowing White's king to successfully attack the h-pawn. However, it's more than doubtful whether 31...c5 (which was comparatively the best) could save the game. White would then play *not* 32.g4 due to 32...f×g4+ 33.♔×g4 ♔g6+ followed by 34...♘f5 with sufficient counter-chances - but first 32.h5! and only after this preparation g4, freeing his g-Pawn with disastrous effects for Black.

See the next Diagram

32.♗d3!

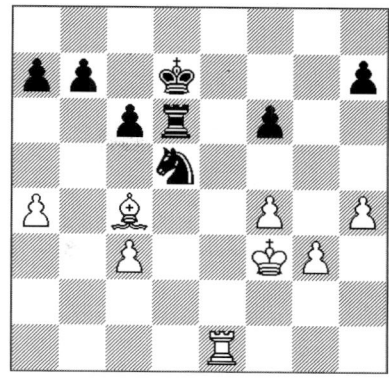

The decisive maneuver, forcing a subsequent weakening of the position of Black's Pawns on the King's wing. Any Pawn losses on the other wing will not matter, as the passive position of Black's pieces prevents them from launching any serious counterdemonstration.

32...h6 33.♗f5+ ♔d8 34.♔g4!

If now 34...♘×c3 then 35.♔h5 ♘×a4 36.♔×h6 would win easily.

34...♘e7 35.♗b1 ♔e8

Or 35...♖d5 36.f5, etc.

36.♔h5 ♔f7 37.♗a2+ ♔f8 38.♔×h6 ♖d2

The main variant was 38...♘f5+ 39.♔g6 ♘×g3 40.f5 followed by the advance of the h-pawn.

39.♗e6 ♖d3 40.g4 ♖×c3 41.g5

Even simpler than 41.♖d1 ♘d5. If now 41...f×g5, then 42.f×g5 etc., winning. Black resigned.

Game 98
A.Alekhine-M.Euwe
World Championship (6), Haarlem
October 1937
Slav Defense [D10]

1.d4 d5 2.c4 c6 3.♘c3

In my opinion this move gives White more chances of gaining an advantage in the opening, and this for the following reasons: (1) The dangers of the continuation 3...d×c4 in *conjunction with* 4...e5 are clearly shown in the present game; (2) Winaver's counterattack ...e5 can be dealt with in a simple and effective way by 4.c×d5 c×d5 *5.e4!* and if 5...d×e4 6.♗b5+ with advantage; (3) In response to 3...♘f6 4.e3 g6 I suggest *5.f3*, which after 5...♗g7 6.e4 d×e4 7.f×e4 e5! 8.d5 0–0 9.♘f3 leads to a rather complicated position, positionally still favorable to White.

3...d×c4 4.e4!

It's almost unbelievable that this natural move hasn't been considered by the so-called theoreticians. White now has an appreciable advantage in development, no matter how Black responds.

4...e5

The alternative is 4...b5 5.a4 e5 (or 5...b4 6.♘a2 ♘f6 7.e5 ♘d5 8.♗×c4 with advantage) 6.a×b5 e×d4 7.♗×c4! ♗b4! 8.♖a4 a5 9.b×a6, and White would emerge with an extra Pawn.

5.♗×c4

This combination with sacrifice is certainly very tempting and, especially on the board, extremely difficult to refute. But this is by no means the necessary consequence of White's previous move, which has a value independent of the correctness of the sacrificed piece. The *positional* exploitation of White's space advantage consists of 5.♘f3! e×d4 6.♕×d4 ♕×d4 7.♘×d4 after which Black would only get into further trouble to protect the gambit Pawn - for example: 7...b5 8.a4 b4 9.♘d1 ♗a6 10.♗e3 ♘f6 11.f3, followed by ♖c1 and ♗×c4, with a clear positional advantage.

5...e×d4

It would be fatal to 5...♕×d4 6.♕b3 ♕d7 7.♗g5! with a winning attack.

6.♘f3

Posing a very difficult practical problem for the black Queen...

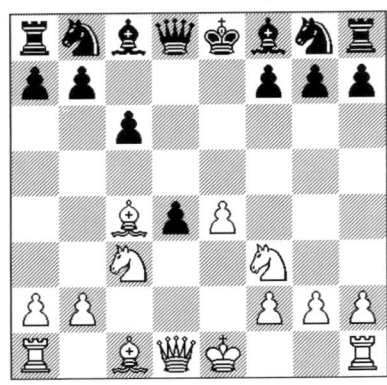

6...b5?

Which they not only fail to solve, but even choose a move that immediately puts them at a decisive disadvantage. In fact, the offer could be accepted if Black had at his disposal a more effective line than the one I analyzed when I proposed it. My "main" variant was as follows: 6...d×c3 7.♗×f7+ ♔e7 8.♕b3 ♘f6 9.e5 ♘e4 10.0–0! ♕b6 (or 10...♘a6 11.♕c4! ♘ac5 12.♗g5+! ♘×g5 13.♘×g5 with a winning attack) 11.♕c4! c×b2 12.♗×b2 ♕×b2 13.♕×e4 ♔×f7 14.♘g5+ ♔e8 15.♕c4 ♗e7 16.♕f7+ ♔d8 17.♖ad1+ ♗d7 18.♘e6+ ♔c8 19.♕×e7 ♕×e5 20.♖fe1 ♕f6 21.♖×d7 ♕×e7 (21...♘×d7 22.♕d6 winning) 22.♖×e7 with a winning position. But instead of 8...♘f6 Black could play *8...c×b2! 9.♗×b2 ♕b6! 10.♗×g8 ♔×g8 11.♕×g8* (or 11.♗a3+ c5) *11...♕b4+ 12.♘d2 ♕×b2,* after which their chances in the middlegame, despite the approximate equality of forces, would be estimated to be decidedly greater than the remaining possibilities of a direct White attack. Consequently, unless an improvement can be found in this last line of the game, White's knight offer could hardly be repeated, at least in serious chess practice.

7.♘×b5!

Dr. Euwe admits he simply didn't understand that answer. *At that point the knight obviously can't be taken due to 8.♗d5, etc.*

7...♗a6 8.♕b3!

An important move, with a triple objective: (a) to protect the King's Bishop; (b) to avoid Black's check on b4; (c) to strengthen the pressure against Black's f7 square.

8...♕e7

If 8...♗×b5 then 9.♗×f7+ ♔d7 10.♘×d4! (not 10.♗×g8 ♔×g8) etc., with an easy win.

9.0–0 ♗×b5 10.♗×b5 ♘f6

Of course, not 10...c×b5 due to 11.♕d5.

11.♗c4 ♘bd7 12.♘×d4

Another winning method would be 12.e5 ♘×e5 (if 12...♘g4 13.♕b7) 13.♘×e5 ♕×e5 14.♕b7 ♖b8 15.♕×f7+ ♔d8 16.♕×a7; but after 16...♗d6 Black would be able to put up at least that much more resistance than with the simple text move.

12...♖b8 13.♕c2 ♕c5

From now on, White will just have to avoid a small trap in order to win.

14.♘f5

Here, for example, 14.♘×c6 would be wrong because of 14...♔c8.

14...♘e5 15.♗f4!

And now, after the tempting 15.♘×g7+ ♔d8! (15...♗×g7? 16.♗×f7+) 16.♖d1+ ♔c7 White would be resigned with two pieces *en prise*.

15...♘h5

See the next Diagram

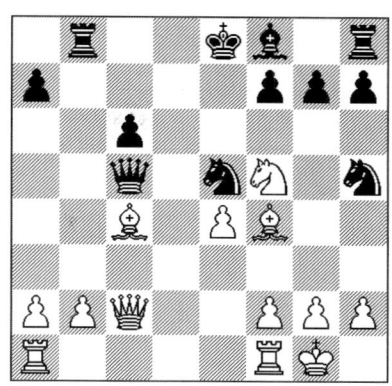

16.♗×f7+!

A very profitable simplification. It would be less convincing instead 16.♗×e5 ♕×e5 17.♗e2 ♕c5 18.♕×c5 ♗×c5 19.♗×h5 g6, etc.

16...♔×f7 17.♕×c5 ♗×c5 18.♗×e5 ♖b5 19.♗d6

Threatening 20.a4.

19...♗b6 20.b4!

And now the Rook is in danger. Black cannot avoid further loss of material.

20...♖d8 21.♖ad1 c5 22.b×c5 ♗×c5 23.♖d5!, and Black resigned.

Game 99
A.Alekhine–M.Euwe
World Championship (8), Leyden, October 1937
Nimzowitsch Defense [E34]

1.d4 ♘f6 2.c4 e6 3.♘c3 ♗b4 4.♕c2

I believe that this move is the most logical of the many possible moves (4.♕b3, 4.a3, 4.♗d2, 4.♗g5, 4.e3, 4.♘f3, 4.g3 or even 4.♗f4), as it achieves two important objectives: it takes control of e4 and at least temporarily prevents the Pawns from doubling on the c-file.

4...d5 5.c×d5

If 5.a3 ♗×c3+ 6.♕×c3 ♘e4 7.♕c2 c5 8.d×c5 ♘c6 9.e3 Black would get an equal game through

9...♕a5+ 10.♗d2 ♘xd2 11.♕xd2 dxc4! and if 12.♕xa5 ♘xa5 13.♔c1 then 13...b5! 14.cxb6 ♗b7!.

5...♕xd5 6.e3

If 6.♘f3, then for example 6...c5 7.♗d2 ♗xc3 8.♗xc3 cxd4 9.♘xd4 e5! (Loevenfisch - Botvinnik, 7th Game of the game, 1937).

6...c5 7.a3 ♗xc3+ 8.bxc3 ♘bd7

There's no hurry about this Knight development here. More appropriate for equalizing seems to be 8...0–0 9.♘f3 b6! – and if 10.♗e2, then 10...cxd4 11.cxd4 ♗a6! As, for example, I played with Black against Grau in Montevideo, 1938.

9.f3

A sound strategic system: White wants to deal with the eventual ...e5 by counter-advancing e4. Even more accurate, however, would be *first* 9.♘e2, because then 9...cxd4 10.cxd4 ♘b6 would not be satisfactory due to 11.♘c3.

9...cxd4 10.cxd4 ♘b6 11.♘e2 ♗d7 12.♘f4

Played to get a slightly higher endgame after 12...♕c6 13.♕xc6, etc. If, instead, 12.♘c3, then 12...♕c6 with a very satisfactory game.

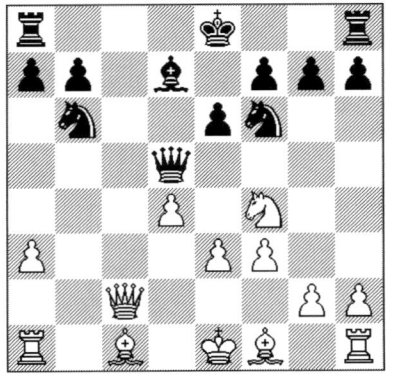

12...♕d6 13.♗d2 ♖c8 14.♕b2 ♘fd5

Undoubtedly the best move, eliminating any immediate danger in the center.

15.♘xd5 exd5 16.♗b4 ♕e6

If 16...♕g3 then 17.♔c1.

17.♔f2

The first move of the "Indian Castling" (see my game with Sultan Kahn, *Game 53*). Indeed, in this position the King is quite comfortable on f2.

17...♘a4

The first derivation of the logical path. By far the best chance of a draw consisted of 17...♘c4 (but not 17...f5 18.♗c5!, with advantage) 18.♗xc4 ♖xc4 thus obtaining Bishops of opposite colors; if, for example 19.♖ac1, then 19...♖xc1 20.♖xc1 ♗c6 21.♕c3 f6 22.♕c5 a6 23.♕b6 ♕d7, with an adequate defense.

18.♕d2 b6?

A fatal mistake, allowing White to win by force. 18...f5 was needed, although White's advantage after 19.♗d3 followed by ♖e1 and eventually e4 would already be evident.

19.♗a6! ♖b8

As the sequence shows, the threat of trapping the Bishop with ...g5 is by no means effective. But 19...♔c7 20.♖ac1 would be equally hopeless.

20.e4

This simple opening in the center leaves the blacks without the slightest saving grace.

20...b5

If 20...f6, then 21.exd5 ♕xd5 22.♕e2+! ♕e6 23.♖he1 ♕xe2+ 24.♖xe2+ ♔d8 25.♗e7+ ♔c7 26.♖c1+ winning.

See the next Diagram

21.♕f4!

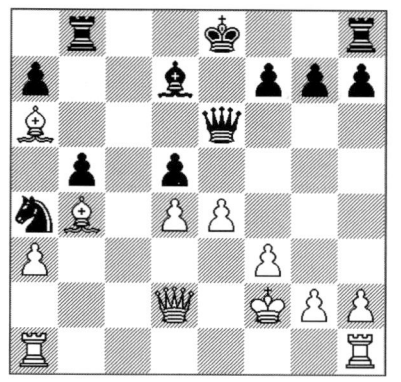

This powerful intermediate move destroys Black's last hopes of taking the opponent's King's Bishop. If now 21...♖d8, then 22.e×d5 ♕×d5 23.♖he1+ ♗e6 24.♖e5 ♕×d4+ 25.♕×d4 ♖×d4 26.♗×b5+ winning.

21...♖b6 22.e×d5

More precise than 22.♖he1 which could be answered by 22...♘b2!

22...♕×d5   23.♖he1+   ♗e6 24.♖ac1

With the terrible threat of 25.♖c8+.

24...f6 25.♖c7!

More convincing than winning the exchange with 25.♗c8+.

25...♔d8 26.♖×a7

After that mate was inevitable in a few moves. Black resigned.

Game 100
A.Alekhine-M.Euwe
World Championship (14), Zwole,
November 1937
Catalan Opening [E02]

1.d4 ♘f6 2.c4 e6 3.g3 d5

The Soviet grandmaster Loevenfish played in a tournament game in Tbilisi 1937 3...♗b4+ 4.♗d2 ♗×d2+ 5.♕×d2 ♘e4 6.♕c2 d5 7.♗g2 ♕e7 8.a3 c5 – and got a very satisfactory position. The text move in conjunction with the next one leads to a modern version of the Accepted Queen's Gambit that is slightly in White's favor.

4.♘f3

White needs to avoid exchanging queens, playing 4.♗g2 d×c4 5.♕a4+ ♕d7 6.♕×c4 ♕c6 7.♘d2 etc., and gaining an advantage in both space and development.

4...d×c4 5.♕a4+ ♘bd7 6.♕×c4

There is no advantage in delaying this capture, for example 6.♗g2 a6 7.♘c3 ♖b8! 8.♕×c4 b5, with at least equality.

6...c5

If now 6...a6, then 7.♕c2 to answer 7...b5 with 8.a4! The same maneuver would apply if Black had played ...a6 on his seventh move.

7.♗g2 ♘b6

This method of play has the disadvantage of not solving the Queen's Bishop development problem. It would be more advisable to first play 7...c×d4, and if 8.♘×d4 ♘b6 followed by ...♗b4+; and if 8.♕×d4 then 8...♗c5 9.♕h4 ♗e7 etc., still harassing White's adventurous Queen.

8.♕d3 c×d4 9.0-0!

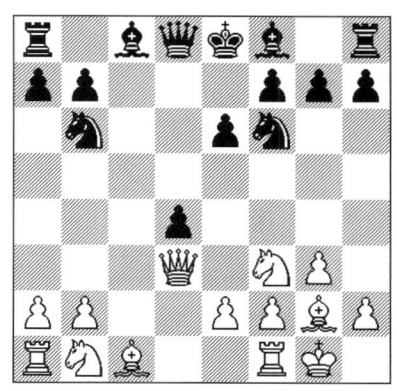

To prevent 9...♗b4+, possible for example after 9.♘×d4. Black's extra pawn can't be protected due to (9...c5) 10.b4!.

9...♗e7 10.♘×d4 0-0

Of course, not 10...e5 due to

11.♕b5+ ♘bd7 12.♘f5 with a clear advantage.

11.♘c3 e5

The next double exchange is quite risky and the slight disturbance of White's Pawn position on the Queen's wing will be more than compensated for by the advantage of the pair of Bishops. An interesting attempt would be 11...♕d7 aiming for both 12...e5 and 12...♖d8.

12.♘f5 ♗b4 13.♕c2! ♗×c3 14.b×c3 ♗×f5?

This exchange - it's true - would be necessary sooner or later - but why rush? As Black intends to play ...♕c7 he would be better advised to do it straight away, thus not giving White so many choices of attacking moves.

15.♕×f5 ♕c7 16.♗h6

The main aim of this rather difficult move is to avoid the Knight move on d5, which would be possible, for example, after 16.♗g5. If *now* 16...♘fd5 then 17.♗e4! g6 18.♕f3 ♔fd8 19.♖fd1 etc., with White's advantage.

16...♘bd7 17.♕g5?

But by leaving their Bishop so dangerously positioned, White certainly complicates things unnecessarily. Simple and strong would be 17.♗e3 and if 17...g6 then 18.♕g5 etc., with a considerable positional advantage.

17...♘e8 18.♖ab1

It was also possible to play 18.♗h3, a move that I intended to play later as a response to, for example, 18...♔b8.

18...♘c5

The tempting 18...♘b6 would be answered by 19.a4! and if 19...f6 then 20.♕f5! g×h6 21.a5 ♕d7 22.♕h5 – and Black would be in serious trouble if he tried to keep the extra piece for too long.

19.♕g4 ♖d8

It would hardly be a wise policy to force the exchange of the queens through 19...♕c8, as after 20.♕×c8 ♔×c8 21.♗g5 f6 22.♗d5+ followed by 23.♗e3 the bishops would certainly play a vital role in the endgame.

20.♗g5 ♖d6 21.♕c4

Preparing the advance of the f-pawn, which at that point would be premature - for example 21.f4 h6 22.f×e5? ♔g6 with an advantage.

21...b6

White also threatened 22.♗×b7.

22.f4 ♖g6!

With this and the next few moves Black eliminates any immediate danger.

23.♖bd1

Threatening 24.♗d8 followed by f5.

23...e4

Avoiding the above threat, as 24.♗d8 ♘d6! 25.♗×c7 ♘×c4 would now be in Black's favor.

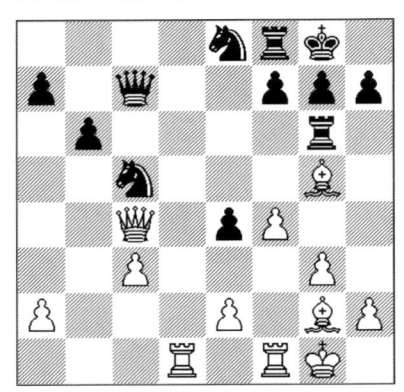

24.♗h4!

After this timely retreat, Black's position begins to look very precarious, as for example 24...♘d6 25.♕d5 ♘b5 26.♔c1 ♖d6 27.♕c4 would be favorable to White. Through the interesting Pawn offer that follows, Black manages to remove White's Queen to a less active square - but at the high price of a serious weakening of his Knight's position on c5.

24...b5!? 25.♕b4!

The only correct answer, because 25.♕×b5 would allow Black to put a knight on f5 via d6, with the threats ...♘×h4 and ...♘e3, which would secure them a promising initiative.

25...a5 26.♕a3

And not 26.♕b2 or on b1 due to 26...♘a4.

26...f5?

The desire to avoid f5 and at the same time secure the e-Pawn is very understandable. But the move has the serious drawback of making Black's position in the center even more unstable than it was before. A perfectly satisfactory line was, however, difficult to find. If, for example, 26...♖d6 (recommended by the great theoretician Prof. Becker, who even gave Black an advantage!) then 27.♗e7! ♔×d1 (27...♕×e7 28.♕×c5) 28.♗×c5! ♔×f1+ 29.♔×f1, after which Black would suffer further material loss. Also after the relatively better 26...♘d6 White would secure a definite positional advantage through the important intermediate move 27.♖d5!, and Black would then only have the choice between unpleasant alternatives.

27.♗d8!

A very unpleasant clash: White gets his threat first and thus prevents the harmonious collaboration of Black's forces.

27...♕a7 28.♔h1 ♖a6 29.♖d5

The simple domination of the central column through the Rooks will soon prove decisive due to the various weaknesses created by Black's Pawn moves 23 to 26.

29...♘e6 30.♖fd1 ♘×d8

If instead 30...♕e3, then simply 31.♕b2 and the threats would remain.

31.♖×d8 ♕f7 32.♖1d5

More effective than 32.♗1d7 ♕c4.

32...♖c6 33.♖×b5 ♕c4

34.♖×f5!

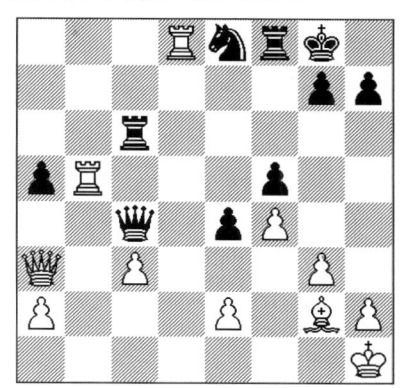

Conclusive, because 34...♖×f5 35.♖×e8+ ♔f7 36.♕e7+ ♔g6 37.♗×e4 etc. would be absolutely hopeless for Black.

34...♖cf6 35.♖×f6 g×f6 36.♖d4?

A typical time-honored calculation. I was happy to have found a practically forced sequence of moves that would lead me undamaged to the threatening 40th move - and paid no attention to the simple 36.♕b3 forcing an ending with two extra Pawns and most likely an immediate surrender!

36...♕×e2 37.♕b3+ ♔h8 38.♖×e4 ♕d2 39.♕b1!

Easier technically than 39.h6 ♘d6 with slight fighting possibilities for Black.

39...♕×c3 40.♕e1 ♕×e1+

Or 40...♕c8 41.♕×a5.

41.♖×e1

The ending is easily winning because White, in addition to his Pawn a plus, has a very strong Bishop against a Knight completely lacking in safe squares in the center of the board.

41...♘d6 42.♗c6!

Immobilizing the knight (due to a possible exchange of the rooks through ♖e8) and preventing a later advance of the pawn to black.

42...♖b8

Or 42...♖c8 43.♗a4.

43.♖e6 ♖b1+ 44.♔g2 ♖b2+ 45.♔h3 ♘f5 46.♖xf6 ♘e7 47.♗e4 ♔g7 48.♖e6 ♔f7 49.♖h6 ♖xa2 50.♖xh7+ ♔f6 51.♖h6+ ♔f7 52.♖a6, and Black resigned.

Game 101
M.Euwe–A.Alekhine
World Championship (21), Amsterdam,
November 1937
Queen's Indian Defense [E18]

1.d4 ♘f6 2.c4 e6 3.♘f3 b6 4.g3 ♗b7 5.♗g2 ♗b4+ 6.♗d2 ♗e7

To the best of my knowledge, this move had not been played before; but an analogous idea in the Dutch Defense had already been tried - first by Soviet players and then by myself, most of the time with very satisfactory results. The idea of the Bishop's retreat is to take advantage of the somewhat unusual position of White's Queen's Bishop. So, after the game I came to the conclusion that the old 5...♗e7 (instead of 5...♗b4+) that I adopted in the 23rd Game of the game is at least as good as the maneuver in the text.

7.♘c3 ♘e4

Allowing White to gain a slight advantage in space. It was safer 7...0-0 8.0-0 d5 and if 9.♘e5, then ...♕c8 with roughly equal play.

8.0-0

White could also play straight d5.

8...0-0 9.d5! ♘xd2 10.♕xd2

10.♘xd2 would also be good, as it would hardly leave Black with anything better than 10...♕c8, stopping the threat of 11.d6!

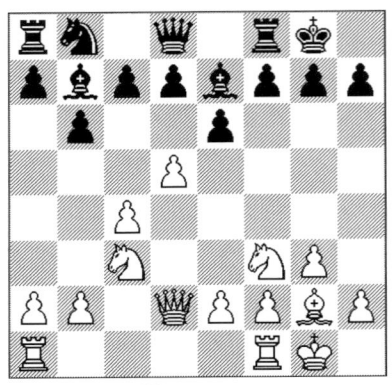

10...♗f6 11.♖ad1

Wasting precious time. After 11.♘d4 White's game would definitely remain preferable.

11...d6 12.dxe6

If now 12.♘d4, then 12...♗xd4 followed by ...e5 with satisfactory play for Black. Exchanging the text also only leads to equality, as Black can easily protect his Pawn e6.

12...fxe6 13.♘d4 ♗xg2 14.♔xg2

Of course, not 14.♘xe6? due to 14...♕e7 15.♘xf8 ♗xc3 16.bxc3 (16.♕xc3 ♗xf1) 16...♗b7! remaining with two minor pieces for the Rook.

14...♕c8

In some variants he wants to use the b7 square, for example, 15.f4 ♘c6! 16.♘xc6 ♕b7, with an advantage for Black.

15.♕e3 ♗xd4 16.♖xd4 ♘c6 17.♖e4

The start of a totally mistaken plan that quickly turns a playable position into a losing one. A solid move would be 17.♖d2, but even simpler would be 17.♔f4; so after the exchange of the Rooks, Black's attacking chances would be reduced to a minimum.

17...♖f6 18.f4?

Leaving the Rook in a drowned position. The move 18.♔f4 was still correct.

18...♕d7 19.g4

Weakening the f-pawn and thus adding to all White's other problems. Instead, 19.♖d1 would give them some chances of salvation.

19...♖af8 20.g5

Useless, as the answer shows. But that game was already strategically lost.

20...♖f5!

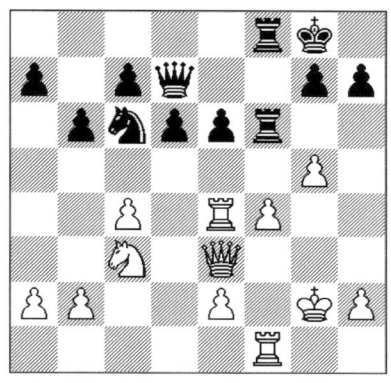

Black doesn't need to protect his Pawn and, after 21.♔×e6, 21...♘e5 would win the exchange.

21.h4 ♕f7 22.♖f3 ♔h8!

An important preparation for the central advance afterwards, rather that the immediate 22...d5 would be slightly premature due to 23.♔×e6 d4 24.♕e4 d×c3 25.b×c3! ♘d8 26.♖e7, with some fighting chances for White. And how 22...e5 could also be unconvincing due to 23.♘d5 ♘d4 24.♘e7+! ♕×e7 25.♔×d4 etc., I decided to hold back the advance of my central Pawns until it was absolutely decisive.

23.♕d3 d5!

Now the time has come, because 24.c×d5 e×d5 25.♖a4 d4 would be quite desperate for White.

24.♖×e6 ♘b4!

Obviously stronger than 24...♕×e6.

25.♕e3 ♘c2

Instead, 25...d4 26.♕e4 d×c3 27.b×c3 etc. would allow a long resistance.

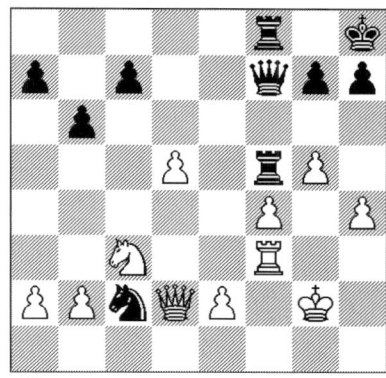

26.♕d2 ♕×e6 27.c×d5 ♕f7

28.♕×c2

After this move Black easily won with a direct attack. I expected, on the contrary, the more subtle 28.♔g3 (also threatening 29.e4), after which the impressive variant 28...♘e1! 29.♖f2 ♘g2 30.e3 (still fighting for the Pawn f) 30...♘×h4 31.♔×h4 h6! etc. would occur, with decisive threats.

28...♖×f4 29.♕d3 ♕h5 30.♖×f4 ♖×f4 31.♕h3 ♖g4+ 32.♔f2 h6!

If now 33.g×h6, then 33...♕f5+, after which checkmating with the Rook would win the queen.

The whites resigned.

Game 102
A.Alekhine-M.Euwe
World Championship (22), Delft, November 1937
Réti Opening [A09]

1.♘f3 d5 2.c4 d4 3.e3

After 3.b4 Black can play 3...f6 followed by ...e5 with good prospects. The move chosen avoids this possibility, because after 3...c5 4.b4 f6 White can play - *not* 5.b×c5 e5! with almost equal chances, but *5.e×d4 c×d4 6.c5!* (this last move, which seems very effective, was discovered by myself in the preparations for the game) - after which the weakness of the g1–a7 diagonal will cause considerable problems for Black: if 6...e5, then 7.♗c4; if 6...♕d5 then 7.♕b2 with advantage; if 6...a5, then 7.♕a4+ ♗d7 8.b5 e5 9.♗c4 and Black can't play 9...♗×c5 due to 10.♗×g8 followed by ♕c4. In other words, the consequences of 3...c5 seem to be decidedly in White's favor.

3...♘c6

On the contrary, after this move White will find it very difficult (if possible) to gain any advantage in the opening.

4.e×d4 ♘×d4 5.♘×d4 ♕×d4 6.♘c3 ♘f6

Even simpler is immediately 6...e5, but as Black can make this advance through his next move, the continuation of the text still doesn't hurt anything.

7.d3

It would be pointless 7.♘b5 ♕b6 8.d4 e5 9.c5 ♕c6 10.♘c3 a6.

7...c6?

A serious waste of time, instead of 7...e5 which would be quite sufficient. If then 8.♗e3, simply 8...♕d8 9.d4 ♘g4; or if 9.♗e2, then 9...c5 (or even, more solidly, 9...♗e7), with an approximately equal game.

8.♗e3 ♕d7

With the intention of developing the Bishops on the great diagonals. But White's advantage in space became clear with every move.

9.d4 g6 10.♗e2 ♗g7

Threatening ...♘g4, which would be useless immediately due to 11.♗f4 followed by h3.

11.h3 0–0 12.0–0 b6 13.♗f3 ♗b7

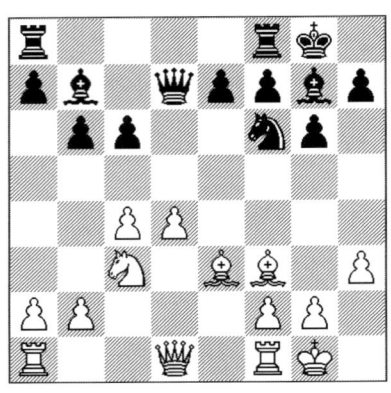

14.a4!

To make a more effective break in the center, White first tries to weaken Black's b6 square. The continuation will prove the depth of this scheme.

14...♖ad8

In connection with his eighteenth move, this seems like a waste of time, but in reality, it's almost a sad necessity, because after a5 Black would have to deal with the threat of a6, while, on the other hand, after the exchange on square b6 he would be obliged to offer the exchange of at least a pair of rooks.

15.a5 ♕c7

This and the next move are necessary to give sufficient protection to the weak square b6.

16.♕b3 ♘d7 17.a×b6 a×b6 18.♖a7 ♖a8

White's main threat was 10.d5.

19.♖fa1 e6

Otherwise the imminent d5 would be even more unpleasant than it proved to be in the current game.

20.♖×a8 ♗×a8

This move was unfairly criticized. After 20...♖×a8 21.♖×a8+ ♗×a8 22.♕a3 ♗b7 23.b4, White had a technically easier problem than in the game.

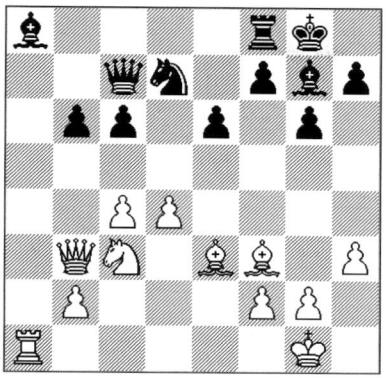

21.d5!

It wasn't an easy decision, as I was very careful that the resulting exchanges didn't give up important central squares to Black. It was also necessary to launch something definitive at this point, because (1) White has no means of improving the excellent position of his pieces; (2) Black, on the other hand, could possibly try to form an attack against the d-Pawn, starting with ...♖d8; and (3) this is the only possibility of taking advantage of Black's b6 weakness, created by the advance of White's a-Pawn.

21...cxd5 22.cxd5 ♘c5

The logical justification for move 21.d5 lies in the variant 22...♗xc3 23.d6! ♕xd6 24.♕xc3 ♗xf3 25.♗h6!, winning the quality. And if 22...♘e5, then 23.♗e4 still threatens d6.

23.♕c4

If 23.♗xc5 ♕xc5 24.dxe6 ♗xf3 25.exf7+ ♖xf7 26.gxf3 ♗xc3 27.♖a7 ♕g5+ with perpetual check.

23...exd5 24.♗xd5 ♗xd5 25.♘xd5 ♕e5

Black chooses the more aggressive line, which is certainly more promising than the passive 25...♕b7 26.♖b1 ♘d7 27.♕b5!, with a clear space advantage for White.

26.♖b1 ♘a4!

An ingenious way of taking the sick pawn, at least temporarily. The text move had to be precisely calculated by both sides.

27.b3 ♘b2 28.♕c6 b5!

The point of the Knight's previous move because the Pawn can't be taken due to the response 29...♖d8.

29.♗f4! ♕e6

After that White, as the next moves will show, could take the Pawn. The only adequate defense consisted of 29...♕e7! which could be answered by 30.♔f1!, leaving Black with the following weak points: (a) the b-Pawn; (b) the f6-square; (c) last but not least, the insecure position of the Knight on b2.

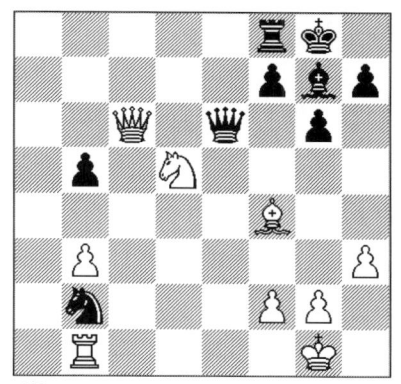

30.♕xb5!

This seemingly very risky capture gives White a material advantage that he will be able to maintain until the end. If now 30...♖d8, then 31.♔c1! ♔xd5 32.♕b8+ (this required 29.♗f4) 32...♗f8 33.♗h6 ♕d6 (or 33...♕e7) 34.♕xd6 ♔xd6 35.♔c8 winning.

30...♕e4 31.♖c1 ♘d3

Or 31...♖d8 32.♗g5 with variants similar to those mentioned above.

32.♕c4!

Again the only move, but it was enough to keep the lead.

32...♕e2

It would be a serious mistake 32...♗e4 because of 33.♘f6+.

33.♖f1 ♘xf4

Black has practically no choice, as 33...♖e8 (threatening 34...♕xf1+) would be easily met by 34.♗e3.

34.♕xf4

And not 34.♘xf4 ♕xc4 35.bxc4 ♔c8 36.♖c1 ♗h6 – with a probable draw.

34...♕b5 35.♕f3!

White still must be careful. Here, for example, the most "natural" move 35.♕c4 would lead to a quick draw after 35...♔b8.

35...♖b8 36.♖b1 ♕a6 37.♖d1

This attempt to repeat moves is due to the slight shortage of time caused by the extremely interesting complications. After the simple 37.b4 White wouldn't have much trouble getting the advantage of a passed Pawn. A plausible variant would be, for example 37.b4 ♕c4 38.♘e7+ ♔f8 39.♘c6 ♔b6 40.b5! ♔xb5 41.♕a3+, winning.

37...♕a3 38.♖b1 ♕a2 39.♕d3 ♗d4

This counterattack only compromises the position of Black's King. But it's difficult to suggest a satisfactory line of play, for White is simply to advance his passed Pawn.

40.♖f1 ♕b2

The alternative 40...♕a7 would also be unsatisfactory due to 41.b4, etc.

See the next Diagram

41.♘e7+!

This secret move initiates the final attack, which after a dozen moves leads to a practically forced Queen win by two pieces.

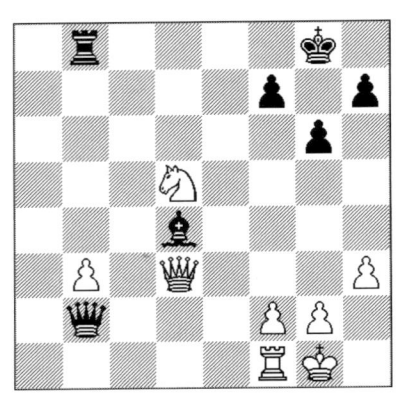

41...♔f8

The only move. It would be hopeless 41...♔g7 42.♘f5+ gxf5 43.♕g3+ and ♕xb8 – or 41...♔h8 42.♘c6 ♗xf2+ 43.♖xf2 ♕c1+ 44.♔h2 ♕xc6 45.♖xf7, etc.

42.♘c6 ♗xf2+ 43.♔h2!

The idea of this Pawn sacrifice (instead of 43.♖xf2 ♕c1+ 44.♕f1 ♕xc6 45.♖xf7+ ♔g8 46.♕f3, with rather problematic winning chances) will become apparent only after the 48th move. Knight's next move is quite spectacular.

43...♖e8

If 43...♔b7, then 44.♕f3 ♗b6 (or 44...♗c5 45.♕d5) 45.♘d8, winning at least the quality.

44.♕f3 ♖e2

Again, the only move, as well as the next move. But if White's king had gone for h1 on the 43rd move, then 44.♖e8 would have saved White.

45.♘d4! ♖d2 46.♘e6+ ♔e7 47.♘f4

Threatening 48.♘d3.

47...♕d4

Or 47...♕c2 48.♖a1 and Black's king would succumb to the continuous combined attack of the three white pieces.

My Best Games 1924-1937

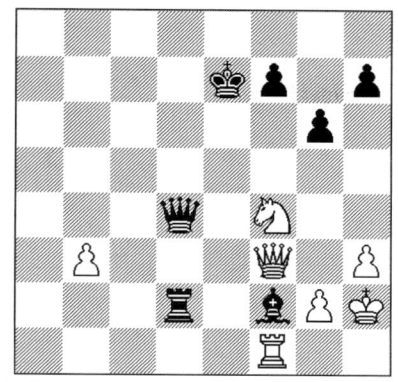

48.♔h1!

Only this "smooth" move, which had to be calculated a long time in advance, justifies the attack launched with 43.♔h2. White now threatens 49.♘e2, and if Black tries to prevent this with 48...♗h4, he loses as follows: 49.♕b7+ ♕d7 50.♕b4+ ♔e8 51.♘e6! (stronger than 51.♘×g6 h×g6 52.♕×h4 ♖d1! etc.) 51...♗e7 52.♕b8+ ♗d8 53.♘×d8 ♕×d8 54.♕e5+ ♕e7 55.♕h8+ ♔d7 56.♕×h7 ♗f2 57.♖d1+ ♔c7 58.♕h8 etc.

48...♖a2

Or 48...h5 49.♘e2 ♖d1 etc., which wouldn't be very different from the line actually played in the game.

49.♘e2 ♖a1 50.♕b7+

Of course, not 50.♘×d4 ♖×f1+ followed by ...♗g1+ taking back the queen.

50...♔f6?

The game is lost anyway, but 50...♔f8 would prolong the battle - for example 51.♘×d4 ♗×f1+ 52.♔h2 ♗g1+ 53.♔g3 ♗f2+ 54.♔f3 ♗×d4+ 55.♔e4 ♗f6, or 55.♔e2 ♖f2+ 56.♔e1 ♔g7! In this variant, to force the resignation, White would be forced to use his reserve trump - the passed Pawn-b.

51.♘×d4 ♖×f1+ 52.♔h2 ♗g1+ 53.♔g3 ♗f2+ 54.♔f3 ♗×d4+ 55.♔e4 ♖d1

Now forced, as White threatened 56.♕a6+.

56.♕d5?

Here there was really no need to bother calculating the (winning) Pawn ending after 56...♖e1+ 57.♔×d4 ♖d1+ 58.♔c5 ♖×d5+ 59.♔×d5 ♔e7 60.♔c6 etc., as a simple 56.♕c6+ followed by 57.♕c2 would win straight away! That was the only (fortunately negligible) omission I made in this unusually difficult game.

56...♔e7 57.g4 h5

Despair.

58.g×h5 f5+ 59.♔f3 ♖d3+ 60.♔e2 ♖e3+ 61.♔d2 ♖e4 62.h×g6, and Black resigned.

Game 103
A.Alekhine-M.Euwe
World Championship (24), Rotterdam, November 1937
Queen's Gambit Declined
Semi-Tarrasch Defense [D41]

1.♘f3 d5 2.c4 e6

For 2...d5, see *Game 102*.

3.d4 ♘f6 4.♘c3 c5 5.c×d5 ♘×d5 6.g3

A harmless derivation of the usual 6.e4. In both cases Black has very little difficulty in developing his pieces.

6...c×d4

Also quite good is 6...♘c6 7.♗g2 ♘×d4 8.♘×d4 ♘×c3 9.b×c3 c×d4 10.♕×d4 ♕×d4 11.c×d4 ♗d6 12.a4 ♔e7 with equality, as played in the last of the exhibition games organized after the game.

7.♘×d5 ♕×d5 8.♕×d4 ♕×d4 9.♘×d4 ♗b4+

There's nothing to talk about this sheikh and the subsequent exchange.

221

10.♗d2 ♗xd2+ 11.♔xd2 ♔e7?

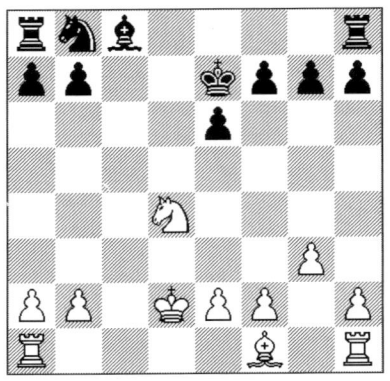

But neglecting to develop the pieces on the Queen's wing from now on will cause all the problems. It was indicated 11...♗d7 12.♔g2 ♘c6 13.♘xc6 ♗xc6 14.♗xc6+ bxc6 15.♖ac1 0-0-0+ 16.♔e3 ♔c7 with an easily defensible Rooks ending.

12.♔g2 ♖d8 13.♔e3 ♘a6

Practically forced, as the c7 square needs protection. But the knight on a6 would not only be out of the game, but as the next section will show, dangerously exposed. The next part of the game, which ends with White winning a Pawn, is easy to understand, but still quite instructive.

14.♖ac1 ♖b8 15.a3

15.♘b5 would be useless because of 15...♗d7 (16.♘xa7? ♖a8).

15...♗d7

Now threatening 16...e5, which White avoids with his next move.

16.f4 f6

This move has been criticized a lot, in my opinion without much reason, because in the long run Black wouldn't be able to avoid material loss anyway. If, for example, 16...♗e8, then 17.b4 ♖d7 18.♘b5 ♖a8 19.♖c3 followed by 20.♖hc1 followed by 21.♖c8 or 21.♘c7. As happened in the present game, Black, despite being a Pawn down, would still have some chances of a draw.

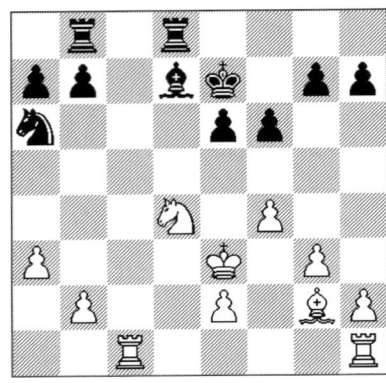

17.♗e4!

A typical "centralization" that the late Nimzowitsch would surely have appreciated. White not only attacks the h-Pawn but in some variants threatens ♗d3 and (more importantly) avoids 17...e5 due to 18.fxe5 fxe5 19.♘f3 winning a Pawn.

17...♗e8

Avoiding 18.♗xh7, because the reply 18...g6 with the threats (a) ...♗f7 followed by ...♖h8, or (b) ...♖bc8 followed by ...♘c7, would give Black enough resources. But with his next two moves White manages to take advantage of Black's weakness on e6.

18.b4! ♖d7 19.f5! ♘c7

Comparatively better than 19...e5 20.♘e6, or 19...exf5 20.♗xf5 ♖d5 21.♗xh7 - in both cases with a considerable advantage for White.

20.fxe6 ♘xe6 21.♘xe6 ♔xe6 22.♗xh7

So White has gained a material advantage, but his positional advantage has meanwhile almost disappeared, and Black even manages to get some pressure on the e column.

22...f5 23.♖c5!

Preparing for the change of Bishops in d5.

23...g6 24.♗g8+ ♔f6 25.♖hc1 ♖e7+ 26.♔f2 ♗c6 27.♗d5 ♖be8 28.♖e1!

By far the best, as 28.♖1c2 ♗a4 29.♖d2 b6 30.♖c3 ♖d8 would lead to an unpleasant pin.

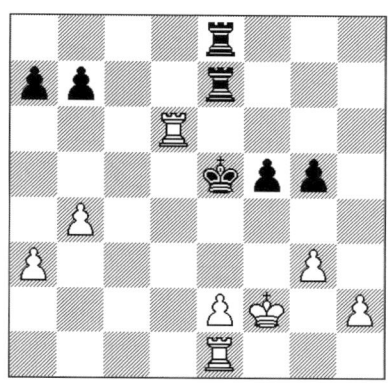

28...♗×d5 29.♖×d5 g5 30.♖d6+ ♔e5

After this desperate advance the game quickly becomes hopeless. The natural course would be 30...♔f7 31.h4 g×h4 32.g×h4 ♖h8 33.♖d4 and White would still have some technical difficulties to force a win.

31.♖ed1 g4

It would be equally hopeless 31...♖e6 32.♖d7 ♔e7 33.h4, etc.

32.♖1d5+ ♔e4 33.♖d4+♔e5 34.♔e3

Also possible was 34.e4, which would lead to the winning of a second Pawn, but still allow Black a longer resistance than in the game - for example (34.e4) ♖c8! 35.♔6d5+ ♔e6 36.e×f5+ ♔f6, etc. The chosen path is quite simple.

34...♖e6

Or 34...f4+ 35.♔d3! still threatening mate.

35.♖4d5+ ♔f6+ 36.♔f4 ♔g6 37.♖×e6+ ♖×e6 38.♖e5 ♖a6

If 38...♔f6, then 39.e4 f×e4+ 40.♔×g4 ♔f7 41.h4 winning quickly.

39.♖×f5 ♖×a3 40.♖b5!

The immediate 40.♔×g4 would probably win too - but the move in the text is more accurate.

40...b6 41.♔×g4

If now 41...♖e3, then 42.♖g5+ ♔h6 43.b5! (the point of the 40th move) ♖×e2 44.h4, after which there would be no more fighting chances for Black.

Black resigned.

Game 104
M.Euwe-A.Alekhine
World Championship (25), The Hague, December 1937, Final Game
Nimzowitsch Defense [E46]

1.d4 ♘f6 2.c4 e6 3.♘c3 ♗b4 4.e3 0-0 5.♘ge2

This is one of the less happy inventions of the great opening artist Rubinstein. Its weak point is that the knight doesn't have much of a future, either on f4 or g3, and that Black, by making the simplest move, will get a slight development advantage. So 5.♗d3 is preferable first, and if 5...b6 then 6.♘e2 (or even 6.♕f3); or if 5...d5, then 6.♘f3, with quite good prospects.

5...d5 6.a3 ♗e7 7.c×d5

Since White intends to play ♘g3, it would be better to delay this exchange. Indeed, after 7.♘g3 c5 8.d×c5 ♗×c5 9.b4 the move 9...d4 would be wrong because of 10.♕b3, and if 10...♗b6 then 11.c5, etc. Consequently, Black would be forced to change his development plan.

7...e×d5 8.♘g3

Rubinstein used to play 8.♘f4 here, obviously to avoid Black's next move, after which the second player experiences no more difficulties in the opening.

8...c5 9.d×c5

Preparing for the blunder of the next move. As Black's move ...c4 is not to be feared, White's normal course was 9.♗d3 ♘c6 10.d×c5 ♗×c5 11.0–0, etc.

9...♗×c5 10.b4?

Obviously not predicting the answer, otherwise they would play 10.♗d3.

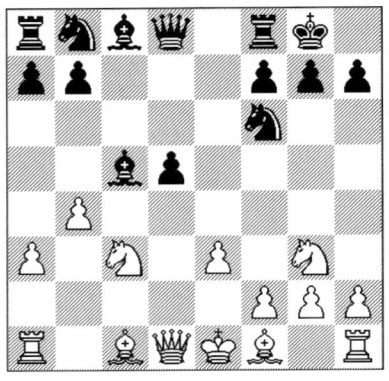

10.d4!

The point of this interesting move is that White can't respond well with 11.♘a4 due to 11...d×e3! 12.♕×d8 (12.♘ or ♙×c5? e×f2+ 13.♔e2 ♗g4+ winning) 12...e×f2+ 13.♔e2 ♗g4! forcing the King's move to the d-file, after which the Queen will be taken with check, thus saving the King's Bishop. And since 11.♘ce4 ♘×e4 12.♘×e4 ♗b6 etc. would also favor Black, White's next move is comparatively the best.

11.b×c5 d×c3 12.♕c2

White is in a very optimistic mood and underestimates Black's threats. Otherwise, they would have tried to simplify things with 12.♕×d8 ♔×d8 13.♘e2 ♘e4 14.f3 ♘×c5 15.♘×c3 ♘c6, after which, however, Black, due to his majority of Pawns on the Queen's wing and better development, would still have a slight advantage.

12...♕a5 13.♖b1

Now 13.♘e2 wouldn't be enough due to 13...♘d5 14.e4 ♘b4! etc., winning the exchange.

13...♗d7!

The threat 14...♗a4 is now difficult to deal with. If, for example, 14.♗c4 ♗a4 15.♗b3 then 15...♗b5, etc.; and if 14.♗b4 (which has been suggested by many commentators), then 14...♘a6! 15.♗×a6 ♕×a6 16.e4 ♔fe8 and White can neither castle nor take the threatening Pawn c due to ...♘d5. White's decision to give up the quality for a Pawn to finally finish the development of his pieces seems comparatively the wisest.

14.♖b3 ♗a4 15.♕×c3 ♕d8!

The point of the thirteenth move. Despite their material advantage, it won't be easy for Black to force a win. The next phase of the game is particularly instructive from a tactical point of view.

16.♗c4 ♘a6!

Instead of 16...♗×b3 17.♕×b3 ♘a6 18.♕×b7 ♘×c5 etc., which would allow White to keep his two bishops.

17.♗×a6 b×a6

And not 17...♗×b3 18.♗d3! with comparatively more chances than in the game.

18.0–0 ♗×b3 19.♕×b3 ♖b8

The d-file will soon become a very important factor. After the more obvious 19...♕d5 White, playing 20.♕×d5 ♘×d5 21.e4 etc., would have even more chances of saving the endgame.

20.♕c2 ♕d5 21.e4 ♕b3 22.♕e2

Now, on the other hand, the ending after 22.♕×b3 ♖×b3 would be rather hopeless due to the weakness of

White's Pawn.

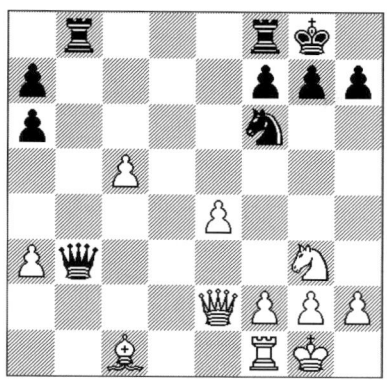

22...♛b5! 23.♛f3

Relatively better than 23.♛e3 ♞d7. If White wants to avoid exchanging Queens he needs to forget his c-pawn.

23...♛×c5 24.♞f5?

But here 24.♗f4, to avoid the pin afterwards, would offer slightly better fighting chances. The right answer for Black would be 24...♖be8 and if 25.e5 (25.♔c1 ♛b5! 26.♗d6 ♔c8 etc.) then 25...♞d7 26.♞e4 ♛c2 27.♔c1 ♛b2 etc., taking the advantage material.

24...♖b1 25.♛f4

Or 25.♛g3 ♞h5 26.♛g5 ♔h8! etc., with an easy defense. But now they threaten to win the queen by playing 26.♛g5.

25...♞×e4

It might have been assumed that after the capture of this important Pawn the fight would soon be over. But White manages to find new attacking moves again and again.

26.h4 ♖e8

Not convincing enough would be 26...♞×f2 due to 27.♔h2!

27.♖e1 ♛c3 28.♖d1

Threatening 29.♛×e4.

See the next Diagram

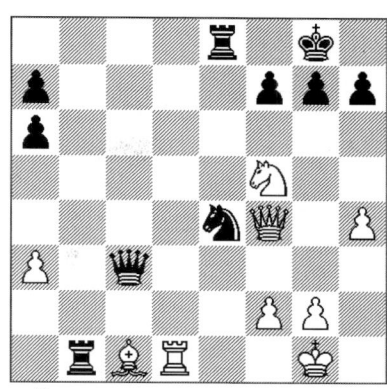

28...♞d2!

This spectacular move forces a subsequent, very welcome simplification, after which there will be practically no fight resigned.

29.♖×d2 ♖×c1+

But not 29...♛×c1+ 30.♔h2 ♔b2? 31.♛g5! with a win for White!

30.♔h2 ♛c7 31.♖d6 ♖c5 32.g3!

A very ingenious idea, worthy of a better fate. If Black carries out his threat (32...♔×f5) he would be forced after 33.♖e6!! to give up the queen for two rooks (33...f×e6 34.♛×c7 ♔×f2+ 35.♔h3 e5) after which he would be able to put up a stubborn resistance.

32...♖f8!

But this simple answer puts an end to the last hopes of salvation. What follows is agony.

33.g4

Instead 33.♞×g7 ♔×g7 34.♛f6+ ♔g8 35.♖d4 h5 etc. wouldn't work.

33...f6 34.♔h3 h5

The start of the counterattack.

35.♛d2 h×g4+ 36.♔×g4 ♛f7 37.h5

See the next Diagram

37...♖×f5!

Finally, the most hated knight in the game could be eliminated with deci-

225

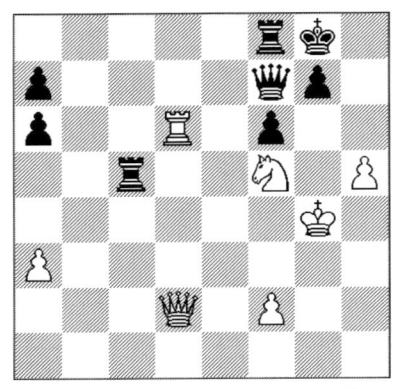

sive effect, and Black, in addition to the two extra pawns, quickly got a mate attack. It was an exciting fight!

38.♔xf5 ♕xh5+ 39.♔f4 ♕h4+ 40.♔f3

If 40.♔f5, then mate in four: 40...g6+ 41.♔e6 (41.♔xg6 ♕h7 mate) 41...♕e4+ 42.♔d7 ♕b7+ 43.♔e6 ♕f7 mate.

40...♕h3+ 41.♔e4

Or 41.♔f4 ♖e8 with the deadly threat of 42...g5 mate.

41...♖e8+ 42.♔d5 ♕b3+ 43.♔d4 ♕xa3, and White resigned.

Alexander Alekhine

CHAPTER 4
Simultaneous and Blind Games
Exhibitions and Games
with consultations

Game 105
A.Alekhine-A.Kussman
Simultaneous, New York, January 1924
Semi-Tarrasch Defense

1.d4 d5 2.♘f3 ♘f6 3.c4 e6 4.♘c3 c5 5.c×d5 e×d5?

Nowadays "theory" considers - and rightly so, playing straight - 5...♘×d5 as the only correct answer. But when this game was played, even the masters couldn't imagine the danger of the move in the text. For example, Dr. Vidmar played it against me in the 1922 London Tournament.

6.♗g5!

Much more effective here than 6.g3, which in regular Tarrasch Defense (with Black's Queen's Knight on c6 and the King's Knight undeveloped) would be the most promising line.

6...♗e6 7.♗×f6 ♕×f6 8.e4! d×e4 9.♗b5+ ♗d7

Or 9...♘d7 10.♘×e4 ♕g6 11.♗×d7+ ♗×d7 12.0-0 etc., with an advantage.

10.♘×e4 ♕b6 11.♗×d7+ ♘×d7 12.0-0 c×d4

Facilitating White's attack. A lesser evil would be to allow the unpleasant d5.

13.♘×d4 ♖d8

After White's next move, Black's d6 square will need further protection.

14.♘f5 ♘e5 15.♕e2 g6

Allowing for an elegant ending. But the position was, of course, already a loser.

See the next Diagram

16.♕b5+! ♘d7

The queen can't be taken due to 17.♘c6 mate.

17.♖fe1

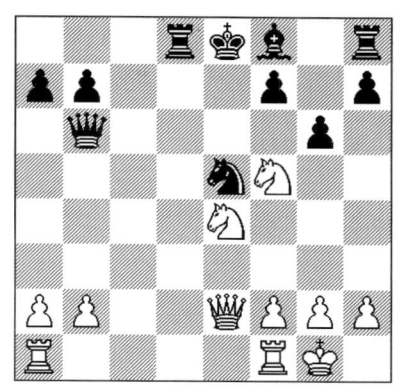

Again threatening mate.

17...♗b4 18.♘f6+ ♔f8 19.♘×d7+ ♖×d7 20.♕e5!

This time threatening three different kills. That's awesome.

Black resigned.

Game 106
A.Alekhine-S.Freeman
Blind Simultaneous against 24 opponents
New York, May 1924
Central Gambit

1.e4 e5 2.d4 e×d4 3.c3 d5

Undoubtedly the best defense, allowing Black to get an even game.

4.e×d5 ♕×d5

But here 4...♘c6 is even better.

5.c×d4 ♗b4+ 6.♘c3 ♘c6 7.♘f3 ♘f6 8.♗e2 0-0 9.0-0 ♗×c3

So far Black has made the right moves, but this exchange is wrong because it strengthens White's center. It was correct 9...♕a5.

10.b×c3 b6

This isn't good either, as White's pawns will now advance with an advantage in both time and space. It would be better 10...♗g4.

11.c4 ♕d8 12.d5 ♘e7 13.♘d4

Avoiding an effective development of Black's bishop on the c8–h3 diagonal.

13...♗b7 14.♗b2

It would have been simpler to go for 14.♗f3 or 14.♗g5. Still, the idea of sacrificing the central Pawn to increase the advantage in development was quite tempting.

14...c6 15.♗f3! c×d5 16.♖e1 ♖e8

Instead, surely 16...♕d7 17.♘b5!

17.♕d2 ♖b8 18.♕g5

Threatening 19.♘e6!

18...♘g6 19.♘f5

After this move the attack can hardly be stopped. White's next threat is the simple 20.c×d5.

19...♖×e1+ 20.♖×e1 d×c4

If 20...h6 then 21.♕g3, threatening both 22.♗×f6 and 22.♘e7+, etc.

21.♗×b7 ♖×b7 22.♗×f6 ♕×f6

Or 22...g×f6 23.♕h6 ♕f8 24.♖e8, followed by mate.

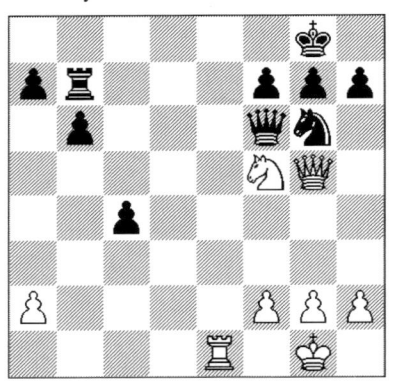

White announces mate in four moves: 23.♖e8+ ♘f8 24.♘h6+ ♕×h6 25.♖×f8+ ♔×f8 26.♕d8 mate.

Game 107
A.Alekhine-P.Potemkin
Blind Simultaneous against 26 opponents
Paris, May 1925
Alekhine Defence

1.e4 ♘f6 2.♘c3 d5 3.e×d5 ♘×d5 4.♗c4 ♘b6

White's treatment of the opening was in no way a refutation of Black's defense. In addition to the move in the text, the second player could also reply simply 4...♘×c3 with excellent prospects. If in that case 5.♕f3, then 5...e6 6.♕×c3 ♘c6 7.♘f3 ♕f6! 8.♕×f6 g×f6 9.d4 ♔g8 followed by ...♗d7 and ...0–0–0 etc.

5.♗b3 c5 6.d3 ♘c6 7.♘f3 ♘a5

Black overestimated the value of his pair of bishops. 7...e6 was indicated, followed by ...♗e7 and ...0–0, with very good play.

8.♘e5! ♘×b3

If 8...e6, then 9.♕f3 with advantage.

9.a×b3 ♘d7

It would be slightly better 9...♗e6 followed by ...g6 etc.

10.♘c4! ♘b6

It would be equally unsatisfactory to play 10...e6 11.♘b5 (threatening 12.♗f4) or 10...e5 11.♕e2! But by playing 10...g6 11.♕e2 (threatening mate) 11...♗g7 12.♗f4 a6 13.♘d5 ♔f8 Black would still retain some chances of consolidating his position.

11.♗f4 ♘d5

Instead, 11...a6 12.0–0 e6 would stop the immediate threats, but the position would still be compromised. After the move, there's practically no salvation for Black.

12.♘×d5 ♕×d5 13.0–0

Now threatening 14.♘b6.

13...b5 14.♘e3 ♕c6 15.d4! e6

If instead 15...♗b7 then simply 15.♖e1.

16.d5 e×d5 17.♘×d5

Also 17.♕×d5 would be quite effective.

17...♗d6 18.♖e1+

And not 18.♘f6+ ♔e7!.

18...♗e6 19.♗×d6

Simpler than the perhaps more accurate 19.♕f3 ♔c8 20.♗×a7 etc.

19...♕xd6

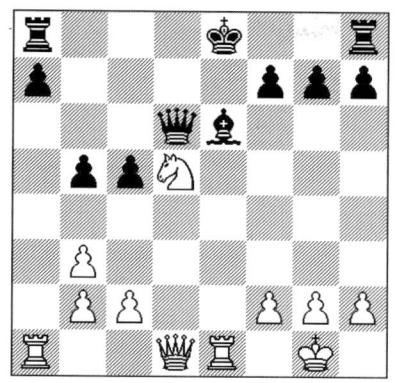

20.♖a6!
The combination started with this move wins faster than with the prosaic 20.♘f6+ ♔e7 21.♕xd6+ ♔xd6 22.♘e4+, winning a Pawn and with a long ending afterwards.
20...♕d8
Also after 20...♕d7 the answer 21.♖axe6+ would win easily: for example, 21...fxe6 22.♖xe6+ ♔d8 23.♖e7 ♕d6 24.♕d2 a5 25.♖xg7 h6 26.♖g6! ♕d7 27.♕f4, etc.
21.♖exe6+ fxe6 22.♖xe6+ ♔f7 23.♖e7+ ♕xe7
Or 23...♔g8 24.♕g4 winning immediately.
24.♘xe7 ♔xe7 25.♕e2+ ♔f7 26.♕h5+
A small subtlety: White not only wins a Pawn but also forces the King to remain in the center.
26...♔f6 27.♕xc5 ♖he8 28.g4!
Threatening 29.♕f5 and thus winning a third Pawn.
Black abandon.

Game 108
A.Alekhine-N.Schwartz
Blind Simultaneous, London, January 1926
King's Indian Defense [E62]

1.d4 ♘f6 2.c4 g6 3.g3 ♗g7 4.♗g2 0–0 5.♘c3 d6
If instead 5...c6 then 6.d5.
6.♘f3 ♘c6 7.d5 ♘a5
This knight position will become the cause of problems. But 7...♘b8 isn't satisfactory either, as was shown in my games against Sir G. Thomas in Carlsbad 1923 (*My Best Chess Games 1908-1923*) and against Réti, New York 1924 (*Game 1* in this book).
8.♕d3 b6
Wanting to get the Knight to c5 as quickly as possible. It would be slightly better to go for 8...e5 first, as the reply 9.b4 wouldn't be effective due to 9...e4, etc.
9.♘d4 ♗b7 10.♘c6 ♕d7 11.0–0 a5 12.b3
The routine method for dislodging the Knight from c5.
12...♘c5 13.♕c2 ♗b7 14.h3
Preventing Black's maneuver ♘–g4–e4.
14...♖ae8
Neither this move nor the next exchange is advisable. Instead Black with 14...♘fe4 15.♗b2 ♘xc3 could try to facilitate the defense by eliminating some material.
15.a3 ♗xc6 16.dxc6 ♕c8 17.b4 axb4 18.axb4 ♘a6
After this move, the knight will be buried alive. But 18...♘ce4 19.♘b5! wouldn't be pleasant either.
19.♖a4! ♘b8
Otherwise White would have forced this retreat with 20.♕a2.
20.b5 h6 21.♖a7 e5 22.♔h2
In order not to have to rely on ...♘h5 in the case of g4.
22...♔h7 23.f4 ♖e7 24.fxe5 ♖xe5 25.♗f4 ♖ee8
After 25...♖h5 26.♘d5 ♘xd5 27.cxd5, the Rook would finally be trapped.

26.♘d5 ♘xd5 27.♗xd5 ♕d8 28.h4 ♕e7 29.e3 ♔h8 30.♔g2

Preventing 30...g5 through the possible threat (after 31.hxg5 hxg5) 32.♖h1+.

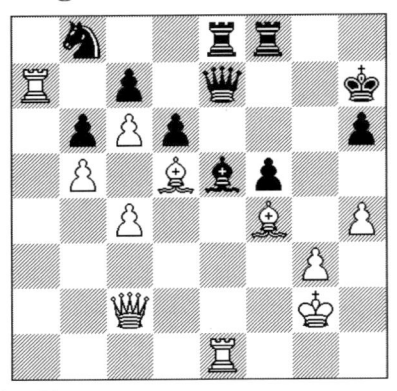

30...f5 31.♖e1 ♔h7 32.e4 ♗e5 33.exf5 gxf5

34.c5!

The start of a 10-move combination (in which the point is 43.♗e6!) forcing a piece win.

34...bxc5 35.b6 ♖c8 36.♕c3! ♖fe8

It's quite obvious that 36...♗xc3 37.♗xe7+ etc. would be hopeless.

37.♗xe5 dxe5 38.♕xe5!

Without this possibility, the previous moves would be meaningless.

38...♕xe5 39.♖xe5 ♖xe5 40.♖xc7+ ♖xc7 41.bxc7 ♖e8 42.cxb8♕ ♖xb8 43.♗e6!

Decisive.

43...♔g6 44.c7 ♖f8 45.c8♕ ♖xc8 46.♗xc8 c4 47.♗a6 c3 48.♗d3 ♔f6 49.♔f3 ♔e5 50.♔e3 h5 51.♗c2 ♔f6 52.♔f4 ♔g7 53.♔xf5 ♔h6

Still waiting for his blind opponent to drown his king with 54.♔f5...

54.♔f4!, and Black resigned.

I consider this game to be one of my best achievements in blindfold chess.

Game 109
M.Euwe-A.Alekhine
2nd Exhibition Game, Amstredam
December 1926
Nimzowitsch Defense [E21]

1.d4 ♘f6 2.c4 e6 3.♘c3 ♗b4 4.♘f3

In the second exhibition game, played after our game in 1937, Dr. Euwe played 5.♗g5, but after the correct answer (5...h6 and 6.♗xf6 ♗xc3+ 7.bxc3 ♕xf6, etc.) he had to play very accurately to avoid being disadvantaged. But also, the fianchetto development of the text is quite harmless.

5...b6 5.g3 ♗b7 6.♗g2 0–0 7.0–0 ♗xc3 8.bxc3 d6?

After this move, White takes advantage of the fact that Black's queen bishop is unprotected and forces an advantageous exchange in the center. Had Black made the correct move (8...♕c8), he would have resigned the opening stage with much better prospects.

9.d5! exd5

Although this Pawn can't be held, it's still better to start an open halfgame fight than to allow, after 9...e5, the formation 10.♘h4, followed by e4, f4 etc., with an advantage.

10.♘h4 ♘e4

After 10...c6 11.cxd5 ♘xd5 12.c4 ♘b4 13.a3 ♘4a6 14.♗b2 etc., White would dominate the board.

11.cxd5 ♖e8

If 11...♘xc3, then 12.♕d3 ♘a4 13.♗e4! g6 14.♕d4 ♘c5 15.♘f5 f6 16.♗c2 etc., with a decisive positional advantage.

12.♗b2

See the next Diagram

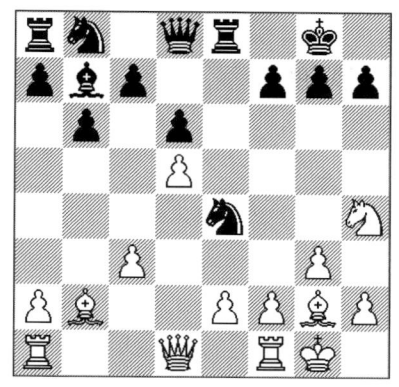

Here I don't agree with Dr. Euwe, who in the Dutch libretto devoted rather harsh criticism to the game's 12th and 13th moves. In any case, the Pawn sacrifice he suggests instead of the move in the text is anything but convincing; then after 12.♕d3 ♘c5 13.♕c2 b5 14.c4, Black would have an adequate defense through the continuation 14...b×c4 15.♗b2 ♘bd7 16.♘f5 ♘f6, etc.

12...b5

As 12...♕f6 (or 12...♘g5) would be inferior, due to the reply 13.♕a4, Black has practically no other way to avoid c4.

13.a4

A natural and good move. After 13.♕d4, recommended by Dr. Euwe, Black would have the choice between (a) sacrificing a Pawn, to keep control of the c4 square; 13...c5 14.d×c6 ♘×c6 15.♕d3 ♘e5 16.♕×b5 ♕b6! 17.a4 ♗c6, etc.; (b) the exchange of the queens, which would offer them good defensive possibilities: 13...♕f6 14.f3 ♕×d4+ 15.c×d4 ♘d2 16.♔f2 ♘c4 17.e4 ♘d7, etc.

13...♕g5!

Correctly deciding to eliminate White's Pawn at the cost of a subsequent delay in development on the Queen's wing.

14.a×b5 ♕×d5 15.♕a4?

But here White overestimated his chances. They could instead, by exchanging queens, force a favorable ending, which, however, would be far from hopeless for Black. For example, 15.♕×d5 ♗×d5 16.♖a4! ♘f6 17.e3 ♗×g2 18.♔×g2 ♘bd7 19.♖fa1 ♖eb8 20.c4 ♖b7 21.♗d4 ♘b6 22.♖b4 ♘fd7 23.♘f5 (finally!) 23...g6 24.♘e7+ ♔f8 25.♘c6 ♘c5, with sufficient defense. And if 14.c4 (instead of 15.♕×d5), Black wouldn't take the poisoned Pawn, but would simply reply 16...a6! with an easy defense. After the text move, which only contains an obvious trap, White's advantage instantly disappears.

15...♘d7

Of course, not 15...♕d2? 16.b6 ♗c6 17.b7!, winning.

16.c4 ♕d2 17.♕a2

Under the circumstances, comparatively the best.

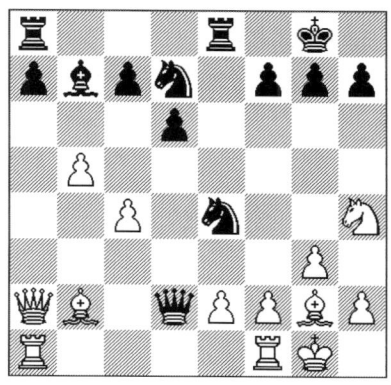

17...a6!

Then forcing a simplification. It would be inferior 17...♕×e2 due to 18.♘f5 f6 19.♘×g7!, etc.

18.♗c1

It would be ineffective to sacrifice Pawn 18.b6, for example 18...♘×b6 19.♘f5 ♕g5 20.♘×g7 ♖e7 21.♗h3 ♗c8, followed by ...f6 etc, with advantage.

18...♕xa2 19.♖xa2 axb5 20.♖b2

Slightly better than 20.♔xa8 ♗xa8 21.cxb5 ♘c3, etc.

20...♖ab8 21.cxb5?

After this move, Black manages to emerge from the complications with a Pawn advantage. After 21.♗xe4 ♗xe4 22.cxb5 ♗d5! etc., they would remain with only a positional advantage.

21...♘c3 22.♗c6

Now the only way is to try to maintain the balance of the position.

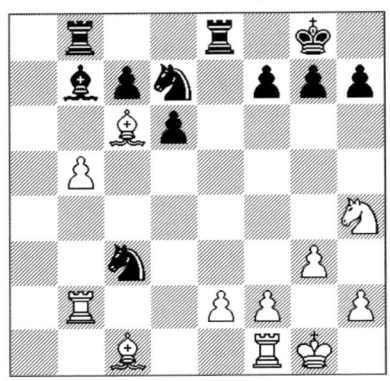

22...♖xe2!

An unpleasant surprise for White, justified by the variant 23.♗xd7 ♔xb2 24.♗xb2 ♘e2 mate!

23.♖b3

23.♗d2 ♘a4 24.♖a2 ♘dc5, etc. would hardly be preferable.

23...♗xc6 24.♖xc3 ♗xb5 25.♖xc7 ♘e5

Not the most effective way to take advantage of the material advantage. Through 25...h6!, Black would avoid both 26.♘f5 (due to 26...♖e5) and 26.♗f4 (due to 26...g5), thus leaving White practically without an efficient response.

26.♘f5?

The complications introduced by this move end decisively in Black's favor. It required 26.♗f4 h6 27.♗xe5 ♖xe5 28.♖b1 ♖be8 29.♘f3 ♖d5, after which Black would win - but only after a prolonged ending.

26...♘f3+ 27.♔g2

Or 27.♔h1 ♖e5, etc.

27...♘e1+! 28.♔h3 ♖e5

That would also be the answer to 28.♔g1.

29.♖h1

White could resist more - but without any real hope - by immediately giving up the quality: 29.♔xe1 ♗xe1 30.♘xd6, etc.

29...♘d3 30.♘e7+ ♔f8 31.♗a3

The last convulsions!

31...♘xf2+ 32.♔g2 ♘xh1 33.♗xd6 ♖e6 34.♗c5

Or 34.♘c6+ ♖xd6 35.♘xb8 ♖d8 etc., with a decisive advantage.

34...♖e8! 35.♘f5+ ♔g8 36.♘e7+

If 36.♘d6, then 36...♗d3! 37.♔xh1 ♖e1+ 38.♔g2 ♖8e2+ 39.♔h3 h6 40.♖xf7 ♖c2 41.♗f2 ♖e6, winning.

36...♔h8 37.♔xh1 ♗d3 38.♔g2 h6 39.♔f3 ♔h7 40.h4 h5, and White resigned.

Game 110
A.Alekhine-M.Euwe
3rd Exhibition Game, Amsterdam
December 1926
King's Indian Defense [E88]

1.d4 ♘f6 2.c4 g6 3.♘c3 ♗g7

At the time this game was played, the Grunfeld Variant was somewhat out of fashion. Nowadays, thanks to Botvinnik, Flohr, Keres and other masters of the new generation, it is played more often, although without any notable success.

4.e4 0-0 5.♗e3

If 5.f4 d6 6.♘f3, then 6...c5! with good play for Black.

5...d6 6.f3 e5 7.d5

Better 7.♘ge2, and only after

7...♘c6 (or 7...♗e6) 8.d5, buying time. In that case, Black would face unpleasant development problems.

7...c6 8.♕d2 c×d5 9.c×d5 ♘e8

Preparing the counterattack ...f5 and at the same time preventing White's attempt to open up the h-file (10.h4 f5 11.h5 f4, followed by ...g5, etc.).

10.0–0–0 f5 11.♔b1

It's obvious that the King needs to be removed as soon as possible from the open column.

11...♘d7?

Giving White the opportunity to create - without giving too many chances - interesting complications by temporarily sacrificing some material. By continuing with 11...a6 12.♗d3 b5 13.♘ge2 f4 14.♗f2 ♘d7, followed by ...♘ef6 Black would obtain a perfectly satisfactory position.

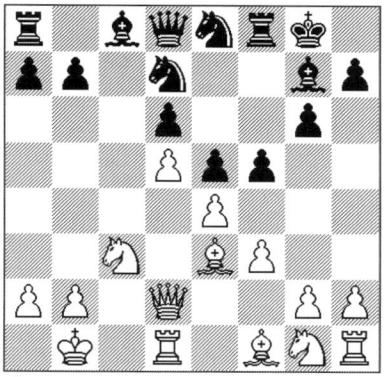

12.♘h3!

To answer either 12...♘ef6 or 12...♘df6 via 13.♘g5, for example: 12...♘b6 13.♘g5 f4 14.♗×b6 ♕×g5 15.♗f2 ♗d7 16.♔c1 ♘c7 17.g4! or 16...a6 17.♗b6 etc, with excellent prospects due to the open c-column.

12...a6

Even if Black were to prevent the next move with 12...f4, White's prospects would remain the most favorable.

13.e×f5 g×f5 14.g4!

The point of his 12th move, through which White obtained the very important square e4 for his pieces.

14...f×g4

Comparatively better than 14...f4 15.♗f2 etc., without any counter-chances for Black.

15.♘g5 ♘df6 16.♗d3 ♕e7

In the case of 16...g×f3, I would continue the attack with 17.♖df1!, and if 17...h6 18.♘e6 ♗×e6 19.d×e6 ♘g4 20.♘d5, with enough threats to scare an elephant to death.

17.f4

Both 17.♖df1 and 17.♖hg1 were also considered. But the prospects associated with the chosen move (the eventual opening of the g-file or g5 followed by ♘e6) were extremely tempting.

17...e4

Through this counter-sacrifice Dr. Euwe secures the h8–a1 diagonal for his Bishop, and at the same time reduces the danger threatening his King by forcing the exchange of a pair of minor pieces. Even so, White's chances after recapturing the sacrificed Pawn remain the best.

18.♘g×e4

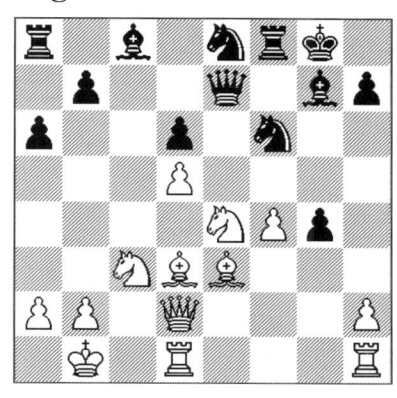

But this is not the most energetic method. The Pawn should be taken by the other Knight, and if in that case 18...♘xe4 19.♗xe4 h6, then 20.♘e6 with advantage; or 18...h6 19.♘e6 ♗xe6 20.dxe6 ♕xe6 21.♘g3 threatening 22.f5, etc. Black could hardly find a way to sufficiently protect his various weaknesses.

18...♘xe4 19.♘xe4

Now forced as 19.♗xe4? doesn't work because of 19...♗xc3.

19...♗f5 20.♘g3

Blocking the g Pawn to play h3 at the earliest opportunity. After 20.♘g5 Black would protect e6 with ...♘c7.

20...♗xd3+ 21.♕xd3 ♕f6

A refined tactical maneuver, very much in the style of Dr. Euwe. He provokes White's ♖d2 move to remove (after h3 gxh3 ♖xh3) the natural protection of the first rank. But with the right response, all this refinement will prove useless.

22.♖d2 ♕f7

Due to the threat 23.♘h5.

23.h3 gxh3 24.♖xh3 ♕g6 25.f5?

Only after this second inaccuracy does Black suddenly get some kind of counterattack. Here 25.♘e4! would be very strong, and in the case of 25...♘f6 simply 26.♘xd6 ♖ad8 27.♗c5 etc; and other responses would allow White to strengthen his position later through ♖g3 or ♖dh2 etc.

25...♕g4 26.♖dh2 ♖c8!

In the case of 26.♘f6 (which apparently protects everything), White would play 27.♗c1! with the strong threat 28.♔h4. Occupying the c-file gives Black some new opportunities.

See the next Diagram

27.f6!

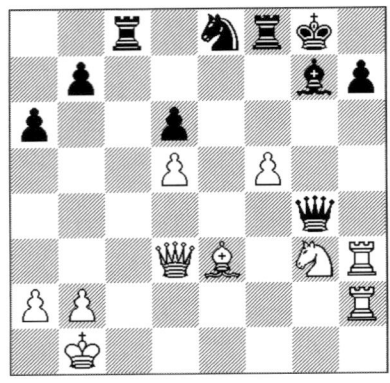

The main idea of this move is shown in the following variant: 27...♘xf6 28.♘f5 ♕c4 29.♘e7+ ♔f7 30.♕f5 ♔xe7 31.♕e6+ ♔d8 32.♗b6+ ♔c7 33.♖c3 ♕f1+ 34.♔c2, winning.

27...♖xf6! 28.♕xh7+ ♔f8 29.♖h1

This rather sad necessity is the direct consequence of Black's fine 21st move. But despite this partial success, the second player's position is still fraught with danger. If, for example, 29...♕b4, then simply 30.a3 and 30...♔f1+? would be refuted by 31.♗xf1+. And 29...♔f3 would also be unsatisfactory due to 30.♗h6! (30...♔xg3? 31.♔xg3 ♕xg3 32.♕f5+, etc.). Consequently, Black decided to simplify things.

29...♕g6+

It would be slightly better to delay this exchange by playing 29...♔c7 first, in which case White, by continuing with 30.♘h5 ♕f5+ 31.♕xf5 ♔xf5 32.♘f4 etc., would maintain strong pressure. After the text move, they have a straightforward win.

30.♕xg6 ♖xg6 31.♘f5!

Simply threatening 32...♘xg7, etc. If now 31...♔c7, then 32.♗d4! ♗xd4 33.♘xd4 and Black is out of resources.

31...♗e5 32.♖f3! ♘f6

Or 32...♖f6 33.♗g5 ♖f7 34.♗e7+! ♔xe7 35.♞xd6+, winning.
33.♖h8+ ♖g8 34.♖xg8+ ♔xg8 35.♞e7+, and Black resigned.

> **Game 111**
> **F.Marshall-A.Alekhine**
> *Exhibition Game, New York, June 1929*
> Queen's Indian Defense [E11]

1.d4 ♞f6 2.c4 e6 3.♞f3 ♗b4+ 4.♗d2 ♕e7 5.e3

White can gain control of e4 here by playing 5.♕c2, but in that case Black would choose another system: 5...♗xd2+ 6.♞bxd2 d6, followed by ...e5 etc.

50...b6 6.♗d3 ♗b7 7.♕c2 ♗xd2+

To advance a Pawn to the center and thus indirectly avoid White's e4 move.

8.♞bxd2 c5

If now 9.e4, then 9...♞c6 with advantage.

9.0-0 ♞c6 10.a3 0-0 11.♖ad1 g6

Avoiding d5, which, especially after White's last move with the Rook, would eventually be unpleasant.

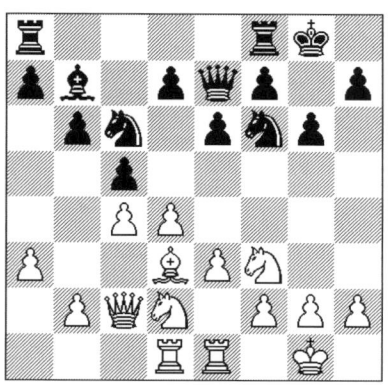

12.♖fe1

A refined preparation for ♞e4, which at this point would not be satisfactory due to 12...♞xe4 13.♗xe4 d5! 14.cxd5 exd5 15.♗xd5 ♞xd4 etc., with Black's advantage.

12...♖ac8 13.♞e4 ♖fd8

It would technically be simpler to make 13...♖fe8, because after 14.d5 exd5 White himself would be forced to exchange the knights. But the move chosen is at least good enough to maintain the balance of the position.

14.d5

Very brave - and very much in Marshall's style: he gives Black most of the Pawns on the Queen's wing without getting any real compensation anywhere, because his pieces aren't coordinated enough to support an effective central action. It can be admitted, however, that White's position, *due to the elasticity of Black's Pawn structure (compare with Game 50 with Miss Menchik)*, was already slightly inferior. Black threatened - after some further preparations, such as ...d6 - to start an action on the c-file with ...dxc4 followed by ...♞a5.

14...exd5 15.cxd5! ♞xe4

The move 15...♞xd5 would have sad consequences, for example 16.♗c4 ♞db4 17.♕c3! ♕xe4 18.♗xf7+ ♔f8 19.axb4 etc., with advantage.

16.♗xe4 ♞a5

Of course, not 16...♞e4 because of 17.d6, etc.

17.♞d2

Black threatened 17...f5.

17...c4!

Taking advantage of the fact that d6 is still no good. It's obvious that the move started by White's 14th move was more favorable to his opponent.

18.♗f3 ♕e5

Threatening 19...c3, etc.

19.♞e4 d6

Black would also avoid the Rook's next move by playing 19...♞b3, after which White would hardly have anything better than 20.♕c3; but they didn't think this was necessary, because due to their space advantage, the complications of the middlegame would normally end in their favor.

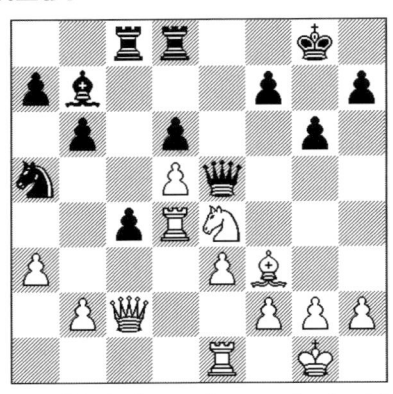

20.♖d4

It wouldn't have been desirable for Marshall to trade the queens through 20.♕c3 to get a distinctly inferior endgame. Looking at that Rook, no one could believe that, at the height of his existence, he intended soon to commit suicide - and yet that's how it is!

20...b5

Now threatening 21...♘b3.

21.♘d2 ♗a6

To leave the home to the knight in the case of ♕c3.

22.♖e4 ♕g7 23.♖e7

The road to death.

23...♘b7! 24.♘e4

Probably a difficult decision - but under the circumstances the most sensible, as the alternative 24.♗g4 ♖c5! (not 24...c3 25.♗×c8 c×d2 26.♖d1 with an advantage for White) 25.e4 ♕f6 26.♖d7 ♖×d7 27.♗×d7 ♕e7 (also threatening ...♖×d5) 28.♗c6 ♘a5 etc. would lead to a loss of material without any hope of a counterattack.

24...♔f8!

It would be a mistake 24...♕f8 25.♘f6+ ♔g7 due to 26.♕c3 etc., with White's advantage.

25.♖×b7 ♗×b7 26.♖d1

Although Black now has a clear extra quality and his majority on the queen's wing is more threatening than ever, the problem of winning is by no means as easy or quick to solve as one might imagine. White is in a position - in the case of 26...♕e5 for example - to build a good defensive position with the possibility of a Pawn counterattack on the King's wing through 27.♘c3 a6 28.♖d4, etc. Furthermore, through this line Black, with subsequent circumspection and patience, would probably increase his advantage decisively, without having to suffer the melodramatic complications that arose from his risky next move.

26...a5?

Preventing 27.♘c3 (due to 27...e4) and looking for a quick win. But from here on Marshall takes advantage of the hidden possibilities of his position in a remarkable way, recalling his most glorious performances.

27.♗g4! ♖c7

Of course, not 27...c5 due to 28.♘g5, but also not for example 27...♖a8 due to 28.a4! etc.

28.♕d2!

After this move, the situation starts to look quite dangerous for Black, as the a-awn cannot be defended directly.

28...h6!

This is temporary salvation, because by preventing ♘g5 Black threatens 29...c5.

29.♗f3 ♖cc8

And after this move 30.♕×a5 can be answered simply by 30...♕×b2.

See the next Diagram

238

My Best Games 1924-1937

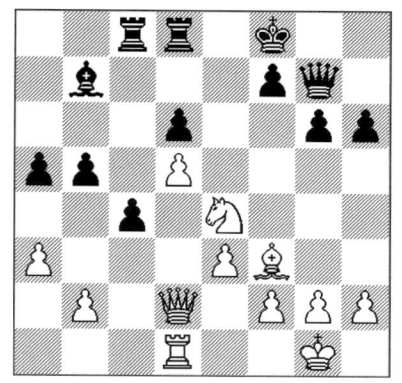

30.h4!
A new attacking idea, which the Blacks are trying to tackle in an equally energetic way.
30...♕e5
If instead 30...f5, then 31.♘c3 b4 32.a×b4 a×b4 33.♘e2 c3 34.b×c3 b×c3 35.♕c2, followed by the promising Knight move - ♘d4 (or f4) and ♘e6.
31.h5! g×h5
Also, after 31...g5 32.g4 followed by ♘-g3-f5 or ♗g2 and f4 Black's defense would remain difficult.
32.♘g3 c3 33.b×c3 ♕×c3
If 33...♔×c3, the answer would be 34.e4!
34.♕e2 b4 35.a×b4 a×b4
Finally Black manages to get the "winning" passed Pawn, but in the meantime White's forces have concentrated against the hostile King, which can only be defended by the Queen and Black's other pieces are, for the moment, mere spectators.
36.♗e4!
Covering the b1–h7 diagonal and opening prospects for the queen. In this second half of the game Marshall always finds the best moves, and it's a bit of bad luck that Black's resources at the end prove sufficient to cope with his furious assault.

36...♕e5!
From here on in, a very difficult Queen maneuver begins, the aim of which is to provoke moves by White's Pawns in order to allow at least one Rook to participate in a counter-attack.
37.f4 ♕f6
Otherwise, White plays 38.♕×h5 to gain time.
38.♘×h5 ♕h4!
And not 38...♕e7 39.♕b2! ♕×e4 40.♕h8+ ♔e7 41.♕f6+ ♔e8 42.♕h8+ ♔d7 43.♘f6+ followed by 44.♕×d8+ and ♘×e4.
39.g3
The weakening of the second rank will finally prove fatal, but if 39.♗f3 the reply 39...♕e7 would now offer sufficient defense, as 40.♕b2 is met by 40...♕×e3+.
39...♕h3!
Possible and good, because 40.♗g2 can be answered by 40...♗a6.
40.♗f3!

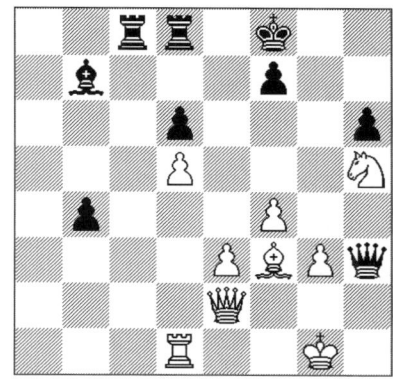

40...♖c3!
An unexpected defense against White's two main threats - 41.♗g4 and 41.♘b2 - and which involves, in the first case, a possible sacrifice of two qualities: to 41.♗g4 Black would respond 41...♖×e3! 42.♕×e3 ♕×g4 43.♖e1 ♕×h5! 44.♕e7+ ♔g7

239

45.♕xd8 (or 45.♕xb7 ♕f3 with a winning position) 45...♕xd5 winning. With his next move the then American Champion presents a new trump, which, however, this time will prove to be his last.

41.♕d2!

How do I now face the threat of 42.♕d4 without losing the passed Pawn? My lucky star - or Marshall's unlucky one - helped me find the right answer - but it took me no less than half an hour.

41...♖e8!

The value of this sealed response is well illustrated by comparing the consequences with the possible outcome of another plausible secret move: 41...♗a6 42.♕d4 ♗c2! 43.♕h8+ ♔e7 44.♕f6+ ♔d7 (44...♔e8 45.♘g7+ etc.) 45.♕xf7+ ♔c8 46.♕e6+ ♕xe6 47.dxe6 b3 48.♗e4 and, to say the least, White wouldn't lose.

42.♕d4

Instead, 42.♕b2 wouldn't help either, because of 42...♗a6, etc.

42...♖c2 43.♖d2

Simplification is almost always sad for the materially weaker party, but here there is no choice, as is shown by the variant 43.♕h8+ ♔e7 44.♕f6+ ♔d7 45.♗g4+! ♕xg4 46.♕xf7+ ♔d8 47.♕xe8+ ♔xe8 48.♘f6+ ♔e7 49.♘xg4 b3, winning.

43...♖xd2 44.♕xd2 ♗a6! 45.♕e1

Practically resigning. Almost an hour's reflection persuaded Marshall that the intended 45.♕xb4 would lead forcibly to defeat, as follows: 45...♕f1+ 46.♔h2 ♕f2+! (but not 46...♕xf3 47.♕xd6+ ♔g8 48.♘f6+ ♔h8 49.♕xa6! and Black wouldn't win) 47.♔h3 (or 47.♗g2 ♗f1 48.♕xd6+ ♔g8 49.♘f6+ ♔h8 winning) 47...♗c8+ 48.♗g4 ♗xg4+ 49.♔xg4 ♕e2+ 50.♔h4 ♕h2+ 51.♔g4 f5+!, winning.

45...b3

The last day of the Pawn festival!

46.♗d1 b2 47.♕b4

It leads to an ending like the one indicated.

47...♕f1+ 48.♔h2 ♕f2+ 49.♔h3 ♗c8+ 50.f5 ♗xf5+ 51.♗g4 ♗xg4+ 52.♔xg4 ♕e2+ 53.♔h4 ♕h2+ 54.♔g4 f5+, and White resigned.

In this kind of game, the loser certainly deserves as much credit as the winner.

Game 112

A.Kewitz & A.Pinkus–A.Alekhine

Simultaneous with consultation
New York, March 1929
Réti Opening [A15]

1.♘f3 ♘f6 2.c4 b6

One of the different ways of properly tackling White's opening game. With this Black aims to turn the game into a typical Indian Queen Defense.

3.g3 ♗b7 4.♗g2

Allowing Black to choose a more aggressive form of development. Instead, 4.d4 e6 5.♗g2 etc. would lead to well-known variants.

4...e5

This move has its advantages and defects, as the central pawn can become exposed. Still, it's worth a try, as there's not much risk in attacking it.

5.♘c3 ♗b4 6.0–0

Decidedly too optimistic, as the doubled Pawn on the c-file is much more often a serious fault in the position than is generally believed, and in this case this fault is in no way compensated for by the pair of Bishops. It would be natural and good enough for

6.♕b3.

6...♗×c3! 7.b×c3

It would even be more satisfying 7.d×c3 d6 etc.

7...d6

Black's pawn structure being on black squares, there's obviously no need for Black to keep the king's bishop.

8.d4 e4

Correctly calculating that the f column that White will now be able to open will not compensate for a new weakness thus created in the e column.

9.♘h4 0-0 10.f3 e×f3

Black is already in the pleasant position of being able to proceed in the simplest way. White's problem now is that he can't retake the Pawn well due to 11...♗a6! 12.f4 c6 followed by ...d5 with some material gain. And after his next move the e-Pawn remains extremely weak.

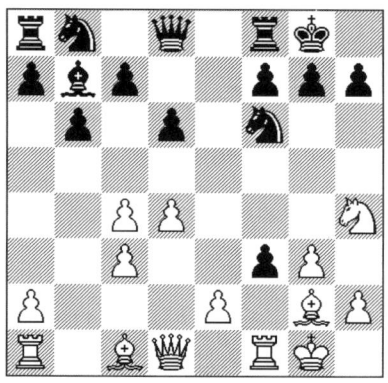

11.♗×f3 ♘e4 12.♕d3 ♖e8 13.d5

The counterattack now launched will be very short-lived. But if White had decided to restrict Black's bishop action on the big diagonal, he had to do it now, because after ...♘d7 Black obviously wouldn't be forced to give up the e4 square.

13...♘c5 14.♕d4 ♘bd7 15.♗h5

White hopes to provoke the response ...g6 with one of the next moves, which would eventually give him a real chance on the f-file. But Black resists all temptations and calmly prepares a complete blockade.

15...♘e5 16.♗f4 ♕d7!

If on the contrary 16...g6 17.♗f3 g5 18.♗×e5 d×e5 19.♕g4 h5 20.♕×h5 g×h4 21.♗e4! ♘×e4 22.♕×f7+ ♔h8 23.♕h5+ ♔g8 24.♔f7 and White wins!

17.♘f3 ♘g6 18.♘d2 ♕h3 19.♗×g6

The attempt to capture the aggressive queen - 19.♗h6 g×h6 20.♗g4 would fail miserably due to the simple 20...♖e4.

19...h×g6 20.e4

The Pawn is weaker here - if possible - than on e2, but White already had a difficult choice.

20...f6

By fixing the Pawn forever - and by bringing the last Pawn to a black square - increasing your Bishop's radius of action.

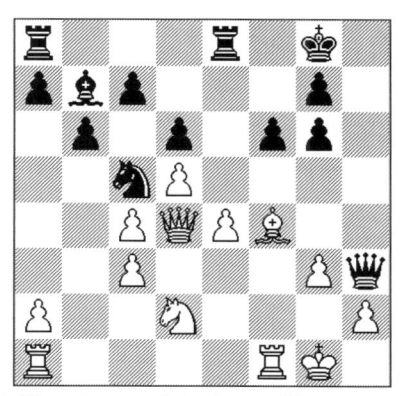

21.♖ae1 g5 22.♗e3 ♖e7 23.♔h1 ♖ae8 24.♗g1 ♗c8

Of course, it would be premature to 24...♘×e4 25.♘×e4 ♗×e4 26.♗×e4 ♖×e4 27.♕×e4 ♕×f1 28.♕e8+ etc., with perpetual check. What's more,

Black doesn't need to rush with the liquidation on e4 after all - *since the position should bring much more than a Pawn over time.*

25.♖f3 ♗g4 26.♖fe3

White now has weaknesses in several places: (a) on the queen's wing - the doubled pawn; (b) in the center - the pawn and backward; (c) on the king's wing - the weakness in the white squares. As a direct consequence of this sad situation, almost all the white pieces are drowned, and they have practically nothing better to do than move their Bishop back and forth. No wonder that instead of adopting the most obvious plan - a five-piece attack on the Pawn with ...♕h7 followed by ...♗-h5-g6, which would finally force an ending with an extra Pawn - Black prefers to prepare a decisive advance of the Pawn in the center. It's true that the preliminary maneuvers take another fifteen moves, but the success of the scheme gives the game an artistic touch that is absent in the first mode.

26...♕h5

Before launching the King's long journey, Black reverses the places of his Queen and Bishop to "observe" the central weak point with one more piece.

27.♔g2 ♗h3+ 28.♔h1 ♕g4 29.♗f2 a5 30.♗g1 a4

This could be used to eventually avoid ♘b3.

31.♗f2 ♖e5 32.♗g1 ♖8e7 33.♗f2 ♔f7

Now it's time to bring the King to the safest square on the board - a6!

34.♗g1 ♔e8 35.♗f2 ♔d8 36.♗g1 ♔c8 37.♗f2 ♔b7 38.♗g1 ♔a6 39.♗f2 ♕h5

The final preparation: the decisive combination needs the prior configuration of the Queen and the Bishop!

40.♗g1 ♗g4 41.♔g2 ♕h3+ 42.♔h1 g6

Finally revealing the winning idea.

43.♗f2

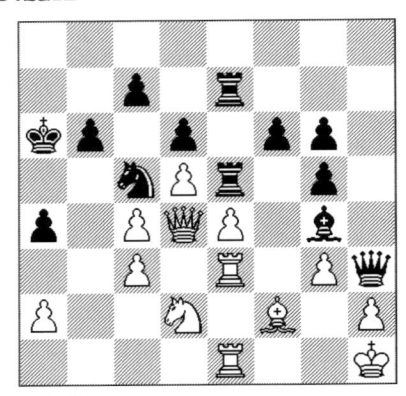

43...f5!

The battle should be decided not by winning a Pawn, but by direct threats to the King. If, after 44.exf5 gxf5 again 45.♗g1, then 45...♘e4 46.♘xe4 ♔xe4 followed inevitably by ...♗f3 winning.

44.exf5 gxf5 45.♖xe5 dxe5 46.♕e3

The main variant calculated by Black was 46.♔xe5 ♔xe5 47.♕xe5 ♗f3+! 48.♘xf3 ♕f1+ 49.♘g1 ♘e4! winning. This possibility clearly proved the usefulness of King's journey from as far away as h8.

46...e4 47.d6!

Not merely to make a move, but with a very definite purpose.

47...cxd6 48.♗g1

Which is seen in the following case: 48...♗f3+ 49.♘xf3 exf3 50.♕xf3 ♔xe1 51.♕a8 mate! But Black had a powerful intermediate move at his disposal.

48...f4!

If now 40.gxf5, then ...♗f3+ etc. wins immediately. White has resigned.

On the same occasion, the following short game was played, which dramatically shows the effects of excessive greed in chess; Black I. Kashdan and H. Steiner.

1.d4 d5 2.c4 e6 3.♘c3 c6 4.♘f3 dxc4 5.a4 ♗b4 6.e3 b5 7.♗d2 ♕b6 8.♘e5 ♘d7 9.axb5 ♘xe5 10.dxe5 cxb5 11.♘e4 ♗e7 12.♕g4 ♔f8 13.♕f4 a5 14.♗e2 ♗b7 15.0-0 h5 16.♘g5 ♗xg5 17.♕xg5 ♖h6 18.e4 h4 19.♖xa5 f6 20.exf6 ♘xf6 21.♕xb5 1-0

> **Game 113**
> **Alekhine/Monosson-Stoltz/Reilly**
> *Game with consultation, Nice, May 1931*
> Queen's Indian Defense [E17]

1.d4 ♘f6 2.c4 e6 3.♘f3 b6 4.g3 ♗b7 5.♗g2 ♗e7 6.0-0 0-0 7.b3

Leading to more complicated positions - or at least the least exploited - than the usual 7.♘c3, which is nevertheless very favorable to White, for example 7...♘e4 8.♕c2 ♘xc3 9.♕xc3 c5 10.♗e3, and in the case of subsequent exchanges Black will always remain with some weak point in the center.

7...♕c8

Against Dr. Euwe (23rd Game of 1937), here I played 7...d5 8.♘e5 c5 and got a fighting game full of possibilities for both sides. Black's idea of exchanging only a Pawn in the center gives White time to take advantage of the open c-file without allowing any counterplay.

8.♘c3 d5

See the next Diagram

9.cxd5!

At the right moment, because if 9...dxc4 Black's queen bishop can develop with an advantage on f5.

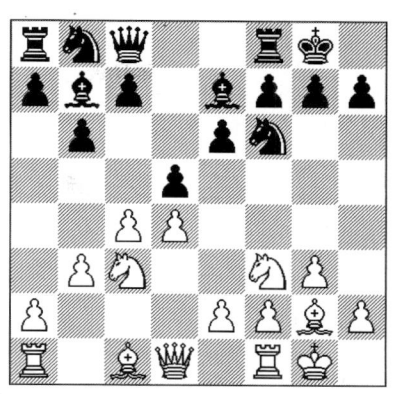

9...♘xd5 10.♗b2 c5

Positionally unfeasible, but from now on Black's queen will "feel" (as modern analysts say) uncomfortable *vis-a-vis* White's rook.

11.♖c1

Possibly threatening ♘a4.

11...♘xc3 12.♗xc3 ♖d8

White wants 13.dxc5 bxc5, leading to the weakening of the half-open column. The text move stops this possibility, but only temporarily, and so they would do better to replace it with 12...♕d8.

13.♕d2!

With the aim, in the case of 13...♘d7, for example, of placing the queen on the comfortable square b2. But Black kept trying to secure for his queen the square corresponding to my other, more aggressive ideas.

13...♗d5 14.♕f4 ♕b7?

Somewhat consistently, but neglecting the development on the queen's wing, which will now prove immediately fatal. After 14...♘d7 15.e4 ♗b7 16.d5! exd5 17.exd5 ♗f6 (not 17...♗xd5 18.♘g5 winning) Black would suffer longer, but die just the same.

15.dxc5 bxc5

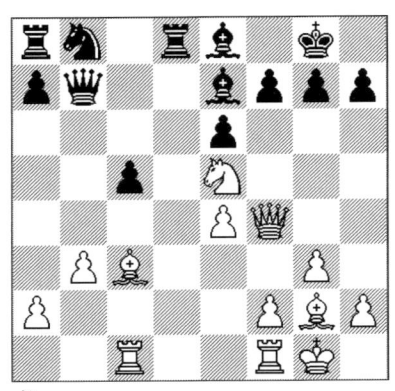

If 15...♗xc5, then 16.♗xg7! etc.
16.e4! ♗c6
Or 16...♗xe4 17.♘g5, winning.
17.♘e5 ♗e8

18.♘g4!
The peculiarity of this sudden attack on the King lies in the fact that it is not facilitated by any weakening resulting from Black's Pawn move in this part of the board.
18...♘a6
There were very few desperate choices resigned, as the "natural" answer 18...♘c6 19.♗xg7! ♔xg7 20.♕h6+ ♔g8 (or 20...♔h8 21.♘f6 and mate next) 21.e5 f6 22.♗e4 f5 23.♕xe6+, followed by 24.♕xf5 winning; and 18...♗c6 would allow 19.♗xg7 ♔xg7 20.♕h6+ ♔g8 21.♖xc5! etc.
19.♗xg7!, and Black resigned.
The main variant now is 19...♔xg7 20.♕h6+ ♔g8 21.e5 ♗c6 22.♘f6+ ♗xf6 23.exf6, followed by mate.

Game 114
Alekhine/Monosson-Flohr/Reilly
Game with consultation, Nice, May 1931
Nimzowitsch Defense [E24]

1.d4 ♘f6 2.c4 e6 3.♘c3 ♗b4 4.a3
Nowadays this move by Saemisch is completely out of fashion - not only because it wastes time to force an exchange that is not so unpleasant for the opponent, but mainly because it occupies the a3 square, which could otherwise be useful for the queen bishop.
4...♗xc3+ 5.bxc3 c5 6.♕c2
To prevent a possible ...♘e4. Black can now obtain by playing 6...d5 7.cxd5 ♕xd5 a position known from my recent title game, which is to their advantage. But this text move doesn't spoil anything either.
6...♘c6 7.♘f3 d5 8.e3 0–0 9.cxd5 exd5
But here Black misjudges the characteristic of the position: as the sequence will clearly show, the isolation of the Pawn d is too high a price for the Bishop's diagonal c8–h3. By resuming with the queen, they would then get 10.c4 ♕d6 11.♗b2, the position from my 10th Game against Euwe (The Hague, October 1937) in which some theorists (e.g. Fine) considered it even more advantageous for the second player. Without going that far, it can be admitted that this line would provide a fighting game, with possibilities for both sides.
10.dxc5!
Ending any hopes Black had of blocking with an eventual ...c4.
10...♕a5 11.♗d3 ♘e4
After this unnecessary effort (since the Pawn on c3 cannot be taken), Black's position is already critical. Also 11...♗g4 wouldn't be enough to reestablish the balance, as White would allow the exchange of his Knight and simply respond 12.♔b1 or 12.a4; but 11...♕xc5 could and should be played.
12.0–0
Of course, the right move, because

Black can play neither 12...♕×c3, due to 13.♗×e4, nor 12...♘×c3, due to 13.♗d2.

12...♕×c5 13.a4!

White finally has the chance to correct his 4th move and thus eliminate the only serious flaw in his position.

13...♖e8 14.♗a3 ♕a5 15.♖ab1!

If now 15...a6, then 16.c4 ♘f6 17.♘g5 (threatening mate in two) 17...h6 18.c×d5 ♕×d5 19.f4! threatening ♗c4 etc., with a winning attack. In this way, Black's next move should be considered a desperate attempt to alter the normal course of the battle.

15...♕×c3   16.♗×e4   ♕×a3 17.♗×h7+ ♔h8

It's certainly surprising that this move, which seems more natural than ...♔f8, quickly lost its force, while after the best move White had to satisfy himself with a (very tangible, it's true) positional advantage by playing 18.♗f5, etc.

18.♘g5!

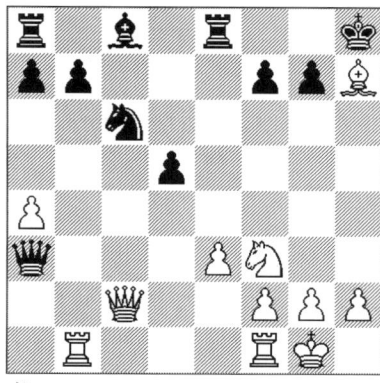

As in the previous game against Stoltz, mate's attack starts rather spontaneously and succeeds in very few moves. Flohr at the start of his career was sometimes superficial in defending his kingside position - compare, for example, his famous defeat by Mikenas in Folkestone. But he has certainly now become one of the most cautious (if not *the* most) of living masters!

18...g6

The consequences of this move are easy to calculate, as 18...♔f8 19.♗g8 or 18...♘d8 19.♗f5! The only more or less complicated variant is after 18...♕e7!, which would lead to the following ending: 19.f4! f6 20.♗g8 g6 21.♕×g6 f×g5 22.♗f7 ♗f5! 23.♕h6+ ♗h7 24.♖×b7! ♕f8 25.♕f6+ ♕g7 26.♕×g7+ ♔×g7 27.♗×e8+, followed by 28.♗×c6, winning.

19.♗×g6

Of course!

19...f×g6 20.♕×g6 ♖e7 21.e4!

A nice *coup de grace*. If now 21...d4 (there's nothing resigned), then 22.♖b5 ♗g4 (again the only move) 23.♕f6+ ♖g7 (or 23...♔g8 24.♘e6) 24.♖×b7 ♕f8 25.♖f7 etc., winning.

The black abandoned.

Game 115
A.Alekhine-A.Asgeirsson
Simultaneous in Reykjavik, August 1931
French Defense

1.e4 e6 2.d4 d5 3.♘c3 ♘f6 4.♗g5 ♗e7 5.♗×f6

This variant was recently favored by the talented German master, K. Richter - but only in conjunction with 6.e5 followed by 7.♕g4. The idea here was quite different - to keep the tension in the center for as long as possible, ending the mobilization of forces first.

5...♗×f6 6.♘f3 0-0 7.♗d3 ♖e8

A waste of time. Instead, 7...c5 was indicated. White would then hardly have anything better than 8.d×c5 ♕a5 9.♕d2 etc., with practically balanced prospects.

8.e5 ♗e7 9.h4!

Intending, of course, to sacrifice on h7. But is this sacrifice absolutely, correct? My opponent, once the Icelandic Champion, was waiting for a negative to launch a counterattack. If 9...h6, White would also have a distinct advantage by continuing with 10.♘e2 c5 11.c3, etc.

9...c5 10.♗×h7+

The solidity of this stereotypical offer is based on the possibility of White *also* exploiting the central columns for attacking purposes. Only the few checkmates on the King's wing, as can easily be seen, will still not have a decisive effect.

10...♔×h7 11.♘g5+ ♔g8 12.♕h5 ♗×g5 13.h×g5 ♔f8

Black now expects to get out of trouble easily after 14.♕h8+ ♔e7 15.♕×g7 ♔g8 16.♕f6+ ♔e8 etc., but White's next move shows them that the situation was much more serious than they thought.

14.g6!

That Pawn can't be taken, because after 15.♕×g6 there would be no defense against 16.♖h8+, etc.

14...♔e7 15.g×f7 ♖f8 16.0–0–0

By no means an automatic development move: White now threatens 17.♘b5, which wouldn't have worked before because of 17...♕a5+.

16...a6 17.d×c5

Threatening 18.♘e4.

17...♘d7

See the next Diagram

18.♖×d5!!

This ensures the participation of all White's forces in the final attack. The main variant if Black accepts this new offer is beautiful: 18...e×d5 19.♘×d5+ ♔e6 20.♘f4+ ♔e7 21.e6 ♘f6 22.♕e5! ♔×f7 23.♘d5+, followed by mate in three moves.

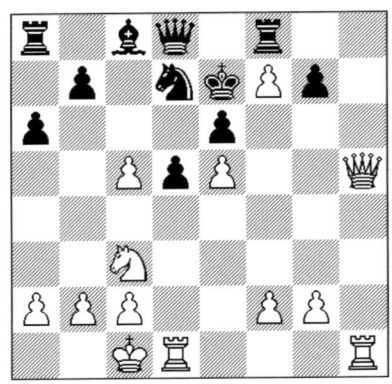

18...♕a5 19.♕g5+

Preventing Black's kingside escape on d8.

19...♔×f7 20.♖h7 ♖g8 21.♖d4!

Not immediately 21.♔×d7+ ♗×d7 22.♘e4? because of 22...♕e1mate.

21...♕×c5 22.♖×d7+! ♗×d7 23.♘e4 ♕b4

Again threatening to kill, but...

24.♘d6+ ♔f8 25.♕f6+! g×f6 26.♖f7 mate.

The mate position is "pure" and, for a practical game, quite economical.

Game 116
Dr.Tartakower&–Dr.Alekhine&
Game with consultation, Paris, October 1932
Queen's Indian Defense

1.d4 ♘f6 2.♘f3 b6 3.e3 ♗b7 4.♗d3 e6 5.♘bd2 c5

Strategically important to counterbalance the now possible advance of the Pawn and White.

6.0–0 ♘c6 7.c4

Instead of 7.c3 or 7.a3 eventually followed by b3 and ♗b2 (Rubinstein). White here adopts a third plan, which has the slight disadvantage of the total absence of immediate threats in the center - a circumstance that allows

Black to calmly finish his development and get an equal game.

7...♗e7 8.b3 c×d4

The simple 7...0–0 followed by ...d6 was also quite good. Through the maneuver in the text, Black secures White's d-pawn - which could become weak - but opens the e-file for his opponent and gives up the e5 square to his opponent.

9.e×d4 d5 10.♗b2 ♘b4

Less harmless than it seems at first glance: Black hopes to provoke a3 sooner or later, after which the ...♘–c6–a5 maneuver will become strong. In addition, White would have to rely on the possible ...♘e4.

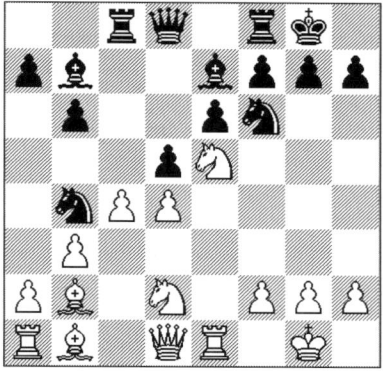

11.♗b1 0–0 12.♖e1 ♖c8 13.♘e5

13...♘c6!

By no means a waste of time, as White's last two moves completely changed the situation: (1) Due to the position of the Rook on e1, Black's King's Bishop acquired some perspective on b4; (2) White's Knight exposed in the center can, in some circumstances, be exchanged with advantage. By comparison, the best for White here would still be 14.a3, which would be answered by 14...♕c7, followed by ...♖fd8.

14.♘df3

White seems to think that the preemptive move 14.a3 would somehow justify Black's last knight move and that this is to punish his opponent for his "unscientific" play. But only a few moves will be needed to show whose assessment of the position was correct.

14...♗b4 15.♖e3?

Logical, but too risky. An almost equal game would still be obtained through 15.♘×c6 ♗×c6 16.♖e3 ♘e4 17.♘e5 ♗b7, etc.

15...♘e7

This knight is certainly trying to make itself useful: instead of being exchanged for a knight, it will now position itself on a very efficient point - f5 - or offer its life for White's dangerous king's bishop.

16.♘g5

Threatening the obvious sacrifice 17.♗×h7+ ♘×h7 18.♘×h7 ♔×h7 19.♕h5+ followed by 20.♖h3 - and at the same time trying to weaken the effect of Black's possible move ...♘e5.

16...h6 17.♘h3

A sad necessity: the combination starting with 17.♔h3 wouldn't work because of the simple answer 17...♘f5!

17...♗d6

It's instructive to see how Black's pieces, having taken advantage of the b4 square, give it up without being forced to.

18.♕e2 ♘f5

The moment is well chosen, as the Rook cannot return and there are no safe houses in the third row.

19.♗×f5 e×f5

Here the pair of Bishops is of great value, because as White doesn't have permanent central squares for his Knights, Black will always be able to

prepare and play ...f6.
20.♖c1 ♖c7
With the main aim of giving more space to the Queen.
21.f3 ♕c8 22.♖cc3 ♖e8
Simply threatening ...♘d7 followed by ...f6 and thus inducing White to simplify with positional cost.
23.c×d5 ♘×d5 24.♖×c7 ♗×c7 25.♕c4
Eventually threatening ♘f4; but this threat - like some of White's other threats in this game - is both obvious and harmless.
25...♕e6 26.♖e1 ♕d6!
From now on the threat of ...f6 becomes acute.
27.♕a4 ♗c6 28.♕a3
A harmless attempt to save the day by swapping the queens. Black, of course, kindly rejects this transaction.
28...♘b4! 29.♖c1
There is no more adequate defense against Black's next move.

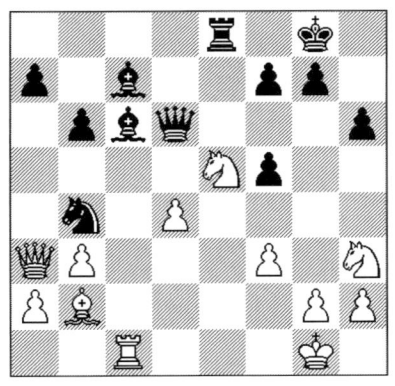

29...f6!
In making this move, Black had the following variants: I. 30.♖×c6 ♘×c6 31.♕×d6 ♗×d6 32.♘×c6 ♖e1+ 33.♔f2 ♖b1 34.♗c3 ♖c1, winning.
II. 30.♘×c6 ♕×h2+ 31.♔f1 (or 31.♔f2 ♘d3+, etc.) 31...♕h1+ 32.♘g1 (or 32.♔f2 ♘d3 mate) 32...♗h2 winning. And also, White's next desperate sacrifice allows for a quick and tidy ending.
30.f4 f×e5 31.f×e5 ♖×e5!
The prosaic 31...♕e7 32.♘f4 a5 etc. would also suffice in the long run - but the Rook's sacrifice is much more forcible.
32.d×e5 ♕d2 33.♘f2
Since 33.♔×c6 ♕e1 mate can't be played, it's forced.
33...♘d3! 34.♔f1 ♘×b2 35.♕e7 ♕d5 36.♘e4 ♗×e5!, and White resigned.

> **Game 117**
> **A.Alekhine-H.Borochow**
> *Blind Simultaneous, Hollywood, November 1932*
> Spanish Opening

1.e4 e5 2.♘f3 ♘c6 3.♗b5 a6 4.♗a4 ♘f6 5.0–0 ♘×e4 6.d4 b5 7.♗b3 d5 8.♘×e5

I've adopted this old move here for one reason in particular: my opponent - one of the best players in California - had played the Ruy Lopez against me in exactly the same way in the Pasadena Magistral Tournament, and achieved a very satisfactory position after 8.d×e5. Consequently, in the present blindfold game, I took the first opportunity to leave the over-explored paths of theory. Although the move in the text isn't the best - White's knight having more value at this point than Black's knight - this is by no means a mistake.

8...♘×e5 9.d×e5 ♗e6

The two other playable moves here are 9...♗b7 and 9...c6.

10.a4

This ward diversion is rather slow - especially in view of White's insufficient development. More advisable seems to be 10.♗e3 followed by f4 or

♘d2.

10...♘c5 11.♘d2 ♗e7

Quite right because the whites don't threaten anything.

12.♕e2 c6 13.c3 ♘xb3

The exchange is the result of an instructive misjudgment of the position. Having obtained a very satisfactory game, Black believes he can now dictate the rules. They should instead secure their King's position by castling, or even first play 13...♗f5, with excellent fighting chances.

14.♘xb3 bxa4

Of course, 14...d4 15.♘xd4 ♗c4 16.♕f3 ♗xf1 17.♕xc6+ ♔f8 18.♔xf1 would be a very bad speculation. After the text move, which is the logical consequence of the previous one, Black expected 15.♔xa4 ♕b6 16.♘d4 c5 17.♘xe6 ♕xe6 18.f4 f5, followed by ...0–0, etc., with prospects of an initiative in the center. But the next "intermediate" move shows them that the problem to be solved would be much less easy than they imagined.

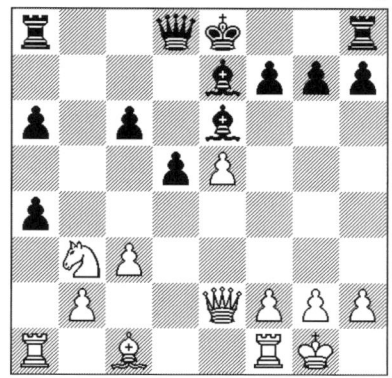

15.♘d4!

If now 15...♕c8 16.f4 c5 17.♘xe6 fxe6 18.♖xa4 0–0 19.♗e3 etc., with White's positional advantage. Black's response, although it allows the opening of the central column, is comparatively better.

15...♗d7 16.e6 fxe6 17.♖xa4!

A second surprise for Black: after 17.♘xe6 ♗xe6 18.♕xe6 ♕d7 White's initiative would quickly disappear.

17...♕c8

But if now 17...c5, then 18.♘xe6 ♗xe6 19.♕xe6 *with an attack against the Pawn a:* and also 17.0–0, as can easily be seen, would lose material.

18.♖e1 ♔f7

This attempt to keep all the goods in the land will be convincingly refuted. The only form of resistance consisted of 18...0–0 19.♘xe6 ♗xe6 20.♕xe6+ ♕xe6 21.♖xe6 ♗c5! 22.♗f4 ♖f6 23.♖xf6 gxf6, after which White, despite his great positional superiority in Pawns, would not easily find a way to decisively increase his advantage.

19.♘f5!

Threatening not only 20.♘xe7, but also - in many variants - 20.♘xg7! etc. And if 19...♕f8, then 20.♘h6+! ♔e8 (20...gxh6 21.♕h5+ etc.) 21.♘g4, followed by ♘e5 etc., with a winning position.

19...♖e8

Also 19...exf5 20.♕xe7+ followed by ♖e3 etc. would be perfectly hopeless.

20.♕h5+ ♔g8 21.♘xg7! ♖f8

If 21...♔xg7, then 22.♗h6+, followed by mate in three.

22.♖g4 ♔h8 23.♖e3! e5

This delayed attempt to bring the unfortunate queen's bishop back to life at first sight seems to temporarily protect everything (24.♕xe5 ♗f6 or 24.♖h3 ♗f5!). But the next reply brings death.

See the next Diagram

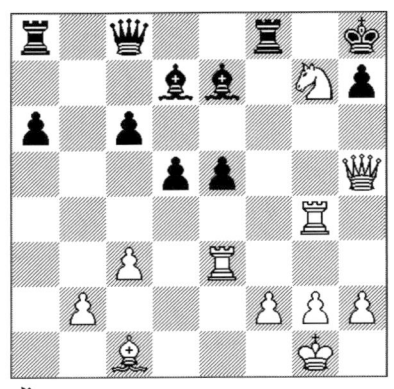

24.♘e6!

Not being a composer of problems, I'm not sure if this is really *the* "problem move". In any case, it's quite effective, as 24...♗xe6 would be followed by 25.♕xh7+ ♔xh7 26.♖h3+ ♗h4 27.♖hxh4 mate.

> **Game 118**
> **A.Alekhine-Kimura**
> *Blind Simultaneous, 15 Tables*
> *Tokyo, January 1933*
> Spanish Opening

1.e4 e5 2.♘f3 ♘c6 3.♗b5 a6 4.♗xc6 bxc6

Although playable, this move is rarely adopted, as 4...dxc6 gives the second player a very satisfactory game.

5.d4 exd4 6.♕xd4 d6

More natural than 6...♕f6 attempted by me against Duras in Mannheim 1914 (see *"My Best Plays 1908-1923"*), a move that could be answered with advantage by 7.e5! ♕g6 8.0–0 etc. - accepting the Pawn sacrifice (8...♕xc2) would be decidedly too dangerous for Black.

7.0–0 ♗e6 8.♘c3 ♘f6 9.♗g5

The positional advantage White would gain by playing e5 ♘d5 etc. here or on the next move didn't seem very convincing.

9...♗e7 10.♕a4 ♗d7 11.♖ad1 0–0

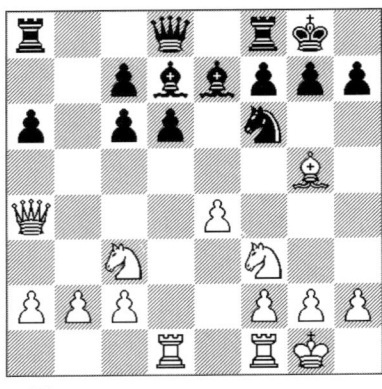

12.e5!

Now this advance ensures White's clear supremacy in one way or another. The main variant I considered here was 12...♘d5 13.♗xe7 ♕xe7 (or 13...♘xc3 14.♕h4!) 14.♘xd5 cxd5 15.♕a3! etc., bringing confusion to Black.

12...♘e8 13.♗xe7 ♕xe7 14.exd6 cxd6 15.♖fe1 ♕d8

A sad necessity, since after 15...♕f6 the reply 16.♘e5! would be practically decisive.

16.♘d4!

If now 16...c5, then 17.♘c6 ♕c7 18.♘d5 ♕b7 19.♘ce7+ ♔h8 20.♕h4 (threatening ♖e4 followed by ♕xh7+!) followed by a strong attack on the King.

16...♕c7 17.♖e7 ♘f6 18.♘f5!

The simpler 18.♖de1 would keep the lead without complications, but the line chosen was tempting - and proved correct.

18...♕d8

The comparatively more embarrassing response for White, whose pieces are beginning to "hang". The alternative 18...♖fe8 would give them an easy job: 19.♘e4! ♘xe4 20.♕xe4 ♔xe7 21.♕xe7! ♖e8 22.♕xd6 ♕xd6 23.♘xd6 ♖e2 24.♘c4 ♖xc2 25.♘e3, winning.

19.♖×d6 ♖e8

Apparently it forces the variant 20.♔×e8+ ♕×e8 21.♘e3, after which Black playing, for example, 21...♔b8 would still pose some problems for his "blindfolded" opponent. More surprising is that the maneuver that follows, with a double move, removes any fighting chance for Black.

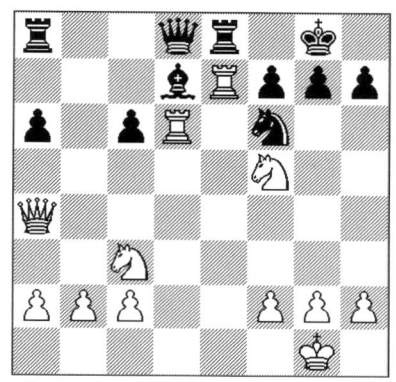

20.♘e4!

The first point of the attack started with 18.♘f5, in which only apparently White allowed a desirable exchange for Black.

20...♖×e7

Forced, because 20...♘×e4 21.♖×d7 etc. would be hopeless.

21.♘×f6+ ♔h8

Or 21...♔f8 22.♘×h7+ ♔g8 23.♘f6+ ♔f8 24.♘×e7 g×f6 25.♘×c6 ♕e8 26.♕b4! a5 27.♕c3, winning.

22.♘×e7 ♕×e7

Waiting not without pleasure for the variant 23.♘e4 ♗f5 24.♖d4 c5 25.♖c4 ♖d8 etc., with a counterattack.

23.♕e4!

A very unpleasant surprise for Black: not only is mate protected, but White himself threatens mate on h7, thus forcing the simplification.

23...♕×e4 24.♘×e4 ♗e6 25.b3 g6

Still waiting for 26.♖×c6? ♗d5. But after White avoided that trap too, Black could just as easily resign.

26.♘c5 ♗f5 27.♖×c6 ♖e8

I was wrong - this was still the chance to give mate in the first row...

28.f3 ♖e2 29.♖×a6 ♗×c2 30.♘e4 ♗e6 31.h4 ♔g7 32.♔h2 ♔h6 33.♔g3 ♗d7 34.a4 f5 35.♘g5 ♖c3 36.♖a7 ♖d3 37.a5 ♔h5 38.♘×h7, and Black resigned.

Game 119
I.Kashdan & - A.Alekhine &
Game with consultation
New York, September 1933
Spanish Opening

1.e4 e5 2.♘f3 ♘c6 3.♗b5 a6 4.♗a4 d6 5.c3 ♗d7 6.d4 ♘f6 7.♕e2

The protection of the Pawn and Queen usually brings White more disadvantages than advantages, so it would be better to replace it with 7.0–0 ♗e7 8.♖e1, etc.

7...♗e7 8.0–0 0–0 9.d5

Here there is hardly anything more advisable than this blocking procedure, as Black threatens 9...♘×d4 etc., and on the other hand 9.♗b3 (or c2) can be advantageously answered by 9...e×d4 followed by ...♘a5 (or ...b4), etc.

9...♘b8 10.♗c2

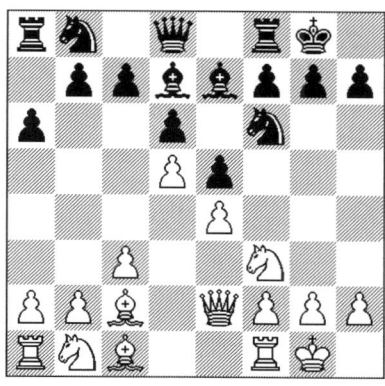

10...a5!

251

The idea of developing the knight by c5, analogous to many variants of Indian defenses - is both tempting and positionally justified. A good alternative, however, would be the dynamic 10...c6 to open columns on the queen's wing before White finishes his mobilization.

11.c4 ♘a6 12.♘c3 ♘c5 13.♗e3 b6 14.h3 g6

Aiming for ...♘-h5-f4. White's next "attacking" moves are apparently played to avoid this possibility.

15.♗h6 ♖e8 16.g4 ♗f8 17.♗×f8

If 17.♕d2, then 17...♗g7 and White would eventually be forced to trade even under less favorable conditions.

17...♖×f8 18.♘h2

The move planned here, f4, which would further weaken Black's squares from White's position, still needs to be considered again as a kind of indirect defense against Black's initiative threats on the h-file. White's bad luck is that he no longer has time for the otherwise indicated Pawn advance on the Queen's wing - b3 followed by a3, b4, etc.

18...♕e7

There's no rush to play ...h5, as White can't avoid it anyway.

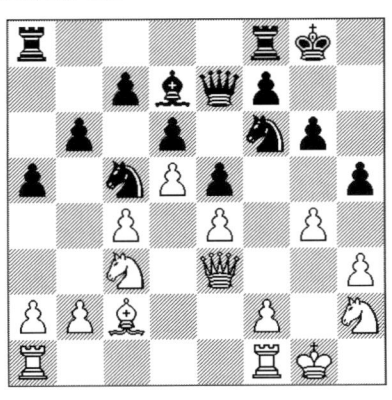

19.♕e3 h5

20.f4!

A purely passive defense starting with 20.f3 would prove, after 20...♔g7 followed by ...♖h8 etc., to be practically hopeless - and the Pawn sacrifice intended by the move in the text is tactically justified. The only problem is that Black doesn't have to accept it, and White's g-Pawn remains weak!

20...h×g4 21.h×g4 e×f4

After 21...♘×g4? 22.♘×g4 ♗×g4 23.♕g3 ♗h5 24.f5 White would get a strong attack.

22.♕×f4 ♔g7 23.♖ae1 ♖ae8 24.♔g2

Probably played in view of a possible exchange of the queens in the case of ...♕e4. But Black rightly prefers to first increase his pressure by taking advantage of the open h-file - especially as he sees that a triple attack on his knight on f6 can be successfully met by a counterattack.

24...♖h8 25.♖e2 ♖h4 26.♖ef2 ♖eh8 27.♔g1

Now it may seem for a moment that White's pressure against Black's f7 and f6 squares is more effective than the counter-threats on the h-file, but the next two moves bring the situation into focus.

27...♗e8!

Not only defending the Pawn f, but also giving space to the Queen's Knight.

28.♕g5

The ending after 28.♕×f6+ etc. would be clearly in Black's favor due to the powerful central e5 for his knight.

28...♔f8!

In its simplicity, it's probably the most difficult move of the whole game: having protected their queen, Black now threatens 29...♘×g4! etc.

29.♖g2 ♘cd7

This withdrawal, which allows the seemingly dangerous response to follow, also had to be calculated precisely.

30.♘b5

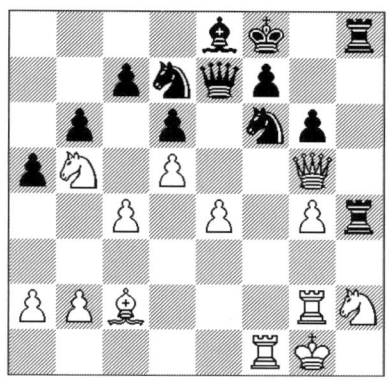

30...♘e5!

The occupation of the dominant central square coincides here with the tactical decision of the game. Since 31.♘xc7 would be refuted by 31...♕xh2! 32.♖xh2 ♖xh2 33.♘xe8 ♘fxg4! 34.♕xe7+ ♔xe7 35.♗a4 ♔xb2 etc., White had nothing better to do than simplify and hope for a miracle in the endgame afterwards.

31.♕xf6 ♕xf6 32.♖xf6 ♗xb5!

A very important midfield exchange, the omission of which would have resigned White with an excellent chance of an equalizer.

33.cxb5 ♖xh2

In so many ways, the decisive point.

34.♖xh2 ♖xh2 35.♖xf7+

The only way to temporarily avoid losing material.

35...♔xf7 36.♔xh2 ♘xg4+ 37.♔g3 ♘e5

Despite the material balance, Black has an easy job, because in addition to the passed Pawn, he has an obvious supremacy (two pieces against one) on the Black squares.

38.b3 ♔f6 39.♗d1 ♘d3 40.♔f3 ♔e5 41.♔e3 ♘c5 42.♗f3 g5 43.♗h1 ♘d7

The immediate 43...g4 was also quite good.

44.♗g2 ♘f6 45.♗f3 g4 46.♗e2

In the case of 46.♗g2 Black could easily win with 46...♘h5 followed by ...♘f4.

46...♘xe4 47.♗xg4 ♘c3 48.♗f3 ♘xd5+ 49.♔d2 ♔d4 50.a3 ♘c3 51.♗c6 a4! 52.♔c2 d5 53.bxa4 ♔c4!, and White resigned.

Game 120
A.Alekhine-A.Mindeno
Simultaneous in Holland, October 1933
Spanish Opening

1.e4 e5 2.♘f3 ♘c6 3.♗b5 d6

The Steinitz Defense, which was fashionable in the days of the 1921 Lasker-Capablanca game, has now completely disappeared from masterly practice. In fact, the modern treatment with the intermediate 3...a6 (the so-called deferred Steinitz) gives Black, after 4.♗a4 d6, considerably more choice of development plans than the self-restrictive move of the text.

4.d4 exd4

After 4...♗d7 the most promising line for White would be 5.♘c3 ♘f6 6.♗xc6 ♗xc6 7.♕d3!

5.♕xd4

Of course, 5.♘xd4 is also good. Through the text move, White is already planning 0-0-0.

5...♗d7 6.♗xc6 ♗xc6 7.♘c3 ♘f6 8.♗g5 ♗e7 9.0-0-0 10.h4

This position had already occurred a long time ago in a game by Anderssen in the 1870 Baden-Baden Tournament, in which the German Champion here played 10.♖he1, drawing at the end. I played this in

Folkestone 1933, against Anderssen's namesake, the late Danish master E. Andersen, but although the game ended in my favor, its early stage (after 10...♘d7 11.♗xe7 ♕xe7 12.♖e3 ♕f6 13.♘d5 ♗xd5 14.exd5 ♕xd4, etc.) was not unsatisfactory for Black. The move in the text is more acute, as Black needs to try to dislodge White's bishop on g5.

10...h6

There is nothing to condemn, as Black is not obliged to take the Bishop with the Pawn and can only do so when it is perfectly safe.

11.♘d5

A correct and exactly calculated offer that Black cannot accept. Even more appropriate for maintaining tension would be 11.♔b1 first.

11...hxg5?

Although the end point of the sacrifice was very difficult to foresee, its acceptance must be decisively condemned: it was quite obvious that the opening of the h-file meant mortal danger here, and, more importantly, Black had a perfectly safe defense here (for the moment, anyway) by continuing with 11...♘xd5 12.exd5 ♗d7, etc.

12.♘xe7+!

Of course, not 12.hxg5 ♘xd5 13.exd5 ♗xg5+, etc. with sufficient defense.

12...♕xe7 13.hxg5 ♘xe4

Also, after other knight moves the doubled rooks on the h-file would prove decisive. And if 13...♕xe4, then 14.gxf6 ♕xd4 15.♔xd4 ♗xf3 16.gxf3 ♔fe8 17.♖g4! g6 18.♖gh4 with mate next.

14.♖h5 ♕e6

In the immediate case of 14...f5 Black would force a win in a similar way to the text: 15.g6 ♕e6 16.♘e5! ♘f6 (otherwise 17.♖dh1) 17.♖h8+! ♔xh8 18.♕h4+ ♔g8 19.♖h1 etc., with mate inevitable.

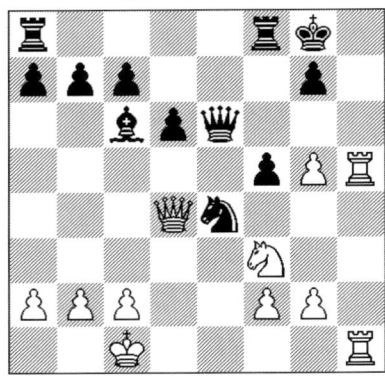

15.♖dh1 f5

After this move Black seems to be temporarily safe, because after 16.g6 ♕xg6 17.♘e5 he would get the Rook and two minor pieces for the Queen through 17...♕xh5 18.♖xh5 dxe5 etc. But a spectacular move transposition ruins their hopes.

16.♘e5!!

A surprise move aimed at weakening the protection of Black's d5 square.

16...dxe5

As 16...♕xe5 17.♕xe5 dxe5 18.g6 loses immediately, Black had no choice.

17.g6!

The point: if now 17...♕xg6, then 18.♕c4+ followed by mate in three moves. Without the preliminary 16.♘e5 dxe5 Black would still have the defense ...d5.

Black resigned.

Alexander Alekhine

Appendix
Biographical notes of Alekhine's opponents in this Book

Ahues, Karl Oscar - **Games 36, 77**
Born on December 26, 1883, in Bremen (Germany), he died at the age of 83 on December 31, 1968, in Hamburg (Germany).

Was awarded the title of International Master in 1950; Berlin champion (1910), German champion (1929), 6th place in the San Remo Tournament (1930), winner of lightning chess tournaments in Germany as an octogenarian, ranked world no. 11 in 1931.

Represented Germany at two World Chess Olympiads: 1930 (Hamburg), 1931 (Prague) and at an unofficial one in 1936 (Munich).

His son, Herbert Ahues (1922-2015), became Grandmaster of Chess Problem Composition in 1989.

Alexander, Conel Hugh O'Donel - **Game 86**
Born on April 19, 1909, in Cork (Ireland), he died at the age of 64 on February 15, 1974, in Cheltenham (England).

Also known as Hugh Alexander, he was a cryptanalyst, chess player and author of chess books. He was awarded the title of International Master in 1950 and was twice British Chess Champion (1938 and 1956). He won the Hastings tournament in 1946/47 and was co-champion of the same tournament in 1953/54. He was a chess columnist for The Sunday Times in the 60s and 70s. He made important theoRetical contributions to the Dutch and Petroff defenses.

He represented England in six World Chess Olympiads: 1933, 1935, 1937, 1939, 1954 and 1958; he also captained the English team between 1964 and 1970.

In February 1940, he joined Bletchley Park, the British decoding center that brought together the Allies during World War II. There, Alexander worked with Alan Turing to break the codes of the German Enigma Machine, in a story later featured in the film The Imitation Game (2014). He was head of the cryptanalysis division of the British Intelligence Service for 25 years.

Andersen, Erik - **Game 39**
Born on April 10, 1904, in Gentofte (Denmark), he died at the age of 33 on February 27, 1938, in Copenhagen (Denmark).

He was Danish champion twelve times (1923, 1925 to 1927, 1929, 1930 to 1936) and won the Nordic Championship in 1930 (Stockholm).

He represented Denmark in the first six World Chess Olympiads: 1927 (London), in which Denmark won the silver medal, 1928 (The Hague), 1930 (Hamburg), 1931 (Prague), 1933 (Folkestone), 1935 (Warsaw) and in an unofficial one in 1936 (Munich).

Asgeirsson, Asmundur - **Game 115**
Born on March 14, 1906, in (Iceland). Won the Icelandic chess championship in 1931, 1933, 1934, 1944, 1945 and 1946.

Asztalos, Lajos - **Game 17**
Born on July 29, 1889, in Pecs, he died at the age of 67 on November 1, 1956, in Budapest during the Hungarian Revolution against the Soviet Union. He was a Hungarian International Master and a teacher of philosophy and languages. After participating prominently in several tournaments in Hungary. Austria and Poland, winning

257

the Hungarian Championship in 1913, he moved after WWI to the Kingdom of Serbia, Croatia, and Slovenia (later known as Yugoslavia). He took part in several post-war tournaments, including the one in Kecskemet in 1927, won by Alekhine, where he came 4th. He represented Yugoslavia at the Olympics in Budapest, London, Prague, and Munich. He returned to Hungary in 1942 and became Vice-President of the Hungarian Chess Union and Secretary of the FIDE Rating Committee. He was awarded the title of International Master in 1950 and the FIDE International Arbiter in 1951. Author of the book Elements of the Game of Chess (1951). The Asztalos Memorial Tournament was played regularly in Hungary between 1958 and 1971.

Bogoljubov Efim Dmitriyevich, *Games 26, 27, 28, 29, 30, 61, 62, 63, 64, 65, 66, 78, 79, 87, 95*

A Russian, Ukrainian, and German Grandmaster, was born on April 14, 1889, in the town of Stanislavchyk, near Kiev, Ukraine, and died suddenly at the age of 67 on June 18, 1952, in Belgrade, just after giving a session of simultaneous games. He won numerous tournaments and faced Alekhine in two world title games - in 1929 and 1934. He took up chess after attending a seminary when he switched his studies to a polytechnic. From 1909 he began to take part in local and national Russian tournaments. In 1911 he took first place in the Kiev Championship. In 1913-1914 he finished eighth in the All-Russia Masters Tournament, won by Alekhine and Nimzowitsch. Between July and August 1914 he took part in the Mannheim Tournament, which had special significance in his life: this tournament was interrupted by the outbreak of World War I and, after the German declaration of war on Russia, eleven "Russian players" (Alekhine, Bogoljubov, Fedor Bogatyrchuk, Alexander Flamberg, N. Koppelman, Boris Maliutin, Ilya Rabinovich, Peter Romanovsky, Peter Petrovich Saburov, Alexey Selezniev and Samuil Winstein) who were taking part in the tournament were arrested by the German authorities. In September, four of them (Alekhine, Bogatyrchuk, Saburov and Koppelman) were allowed to return home via Switzerland. The other Russian prisoners played eight tournaments, the first in Baden-Baden in 1914 and the others in Triberg (1914-1917). Bogoljubov came second in Baden-Baden and won the Triberg Tournament five times (1914-1916). During World War I he stayed in Triberg, married a local teacher, and spent the rest of his life living in Germany.

After the First World War, he won several international tournaments: Berlin 1919, Stockholm 1919, Kiel 1921, Pistyan 1922. He took 1st-3rd places in Karlsbad 1923.

In 1924 Bogoljubov quickly returned to Russia, which had then become the Soviet Union, and consecutively won the 1924 and 1925 Soviet Championships. He also won the 1925 Breslau Tournament and the 1925 Moscow Tournament, ahead of Capablanca and Lasker. He emigrated permanently to Germany in 1926 and that year won the Berlin Tournament against Rubinstein. In Kissingen 1928 he triumphed once again against Capablanca, Nimzowitsch and Tartakower. In 1928 and 1928/1929 he won two games against Dr. Max Euwe, both by 5.5-4.5, and lost to Alekhine in two World Championship games (15.5-9.5 in 1929 and 15.5-10.5 in 1934). Still in 1929, he received German citizenship.

In 1930 he twice shared 2nd/3rd places - with Nimzowitsch in San Remo (won by Alekhine) and in Stockholm - with Stoltz (won by Kashdan). In 1931 he shared 1st/2nd place in Swinemünde and in 1933 he won in Bad Pyrmont. In 1935 he won in Bad Nauheim and Bad Saarov. He won in Berlin 1935, Bas Elster 1936, 1937 and 1938 in Bremen 1937 and Stuttgart 1939.

Represented Germany on the first board at the 4th Chess Olympiad in Prague 1931, winning the silver medal.

During World War II, he lost a match to Euwe (+2-5=3) in Krefeld and drew a mini-match with Alekhine (+1-1=0) in Warsaw 1943. He played several tournaments in Germany and the occupied territories during World War II. In 1940 he won in Berlin and shared 1st/2nd place in Warsaw. In 1941 he came 4th in Munich and 3rd in Warsaw (won by Alekhine). In 1942 he came 5th in Salzburg (won by Alekhine) and shared 3rd-5th places in Munich (also won by Alekhine). In 1943 he came 4th in Salzburg (won by Alekhine and Keres) and 2nd/3rd in Krynica and in 1944 he won the Radom tournament ahead of his former prison mate Fedor Bogatyrchuk.

After the war he lived in West Germany. Although his level of play declined significantly, he won the Lünenburg and Kassel tournaments in 1947. In 1949 he won in Pyrmont (3rd West German Championship) and shared 1st/2nd place in Oldemburg. In 1951 he won in Augsburg and Saarbrücken.

Awarded with the title of FIDE International Grandmaster in 1951.

Bogoljubov was one of the most important players of the 20th century. His affable and humorous temperament won him many admirers. Some anecdotes are famous, mainly linked to his optimism, fearlessness, and overestimation of his possibilities on the board. To illustrate, here are a few:

- During the Bled Tournament (Slovenia) in 1931, Bogoljubov was facing Aszatlov and announced, "mate in two moves!". But his calculation was wrong, and he had to postpone the game in a disadvantageous position. His opponent was able to tell him: "The dead you kill are in perfect health" ...

- Bogoljubov was famous for his humor, which was not always politically correct. One day Bogoljubov faced Tarrash and succeeded in beating the "Professor from Germany". A few days later, unfortunately, Dr. Tarrasch died. *Bogol* published the match and could think of no other title for the article than *The game that killed Dr. Tarrasch*.

Believing in God and in himself, he coined the famous phrase: "If I have white, I will win because I have white; if I have black, I will win because I am Bogoljubov".

Capablanca, José Raul — **Games 20, 21, 22, 23, 24**

One of the greatest chess players of all time, his importance to chess goes beyond the mere biographical notes in this book. We then present his obituary written by Alekhine, a text that unites these two legendary players:

"The first time I heard of Capablanca was in 1909, as indeed did all my contemporaries, when he won his match with Marshall in such an astonishing manner. Capablanca was then twenty years old, and I was sixteen. Neither his chess performance nor his style impressed me at the time. His game seemed 'new' but lacked uniformity. And then when he won such a competitively good victory in San Sebastian 1911, many of his games were won through surprising tactical resources. His first real and incomparable gift began to manifest itself at the time of the 1914 St. Petersburg Tournament, when I also came to know him personally. Neither before nor since have I seen - and I really couldn't have imagined - such a quick grasp of chess as Capablanca possessed at the time. Suffice it to say that he gave all the masters in St. Petersburg a 5-1 lead in rapid games - and won! He was always in a good mood with everyone, loved by women, and in perfect health - truly a dazzling presence. The fact that he came second after Lasker must be attributed entirely to his youth - Capablanca was already playing as well as Lasker."

"I met Capablanca for the second time in London in 1922. He was already the World Champion and had every intention of remaining so for a long time. In fact, at that time his chess potential had reached its peak; a crystal-clear handling of the opening and the middlegame, coupled with an unsurpassed endgame technique. His temperament, however, became a little more nervous, and this nervousness manifested itself to avoid putting his title on the line as much as possible, or even to avoid it. For this reason, he became involved in the "London Rules", which established a purse of 10,000 gold dollars for the match. At the time, it was hard for him to imagine that one of his rivals could raise such a large sum. And in this he was right; it was not by his rivals (me included), but by Capablanca himself that this sum was raised in Buenos Aires in 1927 - in fact in anticipation of being awarded the World Championship once again in a city he had already visited twice, and in which he was very popular. The people there were, of course, convinced that he could win a match against me. What happened to make him lose? I must confess that even now I can't answer that question with much certainty, because in 1927 I didn't believe I was superior to him. Perhaps the main reason for his defeat was that he overestimated his chess powers after his landslide victory in New York 1927 and underestimated me.

Whatever the reason, with the loss of the title Capablanca also lost form for a while, and began to pursue a policy that, if he once really wanted the match rematch, was not calculated in any way for it, to say the least. Immediately after his defeat, he sought to bring in through FIDE (the chess counterpart to the League of Nations) new conditions for a World Title match, and this without consulting me. That was the kind of procedure I couldn't tolerate, and so there was a cooling off and a difference between us.

A few years later, Capablanca made the right decision, namely, to try to show the chess world that he was the best candidate for the world title through his actual performance. And indeed, he went a long way in this respect, winning two very important tournaments in 1936 (Moscow and Notthingham). Then, however, his powers waned, from a competitive and not purely chess point of view. His split third place (out of eight participants) in Semmering-Baden 1937, and his seventh place (out of eight) in the AVRO Tournament showed the chess world that his title hopes were finally over.

And until the end, for example in Buenos Aires 1939, as I'm demonstrating, he could still produce true pearls of chess art, but he didn't have enough stamina to achieve practical success in major tournaments. However, Capablanca was removed from the chess world too soon. With his death, we have lost a great chess genius, the like of whom we will never see again."

Colle, Edgard - **Game 8**

Edgard Colle born 18/05/1897 in Ghent, died in the same city at the age of 33 on 20/04/1932, was a Belgian chess master. He achieved excellent results in major international tournaments, including 1st place in Amsterdam 1926, ahead of Tartakower and future world champion Max Euwe; 1st place in Merano 1926 in a strong tournament, ahead of Esteban Canal and won twice in Scarborough in 1927 and again in 1930, ahead of Maróczy and Rubinstein.

Colle's career was greatly affected by his health. He survived three very delicate operations due to a gastric ulcer and died after the fourth operation.

Colle is remembered today primarily for his introduction of the chess opening now known as the Colle System: 1.d4 d5 2.♘f3 ♘f6 3.e3. White normally follows up with ♗d3, 0-0, and ♘bd2, playing for a central pawn break with e4. The opening is in effect a reversed Semi-Slav Defense. In response to ...c5 by Black, White typically plays c3. The Colle System was most often played in the late 1920s and 1930s. Colle himself played it from 1925 until his death in 1932. He won many games with the opening, including several brilliancies. Colle-O'Hanlon, Nice 1930, featuring one of the best-known examples of a Greek gift sacrifice, is especially famous.

Colle's playing career was hampered by ill health. He survived three difficult operations for a gastric ulcer and died after a fourth at the age of 34 in Ghent.

Davidson, J. - *Game 10*
Jacques Davidson (born 11/14/1890 in Amsterdam and died at the age of 79 on 11/14/1969 in the same city) November 14, 1890, Amsterdam - January 13, 1969, Amsterdam) was a Dutch chess master. Before the First World War, he lived for many years in London. Jacques used to gamble with his father, and although he didn't get paid, it occurred to him that it might be useful to play chess with rich Englishmen. He learned how to do this from another Dutchman, Rudolf Loman. In the 1920s Davidson was twice Dutch runner-up to Max Euwe. In 1911 he won a match against Edward Seargeant (2.5-0.5) in London; in the following years he played several tournaments in Holland, England, and Germany, with average results. He also played a few games: a draw against Teichmann in Berlin 1922 and losses to Euwe 1924 and 1927 and to Spielmann 1932 and 1933, all in Amsterdam.

Curiously, his tombstone in Amsterdam features a chess problem to challenge visitors, with the information "mate in one move". Can the reader find the solution?

MAT IN EEN ZET

HIER RUST
MIJN LIEVE MAN
ONZE VADER EN OPA
JACQUES DAVIDSON
INTERNATIONAAL SCHAAKMEESTER
14 NOV. 1890   13 JAN. 1969

Before World War I, he had lived in London for several years. Jacques had played with his father for a stake, he had won, and though he was not paid, the idea had occurred to him that it could be profitable to play chess against wealthy Englishmen. He learned how to proceed from another Dutchman, Rudolf Loman. In the

1920s, Davidson would finish second in the Dutch championship twice, behind Max Euwe.

In 1911, he won a match against Edward Sergeant (2,5:0,5) in London. He tied for 3rd-5th at Tunbridge Wells 1911 (Frederick Yates won); took 15th at Cologne 1911 (Moishe Lowtzky won); tied for 2nd-3rd at London 1912 (Harold Godfrey Cole won); took 6th at London 1912 (George Alan Thomas won); tied for 4-7th at London 1913 (Edward Lasker won).[2]

He took 2nd at Nijmegen 1921 (Euwe won); took 8th at The Hague 1921 (Alexander Alekhine won); took 16th at Scheveningen 1923 (10+10, Paul Johner and Rudolf Spielmann won);[3] twice took 2nd, behind Euwe, in Amsterdam (1923, 1924). Davidson won at Amsterdam 1925 (Quadrangular); took 16th at Semmering 1926 (Spielmann won); took 8th at Spa 1926 (Friedrich Saemisch and Thomas won); took 2nd at Utrecht 1927 (Quadrangular, Euwe won); shared 1st with Hartingsvelt at Amsterdam 1927; tied for 5-6th at Amsterdam 1929 (Euwe won).[4]

He played several games; drew with Richard Teichmann at Berlin 1922, and lost to Euwe (1924, 1927) and Spielmann (1932, 1933), all in Amsterdam.[5]

Eliskases, E. - *Game 80*
Erich Gottlieb Eliskases (15 February 1913 - 2 February 1997) was a chess Grandmaster of the 1930s and 1940s, who represented Austria, Germany, and Argentina in international competitions.

He learned to play chess at the age of 12 and quickly showed a great aptitude for the game, winning the Schlechter Chess Club championship in his first year at the club, aged just 14. At 15 he was champion of Tyrol and at 16 co-champion of Austria.

His schooling in Innsbruck and Vienna focused on Business and Administration. It was chess, however, that captured his imagination and Eliskases achieved exceptional results at the 1930, 1933 and 1935 Olympiads. After the annexation of Austria by the Nazis in March 1938, he won the German National Championship in Bas Oeynhausen in 1938 and 1939. He played under the German flag at the 1939 Olympics in Buenos Aires, during which World War II began. Eliskases, like many other players, decided to stay in Argentina (and for a while in Brazil) rather than return to the scene of the conflict. Brazilian authorities threatened to arrest and deport him, as he had many links to Nazi Germany. Some Brazilian chess enthusiasts protected him from this fate by hiring him as a chess teacher - for a few years Eliskases taught at the São Paulo Chess Club. After a few years Eliskases became an Argentine citizen, and represented his new country at the 1952, 1958, 1960 and 1964 Olympiads.

FIDE awarded Elikases the title of International Master in 1950 and International Grandmaster in 1952. He won many memorable tournaments, including first place in Budapest 1934, Linz 1934, Zurich 1935, Milan 1937, Noordwijk 1938 (his great success, ahead of Euwe and Keres), Krefeld 1938, Bad Harzburg 1939, Bas Elster 1939, Vienna 1939, Aguas de São Pedro/São Paulo 1941, São Paulo 1947, Mar del Plata 1948,

Punta del Este 1951 and Córboba 1959. His victory in Noordwijk began a run of eight consecutive tournaments in which he remained unbeaten.

He won games against Efim Bogoljubov (1939) and Rudolf Spielmann (three times, in 1932, 1936 and 1937).

At the end of the 1930s Eliskases was considered, along with Capablanca, Keres and Botvinnik, as potential candidates in a World Title fight against Alekhine. It even spoke in his favor after the match against Euwe in 1937 when he regained the title, in which Eliskases was his second.

Dutch Grandmaster Hans Ree noted that Elikases was one of only four players (Keres, Reshevsky and Euwe are the others) to beat both Capablanca and Bobby Fischer.

Euwe, Max - **Games 72, 73, 74, 75, 76, 84, 97, 98, 99, 100, 101, 102, 103, 104, 109, 110**

Machgielis Euwe is better known by the name Max Euwe, and he is better known as the world chess champion from 1935 to 1937 than as a mathematician. However, Euwe was indeed a very fine mathematician who concentrated more on his mathematics throughout his life than on his chess.

Max Euwe's parents were Elisabeth and Cornelius Euwe. Cornelius was a teacher and he often played chess with his wife who loved the game. By the time Max was five years old his parents had taught him to play and soon he was able to beat them. Max attended school in Amsterdam where he excelled in mathematics, and he began to play chess at ever more advanced levels. In 1911, when he was ten years old, Max entered his first chess tournament, a one-day Christmas congress, and won every game. He became a member of the Amsterdam chess club when he was twelve years old and by the time, he was fourteen he was playing in the Dutch Chess Federation tournaments. This was a difficult time in most European countries as World War I was totally disrupting normal life in most places, but The Netherlands remained neutral, so life in Amsterdam was relatively comfortable.

When he was eighteen years old Euwe was awarded his Abitur after attending a six-form High School in Amsterdam. By this time World War I had ended, and international travel became possible again. Euwe made his first trip abroad, going to England to play in the famous Hastings Chess Tournament where he took fourth place. There had been little doubt in his mind what subject he should study at university, and he entered Amsterdam University to begin his study of mathematics. It should not be thought that Euwe kept his study of chess distinct from his mathematical studies. On the contrary he saw mathematics as being able to provide him with a logical, precise, even algebraic, approach to the game. We mention below an interesting mathematics paper he wrote which was motivated by chess.

By 1920 he was the leading Dutch player, and he won the Dutch Championship for the first time in August 1921. In 1923 he was awarded an Honors Degree in mathematics from Amsterdam University. He then undertook research in mathematics which led to him being awarded a doctorate in 1926 from the University of Amsterdam.

In 1930 he won the Hastings tournament ahead of Capablanca. However, in an Euwe - Capablanca match which was played later Euwe lost 0 wins to 2 with 8 draws. The year 1932 was a very successful one beating Spielmann, drawing twice with Flohr and taking second place behind Alekhine in a tournament in Berne.

During 1933-34 he played very little chess while he concentrated on mathematics. Then, in the summer of 1935, he challenged Alekhine; the match began on 3 October. It was held at twenty-three different locations in Amsterdam, The Hague, Delft, Rotterdam, Utrecht, Gouda, Groningen, Baarn, Hertogenbosch, Eindhoven, Zeist, Ermelo, and Zandvoort.

The dramatic result of his first match against Alekhine is old history. Three points down after seven games, he pulled up to equality, only to see his redoubtable opponent draw away again. Battling gamely, he was still two down at the two-thirds stage, but won the twentieth, twenty-first, twenty-fifth, and twenty-sixth games and retained his grip on a now desperate adversary to the end.

Euwe's great characteristic is economy of force. He is logic personified, a genius of law and order. His play is accurate and aggressive. One would hardly call him an attacking player, yet when his genius is functioning at its smoothest, he strides confidently into some extraordinary complex positions: he is no disciple of simplicity. His greatest weakness is a tendency to blunder.

Euwe played the Nottingham International Chess Tournament from 10 August to 28 August 1936 while he was World Champion. In the Introduction to the Book of the Tournament, W H Watts writes:

Euwe is the essence of caution. To win the world's championship and to secure a place only half a point behind the winner on caution alone is impossible, there must be depth and imagination, but the outstanding impression to be gained from his games is caution and dogged perseverance.

Despite this overall impression of caution, it is worth noting that Euwe shared the prize for the most wins in his score during the tournament.

While Euwe was World Champion he changed the way that players competed for the title. From that time on the rights to organize World Championship games was given to FIDE (Fédération Internationale des échecs - the World Chess Federation). The one exception was the return match between Euwe and Alekhine which went ahead according to the conditions already arranged at the time of the first match.

In his return match with Alekhine things went badly for Euwe after winning the first game, and he lost the match by a margin of five points. Various reasons have been put forward as to why he was defeated so heavily, but the main reason was almost certainly the fact that his advisor, Reuben Fine, had taken ill with appendicitis and could not assist him.

Played at Hastings at Christmas 1938-39 and won the Dutch Championship again in 1939 but the onset of war made international play difficult over the next few years. During the war Euwe led work to provide food for people through an underground charity organization.

After the war he won the London Tournament in 1946 and it looked for a while as though he might challenge again for the World Championship. However, after some impressive play in the couple of years following the war, he then began to look past his best. Euwe became interested in electronic data processing and was appointed as Professor of Cybernetics in 1954. In 1957 he visited the United States to study computer technology in that country. While in the United States he played two unofficial chess games in New York against Bobby Fischer, winning one and drawing the second. Was appointed director of The Netherlands Automatic Data Processing Research Centre in 1959. He was chairman, from 1961 to 1963, of a committee set up by Euratom to examine the feasibility of programming computers to play chess. Then, in 1964, he was appointed to a chair in an automatic information processing in Rotterdam University and, following that, at Tilburg University. He retired as a professor at Tilburg in 1971.

In 1970 Euwe was elected the president of FIDE and held that position until 1978. His role of the Fischer - Spassky World Championship match in Reykjavik, Iceland in 1972 was a very difficult one which he carried out with great tact and skill. He was unfortunate that during his time as president negotiations for the World Championship match between Fischer and Karpov became extremely difficult. Euwe made huge efforts to ensure that the match was played but, unfortunately, despite every effort eventually the match had to be awarded to Karpov by default.

Fine, R. - *Games 90, 94*
Reuben Fine (born 11/10/1914 in New York, died in the same city at the age of 78 on 26/03/1993) was a chess grandmaster, psychologist, university professor and author of many books, both on chess and psychology. He was one of the strongest players in the world from the mid-1930s until his retirement from chess in 1951. The best result of Fine's chess career was his shared victory (with Paul Keres) in the AVRO Tournament in 1938, one of the strongest tournaments of all time, among the eight participants were three World Champions - Capablanca, Alekhine and Euwe.

After the death of World Champion Alekhine in 1946, Fine was one of six players invited to compete for the vacant title at the World Chess Championship in 1948. Fine declined the invitation to that tournament, and despite being withdrawn from the most important tournaments of that time, he continued to play a few tournaments until 1951.

Fine won five medals (four gold) at the Chess Olympiad for the United States team. He won the U.S. Open Chess Championship seven times (1932, 1933, 1934, 1935, 1939, 1940, 1941). He is considered one of the greatest American players of the 20th century, alongside Marshall, Reshevsky and Fischer. He was the author of several chess books that are still very popular, including some very important ones on the three phases of the game - openings, middlegames and endgames.

Flohr, S. - *Games 46, 55, 114* (and amateur)
Salomon Mikhailovich Flohr (born 21/11/1908 in Horodenka - now located in Ukraine - and died aged 74 in Moscow on 18/07/1983) was a prominent Czech grandmaster of the mid-20th century, who became a national hero in what was then Czechoslovakia during the 1930s. His name was used to sell various luxury goods, such as Salo Flohr cigarettes, slippers, and perfumes. Flohr dominated several tournaments in the pre-World War II phase and by the end of the 1930s he was considered a potential challenger for the World Championship, even becoming FIDE's nominee. However, his patient positional style was overtaken by the more precise and more tactical methods of the young Soviet battalion after the Second World War. Flohr was also an important author of chess books and an International Arbiter.

His performance at the Chess Olympiad defending his adopted country was impressive: first board in Hamburg 1930 - silver medal with 14.5 out of 17; at home, Prague 1931, again on the first board, he scored 11 points out of 18, leading his team to the bronze medal; in Folkestone 1933, again on the first board, he scored 9 out of 14 points, and won himself the bronze medal and the silver medal with the Czech team; in Warsaw 1935 he scored 13 out of 17 points, remaining undefeated, and won the individual gold medal; in Stockholm 1937 he again won the individual gold medal on the first board, with 12.5 out of 16 points. Adding his Olympic results, his score is 60 points out of a possible 82, i.e., 73% against the strongest players in the world.

Flohr became a Soviet citizen in 1942 and developed his writing career in his new country, contributing articles to various Soviet newspapers and magazines, including the famous Ogonek. As the Soviet Union stopped and later reversed the Nazi invasion, some chess activities resumed and in 1943 Flohr won a small but strong tournament in Baku. In 1944 he won again in Kiev and in 1945 he abandoned the USSR Championship after just three rounds. He remained a successful tournament player until the mid-1960s when he concentrated on journalism.

He became a naturalized Soviet citizen in 1942, and developed his writing career in his new country, contributing articles to several Soviet newspapers and magazines, including Ogonek. As the Soviet Union first stopped then reversed the Nazi invasion, some chess activity started up again, and in 1943 Flohr won a small but strong tournament in Baku. In 1944 he was again victorious in a Bolshevik Society tournament at Kiev, tied with Alexei Sokolsky. He withdrew from the 1945 USSR Championship after only three games.

After the War, he was still a contender for a possible World Championship match, and finished 6th at the 1948 Interzonal in Saltsjöbaden, thereby qualifying to play in the 1950 Candidates Tournament in Budapest. However, he finished joint last with 7 out of 18, and never entered the World Championship cycle again, preferring to concentrate on journalism. He also developed a role as a chess organizer. He did play periodically at high levels, both within the Soviet Union and abroad, with some success, until the late 1960s. He was awarded the title of International Arbiter in 1963.

Foltys, J. - *Games 82, 92*.
Jan Foltys (born 13/10/1908 in Svinov and died aged 43 on 11/03/1952 in Ostravana in the Czech Republic) was an international chess master.

He played on the first board for Czechoslovakia at the 3rd unofficial Chess Olympiad in Munich 1936 (+7-1=11), on the second board at the Chess Olympiad in Stockholm 1937 (+7-2-9) and on the second board at the Chess Olympiad in Buenos Aires 1939 (+8-3=5). In these three events, in 53 games, he scored 34.5 points (+22-6=25) with a score of 65.1%.

Foltys achieved his best result in tournaments by winning in Karlov Vary 1948. That same year he finished 3rd in Budapest. In 1949 he shared first place in the 3rd Memorial Schlechter in Vienna. In 1951 he qualified for the 1952 Stockholm Interzonal, but died of leukemia in 1952, before the Interzonal. He was awarded the title of FIDE International Master in 1950.

Frydman, P. - *Game 81*
Polish International Master (1955) of almost Grandmaster strength. Frydman had an almost consistent record in the Olympiads before the Second World War and played for his country in all of them from 1928 to 1939, except for London in 1927.

He had excellent tournament results in the period from 1934 to 1941. He came third to Salomon Flohr in Budapest in 1934 and this was followed by a third to Henryk Friedman in Warsaw in 1935. He had a triumph in Helsinki 1936, winning +7 = 1 ahead of Paul Keres and Gideon Stahlberg, and in the strong tournament in Podebrady that year he came sixth, with eighteen-year-old Erich Eliskases. His last good tournament in Europe was in Lodz in 1938, where he came seventh out of sixteen. He settled in Argentina after being imprisoned in 1939 following the outbreak of the Second World War. In Buenos Aires, he played his last tournament in 1941, finishing third behind Miguel Najdorf and Stahlberg. After this event, he gave up international chess tournaments for health reasons and lived the rest of his life in Argentina. He died in Buenos Aires.

Grob, H. - *Game 54*
Henri Grob, born on June 4, 1904, and died at the age of 70 on July 5, 1974, was a Swiss International Master, artist, and painter. He pioneered eccentric chess openings such as 1.g4

(*Angriff* book g2-g4, Zurich), also known as the Grob Attack. He was awarded the FIDE International Master Title at the institution of that title in 1950.

Grob was considered the leading Swiss player between the years 1930-1950, during which time he was invited to several closed tournaments. His results in these tournaments were average, with his best performances coming in Barcelona 1935 (3rd place, after Flohr and Koltanowski) and 2nd in Ostend 1936, won by Erik Lundin. In 1937 he won the Ostend tournament in a tie-break, beating Reuben Fine and Paul Keres, winners the following year of the legendary AVRO 1938 Tournament. He played for Switzerland in four Olympic Games (London 1927, Warsaw 1935, Munich 1936, and Helsinki 1952).

Between 1946 and 1972, Grob played 3,614 correspondence games. He won 2,703, lost 430 and drew 481. All the games were played against readers of the Neue Zürcher Zeitung, one of Switzerland's leading newspapers.

Grob has been married nine times. When asked if he was married, he replied "Fast immer" - "Almost always".

Grunfeld, E. - *Game 12*

Grunfeld lost a leg in his povertystricken childhood. Then he discovered chess, studied it intensively and quickly gained a reputation as a skilled player in the local chess club, the *Wiener Schach-Klub*.

The First World War (1914-1918) seriously affected Grunfeld's chances of playing among the best in the world, as few tournaments were played during this troubled period. Grunfeld consoled himself with playing correspondence games and spent much of his free time studying opening variants. He began to build up a library of chess articles which he kept in his small Viennese apartment until his death.

He developed a reputation as an opening specialist during the 1920s and success soon followed. He came 1st in Vienna (1920) with Savielly Tartakower; 1st in Margate (1923); 1st in Merano (1924); 1st in Budapest (1926) with Mario Monticelli; 1st in Vienna (1927) and shared first place in the Vienna tournaments of 1928 and 1933 (Trebitsch Memorial) - the former with Sándor Takács and the latter with Hans Müller; and finally came first in the tournament in Ostrava in 1933. He also won at the 23rd DSB Congress in Frankfurt 1923.

During the Bad Pistyan (Piestany) tournament in April 1922, Grunfeld presented his most important contribution to opening theory - the Grunfeld defense. He played the defense against Friedrich Saemisch in the 7th round, winning in 22 moves, and later that year used it successfully against Alexander Alekhine in the Vienna tournament. However, Grunfeld didn't play this opening very often.

Between the late 1920s and the 1930s, Grunfeld played on the 1st board of the Austrian team in four Chess Olympiads (1927, 1931, 1933, 1935), and his best year was in 1927, when he scored 9.5 out of 12 points. According to the Chessmetrics website, his Elo rating would have been around 2715 at the peak of his career (December 1924).

In May 1943, he came second behind Paul Keres in Posen and won in December 1943 in Vienna. After the Second World War, he shared 3rd-4th places in Vienna in 1951 (Memorial Schlechter, won by Moshe Czerniak). Grunfeld became an International Grandmaster in 1950. By the end of the 1950s, he played very little and worked mainly on his prodigious library, which had completely taken over the living room of his apartment, which he shared with his wife and daughter. His last tournament was Beverwijk (Hoogovens) in 1961, where in a group with five other grandmasters, he finished with a score of 3 points out of 9 (with only one win, against Jan Hein Donner).

He died in Ottakring, Vienna on April 3, 1962.

Gygli, F. - *Game 69*
Fritz Gygli, born on 12/11/1896 in Villachern - and died at the age of 83 on 27/04/1980 in Zurich) was a Swiss chess master, present at several events in the period 1920-1950. In 1920 he came 3rd-4th in St. Gallen, 4th-8th in Neuchâtel 1922, 2nd in Interlaken 1924, 2nd in Zurich 1925, 3rd-4th in Geneva 1926, 5th-6th in Biel 1927, 4th-5th in Basel 1928, 3rd in Schaffhausen and 5th in Lausanne 1930. In the 1930s he came 4th in Bern 1932, 15th in Bern 1932 (tournament won by Alekhine) 3rd in Bern 1933, 11th in Zurich 1934 (tournament won by Alekhine) and 6th in Montreaux 1939.

Gygli represented Switzerland at the chess Olympiads in The Hague 1928, Warsaw 1935, and Munich 1936. Gygli was Swiss Champion in 1941.

Janowski, D. - *Game 2*

Born on 25/05/1868 in Wołkowysk, Russian Empire (now Belarus and died at the age of 58 on 15/01/1927 in Paris, David Janowski came from a Polish family, and settled in Paris around 1890, beginning his professional chess career in 1894. He won the Monte Carlo 1901, Hanover 1902 tournaments and shared first place in Vienna 1902 and Barmen 1905. In 1915 he left Europe to live in the United States, where he spent the next nine years before returning to Paris.

Janowski was devastating against the older masters, such as Wilhelm Steinitz (+ 5-2), Mikhail Chigorin (+ 17-4 = 4) and Joseph Henry Blackburne (+ 6-2 = 2). However, he had fewer points against younger players such as Siegbert Tarrasch (+5-9 = 3), Frank Marshall (+ 28-34 = 18), Akiba Rubinstein (+3-5), Géza Maróczy (+5-10 = 5) and Carl Schlechter (+ 13-20 = 13). He was outplayed by world champions Emanuel Lasker (+4-25 =7) and José Raúl Capablanca (+1-9 =1) but had a respectable score against Alexander

Alekhine (+2 -4 =2). In particular, he was able to beat each of the first four world champions at least once, a feat shared only with Siegbert Tarrasch.

Janowski played very quickly and was famous as a strategist who was devastating with the bishop pair. Capablanca commented on some of Janowski's games with great admiration and said: "When fit, he is one of the most fearsome opponents you can have". Capablanca noted that Janowski's greatest weakness as a player was in the ending, and Janowski told him: "I hate the final phase of the match". American champion Frank Marshall recalled Janowski's talent and his stubbornness. In "Marshall's Best Chess Games", he wrote that Janowski "could go the wrong way with greater determination than any man I have ever met!". Reuben Fine remembered Janowski as a player of considerable talent, but a "master of the alibi" about his defeats. Fine said that his losses invariably occurred because it was too hot or too cold, or that the windows were open too much, or not enough. He also noted that Janowski was sometimes unpleasant with his colleagues because of his predilection to play obstinately, even in an obviously losing position, waiting for his opponent to blunder. Edward Lasker in his book Chess Secrets I learned from the master's recalled that Janowski was an inveterate but undisciplined player, and that he often lost all his chess winnings at roulette.

Janowski played three games against Emanuel Lasker: two friendly games in 1909 (+2 -2 and +1 =2 -7) and a World Chess Championship match in 1910 (=3 -8). The 1909 match is sometimes called the world championship, but Edward Winter's research indicates that the title was not at stake.

In July-August 1914, he was playing in an international chess tournament, the 19th DSB Congress (German Chess Federation Congress) in Mannheim, Germany, with four wins, four draws and three losses (seventh place), when the First World War broke out. Players in Mannheim representing countries now at war with Germany were arrested. Janowski, like Alexander Alekhine, was arrested but released to Switzerland after a short period in prison. That's when he moved to the United States. In New York in 1916, he came second to Oscar Chajes, after José Raúl Capablanca. He won in Atlantic City in 1921 (the eighth American Chess Congress) and came third in Lake Hopatcong in 1923 (the ninth ACC - American Chess Council). Janowski died in France in 1927 of tuberculosis.

Johner, H. - *Game 68*

Hans Johner, born on 07/01/1889 in Basel and who died on 02/12/1975 in Thalwil at the age of 86, was a Swiss chess player who was awarded the title of International Master in 1950. He was Swiss Champion on several occasions, most notably in the 1930s, when he won the title on six occasions - 1931, 1932, 1934, 1935, 1937 and 1938. He played for Switzerland in the first unofficial chess Olympiad in Paris in 1924 and three times in the official chess Olympiads (1927, 1931 and 1956). He was the younger brother of Paul Johner, another important Swiss player of the 1920s and 1930s.

Kashdan, I. - *Game 119* (and amateur)

Isaac Kashdan, born in New York on 19/11/1905 and died at the age of 79 on 20/02/1982 in Los Angeles) was an American grandmaster and chess writer. He was twice US Open champion (1938, 1947) and played five times for the United States in the Chess Olympiad, winning a total of nine medals, and his Olympiad record is the best among American players.

Kashdan was often called *der Kleine Capablanca* (in German, "Little Capablanca") in Europe because of his ability to extract victories from seemingly tied positions. Alexander Alekhine named him one of the most likely players to succeed him as World Champion. Kashdan could not, however, seriously engage in a chess career for financial reasons; his chess heyday coincided with the years of the Great Depression. To earn a living and support his family, he turned to jobs as an insurance agent and administrator. On February 9, 1956, Kashdan took part in the TV edition of Groucho Marx's show, You Bet Your Life, where the host referred to him as "Mr. Ashcan" and challenged him to a game for $500 (but only if cheating was allowed). Kashdan and his partner, Helen Schwartz (mother of the late actor Tony Curtis), won $175 on the show.

In Match 71 presented in this book, at an exhibition with consultation in New York in 1933, Alekhine faces Kashdan in a doubles match, each accompanied by an amateur player.

Kevitz, A. and **Pinkus**, A. - *Game 112*

Alexander Kevitz, who was born on 01/09/1902 and died at the age of 79 on 24/10/1981 in New York, was an American chess master. Kevitz also played correspondence chess and was a creative chess analyst and theoretician. He was a pharmacist by profession.

Kevitz defeated world champion José Raúl Capablanca in a simultaneous exhibition in New York in 1924, and in another simultaneous exhibition he defeated former world champion Emanuel Lasker in 1928, also in New York. He won the Manhattan Chess Club Championship six times: in 1929, 1936, 1946, 1955, 1974 and 1977. Kevitz also represented the Manhattan Chess Club in the Metropolitan Chess League.

In the United States Chess Federation's first official rating list, on July 31, 1950, Kevitz came in third place with a rating of 2610, behind only Reuben Fine and Samuel Reshevsky.

In his later years, Kevitz was very active in correspondence chess, often playing under the pseudonym "Palmer Phar" (he worked at Palmer Pharmacy).

Albert Sidney Pinkus, born on March 20, 1903, and died on February 4, 1984, in New York at the age of 80, was an American chess master and writer. Pinkus won the Hallgarten Tournament in 1925 and the Junior Masters Tournament in 1927. In both events, he beat Isaac Kashdan.

In 1943 and 1944, he published an analysis of the Two Knight Defense. His main career was as an explorer of remote regions, from where he brought back zoological and botanical specimens. In 1932 he embarked on a series of ten expeditions to the jungles of British Guiana and Venezuela to collect zoological and botanical specimens.

In 1939, he returned to New York to work on Wall Street as a stockbroker and resumed his chess career. Pinkus won the Manhattan Chess Club Championship twice (1941 and 1945) and shared second place in 1955. He also won the New York State Chess Championship in 1947. He played in several radio games: USA vs USSR (1945), New York vs La Plata (1947) and USA vs Yugoslavia (1950).

Although he never received an international chess title, his peak of strength put him in the category of International Master.

Kimura, Yoshio - **Game 118**
"Representing the Japan Shogi Federation at the welcome party on January 20th at the Imperial Hotel were Meijin (shogi champion) Sekine, Doi 8th dan, Kon 8th dan, Hanada 8th dan and Mr. Nakajima. The party was also attended by chess lovers from both Japan and abroad, who wanted to witness the incredible feat that the world champion was about to accomplish, and this made for a very pleasant atmosphere. On behalf of the Japan Shogi Federation, Mr. Nakajima gave a welcoming speech in fluent English, stating that shogi and chess came from the same roots and expressing the hope that we could cooperate for their mutual development. Alekhine said that although chess and shogi may only constitute a small part of our respective cultures, they can play a significant role in promoting friendship between the peoples of the world. Alekhine promised to introduce shogi to the West with this goal in mind.

Now it was time for the final event of the program, the simultaneous exhibition of blindfold chess. In addition to Dr. Ishida and Professor Kitamura, Kon 8th dan and I participated as professional shogi players and chess students. Foreign chess enthusiasts Clausnitze, Alexander, Mosler, Baumfeld, Kramer and Gotzscheke also took part.

All the games were played with no possibility of seeing Dr. Alekhine. Figuring that I had no chance of winning if I activated my pieces too early in the opening, I adopted a strategy of defending and waiting for my opponent to make a mistake. In the end, all 14 of us lost without much of a fight. Considering my initial hopes, I felt quite ashamed of my inability to seriously resist, but I was also deeply impressed by the world champion's extraordinary display of chess skill. On the way home, Kon 8th dan said that he considered Alekhine's achievement to be almost beyond human capacity.

Mr. Alekhine later told Professor Mitamura that, in view of my shogi experience, I could become a strong chess player if I studied intensively for six months. He said that he would like to visit Japan again next year, and so it seems that he also wants to study shogi. I showed him all the hospitality I could during the remainder of his stay in Tokyo until his game for Shanghai on the morning of January 22.

Finally, I would also like to thank the foreigners who took part in the simultaneous screening and everyone who attended the event."

Kmoch, H. - **Games 19, 37**
Johann "Hans" Joseph Kmoch, born on July 25, 1894, in Vienna and who died on February 13, 1973, in New

York at the age of 78, was an Austrian-Dutch American chess master (1950), International Arbiter (1951), chess journalist and author of several books, for which he is best known.

Kmoch had most of his best competitive results between 1925 and 1931. He won in Debrecen 1925 with 10 points out of 13. In Budapest 1926 he shared 3rd and 5th place, behind winners Ernst Grunfeld and Mario Monticelli. In Vienna 1928, Kmoch came 6th with 8 points out of 13, when Richard Réti won. Then, at the Trebitsch Memorial in Vienna 1928, Kmoch shared 3rd and 6th places with 6 points out of 10, half a point behind Grunfeld and Sandor Takacs. In Brno 1928, Kmoch came 3rd with 6 points out of 9, with Réti and Friedrich Saemisch winning. Kmoch won at Ebensee in 1930 with 6 points out of 7, ahead of Erich Eliskases.

Kmoch represented Austria three times at the Chess Olympiad. In London 1927, Hamburg 1930, and Prague 1931. His total Olympic score is 23.5 points from 41 games (+14 = 19 -8), 57.3 percent.

His last good tournament result was second in Baarn 1941 with 5.5 points out of 7, behind Max Euwe. Kmoch gave up competitive chess that year.

Kmoch wrote for the magazine *Wiener Schachzeitung* in the early 1920s. His *Die Kunst der Verteidigung* (The Art of Defense) was the first chess book dedicated to this subject. In 1930, Kmoch updated the Bilguer manual and wrote the 1929 Carlsbad tournament book.

In 1929 and 1934, Kmoch acted as Alexander Alekhine's second in his World Championship games against Efim Bogoljubov. Kmoch and his wife Trudy lived in the Netherlands from 1932 to 1947. He also acted as Alekhine's second in the 1935 title match against Max Euwe and wrote a book about the match. In 1941 he wrote a book about Akiba Rubinstein's best games.

After the end of the Second World War, Kmoch and his wife moved to the United States, settling in New York. Kmoch served as secretary and manager of the Manhattan Chess Club and directed numerous tournaments. He also wrote for Chess Review, then one of the leading American chess magazines.

In 1959, he wrote his most famous book, *Pawn Power in Chess*, notable for its use of neologisms.

Koltanowski, G. - *Game 51*

George Koltanowski, born in Antwerp on 17/09/1903 and died at the age of 96 on 05/02/2000 in San Francisco, was a Belgian-born American chess player, promoter and writer. He was informally known as "Kolty". Koltanowski set the world record for blindfold chess on September 20, 1937, in Edinburgh, playing 34 games of chess simultaneously while blindfolded, with headlines in newspapers all over the world. He also set a record in 1960 by playing

56 consecutive games blindfolded, with ten seconds per move.

Born into a Polish Jewish family in Antwerp, Belgium, Koltanowski learned to play chess by watching his father and brother play. He took the game seriously, becoming the best Belgian player when Edgar Colle died in 1932.

He got his first big break in chess at the age of 21, when he visited an international tournament in Merano, planning to take part in one of the lower divisions. The organizers were apparently confused about his identity and asked him to play in the grandmasters' division, to replace an invited player who didn't show up. Koltanowski gladly accepted and finished near the bottom of the table but tied with Grandmaster Tarrasch and gained valuable experience.

He played in at least 25 international tournaments. He was Belgian Chess Champion in 1923, 1927, 1930 and 1936. However, Koltanowski became best known for touring and playing simultaneous and blindfolded exhibitions.

Based on his results during the period 1932-37, Professor Arpad Elo gave Koltanowski a rating of 2450 in The Rating of Chess Players. Koltanowski was awarded the title of International Master in 1950, when this title was officially established by FIDE, and won the title of Honorary Grandmaster in 1988. FIDE appointed him International Arbiter in 1960. However, Koltanowski record as a tournament player was not particularly distinguished. He appeared for the 1946 US Open in Pittsburgh but was eliminated in the preliminary section and did not qualify for the finals.

In those years, the US Open was played in preliminary sections and round-robin finals. However, the following year Koltanowski returned, not as a player but as a director, introducing the Swiss system to the US Open. He directed the 1947 US Open in Corpus Christi, Texas, using the Swiss system for the first time in an American chess tournament. After that, he crisscrossed the country, running Swiss tournaments everywhere. Before long, the Swiss system was adopted as the standard for most chess tournaments in America.

Koltanowski toured the United States tirelessly for years, organizing chess tournaments and giving simultaneous exhibitions everywhere. After his failure at the 1946 US Open in Pittsburgh, he never played tournament chess again, except for two games as a member of the US team at the 10th Chess Olympiad (Helsinki 1952), winning a draw with the Soviet Alexander Kotov, one of the strongest players in the world, and a draw with the Hungarian international master Tibor Florian, in a game that Koltanowski seemed to be better at.

Many of Koltanowski relatives died in the Holocaust. Koltanowski survived because he was on a chess tour in South America, and in Guatemala when WWII broke out. In 1940, the US Consul in Cuba saw Koltanowski giving a chess exhibition in Havana and decided to grant him an American visa.

Koltanowski met his wife Leah on a blind date in New York in 1944. They settled in San Francisco in 1947. Koltanowski became the chess columnist for the San Francisco Chronicle, which carried his chess column every day for the next 52 years, until his death. In total, some 19,000 columns were published.

In the 1960s, Koltanowski promoted a match for the newspaper, following a system like that adopted by Kasparov versus the rest of the world, in which Chronicle readers would face Grandmaster Paul Keres. There would be a vote on the moves and the one with the most votes would be adopted in the match against Keres. Readers would win points and prizes would be awarded at the end of the match. However, after only about 25 moves, Keres abruptly stopped the game and declared himself the winner by adjudication. Koltanowski disagreed and showed an analysis that seemed to give him at least an even game. Keres, an Estonian, may have been ordered by his Soviet handlers to stop playing.

Koltanowski had his own organization, the Northern California Friends of Chess, which resisted the USCF rating system and dominated Northern California chess until the mid-1960s. Koltanowski later decided "if you can't beat them, join them". He won the election for President of the United States Chess Federation in 1974. He also directed all the US Open's from 1947 until the late 1970s. He was named the "Dean of American Chess".

Perhaps Koltanowski most remarkable achievement was that he lived entirely from chess. He wrote many books; his best-known work is Adventures of a Chess Master. In this book he mainly recounts his tours giving simultaneous blindfold exhibitions. He also wrote books on the Colle System, which he sold by mail order. He taught a system that would allow even beginners to leave the opening with a playable game. This saved his students the trouble of memorizing large amounts of moves in chess opening theory. However, he never played this system against strong opponents.

Koltanowski died of congestive heart failure in San Francisco in 2000, at the age of 96.

Koltanowski most sensational chess challenge was the ancient exercise known as the Knight's journey, in which a lone knight traverses an empty board, visiting each square only once. Of the countless patterns for achieving this feat, there are trillions of sequences for executing the most restricted version, known as the re-entry journey, in which the knight on its 64th move lands on its original starting square. For Koltanowski, who claimed to have a "phonographic memory" (a large memory for sequences), the trick depended only on a re-entrant pattern. He could start at any square in the sequence and complete the journey mechanically. However, it was the original presentation that gave Koltanowski's dramatic performance much more than a mechanical movement of the knight through the memorized sequence.

Koltanowski began his journey with a large blackboard divided by lines into a grid of eight-by-eight squares. As he solved problems on a large demonstration board, members of the audience were encouraged to enter the stage to insert words and numbers into the squares. By the time all 64 squares were filled in, it was common to see names of streets and cities, names of months or days of the week, names of famous chess players, names of audience members, names of movie stars or TV personalities, telephone numbers and addresses, dates of birth, serial numbers of bank notes, etc.

After completing his problem-solving challenges on the demonstration board, Koltanowski would turn his back to the audience and examine the blackboard for three or four minutes. Then he would sit with his back to the board and ask any member of the audience to call out a square, for example e4. Then he would recite from memory the contents of that square, which was cut out by an assistant with a chalk mark. Making imaginary knight movements through his re-entry sequence, Koltanowski would recite the contents of each square when the knight landed on it.

As incredible as this demonstration was, if time permitted, Koltanowski would occasionally demonstrate his mental understanding of the board by reciting the information contained in the squares by row or column, or even the two large diagonals. He occasionally made the journey on two boards simultaneously. In Palo Alto, California, he conducted his performance on three boards, jumping the knight back and forth between the boards in the middle of the move, until all 192 squares were completed. He made two mistakes and immediately corrected them both times. At the time of this performance, Koltanowski was 80 years old.

Kussman, A. - *Game 105*

American amateur player, born in Mitava, Latvia on 11/01/1884 and died at the age of 90 in April 1974 in New York. He was a poet, short story writer, playwright, and teacher. He traveled to London in 1911 and immigrated to the USA in 1913.

Lasker, Emanuel - *Game 70*

Emanuel Lasker, born on 24/12/1868 in Berlinchen - Neumark (now Barlinek in Poland) and who died at the age of 72 in New York on 11/01/1941, was a German chess player, mathematician and philosopher who was World Chess Champion for 27 years (from 1894 to 1921). At his peak, Lasker was one of the most dominant champions, and is still considered one of the strongest players of all time.

His contemporaries used to say that Lasker used a "psychological" approach to the game, and even that he sometimes deliberately played inferior moves to confuse his opponents. Recent analysis, however, indicates that he was ahead of his time and used a more flexible approach than his contemporaries, which mystified many of them. Lasker was aware of contemporary analysis of openings but disagreed with many of them. He published chess magazines and five chess books, but players and commentators found it difficult to draw lessons from his methods.

Lasker contributed to the development of other games. He was a first-class bridge player and wrote about bridge and other games, including Go and one of his own inventions, the *Lasca*. His books on games present a problem that is still considered remarkable in the mathematical analysis of card games. Lasker was also a research mathematician who was known for his contributions to commutative algebra. On the other hand, his philosophical works, and a drama he co-wrote have received little attention.

Emanuel Lasker was the son of a Jewish cantor. At the age of eleven he was sent to Berlin to study mathematics, where he lived with his brother Berthold, eight years his senior, who taught him to play chess. According to the Chessmetrics website, Berthold was among the top ten players in the world in the early 1890s. To supplement his income, Emanuel Lasker played chess and card games with small stakes, especially at the Café Kaiserhof.

Lasker rose through the chess ranks in 1889, when he won the annual winter tournament at the Café Kaiserhof 1888/89 and the Hauptturnier A ("second division" tournament) at the sixth DSB Congress (congress of the German Chess Federation) held in Breslau. Winning the Hauptturnier gave Lasker the title of "master". The candidates were divided into two groups of ten. The top four from each group competed in a final. Lasker won his section, with 2.5 points more than his nearest rival. However, the scores were reset to 0 in the final. With two rounds to go, Lasker trailed the leader, Viennese amateur von Feierfeil, by 1.5 points. Lasker won both of his last games, while von Feierfeil lost in the penultimate round and drew in the last. The two players were now tied. Lasker won a playoff and won the master's title. This allowed him to play in master-level tournaments and thus began his chess career.

Lasker finished second in an international tournament in Amsterdam, ahead of some well-known masters, including Isidore Gunsberg (considered the second strongest player in the world at the time by Chessmetrics). In 1890 he finished third in Graz, then shared first prize with his brother Berthold in a tournament in Berlin. In the spring of 1892, he won two tournaments in London, the second and strongest without losing a game. In New York in 1893, he won all thirteen games, one of the few times in the history of chess that a player achieved a perfect score in a significant tournament.

His record in games was equally impressive: in Berlin in 1890, he drew a playoff match against his brother Berthold; and he won all his other games from 1889 to 1893, mainly against top-class opponents: Curt von Bardeleben (1889; 9th best player in the world by Chessmetrics at the time), Jacques Mieses (1889; 11th place), Henry Edward Bird (1890; 29th place), Berthold Englisch (1890; 18th), Joseph Henry Blackburne (1892, undefeated; Blackburne at 51, but still 9th in the world), Jackson Showalter (1892-93; 22nd) and Celso Golmayo Zúpide (1893; 29th). The Chessmetrics website calculates that Emanuel Lasker became the strongest player in the world in the mid-1890s, and that he was in the top ten from the start of his career in 1889.

In 1892, Lasker founded the first of his chess magazines, The London Chess Fifnightly, published from August 1892 to July 1893. In the second quarter of 1893, there was a ten-week gap between issues, supposedly due to problems with the printer. Shortly after the last issue, Lasker traveled to the USA, where he spent the next two years.

Lasker challenged Siegbert Tarrasch, who had won three strong international tournaments in a row (Breslau 1889, Manchester 1890, and Dresden 1892), to a match. Tarrasch proudly declined, saying that Lasker should first prove his worth by winning one or two major international events.

Rebuffed by Tarrasch, Lasker challenged the then world champion Wilhelm Steinitz to a title match. Initially, Lasker wanted to play for $5,000 and a match was agreed with a purse of $3,000, but Steinitz agreed to a series of reductions when Lasker found it difficult to raise that amount. The final amount was $2,000, which was less than in some of Steinitz's previous games (the purse in previous games of $4,000 would have been worth more than $510,000 in 2020 values). Although this has been publicly praised as an act of sportsmanship on Steinitz's part, the truth is that he may have desperately needed the money. The match was played in 1894, at venues in New York, Philadelphia, and Montreal. Steinitz had already declared that he would win without a doubt, so it was a shock when Lasker won the first game. Steinitz responded by winning the second and maintained the balance throughout the sixth. However, Lasker won every game from the seventh to the eleventh, and Steinitz asked for a week's rest. When the match resumed, Steinitz looked in better shape and won the 13th and 14th games. Lasker fought back in the 15th and 16th, and Steinitz didn't make up for his losses in the middle of the match. In this way, Lasker won convincingly with ten wins, five losses and four draws, thus becoming the second formally recognized World Chess Champion, and confirmed his title by defeating Steinitz even more convincingly in their rematch in Moscow in 1896-97 (ten wins, two losses and five draws).

Influential players and journalists disparaged the 1894 match, both before and afterwards. Lasker's difficulty in gaining support may have been caused by hostile pre-match comments from Gunsberg and Leopold Hoffer, who had long been fierce enemies of Steinitz. One of the complaints was that Lasker had never faced two of the four best players of the time, Siegbert Tarrasch and Mikhail Chigorin, although Tarrasch had rejected a challenge from Lasker in 1892. After the match, some commentators, notably Tarrasch, said that Lasker had won mainly because Steinitz was old (58 in 1894).

Emanuel Lasker responded to this criticism by creating an even more impressive match record. Before the outbreak of the First World War, his most serious "setbacks" were third place at Hastings in 1895 (where he may have been suffering the after-effects of typhoid fever), a draw at Cambridge in 1904 and a first-ever draw at the Memorial Chigorin in St. Petersburg in 1909. Lasker won first prizes in very strong tournaments in St. Petersburg (1895 - 96, Quadrangular), Nuremberg (1896), London (1899), Paris (1900) and St. Petersburg (1914), where he overcame a 1.5-point gap to finish ahead of rising stars Capablanca and Alexander Alekhine, who later became the next two world champions. For decades, chess writers have reported that Tsar Nicholas II of Russia conferred the title of "Grandmaster of Chess" on each of the five finalists in St Petersburg in 1914 (Lasker, Capablanca, Alekhine, Tarrasch and Marshall), but historian Edward Winter has questioned this, stating that the first known sources supporting this story were published in 1940 and 1942.

Lasker's match record was impressive between his 1896-97 rematch with Steinitz and 1914: he won all but one of his regular games, and three of them were convincing defenses of his title. He faced Marshall for the first time in the 1907 World Chess Championship, when, despite his aggressive style, Marshall failed to win a single game, losing eight and drawing seven (final score: 11.5 - 3.5).

He then played Tarrasch in the 1908 World Chess Championship, first in Düsseldorf and then in Munich. Tarrasch firmly believed that the game of chess was governed by a precise set of principles. For him, the strength of a chess move lay in its logic, not its efficiency. Because of his stubborn principles, he considered Lasker a *café* player who only won his games thanks to dubious tricks, while Lasker ridiculed the arrogance of Tarrasch, who, in his opinion, shone more in the salons than on the chessboard. At the opening ceremony, Tarrasch refused to speak to Lasker, saying only: "Mr. Lasker, I have only three words to say to you: check and mate!".

Lasker gave a brilliant response on the chessboard, winning four of the first five games and playing a type of chess that Tarrasch couldn't understand. Lasker won the match 10.5-5.5 (eight wins, five draws and three losses). Tarrasch claimed that the rainy weather was the cause of his defeat.

In 1909, Lasker played a mini match (two wins, two losses) against Dawid Janowski, a Polish expatriate attacking player. Several months later, they played a longer match in Paris, and chess historians still debate whether this was for the World Chess Championship. Understanding Janowski's style, Lasker chose to defend solidly so that Janowski would unleash his attacks too early and leave himself vulnerable. Lasker easily won the match 8-2 (seven wins, two draws and one loss). This victory was convincing for everyone except Janowski, who asked for a rematch. Lasker accepted and played a match for the World Chess Championship in Berlin in November-December 1910. Lasker crushed his opponent, winning 9.5 - 1.5 (eight wins, three draws, no defeats). Janowski didn't understand Lasker's moves, and after his first three defeats he declared to Edward Lasker: "Your namesake plays so stupidly well that I can't even look at the chessboard when he thinks. I'm afraid I won't do any good in this match".

Between his two games against Janowski, Lasker organized another World Chess Championship in January-February 1910 against Carl Schlechter, who was a modest man, and was unlikely to win major chess tournaments due to his peaceful inclination, his lack of aggression and his willingness to accept most of his opponents' draw offers (around 80% of his games ended in a draw). The conditions of the match against Lasker are still debated among chess historians, but it seems that Schlechter agreed to play under very unfavorable conditions, notably that he would need to finish two points ahead of Lasker to be declared the winner of the match and would still need to win a rematch to be declared World Champion. The match was initially designed to have 30 games, but when it became clear that there wouldn't be enough funding (Lasker demanded 1,000 marks per game), the number of games was reduced to ten, making the two-point margin even more difficult.

In 1911, Lasker received a challenge for a world title match against rising star José Raúl Capablanca. Lasker was unwilling to play the traditional "first to win ten games" in the semi-tropical conditions of Havana, and the match could last more than six months. So he made a counter-proposal: if neither player had a lead of at least two games by the end of the match, it should be considered a draw; the match would be limited to the best of thirty games, counting draws; if one of the players won six games and had a lead of at least two games before the thirty games were completed, he would be declared the winner; the champion would decide the venue and the purse, and would have the exclusive right to publish the games. The challenger would have to deposit $2,000 (equivalent to more than $200,000 in 2020 values); the time limit would be twelve moves per hour; the match would be limited to two sessions of two and a half hours a day, five days a week. Capablanca objected to the time limit, the short playing times, the 30-game limit and especially the requirement that he win by two games to claim the title, which he considered unfair. Lasker took offense at the terms in which Capablanca criticized the two-game condition and broke off negotiations. Until 1914 Lasker and Capablanca didn't speak to each other. However, at the St. Petersburg tournament in 1914, Capablanca proposed a set of rules for the conduct of the World Championship games, which was accepted by the leading players, including Lasker.

At the end of 1912, Lasker entered negotiations for a world title match with Akiba Rubinstein, whose tournament record in previous years had been equal to Lasker's and slightly ahead of Capablanca. The two players agreed to play a match if Rubinstein could raise the money, but Rubinstein had few wealthy friends to support him, and the match was never held. This situation demonstrated some of the inherent flaws in the championship system that was used at the time. The outbreak of the First World War in the summer of 1914 put an end to hopes of Lasker playing Rubinstein or Capablanca for the World Championship soon. During the entire First World War (1914-1918), Lasker played only two serious chess events. He convincingly won (5.5 - 1.5) a non-title match against Tarrasch in 1916. In September-October 1918, just before the armistice, Lasker won a quadrangular tournament half a point ahead of Rubinstein.

In January 1920 Lasker and José Raúl Capablanca signed an agreement to play a World Championship match in 1921, considering that Capablanca was not free to play in 1920. Because of the delay, Lasker insisted on a final clause that would allow him to play anyone else in the championship in 1920, that would void the contract with Capablanca if Lasker lost a title match in 1920, and that would stipulate that if Lasker relinquished the title, Capablanca would become World Champion. Lasker had already included in his pre-World War I agreement to play Akiba Rubinstein for the title a similar clause that, if he relinquished the title, the World Champion would be Rubinstein.

An article in the American Chess Bulletin (July and August 1920 issue) reported that Lasker had renounced the world title in favor of Capablanca, because the conditions of the match displeased the chess world. The American Chess Bulletin speculated that the conditions were not unpopular enough to justify relinquishing the title, and that Lasker's real concern was that there was not enough financial backing to justify his nine-month dedication to the match. At the time, Lasker didn't know that enthusiasts in Havana had raised $20,000 to finance the match, provided it was held there. When Capablanca heard about the possibility of Lasker's resignation, he went to Holland, where Lasker was living at the time, to inform him that Havana would finance the match. In August 1920, Lasker agreed to play in Havana, but insisted that he was the challenger because, due to his resignation, Capablanca was currently the champion. Capablanca signed an agreement accepting this point, and soon after published a letter confirming this. Lasker also stated that if he defeated Capablanca, he would relinquish the title again so that younger masters could compete for it.

The match was played in March-April 1921. After four draws, the fifth game saw Lasker blunder with Black in an equal ending. Capablanca's solid style allowed him to easily design the next four games without taking any risks. In the tenth game, Lasker with white played a position with a passed queen's pawn but didn't create the necessary activity and Capablanca got a superior ending, which he duly won. The 11th and 14th games were also won by Capablanca, and Lasker abandoned the match.

Lasker was shocked by the poverty in which Wilhelm Steinitz died and did not intend to die in similar circumstances. He became notorious for demanding high fees to play games and tournaments and argued that players should own the copyright in their games, rather than allowing publishers to make all the profits. These demands initially infuriated publishers and other players but helped pave the way for the emergence of full-time chess professionals who spend most of their time playing, writing and teaching. Copyright in chess games had been contentious since at least the mid-1840s, and Steinitz and Lasker vigorously asserted that players should own the copyright and wrote copyright clauses into their game contracts. However, Lasker's demands that opponents should raise large purses prevented or delayed some eagerly awaited World Championship games - for example, Frank James Marshall challenged him in 1904 to a World Championship match but failed to raise the purse demanded by Lasker until 1907. This problem continued during the reign of his successor Capablanca.

Some of the controversial conditions that Lasker insisted on to play in the World Championship led Capablanca to try twice (1914 and 1922) to publish the rules for these games, which other top players readily agreed to.

Lasker was a good friend of Albert Einstein, who wrote the introduction to the posthumous biography Emanuel Lasker, the life of a Chess Master, by Dr. Jacques Hannak (1952). In this preface, Einstein expressed his satisfaction at having met Lasker, writing: "Emanuel Lasker was undoubtedly one of the most interesting people I have met in recent years. We should be grateful to those who have written the story of his life for this and future generations, for there are few men who have taken a warm interest in all the great human problems and at the same time kept their personality so uniquely independent."

Lundin, E. - *Game 71*

Erik Ruben Lundin, who was born in Stockholm on July 2, 1904, and died on December 5, 1988, in Stockholm at the age of 84, was a Swedish chess master. In 1928, he won in Oslo, came 5th in Helsingborg and shared 2nd and 3rd place in Stockholm (Quadrangular, won by Ricardo Réti). In 1929, he came 2nd in Gothenburg (Nordic Chess Championship, won by Gideon Stahlberg) and 3rd in Vasteras. In 1930, he came 7th in Stockholm (Isaac Kashdan won). In 1931, Lundin tied for 1st and 3rd place with Salo Flohr and Gosta Stoltz in Gothenburg. In 1932, he tied for 1st with Stahlberg in Karlskrona. In 1933, he won a match against Rudolf Spielmann (+1 -0 = 5) in Stockholm. In 1934, he won in Stockholm, and took 2nd place in Copenhagen (Nordic-ch; Aron Nimzowitsch won). In 1935, he came 2nd with a score of 7.5 out of 9 points, behind Alexander Alekhine with 8.5 points, in Orebro, after losing to Alekhine in the final round. In 1936, he came 4th in Margate (Flohr won), won in Ostend and won in Helsinki (Nordic-ch). In 1937, he came 7th in Stockholm (Reuben Fine won), won in Copenhagen (Nordic-ch) and won a match for the Nordic Champion title against Erik Andersen 3.5 - 2.5.

In 1938, he won in Kalmar and tied for 2nd to 3rd with Henrik Carlsson, behind Stahlberg, in Orebro (Nordic-ch). In 1939 he came 4th in Alingsas (Swedish Championship, won by Stahlberg), and shared 1st place with Stahlberg in Oslo (Nordic-ch).

During the Second World War, Lundin won in Gothenburg 1941 (Swedish Chess Championship). He shared 2nd and 3rd place with Alekhine, behind Stoltz, in Munich 1941 (2nd Europaturnier). In 1942, he shared 3rd and 4th place with Stoltz in Stockholm (Folke Ekstrom and Stig Lundholm won). In 1942, he won in Ostersund (Swedish Championship). In 1943, he shared 2nd and 3rd places with Olof Kinnmark, behind Bengt Ekenberg, in Malmo (Swedish Championship).

In 1945, he won at Visby (Swedish Championship). In 1946, he won in Motala (Swedish Championship) and tied for 8th and 9th places in Groningen (Mikhail Botvinnik won). In 1947, he tied for 5th - 6th places in Helsinki (zonal; Eero Book and Stoltz won). In 1948, he came 20th in Saltsjobaden (interzonal; David Bronstein won) and won in Bad Gastein.

In 1951, he came 2nd behind Moshe Czerniak in Vienna. In 1952, he won in Zurich ahead of Max Euwe. In 1954, he came 7th in Marianske Lazne (Marienbad). The zonal event was won by Luděk Pachman. In 1960, he won in Kiruna (Swedish Championship). In 1961, he won in Avesta (Swedish Championship). In 1964, he won in Gothenburg -Swedish Championship.

Lundin played for Sweden in nine official chess Olympiads and once in the third unofficial chess Olympiad in Munich in 1936. He was awarded the title of International Master in 1950, and the title of Honorary Grandmaster in 1983. Throughout his career, he beat world-class players such as David Bronstein, Max Euwe, Reuben Fine, Salo Flohr and Miguel Najdorf at least once.

Maróczy, G. - *Games 34, 48*
Géza Maróczy was born in Szeged, Hungary, on 03/03/1870 and died at the age of 81 on 29/05/1951 in Budapest. He won the "minor" tournament in Hastings in 1895, and over the next ten years he took several first places in international events. Between 1902 and 1908, Maróczy took part in thirteen tournaments and won five first prizes and five second prizes. In 1906, he agreed to the terms of a World Championship match with Emanuel Lasker, but political problems in Cuba, where the match was to be played, caused the agreements to be canceled.

After 1908, Maróczy retired from international chess to devote more time to his profession as a civil servant. He worked as an auditor and had a good career at the Center for Trade Unions and Social Insurance. When the communists briefly came to power, he was chief auditor at the Ministry of Education. After the communist government was overthrown, Maróczy couldn't find a job. He briefly returned to chess after World War I with some success, and today the Maróczy formation (a pawn formation, created by Maróczy against the Sicilian Defense, characterized by white pawns on c4 and e4, with white's d pawn exchanged for black's c pawn) is one of the most used Sicilian lines. At the turn of the year 1927 - 1928 he demolished Hungary's 1924 champion Géza Nagy in a match by +5 -0 = 3. With him at the helm, Hungary won the first Chess Olympiad in London (1927).

In 1950, FIDE instituted the title of Grandmaster. Maróczy was one of the players who received the title based on his past achievements.

Maróczy's style, although solid, was very defensive in nature. His successful Danish Gambit defenses against Jacques Mieses and Karl Helling, involving obligatory return of material sacrificed for the initiative, were used as models of defensive play by Max Euwe and Kramer in their two-volume series on the middlegame. Aron Nimzowitsch, in My System, used Maróczy's victory against Hugo Süchting (in Barmen 1905) as a model for blocking the opponent before the break. But Maróczy also played spectacular chess on occasions, such as his famous victory over the famous attacker David Janowski (Munich 1900).

His handling of queen endgames was also highly respected, as against Frank Marshall of Karlsbad in 1907, showing superior technique in this type of ending.

Maróczy had respectable lifetime scores against most of the best players of his time. However, he had negative scores against the world chess champions: Wilhelm Steinitz (+1 -2 =1), Emanuel Lasker (+0 -4 =2), José Raúl Capablanca (+0 -3 =5) and Alexander Alekhine (+0 -6 =5); except Max Euwe, whom he beat (+4 -3 =15). But Maróczy's defensive style was enough to defeat the leading attacking players of the time, such as Joseph Henry Blackburne (+5 -0 =3), Mikhail Chigorin (+6 -4 =7), Frank Marshall (+11 -6 =8), David Janowski (+10 -5 =5), Efim Bogoljubov (+7 -4 =4) and Frederick Yates (+8 -0 =1).

Capablanca held Maróczy in high esteem. In a lecture given in the early 1940s, Capablanca called Maróczy "very kind and correct" and "a gentle figure", praised Maróczy's training as an important contribution to opening theory, credited him as a "good teacher" who greatly helped Vera Menchik reach the top of women's chess and "one of the greatest masters of his time". Capablanca wrote, as quoted by Edward Winter Capablanca's book: "As a chess player, he was somewhat unimaginative and aggressive-minded. His positional judgment, the greatest quality of the true master, was excellent. A very precise player and an excellent endgame artist, he became famous as a specialist in Queen endgames. In a tournament many years ago, he won a champion's ending against the Viennese master Marco, which has gone down in history as one of the classic endgames of its kind (Marco-Maróczy, 1899). As far as the relative strength of Maróczy and the best young master of today is concerned, my opinion is that, with the exception of Botvinnik and Keres, Maróczy in his time was superior to all the other players of today."

Marshall, F. - *Games 9, 16, 111*

Frank James Marshall, born in New York on 10/08/1887, died at the age of 67 in Jersey on 09/11/1944, was the US Chess Champion from 1909 to 1936 and one of the strongest chess players in the world at the beginning of the 20th century.

Marshall was born in New York and lived in Montreal, Quebec, Canada, from the age of 8 to 19. He started playing chess at the age of 10 and by 1890 (age 13) he was one of Montreal's leading players.

Marshall won the Cambridge Springs International Chess Congress in 1904 (with 13 points out of 15, ahead of World Champion Emanuel Lasker) and the American Congress in 1904 but failed to win the national title because American champion Harry Nelson Pillsbury did not compete. In 1906, Pillsbury died, and Marshall again refused the championship title until he won it in 1909.

In 1907 Marshall played a match against World Champion Emanuel Lasker for the title and lost eight games, winning none, with seven draws. The match was played in New York, Philadelphia, Washington DC, Baltimore, Chicago, and Memphis from January 26 to April 8, 1907.

In 1909, he agreed to play a match with the then young Cuban chess player José Capablanca, and to most people's surprise, he lost eight games, drew fourteen and won only one. After this defeat, Marshall didn't resent Capablanca; instead, he realized that the young man had immense talent and deserved recognition. The American champion worked hard to ensure that Capablanca had the chance to play at the highest levels of chess. Marshall insisted that Capablanca be allowed to enter the San Sebastián tournament in 1911, an exclusive championship that promised to be one of the strongest in history. Despite many protests over his inclusion, Capablanca won the tournament.

Marshall finished fifth in the St. Petersburg tournament in 1914, behind world champion Lasker, future world champions Capablanca and Alekhine and former World Championship challenger Tarrasch, but ahead of the players who didn't qualify for the final: Ossip Bernstein, Rubinstein, Nimzowitsch, Blackburne, Janowski and Gunsberg. According to Marshall's 1942 autobiography, allegedly written by Fred Reinfeld, Tsar Nicholas II conferred the title of "Grandmaster" on Marshall and the other four finalists. Chess historian Edward Winter questioned this, stating that the first known sources to support this story are Marshall's autobiography and an article by Robert Lewis Taylor in the June 15, 1940, issue of The New Yorker magazine.

In 1915, Marshall opened the Marshall Chess Club in New York. In 1925, Marshall appeared in the short Soviet film Chess Fever, in a cameo appearance alongside Capablanca.

In the 1930s, Marshall captained the US team to four gold medals in four Chess Olympiads. During one round, he returned to the tables and discovered that his teammates had agreed to three draws. After he finished his own game, he gave each of them individually a stern lecture on how draws don't win games.

In 1936, after having held the title of US champion for 27 years, he gave it to the winner of a championship. The first of these tournaments was sponsored by the National Chess Federation and held in New York. The Marshall Chess Club donated the trophy, and the first winner was Samuel Reshevsky.

Menchik, Vera (Mrs.) - *Games 50, 83*
Vera Frantsevna Menchik, born in Moscow on February 16, 1906, and died in London at the age of 38 on

June 27, 1944, was a British-Czechoslovak-Russian chess player who gained fame as the world's first female chess champion. She also competed in chess tournaments with some of the world's leading male chess masters at the time, defeating many of them, including future world champion Max Euwe.

His father, Frantisek Menchik, was born in Bystra nad Jizerou, Bohemia, and his mother, Olga Illingworth (1885-1944), was English. His father was the manager of several estates owned by a member of the nobility in Russia, and his wife was governess to the estate owner's children.

Vera Menchik was born in Moscow in 1906 and her sister Olga Menchik was born in 1907.

When Vera was nine years old, her father gave her a chess set and taught her how to play. When she was 15, the school club organized a chess tournament, and she came second.

After the Russian revolution, her father lost a mill he owned and, incidentally, the large house where the family lived. The marriage collapsed; her father returned to Bohemia and, in the fall of 1921, Olga and her daughters went to Hastings, England, to live with Olga's mother.

As Vera spoke only Russian, she hesitated to join the local chess club, but finally, on March 18, 1923, she joined the Hastings Chess Club and began taking lessons with John Drewitt. She then became a pupil of grandmaster Géza Maróczy. During 1923 Vera played in several team games.

In December 1923, she played in her first Hastings Tournament and got a draw against Edith Price, the then British checkers' champion.

In the next Hastings Christmas Chess Congress, in 1924/25, Vera played again in Group A, in the first class, and finished second with five points out of seven. She met Miss Price in the final round of the Winners' Group and again drew.

In 1925 Vera played two games against Edith Price, winning both, and was considered the strongest player in the country, but as she wasn't British, she couldn't enter the national competition.

In January 1926, Vera won the first Women's Open Championship at the Imperial Club in London, with her sister Olga coming third. In 1927, she retained this title and Olga came second. The following year, Vera was over the age to play, and Olga came second.

The biggest and strongest tournament Menchik played in was the 1935 Moscow tournament, which featured world champions Botvinnik, Capablanca and Lasker, as well as a host of elite players and masters such as Flohr, Ragozin, Spielmann, Levenfish, Lilienthal, etc. Here, Menchik finished in last place, 20th out of 20 competitors, with a score of (+0 -16 =3).

Other major international tournaments include Karlsbad in 1929, where he finished 22nd out of 22 players, with a score of (+2 -17 =2), and Lodz in 1938, where he finished 15th out of 16 players, with a score of (+1 -9 =5).

Menchik's best results in international tournaments came in Ramsgate in 1929. This was a good match themed on the Scheveningen system of Sicilian Defense, with 7 players from one team competing against 7 from another. Menchik finished with an unbeaten score of (+3 -0 =4). In 1934 she finished 3rd out of 9 players in Maribor, behind Lajos Steiner and Vasja Pirc, but ahead of Rudolph Spielmann and Milan Vidmar, with a score of (+3 -1 =4). In 1942, Vera won a match against Jacques Mieses (+4 -1 =5). It should be noted, however, that Mieses was 77 at the time and no longer an active participant in tournaments.

When Menchik entered Carlsbad in 1929, Viennese master Albert Becker ridiculed his entry, proposing that any player Menchik defeated in tournaments should be a member of the Vera Menchik Club. At the same tournament, Becker himself became the first member of the "club". In addition to Becker, the "club" eventually included Conel Hugh O'Donel Alexander, Abraham Baratz, Eero Book, Edgard Colle, Max Euwe, Harry Golombek, Mir Sultan Khan, Frederic Lazard, Jacques Mieses, Stuart Milner-Barry, and Karel Opocensky. He also worked with Brian Reilly, Samuel Reshevsky, Friedrich Saemisch, Lajos Steiner, George Alan Thomas, William Winter, and Frederick Yates.

In 1937, at the age of 31, Vera Menchik married Rufus Henry Streatfeild Stevenson (1878-1943), twenty-eight years her senior, who was editor of the British Chess Magazine, a member of the West London Chess Club and later honorary secretary of the British Chess Federation.

In 1944, the United Kingdom was approaching its sixth year in the Second World War, and 38-year-old Vera, who had been widowed since the previous year, still held the title of women's world champion. On June 27, she, her sister Olga and their mother were killed in a V-1 bomb attack that destroyed their home at 47 Gauden Road, in the Clapham area of south London. All three were cremated at Streatham Park Crematorium on July 4, 1944.

The trophy of the winning team in the Women's Chess Olympiad is named the Vera Menchik Cup.

Vera Menchik is the oldest world chess champion in history, holding the title for 17 years. Her dominance over her contemporaries can be seen in her games against Sonja Graf. Graf was the second strongest female player in the world at the time and had been coached by the legendary Siegbert Tarrasch. But looking at the two games and the result, their levels of play were completely different. In the two games, Menchik won twelve games to three, with five draws. The fourth world champion, Alekhine, wrote after one of his victories against Sonja Graf in 1939 that "it is totally unfair to persuade a player of a recognized superclass like Miss Menchik to defend her title year after year in tournaments composed of very inferior players." The specific tournament in question is the seventh Women's World Chess Championship. However, against the best male players, Menchik did not fare well. She was beaten by Jose Raul Capablanca (9-0), Alexander Alekhine (7-0), Mikhail Botvinnik (2-0), Paul Keres (2-0), Reuben Fine (2-0) and Emanuel Lasker (1-0).

Vera Menchik entered the World Chess Hall of Fame in 2011.

Mikenas, V. - *Game 57*
Vladas Mikenas, born on 17/04/1910 in Tallinn, Estonia, and died at the age of 82 in Vilnius, Lithuania, was a Lithuanian international chess master, honorary Grandmaster, and journalist.

In 1930 he won the 3rd Estonian Championship in Tallinn; in 1931 he shared 2nd to 5th places in the first Baltic Championship, held in Klaipeda, won by Isakas Vistaneckis. That same year, Mikenas emigrated from Estonia to Lithuania. In 1934, he won a match against Povilas Vaitonis (6 - 2). In 1935, he came tenth in Lodz (Savielly Tartakower won) and drew with Vistaneckis (8 - 8). In 1936 he won the Lithuanian Championship. In 1937, he won a match against Vaitonis (5.5 - 4.5). In 1937, he came 10th in Kemeri; despite his placing, in this tournament Mikenas beat Alexander Alekhine. In 1937/38, he came 6th in Hastings (Samuel Reshevsky won). In 1938, he won a match against Vaitonis (9 - 3). In 1939, he came 4th in Kemeri-Riga (Salo Flohr won). In September 1939, he came 3rd in Rosario (Vladimirs Petrovs won).

On September 28, 1939, the Soviet Union and Germany changed the secret terms of the Molotov-Ribbentrop Pact. Lithuania was then transferred to the Soviet sphere of influence and annexed to the USSR on August 3, 1940.

In September and October 1940, Mikenas finished 13th to 16th in Moscow (12th USSR Championship). In 1941, he came 3rd in Kutaisi. In February and March 1942, he took 3rd to 6th places in Moscow. In March and April 1942, he took 4th-7th places in Sverdlovsk. In July and August 1942, it took 3rd-5th places in Kuibyshev. In 1943 and 1944, he took 7th to 23rd places at the Moscow Championships. In 1944, he won in Tbilisi. In 1944, he won a classification match against Ljublinsky (8 - 6). In 1944, he took 5th - 6th places in Moscow (13th USSR Championship). In July 1945, Mikenas won in Kaunas (13th Lithuanian Championship). In September-October 1945, he came 7th in Tallinn (Estonian Championship - Paul Keres won). In October and November 1945, he won in Riga (Baltic Chess Championship). In June and July 1946, he came 3rd behind Yuri Averbakh and Vistaneckis in Vilna (Baltic Republics Championship). In 1946, he finished 2nd in Tbilisi (7th Georgian Championship). In 1947, he finished 2nd in Minsk (13th Belarusian Championship). In 1948, he drew a qualifying match against Rashid Nezhmetdinov (7 - 7).

Mikenas played several times in the Lithuanian championships in Vilnius.

He won in 1947, 1961, 1965 and 1968.

In 1954, Mikenas won the Vilnius Quadrangular against Ratmir Kholmov, Vistaneckis and Viacheslav Ragozin. In 1955, he shared 3rd to 6th places in Parnu (Keres won). In 1959 he came 2nd behind Boris Spassky in Riga. In 1960 he finished 10th in Parnu (Baltic Rep., Keres won) and shared 4th place in Leningrad (Mark Taimanov won). In 1964 he finished 2nd to 3rd behind Iivo Nei in Parnu (Baltic Rep.). In 1965 he won in Palanga (Baltic Republic Championships). In 1971 he won in Lublin, Poland.

Vladas Mikenas received the title of International Master in 1950 (the year the title was instituted) and was awarded the title of Honorary Grand Master in 1987.

Mikenas was the arbiter of the World Championship match between Anatoly Karpov and Garry Kasparov in 1985.

Mindeno, A. - *Game 120*
I haven't found any definitive confirmation, but it could be Siegfried Bernard van Mindeno, born on March 26, 1905, in Berlin. Youngest son of Bernard van Mindeno from Rotterdam and Kaatje Elias Zeldenrust. He may have been an uncle of Heinz Erwin van Mindeno.

The original family name was Van Minden, probably after the town of Minden in Westphalia, a region of Germany. In the middle of the 19th century, a Van Minden woman, for some inexplicable but undoubtedly very good reason, added to her name. Somehow, she managed to pass on this mutated name to her husband and children.

Nimzowitsch, A. - *Games 15, 32, 43*
Aaron Isayevich Nimzowitsch, born in Riga, Latvia on 07/11/1886 and died in Copenhagen at the age of 48 on 16/03/1935, was a Chess Grandmaster, an influential writer, and one of the most important chess players of the 20th century. He was also the most important figure in the Hypermodern School of Chess.

Born in Riga, Latvia, then part of the Russian Empire, Nimzowitsch, whose native language was Yiddish, was born into a wealthy family, where he learned chess from his father Shaya Abramovich Nimtsovich, a timber merchant. In 1897, the family lived in Dvinsk. In 1904, Aaron traveled to Berlin to study philosophy, but put aside his formal studies and began a career as a professional chess player that same year. He won his first international tournament in Munich in 1906. He shared first place with Alexander Alekhine in St. Petersburg

1913 - 1914 (the eighth all-Russian master's tournament).

During the Russian Revolution of 1917, Nimzowitsch was in the Baltic war zone. He escaped being drafted into one of the armies by feigning madness, insisting that a fly was on his head. He then fled to Berlin and gave his first name as Arnold, possibly to avoid anti-Semitic persecution.

Nimzowitsch moved to Copenhagen in 1922, which coincided with his rise to the world chess elite. He lived in the Danish city for the rest of his life in a small, rented room. In Copenhagen he won the Nordic Chess Championship twice (1924 and 1934). He obtained Danish citizenship and lived in Denmark until his death in 1935.

The peak of Nimzowitsch's career was the late 1920s and early 1930s. Chessmetrcs.com ranks him as the third best player in the world between 1927 and 1931, behind Alexander Alekhine and José Capablanca. His most notable successes were first places in Copenhagen 1923, Marienbad 1925, Dresden 1926, Hanover 1926, the Carlsbad 1929 chess tournament and second place behind Alekhine in the San Remo 1930 chess tournament. However, Nimzowitsch never developed a talent for games; his best result was a draw with Alekhine, but the match consisted of only two games and took place in 1914, thirteen years before Alekhine became world champion.

Nimzowitsch never beat Capablanca, but he did better against Alekhine. He beat Alekhine with the black pieces in the short 1914 match in St. Petersburg. One of Nimzowitsch's most famous games is his immortal zugzwang against Saemisch in Copenhagen in 1923. Another game on this theme is his victory over Paul Johner in Dresden 1926. When in good form, Nimzowitsch was very dangerous with black, scoring great victories over the best players.

Nimzowitsch is considered one of the most important players and writers in the history of chess. His works influenced countless other players, including Savielly Tartakower, Milan Vidmar, Richard Réti, Akiba Rubinstein, Bent Larsen and Tigran Petrosian, and his influence is still felt today.

Nimzowitsch wrote three books on chess strategy: *Mein System* (My System - 1925), *Die Praxis Meines Systems* (The Practice of My System - 1929), and *Die Blockade* (The Blockade - 1925), although for many the last book is generally considered a repetition of the material already presented in My System, which is considered one of the most influential chess books of all time. In that book, Nimzowitsch presents the most important ideas, while his second most influential work, The Practice of My System develops those ideas, adds some new ones, and is immensely valuable as a stimulating collection of Nimzowitsch's own games, accompanied by his idiosyncratic and hyperbolic comments, which are often as entertaining as they are instructive.

Nimzowitsch's chess theories, when first proposed, opposed the widespread orthodoxies enunciated by the dominant theoRétician of the time, Dr. Siegbert Tarrasch, and his disciples. Tarrasch rigid generalizations were based on the earlier work of Wilhelm Steinitz and were confirmed by Tarrasch sharp tongue in dismissing the opinions of doubters. While the greatest players of the time, including Alekhine, Emanuel Lasker and Capablanca, clearly did not allow their moves to be hampered by blind adherence to general concepts. The central ideas of Tarrasch chess philosophy as popularly understood - the occupation of the center by pawns, the central support of rooks, preferential development in wards - beginners were taught to think of these generalizations as unalterable principles.

Nimzowitsch supplemented many of the previous simplistic assumptions about chess strategy, in turn enunciating several general concepts of defensive play aimed at achieving one's own goals by preventing the realization of the opponent's plans. Notable in his "system" were concepts such as overprotection of pieces and pawns under attack, control of the center by pieces instead of pawns, blocking of opposing pieces (notably passed pawns) and prophylaxis. Nimzowitsch was also one of the main exponents of the development of the bishops' fianchetto. Perhaps most importantly, Nimzowitsch formulated the terminology still in use for several complex chess strategies. Other theorists and players have used these ideas in practice, but he was the first to present them systematically, as a lexicon of themes accompanied by extensive taxonomic observations.

GM Raymond Keene writes that Nimzowitsch "was one of the world's greatest masters for a period spanning a quarter of a century, and for a time was the obvious challenger for the world championship. He was also a great and profound chess thinker, second only to Steinitz. His works - The Blockade, My System and The Practice of My System established his reputation as one of the father figures of modern chess". GM Robert Byrne called him "perhaps the most brilliant theoRétician and teacher in the history of the game". GM Jan Hein Donner called Nimzowitsch "a man who was too much of an artist to be proven right and who was considered a madman in his time. He was only understood long after his death".

Many chess openings and variations are named after Nimzowitsch, the most famous being the Nimzo-Indian Defense (1.d4 ♘f6 2.c4 e6 3.♘c3 ♗b4) and the less frequently played Nimzowitsch Defense (1.e4 ♘c6). Nimzowitsch's biographer GM Raymond Keene and others refer to 1.♘f3 followed by 2.b3 as the Nimzowitsch-Larsen attack. Keene wrote a book about the opening with this title. These openings exemplify Nimzowitsch's ideas about controlling the center with pieces instead of pawns. Nimzowitsch was also vital in the development of two important systems in French Defense, the Winawer Variant (in some places called the Nimzowitsch Variant, its moves are 1.e4 e6 2.d4 d5 3.♘c3 ♗b4) and the Advance Variant (1.e4 e6 2.d4 d5 3.e5). Nimzowitsch also pioneered two provocative variants of the Sicilian Defense: the Nimzowitsch Variant, 1.e4 c5 2.♘f3 ♘f6, which invites 3.e5 ♘d5 (similar to the Alekhine Defense) and 1.e4 c5 2.♘f3 ♘c6 3.d4 c×d4 4.♘×d4 d5 ?! (the latter considered dubious today). MI John L. Watson nicknamed the line 1.c4 ♘f6 2.♘c3 e6 3.♘f3 ♗b4, the "English Nimzo", using this designation in Chapter 11 of his book Mastering Chess Openings, Volume 3.

There are many amusing anecdotes about Nimzowitsch - some spicier than others. An article by Hans Kmoch and Fred Reinfeld entitled "Unconventional Surrender" in February 1950 speaks of "...the example of Nimzowitsch, who once lost the first prize in a tournament in Berlin when beaten by Saemisch and, when it became clear that the game was lost, Nimzo stood up and shouted: - *Gegen diesen Idioten muss ich verlieren?!*" (I have to lose to this idiot?!).

Nimzowitsch was annoyed by the smoke of his opponents. A popular story, but probably apocryphal, is that once when an opponent put an unlit cigar on the table, he complained to the tournament referees: "He's threatening to smoke, and as an old player you should know that the threat is stronger than the execution".

Nimzowitsch had long and bitter dogmatic conflicts with Tarrasch over whether their ideas constituted "proper" chess.

Nimzowitsch's vanity and faith in his ideas of overprotection provoked Hans Kmoch to write a parody about him in February 1928 in the Wiener Schachzeitung. This parody consisted of a simulated match against the fictional player "Systemsson", supposedly played and commented on by Nimzowitsch himself. The comments gleefully exaggerate the idea of overprotection, as well as affirming the true genius of the wonderful idea. Kmoch was in fact a great admirer of Nimzowitsch, who had a lot of fun with the parody.

Kmoch also wrote an article about his nine years with Nimzowitsch:

"Nimzowitsch suffered from the illusion that he was not appreciated and that the reason for this was wickedness. All it took to make him a friend, as I learned later, was a little compliment. His paranoia was most evident when he dined with me. Nimzowitsch always thought that he was served much smaller portions than everyone else. He didn't care about the actual quantity, only the imagined affront. I once suggested that he and I order what the other really wanted and, when the food was served, swap plates. After we did that, he shook his head in disbelief, still thinking that he had received the smaller portion."

Nimzowitsch's colleague Tartatakower remarked: "He pretends to be crazy to make us crazy."

Despite suffering from heart problems, his premature death was unexpected; he fell ill suddenly at the end of 1934 and was bedridden for three months before dying of pneumonia. Nimzowitsch is buried at Bispebjerg Cemetery in Copenhagen.

Opocensky, K. - *Game 4*
Karel Opocensky, born in Most, Bohemia on 07/02/1892 and died at the age of 83 in Prague on 16/11/1975, was a Czech chess master. He was Czech champion four times (1927, 1928, 1938 and 1944) and runner-up once in 1919, behind Frantisek Schubert. In 1925, he finished 3rd - 4th in the Paris Tournament (Alexander Alekhine won). In 1933, he won the 10th Vaclav Kautsky Memorial in Prague. In 1935, he came 4th in Bad Nauheim (won by Efim Bogoljubov).

In 1935, he came 4th in Lodz (Savielly Tartakower won). In 1935, he won in Luhacovice. In 1936, he came 2nd behind Henryk Friedman in Vienna. In 1937, he came 2nd behind Karl Gilg in Teplice (Teplitz Schönau). In 1938, he won in Nice.

Karel Opocensky played for Czechoslovakia four times at the Chess Olympiad (1931, 1933, 1935 and 1939). He won individual gold medals, team medals in Folkestone in 1933 and team bronze medals in Prague in 1931.

When World War II broke out, Opocensky, Jan Foltys and Frantisek Zíta were playing for the Bohemia & Moravia team at the 8th Chess Olympiad in Buenos Aires. They chose to return home, while Jiri Pelikán and Karel Skalicka chose to remain in South America.

In 1940, Opocensky came second behind Foltys in Rakovnik (Bohemian and Moravian Championship). In 1941, he drew a match against Foltys in Prague (+4 -4 =4) and came 7th in Trencianske Teplice (Foltys won). He also came 13th in the 1941 Munich chess tournament (Europa Turnier, won by Gosta Stoltz). In 1942, he tied for 4th-5th place in Prague (Duras Jubilee), behind joint winners Alekhine and Klaus Junge. In 1943, he came 3rd in Prague (Bohemian and Moravian Championships, won by Zita). He won the Bohemian and Moravian Championships in Brunn in 1944.

After the war, Opacensky played in several local and international tournaments (Czechoslovakia). In 1945, he tied for 2nd-3rd place behind Emil Richter in Prague. In 1946, he came 4th in (Czechoslovak Championship, won by Ludek Pachman). In 1946, he came 4th in London. In 1946, he shared 1st place with Daniel Yanofsky and Ludek Pachman in Arbon. In 1947, he came 4th in Vienna. In 1949, he shared 3rd place in Vienna. In 1949, he shared 4th-5th place in Arbon. In 1956, he came 3rd in Podebrady (Czechoslovak Championship, won by Ladislav Alster).

In 1951 and 1954, he was the main arbiter of the World Chess Championship games in Moscow, also at the 10th Olympiad in Helsinki in 1952 and at the second Candidates Tournament in Zurich in 1953.

Opocensky is also known as a theoretician. There are two opening variants named after him: the Opocensky Variant in the Grunfeld Defense (1.d4 ♘f6 2.c4 g6 3.♘c3 d5 4.e3 ♗g7 5.♘f3 0–0 6.♗d2) and the Opocensky Variant in the Sicilian Defense (1.e4 c5 2.♘f3 d6 3.d4 c×d4 4.♘×d4 ♘f6 5.♘c3 a6 6.♗e2).

Opocensky was awarded the title of International Master in 1950 and became an International Chess Arbiter in 1951.

Pirc, V. - *Game 45*

Vasja Pirc, born on 19/12/1907 in Idrija, Slovenia, and who died at the age of 72 on 02/06/1980 in Ljubiyana, was an important Yugoslav (Slovenian) chess player. His name is best known to contemporary players as the creator of a strong hypermodern defense, generally known as the Pirc Defense.

Pirc was Yugoslav champion five times: 1935, 1936, 1937, 1951 and 1953. He was awarded the title of International Master in 1950 and Grand Master in 1953. Pirc became an International Arbiter in 1973.

Although Pirc had a negative record against Alexander Alekhine, he defeated Alekhine with the black pieces in a blitz game in Ljubljana in 1930:
1.d4 e6 2.c4 ♘f6 3.♘c3 ♗b4 4.♗d2 b6 5.f3 ♗xc3 6.♗xc3 d5 7.e3 0-0 8.♗d3 c5 9.♘e2 ♘c6 10.0-0 ♗b7 11.♕a4 ♕d7 12.♕c2 ♘b4 13.♗xb4 cxb4 14. b3 ♖ac8 15.e4 h6 16.e5 dxc4 17.bxc4 ♘d5 18.♕d2 ♘c3 19.♖ae1 ♖fd8 20.d5 exd5 21.c5 ♖xc5 22.♘d4 ♗c8 23.e6 ♕c7 24.exf7+ ♔xf7 25. F4 ♘e4 26.♕b2 ♖c3 27.♘f3 ♔g8 28.♘e5 ♕c5+ 29.♔h1 ♕d4 30.♕e2 ♗f5 31.g4 ♘g3+ 32.hxg3 ♗xd3 33.♘xd3 ♖xd3 34.♖d1 ♕e4+ 35.♕g2 ♖c8 36.♖xd3 ♕xd3 37. ♖f2 ♖c1+ 38.♔h2 a5 39.♖d2 ♕e4 40.♕xe4 dxe4 41.♔g2 a4 42.♖d4 ♖c2+ 43.♔f1 ♖xa2 44.♖xb4 e3 45.♖xb6 e2+ 46.♔f2 a3 47.♖a6 ♖a1 48.♔xe2 a2 0-1.

Potemkin, P. - *Game 107*
Peter Petrovich Potemkine, born in Oriol, Russia on 02/05/1886 and died at the age of 40 on 21/10/1926 in Paris, was a Russian chess master. He took 7th place in St. Petersburg in 1904 (Mikhail Chigorin won), 5th place in St. Petersburg in 1907 (Eugene Znosko-Borovsky won) and 8th place in St. Petersburg in 1913 (Andrey Smorodsky won). In the winter of 1912, he played with Alexander Alekhine and Vasily Osipovich Smyslov (Vasily Smyslov's father) in St. Petersburg. In 1920 they shared 3rd - 6th places in the Moscow Tournament (Alexander Alekhine won).

Count Potemkine was a Soviet expatriate living in France. He officially represented Russia at the 1st unofficial chess Olympiad in Paris in 1924.

He took 7th - 8th places in Prague 1923 (Karel Skalicka won), 4th - 7th places in Paris 1924 (Znosko-Borovsky won), 5th - 6th places in Paris 1925 (Victor Kahn won) and shared 1st place with Vitaly Halberstadt in Paris 1926.

In 1926, Le Cercle d'échecs Potemkine opened in Paris.

Reshevsky, S. - *Match 93*

Samuel "Sammy" Herman Reshevsky (born Szmul Rzeszewski on 26/11/1911 in Ozorkow, near Lodz in Poland and died at the age of 80 on 04/04/1992 in New York) was a Polish prodigy and later an American chess Grandmaster. Reshevsky was never a full-time chess professional. He was a strong contender for the World Chess Championship from the mid-1930s to the mid-1960s. He shared 3rd place in the 1948 World Championship tournament and tied for 2nd place in the 1953 Candidates

Tournament. He was an eight-time winner of the US Chess Championship. An excellent player throughout his career, Reshevsky excelled in positional play, and was an excellent strategist when necessary. He played the opening moves slowly, and was often pressed for time, but this often bothered his opponent more than himself.

Sammy was an accountant by profession and was also a renowned chess writer.

Reshevsky was the son of a Jewish family. He learned to play chess at the age of four and was soon recognized as a child prodigy. By the age of eight, he was beating many talented players with ease and giving simultaneous exhibitions. In November 1920, his parents moved to the USA to make a living by publicly displaying their son's talent. Reshevsky played thousands of games in exhibitions all over the USA. He played in the master's tournament in New York in 1922; at the time, he was probably the youngest player ever to compete in such a strong tournament.

For a period in his youth, Reshevsky didn't attend school, and his parents had to appear in District Court in Manhattan to face a charge of improper guardianship. However, Julius Rosenwald, a wealthy partner at Sears Roebuck, and Company in Chicago, soon became Reshevsky's benefactor, and guaranteed Sammy's future on the condition that he complete his education.

Reshevsky never became a truly professional chess player. He gave up more competitive chess games for seven years, from 1924 to 1931, to complete his secondary education while competing successfully in occasional events during this period.

He graduated from the University of Chicago in 1934 with a degree in accounting and supported himself and his family by working as an accountant. He moved to New York, where he lived, or in its suburbs, for the rest of his life. His 1941 marriage to Norma Mindick produced three children. Reshevsky was a devout Orthodox Jew and did not play on the Jewish Sabbath; his games were scheduled to respect this.

Reshevsky won the US Open Chess Championship in 1931 in Tulsa; this event was known as the Western Open at the time. He shared the 1934 US Open title with Reuben Fine in Chicago. Sammy won the US Chess Championship in 1936, 1938, 1940, 1941, 1942, 1946 and 1969. He also finished tied in 1972 but lost the play-off in 1973 to Robert Byrne. He is a record holder with participation in 21 U.S. Championships, and managed a positive score in all of them, except for 1966-1967, when he scored only 4.5 points out of 11. He also holds U.S. Championship records for most top-three finishes (15), the number of games played (269), and the number of games won (127).

Reshevsky competed eight times for the USA in the Chess Olympiad, six times on the first board over a 37-year period, helping the US team win gold in 1937 and bronze in 1974, and winning an individual bronze medal for his performance on the first board in 1950. His complete results were (+39 -12 =49) in 100 games, with a score of 63.5 percent. He played in Stockholm 1937, Dubrovnik 1950, Helsinki 1952, Munich 1958, Tel Aviv 1964, Lugano

1968, Siegen 1970 and Nice 1974. He played for the first US board in its first six Olympics.

When Bobby Fischer made his debut at the age of 14 at the US Championship in 1957-1958, he completely dominated, winning that competition all eight times he took part, leaving Reshevsky, the former champion, seven times in the chasing pack. There was little sympathy between the two players, separated in age by a generation. Before the 1960 Buenos Aires tournament, Reshevsky said: "I'd settle for 19th place - if Fischer finished 20th". Reshevsky did win the 1960 Buenos Aires tournament, with Fischer close behind; this was the only time Sammy finished ahead of Fischer in an international tournament.

In 1961, Reshevsky started a 16-game match with the then American champion, Bobby Fischer. The match was organized jointly between New York and Los Angeles. Despite Fischer's meteoric rise, the prevailing opinion favored Reshevsky as the favorite. After eleven games and one draw (two wins each with seven draws), the match ended due to a scheduling dispute and postponements between Fischer and Jacqueline Piatigorsky, the sponsor of the match. Reshevsky received the winner's share of the prize.

In 1969, at the Interzonal in Sousse, Fischer arrived 53 minutes late (just seven minutes before losing by default) for his match against Reshevsky and made his opening move without saying a word of apology. Reshevsky, who was convinced that Fischer had abandoned the tournament, lost the game, and complained furiously to the organizers. Despite losing that match, Reshevsky advanced to the next stage of the world cycle.

Reshevsky refused to play for the US team at the 1960, 1962 and 1966 Chess Olympiads because Fischer, as US champion, was chosen as the team's first board. However, he finally consented to play on an inferior board in 1970, the only time the two players appeared on the same team.

Although Reshevsky and Fischer had one of the fiercest rivalries in chess history, Fischer greatly respected the former champion, saying in the late 1960s that he thought Reshevsky was the strongest player in the world in the mid-1950s, when he defeated World Champion Mikhail Botvinnik in their four-game mini-match, which was the pinnacle of the USA vs USSR team match held in Moscow.

It wasn't until 1968, at the age of 57, that Sammy finally lost a match for which he had time for extensive preparation. That was against Viktor Korchnoi in Amsterdam, in the first round of the Candidates Tournament. The match was scheduled for ten games, but the young Russian Grandmaster proved too much for Reshevsky, who didn't win a single game and lost by the final score of 5.5-2.5.

During his long chess career, Reshevsky faced the first twelve World Champions, from Emanuel Lasker to Anatoly Karpov, the only player to do so (Sammy also met Garry Kasparov, but never played him). Reshevsky defeated seven World Champions: Emanuel Lasker, José Raúl Capablanca, Alexandre Alekhine, Max Euwe, Mikhail Botvinnik, Vasili Smyslov and Bobby Fischer.

Réti, R - *Games 1, 6*

Ricardo Réti, born on 28/05/1889 in Pezinok (now Slovakia), died at the age of 40 on 06/06/1929 in Prague. Although he was born in what was then Hungary, Réti considered himself Viennese, born into a wealthy Hungarian Jewish family. He had a great sense of humor and was always smiling, except when he saw a car, because he was afraid of them.

One of the world's greatest players during the 1910s and 1920s, Réti began his career as a classic, fiercely combinatorial player, using openings such as the King's Gambit. However, after the end of the First World War, his style underwent a radical change and Réti became one of the main authors of hypermodernism, along with Aron Nimzowitsch and others. In fact, with the notable exception of Nimzowitsch's acclaimed book My System, Réti is considered the greatest literary contributor to this movement.

The Réti opening (1. ♘f3 d5 2.c4), with which Réti defeated the then world champion José Raúl Capablanca in New York in 1924 - Capablanca's first defeat in eight years and his first after winning the Champion's title - is named after him. Tartakower called this opening "the opening of the future".

Réti was also a notable player at the end of games. In 1924 and 1925, he was in Montevideo, Uruguay, where he gave simultaneous lectures and exhibitions, also blindfolded. In 1925, in São Paulo, he broke the world record for blindfold chess, with 29 simultaneous games. Incredibly, Réti won 21 games, drew six and lost only two. Old photos in the archives of the São Paulo Chess Club show a picture of Ricardo Réti on the Club's wall, during the simultaneous exhibition of Capablanca held there in 1927.

Ricardo Réti's books are considered classics by the chess world: *New Ideas in Chess* (1922) and *The Masters of the Chessboard* (1930) are still studied today.

Ricardo Réti died in Prague in 1929 of scarlet fever. He is the great-great-grandfather of the German painter Elias Maria Réti.

Roselli del Turco, Stefano - *Game 67*

The Marquis Stefano Rosselli del Turco, born on 27/07/1877 in Florence and died at the age of 70 on 18/08/1947 in the same city, was an Italian chess master. He played in all the top ten Italian championships and was twice Italian champion. He drew 7-8 in Viareggio 1921 (1st ITA-ch, Davide Marotti won); won a title match against Marotti (8.5: 4.5) in Napoli 1923; lost a title match to Mario Monticelli (6: 8) at Firenze 1929; won at Milan 1931 (4th ITA-ch); took 6th at Milan 1934 (Monticelli won); drew 2-3 at Firenze 1935

(Antonio Sacconi won); drew 7-9 at Firenze 1936 (Vincenzo Castaldi won); took 12th in Napoli 1937 (Castaldi won); drew 7-8 in Rome 1939 (Monticelli won), and drew 7-8 in Firenze 1943 (10 ITA-ch, Vincenzo Nestler won). [1]

He drew 8-9 in San Remo in 1911 (Hans Fahrni won); took 5th in Trieste 1923 (Paul Johner won); drew 12-13 in Meran 1924 (Ernst Grunfeld won); came 9th in Meran 1926 (Edgar Colle won). Rosselli won in Livorno in 1926; came 6th in Venice in 1929 (Rudolf Pitschak won); [2] tied for 2nd and 3rd with Abraham Baratz, behind Brian Reilly, in Nice in 1931. [3]

Rosselli del Turco represented Italy at the Chess Olympiads: 1924 in Paris; 1927 in London; 1931 in Prague; 1933 in Folkestone; 1935 in Warsaw (+1-11 = 3); 1936 in Munich and 1937 in Stockholm. In 1911-1916 and 1924-1943, he was the founder and editor of *L'Italia Scacchistica*.

Rubinstein, A. - *Games 11, 14*

Akiba Kiwelowicz Rubinstein, born on December 1, 1880, in Stawiski, Poland and died at the age of 80 on March 14, 1961, in Antwerp, Belgium, was a chess genius and one of the most influential players in chess history. Born into a Jewish family, he had several brothers, but only one sister survived to adulthood. Rubinstein learned to play chess relatively late, at the age of 16, and his family planned for him to become a rabbi. Rubinstein trained and played with the strong master Gersz Salwe in Lodz and in 1903, after finishing 5th in a tournament in Kiev, he decided to abandon his rabbinical studies and devote himself entirely to chess.

Between 1907 and 1912, Rubinstein established himself as one of the strongest players in the world. In 1907, he won the Carlsbad tournament and shared first place in St. Petersburg. In 1912 he went on a winning streak, finishing first in five consecutive major tournaments: San Sebastian, Pistyan, Breslau, Warsaw, and Vilnius, although none of these events included the participation of Lasker or Capablanca. Some sources believe that at this time Rubinstein was stronger than World Champion Emanuel Lasker. The Chessmetrics rankings support this conclusion, placing him as number 1 in the world between mid-1912 and mid-1914.

During the first decade of the 20th century, the playing field for competitive chess was relatively small. Wilhelm Steinitz, the first universally recognized world champion, died in 1900 after being away from chess for several years, Russian master Mikhail Chigorin was coming to the end of his life, while American master Frank Marshall lived on the other side of the

Atlantic, far from the center of chess activity in Europe. Another promising American master, Harry Nelson Pillsbury, died in 1906 aged just 33. In the pre-FIDE era, the then world champion chose his opponent, and Emanuel Lasker demanded a large sum of money to face Rubinstein. That sum was not forthcoming from the challenger. At the tournament in St. Petersburg in 1909, Rubinstein drew level in the final standings with Lasker and beat him in their individual encounter. However, Rubinstein performed poorly at the St. Petersburg tournament in 1914, not making the top five. A match with Lasker was scheduled for October 1914, but didn't take place due to the outbreak of the First World War.

Rubinstein's peak as a player is generally considered to have been between 1907 and 1914. During World War I, he was confined to Poland, although he did take part in some organized chess events and travelled to Berlin in early 1918 for a tournament. His play after the war never regained the same consistency as before 1914, although it remained quite strong in the 1920s. Rubinstein and his family moved to Sweden after the Armistice in November 1918, where they stayed until 1922 and then moved to Germany. Rubinstein won in Vienna in 1922, ahead of future world champion Alexander Alekhine, and was the leader of the Polish team that won the 1930 Chess Olympiad in Hamburg with a record of thirteen wins and four draws. He also won an Olympic silver medal at the 1931 Chess Olympiad, again leading the Polish team.

Rubinstein came fourth in the 1922 London tournament, after which the new world champion, José Raul Capablanca, offered to play him in a match if he could raise the money, which he again failed to do. In Hastings 1922, he came second, followed by a fifth place in the Teplitz-Schönau at the end of the year, and then won in Vienna brilliantly. This triumph, however, was soured when the Austrian border guards confiscated most of the prize money he had won. Rubinstein closed out 1922 with another appearance in Hastings, which he won, but his tournament record in 1923 was disappointing, as he came twelfth in Carlsbad and tenth in the Maehrisch-Ostrau.

His first tournament in 1924, in Merano, saw him come third. He tried to take part in the New York tournament that spring but was excluded from the event due to the limited number of places available, all of which were filled and, in any case, former world champion Lasker dominated the event by a large margin. Rubinstein's 1925 tournament record was reasonably good, but his appearance at the end of the year in Moscow saw him come 14th. His record in 1926 was fair, but not exceptional. That year, the Rubinstein family moved to Belgium permanently.

In 1927, Rubinstein visited his birthplace in Poland, where he won the Polish championship in Lodz. He embarked on an exhibition tour of the United States in early 1928. Although a match with the then US chess champion Frank Marshall was proposed along with an international tournament, it never materialized. He drew third with Max Euwe in Bad Kissingen and then performed poorly in Berlin.

Rubinstein had his best post-World War I showing in 1929, when he dominated the Ramsgate tournament in Great Britain and had excellent showings in Carlsbad and Budapest. He also won in Rogaska-Slatina.

When the 1930s began, Rubinstein played in the San Remo tournament, coming fourth. He played well in a few Belgian events that year and then took third place in Scarborough. His performance in Liège was poor, possibly due to exhaustion. He didn't take part in Bled in 1931 despite an invitation, played well in Antwerp but came last in Rotterdam. This was the last major chess event in which he took part.

After 1932, Rubinstein withdrew from tournaments as his noted anthropophobia showed traces of schizophrenia during a mental breakdown. In one period, after making a move in a game, he would hide in the corner of the tournament hall while waiting for his opponent to respond. Regardless, his former strength was recognized by FIDE when he was one of 27 players awarded the inaugural Grandmaster title in 1950. Unlike many other grandmasters, he left no literary legacy, which can be attributed to his mental problems. He spent the last 29 years of his life suffering from severe mental illness, alternating between times at home with his family and times in a sanatorium. It is unclear how the great Jewish master survived World War II in Nazi-occupied Belgium.

Rubinstein was one of the first chess players to consider the endgame when choosing and playing the opening. He was exceptionally talented in the endgame, particularly rook endings, where he innovated general knowledge. Jeremy Silman rated him as one of the five best endgame players of all time, and a master of rook endings.

He created the Rubinstein System against the Tarrasch Defense variant in the Queen's Gambit: 1.d4 d5 2.♘f3 c5 3.c4 e6 4.cxd5 exd5 5.♘c3 ♘c6 6.g3 ♘f6 7.♗g2 (Rubinstein-Tarrasch, 1912). He also created the Merano System, which stems from the Queen's Gambit Rejected, but reaches a Queen's Gambit Accepted position with a tempo gain for Black.

Many opening variants bear his name. According to Grandmaster Boris Gelfand, "most modern openings are based on Rubinstein". The "Rubinstein attack" often refers to 1.d4 d5 2.c4 e6 3.♘c3 ♘f6 4.♗g5 ♗e7 5.e3 0–0 6.♘f3 ♘bd7 7.♕c2. The Rubinstein Variant of the French Defense appears after 1.e4 e6 2.d4 d5 3.♘c3 (or 3.♘d2) dxe4 4.♘xe4. As well as 4.♕c2, Rubinstein's variant in the Nimzo-Indians: 1.d4 ♘f6 2.c4 e6 3.♘c3 ♗b4 4.e3. There is also the Variant in the Four Knights Opening, which comes after 1.e4 e5 2.♘f3 ♘c6 3.♘c3 ♘f6 4.♗b5 ♘d4, and the Rubinstein Variant of the Symmetrical English 1.c4 c5 2.♘c3 ♘f6 3.g3 d5 4.cxd5 ♘xd5 5.♗g2 ♘c7, a complex system that is very popular at masters' level.

Rubinstein's Trap, an opening trap in the Queen's Gambit Declined, in which Black loses at least one Pawn, also bears his name: 1.d4 d5 2.c4 e6 3.♘c3 ♘f6 4.cxd5 exd5 5.♗g5 ♗e7 6.e3 0-0 7.♘f3 ♘bd7 8.♗d3 c6 9.cxd5 exd5 10.0–0 ♖e8 11.♖c1 h6 12.♗f4 ♘h5 13.♘xd5! Now 13 ... cxd5 ?? is met by 14.♗c7, winning the queen, while 13... ♘xf4 14.♘xf4 leaves White with a Pawn advantage.

The Rubinstein Memorial tournament in his honor has been held annually since 1963 in Polanica Zdrój, with a glittering list of top-class winners. Boris Gelfand named Rubinstein as his favorite player, and once said: "What I like about chess... comes from Akiba! comes from Akiba!". In 1917, Rubinstein married Eugénie Lew and they had two sons, Jonas in 1918 and Sammy in 1927. For a while, they lived in the basement of the restaurant where Eugénie worked. After Eugénie's death in 1954, Rubinstein lived in a nursing home until his death in 1961 at the age of 80.

Rubinstein still followed chess in the last years of his life: his children recalled replaying the games of the 1954 Botvinnik-Smyslov World Championship match with their father.

Saemisch, F. - *Games 13, 96*
Friedrich Saemisch, born in Charlottenburg on September 20, 1896, and died on August 16, 1975, in Berlin at the age of 78, was a German chess Grandmaster.

Saemisch won a match against Réti (+4 -1 =3) in Berlin in 1922. Perhaps his most famous match was his defeat by Nimzowitsch in Copenhagen in 1923, known as "The Immortal of the Zugzwang". Saemisch also played many beautiful games, one of them being his victory against Grunfeld in Carlsbad 1929, which won the beauty prize. In the same tournament Saemisch also beat Capablanca. The former world champion lost a piece in the opening, but didn't abandon, which usually happens in such cases in grandmaster games. He resisted in vain, this handicap being too much even for a player of Capablanca's class.

At the age of 73, in 1969, Saemisch played in a tournament in memoriam of Adolf Anderssen in Büsum, Germany, and another tournament in Linköping, Sweden, but lost all the games in both events (fifteen in the former and thirteen in the latter) due to time control.

During World War II, Saemisch was appointed as a "Betreuer" (caretaker) for the troops, and his task was to give chess demonstrations and play simultaneous exhibitions with German soldiers throughout Europe. Arriving in Spain in 1944 for a tournament, Saemisch proposed to the British ambassador to play a simultaneous game for the British troops in Gibraltar, but his well-meaning offer was turned down. Saemisch then criticized Adolf Hitler at the closing banquet of the Madrid tournament in the summer of 1944. On his return to the German border, he was arrested and transported to a concentration camp. It wasn't his first transgression, as he had said out loud in the Luxor café in Prague: "Isn't Hitler a fool? He thinks he can win the war with the Russians!" recounts the great master Ludek Pachman, who accompanied him at the Café: "Prague was full of Gestapo officers and soldiers, and Saemisch was heard at least at the nearest tables. I asked him to keep his voice down. 'Don't you agree that Hitler is a fool?' was Saemisch's nonchalant reply.

Schwartz, N. - *Game 108*
Nicholas Schwartz (São Paulo, Brazil): My paternal grandfather, Nicolai Eugen Schwartz, was born in Riga on November 20, 1893. He came from a

mercantile and banking family with business interests in the Baltic States, Russia, Germany, and Great Britain, and was sent to Scotland in November 1913 to study the flax, jute and hemp industries and look for possible business contacts. Dundee was chosen as his base because of the city's association with these fiber industries and because Henry W. Rennie, a very prosperous merchant and boat owner in Dundee, was my grandfather's godfather. Above all, Nicolai Schwartz was sent to Dundee to invest a substantial sum in Rennie's firm.

My grandmother's maiden name was Jeanne Catherine Carolina and Marie Vernon Le Cocq: her father, John Le Cocq, from Jersey and Alderney, had married Rose Vernon.

My grandfather never returned to Riga but remained in Dundee. He had three children: Olga Stella, who was born in 1917, Alexander Nicolai (my father), born in 1918, and Nicolai Roy (born in 1920 and killed in 1944 while flying for the RAF). In the 1920s, the family moved to London, first to Norwood, then to Streatham and finally to Clapham.

In London, Nicolai Schwartz attended the Gambit Chess Rooms and Simpson's Divan. He was brought up to live a very easy life and never went to work. I well remember him sitting all day solving chess problems and bridges in books and newspapers, while smoking and drinking tea non-stop. He was always discreetly and impeccably dressed, exceptionally well-mannered, invariably kind, and absolutely devoted to my grandmother until the day he died, in Putney, London, on March 20, 1965.

He talked about chess most of the time, and most of his gifts to me, when I was seven or eight, were books about chess problems. I still own his Staunton chess sets, his chess boards, one of them rolled up for traveling, and his Jaques chess set, the wallet kind.

Stahlberg, G. - *Game 38*
Anders Gideon Tom Stahlberg, born on 26/01/1908 in Surte, near Gothenburg, and died at the age of 59 on 26/05/1967 in Leningrad, was a Swedish chess grandmaster. He won the Swedish Chess Championship in 1927, became Nordic Champion in 1929 and held the title until 1939.

Stahlberg became famous when he won games against stars Rudolf Spielmann and Aron Nimzowitsch in 1933 and 1934 respectively and came third (after Alekhine) in Dresden 1936, and second (after Fine) in Stockholm 1937. In 1938 he tied with Keres.

After the Chess Olympiad in Buenos Aires in 1939, he stayed in Argentina until 1948, where he won many tournaments, some of them with Miguel Najdorf: Mar del Plata 1941 (ahead of Najdorf and Eliskases), Buenos Aires 1941 (tied with Najdorf), Buenos Aires 1947 (ahead of Najdorf, Eliskases and Euwe).

His best results after returning to Europe were the Saltsjobaden Interzonal in 1948 (6th, qualifying for the Candidates), the Budapest Candidates tournament in 1950 (7th place), Amsterdam 1950 (3rd place), Budapest 1952 (3rd place), the Saltsjobaden Interzonal in 1952 (5th place, again qualifying for the Candidates).

Stahlberg took part in five World Cycles between 1957 and 1963.

In 1967 he traveled to Leningrad to take part in an international tournament but died before playing his first game. Stahlberg is buried in Gothenburg.

Ståhlberg published more than ten chess books (some of them originally in Spanish):

Steiner, E. - *Game 41*
Endre Steiner was born on June 27, 1901, in Budapest and died on December 29, 1944, in a Nazi concentration camp near Budapest, Hungary. He played in 6 Hungarian Olympic teams from 1924 - 1937, came 3rd in Portsmouth 1923, 2nd in Trencianske Teplice 1928 and won in Kecskemet 1933. He was Lajos Steiner's older brother.

Steiner, H. - *Games 25, 56*
Herman Steiner, born on 15/04/1905 in Dunajská Strega, Slovakia and died at the age of 50 on 25/11/1955 in Los Angeles, was a chess player, organizer, and columnist from the United States. He won the US Chess Championship in 1948 and became an International Master in 1950. Even more important than his playing career were his efforts to promote chess in the USA, particularly on the West Coast. An exemplar of the Romantic School of chess, Steiner was a successor to the American chess tradition of Paul Morphy, Harry Nelson Pillsbury, and Frank Marshall. Born in Slovakia, Steiner came to New York City at a young age. For a time, he was an active boxer. At 16, he was a member of the Hungarian Chess Club and the Stuyvesant Chess Club. With the experience gained in New York City's active chess scene, Steiner quickly developed his chess skills and in 1929 tied for first place (with Jacob Bernstein) in the New York State championship tournament in Buffalo. In the same year, he came first in the Premier Reserve in Hastings, England.

Steiner left New York for the West, settling in Los Angeles in 1932. He became chess editor of the Los Angeles Times that year, writing a chess column until his death. He formed the Steiner Chess Club, later called the Hollywood Chess Group, based in a club next to Steiner's home. The Hollywood Chess Group was visited by many movie stars, including Humphrey Bogart, Lauren Bacall, Charles Boyer, and José Ferrer. Steiner and the Hollywood Chess Group organized the Pan-American International Tournament in 1945 and the second Pan-American Chess Congress in 1954.

Steiner played three challenge games against Reuben Fine, one of the best players in the world. Fine won all three games: by 5.5-4.5 in New York in 1932, by 3.5-0.5 in Washington, D.C. 1944, and by 5-1 in Los Angeles in 1947.

One of his biggest international victories came in the 1946 London Victory Invitational, the first major European tournament held after the end of the Second World War. Steiner challenged Arnold Denker in 1946 to a match for the United States Chess Championship in Los Angeles but lost 6 - 4. In 1948, Steiner won the United States Chess Championship in South Fallsburg, New York, ahead of Isaac Kashdan.

Steiner was a member of the United

States Chess Federation teams sent abroad to the Chess Olympiads in The Hague 1928, Hamburg 1930, Prague 1931, and Dubrovnik 1950. As US champion, he captained the 1950 team.

In the historic 1945 US-USSR radio match between the US and Soviet teams, Steiner was the only US player to get a positive score. Although the American team, including Reuben Fine, Samuel Reshevsky, Arnold Denker, and Isaac Kashdan, was defeated, Steiner scored 1.5 - 0.5 against Igor Bondarevsky.

Steiner was very active as a player in West Coast tournaments, winning the only two California Open tournaments he took part in, in 1954 and 1955, and winning the California State Championship in 1953 and 1954. He was defending his State Championship in Los Angeles in 1955, and after finishing his fifth round (a 62-move draw against William Addison), Steiner felt unwell, and his afternoon match was postponed. About two hours later, at around 9:30 in the evening, Steiner died suddenly of a massive coronary occlusion while being attended to by a doctor. By agreement between the players, the 1955 California State Championship tournament was canceled.

Steiner, Lajos

Lajos Steiner, born in Oradea, Hungary on June 14, 1903, and died at the age of 71 in Sydney, Australia on April 22, 1975, was a chess master. Steiner was one of four children of Bernat Steiner, a math teacher, and his wife Cecilia, and the youngest of Endre Steiner. He was educated at the Technical High School in Budapest and obtained a diploma in mechanical engineering (1926) from the Technikum Mittweida, Germany.

In 1923, he took 4th - 5th places in Vienna. In 1925, he came second to Sandor Takacs in Budapest. In 1927, he won in Schandau and tied for 2nd and 3rd place in Kecskemet. In 1929, he came 2nd in Bradley Beach. In 1931, he won in Budapest (Hungarian Championship), came 5th in Vienna and tied for 5th - 6th places in Berlin, won by Herman Steiner. In 1932-1933, he tied for 3rd - 4th places in Hastings (Salo Flohr won). In 1933, he shared 2nd and 3rd place in Ostrava, won by Ernst Grunfeld. In 1933, came 4th in Budapest.

In 1934, he shared 1st and 2nd place with Vasja Pirc in Maribor. In 1935, he tied for 1st and 2nd place with Erich Eliskases in Vienna (18th Trebitsch Memorial). In 1935, he shared 5th - 6th places in Lodz (Savielly Tartakower won) and came 4th in Tatatovaros (László Szabó won). In 1936, he won with Mieczysław Najdorf in Budapest (Hungarian Championship). In 1937, he came 2nd in Brno and 3rd in Sopot. In 1937-1938, he won in Vienna (the 20th Trebitsch Memorial). In 1938, he shared 3rd - 4th places in Ljubljana, won by Borislav Kostic. In 1938, they shared 8th - 9th places in Lodz, where Pirc won.

Lajos Steiner played a few games. In 1930 he lost (+3 -5 = 2) to Isaac Kashdan. In 1934 he won (+7 -3) against Pal Rethy. In 1935 he beat (+3 -1) Henri Grob.

He played for Hungary in four Chess Olympiads: 1931 in Prague, 1933 in Folkestone, 1935 in Warsaw and 1936 in Munich. He won the individual bronze medal in Prague and the individual silver medal in Munich.

Steiner emigrated to Australia in 1939. He won the Australian Chess Championship four times in 1945, 1946-1947, 1952-1953 and 1958-1959. He won in nine of his ten attempts at the New South Wales title (1940-1941, 1943, 1944, 1945-1946, 1953, 1955, 1958). He came 3rd in Karlovy Vary - Marianske Lazne in 1948, won by Jan Foltys. He came 19th in the 1st Interzonal Tournament in Saltsjöbaden in 1948, won by David Bronstein.

Lajos Steiner was awarded the title of International Master in 1950.

Stoltz, J. - *Games 42, 47, 113* (and amateur)
Gösta Leonard Stoltz, born in Stockholm on May 9, 1904, and died at the age of 59 on July 25, 1963, in the same city, was a Swedish chess Grandmaster.

Stoltz played some games against strong chess masters. In 1926, he lost to Mikhail Botvinnik (+0 -1 =1) in a Stockholm - Leningrad team match. In 1927, he drew with Allan Nilsson (+2 -2 =1) in Gothenburg (Swedish Chess Championship). In 1930, he won the match against Isaac Kashdan (+3 -2 =1) in Stockholm. In 1930, he lost to Rudolf Spielmann (+2 -3 =1) in Stockholm. In 1931, he won against Salo Flohr (+4 -3 =1) in Gothenburg. In 1931, he lost to Flohr (+1 -4 =3) in Prague. In 1931, he drew with Gideon Stahlberg (+2 -2 = 2) in Gothenburg. In 1934, he lost to Aron Nimzowitsch (+1 -2 =3) in Stockholm. In September 1935, he played in a match between Sweden and Germany and obtained the 2nd individual result, behind Stahlberg, in Sopot.

Stoltz played for Sweden in nine Chess Olympiads (1927-1937, 1952, 1954) and in the 3rd unofficial Chess Olympiad in Munich in 1936.

Stoltz shared 11th - 13th place in Berlin in 1928, won by Efim Bogoljubov. In 1930, he shared 2nd - 3rd places with Bogoljubov, behind Kashdan, in Stockholm. In 1931, he tied for 4th-7th places in Bled (Alexander Alekhine won). In 1931-1932, tied for 5th - 8th places in Hastings (Flohr won). In 1932, he won in Swinoujscie. In 1933, he came 2nd behind Nimzowitsch in Copenhagen. In 1934, he came 3rd in Stockholm (Erik Lundin won). In 1935, he tied for 1st place with Lindberg in Harnosand. In 1935, he came 4th in Orebro (Alekhine won). In 1935, he tied for 5th - 6th place in Bad Nauheim (Bogoljubov won). In 1936, he tied for 2nd and 3rd place with Böök, behind Vladimir Petrov in Helsinki (Helsingfors). In 1936, he came 3rd in Helsinki (Lundin won). In 1937, he tied for 3rd-4th places in Stockholm (Reuben Fine won). In 1938, won in Stockholm (Swedish Championship). In 1939, he came 5th in Stockholm (Swedish Championship - Stahlberg won).

During the Second World War, Stoltz played in Sweden and Germany. In 1940, he tied for 4th - 5th in the Stockholm championship, won by Nils Bergqvist. In September 1941, he won the 1941 Munich chess tournament ahead of Lundin and Alekhine (the second Europaturnier). In June 1942, he came 6th in the Salzburg 1942 chess tournament (Alekhine won). In September 1942, he tied for 9th - 10th places in Munich (European

Championship, won by Alexander Alekhine). In 1943, he tied for 1st place with Lundholm in Stockholm. In 1943-1944, came 4th in Stockholm (Folke Ekström won). In 1944, he came 3rd behind Stig Lundholm and Paul Keres in Lidköping (Swedish Championship).

After the war, Stoltz played in some international tournaments. In 1946, he came 2nd behind Albéric O'Kelly from Galway in Beverwijk. In 1946, he came 4th in Zaandam (László Szabó won). In 1946, he tied for 8th - 9th place in the 1946 Groningen chess tournament (Botvinnik won). In 1946, he tied for 2nd and 3rd place in Prague (Miguel Najdorf won). In 1947, he tied for 1st place with Eero Böök in Helsinki (zonal) and drew a playoff match (+1 -1 =6). In 1948, he came 18th in Saltsjöbaden (Interzonal, won by David Bronstein). In 1948, won in Stockholm. In 1948, tied for 4th - 5th places in Karlovy Vary - Marianske Lazne, won by Jan Foltys. In 1950, he tied for 9th to 13th places in Bled (Najdorf won). In 1951, he tied for 8th - 9th places in Dortmund (O'Kelly won). In 1951, he tied for 3rd - 4th place in Marianske Lazne - Zonal, won by Luděk Pachman. In 1952, he came 16th in the Stockholm Interzonal, won by Alexander Kotov. In 1962, he came 12th in Belgrade, won by Herman Pilnik.

Stoltz won the Swedish championships in Halmstad in 1951, Haland in 1952 and Orebro in 1953. He was awarded the title of International Master in 1950, and the title of International Grandmaster in 1954.

Sultan Khan, Mir - *Game 53*

Malik Mir Sultan Khan, born in Sargodha, Pakistan, in 1905 and died there on April 25, 1966, was the strongest chess master of his time of Asian origin. A servant of British India, he traveled with Colonel Nawab Sir Umar Hayat Khan ("Sir Umar"), his master, to Great Britain, where he conquered the chess world. In an international career of less than five years (1929-1933), he won the British Championship three times in four attempts (1929, 1932, 1933) and had results in tournaments and games that placed him among the top ten players in the world. Sir Umar then took him back to his homeland, where he gave up chess and returned to his humble life. David Hooper and Kenneth Whyld called him "perhaps the greatest natural player of modern times". Although he was one of the best players in the world in the early 1930s, FIDE, the International Chess Federation, never awarded him any titles (International Master or

Grandmaster).

Sultan Khan was born in Mittha Tawana, in the United Punjab, in British India, where he learned Indian chess from his father at the age of nine. Under the rules of that game at the time, the laws of pawn promotion were different, and a pawn could not move two squares in the first move. By the age of 21, he was considered the strongest player in Punjab. At the time, Sir Umar took him into his home with the idea of teaching him the European version of the game and introducing him to European chess. In 1928 Sultan Khan won the all-India championship, scoring eight wins, one draw and going undefeated.

In the spring of 1929, Sir Umar took him to London, where a training tournament was organized for his benefit. Due to his inexperience and lack of Theoretical knowledge, Sultan Khan didn't do well, sharing last place with H.G. Conde, behind William Winter and Frederick Yates. After the tournament, Winter and Yates trained with Sultan Khan to help prepare him for the British Chess Championship to be held that summer. To everyone's surprise, Sultan Khan won. Soon after, he traveled to India with Sir Umar.

Returning to Europe in May 1930, Sultan Khan began an international chess career that included victories over many of the world's leading players. His best results were 2nd place after Savielly Tartakower in Liege 1930; 3rd place in Hastings in 1930-1931 (+5 -2 =2), behind future world champion Max Euwe and former world champion José Raúl Capablanca; 4th place in Hastings 1931-1932; 4th place in Bern 1932 (+10 -3 =2); and a tie for 3rd place with Isaac Kashdan in London 1932, behind world champion Alexander Alekhine and Salo Flohr. Sultan Khan won the British Championship again in 1932 and 1933. In games he narrowly beat Tartakower in 1931 (+4 -3 =5) and narrowly lost to Flohr in 1932 (+1 -2 =3).

Sultan Khan played in the Chess Olympiad three times. In Hamburg 1930 there was still no rule that teams had to put their best player at the top of the table, and some teams, unconvinced of his strength, put their second or even third best player against him. Sultan Khan scored nine wins, four draws and four losses (64.7%). In Prague 1931, Sultan Khan faced a much stronger environment. He had an excellent result, scoring eight wins, seven draws and two defeats (67.6%). This included wins against Flohr and Akiba Rubinstein, and draws against Alekhine, Kashdan, Ernst Grunfeld, Gideon Stahlberg and Efim Bogoljubov. In Folkestone 1933, he had his worst result, winning four games, drawing six and losing four. Once again, his opponents included the best players in the world, such as Alekhine, Flohr, Kashdan, Tartakower, Grunfeld, Stahlberg and Lajos Steiner.

Reuben Fine wrote about him: "Sultan Khan's story ended up being one of the most unusual. Sultan" was not the status term we had assumed; it was just a first name. In fact, Sultan Khan was a kind of servant owned by a maharajah when his chess genius was discovered. He spoke poor English and took notes in Hindustani. It was said that he couldn't even read European notation. After the tournament (the 1933 Folkestone Olympiad), the American team was invited to visit Sultan Khan's master's house in London. As we drove up, we were greeted by the maharajah with the remark: "It's an honor for you to be here; normally, I only talk to my greyhounds". Although he was a Muslim, the maharajah had been given special permission to drink alcoholic beverages, and he made liberal use of this dispensation. He gave us a four-page printed biography of his life and exploits. As far as we could see, his greatest achievement was being born a maharaja. Meanwhile, Sultan Khan, who was our real entrée to his presence, was treated as a servant of the maharaja (which, in fact, was according to Indian law), and we found ourselves in the peculiar position of being served at table by a grand chess master.

In December 1933, Sir Umar took Sultan Khan back to India. In 1935, he won a match against V. K. Khadilkar, with only one draw in ten games. The chess world never heard of him again.

Miss Fatima, also a servant of Sir Umar, won the British Women's Championship in 1933 with a remarkable three-point margin, scoring ten wins, one draw and no defeats. She said that Sultan Khan, on his return to India, felt as if he had been released from prison. In the humid climate of England, he was continually afflicted with fever, colds, flu, and throat infections, often playing with his neck wrapped in bandages. Sir Umar died in 1944, leaving Sultan Khan a small farm, where he lived for the rest of his life. Ather Sultan, his eldest son, recalled that Sultan Khan didn't train his sons in chess, telling them that they should do something more useful with their lives.

Sultan Khan died of tuberculosis in Sargodha, Pakistan (the same district where he was born) on April 25, 1966. In his brief but meteoric career, Sultan Khan rose to the top of the chess world, playing on a par with the best players in the world. By Arpad Elo's calculations, his playing strength during his five-year heyday was equivalent to an Elo rating of 2530.

In 1950, when FIDE awarded the first International Grandmaster and International Master titles, Sultan Khan had not played for more than 15 years. Although FIDE awarded titles to some retired players who had recognized careers earlier in their lives, such as Rubinstein and Carlos Torre, it never awarded any titles to Sultan Khan.

Hooper and Whyld write about him: "When Sultan Khan first traveled to Europe, his English was so rudimentary that he needed an interpreter. Unable to read or write, Sultan Khan never studied any books on the game, and was placed in the hands of trainers who were also his rivals in the game. Sultan Khan never mastered openings which, by their empirical nature, cannot be learned by applying common sense alone. Under these adverse circumstances and having known international chess for a mere seven years, only half of which was spent in Europe, Sultan Khan had few equals in the middlegame, was among the best two or three endgame players in the world and was one of the best ten players in the world. This achievement brought admiration from Capablanca, who called him a genius, a compliment he rarely gave".

Probably Sultan Khan's most

famous game is his win with White against Capablanca in Hastings 1930-1931: 1.♘f3 ♘f6 2.d4 b6 3.c4 ♗b7 4.♘c3 e6 5.a3 d5 6.cxd5 exd5 7.♗g5 ♗e7 8.e3 0–0 9.♗d3 ♘e4 10. ♗f4 ♘d7 11.♕c2 f5 12.♘b5 ♗d6 13.♘xd6 cxd6 14.h4 ♔c8 15.♕b3 ♕e7 16.♘d2 ♘df6 17.♘xe4 fxe4 18.♗e2 ♔c6 19. g4 ♖fc8 20.g5 ♘e8 21.♗g4 ♖c1 + 22.♔d2 ♖8c2 + 23.♕xc2 ♖xc2 + 24.♔xc2 ♕c7 + 25. ♔d2 ♕c4 26.♗e2 ♕b3 27.♖ab1 ♔f7 28. ♖hc1 ♔e7 29.♖c3 ♕a4 30.b4 ♕d7 31.♖bc1 a6 32.♖g1 ♕a4 33.♖gc1 ♕d7 34.h5 ♔d8 35.♖1c2 ♕h3 36.♗c1 ♕h4 37. ♔b2 ♕h3 38.♖c1 ♕h4 39.♖3c2 ♕h3 40.a4 ♕h4 41.♔a3 ♕h3 42.♗g3 ♕f5 43.♗h4 g6 44.h6 ♕d7 45.b5 a5 46.♗g3 ♕f5 47. ♗f4 ♕h3 48.♔b2 ♕g2 49.♔b1 ♕h3 50.♔a1 ♕g2 51.♔b2 ♕h3 52.♖g1 ♗c8 53.♖c6 ♕h4 54.♖gc1 ♗g4 55.♗f1 ♕h5 56. ♖e1 ♕h1 57.♖ec1 ♕h5 58.♔c3 ♕h4 59.♗g3 ♕xg5 60.♔d2 ♕h5 61.♖xb6 ♔e7 62.♖b7 + ♔e6 63.b6 ♘f6 64.♗b5 ♕h3 65.♖b8 1–0

Tarrasch, S. - *Game 5*

Siegbert Tarrasch, born in Breslau on March 5, 1862, and died at the age of 71 in Munich on March 5, 1934, was one of the strongest and most influential chess players of the late 19th and early 20th centuries. He was also a chess teacher who was responsible for teaching and spreading the game of chess to several generations and was therefore also called *Praeceptor Germaniae*, which means "Teacher of Germany".

Tarrasch was born in Breslau (Wrocław), Silesia, Prussia. When he finished school in 1880, he left Breslau to study medicine in Halle. With his family, he settled in Nuremberg, Bavaria and later in Munich, establishing a successful medical practice. He had five children. Tarrasch was Jewish, converted to Christianity in 1909, and a patriotic German who lost a son in World War I, but faced anti-Semitism in the early stages of Nazism.

A doctor by profession, Tarrasch was the best player in the world in the early 1890s. He vigorously beat the ageing World Champion Wilhelm Steinitz in tournaments, (+ 3 -0 =1), but turned down the opportunity to challenge Steinitz for the world title in 1892 due to the demands of his medical practice.

Soon after, in St. Petersburg 1893, Tarrasch drew a tough match against Steinitz's opponent Mikhail Chigorin (+9 -9 =4) after leading for most of the match. He also won four major tournaments in a row: Breslau 1889, Manchester 1890, Dresden 1892, and Leipzig 1894. However, after Emanuel Lasker became world chess champion in 1894, Tarrasch was no match for him. Fred Reinfeld wrote: "Tarrasch was destined to play second fiddle for the rest of his life". For example, Lasker scored much better against mutual opponents, such as against Chigorin, - Tarrasch was +2 in 34 games, while Lasker scored +7 in 21; against Akiba Rubinstein Tarrasch was -8 without a win, while Lasker scored +2-1 =2; against David Janowski Tarrasch scored +3 compared to Lasker's fantastic +22; against Géza Maróczy, Tarrasch scored +1 in 16 games, while Lasker scored +4 -0 =1; against Richard Teichmann Tarrasch scored +8 -5 =2, while Lasker won all four games of the match. However, Tarrasch had a higher score against Harry Nelson Pillsbury of +6 -5 =2, while Lasker drew +5 -5 = 4. Still, Tarrasch remained a powerful player, demolishing Frank Marshall in a match in 1905 (+8 -1 =8) and winning Ostend in 1907 over Schlechter, Janowski, Marshall, Burn and Chigorin.

There wasn't much sympathy between the two masters. The story goes that when they were introduced at the opening of the championship in 1908, Tarrasch clicked his heels, bowed stiffly, and said: "To you, Dr. Lasker, I have only three words: check and mate". When Lasker finally agreed to compete for the title in 1908, he defeated Tarrasch convincingly +8 -3 =5.

Tarrasch continued to be one of the world's leading players for some time. He finished fourth in the 1914 St. Petersburg chess tournament, behind only world champion Lasker and future world champions José Raúl Capablanca and Alexander Alekhine, and ahead of Marshall, Ossip Bernstein, Rubinstein, Nimzowitsch, Blackburne, Janowski and Gunsberg.

His victory against Capablanca in the 19th round, although much less famous than Lasker's victory against Capablanca in the previous round, which was essential in allowing Lasker to overtake Capablanca in the tournament standings. St. Petersburg 1914 was probably Tarrasch's swansong, as his chess career wasn't very successful after that, although he still played some highly respected games.

Tarrasch was a very influential chess writer, editor of the magazine Deutsche Schachzeitung in 1897 and wrote several books, including *Die moderne Schachpartie* and *Three Hundred Games of Chess*. Although his teachings became famous throughout the chess world, until recently his books had not been translated into English.

Tarrasch developed some of Wilhelm Steinitz's ideas (e.g., control of the center, pair of bishops, space advantage) and made them more accessible to the average chess player. In other areas, he departed from Steinitz. He emphasized the mobility of the pieces much more than Steinitz, and disliked restricted positions, saying that they "had the germ of defeat".

Tarrasch formulated what is known as the Tarrasch rule, that rooks should be placed behind passed pawns - either yours or your opponent's. Andrew Soltis quotes Tarrasch, saying "Always place the rook behind the pawn... Except when it is incorrect to do so".

Tartakower, S. - *Games 18, 35, 52, 88, 116* (and amateur)
Ksawery Tartakower (also known as Saviely, born in Rostov on Don, Russia, on 22/02/1886 and died at the

age of 68 in Paris on 04/02/1956, was a Polish and French chess grandmaster. He was also an important journalist and author of chess books, written between 1920 and 1930, which are still popular today. Tartakower is remembered for his sharp wit and his famous aphorisms.

Tartakower was born on February 22, 1887, in Rostov-on-Don, Russia, in a colony for Austrian citizens of Jewish origin. His parents were killed in a robbery in Rostov-on-Don in 1911. Tartakower lived mainly in Austria. He graduated from the law faculties of the universities in Geneva and Vienna. He spoke German and French perfectly. During his studies, he became interested in chess and started attending chess meetings at various players' *cafés* in Vienna. He met many notable masters of the time, including Carl Schlechter, Géza Maróczy (against whom he later won probably his most prestigious prize), Milan Vidmar and Richard Réti. His first achievement was first place in a tournament in Nuremberg in 1906. Three years later, Tartakower took second place in a tournament in Vienna, second only to Réti.

During the First World War, he was drafted into the Austro-Hungarian army and served as a staff officer in various positions. He went to the Russian front with the Viennese infantry regiment.

After the war, he emigrated to France and settled in Paris. Although Tartakower didn't even speak Polish, after Poland regained its independence in 1918, he accepted Polish citizenship and became one of Poland's most prominent honorary ambassadors abroad. He was the captain and coach of the Polish chess team in six international tournaments, winning a gold medal for Poland at the Hamburg Olympiad in 1930.

In France, he decided to become a professional chess player. He also began cooperating with various chess-related magazines, as well as writing several chess-related books and pamphlets. The most famous of these, *Die Hypermoderne Schachpartie* ("The Hypermodernist Chess Game") was published in 1924 and has been reprinted in almost a hundred editions since then. Tartakower took part in many of the most important chess tournaments of the time. In 1927 and 1928 he won two tournaments in Hastings and shared first place with Aron Nimzowitsch in London. On the latter occasion, he defeated notable players such as Frank Marshall, Milan Vidmar and Efim Bogoljubov. In 1930 he won the Liege tournament, beating Mir Sultan Khan by two points. Further down the list were, among others, Akiba Rubinstein, Nimzowitsch and Marshall.

He won the Polish Chess Championship twice, in Warsaw in 1935 and in Jurata in 1937. In the 1930s, Tartakower represented Poland in six Chess Olympiads and France in 1950, winning three individual medals (gold in 1931 and bronze in 1933 and 1935), as well as five team medals (gold in 1930, two silver in 1931 and 1939, and two bronze in 1935 and 1937).

In 1939, the outbreak of World War II found him in Buenos Aires, where he was playing in the 8th Chess Olympiad, representing Poland in a team that included Miguel Najdorf, who always referred to Tartakower as "my teacher".

After a short stay in Argentina, Tartakower decided to return to Europe. He arrived in France shortly before its collapse in 1940. Under the pseudonym Cartier, he joined General Charles de Gaulle's forces. After the Second World War and the communist takeover of Poland, Tartakower became a French citizen. He played in the first interzonal tournament in Saltsjöbaden in 1948 but failed to qualify for the Candidates Tournament. He represented France at the 1950 Chess Olympiad. FIDE instituted the title of International Grandmaster in 1950; Tartakower was in the first group of players to receive this title. In 1953, he won the French Chess Championship in Paris.

Tartakower died on February 4, 1956, in Paris, 18 days before his 69th birthday.

Tartakower is considered one of the most remarkable chess personalities of his time. Harry Golombek translated Tartakower's book on his best games and wrote in the preface:

"Dr. Tartakower is by far the most cultured and the most intelligent of all the chess masters I have ever met. His extremely cultured mind and his native and always fluent wit make conversation with him a constant delight. So much so that I consider one of the most brilliant attractions that an international tournament can offer to me to be Dr. Tartakower's participation. His talk and thought are more like a modernized mix of Baruch Spinoza and Voltaire; and all this with a dash of paradoxical originality that is essential, Tartakower."

His famous aphorisms have become maxims for all generations of chess players:

- "It is always better to sacrifice your opponent's pieces".
- "An isolated pawn spreads melancholy all over the chessboard".
- "The mistakes are all on the board, waiting to be made".
- "The winner of the game is the player who makes the penultimate mistake".
- "The move is there, but you have to see it".
- "No match has ever been won by abandonment".
- "I've never beaten a healthy opponent" (this quote refers to players who blame an illness, sometimes imaginary, for their defeat).
- "Tactics are what you do when there's something to do; strategy is what you do when there's nothing to do."
- "Moral victories don't count".
- "Chess is a fairy tale of 1001 blunders".
- "The grandmaster puts a knight on e5; checkmate comes by itself."
- "A master can sometimes play badly, a fan never!".
- "A match shows less than a tournament. But a tournament shows absolutely nothing."
- "Chess is a fight against your own mistakes."
- "Every chess player should have a hobby".
- "A chess game has three phases: the opening, where you hope you're better; the middlegame, where you think you're better; and the ending, where you know you're lost."
- "As long as the opening is considered weak, it can be played."
- "The stalemate is the tragicomedy of chess".

- *"Erro ergo sum"*.

Thomas, G. A. - **Game 8**

Sir George Alan Thomas, 7th Baronet, born on June 14, 1881, in Istanbul and died on July 23, 1972, in London at the age of 91, was a British badminton, tennis and chess player. Thomas was twice British Chess Champion and 21 times All-England Badminton Champion. He also reached the quarterfinals of the men's singles and the semi-finals of the men's doubles at Wimbledon in 1911. The men's badminton world championship cup, equivalent to the Davis Cup, is named the Thomas Cup after him. Thomas lived most of his life in London and Godalming. He never married, so Thomas's hereditary title of baronet ended with his death. Thomas was admired for his great sportsmanship.

Thomas was British Chess Champion in 1923 and 1934. He shared first prize at the Hastings International Chess Congress in 1934 with world chess champion Max Euwe and Czechoslovak leader Salo Flohr, ahead of past and future world champions José Raúl Capablanca and Mikhail. Botvinnik, whom he defeated in their individual games. For Capablanca, this was his first defeat in the tournament for four years, and his first with white in over six years. Also in Hastings, eleven years later, Euwe would become the third world chess champion to be beaten by Thomas in a match.

His "lifetime" scores against the world's elite were, however, less flattering: less against Emanuel Lasker (-1, not counting a win in a simultaneous exhibition by Lasker in 1896), Capablanca (+1 -5 =3), Alekhine (-7 =6), Efim Bogoljubov (-5 =3), Euwe (+1 -9 =2), Flohr (+2 -9 =4) and Savielly Tartakower (+3 -9 =10). He also did badly against Edgard Colle (+1 -9 =8). Thomas also scored points against Botvinnik (+1 -1), Richard Réti (+3 -3 =1) and Siegbert Tarrasch (+1 -1 =3). Against Géza Maróczy, the balance is in Thomas' favor (+3 -1 =5).

Domestically, he had a positive score against his great rival Frederick Yates (+13 -11 =13) but was less successful against Women's World Chess Champion Vera Menchik (+7 -8 =7).

In 1950, Thomas was awarded the title of FIDE International Master and in 1952 he became an International Arbiter. Thomas gave up competitive chess at the age of 69.

Treybal, K. - **Game 7**

Karel Treybal, born on 02/02/1885 in Kotopeky, Czechoslovakia and died at the age of 56 in Prague on 02/10/1941, was a prominent Czech chess player of the early 20th century.

Treybal was born in Kotopeky, a village southwest of Prague in central Bohemia. He trained as a lawyer and became president of the district court in Velvary, a small town on the opposite side of Prague. Although he played chess as an amateur, Treybal was a master who took part in several major international tournaments. He was the younger brother of Frantisek Treybal, who was also a prominent Czech chess player.

In 1905 he tied for 3rd - 4th place in the first Czechoslovak Prague Championship (Oldrich Duras won). In 1907, he tied for 2nd - 4th place in Brno (second Czechoslovak Championship, won by Frantisek Treybal). In 1908, he won in Prague (B tournament). In 1909 he came second behind Duras in Prague (third Czechoslovak Championship). In 1921 he tied Karel Hromádka and Ladislav Prokes for 1st - 3rd place in Brno (seventh Czechoslovak Championship). He played for Czechoslovakia in three Chess Olympiads: 1930 in Hamburg, 1933 in Folkestone and 1935 in Warsaw. He won the team silver medal in Folkestone 1933.

Treybal's greatest international success was sixth place alongside Aron Nimzowitsch in the 1923 tournament in Karlovy Vary (Karlsbad). His performance included a victory against World Champion Alexander Alekhine.

Treybal died during the Nazi occupation of Czechoslovakia. On May 30, 1941, he was arrested, imprisoned, and later charged with hiding weapons for use by the resistance forces and illegal possession of a pistol. It is not known whether these charges were well-founded. Treybal was sentenced to death and executed on October 2. After his execution, his body was not handed over to his family and the whereabouts of his grave or remains are unknown.

In 1945, in a tribute to Treybal that appeared in the Czech chess magazine *Šach*, it was stated that Treybal was executed without trial and that he "never occupied himself with politics". After Treybal's death, Prokes published a monograph about him in 1946.

Tylor, T. H. - *Game 91*
Sir Theodore Henry Tylor, born on 13/05/1900 in Bournville and who died at the age of 68 in Oxford on 23/10/1968, was a lawyer and world-class chess player, despite being almost blind. In 1965, he was decorated for his services to organizations for the blind. He was a fellow and tutor in Jurisprudence at Balliol College, Oxford for almost forty years.

Born in Bournville, Tylor learned to play chess at the age of seven. His chess skills increased while attending Worcester College for the Blind from 1909 to 1918. He studied at Oxford University from 1918 and was captain of the Oxford University Chess Club. Tylor received first class honors in Jurisprudence in 1922 and became an honorary scholar of Balliol College. The following year, he became a Bachelor of Civil Law and a lecturer at Balliol College. Called to the Professional Association of Lawyers for the London Courts with a certificate of honor, he was made a fellow of Balliol College in 1928.

Tylor competed in twelve British championships, finishing fourth in his first appearance in 1925. His best result was in 1933, finishing second to Mir Sultan Khan. He tied for first place in the 1929 - 1930 Hastings Premier Reserves alongside George Koltanowski ahead of Salo Flohr, Josef Rejfir, Ludwig Rellstab, C.H.O'D. Alexander, Daniel Noteboom and Milan Vidmar. Tylor played in the top section, the Hastings Premier, nine times from 1930/1931. His best result was 6th in 1936 - 1937. He was first reserve for the English team at the 1930 Hamburg Chess Olympiad.

Tylor won the British Correspondence Chess Championship in 1932, 1933 and 1934. He shared 5th-6th places in Margate 1936 with P. S. Milner-Barry but won his individual match and drew with second and fourth placed José Raúl Capablanca, Gideon Stahlberg and Erik Lundin (Salo Flohr won). Despite finishing 12th in Nottingham 936, he had the best score of the British participants, ahead of C. H. O' D. Alexander, G. A. Thomas, and William Winter. Mikhail Botvinnik noticed that Tylor was using a tactile chessboard that rang incessantly, as well as a device for counting the number of moves made.

Tylor was president of the Midland Counties Chess Union from 1947 to 1950, but his work for the university and for the welfare of the blind limited the time he had to devote to chess. Tylor also enjoyed bridge. He died in Oxford on October 23, 1968.

Vidmar, M. - *Games 33, 44, 89*
Milan Vidmar, born in Ljubljana on June 22, 1885, and who died on October 9, 1962, in the same city at the age of 77, was a Slovenian electrical engineer, chess master, theoretician and arbiter, philosopher and writer. Vidmar was among the twelve best chess players in the world from 1910 to 1930. He was a specialist in power transformers and electric current transmission.

Vidmar was born into a middle-class family in Lyublyana, Austria-Hungary (now Slovenia). He began his studies in mechanical engineering in 1902 and graduated from the University of Vienna in 1907. He obtained his doctorate in 1911 from the Technical Faculty in Vienna. The study of electrical engineering at the technical faculty didn't begin until 1904, and then Vidmar had to take special exams in the basic field. He was a professor at the University of Ljubljana, a member of the Slovenian Academy of Arts and Sciences and founder of the Faculty of Electrical Engineering. Between 1928 and 1929, Vidmar was the tenth chancellor of the University of Ljubljana. In 1948, he founded the Institute of Electrotechnics, which now bears his name.

Vidmar was also a first-class chess player, probably one of the best players in the world between 1910 and 1930, while remaining an amateur. He was awarded the title of FIDE Grandmaster in 1950.

His successes include high placings in some of the leading chess tournaments of his time, for example 6th place in Carlsbad in 1907, 3rd place in Prague in 1908, Champion in Gothenburg in 1909 (the 7th Nordic Chess Championship), 2nd place in San Sebastián in 1911 (with Akiba Rubinstein behind José Raúl Capablanca), Champion in Budapest in 1912, 2nd place in Mannheim in 1914, Champion in Vienna and Berlin in 1918, 2nd place in Kosice 1928, 3rd place in London 1922, shared first place with Alexander Alekhine in Hastings 1925-1926, 3rd place in Semmering 1926, 4th place in New York 1927, 4th place in London 1927, shared 5th place in Carlsbad 1929, shared 4th - 7th places in Bled 1931, tied for 3rd - 6th places in Stuttgart 1939, 2nd place - to Max Euwe in Budapest 1940, and Champion in Basel 1952.

Vidmar represented Yugoslavia at the Chess Olympiads in Prague in 1931 and Stockholm in 1935. He became an International Arbiter, receiving this title from FIDE and being the main arbiter at the 1948 World Chess Championship in The Hague and Moscow.

Weenink, H. - *Game 40*

Henri Gerard Marie Weenink, born in Amsterdam on 17/10/1892 and died on 02/12/1931 in the same city at the age of 39, was a Dutch chess player and composer of problems. He took 2nd place behind Fick in Amsterdam 1918-1919; shared 4th - 5th places in Amsterdam 1919 (Richard Réti and Max Marchand); tied for 3rd - 6th places in Rotterdam 1919 (Réti won); shared 2nd place behind Abraham Speijer in Amsterdam 1919; took 3rd place in Amsterdam 1920 (Réti won); tied for 2nd - 3rd places in Amsterdam 1921; shared 13th place in Scheveningen 1923 (Paul Johner and Rudolf Spielmann won); shared 3rd - 4th places in Amsterdam 1925 (quadrangular); tied for 2nd - 3rd places with Salo Landau, behind Max Euwe, in Amsterdam 1929 (Dutch Championship), shared 8th - 9th places in Liege 1930 (Savielly Tartakower won), and won, ahead of Euwe and Spielmann, in Amsterdam 1930.

Weenink played four times for the Netherlands in the Chess Olympiad: London 1927, The Hague 1928, Hamburg 1930, and Prague 1931.

As well as being an excellent chess player, Henri Weenink was also a composer of problems. He composed problems in all genres and endgame studies. In 1921 he published *Het schaakprobleem*, of which an improved version appeared in 1926 under the title "The Chess Problem", in the White Christmas series: "a comprehensive treatise with 374 examples and several pictures".

Until his death, Henri Weenink worked on the book "David Przepiórka - A Master of Strategy", which was published posthumously.

Weenink died of tuberculosis at the age of 39.

Winter, W. - *Games 49, 85*

William Winter, born in Medstead on 11/09/1898 and who died aged 57 in London on 18/12/1955, was a British chess player. He won the British Chess Championship in 1934, 1935 and 1936. A disciple of Siegbert Tarrasch, his strategic play allowed him to defeat several of the best players in the world, including David Bronstein, Aron Nimzowitsch and Milan Vidmar Unfortunately, his health and tactical play were not strong enough to allow him to repeat these victories consistently.

Winter was a highly respected author of chess books. He was the nephew of J.M. Barrie, the creator of Peter Pan. Winter was also a communist. His characters on the board and in real life were in sharp contrast. Harry Golombek described his personality as "on the board classic, scientific and sober; away from the board, a revolutionary driven illogically by his emotions (he imagined himself to be a fervent communist and a staunch patriot) and, more often than not, drunk".

Winter had the distinction of being the only British champion to have served time in prison (for his political activities). His memoirs were published in Chess magazine at the end of the 1950s.

With the outbreak of the First World War, Winter had to interrupt his law studies, which he later resumed. During his time there, he was the champion of Cambridge University.

Winter played in four Olympiads in

1930, 1931, 1933 and 1935 and was awarded the title of FIDE International Master in 1950. Winter was a chess columnist for the Manchester Guardian and the Daily Worker.

Yates, F. D. - *Game 31*
Frederick Dewhurst Yates, born on 16/01/1886 in Birstall, England and who died at the age of 46 on 11/11/1932 in London, was an English chess master who won the British Championship on six occasions. Yates began his career as an accountant but abandoned it in 1909 in favor of becoming a journalist and professional chess player.

Yates almost won the British Championship in 1911, when he tied for first place with Henry Atkins, but lost the play-off. He then won the titles in 1913, 1914, 1921, 1926, 1928 and 1931.

Despite considerable domestic success, his record in international tournaments didn't do him justice. Often victorious against his strongest opponents, he would lose to players at the bottom of the table. This was particularly evident at the Budapest 1926 tournament.

His lack of consistency was attributed to health problems and loss of stamina. A constant cough went unchecked, as his resources did not allow him a period of rest in warmer climates, advice given by his doctor. He was also subjected to journalistic pressure, as he frequently reported on the tournaments, he was playing in. However, devoting himself solely to chess would have earned him insufficient money to make a living. Some of his contemporaries believed that his talent could have put him among the candidates for the World Championship if his circumstances had been different. However, at the time he defeated most of his illustrious opponents, except for Emanuel Lasker and José Raúl Capablanca. His victory against Alexander Alekhine in Karlsbad 1923 won the beauty prize, while his win against Milan Vidmar in San Remo in 1930 was described by Alekhine as the best game since the end of the First World War.

As a journalist and writer, he was the chess columnist for the Manchester Guardian and with William Winter, co-author of Modern Master Play (1929). He wrote reports on two World Championship encounters: Alekhine vs. Capablanca and Alekhine vs. Bogoljubov.

In the team competition, he played in three Olympiads, representing the "British Empire" team. On each occasion, he improved on his previous score and in London 1927 he won a team bronze medal.

His life ended prematurely when a leaking gas pipe caused Yates to asphyxiate in his sleep.

According to the inscription on Yates' gravestone, his birth name was actually Fred Dewhirst Yates. However, throughout his chess career, he was known by his surname or simply as F.D. Yates, both of which are featured in his posthumously published and partly biographical collection "My Best Games".

Competing in the British Isles, he came first in Glasgow 1911, Cheltenham 1913, Chester 1914, Malvern 1921, Edinburgh 1926, and Tunbridge Wells 1927. There were second places in Oxford 1910, Richmond

1912, Southport 1924, Hastings 1924 - 1925 and Stratford-upon-Avon 1925.

Abroad, his best results included first place shared with Savielly Tartakower in Kecskemet B 1927 and 5th place in San Remo (the strongest tournament of 1930), when he finished ahead of Spielmann, Vidmar and Tartakower. Yates was second in Ghent 1926, after Tartakower, but ahead of Colle and Janowski.

Znosko-Borovski, E. - Game 60

Eugene Alexandrovich Znosko-Borovsky, born on August 16, 1884, in St. Petersburg and who died at the age of 70 on December 31, 1884 - 31 in Paris, was a Russian chess master, also versed in music and theater criticism, teacher and author. Born in St. Petersburg, he settled in Paris in 1920 and lived there for the rest of his life.

Znosko-Borovsky learned to play chess as a boy. He won prizes in local and regional tournaments, while progressing to a first-class education at the Lyceum Tsarskoye Selo.

Making his debut at the international chess tournament in Ostend in 1906, where he won the prize for brilliance for his match against Amos Burn, Znosko-Borovsky's chess career was often interrupted by other events in his life. Between 1909 and 1912 he was a prominent critic for the modernist magazine Apollo, befriended many Russian poets and writers of the Silver Age, and was Nikolay Gumilev's second in his 1909 duel against Maximilian Voloshin. Decorated and wounded in military conflicts, he initially served as a volunteer in the Russo-Japanese War of 1904 and 1905 and was then called up to serve during the First World War. After the armistice, he was transported by a British ship to Constantinople and from there to Paris, which remained his home from 1920.

As a player, Znosko-Borovsky fell short of the highest level. He had some notable results in international competition, including Paris 1930, where he finished first, undefeated, ahead of Savielly Tartakower, Andor Lilienthal and Jacques Mieses, and 1st place in the first tournament in Folkestone 1933. Success often came in singles against his more distinguished peers; he won impressive games against José Raúl Capablanca, Akiba Rubinstein, Max Euwe and Efim Bogoljubov, as well as a miniature against Edgard Colle in 1922. He was also highly skilled in simultaneous exhibitions.

In conversation and as a chess lecturer, teacher or writer, his skills were widely recognized, particularly in Russia and France, where he contributed regular articles and columns to magazines and newspapers. In fact, it was in the field of writing that Znosko-Borovsky excelled, penning many popular books, including The Evolution of Chess (1910), Capablanca and The Muzio Gambit (both 1911). Capablanca and Alekhine followed World War I and most of his later works were translated into English, notably The Chess Half Game, How Not to Play Chess, How to Play Chess Openings, How to Play Chess Endings (1940), and The Art of Chess Combining.

On hearing the news of Znosko-Borovsky's death, Gerald Abrahams wrote a personal tribute: "Znosko-Borovsky's death deprives the chess world of one of the few survivors of an intellectually rich generation, the Russian masters of the old regime... My own memories of Znosko go back to 1923-1924. I found him then, and at all times thereafter, a stimulating friend and a charming conversationalist on many subjects. His reputation as a theatrical and literary critic was, at one time, considerable in Europe, although England knew little of it. Those who have read his chess works, however, should know that their writer was a kultur mensch in the best sense of the term. On the other hand, he was stoic in adversity (adversity was always his luck) and possessed of great humor and resilience... As a player, he suffered from the demands of a professionalism that is incompatible with great performance: but he leaves records in many games that reveal, if not genius, then a great talent... Those who knew him will agree that his life enriched and greatly inspired the world of chess."

Some of Znosko-Borovsky's aphorisms: "It's not a move, not even the best move, that you should look for, but an achievable plan." "Chess is a game of understanding, not memory".

Zukierman, J. - *Game 59*

Josef Cukierman (Zukierman), born in 1900 in Poland and died in 1941 in Castres, France, was a Polish-born French chess master.

Cukierman was born near Bialystok in 1900. He won the second Moscow city championship (1920 - 1921). In the early 1920s, Cukierman lived in Bialystok, Poland, where he won a chess championship in 1926. He then emigrated to France.

In 1928, he shared 2nd - 3rd places with Leon Schwartzmann, behind Abraham Baratz, in the 4th Paris Championship. In 1929, he tied for 5th - 6th places in Paris (Savielly Tartakower won). In 1930, he won the 6th Paris Championship ahead of Tartakower. In 1931, he won again in Paris. In 1933, he finished sixth in the Paris Tournament (Alexander Alekhine won). In 1938, Cukierman came 3rd behind José Raúl Capablanca and Nicolas Rossolimo in the Paris Tournament. In 1939, he shared 5th - 6th places in Paris (Rossolimo won).

During the Second World War, Josef Zukierman committed suicide in Castres, France, in 1941.

Index of Openings

Opening	Opponent	Game	Page
Catalan Opening	Euwe	100	213
	Tartakower	88	184
Queen's Pawn Opening	Kmoch	19	40
	Marshall	16	36
	Roselli	67	141
Three Knights Opening	Bogoljubov	79	165
Réti Opening	Euwe	102	217
	Kevitz e Pinkus	112	240
	Steiner, E.	41	88
Spanish Opening	Bogoljubov	30	64
	Bogoljubov	64	133
	Borochow	117	248
	Eliskases	80	167
	Fine	90	189
	Grob	54	112
	Johner	68	142
	Kashdan	119	251
	Kimura	118	250
	Koltanowski	51	108
	Mindeno	120	253
	Steiner, H.	56	116
	Steiner, L.	58	120
	Saemisch	96	205
	Stoltz	47	102
	Tylor	91	191
	Yates	31	66
	Znosko-Borovsky	60	123
Viennese Opening	Euwe	76	158
Alekhine Defense	Potemkin	107	230
	Reshevsky	93	197
	Thomas	8	23

Opening	Opponent	Game	Page
Benoni Defense	Bogoljubov	63	131
	Gygli	69	144
Budapest Defense	Tartakower	52	109
Cambridge Springs Defense	Bogoljubov	78	163
	Capablanca	21	44
Caro-Kann Defense	Sultan Khan	53	111
	Tartakower	18	39
	Winter	49	105
Slav Defense	Bogoljubov	26	58
	Bogoljubov	27	59
	Bogoljubov	61	125
	Bogoljubov	62	127
	Bogoljubov	87	182
	Davidson	10	26
	Euwe	72	150
	Euwe	97	207
	Euwe	98	209
	Opocensky	4	16
	Stoltz	42	90
	Weenink	40	86
French Defense	Asgeirsson	115	245
	Capablanca	20	41
	Euwe	73	151
	Euwe	75	156
	Euwe	84	175
	Nimzovitsch	32	69
	Nimzovitsch	43	92
	Winter	85	179
Dutch Defense	Tartakower	35	77
Irregular Defense	Marshall	9	24

Index of Openings

Opening	Opponent	Game	Page
Queen's Indian Defense	Ahues	36	79
	Alexander	86	181
	Andersen	39	85
	Bogoljubov	28	61
	Euwe	101	216
	Marshall	111	237
	Menchik, Vera	50	107
	Menchik, Vera	83	173
	Rubinstein	11	27
	Rubinstein	14	32
	Saemisch	13	30
	Stoltz	113	243
	Tartakower.	116	246
	Janowsky	2	13
King's Indian Defense	Bogoljubov	29	62
	Euwe	74	153
	Euwe	110	234
	Réti	1	11
	Schwartz	108	231
Lasker Defense	Vidmar	44	93
Nimzovitsch Defense	Euwe	99	211
	Euwe	104	223
	Euwe	109	232
	Flohr	114	244
	Kmoch	37	81
	Nimzovitsch	15	33
	Stahlberg	38	83
	Vidmar	33	71
Orthodox Defense	Asztalos	17	37
	Bogoljubov	95	203
	Capablanca	22	47
	Capablanca	23	49

323

Opening	Opponent	Game	Page
Orthodox Defense 2	Capablanca	24	51
	Foltys	82	171
	Lasker	70	146
	Lundin	71	147
	Maroczy	34	75
	Maroczy	48	103
	Treybal	7	21
	Vidmar	89	186
	Zukierman	59	121
Semi-Tarrasch Defense	Euwe	103	221
	Kussman	105	229
Sicilian Defense	Foltys	92	194
	Frydman	81	169
Tarrasch Defense	Pirc	45	99
Chigorin Defense	Colle	3	14
King Fianchetto	Mikenas	57	117
	Reti	6	19
Queen's Gambit Accepted	Ahues	77	161
	Bogoljubov	65	135
	Bogoljubov	66	136
	Fine	94	200
	Flohr	46	100
	Gruenfeld	12	29
	Steiner, H.	25	57
Central Gambit	Freeman	106	229
Giuoco Piano	Tarrasch	5	17
Colle System	Flohr	55	114

Printed in Great Britain
by Amazon